SOCIAL PSYCHOLOGY THROUGH VISUAL KEY CONCEPTS

■ *Visual Key Concepts* aligned with learning objectives provide an interactive demonstration to make key terms and concepts more memorable.

SOCIAL PSYCHOLOGY IN ACTION

■ *Social Psychology in Action* animations promote student comprehension of core content through concrete examples and visual cues.

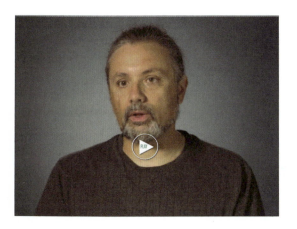

ASK THE EXPERT VIDEOS

• *Ask the Expert* interviews feature popular pioneers and pivotal historical studies from the field.

• Each video is framed with commentary by the authors to stimulate analysis and further discussion.

SOCIAL PSYCHOLOGY THROUGH STORYTELLING

- Historical contexts and contemporary examples help students understand where social psychology has been, where it is going, and how it is part of everyday life.

CONFORMITY IN
MEAN GIRLS AND *THE DUFF*

Social Psychology in Popular Culture

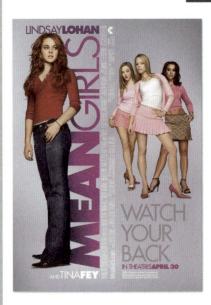

stereotypes and social pressure as she tries to get the attention of a boy.

In *Mean Girls*, the main character, Kady, has to learn how to gain friends quickly as she moves to the United States after being raised in Africa by her scientist parents. She quickly learns that the high school is made up of social cliques such as "Asian nerds," "band geeks," and "varsity jocks." The group of girls in the most popular social group are called "the plastics" by the other groups, because they look like real-life Barbie dolls. The plastics decide to include Kady, but only if she follows certain rules, including the following:

- on Wednesdays you have to wear pink,
- you car
- you car a week,
- jeans or

Kady is to so she can be she sees then of the movie so caught up she becomes thing she orig

In *The DUF social group's embark on a t avoid this lab her world, suc movies have mentary regar of conformity identity and p

Perhaps for many of us, the pressure to conform reached a peak in middle school and high school. Unsure of their identity, teenagers may feel anxiety about fitting into their increasingly complicated social worlds. This pressure and anxiety are highlighted in the comedies *Mean Girls* (2004) and *The DUFF* (2015). In both, a theoretically less attractive girl is thrown into the world of

SELF-DISCREPANCY
THEORY AND WONDER WOMAN

Social Psychology in Popular Culture

Most superheroes have secret identities—but does this complicate how they think about their own self-concept? The most popular female superhero of all time is Wonder Woman, whose secret identity is Diana Prince. But really, both of these identities are costumes; she's really Princess Diana from Paradise Island. When the *Wonder Woman* movie came out in 2017, it broke the record for opening-weekend ticket sales (over $100 million) for a movie with a female director (Lang, 2017). But the original D.C. comics (which started in 1942 for this character) provides an interesting view into the character's original conceptualization.

Applying Tory Higgins's (1987, 2002) self-discrepancy theory, Princess Diana would be her "actual self"—her true identity and the person she is when she's not taking on one of her other identities. Most people would probably say that Wonder Woman is Diana's "ideal self," the self that embodies all of her goals, or the best version of the person she could be. Most regular humans strive for an ideal self in the future, but superheroes usually get to reach their ideals a bit sooner than us mere mortals. Interestingly, though, even Diana has to deal with people judging her, which makes her "ought self" come alive. In the early Wonder Woman comics, both men and women make comments about how her star-spangled outfit is inappropriate and skimpy. When Diana is pretending to be Diana Prince, a modest and gentle military secretary, her love interest Steve Trevor constantly tells her that she's not as attractive, strong, and amazing as Wonder Woman. Diana thus is judged both when she's embodying her Wonder Woman identity (she's too brazen and nonconformist) and when she's embodying her Diana Prince identity (she's too subdued and conformist). It's apparently hard to be a modern woman, even when you have super powers, an invisible plane, and a magic lasso.

[End note: For a more detailed analysis of self-discrepancy theory as applied to Wonder Women, see the book Wonder Woman Psychology: Lassoing the Truth *(2017) and read the chapter "Multiple Identities, Multiple Selves?" by Goodfriend and Formichella-Elsden.]*

SOCIAL PSYCHOLOGY
IN POPULAR CULTURE

- *Social Psychology in Popular Culture* boxes connect concepts to the media readers consume every day, allowing them to relate course material to their own lives.

RESEARCH METHODS IN SOCIAL PSYCHOLOGY

- Heinzen and Goodfriend's highly praised integrated research methods coverage takes students a step further and increases retention by discussing research methods within each chapter in the context of actual studies.

- Marginal icons heighten student awareness of methodology and statistical terms.

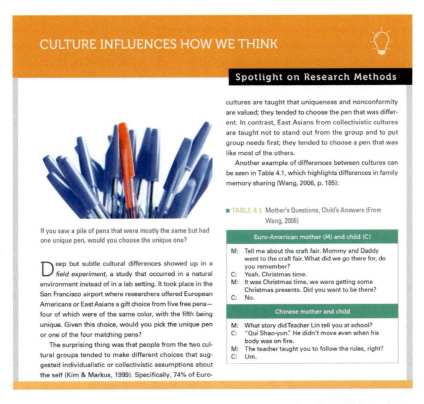

CULTURE INFLUENCES HOW WE THINK

Spotlight on Research Methods

cultures are taught that uniqueness and nonconformity are valued; they tended to choose the pen that was different. In contrast, East Asians from collectivistic cultures are taught not to stand out from the group and to put group needs first; they tended to choose a pen that was like most of the others.

Another example of differences between cultures can be seen in Table 4.1, which highlights differences in family memory sharing (Wang, 2006, p. 185):

If you saw a pile of pens that were mostly the same but had one unique pen, would you choose the unique one?

Deep but subtle cultural differences showed up in a *field experiment*, a study that occurred in a natural environment instead of in a lab setting. It took place in the San Francisco airport where researchers offered European Americans or East Asians a gift choice from five free pens—four of which were of the same color, with the fifth being unique. Given this choice, would you pick the unique pen or one of the four matching pens?

The surprising thing was that people from the two cultural groups tended to make different choices that suggested individualistic or collectivistic assumptions about the self (Kim & Markus, 1999). Specifically, 74% of Euro-

■ **TABLE 4.1** Mother's Questions, Child's Answers (From Wang, 2006)

Euro-American mother (M) and child (C)	
M:	Tell me about the craft fair. Mommy and Daddy went to the craft fair. What did we go there for, do you remember?
C:	Yeah. Christmas time.
M:	It was Christmas time, we were getting some Christmas presents. Did you want to be there?
C:	No.

Chinese mother and child	
M:	What story did Teacher Lin tell you at school?
C:	"Qui Shao-yun." He didn't move even when his body was on fire.
M:	The teacher taught you to follow the rules, right?
C:	Um.

- *Spotlight on Research Methods* boxes give students the opportunity to sharpen skills needed to understand and evaluate social psychological science.

SOCIAL PSYCHOLOGY THROUGH APPLICATION

Heinzen and Goodfriend take a fresh approach by offering more variety in shorter, applied mini-chapters on topics including:

- Behavioral Economics

- Sustainable Environment

- Law and the Courtroom

- Stress and Health

- Positive Psychology, and more.

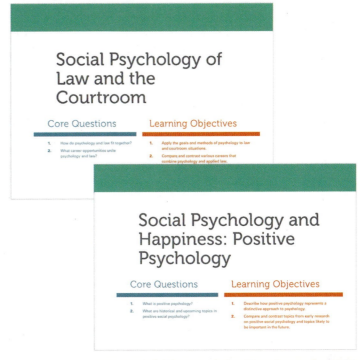

Social Psychology of Law and the Courtroom

Core Questions

1. How do psychology and law fit together?
2. What career opportunities unite psychology and law?

Learning Objectives

1. Apply the goals and methods of psychology to law and courtroom situations.
2. Compare and contrast various careers that combine psychology and applied law.

Social Psychology and Happiness: Positive Psychology

Core Questions

1. What is positive psychology?
2. What are historical and upcoming topics in positive social psychology?

Learning Objectives

1. Describe how positive psychology represents a distinctive approach to psychology.
2. Compare and contrast topics from early research on positive social psychology and topics likely to be important in the future.

- *Applying Social Psychology to Your Life* boxes allow students to take self-report measures of concepts (conformity, rejection sensitivity, belief in a justice world), making concepts more personally relevant.

PRAISE FOR HEINZEN & GOODFRIEND

Good science should tell a story. Heinzen and Goodfriend focus on social psychology as an ever evolving scientific field, emphasizing what questions we've asked and what we've learned as scientists strive to uncover the causes of and factors influencing human social behavior.

–**Jay L. Michaels**, *University of South Florida Sarasota–Manatee*

Provides a unique, modern approach to social psychology. In addition to the fundamentals, the Heinzen and Goodfriend text covers other, relevant to today, topics.

–**Darin Challacombe**, *Fort Hays State University*

This textbook takes a contemporary and conversational approach to social psychology while being able to satisfy a need in the market for social psychology textbooks. This includes greater emphasis on conversational discussions, practical application to the real world, emphasis on research methods, and popular culture references.

–**Amanda ElBassiouny**, *Spring Hill College*

Successfully interweaves theory and relevant applications regarding social psychology, with an emphasis on reflections/applications for the student.

–**Jeannine Stamatakis-Amess**, *Lincoln University*

Takes a modern, interactive approach to teaching Social Psychology. Packed with pop culture references and case studies, students are able to relate concepts to familiar and understandable preexisting structures. However, the emphasis on research methods keeps them thinking critically and cultivates their scientific literacy.

–**Miranda E. Bobrowski**, *University at Buffalo, SUNY*

SOCIAL PSYCHOLOGY

SOCIAL
PSYCHOLOGY

THOMAS HEINZEN
William Paterson University

WIND GOODFRIEND
Buena Vista University

Los Angeles | London | New Delhi
Singapore | Washington DC | Melbourne

FOR INFORMATION:

SAGE Publications, Inc.
2455 Teller Road
Thousand Oaks, California 91320
E-mail: order@sagepub.com

SAGE Publications Ltd.
1 Oliver's Yard
55 City Road
London EC1Y 1SP
United Kingdom

SAGE Publications India Pvt. Ltd.
B 1/I 1 Mohan Cooperative Industrial Area
Mathura Road, New Delhi 110 044
India

SAGE Publications Asia-Pacific Pte. Ltd.
3 Church Street
#10-04 Samsung Hub
Singapore 049483

Printed in Canada.

ISBN 978-1-5063-5751-5

Acquisitions Editor: Lara Parra
Development Editor: Marian Provenzano
Associate Editor: Lucy Berbeo
Editorial Assistant: Zachary Valladon
Production Editor: Olivia Weber-Stenis
Copy Editor: Gillian Dickens
Typesetter: C&M Digitals (P) Ltd.
Proofreader: Theresa Kay
Indexer: Judy Hunt
Cover Designer: Rose Storey
Marketing Manager: Katherine Hepburn

This book is printed on acid-free paper.

MIX
Paper from
responsible sources
FSC® C011825

17 18 19 20 21 10 9 8 7 6 5 4 3 2 1

BRIEF CONTENTS

DETAILED CONTENTS

PREFACE

If social psychology is a roller coaster and we are its passengers, then the recent pace of discovery justifies throwing our hands into the air and screaming. Since the 1930s, the percentage of articles published in PsycINFO (the largest database of psychological research) related to social psychology has quadrupled. This is an impressive growth pattern because when you are actually doing science, the pace of discovery feels more like a race between snails than a careening roller coaster. So why is social psychology growing so fast? Why all the excitement?

THE NUMBER of articles published in journals devoted to social psychology has quickly increased since the 1930s.

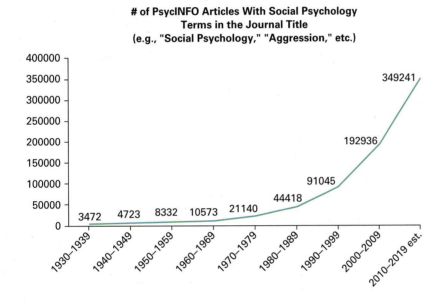

# of PsycINFO Articles With Social Psychology Terms in the Journal Title (e.g., "Social Psychology," "Aggression," etc.)

THREE SOCIAL FORCES

There are three social forces at work that explain the excitement behind what is happening in social psychology: numbers, psychological literacy, and a scientific mission.

Numbers. More than one million students in the United States are taking at least one course in psychology *every year*, and social psychology is among the most popular offerings. It's gone global. In China in the 1970s, there were only three or four departments of psychology; there are now approximately 250–300 (see Halpern, 2010). Social psychology's insights provide practical guidance. The head of a start-up software company finally understood the fundamental attribution error (a major concept within the field) when he said, "You mean . . . if an entire department is unproductive, then the problem might not be with them, but in the situation I created in that department?" Social psychology provides practical guidance to retail consumers and marketers, to trial lawyers and judges, to athletes and coaches, and to politicians and voters. We have a large and growing audience. We can't tell social psychology's distinctive story often enough or well enough. *Numbers = New Opportunities.*

Psychological Literacy. A new term is clarifying our mission as teachers: *psychological literacy* (Cranney & Dunn, 2011; McGovern et al., 2010). A free society requires intelligent citizenship; psychological literacy creates better citizens. We shouldn't be surprised. Everyone benefits from social psychological insights into conformity, aggression, attitudes, attraction, prejudice . . . and much more. A psychologically literate parent will (politely, we hope!) ask, "How do we know whether the D.A.R.E. program really reduces drug abuse . . . that an anger management class really reduces domestic violence . . . that boosting self-esteem solves specific social problems?" Psychological literacy helps citizens ask better questions of people in authority—and helps people in authority make better decisions. *Psychological Literacy = Better Citizenship.*

A Scientific Mission. We college and university teachers of social psychology are the front line soldiers in the ancient war between science and superstition. Science wins every time a student dares to publicly ask, "How do you know that?" But we teachers of social psychology wield unusual weapons in this war. Like Shakespeare, we employ both tragedy and comedy. The motivating tragedies behind scientific social psychology are both obvious (wars and mass murder) and small (stereotyping and prejudices). Social psychology's studies of tragedies are brightened by flashes of humor. (What else can you call a memory-related study about virginity pledgers titled *Reborn a Virgin*?) Social psychology has so many engaging sub-plots that we don't always recognize the beautiful arc to our own story, but here it is: *A Scientific Mission = A Triumph Over Superstition.*

OUR TEACHING APPROACH

Any textbook reflects, to some degree, how its authors tend to teach. Textbook writing is unlike classroom teaching, but there is some overlap. The approach in this textbook synthesizes what we regard as the best teaching and textbook writing we have absorbed from the scholarship of teaching and learning, the excellent practices we have observed in others, and the techniques we have developed based on our own experiences.

A Conversation. This textbook is closer to a conversation with an individual student than a lecture to a class. Every chapter begins with several core questions. Each major heading discusses the science-based answers—with candor when we are uncertain and with conviction when we can. A satisfying conversation also ends when its main points have been clearly understood. So, within each chapter we offer timely summaries of the main points used to answer each of the core questions. Intermittent summaries are a common courtesy extended by most textbook authors, supported by specific learning objectives. Our underlying purpose in these summaries is to give the conversation a chance to breathe, a pause that provides succinct answers to the current question—a natural way to say, "Okay. Got that. What's next?"

The Historical Twists and Turns of Science. When traditional textbooks get to revisions, the authors rightly point out all their updated references. We anticipate that this text, in comparison to others, will have many more references to studies taking place *before* 1950. There is a reason behind this historical sensitivity. We have tried to understand the arc of the stories within social psychology as they evolved into our current state of knowing. (Particular features of the PsychINFO database have made capturing the chronology easier than you might imagine.) So one subtle but distinctive feature of this text is capturing social psychology's story through the chronological twists and turns of its research. Of course, we also make sure to include cutting-edge advances in the field, based on this historical foundation.

Original Features. The potential value of capturing research as a story with a past is that it can usher an informed reader into the present. We want students to experience their present in a personal way, so we created features that would invite them deeper into the world of social psychology.

Feature 1. Applying Social Psychology to Your Life. Feature 1 is a collection of chapter-relevant measurement scales. They appear in every chapter and can provide students with personal self-knowledge. A professor can use these scales in several ways. They can certainly provide students with significant social self-knowledge. But they also can provide practical experience with the insights of statistical reasoning through within-class and between-class comparisons.

Feature 2. Spotlight on Research Methods. There are some experiments that seem to scream, "You can use me to teach about _____." It could be a clear example of why we need to control confounding variables or why ethical constraints require us to use a quasi-experiment. Every chapter features an in-depth discussion of some element of the research methods used in social psychology. The scientific method is not one thing; it is a toolbox of techniques. Consequently, repetition and training in each chapter help students get comfortable with using each of those tools.

Feature 3. Social Psychology in Popular Culture. Historical narratives can deliver students to their present experience. We introduce social psychology's understanding of the present by exploiting (and enjoying) popular culture. Superheroes like Wonder Woman and the relationships in the Harry Potter series engage students through a philosophy that game designers call "serious fun." Applying social psychology to popular culture demands more from professors and students, too, especially if the professor chooses to lead in-depth discussions. But students prefer difficult courses (if they are well designed) the same way that small children insist on walking up a slippery slide rather than using the stairs to slide down.

There's scant literature about how to write a textbook. Fortunately, there is a wealth of material about good writing. Two sources have been particularly helpful: *On Writing Well* by William Zinsser (1991) and the importance of storytelling in *Talks to Teachers on Psychology and to Students on Some of Life's Ideals* by William James (1899/1983). Although we are proud of what we have produced, we can do it much better next time—we just don't know how right now. But we know we will get better because reviewers will tell us how to get better. Good writing, like good science, grows through candid feedback. And for that, we have many more people to thank.

ACKNOWLEDGMENTS

To Lara, Lucy, Zach, Marian, David, Stephanie, Patrice, all the reviewers, SAGE, and the Amazing Randi.

SAGE Publishing wishes to thank the following reviewers:

Aaron J. Moss, Tulane University

Amanda ElBassiouny, Spring Hill College

Amy E. Sickel, Walden University

Beverly L. Stiles, Midwestern State University

Catherine A. Cottrell, New College of Florida

Corey Hunt, Grand Canyon University

Crystal M. Kreitler, Angelo State University

Daniel W. Barrett, Western Connecticut State University

Darin Challacombe, Fort Hays State University

David E. Oberleitner, University of Bridgeport

Emily A. Leskinen, Carthage College

Gregory D. Webster, University of Florida

James Cornwell, United States Military Academy

Jay L. Michaels, University of South Florida Sarasota-Manatee

John E. Myers, Northern Arizona University

Julee Poole, Kaplan University

Kristina Howansky, Rutgers University

Leah R. Warner, Ramapo College of New Jersey

Maya Aloni, Western Connecticut State University

Melissa Streeter, University of North Carolina Wilmington

Miranda E. Bobrowski, University at Buffalo, SUNY

Okori Uneke, Winston-Salem State University

Pamela Lemons, Salt Lake Community College

Patricia Schoenrade, William Jewell College

R. Shane Westfall, University of Nevada, Las Vegas

Rebekah A. Wanic, University of San Diego

Shayn Lloyd, Tallahassee Community College

Tammy Lowery Zacchilli, Saint Leo University

Wendy P. Heath, Rider University

Yvonne Wells, Suffolk University

SUPPLEMENTS

Original Video

Social Psychology is accompanied by a robust collection of **Ask the Experts** interviews that provide an insider's conversation with the elite experts of social psychology, as well as **Social Psychology in Action** clips, a series of animated videos carefully crafted to engage students with course content. All videos are accessible through the interactive eBook available to pair with the text.

For Instructors

SAGE edge is a robust online environment featuring an impressive array of free tools and resources. At **edge.sagepub.com/heinzen**, instructors using this book can access customizable PowerPoint slides, along with an extensive test bank built on Bloom's taxonomy that features multiple-choice, true/false, essay, and short answer questions for each chapter. The instructor's manual is mapped to learning objectives and features lecture notes, discussion questions, chapter exercises, class assignments, and more.

For Students

Multimedia Resources available at **edge.sagepub.com/heinzen** are designed to promote mastery of course material. **Visual Key Concepts** demonstrations provide an interactive look at social psychology's key terms and concepts to make them more memorable. Students are encouraged to access articles from award-winning SAGE journals, listen to podcasts, and watch open-access video resources. The text can also be paired with an **interactive eBook** that offers one-click access to these study tools and to the book's **Original Video** package for a seamless learning experience. Students can then practice with mobile-friendly **eFlashcards** and **eQuizzes** to find out what they've learned.

ABOUT THE AUTHORS

Thomas Heinzen is a full-time teacher/researcher at William Paterson University of New Jersey. He conducted evaluation research for the Rockefeller College of Public Affairs and Policy, consulted on preventing tractor roll-overs at the New York Center of Agricultural Health and Medicine in Cooperstown, New York, and conducted statistical analyses for a temporary commission on homeless veterans in New York State. He has invested in students' lives by mentoring more than 60 student articles and presentations, designing a novel internship program, and creating a lab testing game-based interventions to increase rates of college completion among at-risk students.

Wind Goodfriend has been teaching psychology at Buena Vista University, a Midwestern liberal arts school of 800 students, for twelve years. In that time, she has won the Faculty of the Year award three times and was named Assistant Dean of Graduate Programs. She also serves as the co-director of the trauma advocacy program and volunteers as the chief research officer for the Institute for the Prevention of Relationship Violence. Wind has written 13 book chapters on psychology in pop culture, covering topics including *Game of Thrones, Wonder Woman, Doctor Who, Star Trek*, and more. She has developed sixteen different courses including special topics classes such as Psychology of Colonialism, Psychology in Popular Film, and Relationship Violence. She received her B.A. from Buena Vista University and both her master's and Ph.D. in Social Psychology from Purdue University.

1 An Introduction to Social Psychology

Core Questions

1. What is social psychology?
2. What are the big questions within social psychology?
3. Is science a valid way to learn about complex social behavior?
4. How can social psychology make my life better now?

Learning Objectives

1.1 Explain what social psychology is and what social psychologists do.

1.2 Analyze important questions about social thought and behavior.

1.3 Describe how the science of social psychology provides insight into our behavior, as well as social benefits.

1.4 Apply social psychology concepts to your own life and experiences.

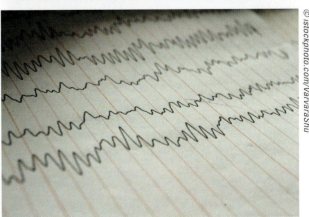

- A man on the street suddenly appears to have a seizure, but none of the people around you seem concerned. What would you do—stop to help or just keep walking?
- You and seven other people seated around a table are all looking at several lines on a board. A man asks each person in the group to identify which line is the longest, and you can tell immediately that it's the fourth line. However, the first person to answer says it's the second line—and so does everyone else. Your turn to answer is coming up. What would you do—say what you think is correct or go along with the group to avoid social embarrassment?
- After volunteering to help a research study on memory and learning, you're told that you have to give another volunteer higher levels of electric shocks each time he or she gets a question wrong—even if this person starts crying out that he or she has a heart condition. What would you do?

These scenes aren't from the popular reality television show, *What Would You Do?* on ABC. They are real experiments in social psychology. So . . . what do you think that *you* would do in each situation? If you are like most people, you probably answered, "I would help the man who collapsed even if no one else appeared concerned," "I would report the correct line despite everyone else," and "I would not administer painful electric shocks to an innocent person!" Your beliefs about yourself would probably be noble, flattering, self-esteem enhancing—and they might be wrong.

When these situations were presented to real people in controlled experiments, a high percentage did not help the man who had a seizure when other people were around (Darley & Latané, 1968). Many people did cave to peer pressure when reporting the length of the line (Asch, 1956).

Reuters/Claro Cortes

Shutterstock / Jacob Lund

© istockphoto.com/VarvaraShu

And a frightening number of people delivered what they believed were increasingly severe levels of painful electric shocks (Milgram, 1963, 1974). Would your behavior be different from theirs?

Get ready for an exciting ride of self-discovery as you enter the strange, fascinating, revealing—and perhaps familiar—world of social psychology.

WHAT IS SOCIAL PSYCHOLOGY?

LO 1.1: Explain what social psychology is and what social psychologists do.

When most people think about psychology, two images come to mind. The first and most common is probably people with mental illnesses or personal problems in a therapy setting, perhaps talking about their concerns while they recline on a couch. The second might be scientists in lab coats, watching mice run through mazes and timing how quickly they find a reward of cheese. Both images represent important chapters in psychology's story, but neither one is social psychology.

Defining Social Psychology

Social psychology is the scientific study of how people influence each other's thoughts, feelings, and behaviors. Social influence can be obvious; a robber with a gun clearly wants to influence you to hand over your money. But it can also be subtle; advertisers try to influence you with simple images or jingles that get stuck in your head. We can even be influenced by people who are not physically present; the memory of our parents' or friends' proud smiles and wishes for our future may change how we act in morally ambiguous situations. In addition, we are often influenced without even realizing it by our culture, national standards, social expectations, and our local community norms.

Social Thinking, Social Influence, and Social Behavior. Social psychology focuses on three main areas: social thinking, social influence, and social behavior. Each of these overlapping areas of study is displayed in Figure 1.1. The circles overlap because, in our everyday lives, these three forces blend together as they influence us. The first section of this book covers social thinking, including topics such as how we define the self and how we think about people in the world around us. The second section covers social influence and asks questions about conformity, prejudice, and persuasion. Third, chapters on social behavior discuss helping, aggression, and romantic relationships. This book thus explores each part individually and then reunites them in several mini-chapters on various applied psychology topics.

Social psychology is popular as both a college course and as a career path. But, it is still a young science compared to many other disciplines; it's only been around for about 100 years, give or take a few decades. The American Psychological Association has a separate division for social and personality psychology, and there are two separate professional organizations just for social psychologists (the Society for Personality and Social Psychology and the Society of Experimental Social Psychology). There are over 200 textbooks just on social psychology (including this one!), and 185 schools offered graduate degrees in social psychology at the time this book was published—and that's counting only programs in the United States!

Ask the Experts: Roy Baumeister on Free Will

©SAGE Publications

Social psychology: The scientific study of how people influence each other's thoughts, feelings, and behaviors.

■ FIGURE 1.1 There are three big areas of study within social psychology, and they combine to form concepts that apply to thoughts and decisions people make every day in their lives.

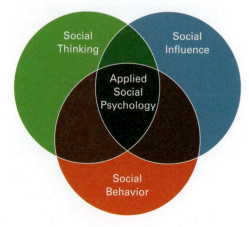

Social psychologists are active around the world, and collaborations across different cultures are becoming more frequent now that we can communicate and share data electronically. It is an exciting time to be engaged with social psychology, both personally and professionally. Who knows? By the end of this book, you may even want to become a social psychologist.

Similar, but Different, Fields That Study Human Social Behavior. Another way to understand the field of social psychology is to compare and contrast it with other academic disciplines that study human social relationships. For example, **sociology** also studies social behaviors but does so from a group level. Sociologists focus on how groups change over time, how cultures evolve, how stereotypes affect social norms, and so on. Social psychologists study the same concepts but measure their effects on individuals. While a sociologist might consider examples of how a particular subculture is geared toward cooperation or aggression, social psychology will measure how cooperative or aggressive each person is and attempt to investigate causes and outcomes on the individual level.

Another field that's similar is **anthropology**, which is the study of culture and human behavior over time. Anthropologists typically focus on one particular culture at a time and try to understand it by describing it in detail—that is why their research methods are typically observational. In contrast, social psychology's research methods again usually focus on individual behaviors and ideally make use of experimental methods (see Chapter 2 for more on research methods). Thus, an anthropologist might observe a particular village of children in terms of their aggressive behavior and consider how culture affects aggression. A social psychologist might form a hypothesis about what increases aggression and then attempt to manipulate aggression (temporarily and safely, of course) through experimental research designs.

Finally, even within psychology, there are divisions and subfields that focus on different aspects of human behavior. When most people think of psychology, they think of **clinical or counseling psychology**, which helps people who have mental illnesses or problematic thoughts and behaviors to be healthier. If mental illness and unhealthy patterns are considered "abnormal psychology," then social psychology is the focus on "normal" behaviors seen in everyone. Importantly, this means that social psychology focuses on negative, problematic behaviors such as aggression, discrimination, and so forth—but it also includes positive behaviors such as empathy, cooperation, creativity, positive self-esteem, systematic group decision making, and overcoming social obstacles. Throughout its history, social psychologists have consistently studied what is now called **positive psychology**, the scientific study of human strengths and virtues.

Sociology: The study of human society and social behavior at the group level.

Anthropology: The study of culture and human behavior over time.

Clinical or counseling psychology: A subfield of psychology that helps people who have maladaptive or problematic thoughts and behaviors.

Positive psychology: The scientific study of human strengths, virtues, positive emotions, and achievements.

How Social Psychology Was Born: A Brief History

If there's a birthplace for psychology, it's Germany and Austria. About 150 years ago, Wilhelm Wundt started the first scientific laboratory specifically designed to apply the scientific method to understanding human thought and experience. Due to this pioneering research, many now consider Wundt the informal "father of psychology." About 20 years later, Sigmund Freud was becoming famous in Vienna, Austria, for his controversial theories about how childhood experiences change adult personality and how our hidden thoughts come out in dreams.

Weltrundschau zu Reclams Universum 1902

Wilhelm Wundt (1832–1920), now largely considered the "father of psychology."

Both Wundt and Freud were asking questions about personality, individual perceptions of the world, and how culture affects thought. Over the next few decades, most Europeans who considered themselves psychologists were interested in explaining abnormal behavior (like Freud) or in basic thought processes like sensory perceptions or memory (like Wundt). Meanwhile, most psychologists in the United States studied nonhuman animals (usually pigeons and rats) because their behavior was easy to observe and measure. These "behaviorists" believed that this more scientific approach would be a better strategy for understanding human behavior than speculating about hidden, internal concepts such as the superego or collective unconscious or even more familiar concepts such as personality, prejudice, or persuasion. But World Wars I and II changed the trajectory of psychology forever.

Kurt Lewin: Social Psychology's Pioneer

If Wilhelm Wundt is the "father of psychology," then perhaps the "father of social psychology" is Kurt Lewin. Lewin was born in Poland and came from a conventional, Jewish, middle-class family that valued education (see Marrow, 1969). However, Lewin did not start out as a great student. Instead, he was an absent-minded, habitually late, mechanically inclined tinkerer who loved long, friendly conversations. He began to show some academic promise late in high school and first considered becoming a country doctor. But Lewin's interests wandered across many topics (which should be comforting to anyone reading this book who is struggling to find a career path). He was also a courageous college activist who organized students to teach working-class people—including women, which was controversial at the time—for free. Those were dangerous activities, especially for a Jewish student.

World War I arrived as a shock when it gave the world its first taste of industrialized warfare. That war started with lances carried by soldiers charging forward on horses and ended with long-distance snipers, terrifying tanks, planes dropping bombs, and the horror of poison gas spreading with the wind across a battlefield. Having completed most of his studies, Lewin joined the German army, where he became a trench soldier for 4 years. He was wounded and awarded the Iron Cross, but his brother died in that conflict. Germany lost the war. As the Nazis then rose to power in the buildup to World War II, Lewin sensed the growing danger and urged his mother to flee with him to America. She refused, confident that Germany would respect a mother who had lost one son and claimed a second as a wounded war hero. Sadly, she probably died in one of the concentration camps.

As a World War I soldier, Lewin had published his thoughts about what today we call "social perception." He observed that the land that many soldiers experienced as a terrifying battlefield was merely a pleasant nature scene to a civilian viewing it from a distance. Nothing had changed except the individual's perceptions. Lewin also pointed out that burning fine furniture made sense for a soldier trying to survive a bitterly cold night but it was a terrible, destructive deed in peacetime. One of social psychology's central insights is that the same behavior can have different meanings depending on the situation and the private viewpoint of the individual.

After the first war, Lewin became a teacher who inspired loyalty in colleagues and students in ways that would have astonished Wilhelm Wundt and Sigmund Freud. Lewin encouraged everyone to "express different (and differing) opinions [and] never imposed either discipline or loyalty on his students and colleagues" (Marrow, 1969, p. 27). Instead, Lewin won people's respect without trying to by listening carefully, honoring their perceptions,

Kurt Lewin (1890–1947), whom some consider the "father of social psychology."

and then connecting their ideas to his own intellectual enthusiasms. A simple conversation with Kurt Lewin could become a memorable experience. British psychologist Eric Trist described Lewin as having "a sense of musical delight in ideas." He also reported once having to push Lewin onto a moving train that he was about to miss because he was too distracted by their conversation (Marrow, 1969, p. 69).

The shadow of World War I and the growing cruelty of anti-Semitism in Europe propelled Lewin (and several influential colleagues) to immigrate to the United States. He became one of the first people to experimentally study how people's behavior changes based on their group environment. For example, Lewin asked young boys to work on group projects with adult leaders who exhibited three very different leadership styles: (1) democratic, where the leader provided a lot of structure but the boys were allowed to give input; (2) laissez-faire, where the leader was generally absent and provided no guidance at all; and (3) authoritarian or fascist, where the leader commanded the boys with orders and maintained tight control.

If those three comparison groups sound familiar, it is because Lewin was both personally and professionally interested in comparing the democratic leadership of the United States—Lewin's newly adopted home—to the fascist regime of Hitler. As Lewin hoped and hypothesized, when the boys worked under the democratic leader, they were the happiest and performed good-quality work—although they also were less efficient than the authoritarian-led group at finishing their work (Lewin, 1939).

$$\text{Lewin's equation: } B = f(P, E)$$

■ TABLE 1.1 Many Important Social Psychologists Have Been Women and/or People of Color

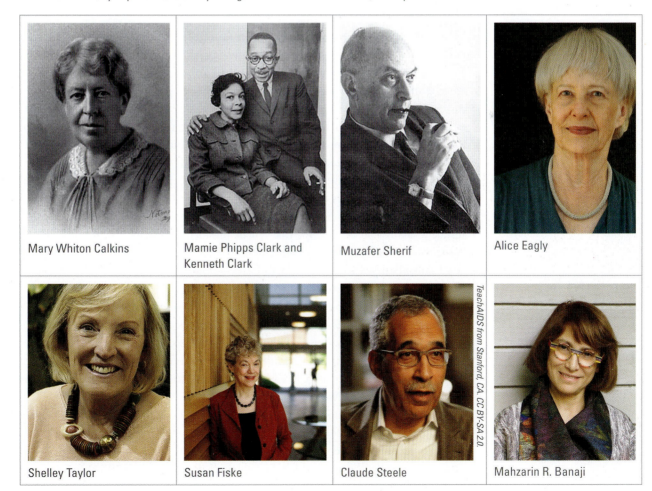

Mary Whiton Calkins

Mamie Phipps Clark and Kenneth Clark

Muzafer Sherif

Alice Eagly

Shelley Taylor

Susan Fiske

Claude Steele

Mahzarin R. Banaji

TeachAIDS from Stanford, CA. CC BY-SA 2.0

Behavior (B) is a function of both personality (P) and the environment (E). Social psychologists use these two criteria to predict behavior but usually start with "environment" and use "personality" to get even more specific.

Lewin unfortunately died in 1947, only a few years after the war ended. However, the effects of war on Lewin's pioneering work are reflected in the chapter contents of this and every other social psychology textbook: aggression, prejudice, persuasion, and prosocial behavior. Lewin's famous conclusion was that every person's behavior is based on "the state of the person and at the same time on the environment" (Lewin, 1936, p. 12). These two factors are your personality (P) and the demands of your current situation or environment (E). Lewin used scientific methods to apply those two factors to socially relevant topics—and he inspired many others to follow his lead.

Different Perspectives: Women and People of Color Join Social Psychology

Valuing diversity is important to social psychologists; it has to be. Half of the human race is female, so gender diversity is critical. There are approximately 200 countries in the world with unique identities and multiple subcultures. Social psychologists are compelled to study the influence of culture on individual thoughts, emotions, and behaviors. We feature entire chapters about prejudice, cooperation, persuasion, and so on. Psychology evolved out of particular cultural and historical contexts. Consequently, social psychology has had to put forth extra effort to advance diversity among the people in our research studies. What's the point of trying to learn something about human nature if the data apply to only a tiny sliver of humanity?

Diversity also means making sure that the researchers themselves come from a variety of backgrounds and perspectives. Robert Guthrie (1976/2004) examined psychology's history of diversity—or, sometimes, the lack of it—in a book (colorfully!) titled *Even the Rat Was White.* The positive effects of diversity can be highlighted by briefly considering some of the women and people of color who have had an important role in advancing theory and research in social psychology (see Table 1.1). Of course, many more examples could have been used to make this point; this list is just a few highlights.

Born during the American Civil War, Mary Whiton Calkins fought to study psychology at Harvard even though the school had a policy blocking women from enrolling. Despite several obstacles based on sexist policies at the time, she succeeded in achieving a prestigious career, including the publication of four books and over a hundred research papers. She focused on memory, the concept of the self, and social justice. Calkins later became the first female president of the American Psychological Association *and* of the American Philosophical Association.

Mamie Phipps Clark and Kenneth Clark were a married African American couple who became nationally known when their research led them to be expert witnesses in one of the cases related to *Brown v. Board of Education* (see Benjamin & Crouse, 2002). This was the Supreme Court case in the United States dealing with desegregation of public schools. The Clarks' research, known as "the doll studies," highlighted the problems of internalized racism and negative self-esteem in some children at the time (see Chapter 9 for more). Kenneth Clark became the first African American president of the American Psychological Association.

Perhaps the most famous study on prejudice was conducted by Muzafer Sherif, who was born in Turkey in 1906. Sherif's study brought young boys to a "summer camp" run by psychologists where they were led to form prejudices toward each other—and Sherif then studied how to reduce those prejudices (see Chapter 9). Alice Eagly has also devoted her research career to studying how to understand and reduce prejudice, with a particular focus on sexism (this theory is also covered in Chapter 9). Her model of sexism, called social role theory, continues to inspire research today and is used to understand several applied problems, such as how to get girls and women more involved in science, technology, and math careers.

Shelly Taylor and Susan Fiske together wrote the book *Social Cognition*. Social cognition is a subarea of social psychology in which researchers try to understand how individuals think about and remember other people and social situations. Their work resulted in the idea that most of us are "cognitive misers," meaning we only think as hard as we have to. For more about cognitive misers and social cognition in general, read Chapter 4.

Finally, both Claude Steele and Mahzarin Banaji are important social psychologists in the lines of research attempting to understand how culture and stereotypes affect people of color. Steele, an African American professor who served as the provost at the University of California, Berkeley, introduced the idea of stereotype threat. He wondered whether students of color were performing worse on some college-level tests because of stereotypes and anxiety. Banaji is interested in how stereotypes and prejudice might affect all of us without us even realizing it, and she helped to develop one of the most controversial tests to measure prejudice in the field of social psychology. You can learn more about both of these researchers and their ideas in Chapter 9.

The Main Ideas

- Social psychology is a subfield of psychology that scientifically studies how individual thought and behavior are influenced by the other people in our world.

- Social psychology can be broken up into topics focused on social thinking, social influence, and social behavior, and each topic has concepts that can be applied to everyday people in the real world.

- Kurt Lewin is considered by many to be the "father of social psychology," and he believed individual behaviors are determined by both someone's personality and by the social situation or environment.

- Many other important social psychologists have been women and/or people of color, including the Clarks, Sherif, Eagly, Taylor, Fiske, Steele, Banaji, and more.

⚡ CRITICAL THINKING CHALLENGE

- If World War II and the Holocaust had never happened, would psychology be where it is today? Would social psychology exist or be as popular if the world hadn't been inspired to understand the events leading up to and ending that war? What other topics might be considered more important?

- Lewin suggested that behavior is determined by both personality and the given social situation or environment. Which do you think is more influential? When you consider your own behavior across a variety of situations (such as in class, at a religious event, or when you're hanging out with friends), is your behavior fairly consistent due to a strong personality, or do you change how you act to better fit it with what's expected, given the environment?

- One of Lewin's most famous studies explored how members of groups change based on their leader. When you are the leader of a group, what kind of style do you tend to have? Do you think your leadership style affects the members of your group in a positive or negative way?

WHAT ARE THE BIG QUESTIONS WITHIN SOCIAL PSYCHOLOGY?

LO 1.2: Analyze important questions about social thought and behavior.

Social psychology's central mission is to understand how our thoughts, feelings, and actions are influenced by other people. To achieve its mission, social psychologists have focused attention on the big questions listed in Figure 1.2. It's important to know that the entire field cannot be encapsulated into *only* these questions—there are many other research topics not specifically covered here. But, thinking about these questions might help you see at least some of the major issues that have led to advances in theory and application.

Each of the questions in Figure 1.2 is somewhat subjective and philosophical—and social psychology's methods are designed to answer objective, specific questions. Social psychology probably can't answer these big questions directly. However, every day, we discover dozens of small answers. Sometimes you can only see these big questions by reading carefully between the lines of scientific reports, but make no mistake: Social psychologists are chasing down the answers. Keep these big questions in mind throughout this text because they serve a practical purpose: They help you understand what motivates many social psychologists and what we hope to accomplish.

■ FIGURE 1.2 Social psychology's big questions motivate researchers and provide a framework for understanding what social psychologists do.

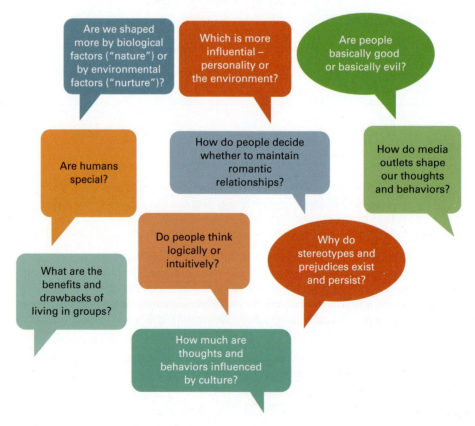

Big Question 1: Which Is More Influential—Personality or the Environment?

Kurt Lewin, the observant trench soldier with "a musical delight in ideas," created a simple intellectual framework that has endured for a century. Lewin's framework continues to help modern social psychologists design small experiments that answer this first big question. Lewin proposed that behavior (B) is a function (f) of both personality (P) and the situation or environment (E), leading to the equation $B = f(P, E)$. You can think of that equation as meaning that behavior is influenced by both personality and the environment . . . but is one more influential than the other?

First, think about the "P" in Lewin's equation. When you describe your own personality, what traits come to mind? Are you shy, agreeable, and cooperative? Or are you extraverted, argumentative, and competitive? Your personality can tell us how you are likely to act across many different situations. If you tend to talk a lot and enjoy attention, this pattern probably follows you in many areas of your life. But does your personality determine your behavior in every situation? No. A great deal of human behavior is governed by specific social expectations about the situation or environment. So, what about the "E" in Lewin's equation?

Even people who tend to be loud and energetic may become quiet and still in certain environments. For example, quiet and stillness are the social norm during many religious ceremonies—so noisy people will modify their behavior to that norm even if they don't belong or believe in that particular faith. On the other hand, someone attending a church, synagogue, or mosque with noisy, energetic worship is likely to be a bit more demonstrative in that setting. The same is true of your classroom behavior. A professor who only lectures will invite different standards of behavior than a professor who seeks discussion, disagreement, and active participation.

In real life, both "P" and "E" influence how you act most of the time, an interaction between variables. **Interactions**, or the combination of several influences on an outcome, are often the most exciting part of social psychology, and you'll see them in many places throughout this book. Social psychologists study how both "P" and "E" constantly interact to influence how any person is likely to think, feel, and act. This question will be addressed in several chapters in the book, including Chapters 3, 5, and 7.

Big Question 2: Are We Shaped More by Biological Factors ("Nature") or by Environmental Factors ("Nurture")?

A parallel question to "personality or the environment" is our second big question, which also asks about the origins of thought and behavior but in a slightly different way. One of the most pervasive debates within all of psychology—not just social psychology—is framed as the "nature versus nurture" debate. This question will be addressed in several chapters throughout the book.

Nature refers to influences on our thoughts and behaviors that come from biology or physiology, such as genetics, hormones, or brain differences among different types of people. These biological influences are largely out of our control. On the other hand, **nurture** refers to influences on our thoughts and behaviors that come from our life circumstances, how we were raised, experiences we've had, and our environment in general. The nature versus nurture question can be applied to personality, for example. If you are relatively extraverted, is that because you come from a long line of extraverted relatives and it genetically runs in your family? Or is it because as a child, you were rewarded for being extraverted by getting more positive attention from teachers and peers?

Interactions: The combination of several influences on an outcome, such as the influence of both personality and environment on behavior.

Nature: Influences on our thoughts and behaviors that come from biology or physiology, such as genetics, hormones, or brain differences.

Nurture: Influences on our thoughts and behaviors that come from our life circumstances, how we were raised, experiences we've had, and our environment in general.

Many psychologists will actually note that pitting "nature" and "nurture" against each other is what we call a **false dichotomy**, which means a situation presented as two opposing and mutually exclusive options when really there are other ways to think about what's going on. For example, most behaviors are probably influenced by *both* nature and nurture, and it's a question of degree of influence. In addition, sometimes the two "sides" of this debate influence each other. More physically attractive people may have been lucky to get a certain set of genes that make them beautiful—but their good looks probably also led to more social praise, popularity, and other opportunities; thus, both nature and nurture have influenced their fate.

Big Question 3: Are People Basically Good or Basically Evil?

For social psychologists, figuring out whether humans are basically good or evil is both a practical and a philosophical question. For example, imagine someone you don't know well discovers he left his wallet at home and asks you to borrow some money. Do you believe that this person tends to be good (and thus trustworthy about your money) or evil (and thus unlikely to ever repay you)? What you believe about yourself and others is an important social question. Without laws and social punishments for crime, would human society turn into an animalistic anarchy?

Exploring whether people are good or evil is a popular topic in literature and movies, such as the classic *Lord of the Flies* (Golding, 1954), in which a group of young boys on a deserted island become savage murderers. Good and evil were explored in almost the same way by social psychologists in a famous experiment. It was called the Robbers Cave study (Sherif, 1956), and it had just as much drama, tension, and uncertainty—and it also involved quickly escalating dynamics among a group of young boys in an isolated environment. Fortunately, some social psychological interventions transformed the boys' dangerous brush with evil and violence back into a pleasant summer camp experience before anyone got seriously hurt. But these innocent, well-raised young boys were stockpiling rocks in socks and preparing for a major conflict before the social psychologists stepped in (you'll read more about this study in Chapter 9).

The Robbers Cave study highlights how social psychologists use smaller, more manageable questions to study bigger questions about good, evil, and human nature. We study thoughts and behaviors that might predict "evil" acts such as harmful aggression and blind obedience to charismatic leaders. These topics are covered in Chapters 7 and 11. However, social psychologists also explore the sources of human goodness. For example, perhaps people are actually more civilized than the boys in *Lord of the Flies*. Even famously evil people are occasionally good, hopeful, and loving. We will explore this happier part of human nature in Chapter 10, where we discuss altruism and helping behaviors.

Big Question 4: How Do People Decide Whether to Maintain Romantic Relationships?

One of the most important parts of anyone's social encounters is probably their romantic relationships. Throughout middle school, high school, and college, many of us experiment with dating different kinds of people to see what seems like a good match.

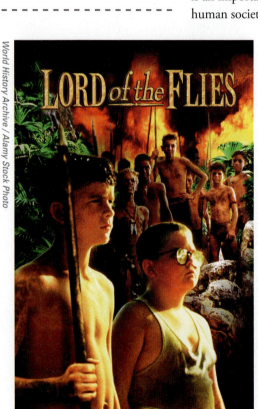

If the classic book *Lord of the Flies* is right, then humans are essentially savages, held back only by rules and laws of society.

False dichotomy: A situation presented as two opposing and mutually exclusive options when both options may work together, such as the role of nature and nurture in determining human behavior.

Even if we don't actually date others, most of us will certainly be attracted to some people more than others.

The scientific study of attraction, how we decide whom to date, and whether we want to commit to a particular relationship is a large area of focus within social psychology. Entire conferences occur across the world every year on just the study of relationships and sexual behaviors. You can read an entire chapter devoted to this subject in this book (see Chapter 12), where we'll cover variables that predict attraction and several theories regarding how relationship dynamics unfold once two people form a romantic relationship.

How do any two people decide whether they should stay in a committed romantic relationship?

Big Question 5: What Are the Benefits and Drawbacks of Living in Groups?

We are intensely social animals. It is so important that our most severe prison punishment (besides death) is sending someone to solitary confinement. The impulse to connect with others can be seen directly in public parks or restaurants, as people sit and laugh together, or indirectly through social media outlets as people connect electronically. Even people living in distant rural communities find ways to regularly connect with others.

We are social animals, and connecting with others consumes enormous amounts of time and energy. Why is group living so important to us? There are certainly huge advantages to forming groups. Other people validate us and help us understand our own sense of self through comparisons to each other, agreeing (or disagreeing) with us, and so on. Cooperating leads us to combine resources to help our survival. Working together also provides the opportunity to make better decisions due to the opportunity to use different people's skills.

Living and working in groups has benefits, but it also involves risks. For example, sometimes group members can reinforce individual opinions that can lead to risky or even foolish decisions. Groups get worse when a conspiracy of silence frightens the most thoughtful members of a group or when a leader makes followers reluctant to voice doubts. In addition, when people feel like they can hide in groups, they might display behaviors they wouldn't enact if they felt they could be tied back to them personally. They might also decide not to put in as much effort, coasting on the work of team members instead. Several chapters in this book discuss how groups affect both our good and our bad decisions and outcomes within a social world, and Chapter 8 focuses especially on group dynamics.

Computers now allow even isolated people to connect to each other.

Big Question 6: How Much Are Thoughts and Behaviors Influenced by Culture?

Can you identify ways that your values and sense of self are influenced by your own culture? Whether we notice it or not, being raised in certain cultures affects our view of the world and of other people in it. Some cultures value independence and competition, sending the message that people who work hard will be personally rewarded. Other cultures value cooperation and self-sacrifice, with social norms that ask individuals to put the needs of their group first.

Cultural norms and values are usually communicated in subtle, informal, and implicit ways. Parents, for example, will praise or punish their children for certain types of behaviors. Culture affects almost everyone; cultural differences in social patterns of thought or behavior will come up repeatedly throughout this book. You will see the influence of culture in chapters about personality, aggression, stereotypes and prejudice, group dynamics, and more. While not everyone in a culture will act exactly the same, people from some cultures may tend to display different behavioral patterns. Time and situations eventually reveal those cultural differences. Subcultures arise within cultures as you can probably see within different majors and social groups on campus. It would be a mistake to say that culture influences people in definite, predestined ways—but it would also be a mistake to deny the influence of culture at all. Cultural influence is such an important topic that it will come up many times throughout this book.

Big Question 7: Why Do Stereotypes and Prejudices Exist and Persist?

An extremely important question within social psychology is why stereotypes and prejudices exist in individuals. Theories that try to answer this question will be covered in Chapter 9. The theories allow us to ask more specific questions: Is it a basic human tendency to group and label people into different categories? If so, why? Do particular stereotypes pop up across different parts of the world and different cultures?

An equally important question is whether stereotypes and prejudices can be reduced or even eliminated. How can people who are racist, sexist, homophobic, and so on change their views of the world to be more respectful of all types of people? How can social psychology help? What motivates people to discriminate against each other—and what can be done about it? These questions have been asked for hundreds of years by philosophers, but the scientific methodologies used by social psychology now offer intriguing and exciting ideas for a more hopeful future.

Big Question 8: How Do Media Outlets Shape Our Thoughts and Behaviors?

Most of us are exposed to hundreds of media messages every day, through Facebook, Twitter, Instagram, television, advertisements, and so on. It's virtually impossible to escape exposure to these forms of media—and most of us don't even try because we enjoy the entertainment. But how are these media messages changing our thoughts and behaviors?

Again, many examples of exposure to media messages will be covered throughout this book. Research has examined whether watching violent television shows makes children more violent. Studies have investigated whether people who use Facebook more are happier or more secure with their friendships and life choices. And of course, how certain types of people are portrayed in the media can contribute to stereotypes. As much as media outlets can be fun distractions from the stress and pressures of daily life, they also might be influencing us in ways we don't realize—and in ways that we might not like to admit.

Big Question 9: Do People Think Logically or Intuitively?

The big question about how we think is also becoming clearer thanks to many small, easy-to-conduct experiments. How we think is another big yet practical question that plays out in our everyday decisions. Do you rely on logic and objective evidence, or do you trust your intuition? This is an important question for everyone, but especially relevant for traditional-aged college students facing several consequential life decisions about careers, personal values, and long-term relationships.

You can probably think of some decisions that seemed like a great idea at the time, but afterward you thought, "I should have known better." Are we motivated to be logical and correct, or do other motivations creep into our decision making? Those questions can be made small enough to put to scientific tests—and that's just what social psychologists have been doing for several decades. Chapter 4 focuses on social thinking, but findings on this question about logic versus intuition will keep popping up as explanations in later chapters as well. For example, the mini-chapter about "behavioral economics" explores real-life questions such as how people make decisions when money is tight but the risk/reward ratio is promising. In addition, Chapter 6 covers research regarding whether we are more likely to be persuaded by logical arguments or by intuitive, emotional attempts to pull at our heartstrings.

Big Question 10: Are Humans Special?

This is really a three-part question.

First, are humans "special" compared to one another? Social psychology answers this question with a "yes" in almost every experiment because it is rare that any two

participants in a study behave in exactly the same way. For example, when you read about the famous Stanford Prison experiment, notice that the trend was for guards to abuse prisoners. However, "personality types" emerged within the group of prisoners and the group of guards. One guard was mean and macho; another tried to help the prisoners. One prisoner was obedient and submissive; another played the role of the rebel. Identifying such individual differences—and there are many—is how social psychology affirms that each individual is special.

The second way of asking whether humans are special is by comparing humans in different cultures. The Center of Intercultural Competence identifies several cultural differences. For example, while the Inuits use at least 10 different words to describe snow, the Zulu employ 39 words to describe shades of green. Gestures also can have significantly different meanings. Using the thumb and forefinger to form an O means "Everything's okay" in Western Europe and the United States. But it means "now we can talk about money" in Japan—and it is an indecent sexual sign in Spain, Eastern Europe, and Russia. Social psychologists recognize human specialness at a cultural level.

The third way of asking whether humans are special is by comparing humans to other species. Social psychology does this through **comparative social psychology**, species-level comparisons of social behavior. Here, the story of human specialness turns in a different direction. Are humans special because they are social? Well, ants demonstrate sophisticated levels of role specialization and cooperation, and wolves employ strategy as they hunt in packs. Do humans hold a patent on goodness? Well, honeybees sacrifice their lives to save the hive; vampire bats will regurgitate precious blood meals for hungry roost mates—but only if they deem the recipient as deserving. What about self-awareness? Surely, that is something that only humans can experience—after all, does your dog think about what it means to be a dog and not a human? Well, not so fast. Dolphins, elephants, chimpanzees—and humans—have all scientifically demonstrated self-awareness. So no, the human animal is not always special in the ways that we like to think make us special. You'll read more about this in Chapter 3.

Yes, every person is unique but somehow similar to others. Yes, each culture is slightly different but similar in some ways to other cultures. No, humans are not unique as a social, caring, self-aware species. Of course, humans may be much better than other species at some of these things. But other species surpass humans by running faster, smelling better, and even mating more efficiently. If all this suggests that the social psychology of humans is a complicated business, then you're right. Unraveling the complicated interactions between people is what makes social psychology fun, fascinating, and difficult.

The Main Ideas

- One way to think about important topics in psychology is to consider the "big questions" asked by the field.

- This book provides evidence on both sides of these questions, but research is still needed to fully understand the complicated nature of human social experiences.

- Social psychology asks these questions because they are interesting from a philosophical or academic perspective but also because they actually affect people's everyday lives.

Comparative social psychology: Species-level comparisons of social behavior usually used to determine the uniqueness of human behavior.

- Go back to each of the "big questions" asked in this section. Think about times in your own life when you've thought or behaved in a way that seems to confirm one side of the debate or the other. Now, try to identify a time in your life that confirms the *other* side of the question. Do you think your behaviors in general provide support for answers to these questions? What about when you think of other people's behaviors?

- Many popular books and movies focus on utopias (perfect societies) or dystopias (malfunctioning societies). Examples of dystopias are *Lord of the Flies* (Golding, 1954), *The Hunger Games* (Collins, 2008), or *Divergent* (Roth, 2011). Why do people like this kind of story? Is it because it makes us feel good—our society is better by comparison—or because it serves as a warning, reminding us of what society could become?

- Which of the "big questions" posed here is the most interesting to you, personally, and why?

IS SCIENCE A VALID WAY TO LEARN ABOUT COMPLEX SOCIAL BEHAVIOR?

LO 1.3: Describe how the science of social psychology provides insight into our behavior, as well as social benefits.

You probably would have liked Kurt Lewin. He was known to miss an occasional class when, after the war, he was teaching at the University of Iowa. The reason? He was deeply involved in a conversation with students at a local café. Perhaps Lewin fit the stereotype of the absent-minded but passionate professor. His brain was full of a brilliant idea and all sorts of ways to make it work. His vision could be summed up in just two words: **action research**, the application of scientific principles to problem solving.

But is science—and experiments in particular—the best way to learn about social psychology? What about the social psychology of graffiti artists, the social commentary of thoughtful politicians, and the social insights from playwrights, movie producers, and film documentaries? Scientific social psychologists love those things! In fact, some of the high-level scientific conferences are occasionally spiced up with performances by social psychologists who perform in rock bands, read poetry, and make films. But science is special, just as those other ways of knowing are special. It's one of your jobs, as a college-educated citizen, to understand what is distinctive and valuable about each of those ways of knowing.

Throughout this book, we bring your attention to the use of the scientific method to answer questions in social psychology in two ways. First, when we talk about how answers were found using different research methods, you'll see a symbol in the margin that looks like gears. Second, each chapter has a feature that highlights one particular study in detail due to interesting or innovative research methodology.

Social Psychology in Action:
Marshmallow Study

©SAGE Publications

Experiments Can Isolate Causality

Experiments accomplish something better than any other research approach: They can isolate a *causal variable*. Experiments do that by using what you can think of as a tool-box of techniques that are all developed to help answer questions about cause-effect relationships. As an undergraduate student, you basically learn that the toolbox exists and you hopefully get to use a few of the tools on a real research project. As a graduate

Action research: The application of scientific principles to social problem solving in the real world.

student, you become an expert at using specific tools to solve specific research problems. You may even get to invent some new tools for new problems that come up.

You may be familiar with some of the research tools (and we will review them more thoroughly in the next chapter). One of the most popular (because it solves so many research problems) is called **random assignment to groups**. This tool isolates causal variables by making all groups in a particular experiment equal before any treatment or intervention takes place. It doesn't take long to use that tool, but you'll waste a lot of time if you don't use it. If it's true that each group in a study is equal to each other except for a *single* difference based on the experimental manipulation, then any differences in the outcome must have been caused by the manipulation. Again, we'll go through several examples of this setup in the next chapter.

Another tool is using *single-blind or double-blind experiments*. That research tool isolates causal variables by making sure that the experimenter does not accidentally bias the outcome of the experiment. In a **single-blind** procedure, the participants don't know which group they are in. In a **double-blind** procedure, neither the participants nor the researchers know which group the participants are in until after the study is done. That way, no one's expectations or hopes can influence the outcomes.

Isolating causality is a tricky business under the best circumstances. We need to use all the appropriate tools available if we really want to learn something about social psychology. As you read through the next chapter on research methods, think about the utility of each tool and technique, and try to think about how you might design your own experiment regarding a question that's important in your own life.

Proving Ourselves Wrong: The Falsification Principle

Weird, right? First, social psychologists come up with an explanation for something. It could be a hypothesis about which personalities are likely to fall in love, how prejudice is communicated, or when people will help one another in an emergency. And then, instead of trying to prove that their idea is a great idea, they immediately try to prove that it is a terrible idea.

Frederick M. Brown / Stringer / Getty Images

The Amazing Randi, a celebrity magician who tried to debunk psychic powers by asking people to prove them.

Random assignment to groups: A technique in which every participant in an experiment has equal probability of being assigned to each group. This means that extraneous variables are also likely to be evenly distributed.

Single-blind experiment: A tool used by psychologists to reduce bias where the participants do not know whether they are in the control group or the experimental group. This reduces the likelihood that hopes or expectations can influence outcomes.

Double-blind experiment: A tool used by psychologists to reduce bias where neither the participants nor the researchers know whether the participants are in the control group or the experimental group. This reduces the likelihood that hopes or expectations can influence outcomes.

Falsification: Testing whether a hypothesis can be disproved. A skeptical approach taken by psychologists used to determine the accuracy of an idea based upon eliminating all other possibilities.

Sir Karl Popper (1959) called this approach **falsification**, the ability to test whether a hypothesis can be disproved. Like a reality show, social psychologists are most likely to believe the last theory still standing after all the others have been proven wrong—not by judges sitting in chairs offering opinions but by open scientific methods that are known and reported to everyone, ideally without bias.

For example, for several decades, the magician called "The Amazing Randi" has offered a prize of one million dollars to anyone who can demonstrate psychic phenomena under controlled scientific conditions. His hypothesis is that there is no such thing as psychic powers. Can anyone prove him wrong? He has tested many applicants in a variety of public settings, and he still hasn't parted with his one million dollars. He is, in his own colorful way, using the falsification principle to test his hypothesis that psychic phenomena are bogus. It requires only one (!) demonstration by any real psychic to falsify his hypothesis and claim the prize.

Just one! So far, there is no evidence that such a person exists. There are three difficulties for all the "psychics" who have come forward. As a magician, the Amazing Randi knows (a) the tricks of the trade, (b) how easily people are distracted, and (c) that people enjoy deceiving themselves.

There's something wonderful about the falsification principle: healthy skepticism. We don't mean cynical assumptions that the whole world stinks. Healthy skepticism encourages you to think twice before following a link that promises you $10 million from a foreign prince in desperate circumstances if you will only send him a few hundred dollars to clear his paperwork. Healthy skepticism questions unlikely assertions such as, "I know we just met five minutes ago but I'm already in love with you and want to get married. Will you come up to my apartment so we can talk it over?" Falsification insists that such statements be tested before you even start to consider believing them. Like you, social psychologists believe in healthy skepticism.

Beyond Experiments: Other Methods and Analysis

Blame Kurt Lewin, if you must, but most social psychologists are trained as experimenters. His experiments, and those of his students, were so compelling that generations of social psychologists became more or less addicted to experiments. It's hard to describe how much fun experiments can be. But we'd like to give it a try because it happens every semester and in the most unlikely setting: statistics class.

Students come to their first statistics class nervous and worried and then, about two thirds of the way into the course, they become ridiculously excited. Why? Because they are just about to click on the last step in a computer program that will statistically analyze *their* data. Everything changes when you feel as if you *own* the idea that is being tested. You start to love statistics the way a custom carpenter comes to love a particular chisel or the way a tennis player loves the right racquet. You come to love the tools that allow you to be creative. One student looked at the data flashing on her screen and called out, "Professor! Come quick! You have to tell me if this means what I think it means!" It's a great moment to be a teacher and, having taught for enough years, Tom and Wind know how to set this moment up. We can predict it and watch for it like a midwife about to deliver a baby.

Experimental techniques are not the only tool we have. We will describe other methods frequently used by social psychologists in the next chapter. For now, you only need to understand that (a) case studies (single instances or examples) have often directed the path of psychological science, (b) archival research (data originally gathered for a different purpose) can tell us things that experiments will never reveal, (c) observational studies can reveal behaviors in their natural environments, and (d) surveys can help us by asking people for their personal and hidden views. In addition, sometimes ethical concerns prohibit us from conducting true experiments.

Doing social psychology is much more fun than reading about it, and your professor can help you experience it. Having fun as a researcher is relatively easy; however, the joy of true discovery can be fairly rare. It involves a coming-together of knowledge created by multiple experiments, case studies, archival data, and any other sources of information. Like a well-designed computer game, there are levels of achievement within the science of social psychology. Only a few scientists get to enjoy an epic win; for the rest of us, it's enough that we are able to admire them and write about them in textbooks.

The Main Ideas

- Experiments are the preferred scientific methodology for studies because they can isolate causal variables.

- An important aspect of good research ideas is falsification, the ability to test whether a hypothesis can be disproved.

- Experiments are just one of the many ways that social psychologists use the scientific method to analyze data; other methods are surveys, case studies, archival data, and more (see the next chapter for details).

⚡ CRITICAL THINKING CHALLENGE

- Do you have any friends or family members who claim to have psychic powers—or have you suspected that you have them yourself? What is a scientific way to test whether they are really present?

- Politicians debate the value of spending millions of tax dollars on funding research within social psychology. What is your view on this issue? Is funding research in social psychology worthwhile? Should tax dollars and government resources be increased, or decreased, and why?

HOW CAN SOCIAL PSYCHOLOGY MAKE MY LIFE BETTER NOW?

LO 1.4: Apply social psychology concepts to your own life and experiences.

As the story about statistics demonstrates, any topic becomes more interesting if you can see how it applies to you, personally. Being able to relate to theoretical ideas also makes them easier to remember later (Craik & Lockhart, 1972), something that will come in handy when you have to take exams in this class. For example, at the beginning of this chapter, we asked you to consider several situations that came from famous psychological studies and to consider what *you* would have done if you had been a participant or encountered that situation in your regular life. Below are some more specific suggestions about how to approach social psychology.

Apply Each Topic to Your Own Life

Take a quick look at this book's table of contents. Are there some chapters that seem more exciting to you than others? That may be because you can already see places where social psychology applies to your own life. Most of us are very interested in romantic attraction and dating partners, for example; Chapter 12 covers a wide variety of theories and scientific studies on this topic. Unfortunately, most of us have also been the victim—or the perpetrator—of stereotypes and prejudice, the focus of Chapter 9. This might be based on race, gender, or sexual orientation, but it could also be based on your family's last name, your hometown, what kinds of activities you enjoyed in school (e.g., "jocks" versus "band geeks"), and a wide variety of other concepts that humans have decided are meaningful.

As we go through each chapter, we suggest you make it a habit to apply the theories and concepts to yourself or to other people in your life. For example, what is *your* hypothesis about why so many high school students in different settings separate themselves into the same sorts of groups? How would you test your hypothesis? Can you see variables or circumstances that might affect what happens in social situations that haven't been previously considered? If so, perhaps you have a future in social psychology.

Use the Self-Report Scales to Compare Yourself to Others

Many of the studies in this book used self-report scales that we provide (at least one in each chapter, starting in Chapter 2). We hope you will jot down the numbers that represent you. Reading and thinking about the actual items within a scale will add to your understanding of the underlying concept. In Chapter 3, for example, you will see one of the most popular scales in all of social psychology, a measure of self-esteem. Really understanding what "self-esteem" is comes from a close examination of the subcomponents of the larger concept, such as being aware of your good qualities and feeling equal to other people.

However, maybe a more exciting reason to offer you these scales is so that you can actually fill them out and score them for yourself. By actually taking the scale, you can think about how participants felt when they were in the studies that created and used the scales. You can also see where you fall on the measure. (Do you have a high score? A low score? How do you compare with your classmates and with people at other colleges?) This all contributes to self-knowledge. In this way, after reading this book, you'll not only gain insight into the world of social psychology on a theoretical level but also gain insight into yourself, on a very practical and personal level.

Critically Analyze Your Opinions After Each Section

Finally, each section of every chapter in the book presents several critical thinking questions. **Critical thinking** is the ability to analyze, apply, and explore ideas in new and open-minded ways. Critically analyzing what you learn will also help you to remember it (Craik & Lockhart, 1972). But again, remember that social psychology progresses through the scientific method, which requires skeptical questioning of what we think we observe and know. Only by having the next generation of thinkers see new hypotheses and new applications can the field improve with a greater understanding of the human social experience.

Albert Einstein, one of the world's most important intellectuals and scientists, is famous for the quotation shown in the caption above. We hope this book allows you to comprehend a little more of the mystery of our social world.

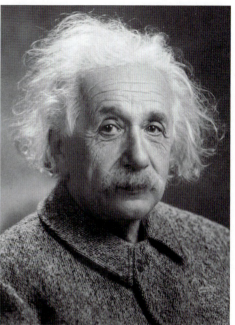

Albert Einstein (1955) said, "The important thing is not to stop questioning. Curiosity has its own reason for existing. One cannot help but be in awe when he contemplates the mysteries of eternity, of life, of the marvelous structure of reality. It is enough if one tries merely to comprehend a little of this mystery every day."

The Main Ideas

- Being able to personally relate to theoretical ideas and to critically analyze them also makes them easier to remember later.

- This book offers several opportunities for readers to apply concepts to themselves, including self-report scales to measure certain topics.

- Social psychology can only progress when new thinkers approach topics with scientific thinking and friendly skepticism.

Critical thinking: The ability to analyze, apply, and explore ideas in new and open-minded ways.

⚡ CRITICAL THINKING CHALLENGE

- Social psychology claims to provide insight into important topics that apply to real people's lives. However, most findings in the field are published in academic journals that only other scientists read. How can social psychologists do a better job of sharing their research with everyday people or with people or organizations that could use the research findings to actually improve the world?

- The beginning of this book discussed a reality show called *What Would You Do?* in which people are put into situations that are manipulated and then recorded without their knowledge to appear later on TV. What are the ethical implications of this type of program? Once people learn that they were essentially "tricked," do you think they can learn from the experience? Do you think that participants in social psychology research studies can do the same thing—learn from the experience?

- Again, look over the table of contents of this book. Do you think there are important topics that are missing? Are there aspects of the social experience that you think social psychology needs to address or spend more time studying?

CHAPTER SUMMARY

What is social psychology?

Social psychology is the scientific study of how people influence each other's thoughts, feelings, and behaviors. It includes the study of (1) social thinking, such as how we define the "self" and how we perceive the world; (2) social influence, such as how we can persuade other people, why we conform, and the dynamics of stereotypes and prejudice; and (3) social behavior, such as helping, aggression, and romantic relationships. All of these areas of social psychology can be applied to a variety of settings.

Social psychology can also be understood by comparing it to similar but different academic fields. Sociology is also the study of social behaviors, but it focuses on analysis of entire groups instead of on individuals within groups (which is how social psychology approaches research). Anthropology is the study of human cultures. Most anthropologists will study a particular culture in depth by observing it in detail; in contrast, social psychologists will study individuals in different cultures using alternative research methods such as experiments or surveys. Finally, while clinical and/or counseling psychology focus on helping people with mental illnesses or who are having unhealthy thoughts and behaviors, social psychology studies "everyday" thoughts and behaviors throughout life, including both negative behaviors (such as discrimination or aggression) and positive behaviors (such as helping or cooperation).

The field of social psychology was pioneered by Kurt Lewin, whom many people consider the "father of social psychology." Lewin was a Jewish man greatly influenced by both World Wars I and II, and when he immigrated to the United States, he devoted his academic career to understanding social dynamics. Lewin famously suggested that each person's social behaviors are influenced by both personality and the social environment. Many other influential social psychologists followed in his footsteps. Some of these later social psychologists were women and/or people of color, which highlights the importance of diversity of perspective in the field.

What are the big questions within social psychology?

The field of social psychology is highly varied, and many important questions cannot be distilled into simple questions. However, by considering the "big questions" listed here, students of social psychology can see several of the major themes or ideas that are studied and can have insight into the motivations or goals that many researchers have. These questions are simplified versions of complicated ideas and do not encompass the entire field. In addition, no research study can find a single or simple answer to these questions, but each study helps us understand one more piece of the puzzle. Ten important "big questions" in social psychology are the following:

1. Which is more influential—personality or the environment?

2. Are we shaped more by biological factors ("nature") or by environmental factors ("nurture")?

3. Are people basically good or basically evil?

4. How do people decide whether to maintain romantic relationships?

5. What are the benefits and drawbacks of living in groups?

6. How much are thoughts and behaviors influenced by culture?

7. Why do stereotypes and prejudices exist and persist?

8. How do media outlets shape our thoughts and behaviors?

9. Do people think logically or intuitively?

10. Are humans special?

Is science a valid way to learn about complex social behavior?

Social psychology uses the scientific method to answer the questions (and more) listed here. More details about scientific procedures and statistical analysis are found in the next chapter. Action research is the application of scientific principles to social problem solving, which many social psychologists attempt to do.

Many social psychologists believe that the best way to investigate questions scientifically is to use true experiments because they can isolate causal variables. In other words, experiments are the only scientific methodology that allows us to make claims about cause and effect. To have a true experiment, people in a study must be assigned to various conditions or groups by random assignment, meaning that any given person has an equal chance of being put into any of the study's groups. Ideally, the participants are not aware of which group they are in, just in case this knowledge would affect their thoughts or behaviors. Not knowing which group you're in is called being in a "single-blind" experiment. If the researcher is also unaware of group assignment until after the study is done, it's called a "double-blind" experiment.

Scientific approaches are also guided by the falsification principle, which is the idea that good theories must be able to be proven wrong. If a hypothesis or theory cannot be disproved using scientific approaches, it cannot be considered particularly useful. That said, there are other procedures beyond experiments to test ideas, such as observing people in their natural environment, examining single people or instances in depth (called case studies), or giving people self-report surveys in which they answer questions about themselves. Each approach has advantages and disadvantages, which are discussed more in the next chapter.

How can social psychology make my life better now?

Each topic in this book is important because it is relevant to thousands, if not millions, of people. Many topics could apply to your own life, and thinking about how each idea is relevant to you can help this book be more interesting and more memorable. To help, each chapter has a "feature" called Applying Social Psychology to Your Life. Here, you can fill out a survey that measures where you fall on one of the variables discussed in that chapter. If you are honest on these surveys, it will help you gain insight into how the topics discussed might affect your choices and actions.

In addition, each section of every chapter ends with critical thinking questions. Instead of skipping these questions, we encourage you to take at least a few minutes to consider them as you read. Evaluate your opinion of different theories. Think about how a new study might test some of the ideas. Analyze whether the theory is missing an important piece of information that should be added so that the field of social psychology could gain even more insight into how people think, feel, and act in a social world. Perhaps you are the next famous social psychologist who will be included in books like this one.

CRITICAL THINKING, ANALYSIS, AND APPLICATION

- As we learn more and more about social psychology, will the field continue to grow in numbers, or will people stop studying it once we have more answers? Do you think spending your life as a social psychologist would be a worthwhile endeavor, or are there more important ways to spend your career?

- Consider the 10 "big questions" covered in this chapter and put them in order of importance. Which would you say is the most essential and urgent question that social psychologists should be studying, and which is less important? Justify your order of importance with historical or personal evidence.

- Do you think that every academic discipline, job, and career benefit from having diverse kinds of people involved? What are some of the advantages of providing opportunities for traditionally minority or marginalized people in any job or field of study?

- What aspects of your own social world do you think would benefit from further analysis by social psychologists? Which chapters of this book sound like the most interesting or intriguing? Which topics are you most excited to study?

PERSONAL REFLECTIONS

As a little girl, I had no friends at all. I was strange. Other children didn't understand me, and I didn't understand them. Why did people lie? Why did some TV and movies portray certain races positively and others negatively? Why did some of the kids have boyfriends or girlfriends and others didn't? Why did some of the kids bully me while others simply ignored me? Even as a young child, I started to study human interactions in an attempt to understand people's perceptions and behaviors. It wasn't until high school when I realized that there was an entire field of science dedicated to answering these questions: psychology. And psychology wasn't just about mental health and therapy—it was also about prejudice, conformity, helping, and so much more. Social psychology really *mattered* to me, which is why I knew I wanted to spend the rest of my life understanding it. And, by the way, I now have lots of friends, a life partner, and a career that's more fun than it is work. All thanks to social psychology. [WG]

I dropped out of college when I was a first-year student in Wisconsin and didn't make it back until I restarted my first year at the age of 29. It was strange and sometimes embarrassing to be so much older than all of the students and even some of my professors at the community college in rural Illinois. But I decided that when I didn't know the meaning of a word or understand a concept, I would raise my hand and ask. At first, I asked some questions that probably made me look pretty stupid, but I no longer cared about that. Instead, I discovered that it didn't take very long until I started asking much better questions and that professors liked discussing the material with me. That was exciting. I shifted my major from business to psychology when I moved to a 4-year college. To my complete surprise, there were two courses that helped me understand the arc of my own life, the lives of those around me, and how to make sense of the larger world: statistics and social psychology. [TH]

PRACTICE AND APPLY WHAT YOU'VE LEARNED

▶ **edge.sagepub.com/heinzen**

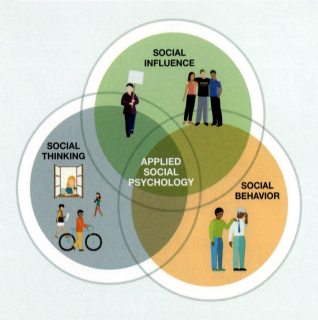

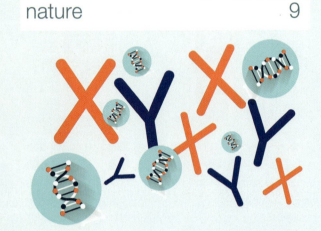

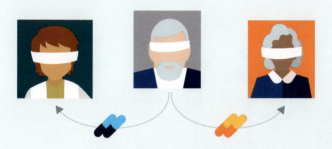

2 Research Methods

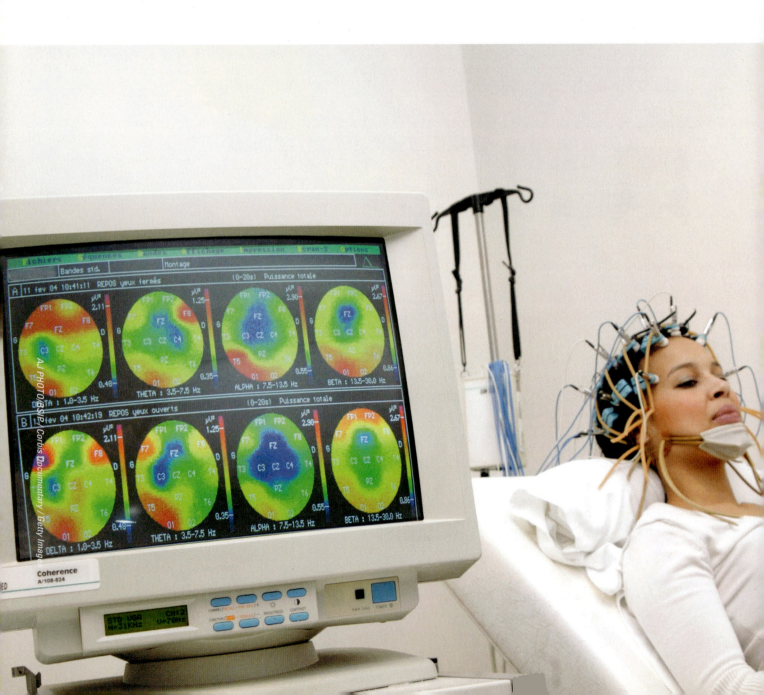

Core Questions

1. What are the elements of the scientific method?

2. How do social psychologists design studies?

3. How do social psychologists analyze their results?

4. How can research be analyzed in terms of quality?

Learning Objectives

2.1 Describe how the scientific method creates knowledge.

2.2 Compare the logic behind preexperiments, true experiments, quasi-experiments, and correlational designs.

2.3 Summarize the most common ways to analyze and interpret data.

2.4 Describe reliability, validity, replication, and ethical standards for research in social psychology.

Like all sciences, social psychology usually moves like snail: steady but slow. It is slow, in part, because what social psychologists study is usually invisible—and therefore difficult to measure. For example, prejudice, persuasion, altruism, and romantic love are all scientific constructs, theoretical ideas that cannot be directly observed. Although the scientific process is slow, social psychology is growing fast. It is growing fast because so many students are attracted to Kurt Lewin's vision of an applied science.

Perhaps social psychology's popularity explains why so many passengers were carrying long plastic or cardboard tubes on a recent plane ride. The plane was full of people presenting at a conference sponsored by the Society for Personality and Social Psychology (SPSP), which happens at the end of every winter. The tubes contained rolled-up posters summarizing the most cutting-edge research in the field. This chapter describes how the professional scientists, graduate students, and even a few undergraduates created those studies—and it invites you to join us.

how to think scientifically

Ask the Experts: Keon West on Research Methods in Psychology

©SAGE Publications

WHAT ARE THE ELEMENTS OF THE SCIENTIFIC METHOD?

LO 2.1: Describe how the scientific method creates knowledge.

Social psychologists tend to describe themselves as belonging to one of two groups. **Basic researchers** increase our understanding by creating and improving the theories that predict social behavior. **Applied researchers** translate those theories into social action. Applied research is where theory confronts reality—but with the understanding that reality always wins. If a theory does not describe reality, then the theory has to change. Basic research is important because, as social psychology's pioneer Kurt Lewin famously said, "There is nothing so practical as a good theory" (Lewin, 1951, p. 169). Applied research has to have a theoretical foundation—and a "good" theory has to describe and explain the real world. How does this balance play out in actual scientific research?

The Cycle of Science: The Scientific Method

Most of the research stories on those conference posters followed the same, easy-to-follow formula. The **scientific method** is a systematic way of creating knowledge by observing, forming a hypothesis, testing a hypothesis, and interpreting the results. Your results lead you to generate a new hypothesis that starts the process all over again. As you can see in Figure 2.1, it cycles endlessly through the same steps (or phases) and demands

Basic researchers:
Psychologists who increase our understanding of psychology by creating and improving the theories that predict social behavior.

Applied researchers:
Psychologists who translate the findings of basic researchers into social action and apply psychological ideas to the real world.

Scientific method:
A systematic way of creating knowledge by observing, forming a hypothesis, testing a hypothesis, and interpreting the results. The scientific method helps psychologists conduct experiments and formulate theories in a logical and objective manner.

■ FIGURE 2.1 In the scientific method, scientists observe the world and notice patterns, then formulate a hypothesis. Next, they create a procedure to scientifically test their hypothesis. After interpreting the results, the process begins again as the hypotheses become more refined or complicated or as they are applied to a wider variety of settings or people.

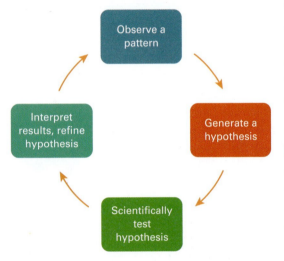

a willingness to change your mind if the data surprise you. Even though properly following the scientific method is sometimes a challenge, the rewards of exploring the fascinating topics within social psychology make it all worthwhile.

There are four phases in the scientific method:

Phase 1: Observe a pattern of behavior. Imagine that you are in a coffee shop quietly observing other customers. You notice that men frequently interrupt people during conversations—and that seems to be especially true when their conversation partner is a woman. Welcome aboard; you've started the scientific journey. Your simple observation got you started as your curiosity prompted you to ask, Is this a pattern? (By the way, this exact observation was tested in coffee shops and drug stores back in 1975 by Zimmerman and West.) Phase 1 of the scientific method occurs when we observe a reliable pattern of behavior.

Phase 2: Generate a hypothesis. After you identify what looks like a pattern, you move on to Phase 2 by generating a formal **hypothesis**, or a specific statement of what you believe will happen in an experiment that tests your observation. Perhaps your hypothesis is that men are more willing to interrupt others than women are, especially in cross-sex interactions. In other words, you expect that (1) men interrupt more than women in general, and (2) men interrupt women more than they interrupt other men. Hypotheses are never stated as questions (such as, "Who interrupts more, men or women?"). As we discussed in Chapter 1, hypotheses are always falsifiable statements that can be proved wrong.

Consider the following hypotheses: (1) Every man on Earth has interrupted someone else at least once, and (2) men have always been more likely to interrupt than women, in every culture throughout history. Neither of these hypotheses stands up to the "falsifiability" rule because they can't be tested and proved wrong. The first hypothesis is untestable because it simply can't be done. Even a crack team of well-funded researchers couldn't locate every single man on the face of the planet and then observe him in an objective social setting. The second hypothesis also can't be falsified because there is no archive of historical records that enables us to ask the question about every historical period for the past thousands of years.

Phase 3: Test the hypothesis. Now that we have a hypothesis, we set up a specific methodology or procedure to test it. For our current example, we might observe people in public places (like the coffee shop) in a more structured way, such as by making a spreadsheet of all the men and women and making tallies for each time someone interrupts. We might also ask people to come to a classroom or lab on a college campus and set them up in groups with a certain number of men and women and then observe who interrupts whom.

Either way, we can gather real, measurable data that will support our hypothesis, allowing us to modify it and move to the next step, or data that cause us to throw it out. We have to be careful, of course, not to ruin our own experiment by staring as we eavesdrop on some innocent couple drinking coffee (later we will discuss this issue in more depth, as well as ethics in research).

Phase 4: Interpret the results and refine your hypothesis. Notice that the final stage of interpreting results is not the end of the road. Once we have our data, we aren't done with science—in fact, we've only just begun! The scientific method cycles back so that we can explore our topic in more complicated and refined ways. Perhaps we

Hypothesis: A specific statement made by a researcher before conducting a study about the expected outcome of the study based on prior observation. Hypotheses are falsifiable statements that researchers believe to be true (see *falsification*).

found support for the basic idea that, overall, men are indeed more likely than women to interrupt someone. However, this general pattern probably varies greatly based on the people involved and the circumstances. In other words, our results have become a new hypothesis that requires us to begin again. Consider the following possible new hypotheses as examples:

- Women with more assertive personalities are more likely to interrupt others, compared to women with less assertive personalities.
- Men are less likely to interrupt women they find physically attractive, compared to women they don't find attractive.
- Men interrupt others more in friendly or informal settings, compared to formal settings such as at work.
- Men from cultures with more traditional gender roles are more likely to interrupt women than are men from more egalitarian cultures.

Can you see why the scientific approach is a constantly unfolding story? That story can only move forward if we remain as objective as possible when forming hypotheses and interpreting results. An individual research study, like the posters at a research conference, is a very small piece of a very big puzzle. But every step we take brings us a tiny bit closer to understanding the complicated world of social interaction.

Constructs: Theoretical ideas that cannot be directly observed, such as attitudes, personality, attraction, or how we think.

Operationalize: The process of specifying how a construct will be defined and measured.

Creating and Measuring Constructs

Many of the things social psychologists are interested in are abstract ideas or **constructs**, theoretical ideas that cannot be directly observed; examples are attitudes, personality, attraction, or how we think. Those measurement challenges—and the passion to conduct meaningful social research—are what has made social psychologists so creative in designing studies.

Because constructs are abstract and sometimes relatively broad ideas, the first step in using them in research is to **operationalize** your variables by specifying how they will be defined and measured. The process is called operationalizing because you must describe the specific operations you will perform to measure each of the variables in your study. If a researcher wanted to investigate the construct of "love," for example, she could operationalize it in a wide variety of ways such as (1) scores on a survey asking people to rate how much they love someone on a scale of 1 to 10; (2) how long they have maintained a committed, monogamous relationship; or even (3) how much their heart rate increases and their pupils dilate when the other person comes into the room.

Once we've operationalized the variables in our hypothesis, we have to decide how to proceed. Here are common methodologies that you'll see in several of the studies featured in this book. It's not a complete list of every possible study design, but it will give you a good idea of how social psychologists do business.

Sisyphus by Titian, 1549

The myth of Sisyphus says that he's constantly trying to roll a heavy boulder uphill. The scientific method can sometimes feel like an uphill battle—but progress requires constant small steps. The top of the scientific mountain may not even exist, but moving up remains satisfying.

Types of Research

Once you've noticed a pattern and generated a hypothesis, there are a lot of different ways you can set up a scientific methodology or procedure to test that hypothesis. This book isn't about research methods, so we'll just cover a few of your options here—these are the most popular methods you'll see throughout the rest of the book and in the field of social psychology. Four options are (1) archival studies, (2) naturalistic observation, (3) surveys, and (4) experiments. We'll cover the first three methods here, and experiments will be discussed in depth in the next section.

Archival Studies. One of the sources of information available to social psychologists requires (almost) no work because the data already exist. **Archival data** are stored information that was originally created for some other purpose not related to research. Newspapers, census data, Facebook posts, and even pop culture are all examples of archival data.

Archival data are being collected every day in every community, and it's up to social scientists to think about hypotheses that might be tested. For example, researchers interested in patterns within domestic violence can look at police records to test hypotheses about whether different types of people report this crime, whether couples who report once are more likely to report again, whether demographic variables such as socioeconomic status or certain neighborhoods have higher or lower rates of violence, and so on.

Naturalistic Observation. Another approach is **naturalistic observation**, or scientific surveillance of people in their natural environments. By "natural," we don't mean in a cornfield or a forest—we mean people doing the behavior of interest where it normally would occur. Observing people in a coffee shop is a good example. If we were interested in whether teachers are nicer to physically attractive children, then we might go to an elementary school to observe classes. If we were interested in leadership styles, we might go to a large corporate office and observe how workers react to different types of managers. Either way, we're simply observing behavior in its natural setting.

You might be thinking, "If some scientist came to my workplace and followed me around, writing down everything I do, then I probably wouldn't react very naturally." If that thought occurred to you, then congratulations—you are thinking like a good scientist. The presence of the researcher is one of the biggest challenges for naturalistic observations. When people change their behavior simply because they're being observed, it's called **reactivity**. But social psychologists are clever people. How do you think they get around this problem?

One creative solution is a technique called **participant observation**, in which scientists disguise themselves as people who belong in that environment. It's kind of like going undercover. You pretend you're not doing research at all and hope to fade into the background—and still find some discreet way to record your observations. For example, when observing schoolchildren, we might pretend to be substitute teachers. If we want to observe people at work, we might pretend to be interns at the company. One set of researchers wanted to photograph boys enjoying themselves at a summer camp (that was secretly run by psychologists). So, one of the camp counselors played the role of a "shutter bug"—someone who is taking pictures all the time. The boys quickly learned to ignore the shutter bug, and the researchers came away with some beautiful, authentic photographs (see the Sherif study described in Chapter 9).

Participant observation may create some ethical problems, so be careful. After all, you are deceiving people about why you are there. And it may be an ethical violation to observe people when they don't know they are being observed. The advantage of this technique—or any form of naturalistic observation—is that hopefully, we get to observe authentic social behaviors.

Archival data: Stored information that was originally created for some other purpose not related to research that can later be used by psychologists, such as census data.

Naturalistic observation: A research design where scientists gather data by observing people in the environment within which the behavior naturally occurs (for instance, observing leadership styles in a corporate office).

Reactivity: When people change their behavior simply because they're being observed (see *social desirability bias* and *good subject bias*).

Participant observation: A technique used during naturalistic observation where scientists covertly disguise themselves as people belonging in an environment in an effort to observe more authentic social behaviors.

AF archive / Alamy Stock Photo & Atlaspix / Alamy Stock Photo

In the movie *Never Been Kissed* (Isaac, Juvonen, & Gosnell, 1999), Drew Barrymore's character is a reporter who wants to write about the life of high schoolers. To get the "true scoop," she pretends to be a high school student herself. In *Imperium* (Taufique, Lee, Ragussis, Walker, & Ragussis, 2016), Daniel Radcliffe works for the FBI and infiltrates a White supremacist group, pretending to be racist. If either one of them had been social psychologists in a real setting, then their technique would have been called participant observation.

Surveys. An alternative approach is simply to ask people to tell us about their own thoughts, emotions, and behaviors in **surveys**. Psychological surveys typically ask people to react to statements about themselves by choosing a number on a scale. It might range from 1 (*strongly disagree*) to 7 (*strongly agree*). These **self-report scales** ask people to give us information about themselves in a straightforward, explicit manner (hence the name "self-report"). There are self-report scales throughout this textbook, so you can see how you score on a variety of social psychological concepts. Those scales will help you understand just how interesting and complicated you are as you navigate your social world.

There are several considerable advantages to the survey method of research. One is that it is relatively inexpensive and you can get hundreds of participants in your study relatively quickly, especially if you put your survey online. This also allows for you to get a wider diversity of participants as you can send your survey's URL to people all over the world. Self-report surveys also can ask people personal questions about their intimate lives that you would never have access to (at least, not legally!) through naturalistic observation.

However, recall that one common problem with naturalistic observation is reactivity, or people changing their behaviors because they know they are being observed. Self-report surveys have their own concerns, and one of the big ones is dishonesty. For example, you might not tell the truth if you were asked whether you've ever treated a romantic partner badly, cheated on a test, stolen something, or had "bad thoughts" about another person. The dishonesty problem is often attributed to the **social desirability bias**, the idea that people shape their responses so that others will have positive impressions of them. (This problem is also sometimes known as impression management.) For one creative way to get around the social desirability bias in survey research, see the Applying Social Psychology to Your Life feature.

Case Studies

In the first three common methods for testing hypotheses—archival studies, naturalistic observation, and surveys—most studies will have several people who serve as the participants. However, before we move on to discuss experiments, there's one more term it would be good for you to know.

Survey: A research design where researchers collect data by asking participants to respond to questions or statements.

Self-report scale: A type of survey item where participants give information about themselves by selecting their own responses (see *survey*).

Social desirability bias: The tendency for participants to provide dishonest responses so that others have positive impressions of them.

Applying Social Psychology to Your Life

Sometimes when people fill out self-report scales in research studies (or on job interviews, or anywhere else), they aren't completely honest. Instead, they answer in a way that they think makes them look good; this tendency in people is called the social desirability bias. One creative way that social psychologists test for this tendency in people is to give them the scale shown here, which is specifically designed to catch people in small lies. Most people *have* done many of the bad behaviors listed here—so if research participants don't admit to them, they are probably showing the social desirability bias; they are changing their answers to look good.

Instructions: Listed below are a number of statements concerning personal attitudes and traits.

Please read each item and decide whether the statement is true or false as it pertains to you personally.

Circle "T" for true statements and "F" for false statements.

T F 1. Before voting I thoroughly investigate the qualifications of all the candidates.

T F 2. I never hesitate to go out of my way to help someone in trouble.

T F 3. I sometimes feel resentful when I don't get my way.

T F 4. I am always careful about my manner of dress.

T F 5. My table manners at home are as good as when I eat out in a restaurant.

T F 6. I like to gossip at times.

T F 7. I can remember "playing sick" to get out of something.

T F 8. There have been occasions when I took advantage of someone.

T F 9. I'm always willing to admit it when I make a mistake.

T F 10. There have been occasions when I felt like smashing things.

T F 11. I am always courteous, even to people who are disagreeable.

T F 12. At times I have really insisted on having things my own way.

Scoring: Give yourself 1 point if you said TRUE for Item 1, 2, 4, 5, 9, or 11. Then, give yourself 1 point if you said FALSE for Item 3, 6, 7, 8, 10, or 12. The more points you have, the more you are trying to manage your impression on others.

Source: Crowne and Marlowe (1960).

When a single example of an event or a single person is used to test a hypothesis or refine it further, it's called a **case study**. A case study represents a single example of the phenomenon of interest. For example, one case study you'll see later (in Chapter 11) describes the level of violence in *The Great Train Robbery,* a 1903 movie that was the first film to tell a story (Porter & Porter, 1903). The case study summarized the story in the film and computed the ratio of violence per minute to analyze how much violence was shown in the movie.

Note that this case study used archival data. The movie itself was preexisting information, sitting in YouTube and waiting to be analyzed. Case studies can be archival, but we might also use naturalistic observation to record behaviors in a particular person over time, or we might give one person a survey to complete—or we might even ask a single person to engage in an experiment (see the next section). So, case studies can be used in any of the forms of research we've covered here.

As we prepared to write this chapter, we became interested in whether case studies were being more or less accepted by modern psychologists. We hypothesized that the rate

Case study: A type of research where scientists conduct an in-depth study on a single example of an event or a single person to test a hypothesis.

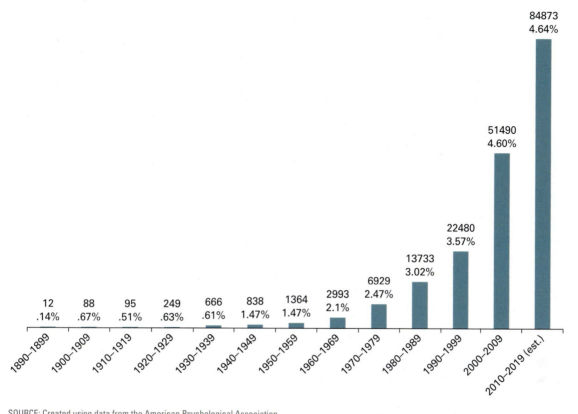

■ FIGURE 2.2 The frequency and percentage of articles referring to case studies in PsycINFO.

SOURCE: Created using data from the American Psychological Association.

of referencing case studies had been declining over time, as the use of online survey software has become more and more popular. To test our hypothesis, we used archival data that existed in the **PsycINFO database**. PsycINFO is the most comprehensive database of research books and journal articles across psychological subdisciplines. It's like Google or any other search engine, except your search collects data from books, chapters, or journal articles published by psychologists around the world. When we searched PsycINFO for publications that made use of case studies, would we see a decline over time?

Our hypothesis was not supported—in other words, we were wrong. Instead, we found a trend of increased referencing of case studies (Figure 2.2). Again, these were archival data, originally created for another purpose, waiting to be mined for insight. (Note: If you do this study again, you probably will get slightly higher numbers, especially for the most recent years, as new articles are admitted into the PsycINFO database.)

The Main Ideas

- The scientific method, which is used by social psychologists who conduct research, includes (1) observing a pattern, (2) generating a hypothesis, (3) scientifically testing the hypothesis, and (4) interpreting results so that the hypothesis can be refined and tested again.

- Abstract ideas or variables are called constructs, and deciding how to define and measure constructs is called operationalization.

- Three ways to gather data are (1) using archival data, or sources originally gathered or created for a different purpose; (2) naturalistic observation, or watching behavior where it would have occurred anyway; and (3) surveys, or asking people directly to report their thoughts, emotions, or behaviors. Any of these methods can use multiple participants or a single participant; single-participant studies are called case studies.

PsycINFO database: The most comprehensive database of research books and journal articles across psychological subdisciplines.

- Think about the classrooms you've been inside recently. Consider the physical aspects of the room (such as size, type of desks, color, art on the walls, and so on). Then consider how people choose to sit in the room during classes (such as whether they prefer the front or back row, how much they spread out, what kinds of people tend to sit together, and so on). Generate three hypotheses about how either the physical environment or the social environment shapes learning.

- Imagine that you want to do a study on how companies support leadership within their organizations. First, describe how you might conduct the study using archival data; then, how you'd do it with naturalistic observation. Finally, describe how you would conduct the study differently if you decided to give people who work there a survey. What kinds of questions would you ask? How would you get people to fill it out honestly?

- Identify three different ways you could operationalize each of the following variables: (1) prejudice, (2) high self-esteem, and (3) empathy toward other people.

HOW DO SOCIAL PSYCHOLOGISTS DESIGN STUDIES?

LO 2.2: Compare the logic behind preexperiments, true experiments, quasi-experiments, and correlational designs.

The working world is full of designers. We have fashion designers, graphic designers, architectural designers, cookware designers, landscape designers, and game designers. To become a clear-thinking social psychologist, you must become an experiment designer.

If the most famous book about experimental designs were going for a big audience in the self-help market, then it might be called *How to Think Clearly.* However, the original book by Donald Campbell and Julian Stanley (1966) had a less dramatic title: *Experimental and Quasi-Experimental Designs for Research.*

Its original target market was the unruly world of education research. Education research had been (and perhaps still is) like a pendulum clock hanging from a swinging rope, lurching back and forth between "a wave of enthusiasm for experimentation [that] gave way to apathy and rejection" (Campbell & Stanley, 1966, p. 2). Campbell and Stanley wanted to calm things down and remind researchers that experimentation takes time, replications, and multiple methods. They organized the world of research design into four categories that we'll cover here: preexperimental designs, true experiments, quasi-experiments, and correlational designs.

Preexperimental Designs

The most basic methodology is called a **preexperiment**, in which a single group of people is tested to see whether some kind of treatment has an effect.

One type of preexperimental design is the **one-shot case study**, which explores one event, person, or group in great detail. This design can be either archival (data originally created for some other reason) or a case study examined specifically for research purposes from the outset. For example, interviewing a particular world leader in depth about how he or she made leadership decisions might be a one-shot case study. In a classroom environment, one teacher who uses a particular new technique—such as playing music in

Social Psychology in Action:
Self-Deception Experiment

©SAGE Publications

Preexperiment: A research design in which a single group of people is tested to see whether some kind of treatment has an effect, such as a one-shot case study or a one-group pretest-posttest.

One-shot case study: A type of preexperimental research design that explores an event, person, or group in great detail by identifying a particular case of something or trying a technique once, then observing the outcome.

the background of the classroom—and then measures how well the students do on a test is another example. You might try a particular approach to studying one time, and your test score will be the measurement of how well that technique worked.

The one-shot case study, then, involves just two elements: (1) identifying a particular case of something or trying a technique once and (2) an observation or outcome.

Another type of preexperimental design is the **one-group pretest-posttest design**, sometimes called a "before-after design." Here, the expected outcome is measured both before and after the treatment so that the researchers can assess how much *change* occurred. The one-group pretest-posttest design is represented this way, with an initial observation (pretest), the presentation of the treatment or technique, and a second observation (posttest):

Notice that neither type of preexperiment counts as a true experiment. The major problem with either type of preexperiment is that you can't be sure that any outcome was really due to the treatment or technique. For example, imagine that a classroom teacher tries a new teaching technique and the students all do very badly. Can the teacher be sure this disappointing outcome was really due to the technique? No, because there are other possible explanations. Maybe the students all would have done badly regardless of how they were taught because the material was particularly difficult. Maybe it was the time of year, or the teacher was badly trained on the technique, or the teacher was sick that week, and so on.

Many studies attempt to establish cause-effect relationships, meaning the researchers want to say, "X caused Y to happen." Preexperiments can't make causal claims because of these alternate explanations (bad weather, someone was sick, etc.). Alternate explanations are called **confounding variables**, which are co-occurring influences that make it impossible to logically determine causality. Fortunately for science, this problem is solved by true experiments.

True Experiments

The "gold standard," or best methodology, for most social psychological studies is an **experiment**, which compares groups that have been created by the researchers on some important outcome. A well-designed experiment extracts meaningful patterns from a chaotic world. (Pretty amazing, if you stop to think about that one!) The main goal of a true experiment is to be able to make claims about causes and effects. Establishing causality is a rich philosophical question. But to the experiment designer, that means ruling out alternative explanations by controlling confounding variables (the "enemy" of good research).

Imagine you wanted to know whether being sleep-deprived makes people anxious. So, you ask 10 people to take a nap and 10 people to not nap, and then you measure

One-group pretest-posttest design: A type of preexperimental research design in which the expected outcome is measured both before and after the treatment to assess change.

Confounding variables: Co-occurring influences that make it impossible to logically determine causality. Confounding variables, such as bad weather or the inability to concentrate on a survey due to illness, provide alternate explanations for the outcome of an experiment that make it impossible to know whether the results are due to the independent variable (see *internal validity*).

Experiment: A research design where scientists randomly assign participants to groups and systematically compare changes in behavior. Experiments allow scientists to control confounding variables and establish cause-effect relationships.

their anxiety. If the freshly napped group is less anxious, can you be sure their relatively relaxed feelings are due to the nap? How do you know that those 10 people weren't already more relaxed and happy-go-lucky than the other 10 people?

The best solution to the problem of confounding variables is **random assignment to experimental condition**, which occurs at the beginning of your study. Each person in the study has an equal chance of being put in the nap or no-nap group based on some determination of chance, such as the flip of a coin. With random assignment, it's statistically likely that people who came into the study already high or low in anxiety will be equally distributed across the two experimental groups, which in essence makes the groups identical. If this is done, then any differences in the measurement at the end must be due to experimental treatment; it's the most plausible explanation. Let's talk about the details of how true experiments work.

Independent and Dependent Variables. All true experiments have two types of variables, called "independent" and "dependent." Researchers use the **independent variable** to make the participant groups different from each other at the start of the experiment. For example, researchers might have some people in the study listen to classical music and have others listen to rock music. So, the independent variable is type of music—it's what makes the groups different from each other from the very beginning of the study.

Of course, we also have to measure some kind of outcome, which is the **dependent variable**. Maybe while our two groups listen to either classical or rock music, everyone reads a passage from a textbook. Then, they take a memory test. If the experiment is trying to establish whether type of music causes better or worse memory, then performance on the memory test at the end is the dependent variable. It's called the "dependent" variable because we are hypothesizing that memory scores are "dependent" on whether participants heard classical or rock music. Does type of music cause people to do better or worse on a memory test? In experiments, the independent variable is the *cause* being tested (here, music) and the dependent variable is the *effect* or outcome (here, memory test scores).

The "studying while listening to different kinds of music" is a popular experiment among new researchers, so we hope that you noticed some other problems. For example, what kind of classical music was it? How well was each type of music performed? Were they played at equal volume? Again, if some of those problems occurred to you, then you are starting to think like a scientist. If any of these other differences by group occurred (such as the rock music was loud and fast but the classical music was soft and slow), then both volume and tempo are confounding variables. Possible criticisms such as these are important in the scientific process, and they are one reason why so many studies need to be done to answer what may have seemed like a simple question at the beginning of the process. Each study helps us refine our hypothesis and begin again.

For several more examples of independent and dependent variables, see Table 2.1.

Types of True Experiment. Just like we saw with preexperiments, there are several different kinds of true experiment. One type of experimental design is called the **pretest-posttest control group design**. This is basically a before-after design because the outcome (or dependent variable) is tested both before and after the experimental manipulation or intervention occurs. For example, memory could be measured in all participants—then they listen to either rock or classical music—and then memory is measured again. The researchers can now measure how much each type of music affects *change* in memory from the pretest to the posttest. The key difference is that in a true

Random assignment to experimental condition: A solution to the problem of confounding variables by creating equivalent groups at the start of an experiment. Random assignment cancels out the influence of confounds by distributing them equally across groups.

Independent variable: A variable that is manipulated at the beginning of an experiment to determine its effect on the dependent variable.

Dependent variable: The measured outcome of an experiment that is affected by the independent variable.

Pretest-posttest control group design: A type of true experiment where the dependent variable is tested both before and after the experimental manipulation.

Study Basics	Independent Variable	Dependent Variable
Students listen to either classical or rock music while they study, to see if music affects their memory on a test later.	Musical style (classical or rock)	Performance on the memory test
People write an essay about either death or puppies, then rate how much anger they feel.	Essay topic (death or puppies)	Level of anger
Children watch a commercial with dolls or with trucks, then are rated on how aggressively they play with clay and crayons.	Commercial topic (dolls or trucks)	Level of aggression
Sports fans see images of athletes wearing black jerseys or green jerseys and are asked to rate how well they expect each player to do that year.	Jersey color (black or green)	Expectations of players' performance

experiment, we now have two groups instead of one, and participants have been placed into one group or the other through random assignment. It looks like this:

You need both groups, made equivalent by random assignment, to control for confounding variables. However, sometimes the different levels of the independent variable are compared to a "neutral" or baseline group. In our example about measuring whether memory scores change after listening to music, imagine that memory scores went up in both conditions. Maybe simply listening to *any* kind of music helps memory. To test this refined hypothesis, we need another group that doesn't listen to music at all. A group that serves as a neutral or baseline group that receives no treatment at all is called a **control group**. That experimental design would look like this:

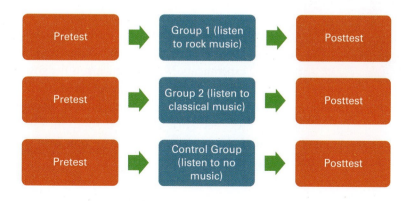

Finally, you will learn about many studies in this book that are *close* to the design described here, with one difference: They sometimes skip the pretest phase. When this happens, it's called a **posttest-only control group design**. Everything else is the

Control group: A group of participants in a true experiment that serves as a neutral or baseline group that receives no treatment.

Posttest-only control group design: A type of true experiment where the dependent variable is measured for two or more groups, including a control group, only after the experimental manipulation.

same—you have two or more groups, including a control group, and you measure outcomes for each group. You just don't have the pretest, which means you compare how the groups are different from each other in only the posttests. This design is perfectly fine as long as you really did use random assignment to put each participant in the different groups. Again, this should logically mean that the groups started out on equal footing, so it's okay to measure the influence of the independent variable by simply looking at how the groups differ on the dependent variable (posttest only).

Between-Participants Versus Within-Participants. The different designs described so far are considered by many to be ideal choices for research. However, sometimes real studies have challenges. For example, there might be limitations to how many people you can get in your study or how you can create the different conditions of your independent variable. So far when we've considered designs with two or more groups, the assumption has been that each group is made up of different people. This approach in general is called a **between-participants design**, meaning that levels or conditions of the independent variable change between groups of different participants. Maybe 20 people listened to rock music, and 20 different people listened to classical music (and maybe 20 others listened to no music). This would require 60 different people!

However, imagine you are a teacher and you want to test your hypothesis, but there are only 20 students in your entire class. In addition, you need to teach all of them the material, but you have only one set of speakers in your classroom, so everyone will have to listen to the same music. With this kind of limitation, you can consider a **within-participants design**, which means that the *same* group of participants all experience each experimental condition. You put each person in every group, one group at a time.

For example, in Unit 1, the entire class listens to rock music; in Unit 2, the entire class listens to classical music; and in Unit 3, there is no music. Ideally, different people would go through all of the groups in different orders (for example, someone might listen to classical music first, while someone else hears rock first; then they switch), but sometimes this just isn't possible. Just like we saw with archival research, naturalistic observation, and surveys, there are advantages and disadvantages to each different design option within true experiments. Within-participants designs have the advantage of needing fewer people (here, it's 20 people compared to 60). But a within-participants design comes with built-in disadvantages. One of them is the possibility of **order effects** that influence the outcome variable just because one condition of the independent variable happened to come first. Choosing the right design is an important step in the research process.

The famous character Quasimodo from Victor Hugo's (1831) novel *The Hunchback of Notre Dame* was known for being "half-formed." Quasi-experiments could be considered "half-formed" versions of true experiments, because they compare groups but are missing the key element of random assignment of people to those groups.

Quasi-Experimental Designs

As we've already indicated, there are many situations in which true experimental designs are impossible, unethical, or impractical. In addition, sometimes the variables of interest aren't things that can be randomly assigned. For example, you can't randomly assign some people to experience a tornado. In these cases, quasi-experiments can help us reach reasonable but still tentative conclusions. *Quasi* is the Latin word for "almost" or "partially." Thus, a quasi-experiment is *almost* like a true experiment.

Quasi-experiments compare outcomes across different groups, just like true experiments—but the key difference is that the groups have not been formed through random assignment. The groups in quasi-experiments formed on their own, naturally. For example, you may want to compare men to women in terms of who interrupts more. Here, the independent variable you're testing is sex (men vs. women), and the dependent variable is frequency of interruptions. However, these variables aren't "true" independent and dependent variables because they were not randomly assigned, and thus the experimental setup hasn't really eliminated any possible confounding variables.

Even if we find that one group interrupts more, we still don't really know *why*. Is it because of genetics? Hormones? How boys versus girls are raised? Because we are not able to eliminate all confounding variables, we can't truly make causal inferences or statements with a quasi-experimental design. But, it's impossible to randomly assign each participant to sex—you'd find it odd to show up to an experiment only to be told, "Today you're going to be a woman."

While participant sex is impossible to randomly assign, other variables may be simply very difficult or unethical to randomly assign. If you want to study the effect of going through a hurricane or being in a terrible car accident, you can't randomly assign half of your participants to experience these traumas. You might also want to study variables such as religion or choice of career—and again, participants would probably protest if you randomly assigned them to either of these important variables. In short, quasi-experiments are needed to study several important variables within social psychology—but we need to be more cautious when interpreting results, especially in regards to any claims about causality.

Correlational Designs

Your head might be spinning with all of the different study designs we've gone through so far—preexperiments, true experiments, quasi-experiments—so we've saved the most simple design for last.

Correlational designs are relatively easy; they involve simply collecting or measuring two pieces of information from each participant in the study, then seeing if there is a pattern. For example, you can ask people (1) how many hours they study each week and (2) what their grade point average (GPA) is. Most people would quickly see the hypothesis being tested: More studying is associated with higher grades. (Note: We'll talk more about how to specifically test for this pattern in the next section.)

Correlational designs thus look for patterns in which two variables have a relationship or association with each other. Height and shoe size are correlated; the general pattern is that taller people have larger feet. Income and size of someone's house are correlated; richer people usually have bigger houses. It's sometimes easy to think of correlations as patterns that indicate a causal relationship: Studying for more hours each week causes a student's GPA to improve, or having more money causes someone to be able to buy a bigger house.

While it is *possible* that some correlations show causal relationships, in social psychology (and in all forms of science), it is very important not to *assume* that correlations indicate causal relationships. This word of caution is summarized in the popular motto, "Correlation does not imply causation." Why not? First, it might be the case that both variables are actually caused by a third variable. In the case of a student who spends many hours studying and has a very good GPA, both of these outcomes might have been caused by the student's (1) motivation to do well, (2) level of pressure from parents, or (3) amount of enjoyment of class subjects.

Between-participants design: An experimental research design where the levels or conditions of the independent variable are different for each group of participants; patterns are found by comparing the responses between groups.

Within-participants design: An experimental research design where the same group of participants all experience each experimental condition; patterns are found by comparing responses for each condition.

Order effects: Variations in participants' responses due to the order in which materials or conditions are presented to them.

Quasi-experiment: A research design where outcomes are compared across different groups that have not been formed through random assignment but instead occur naturally.

Correlational design: A research design where scientists analyze two or more variables to determine their relationship or association with each other.

CORRELATION AND CAUSATION IN
HARRY POTTER

United Archives GmbH / Alamy Stock Photo

Most people are familiar with the Harry Potter series of books and movies, in which a young boy discovers he's a wizard and attends a boarding school to learn spells. In the sixth book, *Harry Potter and the Half-Blood Prince* (Rowling, 2005), Harry first gets the chance to learn the magical power of "apparition," or the ability to disappear and reappear in a different location. Harry's first apparition lesson is an example of his awareness that correlation does not imply causation.

Harry describes his apparition teacher's appearance and how that appearance might be linked to the ability to disappear:

> He was oddly colorless, with transparent eyelashes, wispy hair, and an insubstantial air, as though a single gust of wind might blow him away. Harry wondered whether constant disappearances and reappearances had somehow diminished his substance, or whether his frail build was ideal for anyone wishing to vanish. (p. 382)

Harry doesn't know whether having a wispy appearance caused his teacher to have a greater apparition ability—or whether his talent at apparition has caused him to appear wispy. While Harry suspects there's a correlation or association between the two things, he knows that without more information, he can't know which is the cause and which is the effect. It's also possible that the association is merely a coincidence or that both are caused by something else. Without logical research designs, the secrets of apparition may remain unknown to Muggles (nonmagical folks) and wizards alike.

Consider another example: There is usually a correlation between amount of ice cream sold per year and the number of people who drown that year. Is ice cream consumption causing drowning? Probably not. It's more likely that a third variable explains the correlation: heat. Towns that have hotter temperatures (such as Miami, Florida, and Austin, Texas) sell more ice cream. In addition, more people swim in these towns due to the heat (which unfortunately sometimes leads to more drownings). So, while it might look like the two variables of ice cream and drownings are related, both are actually driven by something else.

It's also important to realize that with a simple correlation, even if there is a causal relationship between the two variables, we don't necessarily know which is the cause and which is the effect. Think about the controversial idea that watching violence on TV causes children to act more violently in real life. This hypothesis makes a lot of intuitive sense, and there are studies showing that amount of violence viewed on TV is related to how violent children are.

However, it's also possible that the causal relationship goes the other way around. Maybe children who are already inclined to have violent personalities and behaviors are more likely to watch violent TV, because they find it interesting. Now, the cause is the violent personality and the effect is watching violence on TV. Simple correlations aren't enough to assume anything about causation; we need more precise methodologies, like experiments, to know the details.

It's fun to be a scientific problem solver, addressing important social issues. But it is much more than that. Research can be a satisfying, meaningful way to spend a life—words you may never thought you would hear in a discussion about research designs.

Cutting-Edge Combinations

Classic studies using naturalistic observation, archival data, surveys, and experiments have now established many foundational theories and concepts in social psychology, and all of these methods continue to provide new insights from research labs around the world. However, social psychology's research methodology is also able to grow and evolve as technology advances. These advances result in new, cutting-edge procedures, many of which will be described in the rest of this book.

One exciting way that social psychology research is becoming more advanced is by joining forces with neuropsychologists to study how social interactions both influence and are influenced by neurons in the brain. For example, one study (Cyders, Dzemidzic, Eiler, & Kareken, 2016) used functional magnetic resonance imaging (fMRI) brain scans to show that men have more neural reaction to sexual images than to nonsexual images and that degree of neural reaction was positively correlated with the men's survey responses on how much they engage in high-risk sexual behaviors. Several other examples of how the brain is connected to social psychology are highlighted in later chapters.

Other researchers examine physiological responses during studies, such as blood pressure (e.g., Hill et al., 2017; Huntley & Goodfriend, 2012; Jennings, Pardini, & Matthews, 2017) or the release of stress hormones such as cortisol in blood or saliva (e.g., Simons, Cillessen, & de Weerth, 2017; Tarullo, St. John, & Meyer, 2017) as ways of measuring participants' biological reactions, in addition to their psychological reactions. One interesting example is pupil dilation, which has been correlated with sexual interest or attraction to other people (see Lick, Cortland, & Johnson, 2016; Savin-Williams, Cash, McCormack, & Rieger, 2017).

Finally, computer software has been specifically designed or updated by researchers in social psychology labs both to create different independent variables and to measure dependent variables; often, this takes the form of video games that participants play in which various aspects of the game are manipulated, and how the participants play and respond serves as the outcome being measured. Again, several examples will be seen in future chapters. As technology advances, our ability to test hypotheses about social psychological phenomena will also advance in exciting new ways.

The Main Ideas

- A preexperiment is a method in which a single group of people is tested to see whether some kind of treatment has an effect.

- A true experiment compares outcomes on two or more groups that have been created by the experimenter through random assignment to condition. True experiments are the only methodology that can lead researchers to make claims about cause-effect relationships between variables.

- A quasi-experiment tests for the effect of a treatment in groups that have formed naturally, such as men versus women or people who prefer different kinds of music.

- Correlational designs look for associations between two variables that are measured in a single group. A correlation between two variables does not necessarily mean that one causes the other.

- Earlier, we discussed challenges to naturalistic observation (reactivity) and to surveys (social desirability bias). What are some challenges to experimental research designs? How could scientists overcome these challenges?

- Imagine that you have a hypothesis that people who drink a lot of caffeine will experience heightened emotions over the course of a day. Explain three different ways you could design a study to test your hypothesis, using three different methods from this section of the chapter.

- Think of a correlation you've observed in the world where it's hard to tell if the relationship is causal because either of the two variables could be the cause or the effect. Which comes first and affects the other? Then, think of a correlation that appears to show a relationship, but both variables are actually being caused by a third variable that wasn't directly measured.

HOW DO SOCIAL PSYCHOLOGISTS ANALYZE THEIR RESULTS?

LO 2.3: Summarize the most common ways to analyze and interpret data.

"I don't like statistics," one of our students declared before class was starting, and then asked his neighbor, "Do you know if the Pittsburgh Pirates won last night? They're only two games out of the lead." He couldn't see the obvious: He already loves numbers, what they mean, and the stories they tell—but only when they are connected to something that he cares about (in this case, baseball). We hope that in this next section, which reviews some basic types of statistics used in social psychology, you can think about how each one might apply to something that you care about.

People who are serious about understanding social psychology need an understanding of **statistics**, or mathematical analyses that reveal patterns in data. They are important, both on an individual level—the pleasure of thinking analytically is satisfying—and on a larger level. Understanding patterns in data and how to interpret them correctly is absolutely necessary for authentic understanding of how to create government policies, how to design effective education, how to plan for a stable financial future, how to respond to global climate change, and more. Critical, scientific, analytical thinking is needed for social psychology to be able to influence the world for the better.

Comparing Groups

Let's think through the hypothetical results (in Figure 2.3) about the effects of different types of music on memory. The horizontal *x*-axis indicates memory scores; higher memory scores are shown to the right. The vertical *y*-axis indicates how many people got that score. The average memory score for people listening to classical music is higher than the average for people listening to rock music. These two averages provide the most important statistical information.

But you also may have noticed something else in Figure 2.3. The shape of the memory curve for people listening to rock music is a little flatter and wider. The flatter, wider distribution of scores means that there was more variability in the memory scores for people in that group (the highest score was further away from the lowest score, meaning a wider range). The amount of variability in a distribution is called the **standard deviation.**

Statistics: Mathematical analyses that reveal patterns in data, such as correlations, *t* tests, and analyses of variance.

Standard deviation: The amount of variability in a distribution. In other words, how widely dispersed the data are.

The two bell-shaped curves in Figure 2.3 also show overlap between the two groups. Some people listening to rock music had higher memory scores than some of the people listening to classical music. If the overlap were small and the average scores were far apart from one another, then we can be more confident that this experiment found a real effect of type of music on memory. But if the overlap is large and the average scores are close to one another, then we could have very little confidence that this was a real difference.

Comparing Two Groups: The *t* Test Statistic.

The **t test** statistic uses both the mean and the standard deviation to test for differences between two groups. William Sealy Gossett, a brewer at Dublin's Guinness Brewing Company, first published how to calculate it anonymously. He wasn't supposed to publish industrial secrets, and the *t* test was one of them. Gossett's statistical invention used small samples to make far-reaching judgments about the quality of Guinness's many ingredients (Mankiewicz, 2000). The *t* test solved many practical problems at Guinness.

One of Gossett's jobs was to test the amount of stout in each batch of beer—think of it as a taste test. It would have been impossible (although a fun challenge, at least for a while) for him to sample from the thousands of casks produced every single day. Imagine that Gossett tasted 10 random samples from one batch made on Monday morning and gave each a taste rating. Then he did the same thing with a second batch made on Monday afternoon. Gossett's *t* test allowed him to compare the quality in thousands of casks even though he only sampled from a total of 20 batches.

There were two critical components to Gossett's statistical invention: (1) the sampling had to be random, and (2) the sample had to be big enough to be representative of all casks of beer. It would not be good for Guinness's business if the morning batch tasted different from the afternoon batch. Gossett's invention of the *t* test statistic for comparing two groups (the morning vs. afternoon batches) ensured consistent quality in Guinness. So, the next time you're sipping a beer and wondering why you're required to learn statistics, you can lift a glass to W. S. Gossett for his liver-saving contributions to science. The secrets of sampling are as important for making far-reaching judgments about human behavior as they are for brewing a better beer.

Comparing Three or More Groups: Analysis of Variance.

You can use the *t* in the *t* test to remind you that it is used to compare two groups. But think back to our example from earlier in the chapter, when we wanted to test the effects of different kinds of music on memory. What if our study involved students listening to three types of music, such as country music, hip hop, or jazz? What if we wanted to compare five types of music? And what if Gossett wanted to compare taste samples from more than two groups of beer—say, one from each day of the week?

The principle for comparing multiple groups is the same as comparing two groups. For each group, we calculate the average score and the standard deviation, just like before. However, when we're comparing three or more groups, the test is called an **analysis of variance**, or "ANOVA" for short. For example, perhaps the classical music group in a three-group experiment does

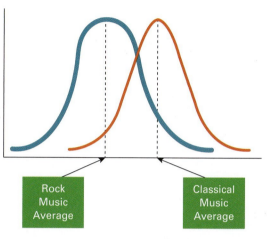

■ **FIGURE 2.3** One way social scientists look for patterns is by comparing average scores within different groups of participants. When we compare two groups, as here, we use a *t* test. When we compare three or more groups, we do an analysis of variance, or "ANOVA."

Rock Music Average

Classical Music Average

We have Guinness to thank for the statistic known as the *t* test.

better than the rock group—and maybe they are both better than the control group with no music at all! ANOVA tests will tell you whether at least one of the groups is different from the others. Different types of comparison groups require different statistical tests. However, they all rely on just two basic ingredients: the average and the standard deviation in each group.

Patterns in a Single Group: Correlations

While *t* tests and ANOVAs compare patterns of results in different groups, **correlations** look for patterns of results in a single group. Specifically, as explained in the preceding section, correlations test whether two different variables are systematically associated with each other. Think about the following questions that all apply to the life of college students:

- Does a student's high school grade point average (GPA) predict his or her college GPA?
- Does the distance between home and chosen college relate to how much homesickness a typical student feels?
- Are the number of hours spent studying related to test scores?
- Are students with more individual interactions with professors going to be more satisfied with their college experience?
- Do hours of sleep in an average week predict levels of stress in that same week?

All of these questions would be tested with correlations. Correlations begin with two variables of interest (for example, hours spent studying and GPA). To test for a pattern, scores on each variable are gathered from as many people as possible and are then charted on a graph called a **scatterplot**. One variable is on the (horizontal) *x*-axis, and the other is on the (vertical) *y*-axis, and each dot on the scatterplot represents one person. Take a look at Figure 2.4 for an example.

The pattern shown in Figure 2.4 indicates that, for most people, more hours studying each week is associated with better grades. As you would expect, as studying increases, so does GPA. Certainly, not everyone will fit the pattern—there might be brilliant people who can get a high GPA without studying and people who study for hours and hours and still struggle with grades. But, the general pattern is fairly stable. The line summarizes the story told in detail by the scatterplot.

When a correlation is calculated, the number you get is called a **correlation coefficient**. It will always be a number between −1.00 and +1.00. How can you tell what the coefficient means? It's basically like a two-part code you can crack to understand what the pattern looks like on a scatterplot. There are two parts to the code: (1) the sign or direction—positive or negative—and (2) the number. Let's talk about each part.

First, the sign will always be either a positive or a negative (unless the correlation is

t test: A statistical test that uses both the mean and the standard deviation to compare the difference between two groups.

Analysis of variance (ANOVA): A statistical test that uses both the mean and the standard deviation to compare the differences between three or more groups.

Correlation: A type of statistical test that determines whether two or more variables are systematically associated with each other by identifying linear patterns in data.

Scatterplot: A graph that demonstrates the relationship between two quantitative variables by displaying plotted participant responses.

Correlation coefficient: A number that indicates the relationship or association between two quantitative variables. It ranges from −1.00 to +1.00.

■ FIGURE 2.4 In this scatterplot, each dot represents one person. For each person, study hours per week fall on the *x*-axis, and GPA falls on the *y*-axis. By looking at the general pattern, we can determine whether the two variables are correlated.

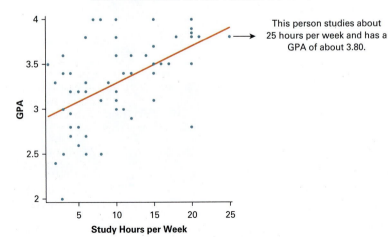

This person studies about 25 hours per week and has a GPA of about 3.80.

exactly zero). A **positive correlation** (between +0.01 and +1.00) indicates that both variables move in the same direction. In other words, if scores or values on one of the variables go up, values on the other variable will also go up. If one goes down, the other will go down. The example in Figure 2.4 shows a positive correlation: As a typical student spends more hours studying each week, grades will go up. Hours and grades are both moving up, in the same direction. Positive correlations are shown in scatterplots when the pattern or summary line moves from the bottom left-hand corner to the upper right-hand corner.

In contrast, a **negative correlation** (between −0.01 and −1.00) indicates that the variables move in opposite directions. As one variable goes up, the other goes down. Instead of hours spent studying, think about hours spent partying. The more hours a student parties, the lower his or her grade might be: Partying moves up, and grades move down. Negative correlations will be shown in scatterplots with a pattern that goes from the upper left-hand corner to the bottom right-hand corner.

The second part of a correlation coefficient is the number, which will always be between zero and 1 (either positive or negative). The number tells you how clear the pattern is on the scatterplot or how well the different dots (which represent people) fall along the summary line. Basically, this number tells you how much variability there is in the data, or whether some people don't fit the pattern. In Figure 2.4, for example, you can see that there is one student who studies an average of about 20 hours per week but only has a GPA of about 2.75. If the dots all fall *exactly* on the line, meaning the pattern is perfect, the number you get will be 1.00. As the number gets closer to zero, it means the pattern becomes slightly less clear.

Note that coefficients of +1.00 and −1.00 are equally strong—both indicate perfect patterns—it's just that in one case, the variables move together (+1.00), and in one case, they move in opposite directions (−1.00). Figure 2.5 shows a summary of how to understand correlations, showing a range of patterns that move from perfect and positive, through no correlation at all, to perfect and negative. A zero correlation coefficient means that the two variables have no relation to each other at all, such as GPA and

■ **FIGURE 2.5** Correlations always range from −1.00 to +1.00. The sign (positive or negative) indicates whether the two variables move in the same direction or in opposite directions. The number (from 0.0 to 1.0) tells you how well each data point fits onto a general pattern. If a correlation is zero, it means there is no pattern or association between the two variables.

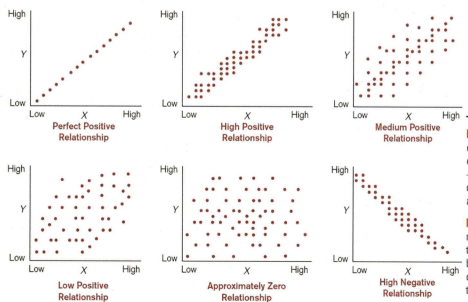

Positive correlation: A positive correlation occurs when the correlation coefficient is between +0.01 and +1.00. In this case, as one variable increases, the other also increases.

Negative correlation: A negative correlation occurs when the correlation coefficient is between −0.01 and −1.00. In this case, as one variable increases, the other decreases.

someone's height or love of chocolate. These variables are not associated with each other at all, so the scatterplot looks like a bunch of random dots.

Testing for Statistical Significance: p Values

So far, you've learned about *t* tests, ANOVA tests, and correlation tests. All of these statistics look for patterns of data. The last statistical concept is to know what it means—and what it does not mean—when your research results approach **statistical significance**. In this case, the word *significance* has nothing at all to do with importance. A finding that is statistically significant might be unimportant, very important, or just a trivial curiosity. Statistical significance only means that a pattern of data identified by any statistical test is strong enough that it probably wouldn't have happened by chance. If it didn't happen by chance, then it probably would happen again if you did the study again. So, you can think of statistical significance as the "happen again estimate."

For example, consider once again the hypothesis that listening to different kinds of music will have an effect on memory. Imagine that the scores on the memory test could range from 0 to 100, and the average scores were 86 for the classical music group versus 85 for the rock music group. Is that difference of 1 point enough for you to be confident that classical music has a better effect on memory than rock music? Probably not.

However, you probably would be more confident if the difference were larger, such as comparing 86 to 46. In addition, it might matter how many people were in the study. If you found a difference between 86 and 46 but you had only a single participant in each group, you probably still wouldn't be very confident—maybe the person who listened to classical music would have done better anyway, due to confounding variables such as intelligence, interest in the material, and so on. And don't forget that standard deviation will matter as well.

When a researcher reports that a result is "statistically significant," that only means that the patterns of data found in *t* tests, ANOVAs, or correlations seems stable, that it is likely to happen again. To determine whether the results of any statistical test reach the level of "statistical significance," a final calculation is usually done.

The last calculation is for a *p* **value**, which results in a number between zero and 1. The *p* value number indicates the probability or likelihood that the pattern of data would have been found by random chance, *if* the pattern doesn't really exist. The *p* in *p* value stands for probability. Let's go back to our example of music and memory. If music has *no effect* on memory, then we'd expect the groups we test to be equal in memory scores. The *p* value tells us how likely it is that the results we actually find would exist if the groups were equal. In other words, it tells us how confident we can be that the groups really are different from each other. We also calculate *p* values for ANOVAs and correlations, and the logic is the same; the number from the *p* value tells us whether the pattern would have been found by chance if the groups are the same (for an ANOVA) or if the two variables we're testing in a correlation have nothing to do with each other.

For several decades, social psychologists (and other scientists) have generally agreed that to be really confident in conclusions based on statistics, we want to say that we're 95% sure that the patterns we find aren't the result of random chance. You will also hear the phrase "$p < .05$" to refer to stable patterns of results. You should know, however, that there are big changes coming to the traditional world of statistics. If you go to graduate school, then you probably will hear much more about "effect sizes," "confidence intervals," "power analyses," "replications," and "Bayesian statistics." Many undergraduate textbooks on statistics are already teaching these new approaches.

Statistical significance: The likelihood that the results of an experiment are due to the independent variable, not chance (see p *value*).

***p* value:** A number that indicates the probability or likelihood that a pattern of data would have been found by random chance. Commonly seen as a variation of "$p < .05$," which, in this example, means there is a less than 5% probability the patterns are due to chance.

The Main Ideas

- Statistics are mathematical analyses that reveal patterns in data. Researchers use *t* tests to compare two groups and analysis of variance (ANOVA) tests to compare three or more groups. Correlations are used to see whether two variables within a single group have a consistent relationship with each other.

- Correlations can be positive (the variables move in the same direction) or negative (the variables move in opposite directions), and they can range from zero (no association between the variables) to a perfect score of 1.00 (all of the scores match the pattern exactly).

- All three of these statistical tests (*t* tests, ANOVAs, and correlations) can have their strength tested with a final test that calculates a *p* value. A statistical test's *p* value indicates the probability that the pattern of data found would have happened by random chance, if the pattern isn't really there. Most social psychologists want a *p* value of .05 or less, meaning a 5% or lower chance that the pattern occurred due to chance.

⚡ CRITICAL THINKING CHALLENGE

- Scatterplots look for patterns in data within a single group. Experiments look for whether different groups of people have different outcomes. How many people do you think need to be included in either research design before we can be confident that the pattern would probably also apply to other people we haven't tested? If we chart the study hours and GPAs of five students at your school, do you think it would be representative of every student? What about 20 students or 100? How do we explain people who don't fit into the "typical" pattern?

- Most social psychologists have decided that a *p* value of .05 or less is the cutoff for "statistical significance." Do you think that a 5% chance of patterns being found by chance is a low enough number? Or, do you think it should be higher—would 10% be good enough for you to feel confident?

HOW CAN RESEARCH BE ANALYZED IN TERMS OF QUALITY?

LO 2.4: Describe reliability, validity, replication, and ethical standards for research in social psychology.

You now know quite a bit about how different studies are designed and even how results are analyzed. Perhaps it is time to start forming and testing your own hypotheses. It may be the best way to figure out how much you can trust the many studies you will read about in this (and every other) psychology textbook. If you were going to assign a grade to each study in this book, what criteria would you use to decide whether a study deserves an A+ or something a bit lower? In this section, we will consider reliability and validity, the importance of replication, and ethical considerations.

Reliability, Validity, and Replication

Imagine this: Your back hurts from lugging around heavy textbooks all day, so you become curious about just how much those suckers weigh. You pile them on top of the scale at your local gym and it gives you a result: 36.8 pounds. No wonder your back

If you use a scale like this one to weigh yourself, how confident are you that the result is correct or that it wouldn't change if you stepped off and back on?

Reliability: Consistency of measurement, over time or multiple testing occasions. A study is said to be reliable if similar results are found when the study is repeated.

Internal validity: The level of confidence researchers have that patterns of data are due to what is being tested, as opposed to flaws in how the experiment was designed.

External validity: The extent to which results of any single study could apply to other people or settings (see *generalizability*).

Generalizability: How much the results of a single study can apply to the general population (see *external validity*).

Random sampling: A sampling technique used to increase a study's generalizability and external validity wherein a researcher randomly chooses people to participate from a larger population of interest.

hurts! But then your friend tells you that the scale is often off by several pounds, which she knows because she sometimes compares what that scale tells her to the scale at her doctor's office on the same day. So, you try again, and this time the scale tells you that the exact same pile of books weighs 33.2 pounds. Surprised, you take the books off and put them back on, and now it says 40.6 pounds! Clearly, you can't trust this scale much because it is unreliable.

This simple example illustrates the first criterion for assessing the quality of a particular research study: reliability. **Reliability** is consistency of measurement, over time or over multiple testing occasions. If you took an intelligence test that said you were smarter than 95% of people in the world but then tried the same test the following week and it said you're only smarter than 52% of people in the world, you'd probably be disappointed—and you wouldn't know what exactly to think about your intelligence. Reliability is important because if measurements are not consistent, researchers won't feel confident that the tests are particularly useful.

In addition to reliability, scientists also want their studies to be high in validity. Two of the most important types of validity are internal and external validity. **Internal validity** is the level of confidence you have that the results you got from a study really mean what you think they mean. In other words, internal validity refers to whether patterns of data are really due to what you're testing, as opposed to flaws in how the study was designed. For example, if you tested the hypothesis about how listening to types of music affect memory but you forgot to use random assignment, you might not have eliminated other explanations (confounding variables). Random assignment of participants to different conditions or levels of your independent variable is one of the best ways to increase the internal validity of a study.

Good studies also want high levels of **external validity**, which is the extent to which results of any single study could apply to other people or settings. Lack of external validity is one of the most common concerns with single research studies. For example, many of the studies you'll read about in this book used participants who were college students. That's great for you in some ways, because it means that you can relate to the people who participated and that the results might apply to you. However, in other ways, it means that the results might be limited in their **generalizability**, or how much they apply to people "in general." Some people have even used the acronym WEIRD to refer to this problem by saying that too many studies in psychology have "WEIRD" participants—meaning they are Western, Educated, and from Industrialized, Rich, Democratic cultures.

If a study only tested a hypothesis on college students from schools in the United States, we don't know if the same results would be found among college students in other countries—or among anyone not in college (children, older people, etc.). The best way to increase generalizability of results—and thus also increase external validity—is to use a technique called **random sampling**. Random sampling means that instead of asking for volunteers to be in your study, you first identify what your "general" population of interest is, and then you randomly choose people from that larger group to participate in the study. Statistically, then, you'll have a good chance of getting a wider variety of people who represent different aspects of the larger group. Consider this each time you think about whether a study has believable results—you can always ask, "Who was in the study? Do they represent everyone, or just one particular type of person?"

Like all the statistical tools we discussed in the previous section, all of the criteria for a good-quality study (reliability, internal validity, and external validity) can be strengthened by **replication**, conducting the same experiment using the same procedures and the same materials. Replication is one of the easiest ways to get started in research, yet some students think that replication is a form of cheating. Replication is not cheating. You can replicate someone else's study by using their published procedures, scales, methodologies, and analyses. You can even e-mail the researchers and ask them to send you their materials, if needed. If you carefully replicate their study, then you should get pretty close to the same results, right? Replication solves all sorts of problems for psychological scientists, because it helps our confidence that our claims are backed up by a reliable pattern of results across different people in different settings.

Ethical Considerations

There's a certain level of trust that happens when anyone shows up to participate in a psychology study. As researchers, we want to remember that we have a solemn responsibility to treat people with respect. Even when we use unobtrusive methodologies like naturalistic observation or archival studies, all people involved in the study of human social behavior should be valued—otherwise, our research would be quite ironic.

Researchers across all the sciences provide ethical and legal guidance about what it means to treat study participants with respect through **institutional review boards (IRBs)**, which are committees of people who consider the ethical implications of any study. Before any of us begin formal research that might affect participants and be published, we are obliged to submit our methods for review. Your local IRB committee is typically composed of representatives from different departments in a college, university, research institute, or corporation—and sometimes from a combination of such organizations. The committees also often have a lawyer as a member, and sometimes they have a member with no background in research at all, to represent the "average person's" perspective.

In psychology, the specific guidelines we follow come from both our local IRB committees and from the **American Psychological Association (APA)**, an organization

The National Archives at Atlanta

Ethical violations in the Tuskegee Syphilis Study helped establish the need for IRBs to prevent future violations of trust. Participants in this study of syphilis were not (a) told the purpose of the study, (b) given a chance to leave the study, or (c) treated with penicillin that might have cured them.

Replication: The process of conducting the same experiment using the same procedures and the same materials multiple times to strengthen reliability, internal validity, and external validity.

Institutional review boards (IRBs): Committees of people who consider the ethical implications of any study before giving the researcher approval to begin formal research.

American Psychological Association (APA): A large organization of professional psychologists who provide those in the field with information in the form of scholarly publications, citation style guidelines, and ethical standards for research.

Spotlight on Research Methods

Institutional review boards (IRBs) are committees that review ethical considerations for any new study; you need to get IRB approval before you can move forward. To know more about this process, consider the questions below; they are the typical types of questions any researcher will need to answer before starting the research process. Researchers are required to type their answers and submit them to the IRB committee for review, along with copies of any materials such as surveys, videos, and so on.

- What is the purpose of your study, and what are the hypotheses?
- What kinds of participants do you plan to use? How many? How will you recruit them? Will they be compensated for their participation through something like money or extra credit?
- Are the participants from any kind of legally protected group, such as children, prisoners, people with disabilities, and so on?
- How will you get informed consent?
- What are the specific questions you will ask or experimental procedures you will use?

- Will there be any deception? If so, what is the justification for that deception?
- How will debriefing occur?
- What are the potential harms (physically, emotionally, or mentally) that participants might experience, short term or long term?
- Will you provide any resources if participants have questions or concerns?
- Are there any potential benefits participants might experience as a result of being in your study?
- How long will your study take? How will you ensure that the data collected will remain confidential and/or anonymous?
- Do you plan to present your results to the public, such as through a conference presentation or publication? If so, will the participants have access to these results themselves if they are interested?

Hopefully, you can see that IRB committees take their jobs very seriously—as they should.

of professionals in the field who have determined what the ethical standards of research should be. Note that the standards currently in effect from the APA, which are described here for you, were not always in place. Some of the studies you'll read about in this book were done before APA standards and IRB committees were standard—and thus, some of those studies have been harshly criticized for being harmful to the people who were in them. Protecting and respecting participants should be the highest priority for anyone conducting research. What are the guidelines?

The American Psychological Association lists several "rights" that they say all participants should have. Again, consider each of these as you read about studies in this book and consider whether you think the study was ethical. In addition, if you have the chance to participate in any studies yourself, it's important for you to know what your rights are—so that you can stop participating at any point if you are uncomfortable or feel like you don't want to continue for any reason. Some of the participant rights identified by the APA are as follows:

Informed consent: Participants' right to be told what they will be asked to do and whether there are any potential dangers or risks involved before a study begins.

- **Informed Consent:** Participants should be told what they will be asked to do and whether there are any potential dangers or risks involved in the study before it begins.

- **Deception:** Participants should be told the truth about the purpose and nature of the study as much as possible. *Deception*, or hiding the true nature of the study, is only allowed when it is necessary because knowing the truth would change how the participants responded.
- **Right to Withdraw:** Participants have the right to stop being in the study at any time, for any reason, or to skip questions on a survey if they are not comfortable answering them.
- **Debriefing:** After completing the study, all participants should be given additional details about the hypotheses of the study, allowed the opportunity to ask questions, and even see the results if they wish. This *debriefing* after the study is complete should definitely include an explanation of any deception that was involved (if deception occurred) so that participants have the right to withdraw their data if they are upset about the deception.

If you want to design your own study, you should consider all of these criteria for the quality of good research. In addition, you'll have to get approval from your school's IRB committee as well before you begin. To learn more about the IRB approval process, see the Spotlight on Research Methods feature.

The Main Ideas

- Reliability, validity, and replication are all criteria regarding the quality of any given research study.

- Reliability is consistency of measurement. Internal validity is the extent to which results are interpreted in an accurate way. External validity is the extent to which results could apply to other people or settings. Replication means repeating a pattern of results over and over, with different people and in different settings.

- Internal validity is increased when participants are randomly assigned to experimental conditions. External validity is increased when participants are selected from a larger population of interest through random sampling, which means the results are more likely to be generalizable.

- Ethical considerations are also very important when evaluating research studies. The American Psychological Association lists several participant rights, such as informed consent and debriefing. In addition, any study must be approved by an IRB before it can be conducted.

⚡ CRITICAL THINKING CHALLENGE

- Imagine a study was done in 1930, before the APA enacted ethical guidelines and before IRB committees were common. If that study were unethical but highly interesting in terms of the results, should textbooks still talk about the study and what we learned from it? Does continuing to talk about the study disrespect the participants, or does learning from it mean that at least we are attempting to get some good from the bad that already occurred?

- Different IRB committees have different levels of strictness regarding ethical thresholds. For example, one committee might be fine with a study that causes participants to temporarily be angry, sad, or aggressive—while another committee might consider the same study unethical. If you were to serve on an IRB committee, how would you decide what the threshold of danger or harm should be? What's the balance between possible risk of harm versus what could be learned from the study?

Deception: Hiding the true nature of an experiment from a participant to prevent a change in how the participant would respond.

Right to withdraw: The right participants have to stop being in a study at any time, for any reason, or to skip questions on a survey if they are not comfortable answering them.

Debriefing: Additional details given to participants after participation in an experiment, including information about the hypotheses, an opportunity to ask questions, an opportunity to see the results, and an explanation of any deception.

CHAPTER SUMMARY

What are the elements of the scientific method?

Basic researchers advance theories, while applied researchers translate those theories into real-world settings or people. Both types of researchers use the scientific method, a systematic way of creating knowledge by (1) observing patterns of behavior, (2) generating a hypothesis, (3) scientifically testing that hypothesis, and (4) interpreting the results to form new, more refined hypotheses. In this way, the scientific method is a circular, never-ending process. Most psychological hypotheses include constructs, which are abstract ideas or concepts. One important step in research is operationalization of variables, in which researchers explicitly define those constructs and decide how to measure them.

There are four common types of research in social psychology. The first is archival research, when data are analyzed that were originally created or gathered for a different purpose (such as newspapers or police records). The second is naturalistic observation, which is carefully watching people behave in their natural environments. A common problem with this method is reactivity, which occurs when the people being observed change their behavior because they are being watched. One specific technique within naturalistic observation is called "participant observation" and occurs when researchers pretend to be part of the natural environment they are observing. A third common method is surveys that include self-report scales, in which participants are explicitly asked to report their thoughts, emotions, and behaviors. While surveys have several advantages, one concern is the social desirability bias, which is when participants answer questions dishonestly to make themselves look better. The fourth type of research is an experimental design, which is described in the next section.

For all of these types of research, a study might have multiple participants or even a single participant. When a study only examines one person or event, it's called a case study. Simple archival data show that the number of case studies being reported in psychology is increasing over time.

How do social psychologists design studies?

In addition to archival data, naturalistic observation, and surveys, researchers can design studies based on experimental or correlational procedures. There are several types of experimental design. Preexperiments test for the effects of a treatment or technique with a single group of people. This can be done with pretests and posttests or with only posttests.

True experiments have more than one group of people who experience different conditions. The different conditions are levels of the independent variable (such as some people who listen to classical music while others listen to rock music). The outcome being measured at the end of the study is called the dependent variable (such as scores on a memory test). Ideally, people have been put into different experimental conditions based on random assignment, meaning everyone has an equal chance of being put in any of the conditions. Random assignment eliminates confounding variables (other explanations for the results). Sometimes control groups are included, which is a baseline or neutral group that receives no treatment at all (for example, a group that listens to no music). When experiments have different people in each condition, it's called a between-participants design.

When the same people go through all of the different conditions, it's called a within-participants design.

Quasi-experiments also compare groups, but the groups are not formed by random assignment. Instead, they are formed naturally. Examples are men versus women, or people who already prefer classical music to rock music. Finally, correlational designs simply measure two variables and then test to see if they seem to have a pattern of association (such as when one goes up, the other also goes up). Height and shoe size are correlated; taller people tend to have bigger feet. Again, it's important to remember that just because two variables are correlated, it doesn't mean that one causes the other.

How do social psychologists analyze and interpret research results?

To analyze the results of any study, researchers use statistics, which are mathematical tests that reveal patterns. When two groups are being compared, a t test will compare the groups' averages and standard deviations to see if they appear different from each other. The same logic is used when comparing three or more groups, but that test is called an analysis of variance (or ANOVA for short).

Correlations are the statistic used to detect patterns within a single group of people but between two variables of interest. For example, a correlation test could tell you if there's a reliable pattern between hours spent studying each week and performance in school. Positive correlations mean the two variables move in the same direction, while negative correlations mean that the two variables move in opposite directions. Correlations also have a coefficient (or number) between zero and 1.00 (either +1.00 or −1.00). A number closer to 1 means a stronger or more reliable association between the two variables. A number closer to zero means that the two variables are weakly associated.

For any of these tests, a p value can tell researchers the probability that the pattern detected in the results would have happened by random chance if the association isn't really there. The p in p value stands for probability, and researchers want it to be as close to zero as possible, meaning the pattern they found wasn't due to chance. Most researchers have agreed that to claim that a pattern of results is "statistically significant," the p value should be between zero and .05, meaning a less than 5% chance of finding the pattern due to chance or luck.

How can research be analyzed in terms of quality?

Reliability, validity, and replication are all important things to consider when trying to evaluate the quality of a research study. Reliability is whether the measures used are consistent. There are several forms of validity, including internal and external validity. Internal validity is the extent to which results are interpreted in an accurate way. For example, causal claims should only be made after true experiments and even then should only be made if people were randomly assigned to the different experimental conditions. External validity is the extent to which results could apply to other people or settings. If a certain pattern of results can only be found within a specific group of people, then the results have low generalizability (they are not true in general for the larger group of interest). The best way to increase generalizability (and thus external validity) is to choose participants randomly from the larger group of interest; this technique is called random sampling. Random sampling will hopefully result in a diverse variety of different kinds of people in the study. Finally, we can only be confident with results if they are replicated (or repeatedly found) across several studies with different people and different settings.

It is also essential to consider the ethical implications of any study. The American Psychological Association has published a list of participant rights that should apply to any psychological study. In addition, local organizations such as universities will have an institutional review board (IRB), a committee that reviews the ethics of any study before it is carried out. Examples of ethical practices are that participants should have informed consent (be told the nature of the study in advance), have the ability to quit the study or skip parts that make them uncomfortable, and that deception (or deceiving the participants) should only be done when necessary. Finally, a debriefing session should occur at the end, which is when participants are given more details about the study and are given the opportunity to ask questions or express concerns.

CRITICAL THINKING, ANALYSIS, AND APPLICATION

- Which of the research methods described in this chapter seem the most appealing to you? Why is that method appealing, and what issues or concerns do you have with the other methods?

- Find a news report that makes a claim that one variable causes another (for example, "Drug X leads to bad behavior," or "Access to birth control leads to risky sex," etc.). Is the causal relationship being suggested one that seems valid? Why or why not? How could this causal claim be scientifically tested?

- How many times does a study have to be replicated in order for researchers—or the general public—to be confident in the results? Even if a study is never replicated, does that mean that the data are useless? What other explanations could there be for results that seem to change (in other words, aren't replicated)? Is it possible that researchers simply haven't identified the exact reason why the pattern happened the first time, for example?

- Ideally, studies have generalizable samples of people who participate. But what if you want to generalize your findings to all of humanity? It's clearly impossible to use random sampling across everyone in the world, so most people just use participants who are nearby volunteers. What's the balance between convenience for the researcher and the need for a diverse, generalizable sample of participants? Are any studies truly high in external validity if they don't have true random sampling?

PERSONAL REFLECTION

Here's the great and terrible thing about thinking like a scientist: It's psychologically addicting. The track behind my house is a weird shape because it circles both the baseball field and the football field. Do runners perform better on this strange-shaped site? I could answer that question with the tools we described in this chapter. But I won't because I don't have time; there are other, even more inviting questions that we can answer. Although it is perfectly safe, the runway for the long jump at another high school in our region is situated so that athletes feel as if they are almost jumping off a cliff. Apparently, my daughter was not alone in jumping her personal best at that site—by almost 16 inches! But I don't have the time for that one either. Right now, I want to know whether the principles that make a well-designed game psychologically addictive can help at-risk students complete college. We're getting answers to that question, too, but every single answer prompts more questions. Research is fun, frustrating, and addictive—you always want more—and more leads to wanting even more. But it's not just a healthy addiction—the scientific method is the engine of innovation across all the sciences. Social psychology, public health, medicine . . . we all are making slow, steady progress by using the scientific method. [TH]

Visit **edge.sagepub.com/heinzen** to help you accomplish your coursework goals in an easy-to-use learning environment.

- **Visual Key Concepts**
- Mobile-friendly **eFlashcards**
- Mobile-friendly practice **quizzes**
- **Video** and **multimedia content**
- EXCLUSIVE! Access to full-text **SAGE journal articles**

$SAGE edge™

L02.3 Summarize the most common ways to analyze and interpret data.

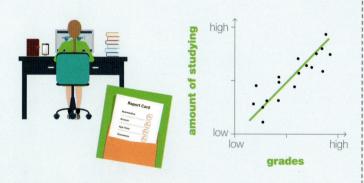

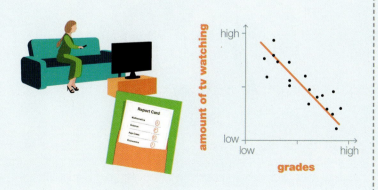

L02.4 Describe reliability, validity, replication, and ethical standards for research in social psychology.

occasionally hits bullseye

misses bullseye

misses bullseye

hits bullseye

reliable not valid **precise** not accurate

not reliable **valid** not precise **accurate**

not reliable not valid not precise not accurate

reliable valid precise accurate

Get a tour of **ALL Visual Key Concepts** and their definitions at **edge.sagepub.com/heinzen**

3 The Social Self

Core Questions

1. What is the "self"?
2. How do we know the self is social?
3. Why do we present different selves in different situations?
4. Is the truth always the self's friend?
5. What is self-esteem and how can we measure it?

Learning Objectives

3.1 Explain how social psychology has defined self-awareness and the self-concept.

3.2 Analyze how our self-perceptions are influenced by others.

3.3 Explain how we adjust our public self-presentation to influence others.

3.4 Articulate why we sometimes benefit from positive illusions and moderate self-deceptions.

3.5 Apply both explicit and implicit methods to the many facets of self-esteem, including its dark side.

Who are you if you have lost your memory? Consider the following movies about memory loss:

Memento (Todd & Todd, 2000): A man finds mysterious tattoos on himself after sustaining brain damage that prevents him from accessing any new memories.

50 First Dates (Giarraputpo, Golin, Juvonen, & Producers, Segal, 2004): A woman has difficulty falling in love because she can't remember the romantic events from the previous day.

The Bourne Ultimatum (F. Marshall, Crowley, Sangberg, & Greengrass, 2007): A CIA agent tries to figure out who he is after suffering long-term amnesia and brainwashing.

Total Recall (Moritz, Jaffe, & Wiseman, 2012): A man in the future discovers his memory has been altered and starts an adventure to discover his true self and history.

Finding Dory (Collins & Stanton, 2016): A friendly but forgetful blue tang fish struggles to be reunited with her long-lost parents.

The characters in these memory-loss movies had to imagine their probable selves into existence. Hollywood scriptwriters are not the only ones using memory loss to imagine the self into existence. The rest of us also have imperfect memories, so we construct our sense of who we are by piecing together fragments of memory, interpreting uncertain evidence, and hoping for the best.

The self is the story we tell ourselves about ourselves. William Swann and Michael Buhrmester (2012) call the self a "functional fiction" because it's a story with a purpose. And even though it's a made-up, pieced-together tale that has an audience of only one person, this solitary self is also a social self. That's because the plot of our self-story always involves family, friends, neighborhood, culture, and much more. To understand how each of us live, think, and behave in a social world, we have to first understand how we define and perceive ourselves.

Infants mirror the expressions of adults while becoming aware of themselves as independent beings.

WHAT IS THE "SELF"?

■■■ LO 3.1: Explain how social psychology has defined self-awareness and the self-concept.

Perhaps the proverbial slap on a newborn baby's backside (or the more likely suction device up the baby's nose) first jars us into self-awareness. Before that moment, we were part of someone else's body. With a snip of the umbilical cord and a sudden breath of air, we became a separate, living creature. But did we know it at that moment? The scientific challenge is to develop a reliable way of discovering how and when we develop **self-awareness** (also called **self-recognition**), the understanding that we are a separate entity from other people and objects in our world. The experience of becoming self-aware (Sedikides & Skowronski, 1997) is not easy to document with the reliability and validity that science requires.

The Scientific Study of Self-Awareness

How we think about ourselves changes over the entire arc of our lives. The creator of psychology's first textbook, William James (1890), wrote that the self "is the sum total of all that a person can call his [today we would add "or her"] own," including

> not only his body and his psychic powers, but his clothes and his house . . . his reputation and works . . . his yacht and his bank-account. All these things give him the same emotions. If they wax and prosper, he feels triumphant; if they dwindle and die away, he feels cast down. (p. 292)

How has science approached the abstract and changing *construct* of self-awareness?

Early Research on Self-Awareness: Darwin and Imitation.
He was really just a proud papa. Charles Darwin couldn't help but notice interesting things about the development of his beautiful new baby. The scientific study of self-awareness began with Darwin's *naturalistic observations* of William, the first of the 10 children of Charles and Emma Darwin. Darwin (1877) carefully observed and reported that his infant son began imitating what he saw and heard:

> When our infant was only four months old I thought that he tried to imitate sounds; but I may have deceived myself, for I was not thoroughly convinced that he did so until he was ten months old. (p. 286)

Since these first observations from Darwin, scientists have been studying imitation as an early sign of self-awareness (Anderson, 1984; Damon & Hart, 1988). A 1977 study documented 2- to 3-week-old infants imitating a mouth opening, a finger moving, or a tongue appearing between the lips (Meltzoff & Moore, 1977). By 1989, the

Charles Darwin noted early signs of mental development in his infant son, William. His "eyes were fixed on a candle as early as the 9th day . . . on the 49th day his attention was attracted by a bright-coloured tassel" (Biographical Sketch of an Infant, p. 286).

same research team had documented imitation among infants who were less than 72 hours old (including a 42-minute-old infant!). Four-month-old infants reliably display a more distinct sense of self by smiling more and looking longer at pictures of others compared to looking at pictures of themselves (Rochat & Striano, 2002).

Testing Self-Awareness: The Mirror Self-Recognition Test. Imitation is interesting to see in infants, but does it really mean that they have self-awareness? To more directly test this, scientists—including Darwin—wanted to come up with a way to test whether people (and animals) seem to realize they are independent, unique entities. Do all animals have a sense of self, or is this perception unique to humans?

Darwin (1872) tried to answer that question with an experiment. He reported that

> many years ago, in the Zoological Gardens, I placed a looking-glass on the floor between two young [orangutans]. . . . They approached close and protruded their lips towards the image, as if to kiss it, in exactly the same manner as they had previously done towards each other. (p. 142)

Those orangutans acted as if the creature in the mirror were another animal, not themselves, suggesting that they did not possess self-awareness.

Almost 100 years later, in 1968, Gordon Gallup followed Darwin's lead by attempting to find out whether some animals respond to their mirror image "as if their image represented another animal" (Gallup, 1968, p. 782). So he created a more controlled version of Darwin's original experiment by first anesthetizing some chimpanzees, macaques, and rhesus monkeys. While they were unconscious, Gallup marked each animal with a nonodorous, nonirritating red dye just above the eyebrow. The animals could not smell, feel, or see the red dye without the help of a mirror.

What would it mean if an animal looked into the mirror, saw the unmistakable red dye, but did not touch the red dye? The animal probably perceived that the creature in the mirror was just some other animal that happened to have a red splotch on its forehead. But what if an animal looked into the mirror and touched the unusual red dye on its own face—not on the mirror? In that case, the animal was telling us, "That's me in the mirror: I am—and I know that I am the one with the red mark." The **mirror self-recognition test** (also called the mark test) creates an opportunity for animals to demonstrate self-awareness. In Gallup's first study, the four chimpanzees (but not the other primates) did indeed touch the red mark on their foreheads. Voila! Gallup had scientifically demonstrated self-awareness among chimpanzees.

More recently, mirror self-recognition studies have also documented self-awareness among Asian elephants (Plotnik, de Waal, & Reiss, 2006), killer whales (Delfour & Marten, 2001), and dolphins (Marino, 2002). Self-awareness among animals is no surprise to dog owners. Misbehaving dogs will slink about and put their tails between their legs in ways that suggest awareness of a guilty self.

Defining and Measuring the Self-Concept

The **self-concept** is the personal summary of who we believe we are; it is how we answer the question, "Who am I?" It includes our assessment of our positive and

Self-awareness: The understanding that we are a separate entity from other people and objects in our world; a state of being conscious of our own existence.

Self-recognition: See *self-awareness*.

Mirror self-recognition test: A scientific paradigm where a mark is placed on an animal's forehead and it is placed in front of a mirror. The animal is assumed to have self-recognition if it touches the mark on its forehead.

Self-concept: The personal summary of who we believe we are, including our assessment of our positive and negative qualities, our relationships to others, and our beliefs and opinions.

© istockphoto.com/Valery Kudryavtsev

Do non-human animals have a sense of self? A YouTube.com search for "animal self-recognition" results in videos on elephants, lions, chimpanzees and others toying with their image in a mirror.

Dogs seem to be aware when they have misbehaved. They appear to demonstrate something like shame—but only when they are caught.

negative qualities, our relationships to others, our beliefs and opinions, and more. We acquire a self-concept in several ways, including the following:

- We compare our self to others (social comparison theory).
- Culture creates expectations about how the self should behave (social identity theory).
- We create mental structures that direct the self's attention (self-schema theory).

Let's consider each of these theories in more detail.

Social Comparison Theory.

Social comparison theory proposes that we use social comparisons to construct our self-concept, especially when we have no other objective standard available to us (Festinger, 1954). How do you know if you are shy, competitive, rich, anxious, or anything else? These subjective ideas only become meaningful in comparison to others.

For example, if you are walking alone on the beach, you may not even be thinking about your physical appearance. But when someone much more attractive walks by, the unflattering social comparison can deliver a small shock to your previously contented self-concept (Bachman & O'Malley, 1986; Marsh, Köller, & Baumert, 2001). At a basic level, there are two types of social comparisons we can make.

- *Upward Social Comparisons.* When we make an **upward social comparison**, we compare ourselves to someone who is better than us. This type of comparison can be useful when we want to improve on a particular skill. Most people who like to watch cooking shows with celebrity chefs enjoy getting tips on how to make their own food taste or look better. The same is true for people who get ideas about home decorating from Martha Stewart or by reading magazines with ideas, or when athletes learn from coaches. However, constantly comparing ourselves to people who have excelled can lead to frustration or even depression—why can't my cupcakes look as good as the ones on Pinterest?
- *Downward Social Comparisons.* That's where the second type of social comparison comes into play: **downward social comparison**. This occurs when we compare ourselves to someone who is worse than we are. This might not help us improve, but it sure feels better. My cupcakes might not win any cupcake reality show contests, sure, but it's better than the cupcake my daughter tried to make, for example. My tennis skills aren't on a professional level, maybe, but I'm better than the guy in the next court who can't hit a single ball over the net.

How we process those social comparisons also makes a difference (Suls & Wheeler, 2000). The W.I.D.E. guide to social comparisons identifies four factors relevant to our subjective processing of what we see around us (see Figure 3.1):

- *Who.* We evaluate our abilities automatically (Gilbert, Giesler, & Morris, 1995) by comparing ourselves to similar others (Gibbons & Buunk, 1999). Tennis players who are about my ability level or a little better give me the most useful social comparison feedback.

Social comparison theory: The use of social comparisons to construct the self-concept when no other objective standard is available.

Upward social comparison: When individuals compare themselves to someone who is better than they are, often to improve on a particular skill.

Downward social comparison: When individuals compare themselves to someone who is worse than they are, often to help them feel better about themselves.

- *Interpretation.* How we interpret social comparisons influences our self-concept. Moving into a group home with sick elderly neighbors could be processed in two very different ways (Michinov, 2007): (1) "Thank goodness that I'm not *that* ill," or (2) "Very soon, I also could be just as needy" (Brandstätter, 2000).

■ FIGURE 3.1 The W.I.D.E. guide suggests that social comparisons are made up of four factors.

W	I	D	E
Who	Interpretation	Direction	Esteem

SOURCE: Adapted from Suls & Wheeler (2000).

- *Direction.* The direction of our social comparison influences our self-concept. Comparing myself to better tennis players is an upward social comparison (that makes me feel worse) and comparing to worse players is a downward social comparison (that makes me feel better). Downward social comparisons tend to enhance our self-concept (Burleson, Leach, & Harrington, 2005; Gibbons et al., 2002; Guimond et al., 2007; Major, Sciacchitano, & Crocker, 1993).

- *Esteem.* Protecting our self-esteem influences our self-concept. The losing tennis player may say to her opponent, "You played extremely well today," implying that her opponent had to play his or her best to beat her (Alicke, LoSchiavo, Zerbst, & Zhang, 1997). We'll talk more about self-esteem—and how we use psychological tricks to protect it—a little later in this chapter.

Social Identity Theory. Henri Tajfel was in a bad situation when he was captured by German soldiers during World War II. He was a Polish-born Jew who had volunteered to join the French army. When the Germans asked who he was, he faced a terrible dilemma; should he admit he was Jewish? He did—but he also falsely presented himself as a French citizen, which probably saved his life. After surviving the war with other French prisoners, Tajfel became a social psychologist who proposed that the self is composed of two general categories:

when acting in groups, we define ourselves in terms of our group membership and seek to have our group evaluated positively relative to other groups

Ask the Experts: Joanne Smith on Social Identity

©SAGE Publications

(1) personal characteristics (serious, funny, grumpy, tall, or rich), and

(2) social role characteristics (son, mother, musician, Catholic, or accountant).

In other words, there are at least these two sides to the self, and they each have many working parts. You are not just "funny"; you are many other things: short-tempered, generous, and so forth. You are not just a student; you are also a daughter or son who has a certain ethnic heritage, religious upbringing, and sexual orientation. Your complicated self is organized around what Tajfel called **social identity theory**, which proposes that our self-concept is composed of a personal identity and a social identity (see Rivenburgh, 2000; Sherif, 1966b; Tajfel, 1981, 1982; Tajfel & Turner, 1986). What are some examples of social identities?

The Regional Self. One social identity is based on where you are from. The well-known social psychologist Roy Baumeister (1986) pointed out that in Medieval times, a person's region was sometimes part of his or her name; "Leonardo da Vinci" means "Leonardo, from Vinci." Regional identity is also apparent in many of the World War II cemeteries in France for soldiers from different countries who died during the Normandy invasion. The cemetery designers organized the soldiers in death—as in life—in regional groups organized first by country and then by region within that country.

- - - - - - - - - - - - - - - - - - - -

Social identity theory: Psychological theory that proposes that our self-concept is composed of two parts: a personal identity that is based on personal characteristics and a social identity that is based on social role characteristics.

- - - - - - - - - - - - - - - - - - - -

The social self is influenced by cultural expectations and traditions that show up in surprising ways in controlled experiments.

Regional affiliations influence how others perceive us *and* how we, in turn, perceive ourselves. For example, one research team found that within the United States, people from Massachusetts are often perceived as intelligent but snobbish, Iowans as hardworking but hicks, Georgians as hospitable but racist, and New Yorkers as ambitious but rude (Berry, Jones, & Kuczaj, 2000). Do you feel proud when someone from *your* country, especially from your region of the country, wins at the Olympics? You probably didn't train, sacrifice, donate money, or even care very much who won until you turned on the television. Nevertheless, our national and regional identity influence our self-concept.

The Cultural Self.

The tricky thing about our cultural self is that we are mostly unaware of it until we happen to bump into another culture. Cultural collisions create humorous situations that have produced some great comedic films such as *My Cousin Vinny* (Launer, Schiff, & Lynn, 1992), *Bend It Like Beckham* (Chadha & Nayar, 2002), *My Big Fat Greek Wedding* (Goetzman, Hanks, Wilson, & Jones, 2002, 2016), and even *Elf* (Berg, Komarnicki, Robertson, & Favreau, 2003). If you have ever traveled to another country, your assumptions, way of life, clothing, and more may have suddenly become salient to you in new ways because you may suddenly realize that your view of the world is changed due to your cultural self.

Independent and Interdependent Self-Construals.

By placing Western and Asian cultures on a cultural continuum, Figure 3.2 adds an additional layer to Tajfel's social identity theory. This continuum is anchored by a personal, **independent self-construal** (many "Western" cultures) at one end and a social, **interdependent self-construal** (many Asian cultures) at the other end.

This means that the ideal self in one culture is very different from the ideal self in another culture. The rugged individualist so valued in the United States will likely be perceived as rude and insensitive in Japan. The conciliatory team player so valued in Japan may be perceived as wimpy and nonassertive in the United States. Table 3.1 helps us understand how cultural norms influence how we think about the self (Markus & Kitayama, 1991).

Self-Schema Theory.

A third way to think about how the self-concept is formed is through **self-schemas**, memory structures that summarize and organize our beliefs about self-relevant information (Markus, 1977).

A **schema** in general is a cognitive and memory structure for organizing the world, so self-schemas transform the raw material from cultural social comparisons into the building blocks of our self-concept (Hewitt & Genest, 1990), creating what Cervone (2004) calls "the architecture of personality."

Independent self-construal: When an individual's ideal self is largely based on internal, personal qualities.

Interdependent self-construal: When an individual's ideal self is largely based on social qualities, especially relationships with others.

Self-schema: A way to think about how the self-concept is formed whereby memory structures that summarize and organize our beliefs about self-relevant information create a cognitive framework within which individuals interpret the events of their lives.

Schema: A cognitive and memory structure for organizing the world.

■ FIGURE 3.2 Identity can be shaped by culture.

Personal Identity (Western)	Social Identity (Asian)
Autonomy	Relatedness
Individualism	Collectivism
Independence	Interdependence
Assertiveness	Self-Effacement

■ TABLE 3.1 Some Examples of How Culture Affects Views of the Self

	To guide group behavior	To get children to finish their food	To improve worker productivity
American culture recommends that . . .	. . . the squeaky wheel gets the grease.	. . . children think of the starving children in Ethiopia and how lucky they are to be American.	. . . workers stand in front of a mirror and repeat: "I am beautiful."
Japanese culture recommends that . . .	. . . the nail that stands up gets pounded down.	. . . children think about the farmer who worked so hard to produce the rice for you and how disappointed he or she will be if it is not eaten.	. . . workers hold a coworker's hand and repeat: "He or she is beautiful."

SOURCE: Data from Markus & Kitayama (1991).

For example, let's say that you wake up late on Wednesday morning. Is your lateness because you are lazy or because you work so hard that you're exhausted? You then speed in traffic heading to your job. Is your speeding because you are a dangerous, careless driver or because you are responsibly trying to get to work as quickly as possible? When you get to work, the first thing you do is get some coffee from the breakroom. Are you addicted and trying to procrastinate, or are you simply trying to get focused so you can be efficient? Instead of chatting with coworkers, you head straight to your desk. Are you rude or simply motivated to accomplish that day's tasks?

Your self-concept creates a coherent self by activating particular self-schemas that help you interpret your own behavior. In this example, your efforts to get to work could lead you to think of yourself in two very different ways: (1) you are lazy, dangerous, addicted, and rude, or (2) you are hard-working, responsible, highly motivated, and determined to succeed. How you interpret the flow of everyday events in your life depends on which self-schemas have been activated, as the schemas create cognitive frameworks for you to interpret the events of your life.

The Main Ideas

- Self-awareness is the understanding that we are a separate entity from other people and objects in our world. One way that scientists have attempted to measure self-awareness is called the mirror self-recognition test.
- Our self-concept is the personal summary of who we believe we are.
- Social comparison theory proposes that our sense of self is influenced by different types of social comparisons, including upward (comparing the self to someone who's better) and downward (comparing the self to someone who's worse).
- Social identity theory describes the self as a mixture of personal and social identities, and self-schema theory suggests that we organize our beliefs about ourselves into mental structures in memory.

⚡ CRITICAL THINKING CHALLENGE

- Identify three activities you enjoy doing, such as sports, hobbies, and studying various subjects. Then, make one upward social comparison and one downward social comparison for each activity. As you identified one person who was better than you and one person who wasn't as advanced, what emotions resulted from each type of comparison?

- List three ways that you typically perceive the world that you think might have been influenced by your regional, national, or specific social cultures. One way to do this might be to think about how your perceptions might be different from the perceptions of people from different cultures.

- Analyze the pros and cons of having a false but positive self-concept. For example, you might delude yourself about how you are now, but would this delusion eventually shape you into a better person?

HOW DO WE KNOW THE SELF IS SOCIAL?

LO 3.2: Analyze how our self-perceptions are influenced by others.

Magnificent? Yes, humans are in many ways. But we are also petty, deceitful, prone to violence, moody, and many other unattractive things. Like winning the lottery, the gift of self-awareness changes our lives in both good and bad ways. We can't *un*-win the lottery once we have won it, and we can't undo having self-awareness and a self-concept once they have evolved. But how do we know that the self is social? You can think of the social self as the storytelling ringmaster in the three-ring circus of our complicated lives. It directs the spotlight of our attention and narrates a story that brings coherence to our otherwise chaotic interactions with others.

Here are three strands of evidence indicating that the self is social: (1) our self-perceptions rely on the behaviors we display to others, (2) self-discrepancy theory describes how different components of the self are influenced by others, and (3) our sense of self often includes other people. Let's talk about each strand.

Self-perception theory: The theory that individuals form their self-concept by observing their own behavior and trying to infer their own motivations, attitudes, values, and core traits.

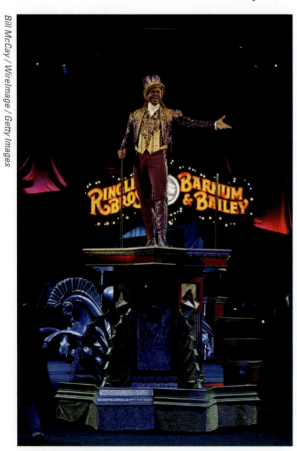

Bill McCay / WireImage / Getty Images

Our "self" sometimes seems like a circus ring master. It usually directs our attention to the most positive self-performances.

Self-Perception Theory: Behaviors Tell Us Who We Are

A friend of mine [Wind's] met my parents a few years ago and was chatting politely with them. My friend casually mentioned to my parents, "Wind really loves waffles!" I was surprised—I don't think I had ever talked to my friend about waffles, and I didn't really consider myself a big waffle fan. When I asked my friend about her statement, though, she said, "Every time we go to brunch, you always order waffles." I thought about it for a second, realized she was right, and realized that yes, I guess I do love waffles! This experience demonstrates self-perception theory.

Self-perception theory proposes that we get help answering the question, "Who am I?" by making inferences about ourselves based on observing our own behaviors (Bem, 1967; Bem & McConnell, 1970). To understand this theory, first think about how you form perceptions of other people. You watch their behaviors and infer—or guess, really—about their motivations, attitudes, values, and core traits based on the behaviors they display to you. You never really know what's going on behind the metaphorical curtain of these outward behaviors.

Self-perception theory proposes that we form our self-concept in very similar ways. Perhaps we don't really have special, privileged access to our inner thoughts and choices all the time—and we thus try to infer our own motivations, attitudes, values, and core traits based on observing *our own* behaviors. If you regularly volunteer at a local dog shelter, then you must be someone who cares about animals. If you love to travel and eat exotic foods, then you must be open to new experiences. We define our self, in part, by how we observe ourselves as we interact with others.

In this way, self-perception theory is the idea that our self-concept forms by observing our own behaviors in a social world. If other people seem to think we're funny, we will likely incorporate "good sense of humor" into our self-concept. If other people look to us to make decisions about where to eat every Friday night, we might come to believe we're decisive leaders. And if you always order waffles when you go to brunch with friends, you probably love waffles. Again, because the self-concept is abstract and subjective, one of the most straightforward ways to decide who we are is by simply observing what we do.

Self-Discrepancy Theory: Are We Trying to Juggle Three Selves?

So far, we've been talking about the self as if we all have a fully formed and single self-concept. Psychologist Tory Higgins (1987, 2002) suggested that in reality, we all have *three* simultaneous selves. We juggle these selves all at once, and they frequently change shape while in the air. As you learn about each one, consider how each contributes to your own self-concept.

The Actual Self. Our first self is our "actual self," which is simply who we think we are, right now. It includes both our good and bad qualities, as well as the qualities we think other people see in us. The actual self is who we are currently, as if someone took a snapshot of our evolving lives. A meaningful actual self can acknowledge our strengths and admit our weaknesses.

The Ideal Self. Higgins hypothesizes that we also have an "ideal self," which is the person we would like to become in the future. It includes enhancing or adding positive qualities that we don't think are maximized in the actual self, and it means eliminating or at least reducing negative qualities we have right now. Our ideal self is our dreams and goals, the person we strive to become. Importantly, our ideal self is truly based on what *we* want, even if that means secret desires we've never been able to admit to anyone else. If you could, for example, have any job in the world, or look a certain way, or live a particular lifestyle, what would it be?

The Ought Self. In contrast with the ideal self, our "ought" self is what we think other people expect of us. The ought self is based on our perception of what our social world hopes for us, perhaps what our parents want us to do or be, what our friends believe would be good for us, or even what our culture tells us is proper and correct. The ought self may influence how we dress, for example, because we know what is expected of us. Interestingly, our ought self might change based on whom our reference is. For example, what you think your parents expect of you might be very different from what you think a first date expects of you.

When Selves Don't Align: Self-Discrepancy. Higgins suggests that not only do we have to juggle these three simultaneous selves, but we also have to deal with times when the selves don't match up. He refers to the mismatch between our three selves as **self-discrepancy**. How do you feel when your actual self doesn't match your ideal self? Are these emotions different from those you experience when your actual self doesn't match your ought self?

Our discrepancies have predictable consequences that Higgins explored in research. He found that when the actual self and ideal self don't match—in other words, when we don't live up to our own ideals or we fail to achieve our dreams—we will experience "dejection-related emotions" such as disappointment, shame, embarrassment, and possibly even depression (Higgins, 1987).

On the other hand, sometimes our actual self doesn't match our ought self. When this happens, we'll feel that we haven't lived up to others' expectations—and that kind of failure produces "agitation-related emotions" such as guilt, fear, self-contempt, and anxiety. Of course, the ideal situation would be that all three selves (actual, ideal, and ought) are exactly in alignment, with perfect overlap. As you can see in Figure 3.3, this would be like a Venn diagram of three circles. Each time the selves get closer together, the circles overlap more until only a single, perfect circle remains because they are all the same self. How likely do you think this is to achieve? Can you see discrepancies between your actual, ideal, and ought selves?

For more on self-discrepancy theory, see the Social Psychology in Popular Culture feature on "Self-Discrepancy Theory and Wonder Woman."

Self-Expansion Theory: Inclusion of Others in the Self

While self-discrepancy theory suggested that we might have more than one self-concept, other social psychologists have suggested that our self-concept might even include other people. Certainly, social identity theory noted that our sense of self includes our group memberships and our relationships with other people. But could our abstract sense of self also actually include specific other individuals in our social world?

Self-expansion theory is the idea that all of us have a basic motivation to grow, improve, and enhance our self-concept; we all want to reach our greatest potential (Aron & Aron, 1996; Aron, Aron, & Norman, 2001). While other theories have noted that we can do that through things like identifying our flaws or working toward our ideal self, self-expansion theory specifically suggests that one common way we attempt to "expand" our self-concept is through close social relationships. If we psychologically bond with others and feel that these individuals now become part of who we are, then their strengths, resources, knowledge, and skills can help us grow and have new opportunities.

Psychologically including others in our self-concept is measured by the **Inclusion of the Other in the Self (IOS) Scale**, which presents people with a series of seven Venn diagrams with increasing overlap between "self" and "other" (see Figure 3.4; Aron, Aron, & Smollan, 1992). Participants simply circle the pair of circles that they feel accurately indicates how much their self-concept now includes the other person. The IOS Scale is most commonly used in research on romantic partners, such as

Self-discrepancy: When a mismatch exists between an individual's actual, ideal, and ought selves.

Self-expansion theory: The idea that all humans have a basic motivation to grow, improve, and enhance our self-concept, specifically through close social relationships.

Inclusion of the Other in the Self (IOS) scale: a scale used to measure psychological inclusion of others in the self-concept where people circle one of many pairs of circles with increasing overlap between "self" and "other" to indicate how much their self-concept includes a specified other person.

■ FIGURE 3.3 Three selves might exist for each of us, according to self-discrepancy theory.

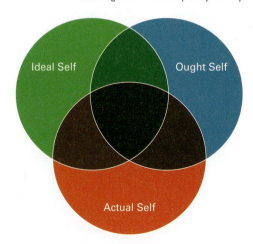

SELF-DISCREPANCY THEORY AND WONDER WOMAN

Social Psychology in Popular Culture

Sabena Jane Blackbird / Alamy Stock Photo

Most superheroes have secret identities—but does this complicate how they think about their own self-concept? The most popular female superhero of all time is Wonder Woman, whose secret identity is Diana Prince. But really, both of these identities are costumes; she's really Princess Diana from Paradise Island. When the *Wonder Woman* movie came out in 2017, it broke the record for opening-weekend ticket sales (over $100 million) for a movie with a female director (Lang, 2017). But the original D.C. comics (which started in 1942 for this character) provides an interesting view into the character's original conceptualization.

Applying Tory Higgins's (1987, 2002) self-discrepancy theory, Princess Diana would be her "actual self"—her true identity and the person she is when she's not taking on one of her other identities. Most people would probably say that Wonder Woman is Diana's "ideal self," the self that embodies all of her goals, or the best version of the person she could be. Most regular humans strive for an ideal self in the future, but superheroes usually get to reach their ideals a bit sooner than us mere mortals. Interestingly, though, even Diana has to deal with people judging her, which makes her "ought self" come alive. In the early Wonder Woman comics, both men and women make comments about how her star-spangled outfit is inappropriate and skimpy. When Diana is pretending to be Diana Prince, a modest and gentle military secretary, her love interest Steve Trevor constantly tells her that she's not as attractive, strong, and amazing as Wonder Woman. Diana thus is judged both when she's embodying her Wonder Woman identity (she's too brazen and nonconformist) and when she's embodying her Diana Prince identity (she's too subdued and conformist). It's apparently hard to be a modern woman, even when you have super powers, an invisible plane, and a magic lasso.

For a more detailed analysis of self-discrepancy theory as applied to Wonder Women, see the book Wonder Woman Psychology: Lassoing the Truth *(2017) and read the chapter "Multiple Identities, Multiple Selves?" by Goodfriend and Formichella-Elsden.*

spouses (e.g., Agnew, Loving, Le, & Goodfriend, 2004; Agnew, Van Lange, Rusbult, & Langston, 1998), but it has also been used to measure how much people see themselves as cognitively including their social groups on a larger scale (e.g., Mashek, Cannaday, & Tangney, 2007; Mattingly & Lewandowski, 2013, 2014).

■ **FIGURE 3.4** Inclusion of the Other in the Self (IOS) Scale

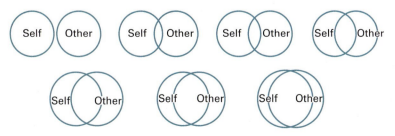

SOURCE: Aron, Aron & Smollan (1992).

The Main Ideas

- Self-perception theory proposes that we form our self-concept by observing our own behaviors, then making assumptions about our internal values, attitudes, and so on based on those behaviors.

- Self-discrepancy theory suggests that instead of a single self, we all have three selves: (1) the actual self (who we are right now), (2) the ideal self (who we'd like to become), and (3) the ought self (who others expect us to be). When our actual self doesn't match our ideal self, we experience dejection-related emotions. When our actual self doesn't match our ought self, we experience agitation-related emotions.

- Self-expansion theory is the idea that we all want to grow and improve, and one way to do that it to cognitively include other people into our self-concept. One way to measure this cognitive self-expansion is through the Inclusion of the Other in the Self Scale, which shows a series of seven progressively overlapping circles; participants choose the one that best represents how they include someone else in their self-concept.

⚡ CRITICAL THINKING CHALLENGE

- Think of at least two times when you realized something about your self-concept by observing your behaviors. Why did you not have this self-insight before you noticed your own behaviors?

- Make a list of traits that make up your actual self, then one for your ideal self, and finally one for your ought self. Mark the traits that match across lists, and mark the traits that don't match. How do you feel about the traits that don't match? Are the emotions you experience in alignment with what self-discrepancy theory hypothesized you would feel?

- Do you think it's healthy for two relationship partners to circle the most-overlapping set of circles, or does this somehow indicate codependency? What do you think would be the "best" pair of circles for couple members to choose, and why?

WHY DO WE PRESENT DIFFERENT SELVES IN DIFFERENT SITUATIONS?

LO 3.3: Explain how we adjust our public self-presentation to influence others.

In the quaint, olden days before mobile phones, a sociology researcher observed that it was not unusual for a college woman living in a dormitory to impress her dorm mates with her popularity by arranging for "herself to be called several times in order to give all the other girls ample opportunity to hear her paged" (Waller, 1937, p. 730). That kind of shallow affirmation probably still happens today when, for example, we may subtly broadcast the number of our social media "friends" to signal our popularity.

Both cases represent behavior that Erving Goffman (1959) describes as a performance—even when we are not fully self-aware that we are performing. People perform in slightly different ways for family, friends, peers, supervisors, professors, and store clerks. This tendency is called **self-presentation theory** or **impression management**, ways that we adjust the self to gain social influence by managing the impressions that we make on others.

Self-presentation theory: The tendency to adjust the self and perform in slightly different ways for varying others to gain social influence.

Impression management: See *self-presentation theory.*

This is not a startling insight, but the routine use of impression management needs to be acknowledged. We do not behave the same way at a funeral as we would at a rock concert or a job interview. Put simply, in different settings, we present different parts of our self-concept. As Kurt Lewin learned while serving as a foot soldier in World War I, our behavior often depends on how we perceive the immediate situation (see Goffman, 1959).

Can a smiling face mask your real feelings when pulled over by police?

We Use Impression Management to Get What We Want

We employ impression management tactics as social power. We might act disappointed to get more attention, pretend to be surprised at a high price hoping for a discount, or even buy a conspicuously fancy sports car to signal sexual availability (Sundie et al., 2011). There are specific tactics associated with impression management.

Ingratiation: Other-Enhancements and Opinion Conformity.
Cynthia Stevens and Amy Kristof (1995) were interested in how job applicants try to influence interviewers by presenting certain aspects of the self. One common tactic was ingratiation. This short-term impression management tactic is designed to increase liking and attraction by complimenting the other person and seeming to admire him or her. One form of ingratiation is **other-enhancement**, praising the interviewer. A variation with the same goal is **opinion conformity**, endorsing the interviewer's perceived attitudes or values.

You can probably think of some of the cruder terms used to describe people who try to ingratiate themselves with people in power by praising everything they do and agreeing with everything they say. No matter what term you use, ingratiation is explicit attempts to present a version of the self that you think the other person will like in an attempt to benefit yourself somehow—such as getting a job offer.

Self-Promotion: Self-Enhancements and Entitlements.
Self-promotion is another short-term impression management tactic that uses positive statements about the self to convey competence. One form of self-promotion is **self-enhancements**; that's when you imply that your actual accomplishments are more significant than they first appear to be. Another common form of self-promotion is **entitlements**; that's when you take credit for positive events even if you had nothing to do with them. These may be effective short-term tactics, but they can backfire. For example, taking credit for someone else's work may turn a friend into a long-term enemy and damage your reputation with important people.

Conspicuous Consumption.
Depending on the type of job, gaining an advantage during a job interview is a short-term tactic. But there are impression management strategies with long-term goals. A young politician with ambitions may carefully calculate the right kind of marriage partner to influence future voters. Others will attempt to influence the impression they make on others by spending money on flashy or high-status items, such as expensive homes, cars, clothes, and jewelry. Publicly displaying the use of expensive products in an attempt to impress others is called **conspicuous consumption**.

In the 19th century, the Norwegian American economist Thorstein Veblen (1899/1918) recognized that some conspicuous consumption is as *un*subtle as a male peacock showing off its extravagant feathers to females (see Darwin, 1871; Møller & Petrie, 2002). Peacocks flash colorful tails to signal their reproductive value to peahens the

Other-enhancement: A short-term impression management tactic where people compliment another person and seem to admire them to increase liking and attraction and gain social influence.

Opinion conformity: A short-term impression management tactic where people endorse the opinion of others to increase liking and attraction and gain social influence.

Self-enhancements: A short-term impression management technique where people imply that their actual accomplishments are more significant than they first appear to be.

Entitlement: A short-term impression management tactic where a person takes credit for positive events he or she was not a part of.

Conspicuous consumption: Publicly displaying the use of expensive products in an attempt to impress others.

same way that some men drive fancy cars to attract females. Most women, by the way, easily decode conspicuous consumption by men as a desire for uncommitted sexual partnerships (Sundie et al., 2011).

Brain Damage Can Limit Self-Presentation Ability

This next part is sad. Some people with advanced cases of Alzheimer's disease can't pass the mirror self-recognition test. They look into the mirror and have no idea who is looking back at them (see Biringer, Anderson, & Strubel, 1988; Bologna & Camp, 1997; Phillips, Howard, & David, 1996). Alzheimer's disease is not the only tragic but useful clue telling us how the self and the brain are connected. Consider one of the most famous case studies in the history of brain research and what it can teach us about our ability to purposefully change how we present ourselves to others.

Phineas Gage: A Landmark Case Study. Phineas Gage's story began on September 13, 1848, when he was working as the foreman of a crew working for the railroad (see Macmillan, 2000). The crew traveled along the path where the railroad was to be built and blew up anything in the way. Apparently, Gage was a very good foreman. Many of the railroad construction workers near Cavendish, Vermont, were Irish immigrants who had carried their ancient regional feuds into America. These were difficult-to-manage men, and an unpopular foreman was subject to "violent attacks . . . some of which ended fatally" (Macmillan, 2000, p. 22). Nevertheless, Dr. John Harlow (Gage's doctor) described the preaccident Gage as a man "who possessed a well-balanced mind," "a shrewd business man," and a man "of temperate habits and possessed of considerable energy of character." He was good at managing people.

On the day of his famous accident, Gage was using his 43-inch, 13-pound iron rod to tamp what he thought was sand on top of blasting powder. The blasting powder had been poured into a hole drilled deep into some rock. The rod was flat at one end but pointed at the end sticking out of the hole. The purpose of the sand was to direct the force of the explosion into the rock rather than back out the hole. The fuse had been set—but this time the sand was missing. Perhaps someone called to Gage to warn him that the sand was not yet in the hole. As Gage turned his head over the hole, the iron rod somehow slipped from his fingers, sparked against the rock, and ignited the blasting powder.

Social Psychology in Action:
Phineas Gage

©SAGE Publications

Phineas Gage's personality changed after his brain accident—but not entirely. He drove a four-horse stage coach in Chile for perhaps seven years. He later told entertaining tall tales about his travels to his nieces and nephews.

The long iron rod shot upward, entered beneath and through Gage's left cheek, passed behind most of his left eye, continued through the front left portion of his brain, and exited out the top of his head. It landed about 23 meters (or 75 feet) away, greasy with Gage's brain matter—and it was still greasy the next day even after some railroad workers rinsed it in a nearby stream. Gage was knocked over, of course, but then surprised everyone by getting up, walking to an oxcart to be taken to a doctor, and writing a note in his foreman's log book—despite a very large hole in his head! Dr. Harlow cleaned the wound, shoved pieces of Gage's skull back into place, and started recording what would become one of the most famous case studies in brain science.

Say Goodbye to Self-Presentation. Was Phineas Gage harmed? Well, he could still recognize his mother and uncle. He understood what had happened to him. And, only a few days after his accident, Gage made plans to return to work. But his physical health cycled between recovery, infection, and delirium for several weeks. As his condition slowly stabilized, Dr. Harlow noticed some odd features about his patient.

Gage's memory was "as perfect as ever" but now the once shrewd businessman "would not take $1000 for a few pebbles." That was odd. Had Gage lost his ability to understand money? About a month after the accident, Harlow wrote that Gage had become "exceedingly capricious and childish . . . will not yield to restraint when it conflicts with his desires." His self-governing mental habits had disappeared. The once effective foreman had been replaced by someone with crude speech and childish impulses. The change in his personality was so great that Gage's friends described the postaccident man as "no longer Gage." Apparently, the damage to Gage's left frontal lobes was linked to a profound change in his self—but not all of his self.

It is easy to imagine Gage's acquaintances saying, "Why doesn't Phineas just stop saying such profane things? Doesn't he know what he's doing?" The answer seems to be no; Gage seemed to have minimal **self-insight**, the ability to self-observe and evaluate our own behavior. Certainly, self-insight is essential if we want to be aware of how we're presenting ourselves in public situations and especially if we want to use impression management to get other people to like us.

In addition to his seeming lack of self-insight, the new Gage was probably less able to notice and adjust his behavior across different social situations. Curiously, patients with similar brain damage (usually due to brain surgery) tell a similar story. When Beer, John, Scabini, and Knight (2006) allowed patients with similar brain damage to see themselves on a video recording, they discovered that they were disclosing personal and inappropriate information. What we call the "self" appears to be connected to particular regions and neural pathways within the brain—and our tendency to display different aspects of our self can be affected by brain damage.

Self-Monitoring: Social Chameleons

After his brain damage, Phineas Gage seemed to lose his ability to **self-monitor**, or change how he acted in different social situations in an attempt to fit in. Self-monitoring suggests an awareness that we have a complicated self that needs monitoring. Some people excel at being "social chameleons" that can blend into almost any environment. Others just don't seem to care. There are benefits and drawbacks to both approaches.

Low Self-Monitors. Some people act the same way no matter where they are or who is around them—they are always shy, for example, or always sarcastic. People who appear to have little change in their personality or self-presentation across time and situations are considered low in self-monitoring. They pay little attention to how they "come across" to other people and act consistently no matter where they are.

Self-insight: Individuals' ability to self-observe and evaluate their own behavior.

Self-monitor: Individuals' ability to notice and adjust their own behavior in an attempt to fit in.

Chameleons can change color to disguise themselves and fit into their environment. Are people capable of similar changes, based on their social environment?

High Self-Monitors. However, other people are high in self-monitoring, and their behavior is the opposite: They change how they act all the time, depending on the situation. In a cooperative environment, they cooperate; in a competitive environment, they compete. High self-monitors are people who look around and assess their environment, then adapt their self-presentation to get whatever they want out of that particular situation.

Adaptability Versus Authenticity: Which Way Is Best? There are advantages and disadvantages to being high in self-monitoring. Certain careers such as sales, politics, and acting require people who can change how they act and appear on cue. It also seems reasonable that people who can easily and comfortably fit in with anyone will be more popular and may advance more quickly in their workplaces. However, sometimes people who are high in self-monitoring can seem inauthentic to others. If they are always changing how they act, others will wonder, who is the "real" person?

The Symphonic Self: The Poetry of Science

Let's take a two-paragraph pause to reflect on Phineas Gage from an artistic perspective. Gage's life illustrates how the self constantly tries to create coherence out of the scattered experiences of our lives. Fernando Pessoa (2002) wrote in *The Book of Disquiet* that "my soul is like a hidden orchestra; I do not know which instruments grind and play away inside of me, strings and harps, timbales and drums. I can only recognize myself as a symphony" (p. 310). The self simultaneously draws on brain regions and neural pathways the same way that a symphony conductor simultaneously draws on multiple sections of an orchestra to produce an overall effect. Gage's self after his accident was like an orchestra missing a few instruments.

One brain scientist, however, believes that what our brain does every day is far more impressive than the most beautiful symphony orchestra. Damasio (2010) continued the metaphor, writing that "the marvel . . . is that the score and conductor become reality only as life unfolds" (p. 24). The self is a symphony orchestra that plays magnificent music only once, without a score, and without any rehearsal—and then flows smoothly into its next performance. What a magnificent, creative self!

The Main Ideas

- Self-presentation (also called impression management) refers to the ways we adjust our self in public to gain social acceptance or influence. Specific ways we alter self-presentation include ingratiation, self-promotion, and conspicuous consumption.

- Phineas Gage's famous accident revealed a connection between the self and the brain. After Gage suffered brain damage, his personality changed, but his ability to change his self-presentation also went away.

- Self-monitoring refers how much we choose to alter our public presentations of self in different social situations, in an attempt to fit in. People who are high self-monitors change across situations, while low self-monitors act consistently regardless of the situation.

- What do the clothes you wear tell others about yourself? For example, do you wear sports logos or clothes with the name of your school? Why do people display parts of their identity in this way?

- Under what circumstances are you more likely to use ingratiation, self-promotion, or conspicuous consumption? Are there situations where attempting to use these self-presentation tactics would backfire?

- How do the goals and tactics of impression management change across different phases of a romantic relationship?

- Do we have a core self (what some call a soul) if we constantly adjust our self to gain social power, impress people, or validate our opinions?

IS THE TRUTH ALWAYS THE SELF'S FRIEND?

LO 3.4: Articulate why we sometimes benefit from positive illusions and moderate self-deceptions.

The self-story is a compelling story, at least to ourselves, because it is *our* version of events (Silvia & Gendolla, 2001). But what if we are telling ourselves a very nice story that is not true? Do people really lie to themselves like that? Steven Pinker compares our storytelling selves to political spin-doctors who are always looking for ways to make their candidates look good (Pinker, 2002). Like some real politicians, we create self-stories that smell a little bit too good to be true. Why not? If I am the screenwriter, producer, director, and final-cut editor of my self-story, I can make the story come out any way that I want. Does that make our self-story fiction or nonfiction?

Optimal Margin Theory: Positive Illusions Can Be Beneficial

Let's be blunt about it: Sometimes we lie to ourselves. Minor self-deceptions show up in many parts of our lives. For example, when our romantic partner asks, "Does this outfit make me look fat?" most partners understand that the desired responses are "No," or, "You look great, but your black top might look even better." But is there anything wrong with believing that we are a little bit more attractive, caring, intelligent, or insightful than we really are? Baumeister (1989) developed **optimal margin theory**, which proposes a slight to moderate range of healthy distortions of reality. A little bit of self-deception can make us feel good—but too much distortion of reality causes problems.

Instead of the "cold, hard truth," we often prefer to believe **positive illusions**, beliefs that depart from reality in ways that influence us to remain optimistic. For example, drivers know that a potential car accident is around every corner, but positive illusions help us manage such chronic stress by maintaining an illusion of more control over our driving fate than we really have (Taylor, Kemeny, Reed, Bower, & Gruenewald, 2000). Shelley Taylor and her colleagues assert that we use three types of self-deceptions that promote our own positive mental health. We:

(1) cling to the belief we can control our own lives more than we can (control),

(2) believe in an unrealistically optimistic view of the future (optimism), and

(3) discover meaning in critical life events, such as bereavement (meaning).

Optimal margin theory: Psychological theory that proposes a slight to moderate range of healthy distortions of reality improves psychological and physiological well-being.

Positive illusions: Beliefs that depart from reality in ways that help us to remain optimistic, especially in relation to the belief we can control our own lives more than we can, the tendency to have an unrealistically optimistic view of the future, and the desire to discover meaning in critical life events.

Age can just be a number—how old you feel is subjective.

For example, one way that many older people use positive illusions to feel more optimistic and in control is called **subjective age**, our sense of how old we feel compared to our chronological age. For example, the chronological age range was between 60 and 95 in a study of more than 800 French retirees (Gana, Alaphilippe, & Bailly, 2004). The researchers wanted to test (a) whether self-deception about their subjective age was harmful or helpful and (b) whether the possible benefits of self-deception stopped when people deceived themselves too much—when they, so to speak, "went off the deep end" of the self-deception continuum.

Optimal margin theory suggests that, like wine, a little self-deception can be a good thing—too much, however, can become dangerous. For the French retirees, those with positive illusions about their age "reported more satisfaction with daily pursuits (leisure time), higher self-worth, and less boredom proneness" (Gana et al., 2004, p. 63). But the people in this sample may not have gotten too close to the edge of unhealthy self-deception. The 85-year-olds, for example, may have thought of themselves as closer to 70 but probably did not think of themselves as 20-year-olds. Subjective age is not the only way we use moderate amounts of self-deception to improve the quality of our lives.

Self-Serving Cognitive Biases

Research has established that a little bit of self-deception—making us feel slightly more intelligent, attractive, funnier, more talented, and so on—has a lot of benefits. These benefits include less anxiety (Brockner, 1984), better coping with stress and setbacks (Steele, 1988), lower levels of depression (Tennen & Herzberger, 1987), and general life satisfaction (Myers & Diener, 1995). Cognitive distortions that enhance our self-concept by making us perceive that we're a little better than we are, objectively, are called **self-serving cognitive biases**. Let's look at three specific examples of how we distort reality, just a little, to maintain these self-serving views.

Biased Views of Our Own Traits. On a piece of scrap paper or in the margin of this book, quickly jot down three of your best traits or qualities and three of your worst. Now, for each trait you wrote down, estimate on a scale from 0 to 100 the percentage of students at your college or university who also possess this trait.

Subjective age: How old individuals feel compared to their chronological age.

Self-serving cognitive biases: Cognitive distortions that enhance people's self-concept by making them perceive that they are a little better than they actually are.

When Marks (1984) had college students do this exact task, people underestimated how many of their peers shared their positive traits and overestimated how many people shared their negative traits. How does this cognitive bias enhance our self-concept? It works because if you think that your positive qualities are rare, that makes you really special. And if your negative qualities are common—hey, everyone has this problem!—then your worst qualities are bad, sure, but not really a big deal.

We underestimate how many people share our talents (Goethals, Messick, & Allison, 1991) and we normalize our negative attitudes or traits so that we don't feel singled out or stigmatized (Suls & Wan, 1987). We can admit fears, such as speaking in front of a group, but we tell ourselves that everyone else shares our anxieties and, thus, these problems are not "fatal flaws." We comfort ourselves by simply framing our "best" and "worst" qualities in this way that makes us feel just a little better.

Biased Views of Our Own Behaviors. Another self-serving cognitive bias emerges when we consider causes for our own successes and failures. Like admitting negative traits we possess, we can admit that we've done bad things or failed at something—but we often protect our view of the self by coming up with an excuse or justification for bad behaviors.

In a review of over 20 studies on this topic, Miller and Ross (1975) found that often, people engage in self-enhancing views of success. When people succeed at a task, they are more likely to perceive that this success is due to their own behaviors, effort, and talent than when they fail. Failures are due to some external, situational factor instead. Did you get an A on the test? You must have studied hard or be really good at this subject! Did you fail the test? It's probably because you were sick, or you stayed up late helping a friend with a crisis, or the test was unfair. By attributing successes to our own efforts—but failures to something we can't control or to something about the situation—we can take credit for doing well and simultaneously avoid blame for doing badly.

Biased Views of Feedback About the Self. A third self-serving cognitive bias is the tendency for people to view feedback about themselves in a skewed manner. Many people enjoy taking little quizzes about themselves on websites like Facebook, for example. When you like the outcome, you might think, "Hey, that was a great quiz! Really insightful." But if you don't like the outcome, it's easy for you to see how the questions were flawed.

People often "discover" validity problems in tests that depict them in a negative or unflattering light; however, they are far less critical of evidence that portrays them positively (Baumeister, 1998; Pyszczynski, Greenberg, & Holt, 1985). For example, one study led participants to either "succeed" or "fail" at a fake social sensitivity test. After seeing their results, participants then saw information that indicated that the test itself was either valid or invalid. Participants who had "succeeded" evaluated the valid conclusion significantly more favorably than people in the invalid condition, and the opposite occurred for people who had "failed" (Pyszczynski et al., 1985).

As usual, more research is needed. But it's interesting that we have several studies with different methodologies that seem to be telling the same story. Optimal margin theory might be right: A little bit of self-deception seems pretty common, and moderate levels can be helpful to maintaining a positive self-concept. To learn about how positive illusions can be applied to social relationships, read the Spotlight on Research Methods feature on "Positive Illusions in Dating Relationships."

Sometimes, our view of our self isn't quite accurate. But is that a bad thing?

POSITIVE ILLUSIONS IN DATING RELATIONSHIPS

One of this book's authors [Wind] focused my graduate school research on positive illusions in romantic couples (Goodfriend, 2005; Goodfriend, Agnew, & Cathey, 2017). I measured positive cognitive biases within relationships in two different ways. First, I asked college students to list the five "best" and five "worst" aspects of their current partner. After making these lists (which everyone could easily do), the participants then considered each of these 10 traits and rated how common or rare they are in general society. As expected, people said their partner's best traits were rare—making them special and "a keeper"—but their worst traits were common and therefore no big deal. In short, the participants showed bias by thinking their partner was "better than average."

In a second study, I asked people to consider six hypothetical positive things their partner might do—such as giving them a surprise gift—and six hypothetical negative behaviors, such as betraying a secret of theirs to a third person. Each hypothetical behavior was presented as the first half of a sentence, and participants were asked to write in the second half of the sentence to explain *why* their partner might have done this. I found that when people were in happy, committed relationships, they wrote that positive behaviors must have been done because their partner was a good person or because they were in love. But, when trying to explain negative behaviors, they wrote that there must have been strange circumstances that required this behavior to protect each other. That trend didn't reach statistical significance for people in unhappy relationships.

In other words, in happy couples, positive behaviors had "dispositional" attributions, while negative behaviors had "situational" attributions. When in love, we give our partners the benefit of the doubt and provide excuses for their bad behavior. My data suggest that the insight attributed to philosopher Francis Bacon 400 years ago is probably still true of modern romantic relationships: "We prefer to believe what we prefer to be true."

The Main Ideas

- The self is a constructed story that we tell our selves about ourselves. Optimal margin theory explains that small to moderate levels of positive illusions can be helpful in maintaining a positive self-concept.

- Three specific types of self-serving cognitive biases are biased views of (1) our own traits, (2) our own behaviors, and (3) feedback about the self.

- Positive illusions can also be seen within social relationships, such as between dating partners.

⚡ CRITICAL THINKING CHALLENGE

- In the movie *Liar Liar* (Grazer & Shadyac, 1997), a lawyer is compelled to always tell the truth, both to others and to himself. How is lying to others different from lying to yourself?

- If optimal margin theory is true, then how will you know when you have gone beyond the boundary of healthy self-deception? Can you identify ways that you are currently engaging in self-deception?

- What topics are we most likely to deceive ourselves about?

- Moderate positive illusions about romantic partners seem to be correlated with relationship satisfaction. How far can this tendency go before it starts to harm people and keep them in relationships that are actually unhealthy or abusive?

WHAT IS SELF-ESTEEM AND HOW CAN WE MEASURE IT?

LO 3.5: Apply both explicit and implicit methods to the many facets of self-esteem, including its dark side.

Let's begin with a practical question: What do we mean by "self-esteem"? Bosson, Swann, and Pennebaker (2000) compare researchers' attempts to define self-esteem to the classic story of six blind men trying to describe an elephant. One feels its trunk and says an elephant is like a large snake; another feels its side and concludes that an elephant is like a wall. A third feels its tail and reports that an elephant is like a broom. Each of the six blind men offers a different description based on their private experience of touching the elephant. Research on self-esteem can be kind of like the story of the blind men; each study or scientist can pick one aspect of the concept and examine in it detail—but encapsulating the entire idea of self-esteem can be difficult.

Defining Self-Esteem

Here's a definition to get us started on the path to understanding: **Self-esteem** is our subjective, personal evaluation of our self-concept. Earlier, we learned that our self-concept is our perception of qualities, relationships, beliefs, and opinions. When we *evaluate* that self-concept and decide that it is good, bad, worthwhile, worthless, or any other type of judgment, that's self-esteem.

Unfortunately, the nonpsychology public's understanding of self-esteem includes many related constructs that, like barnacles on a boat, have attached themselves to the construct of self-esteem—and taken a free ride into our social thinking. Let's start scraping off some of those barnacles by clarifying what self-esteem is *not* (Baumeister, Smart, & Boden, 1996; Crocker & Major, 1989, 2003; Greenwald et al., 2002).

For example, self-esteem is not the same thing as **self-compassion**, an orientation to care for oneself. Leary, Tate, Adams, Allen, and Hancock (2007) describe self-compassion as self-esteem but without "the self-enhancing illusions" (p. 887). Self-esteem is also separate from **narcissism**, an excessive self-love based on unwarranted belief in one's specialness relative to others (Neff & Vonk, 2009). Narcissism is basically arrogance. Self-esteem focuses on whether we regard ourselves as a person of worth; narcissism focuses on whether we regard ourselves as *more* worthy than others (Donnellan, Trzesniewski, Robins, Moffitt, & Caspi, 2005).

Self-esteem is also distinct from **self-efficacy**, the degree to which you believe that you are capable of completing a specific task or achieving a particular goal. Self-efficacy seems to be a good thing, at least most of the time. Self-efficacy contributes to self-esteem (Begue, 2005), helps people cope with failure in the workplace (Newton, Khanna, & Thompson, 2008), and encourages resilience in the face of chronic diseases such as diabetes (Yi, Vitaliano, Smith, Yi, & Weinger, 2008). Self-esteem is not self-compassion, narcissism, or self-efficacy. It's our evaluation of our own worth, based on our assessment of our self-concept.

Self-esteem: Individuals' subjective, personal evaluation of their self-concept, including judgments made about self-worth.

Self-compassion: An orientation to care for oneself.

Narcissism: Excessive self-love based on unwarranted belief in one's specialness relative to others.

Self-efficacy: The degree to which individuals believe that they are capable of completing a specific task or achieving a particular goal.

Two Strategies for Measuring Self-Esteem

Because self-esteem is a complex, abstract, and subjective *construct*, it's important to think about how researchers *operationalize* it in scientific studies. There are two general strategies for measuring self-esteem: explicit, direct measures and implicit, indirect measures (Bosson et al., 2000).

Measuring Explicit Self-Esteem (Directly). One of the most popular self-report scales in the entire field of psychology is a short and simple, 10-item questionnaire created by Rosenberg over 50 years ago (1965). Rosenberg's Self-Esteem Scale is a direct, explicit measure. It has what is called *face validity* because it is obvious (on its face) what the scale is intended to measure: how much you value your self. The Rosenberg scale has clarified many of the connections between self-esteem and related psychological constructs (Brummett, Wade, Ponterotto, Thombs, & Lewis, 2007; Hair, Renaud, & Ramsay, 2007; Penkal & Kurdek, 2007).

Try it for yourself in the Applying Social Psychology to Your Life feature (you will find it easier to understand the material that comes next if you know your own self-esteem score). As we discussed in Chapter 2 (Research Methods), the idea of any direct or *self-report* measure is simple: We ask; you tell. The critical assumption is that you are able and willing to provide a consistent (*reliable*) and accurate (*valid*) response to each item. Notice that some statements indicate high self-esteem and others (such as Question 2) indicate low self-esteem. Researchers often use this technique, called *reverse scoring,* to encourage careful reading of each item on a scale; it prevents people from simply writing the same response to every question without really reading them. Read the scoring instructions to make sure you come up with the correct result.

Measuring Implicit Self-Esteem (Indirectly). As you learned in Chapter 2, sometimes people are neither willing nor able to give researchers an accurate report. A problem called *social desirability* (one type of impression management) may encourage inaccurate responding to topics that, if answered honestly, might trigger an uncomfortable response. For example, social desirability might encourage dishonest responses to self-reports of taboo or personal sexual behavior, family violence, or out-of-favor political loyalties. When this is the case, indirect or *implicit* methodologies may produce more reliable, valid responses than direct, explicit, self-report approaches to collecting data.

The *Implicit Association Test (IAT)* is an indirect way to measure the strength of particular beliefs and constructs (Greenwald & Farnham, 2000; Pinter & Greenwald, 2005). The IAT does not rely on pesky critical assumptions such as being willing and able to accurately respond to each item, as the Rosenberg Self-Esteem Scale does. Instead, the IAT measures our implicit associations between two constructs. It attempts to measure, for example, whether your mental view of "self" is more associated with positive words or with negative words.

The underlying procedures of the IAT are a bit complicated, but faster *reaction times* (*the dependent variable*) suggest a strong mental connection for whatever constructs we are trying to measure (see Schnabel, Asendorpf, & Greenwald, 2008; von Stülpnagel & Steffens, 2010). If you can respond more quickly to a computer task that pairs "self" with positive words (compared to pairs of "self" and negative words), then the IAT results might indicate that you have a positive self-esteem.

This is a game-like measure that most people enjoy experiencing. However, it's important to note that there are many criticisms of the IAT and whether scores on this test can really predict behaviors, whether scores are reliable over time, and so on

Applying Social Psychology to Your Life

Instructions: Below is a list of statements dealing with your general feelings about yourself. If you strongly agree, circle SA. If you agree with the statement, circle A. If you disagree, circle D. If you strongly disagree, circle SD.

1. On the whole, I am satisfied with myself.   SA A D SD

2. At times, I think I am no good at all.   SA A D SD

3. I feel that I have a number of good qualities.   SA A D SD

4. I am able to do things as well as most other people.   SA A D SD

5. I feel I do not have much to be proud of.   SA A D SD

6. I certainly feel useless at times.   SA A D SD

7. I feel that I'm a person of worth, at least on an equal plane with others.   SA A D SD

8. I wish I could have more respect for myself.   SA A D SD

9. All in all, I am inclined to feel that I am a failure.   SA A D SD

10. I take a positive attitude toward myself.   SA A D SD

Scoring Instructions: Assign the following scores to your answers by writing the appropriate number on the blank next to each item. Then, add your scores up:

For Items 1, 3, 4, 7, 10: SA = 3, A = 2, D = 1, SD = 0.

For Items 2, 5, 6, 8, 9: SA = 0, A = 1, D = 2, SD = 3.

Higher scores indicate higher levels of self-reported self-esteem.

Source: Rosenberg, M. (1965). *Society and the adolescent self-image*. Princeton, NJ: Princeton University Press.

(see, e.g., Blanton et al., 2009). You might want to try it for yourself by going to the website https://implicit.harvard.edu/implicit/. You can then compare your score to the averages of thousands of others who have taken the test and think about whether you believe this is a good way to measure people's implicit attitudes about anything, including their self-esteem.

Collective Self-Esteem

Earlier, we learned that the self-concept includes both individual parts of the self (such as our attitudes and personality traits) and our relationships with others—the self is social. Given the fact that our self-concept includes our group memberships, our self-esteem must also then be tied to how we evaluate the worth of our in-groups.

Collective self-esteem is our evaluation of the worth of the social groups in which we are members. Tajfel (1981) defined it as "that aspect of an individual's self-concept which derives from his knowledge of his membership in a social group (or groups) together with the value and emotional significance attached to that membership" (p. 255). You have collective self-esteem for the reputation of your college or university, for example; do you feel proud of your school? What about your religious group, political party, chosen major, and so on? Do you feel good about these groups?

Collective self-esteem:
Individuals' evaluation of the worth of the social groups of which they are a member.

Collective Self-Esteem and Race.
One group of psychologists (Crocker, Luhtanen, Blaine, & Broadnax, 1994) studied collective self-esteem in college students in terms of how they felt about their own racial group; participants were White, Black, and Asian. To do this, they created a new self-report scale to measure collective self-esteem. It includes items such as, "The social groups I belong to are an important reflection of who I am," and, "In general, others respect the social groups that I am a member of."

Their findings showed that on average, people from these three races felt differently about their own status regarding their race (Crocker et al., 2004). Specifically, Asians said that they didn't feel like they were very worthy members of their racial group. Black students perceived that their race was judged most negatively by the general public. White students (members of the dominant group) said that their racial membership didn't matter in terms of how they thought about their identity—but both Asian and Black participants said that race did factor into their self-concept. How we think about our group memberships—and what we think other people think about those groups—seems to have an influence on how we view ourselves.

Sports Fan Psychology: Basking in Reflected Glory.
If evaluation of our social groups affects our self-esteem, then it makes sense that when our groups are successful, we'd want to make our membership more obvious to others. The opposite should also be true; if our group does badly or embarrasses us, we might not be so excited to display our group membership for everyone to see. This general hypothesis can be tested in fascinating ways by exploring one aspect of social psychology tied to many people's lives: the world of sports fans.

Being a sports fan often involves much more than just rooting for your favorite team; hard-core sports fans identify personally with their team and incorporate how well their team does into their collective self-esteem. Robert Cialdini began investigating the connection between fan psychology and our sense of self after he noticed that his Ohio State university students tended to say, "*We* won," after a school victory but, "*They* lost," following a defeat. The pronoun *we* includes the self, as if the person speaker were personally involved. He also noticed that Ohio State students were more likely to wear clothing displaying their school name and colors following a victory compared to a defeat (Cialdini et al., 1976).

Cialdini called this kind of behavior **basking in reflected glory (BIRGing)** because participants' sense of self is enhanced by the success of the groups with whom they identify. We try to make our membership or affiliation with the group more

Basking in reflected glory (BIRGing): A method of self-enhancement that involves affiliating with an ingroup when that group has been successful.

Hero Images / Hero Images / Getty Images

Students are more likely to wear their school colors after a big athletic win. We make our group identity more obvious to others when our group does well.

obvious to others in order to feel good about ourselves—but only when our group has succeeded. One easy way to do that is by wearing clothes showing that we're part of that winning group. However, when the group is getting negative press or has a failure, we tend to try to distance ourselves from the group by choosing to wear more generic clothes or by using pronouns like *they* instead of *we.* These are subtle but fascinating insights into the world of collective self-esteem.

Self-Esteem Has a Dark Side

Our students often express bewilderment and even shock when we suggest that building self-esteem is not necessarily a good idea. Debates about the complexities of self-esteem have been around for a long time (see Hume, 1888). We certainly do not want to dismiss the genuine benefits of high self-esteem (Swann et al., 2007) or the problems associated with low self-esteem (Donnellan et al., 2005). But the evidence is becoming clearer: Self-esteem has a dark side.

The Boosting Self-Esteem Movement. On the surface, the case for boosting self-esteem makes sense. Low self-esteem is associated with a wide range of minor and major social problems, from overusing a cell phone when you can't afford it to child abuse, school failure, teenage pregnancy, crime, welfare dependency, substance abuse, aggression, antisocial behavior, and delinquency. There is a long, impressive list of troubles associated with low self-esteem (Bianchi & Phillips, 2005; Donnellan et al., 2005; Ellison, Steinfield, & Lampe, 2007; Mecca, Smelser, & Vasconcellos, 1989; Phillips, Butt, & Blaszczynski, 2006).

As a psychology student, you understand better than most people that *correlation does not imply causation.* Just because certain behaviors are correlated with low self-esteem does not mean that they were caused by low self-esteem. Being related to a problem is not the same thing as causing the problem, just as being second cousin to a bank robber doesn't make you guilty of robbing a bank. Nevertheless, the self-esteem movement caught fire in the public's imagination. The California State legislature even created a special task force on self-esteem and eventually published a book titled, *The Social Importance of Self-Esteem* (Mecca et al., 1989). Self-esteem was such a nice thing to believe in that its influence didn't stop in people's optimistic imaginations or even at the California State legislature. Twenge (2006) discovered that among elementary schools, the word *self-esteem* is often included in the opening part of the school's mission statement, sometimes listed before reading, writing, and arithmetic. For example:

Cannon Elementary School, Spartanburg, South Carolina: "We are committed to building self-esteem, enhancing creativity and individuality."

The Margaret Gioiosa School, Staten Island, New York City, New York: "We believe that a child's self-esteem directly affects his/her achievement."

Oak Park Elementary, Laurel, Mississippi: "To provide a safe and positive learning environment, promoting high self-esteem and parental involvement. . . ."

Green Lake School, Seattle, Washington: "In pursuing its mission, Green Lake School adheres to these values: Building self-esteem. . . ."

Grant Foreman Elementary School, Muskogee, Oklahoma: "The mission of Grant Foreman Elementary School will be achieved when all exiting sixth grade students possess: A healthy sense of self-esteem. . . ."

Should children receive trophies just for participating or only for winning?

Dangers of Elevated Self-Esteem. But, you might argue, don't we want children to feel good about themselves? Yes, probably—but not to such an extreme that they feel "better," "more deserving," or even "more pure" than other people or other groups (see Baumeister, Campbell, Krueger, & Vohs, 2003).

Elevated self-esteem closely resembles narcissism, especially when it's built on platitudes instead of actual achievements. It probably won't surprise you to learn that school bullies usually have high self-esteem. In fact, Scottish researchers discovered that the self-esteem of 14-year-old bullies was highest when they were comparing themselves to the people they bullied: other 14-year-olds (Karatzias, Power, & Swanson, 2002). It wasn't beating up just anybody that made them feel good about themselves—they evaluated themselves the highest when they were bullying their peers. And, in case you are wondering, bullies don't seem to be putting on a public show of high self-esteem to hide their private or secret low self-esteem. Instead, the crux of the problem appears to be that "what individuals want is not necessarily what society values" (J. I. Krueger, Vohs, & Baumeister, 2008, p. 64).

Negative Feedback Can Help Us Improve. Here's a different way to get at an understanding of the questionable benefits of high self-esteem: If you were about to go into surgery, would you prefer a surgeon with

1. high self-esteem despite low skills,

2. low self-esteem despite high skills, or

3. moderate self-esteem and moderate skills?

The teaching doctors in the department of surgery at the Southern Illinois University School of Medicine were not trying to study self-esteem directly, but they were asking a similar question. They were worried about whether their chronically high-achieving medical students were paying attention to the feedback they were giving them. So they arranged for "an academic surgeon, who was seen by (medical) students as being an expert" (Boehler et al., 2006, p. 747) to provide two different kinds of feedback to medical students learning how to tie two-handed surgical knots.

The surgeon gave one group of medical students self-esteem boosting feedback such as, "Great job," "You're making progress," and "Outstanding"—the kind of praise that high-achieving medical students had probably received most of their lives from their teachers. The *comparison group* of students was given feedback based on their deficiencies, things they were doing wrong. In other words, the *independent variable* was whether the medical students got false but esteem-boosting praise or accurate, specific, but potentially harsh feedback. The *dependent variable* became the quality of their knots by the end of training. Did their ability improve?

How do you fairly evaluate the quality of two-handed surgical knots? In this case, "three faculty evaluators observed and scored blinded videotapes of each performance" and made sure that there was "agreement among expert ratings of performance." This is an example of a *blind study* because the three expert evaluators did not know the experimental group each student belonged to. The goal of this (and all other) procedural tricks of the trade is to produce fair, unbiased assessments. If one of the expert raters wanted the study to come out a certain way, she might unconsciously evaluate knots from one of the two experimental groups in a biased manner.

Figure 3.5 tells a sobering but also amusing story. It's sobering because the group that had been criticized tied better surgical knots than the group receiving complimentary (esteem-boosting) praise. It's amusing because they also measured student satisfaction ratings. Although the self-esteem group was less competent at tying surgical knots, they gave higher ratings to the teacher.

The Self-Esteem Intervention That Backfired. Instead of high-achieving medical students, a second study about the dangers of boosting self-esteem involved low-achieving psychology students who were earning grades of D and F (Forsyth, Lawrence, Burnette, & Baumeister, 2007)—the kind of people that the California State legislature was trying to help by boosting their self-esteem. Their professors sent some

■ FIGURE 3.5 Boosting self-esteem in surgeons might not lead to positive medical consequences.

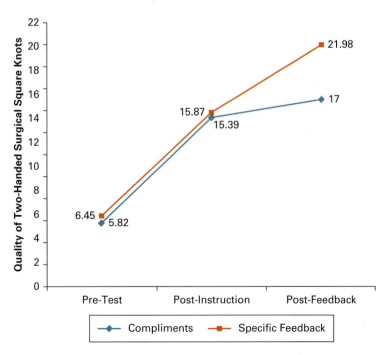

Do Compliments Make Better Surgeons?

SOURCE: Data from Lawrence, Burnette, & Baumeister (2007).

■ FIGURE 3.6 Can too much self-esteem lead to poor academic results?

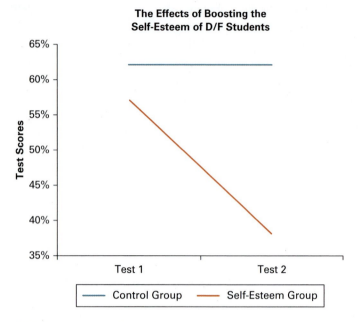

The Effects of Boosting the Self-Esteem of D/F Students

SOURCE: Data from Lawrence, Burnette, & Baumeister (2007).

of them self-esteem boosting email messages such as, "Studies suggest that students who have high self-esteem not only get better grades, but they remain self-confident and assured. . . . Bottom line: Hold your head—and your self-esteem—high." They thought they might be helping students, but the results were so startling that the authors subtitled their paper, "An Intervention That Backfired."

Here's what happened: First of all, the self-esteem boosting messages worked; more than two thirds (70%) of the participants recorded the highest possible self-esteem scores that the scale would allow. But Figure 3.6 tells us that their academic performance actually got *worse*. Promoting self-esteem didn't just fail to help between Test 1 and Test 2—it backfired. The struggling students' scores fell dramatically, from 57% to 38%, while the group that did not receive those messages (the *control group*) stayed the same. This study, unfortunately, is sobering without being amusing. Boosting self-esteem appeared to harm these students—and there is nothing funny about that.

What in the world is going on? Why isn't boosting self-esteem helping high-achieving medical students or struggling psychology students?

The Relentless Pursuit of Self-Esteem May Be Harmful

What if self-esteem itself just isn't all that important to our lives—but the relentless pursuit of self-esteem is harmful? Other research indicates that the relentless pursuit of self-esteem triggers a wide range of negative behaviors: making excuses, self-sabotage, blaming others, arguing, scheming, and cheating (Crocker & Nuer, 2003). Why not? If the goal is to feel good about ourselves by, for example, scoring well on a test, then it is as easy to justify academic cheating as it is speeding in traffic—others are doing it and I have to keep up with them (see Wajda-Johnston, Handal, Brawer, & Fabricatore, 2001).

Insidious Dangers of Overvaluing Self-Esteem. There are other insidious dangers lurking behind the relentless pursuit of self-esteem (see Baumeister et al., 2003; Crocker & Nuer, 2003). Research shows that people with fragile but high self-esteem:

1. Are more reluctant to take intelligent risks

2. Make fewer mistakes from which to learn

3. Substitute competitive social comparisons for cooperative social supports

4. Decrease their academic performance

5. Avoid helpful feedback

6. Increase levels of intergroup prejudice

7. Increase bullying and aggression toward others

Echo and Narcissus, *John William Waterhouse, 1903*

In Greek mythology, Narcissus fell so deeply in love with his own image that he continued to stare at his reflection until he died. The personality disorder called narcissism is not the same thing as self-esteem, a subjective assessment of one's own self-worth.

So, what can we say about the effects of boosting self-esteem? Yes, we can improve self-esteem. But no, boosting self-esteem doesn't solve the social problems that the self-esteem movement hoped it would solve. In fact, there is increasing evidence that, under some circumstances, building self-esteem is an intervention that backfires.

The Dangers of Narcissism. The extreme dark side of high self-esteem is narcissism, an absorbing love of oneself. Narcissism can even be considered a mental health personality disorder when it gets so out of control that it starts interfering with someone's ability to have a happy, healthy life and relationships with other people. This is perhaps fitting given the original Greek myth of Narcissus.

Narcissus was a proud hunter who loved himself more than anyone else. In most versions of this story, Narcissus is out in the forest one day and happens to see his own reflection in a pool of water. He's so arrogant and self-absorbed that he immediately falls in love with himself and stops eating or giving anyone else any attention at all. Narcissus eventually dies because he can't do anything except stare at the reflection of himself with absolute admiration. While the myth is clearly an extreme example of what can happen when self-esteem is too high, the moral of the story is pretty simple: A little humility might go a long way toward building a healthy, resilient, socially productive self.

The Main Ideas

- Self-esteem is our subjective evaluation of our self-concept. It can be measured through explicit, direct tests such as self-report scales or through implicit, indirect tests such as the Implicit Association Test.

- Collective self-esteem is our evaluation of the social groups in which we are members. One example is how we view sports teams; when our favorite team does well, we tend to show our affiliation with that team. This tendency is called Basking in Reflected Glory.

- Despite many attempts to boost self-esteem, some research studies show that elevating self-esteem can lead to negative effects (such as decreased academic performance).

- Considering BIRGing in your own life. Do you tend to show more affiliation with certain groups, such as sports teams, when the group is more successful? Do you distance yourself when the group is failing? In what specific ways does this happen?

- Beyond sports, there are many social groups created for people with similar self-interests, such as *Star Trek* conventions or religious retreats. What is the function of this sort of social gathering in terms of how it strengthens self-reflection and social aspects of the self? How do these types of groups exemplify BIRGing?

- Describe three situations that might lead you to alter your answers while filling out the Rosenberg Self-Esteem Scale.

- How important is having self-esteem to you? Based on the research reviewed above, should elementary and middle schools focus on increasing students' self-esteem? Why or why not?

CHAPTER SUMMARY

What is the "self"?

The self is an abstract and subjective psychological construct that makes it sometimes hard to define and measure. We start with self-awareness, the understanding that we are a separate entity from other people and objects in our world. Infants seem to show self-awareness from very early on when they imitate the facial expressions and sounds they observe. Scientists have created the "mirror self-recognition test" to measure self-awareness; here, they place red dye on an animal's forehead then show the animal a mirror. If the animal touches the dye on its own head—and not on the mirror—this seems to indicate that the animal is aware that the dye is on itself.

The self-concept is a personal summary of who we believe we are, including our qualities (both good and bad), our relationships, beliefs, values, and so on. This book has covered three theories on how our self-concept is formed. The first is social comparison theory, which says that we define subjective traits (such as whether we are "good looking" or "shy") by comparing our self to others. Upward social comparisons are when we compare ourselves to people who are better than us, which can help us improve but don't usually make us feel particularly good about ourselves. Downward social comparisons (when we compare ourselves to people who aren't as good as we are on any given trait) may make us feel better but don't help us improve.

Social identity theory suggests that the self-concept is made up of both personal, individual characteristics (such as our personality traits) and social role characteristics, which include our relationships (e.g., brother, mother) and our social groups (e.g., Muslim, student, Republican). Our social self-concept can include regional or cultural selves or self-construals. Finally, self-schema theory suggests that we interpret our own actions and decisions through schemas, which are cognitive and memory structures for organizing the world. The same action—say, not giving money to a homeless person—can be perceived along a schema that distinguishes between selfish versus generous people, or along a schema that distinguishes between savvy city dwellers versus gullible suckers. Which schemas we use to perceive ourselves form our self-concept.

How do we know the self is social?

Self-perception theory notes that when we form impressions of others, we do so by observing their behaviors, then making guesses about those people's values, opinions, and so on. The theory suggests that we form our self-concept in the same way; we observe *our own* behavior and form our self-concept by inferring what our own values, opinions, and so forth are based on those behaviors.

Self-discrepancy theory is the idea that instead of one, single self-concept, we actually have three self-concepts. Our actual self is our perception of who we are right now, while our ideal self is the person we'd like to be. Finally, our ought self is the self-concept we have that reflects what we think other people in our social world expect of us. Self-discrepancy theory hypothesizes that when our actual self and ideal self don't match, we'll feel dejection-related emotions such as disappointment and shame. On the other hand, when our actual self and ought self don't match, we instead feel agitation-related emotions such as guilt or anxiety.

A third theory, called self-expansion theory, suggests that we all want to grow and improve over time, reaching the best possible self-concept. One way to "expand" our self-concept is to include other people into our cognitive view of our self, which provides us access to other people's skills, memories, perspectives, and so on. A measure of the degree to which we've included someone else into our self-concept is called the Inclusion of the Other in the Self (IOS) Scale, which asks people to choose one pair of overlapping circles out of seven choices. The choices show progressive degrees of overlap, with one circle labeled "self" and the second circle labeled "other."

Why do we present different selves in different situations?

Self-presentation is the tendency to adjust how we publicly display the self to gain social influence; this tendency is also called impression management. For example, ingratiation involves attempts to get others to like us by either praising other people (other-enhancement) or pretending to agree with other people (opinion conformity). Self-promotion is an impression management technique that makes us appear more successful or more significant that we really are, and conspicuous consumption is when we show off the use of expensive, flashy products such as cars or jewelry.

Brain damage can apparently decrease someone's ability to manage self-presentation. A famous case study can be seen in the story of Phineas Gage, a man who experienced an explosion that caused portions of his frontal lobe to be destroyed. This damage caused Gage's personality to change, and it also seems to have prevented him from being able to engage in self-presentation strategies.

People who often look around to assess the current situation to change their self-presentation are called high self-monitors. On the other hand, people who act consistently regardless of the current situation are called low self-monitors. There are advantages and disadvantages to either approach to self-presentation.

Is the truth always the self's friend?

Optimal margin theory is the idea that it can be healthy to maintain a small to moderate distortion of reality when it comes to our self-concept. In other words, maintaining some positive illusions about how wonderful we are may be beneficial. For example, some older individuals seem to be happier when their subjective age (how old they feel) is younger than their actual age.

Specific ways we maintain these positive illusions are called self-serving cognitive biases. One self-serving cognitive bias is that we tend to perceive that our positive qualities or traits are rare (and therefore special), whereas our negative qualities are common (and therefore not particularly stigmatizing). We also tend to attribute successes to something internal about ourselves (such as talent or effort) but attribute failures to something about the situation; in this way, we can take credit for success but avoid blame for failure. Finally, we also question feedback about the self that is negative but happily believe that positive feedback about our self is valid. This type of bias has also been seen in people's views of others, such as current romantic partners.

What is self-esteem and how can we measure it?

Self-esteem is our subjective, personal evaluation of our self-concept. It is not the same thing as self-compassion, narcissism, or self-efficacy. There are two general strategies for measuring self-esteem. The first is explicit, direct tests such as self-report scales that simply ask people about their view of themselves. The second is implicit, indirect tests that measure self-esteem in other ways. For example, the Implicit Association Test measures how quickly people respond on a computer when given different pairs of concepts. If people can respond more quickly when the "self" is paired with positive words or images, compared to negative words or images, then that might indicate a positive self-esteem. There are several criticisms of this approach, however.

Collective self-esteem is our evaluation of the worth of social groups in which we are members, such as our racial groups. Another example of collective self-esteem is seen in sports fans, when people affiliate with certain teams. Researchers have noticed that sports fans are more likely to make their chosen affiliations salient or obvious to others when their team is doing well compared to when it's not; this tendency is called Basking in Reflected Glory.

Despite the popularity of movements to increase self-esteem, several studies have shown that boosting self-esteem can actually lead to negative effects, such as lower academic performance. It seems that receiving negative feedback about one's performance may cause self-esteem to suffer, but it can also lead to improved performance next time the task is attempted.

THEORIES IN REVIEW

- Social comparison theory
- Social identity theory
- Self-schema theory
- Self-perception theory
- Self-discrepancy theory
- Self-expansion theory

- Self-monitoring
- Self-presentation theory/impression management
- Optimal margin theory
- Self-serving cognitive biases
- Collective self-esteem

CRITICAL THINKING, ANALYSIS, AND APPLICATION

- Do you think it's possible for any individual to really achieve full matching between his or her actual, ideal, and ought selves? Would this full matching be a good thing or a bad thing, and why?

- Consider the advantages and disadvantages to presenting different versions of yourself in different settings. Is this simply having social intelligence, or is it being less than authentic? Is the success and popularity that may follow from high self-monitoring worth changing who you appear to be? Or is your changing self always authentic—and you're simply choosing different aspects of yourself to be highlighted, like when stores choose to display certain products in more prominent locations? If you knew that a certain friend, politician, or romantic partner was very high in self-monitoring, could you truly trust that person and feel you knew who he or she "really" is?

- You've probably heard the phrase, "Ignorance is bliss." Would you rather have an extremely positive view of yourself, even if it were completely wrong, or have an accurate view of yourself that showed all of your flaws in glaring detail? On a scale of 0 to 100, how much "positive illusion" do you think would be the ideal amount, with 0 indicating none (potentially unhappy accuracy) and 100 being complete (happy but inaccurate perceptions)?

- What is your personal opinion about cultural or educational programs designed to enhance the next generation's self-esteem? Are the benefits from this type of program going to outweigh the potential drawbacks, such as inflated narcissism or a sense of entitlement?

PERSONAL REFLECTION

Like most small children, I wondered about lots of weird things. For example, could Superman really go backward in time by flying around Earth *really* fast? If I dug a hole all the way through the Earth and jumped in feet-first, would I come out on the other side head-first? I also worried about all those other people who hadn't been as "lucky" as I was to have been born into a particular faith. Things didn't look so good for them. And that made me wonder: What if I had been born in a different part of the world? Would I still be me? Those questions bugged me then and still do today. If I had decided to hitch-hike directly back home instead of impulsively taking a detour to see a friend, then I would not have met my future wife and started a family. I would still be me, but I would have been a very different me. And our children . . . well, they just wouldn't be. But now, here they are—and *their* children are wrestling with the same questions about the self that psychological science is slowly starting to answer. [TH]

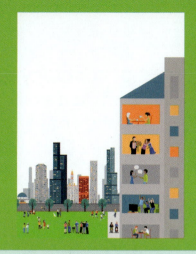

LO3.4 **Articulate** why we sometimes **benefit** from **positive illusions** and **moderate self-deceptions**.

OR

LO3.5 **Apply both explicit** and **implicit** methods to the **many facets** of **self-esteem, including its dark side**.

Get a tour of **ALL Visual Key Concepts** and their definitions at **edge.sagepub.com/heinzen**

4 Social Cognition

Core Questions

1. How do we think?

2. How do we remember social information?

3. Why do our brains sometimes make mistakes?

4. From where does intuition come?

5. Can we trust our intuition?

Learning Objectives

4.1 Discuss how our two thinking systems evolved, interact, and are influenced by culture.

4.2 Describe how memory structures help us process large amounts of social information.

4.3 Summarize why we take mental shortcuts and use magical thinking, and to generate a list of examples.

4.4 Explain how intuition uses mental accessibility that comes from priming, experience, and heuristics.

4.5 Analyze why we can respect, but not always trust, our intuition.

Sgt. First Class Edward Tierney was leading a nine-person patrol in Mosul, Iraq, when they noticed a car parked on the sidewalk, facing the traffic. The windows were rolled up and the faces of two kindergarten-aged boys stared out the back window, their faces close together.

The nearest soldier said to Tierney, "Permission to approach, sir, to give them some water."

"No," Tierney replied and ordered his men to pull back. Something just seemed wrong. Then a bomb exploded, killing the two boys and sending shrapnel across the face of the nearest soldier. Unfortunately, Tierney's intuition could not save the two boys, but it probably prevented an even greater tragedy by saving the lives of some of the men in his patrol (see Carey, 2009). Sgt. Tierney later reported experiencing "that danger feeling" and an urge to move back before he logically knew why.

It doesn't matter whether you call it "going with your gut," "a hunch," or intuition because it all refers to the same idea: knowing something without knowing how you know. It is sometimes a wonderful yet mysterious experience—when it works, as it did for Sgt. Tierney. But when we place too much faith in our intuition, it can lead to disaster. Sometimes, we are better off to rely on logic, a way of knowing based on reasoned, thoughtful analysis of the objective situation. These two types of thinking, intuition and logic, are the basic elements of social cognition, or how we process social information. We can learn more about social cognition and the unavoidable trade-offs between intuition and logic by answering the five core questions and learning objectives shown.

To learn more about Sgt. Tierney, read the *New York Times* piece called "In Battle, Hunches Prove to Be Valuable" (July 2009), found here: http://www.nytimes.com/2009/07/28/health/research/28brain.html.

HOW DO WE THINK?

LO 4.1: Discuss how our two thinking systems evolved, interact, and are influenced by culture.

The combination of intuition and logic is part of the answer to a difficult philosophical question: What, if anything, is so special about humans? Every species, of course, is special in some way, but what makes humans special? We do not run faster than many other creatures. We do not have more fur to protect against the cold. We are not larger or stronger than many other species. And we are not special when it comes to seeing, hearing, smelling, or hiding from predators. However, there is one thing that we humans seem to do exceptionally well: think. We are not unique in our ability to think; instead, our most distinctive ability may be in *how* we think. **Social cognition** is the study of how people combine intuition and logic to process social information.

Social cognition: The study of how people combine intuition and logic to process social information.

The constant interplay between these two ways of thinking helps us synthesize enormous amounts of information quickly and with relative accuracy. Let's look more closely at the two thinking systems of intuition and logic.

Dual Processing: Intuition and Logic

You have just been surprised by a marriage proposal—you need to figure out how to respond—and fast! Will you use logic, intuition, or both? Responding quickly to complex situations is one reason that humans developed the skill of **dual processing**, the ability to process information using both intuition and logic (Bargh & Williams, 2006; DeNeys, 2006; Kahneman, 2003; Schneider & Shiffrin, 1977; Sherman, Gawronski, & Trope, 2014; Simon, 1990). These two styles, forms, or systems of thinking have been labeled in many different ways such as "System 1 versus System 2," "automatic versus effortful," "implicit versus explicit," and more. For this chapter, we will use the terms *intuition versus logic*—but as we discuss each thinking system, keep in mind that they are complex and differ in many ways (see Figure 4.1).

Intuition is the ability to know something quickly and automatically—it could be described as our "gut feelings." Intuition is extremely important when we need to sense and react to potential threats in the environment. Intuition is implicit and requires, at that particular moment, only minimal cognitive effort. Sgt. Tierney, for example, was not aware of the flow of information entering his brain, but his intuition enabled him to make a lightning-quick decision that saved several lives.

Logic, by comparison, enables humans to reason, think systematically, and carefully consider evidence about possible futures. Logic requires mental effort and careful, purposeful reasoning. What appears to separate humans from other species is the fluency with which we combine intuition and logic for decision making.

■ FIGURE 4.1 Two thinking systems: intuition and logic.

Intuition	Logic
Emotional	Analytical
Associative	Rule-Directed
Automatic	Controlled
Effortless	Effortful
Implicit	Explicit
Intuitive	Reasoned
Quick	Slow

Dual processing: The ability to process information using both intuition and logic.

Intuition: The ability to know something quickly and automatically; a "gut feeling" that takes little mental effort.

Logic: The ability of humans to use reason, think systematically, and carefully consider evidence about possible futures.

CBS Photo Archive / CBS / Getty images

Sheldon Cooper and Mr. Spock : Classic characters who are guided by logic instead of emotion or intuition.

Something remarkable must be going on in the human brain, because the brain accounts for about only 2% of our total body weight but consumes about 20% of our energy resources (Dunbar, 1998). As we navigate our everyday lives, intuition serves as our default mode, making automatic decisions, while logic often stays in the background, only stepping in when needed (Kahneman, 2003, 2011; Stanovich & West, 2000, 2002). In this way, we can conserve the extra energy needed to think logically and use it only when we need it.

For example, notice what you do when you try to push your way through a PULL door. As you approach the door, your brain is on automatic pilot and relying on intuition. So, when you get to the door, you use intuition to make the trivial decision about whether to push or to pull. If you successfully pull open a PULL door (or push open a PUSH door), then you just keep on going to your destination. You don't congratulate your intuition or start singing, "We are the champions!"

But what if, based on your intuition, you try to push open a PULL door or vice versa? If you watch people in this situation, many will continue to push, push, push and rattle the door until their logical thinking breaks through with the logical thought, "Hey! What you're doing isn't working. Try something else." That's when you finally change your behavior and pull on the PULL door. We need both intuition and logic to navigate the hundreds of big and little decisions that we make every day, and both types of thinking sometimes lead to errors—such as trying to push your way through a PULL door.

This frustrated woman may need to use logic instead of intuition to realize why the door isn't opening.

Figure 4.1 compares the two thinking systems, and it also summarizes their strengths and weaknesses (Alter, Oppenheimer, Epley, & Eyre, 2007; Gilbert, 1991; Kahneman & Frederick, 2005; Lieberman, 2000). Quick decision making (intuition) makes our lives much easier and may even save our lives—just ask Sgt. Tierney or the soldiers under his command. That's good. But it also risks sometimes making a hurried, catastrophic decision without really considering all of the logical choices and consequences. That's bad—and sometimes very bad. On the other hand, relying on slow, thoughtful logic helps us understand what is happening from an objective point of view. That's good. But it also risks being attacked or missing opportunities through indecision because we are so busy analyzing information. That's bad—and sometimes very bad. The constant trade-offs between intuition and logic describe our daily decision making—and its consequences.

Our Two Thinking Systems Interact

When you first learned to drive, you probably had to put in a lot of effort and concentrate on every tiny movement of the steering wheel and pedals. Over time, we get so used to driving—especially on familiar routes such as between home and work or school—that driving becomes automatic and easy. This "auto pilot" mode of driving becomes our default for routine trips. However, if you have to drive in a new, complicated city with several lanes of traffic, unfamiliar signs, and road construction, your mental effort for driving suddenly kicks in—you concentrate, you pay attention.

Daniel Kahneman (2011) won the Nobel Prize for his research on intuitive versus logical decision making. These two systems of thought often interact beautifully, like dance partners. But sometimes one partner, either intuition or logic, has to take

Daniel Kahneman (right) won the Nobel Prize for his research on how our two thinking systems work together to make everyday decisions.

the lead. The example of driving may help you to understand why you don't want to text and drive. There are limits to your **cognitive load**, the amount of information that our thinking systems can process at one time.

As the driving example suggests, evolving traffic situations require that our two thinking systems interact by smoothly switching back and forth between intuition and logic, a process also called **cognitive load-shifting** (Abel, Krever, & Alberti, 1990; Alain, McDonald, Ostroff, & Schneider, 2004; Jansma, Ramsey, Slagter, & Kahn, 2001; Schneider & Pichora-Fuller, 2001; Velanova, Lustig, Jacoby, & Buckner, 2007). You may be able to drive almost mindlessly, relying on intuition, until you notice another car weaving dangerously up ahead of you. Then, logic springs into action and tells you, "Concentrate! This could be dangerous! Observe, evaluate, and figure out how to avoid that dangerous driver up ahead."

You can get a sense of whether you prefer logic or intuition in the Applying Social Psychology in Your Life feature, "Measuring Need for Cognition." There are times when either preference might pay off. For example, a sports psychology study discovered that some sports tasks are better suited for intuition, while others are more successful when the athlete switches to logical thinking (Furley, Schweizer, & Bertrams, 2015). In football, certain physical actions (like kicking the ball for an extra point after a touchdown) might rely more on practiced intuition. However, running a complicated play among several players probably needs more logical thinking to be successful.

Social Thinking Is Shaped by Cultural Influences

While the focus of this chapter is on types of thinking (such as intuition vs. logic), it's important to point out that social cognition is influenced by culture. What is viewed in one culture as normal and appropriate may be regarded in another culture as strange or deficient. These differences are not necessarily good or bad, better or worse; they simply highlight how our social thinking is shaped by our cultural influences. The accompanying Spotlight on Research Methods feature, "Culture Influences How We Think," describes a cultural difference based on individualistic values versus collectivistic values (we introduced this idea in Chapter 3). Every society is a mixture, of course, but some cultures plainly value one more than the other.

Autobiographical memories about our own upbringing suggest how we may have absorbed an individualistic value or a collectivistic value. For example, even though my [Tom's] athletic abilities peaked in about the fifth grade of a small school, I can still recall momentarily being lifted on my teammates' shoulders after winning a baseball game. That stubborn little vanity memory still reinforces my sense that individual achievement

Cognitive load: The amount of information that an individual's thinking systems can handle at one time.

Cognitive load shifting: When an individual's two thinking systems interact by smoothly shifting back and forth between intuition and logic.

Different people enjoy using the logical, thoughtful part of their brain to different degrees. In your free time, do you think it's fun to complete crossword puzzles, watch documentaries, solve logic problems, and engage in political debates? If so, you might be high in a personality trait called *need for cognition.*

Instructions: To measure your own "need for cognition," write a number next to each statement below using this scale:

1	2	3	4	5
Extremely uncharacteristic of me		Uncertain		Extremely characteristic of me

_____ 1. I prefer complex to simple problems.

_____ 2. I like to have the responsibility of handling a situation that requires a lot of thinking.

_____ 3. Thinking is not my idea of fun.

_____ 4. I would rather do something that requires little thought than something that is sure to challenge my thinking abilities.

_____ 5. I try to anticipate and avoid situations where there is a likely chance I will have to think in depth about something.

_____ 6. I find satisfaction in deliberating hard and for long hours.

_____ 7. I only think as hard as I have to.

_____ 8. I prefer to think about small daily projects to long-term ones.

_____ 9. I like tasks that require little thought once I've learned them.

_____ 10. The idea of relying on thought to make my way to the top appeals to me.

_____ 11. I really enjoy a task that involves coming up with new solutions to problems.

_____ 12. Learning new ways to think doesn't excite me very much.

_____ 13. I prefer my life to be filled with puzzles I must solve.

_____ 14. The notion of thinking abstractly is appealing to me.

_____ 15. I would prefer a task that is intellectual, difficult, and important to one that is somewhat important but does not require much thought.

_____ 16. I feel relief rather than satisfaction after completing a task that requires a lot of mental effort.

_____ 17. It's enough for me that something gets the job done; I don't care how or why it works.

_____ 18. I usually end up deliberating about issues even when they do not affect me personally.

Scoring Instructions: Some of the items need to be "reverse scored," which means that you cross off what you wrote and write a different number instead. For only Items 3, 4, 5, 7, 8, 9, 12, 16, and 17, flip the scale. So, if you wrote a 1, cross it off and write a 5 instead. If you wrote a 2, substitute a 4 instead. If you wrote a 3, it stays the same because it's in the middle of the scale, but a 4 becomes a 2 and a 5 becomes a 1.

After you reverse-score only the items indicated (half of the items should have stayed the same), add up your numbers. Higher scores mean you are higher in "need for cognition," and you prefer to rely on logic. Scores can range from 18 to 90.

Source: Cacioppo, Petty, & Kao (1984).

will be rewarded. As you scan your autobiographical memories, can you identify certain family interactions that encouraged either your individuality or the importance of being part of a group?

CULTURE INFLUENCES HOW WE THINK

If you saw a pile of pens that were mostly the same but had one unique pen, would you choose the unique one?

Deep but subtle cultural differences showed up in a *field experiment,* a study that occurred in a natural environment instead of in a lab setting. It took place in the San Francisco airport where researchers offered European Americans or East Asians a gift choice from five free pens—four of which were of the same color, with the fifth being unique. Given this choice, would you pick the unique pen or one of the four matching pens?

The surprising thing was that people from the two cultural groups tended to make different choices that suggested individualistic or collectivistic assumptions about the self (Kim & Markus, 1999). Specifically, 74% of European Americans preferred the pen that was a different color from all the rest, but 76% of East Asians chose a pen that was the same color. The researchers were careful to control *confounding variables,* co-occurring events that provide alternative explanations for their results. For example, the pens were the same quality and design, came from the same company, and all used black ink. Across different participants, the researchers also changed the color of the pen that was different, to make sure one color wasn't simply more attractive.

Where in the world do such odd little differences come from? Cultural differences in autobiographical memories appear to be part of the explanation (Wang, Koh, Song, & Hou, 2015). European Americans from individualistic

cultures are taught that uniqueness and nonconformity are valued; they tended to choose the pen that was different. In contrast, East Asians from collectivistic cultures are taught not to stand out from the group and to put group needs first; they tended to choose a pen that was like most of the others.

Another example of differences between cultures can be seen in Table 4.1, which highlights differences in family memory sharing (Wang, 2006, p. 185):

■ **TABLE 4.1** Mother's Questions, Child's Answers

Euro-American mother (M) and child (C)
M: Tell me about the craft fair. Mommy and Daddy went to the craft fair. What did we go there for, do you remember?
C: Yeah. Christmas time.
M: It was Christmas time, we were getting some Christmas presents. Did you want to be there?
C: No.

Chinese mother and child
M: What story did Teacher Lin tell you at school?
C: "Qui Shao-yun." He didn't move even when his body was on fire.
M: The teacher taught you to follow the rules, right?
C: Um.

SOURCE: Adapted from Wang, 2008.

Notice how the European American mother encouraged her child to speak up ("Tell me about the craft fair. . . . What did we go there for, do you remember?"). She specifically encouraged her child's individualism ("Did you want to be there?"). This child responded with a blunt but independent "no." By contrast, the Chinese mother emphasized authority and following rules ("What story did Teacher Lin tell you at school. . . . The teacher taught you to follow the rules, right?"). These two children were absorbing very different cultural expectations. Memory researcher and Nobel Prize winner Eric Kandel (2006) has pointed out that, "We are who we are because of what we learn and what we remember" (p. 10).

The Main Ideas

- Social cognition is the study of how people combine intuition and logic to process social information. Intuition is automatic, emotional, and effortless, while logic is controlled, systematic, and analytical.

- There are limits to your cognitive load, the amount of information that our thinking systems can process at one time. Our default thinking process is intuition, and logic is used when needed.

- Social thinking is shaped by cultural influences.

 CRITICAL THINKING CHALLENGE

- We used metaphors and examples (mostly borrowed from other researchers) to describe the relation between intuition and logic, including driving, dancing, and sports. What other metaphors could describe the combination of automatic behavior or thought and controlled, systematic thought serving as a monitor and stepping in when needed? What other specific examples can you identify that show dual processing in your own life?

- Try to identify people you personally know who seem to be high or low in need for cognition. Can you think of examples when they have relied on either intuition or logic? Did those choices work out well or not?

- Think of the popular (but gruesome) fairy tales of Snow White and the Seven Dwarfs and The Little Mermaid. Identify elements of each story that encourage an independent self or an interdependent self. This example becomes even more interesting when you consider the original versions from the Grimm Brothers and from Hans Christian Andersen.

- Think about your own childhood experiences with parents or guardians. Did they encourage you to follow your logic or your intuition more? If you could analyze your own balance between the two systems of thinking, which do you tend to favor more now?

HOW DO WE REMEMBER SOCIAL INFORMATION?

LO 4.2: Describe how memory structures help us process large amounts of social information.

Memory structures have been crucial to the success of the human species. For example, why don't you have to relearn how to read every time you pick up a book? Because you have developed memory structures that maintain your ability to read. You remember the shapes of letters, the sounds they correspond to, the meaning of the sounds, and their grammatical arrangements; you can even apply those rules to new reading situations. In fact, it would be impossible for you to look at a book and *not* read the words because your memory structures for reading are so firmly in place. (You really are rather brilliant in the most important ways, even if you have never been a great student as society has defined it.)

Notice also that you are able to recognize people when you see their faces. At first you need to concentrate on specific features, but after a while you will automatically recognize people—it would be impossible not to immediately identify people after you've known them for a long period of time. So let's learn a little more about your marvelous memory structures.

We have three types of **memory structures** (also called **mental structures**) that organize and interpret social information: schemas, scripts, and stereotypes. These memory structures evolved because they allow us to process large amounts of information quickly—the very thing that we humans seem to do better than other animals. However, there is a trade-off for being able to process so much information: We don't like to change our minds, because even a small change in thinking can have far-reaching implications (see Gawronski & Bodenhausen, 2006). It's similar to rearranging a room. If you move a lamp just a few inches, then suddenly you also may have to shift a bookcase, reorient a chair, and much more, like a mental domino effect. Why are schemas, scripts, and stereotypes so important when processing social information?

Schemas Label and Categorize

A **schema** operates like a spam email filter: It automatically directs and organizes incoming information by labeling and categorizing. A schema automatically ignores some information and forces us to pay attention to other information (Bartlett, 1932; Johnston, 2001). Common schemas people might use in the social world are concepts such as labeling people based on their gender, their religion, or their country of origin. Simply put, schemas are categories we use to understand the world. You will hear people use several other words that describe this same general idea. For example, "templates," "worldviews," and "paradigms" are also attempts to describe mental structures that help us process and remember information. There are two specific *types* of schemas: scripts and stereotypes.

Scripts Create Expectations About What Happens Next

A **script** is a memory structure or type of schema that guides common social behaviors and expectations for particular types of events. We don't have to relearn how to behave every time we go to a sit-down restaurant, for example, because we have a mental script for the expected order of events: (a) waiting to be taken to a table, (b) being seated, (c) reviewing the menu, (d) ordering the meal, (e) eating the meal, (f) paying the bill, and (g) leaving the restaurant. The script is modified for a fast-food restaurant because you have a slightly different memory structure for how to behave in that setting. You would be surprised and confused if the order of expected events somehow changed. For example, you're expected to pay the bill before you get your food at a fast-food restaurant but after the meal at a sit-down restaurant. If you went to a nice steakhouse and they made you pay before you got to eat, you would be startled and might not have a good impression of the restaurant.

Scripts govern a great deal of our lives. For example, your cultural script for a marriage proposal tells you that the photographs shown here are out of order. Knowing how to propose properly within a particular culture is an important social script that shapes marital expectations. A *survey* of over 2,100 college students at the Universities of Iowa and Alaska found that participants, regardless of their sex or age, predicted a stronger marriage if the couple had conformed to a more traditional proposal script (Schweingruber, Cast, & Anahita, 2008). Scripts are comforting to us because they help us feel that we can safely navigate through a complex social world.

Scripts govern other romantic behaviors we often think of as spontaneous. For example, a widely shared script about consensual sex begins with kissing and then

Memory structures: The cognitive structures that form the mind and organize and interpret social information, namely, schemas, scripts, and stereotypes.

Mental structures: See *memory structures.*

Schema: A cognitive and memory structure for organizing the world.

Script: A memory structure or type of schema that guides common social behaviors and expectations for particular types of events; scripts provide individuals with an order of events for common situations and expectations for others' behavior.

Your mental script for how to get married tells you that these photographs are out of order.

proceeds in a very predictable sequence to touching particular parts of the body and in a particular order (see Gagnon & Simon, 1987; Laumann, Gagnon, Michael, & Michaels, 1994). The traditional sexual script includes a "nearly universal sexual double standard that gives men greater sexual freedom" (Blanc, 2001, p. 190). Men who initiate dating or sexual behaviors are seen as normal; women who do so may be negatively judged or seen as "pushy." We use scripts because they are efficient ways of automatically cruising through social situations, but some mental scripts may be harmful. For example, if someone has a script about marriage that includes sexist ideas about male privilege (e.g., the man is the "king of his castle" and therefore can make all the important decisions), this particular misogynistic script can lead to abusive relationships (Johnson, 2007).

The good news is that Dworkin and O'Sullivan (2005) think that harmful sexist scripts may be changing. They found that college men across diverse ethnic backgrounds preferred more egalitarian sexual and relationship scripts. More evidence that sexual scripts are changing comes from *interviews* of 44 heterosexual and sexually active college students in the state of Washington (Masters, Casey, Wells, & Morrison, 2013). They identified three types of scripts related to sexism: (1) conforming (traditional sex roles), (2) "exception finding" (traditional roles but with occasional exceptions), and (3) transforming (traditional roles replaced by egalitarian roles).

That said, most people still expect sexual behavior to follow typical scripts, and they are aware that if their own preferences or interests vary from the expected, then society in general may not be very accepting of straying from the path. Goodfriend (2012) *surveyed* 89 college students in the Midwest regarding two things: (1) whether they personally would consider engaging in nontraditional sexual behaviors and (2) their perceptions of whether these behaviors were socially acceptable. You can see the results in Table 4.2. All mean scores (or averages) were based on a scale of 1 (definitely not acceptable or worth consideration) to 7 (definitely acceptable or worth consideration). The less traditional or scripted the behavior, fewer people seemed to consider it—although there were some exceptions, and some interesting gender

■ **TABLE 4.2** Men's and Women's Views on Possible Sexual Paths, on a Range From 1 (*Not Acceptable*) to 7 (*Definitely Acceptable*).

	Men's Average	Women's Average
Marriage with one person for life		
I would personally consider.	6.47	6.65
Does society accept?	6.18	6.29
Premarital sex		
I would personally consider.	5.58	5.35
Does society accept?	4.95	5.12
Casually dating several people		
I would personally consider.	4.87	5.51
Does society accept?	4.42	5.29
Single and sexually active for life		
I would personally consider.	3.79	3.00
Does society accept?	3.71	3.33
Bisexuality		
I would personally consider.	2.42	3.37
Does society accept?	3.29	3.47
Group marriage or polygamy		
I would personally consider.	2.31	1.27
Does society accept?	2.08	1.84
Prostitution		
I would personally consider.	1.92	1.29
Does society accept?	1.95	2.06

SOURCE: Goodfriend (2012).

differences emerged. While scripts guide our expected or typical behaviors in a variety of different contexts, there are always people who will decide not to follow "the rules."

Stereotypes Ignore Individual Differences Within Groups

A second type of schema is **stereotypes**, which assume everyone in a certain group has the same characteristics. In other words, stereotypes minimize individual differences or diversity within any given group based on the perception that everyone in that group is the same. You may not behave according to the stereotype, but whatever groups you belong to—fraternity, psychology major, garage band, or football team—trigger a stereotype that others use to make judgments about you. Some aspects of a stereotype may be true for *some* members of a particular group, of course, but it's still a logical mistake to assume that *all* members of the group are the same.

This thinking error is called **outgroup homogeneity**, or assuming that every individual in a group outside of your own is the same. Do you think that all students at Harvard are the same? Unless you are a student at Harvard, then Harvard students are your outgroup, and if you believe they all share the same behaviors or characteristics, then you have a stereotype. Stereotypes and prejudice play major roles in social psychology's story. Like other mental shortcuts, stereotypes are efficient ways of making decisions but also can lead to errors in judgment—which sometimes lead to disastrous effects. For more details, see Chapter 9.

Stereotype: A type of oversimplified and overgeneralized schema that occurs when an individual assumes that everyone in a certain group has the same traits.

Outgroup homogeneity: The perception that all members of a particular outgroup are identical to each other.

The Main Ideas

- Schemas, scripts, and stereotypes are memory structures that enable us to process large amounts of social information.

- A schema is a general memory structure that directs our attention by labeling and categorizing.

- A script is a type of schema that guides common, sequential social behaviors for a specific event.

- Stereotypes are a type of schema that makes our memories more efficient by ignoring individual differences between members of a group. This has both advantages and disadvantages.

⚡ CRITICAL THINKING CHALLENGE

- Describe a cultural event such as a holiday or religious celebration involving a group that you did *not* grow up in. Identify how schemas, scripts, and stereotypes influence your understanding of it.

- Identify three of your ingroups (groups in which you are a member) and corresponding stereotypes about your own groups. Do you fit these stereotypes or not? Can you think of other members of your group that either do or don't fit those stereotypes?

- One study summarized above (Masters et al., 2013) found three patterns of scripts in heterosexual relationships, labeled conforming, exception finding, and transforming. When you think about the heterosexual relationships in your world, which patterns do you see? Is the answer different depending on personalities, ages, or other variables you can identify in the couple members?

WHY DO OUR BRAINS SOMETIMES MAKE MISTAKES?

LO 4.3: Summarize why we take mental shortcuts and use magical thinking, and to generate a list of examples.

Our big, busy brains sometimes make mistakes. There seem to be two main sources for our mental errors. You can think of the first source by the familiar shorthand *TMI* for "*t*oo *m*uch *i*nformation," or information overload. For example, we are aggressively confronted—usually without our permission—by advertising when we are on the Web, driving our car, listening to the radio, and even grocery shopping. These advertisers are all fighting for a spot in our thought life—which already has enough to think about. So our brains automatically simplify our world by rejecting most of the incoming information, including some information we actually want or need.

The information overload (TMI) problem is understandable, and so is the second source of mental mistakes: wishing—especially when we substitute wishes for reality. It is tempting to believe that wishing hard enough somehow will make our wishes come true. Unfortunately, no matter how many Disney films take advantage of our fondness for self-deception, the wooden *Pinocchio* will never turn into a real boy, and neither beasts nor frogs turn into princes.

The next time you see a police car with its lights flashing, watch your storytelling brain start spitting out explanations. "Something happened," you tell yourself.

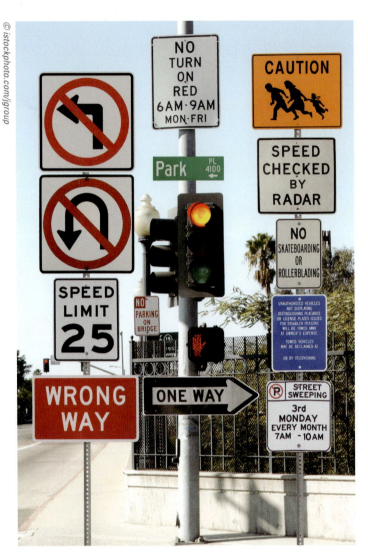

Our brains don't like to process too much information at any given time.

"Maybe it's an accident, a robbery, a speeding motorist. . . ." And your favorite explanation will probably be the one that you wish to believe. You might recognize yourself as we explore these two types of mental mistakes.

Information Overload Leads to Mental Errors

In the face of overwhelming amounts of information, the brain evolved an efficient but imperfect solution: throw most things out and organize what remains. What are some specific ways our brains deal with information overload?

Cognitive Misers. Let's be blunt about it: We are **cognitive misers** who take mental shortcuts whenever possible to minimize the cognitive load (Hansen, 1980; Taylor, 1981). An economic "miser" hates spending money unless absolutely necessary. Likewise, our brains are cognitive "misers" that avoid effortful thinking unless we absolutely have to. It sounds like a lazy way to think, and it is—although *economical* or *efficient* might be a more precise word than *lazy.* Under most circumstances, the brain searches for the shortest, quickest way to solve a problem, partly because logical brainwork is slow, hard work!

For example, Daniel Kahneman (2011) noticed that people will stop walking if you ask them to calculate a difficult arithmetic problem in their heads. Try it for yourself by taking a little stroll and then trying to calculate 23 × 278 in your head. Even a leisurely stroll feels like effort to a brain that is being asked to do too much—so we stop and do one thing at a time. As we pointed out earlier in this chapter, we are generally very bad at "multitasking," and we're also bad at thinking about too much at any given time. We prefer to stick to decisions once we've made them, because reconsidering other options is effortful. It's such a relief once you make up your mind that few people will really stay open to other ideas; our miserly mental habits just say no.

Cognitive miser: The tendency for humans to take mental shortcuts to minimize cognitive load.

Satisficing: A practical solution to the problem of information overload that occurs when an individual takes mental shortcuts to make decisions; criteria are not exhaustively examined but are deemed "good enough" under the circumstances.

Satisficers Versus Maximizers. Our practical solution to the problem of information overload is **satisficing**, decision making based on criteria that are "good enough" under the circumstances (see Nisbett, Krantz, Jepson, & Kunda, 1983). When you buy a car, you won't read every review of every system and subsystem about every car you might purchase; you satisfice. When shopping for shampoo, you won't test every single product available at the megamart; you satisfice. At least some students study only until they believe their knowledge is good enough to achieve whatever grade they desire; they satisfice. Satisficing enables you move on to the next thing demanding your attention.

We satisfice when making both minor decisions, such as what consumer products to buy (Park & Hastak, 1994; Simon, 1955), and major decisions, such as choice of college major or career goals (Starbuck, 1963). We make some errors by satisficing, but we do it anyway because "perfection may not be worth the extra cost" (Haselton & Funder, 2006; Simon, 1956). Of course, some people don't like to satisfice—they enjoy thinking through all the options, or they worry about making the wrong decision so they are more careful. The scale in the Applying Social Psychology to Your Life feature will tell you whether you generally tend to be a satisficer or the opposite—a **maximizer**—when making everyday decisions.

Satisficers, by the way, seem to be happier than maximizers (Snyder & Miene, 1994). Several studies (Polman, 2010; Schwartz et al., 2002; Sparks, Ehrlinger, & Eibach, 2012) suggest that trying to gather all available information for every decision is associated with lower levels of happiness, optimism, life satisfaction, and self-esteem—and with higher levels of depression, perfectionism, and regret. Perhaps that is why another Nobel Prize winner, Herbert Simon, suggested that satisficing directs many, and perhaps all, of our mental shortcuts (Simon, 1956). We tolerate mental errors because being perfect just isn't worth the price.

> " Believing passionately in the palpably not true . . . is the chief occupation of mankind. "
>
> —H. L. Mencken

Magical Thinking Encourages Mental Errors

In her book titled *The Year of Magical Thinking*, Joan Didion (2005) described how her brain refused to accept the death of her husband of 40 years, fellow writer John Gregory Dunne. Her thoughts replayed thousands of little things that she might have done to

Maximizer: An individual who engages a heavier cognitive load by exhaustively examining criteria when making decisions.

THE MAXIMIZATION SCALE

Applying Social Psychology to Your Life

Instructions: Use the following scale to indicate your level of agreement with each statement, then add up all of your answers. The higher your score, the more you tend to maximize rather than satisfice (scores can range from 6 to 42):

1	2	3	4	5	6	7
Completely disagree						Completely agree

1. ____ When I am in the car listening to the radio, I often check other stations to see if something better is playing, even if I am relatively satisfied with what I'm listening to.

2. ____ No matter how satisfied I am with my job, it's only right for me to be on the lookout for better opportunities.

3. ____ I often find it difficult to shop for a gift for a friend.

4. ____ Choosing a show to watch is really difficult. I'm always struggling to pick the best one.

5. ____ No matter what I do, I have the highest standards for myself.

6. ____ I never settle for second best.

Source: Nenkov, Morrin, Ward, Schwartz, and Hulland (2008).

prevent his heart attack. She found herself believing against all rationality that she might somehow find a way to restore him to life. "If only" thinking, she slowly realized during the year after his death, must eventually yield to acceptance. She knew that it was crazy to give in to **magical thinking**, beliefs based on assumptions that do not hold up to reality. But in the throes of her grief, she could not stop thinking, "If only. . . ."

"If Only . . ." Wishes. There are emotional consequences when we try to magically wish bad things away or good things into existence (Boninger, Gleicher, & Strathman, 1994; Bouts, Spears, & van der Pligt, 1992; Kahneman & Tversky, 1982; Roese, 1997). For example, if you are waiting in line for a free ticket to a concert, then you probably will be more disappointed if the person just in front of you got the last ticket than if you were still at the back of the line when tickets ran out. It's easier to imagine that "if only" you had changed one little thing in your schedule, then you would have been going to the concert.

The same kind of "if only" thinking leads Olympic athletes—like those in the photograph below—who finish in third place to feel happier than second place competitors. Why? Second place encourages the magical thinking, "If only I had done one little thing differently, I could have won gold." On the other hand, the bronze medalist reasons that if circumstances had been just a little different, he or she might not have received any medal at all! They can think, "At least I got a medal!" Emotionally, third place might provide a better experience than second place because it leads to happiness and relief rather than frustration and regret.

Counterfactual Thinking: Upward and Downward. **Counterfactual thinking** occurs when we imagine what might have been—alternative facts or events in the past that would have led to a different future (Davis & Lehman, 1995; Davis, Lehman, Silver, Wortman, & Ellard, 1996; Davis, Lehman, Wortman, Silver, & Thompson, 1995; Dunning & Madey, 1995; Dunning & Parpal, 1989; Einhorn & Hogarth, 1986). Counterfactual thinking occurred automatically to a group of tourists who somehow survived the terrible tsunami that took 280,000 lives across Southeast Asia on December 26, 2004.

When Teigen and Jensen (2011) *interviewed* 85 surviving tourists, both parents and children, most survivors comforted themselves, as much as they could, with **downward counterfactuals**, imagined outcomes that are even worse than reality. "Only a matter

Magical thinking: Beliefs based on assumptions that do not hold up to reality, such as "if only" thinking, counterfactual thinking, and optimistic bias.

Counterfactual thinking: The tendency to imagine alternative facts or events that would have led to a different future; imagining "what might have been."

Downward counterfactuals: Imagined outcomes that are worse than reality.

Julian Finney / Getty Images Sport / Getty Images

Which Olympic medalist is the happiest—and which is the second happiest?

The 2004 tsunami as it hit Thailand.

of 1 [minute], one way or the other," reported one interviewee, "and everything would have been different [we might have died]." They can be comforting, like a "silver lining" to tragedy. By contrast, **upward counterfactuals** are imagined outcomes that are better than reality. One interviewee commented, "They could have issued a warning," when imagining what might have led to a better outcome. They lead to anger or regret because you can see what might have been. Downward counterfactuals can be thought of as "at least" thoughts, while upward counterfactuals can be thought of as "if only" thoughts.

For example, upward counterfactual thinking was upsetting to some college students (Leach & Patall, 2013) when they imagined a path that would have led to better test performance or grades. Although not earning a higher grade can't be compared to a devastating tsunami, the underlying psychology was the same. These students were dissatisfied when they had thoughts such as, "If only I had studied more, then my GPA would have improved." On a positive note, however, upward counterfactuals help us learn from our mistakes. The thought, "If only I had studied harder for the exam" might motivate us to study more the next time around. For more on counterfactual thinking—and Spider-Man—see the Social Psychology in Popular Culture feature.

The Optimistic Bias and the Planning Fallacy.
To-do lists suggest another common form of magical thinking. If you keep a to-do list, how often do you actually check off every single item? I [Wind] keep an electronic sticky note on my computer desktop, on which I make a list at the beginning of each week of everything I need to get done. Although I have never, ever completed the entire list in a week, I have been making the list regularly for 7 years. My continued behavior demonstrates the **optimistic bias**, an unrealistic expectation that things will turn out well.

One *survey* suggests that the optimistic bias is a popular way to think. Weinstein (1980) asked more than 250 college students to estimate their chances of experiencing 42 positive and negative events compared to the average probability that their fellow classmates would experience those same events. Positive events included liking your job after graduation, owning your own home, and having a respectable starting salary.

Upward counterfactuals: Imagined outcomes that are better than reality.

Optimistic bias: The unrealistic expectation that things will turn out well.

COUNTERFACTUAL THINKING IN
SPIDER-MAN

Moviestore collection Ltd / Alamy Stock Photo

Even people who aren't big comic book fans could probably tell you that Spider-Man got his superpowers when Peter Parker, a teenager, was bitten by a scientifically altered spider. But when any fictional character suddenly has special, superhuman abilities, what determines whether that character will be a superhero or a supervillain?

For Peter Parker, his choice to use his powers for good may be due to his use of upward counterfactual thinking. In most versions of the Spider-Man origin story, Peter doesn't immediately decide to take the hero route. For example, in one film version (Arad, Tolmach, Ziskin, & Webb, 2012, starring Andrew Garfield), a few days after being bitten, Peter simply stands by as a man robs a convenience store—even though he could easily stop the crime. Unfortunately, the man then shoots Peter's beloved Uncle Ben. Peter's regret over his inaction causes him to start hunting criminals. Upward counterfactual thinking appears to haunt Peter as he imagines that Uncle Ben would still be alive "if only" Peter had done something.

The second half of the film continues this theme. The main antagonist is an evil scientist who morphs into a gigantic lizard only because Peter supplied him with an essential formula to alter his DNA. When several people attempt to tell Peter that it's not his job to stop the man-lizard, he tells them that it is his responsibility because it's his fault. Essentially, Peter is engaging in the upward counterfactual thought, "If only I hadn't provided him the formula he needed, none of this would have happened."

Thus, upward counterfactuals appear to have made Spider-Man choose a superhero's path because of his regret and wish for a better outcome in both situations. It's clear that upward counterfactuals and "if only" thinking have shaped Peter's interpretation of Uncle Ben's parting advice, the famous words of co-creator Stan Lee: "With great power comes great responsibility."

Negative events included having a drinking problem, attempting suicide, and getting divorced shortly after marrying. As the optimistic bias suggests, the students rated their chances of experiencing positive events as above average and their chances of experiencing negative events as below average. There's only one problem: We can't *all* be above average. At least some of these students must have been deceiving themselves about how nicely their lives were going to turn out after graduation.

Students also tend to be overly optimistic about their test performance (Gilovich, Kerr, & Medvec, 1993), and they are not alone in their optimism. Teens underestimate their likelihood of eventually becoming the victim of dating violence (Chapin & Coleman, 2012) or sexual assault (Untied & Dulaney, 2015). Potential blood donors overestimate their probability of actually making a donation (Koehler & Poon, 2006). Students who steal music instead of paying for it underestimate their chances of getting caught (Nandedkar & Midha, 2012). And those who sincerely make extravagant promises in romantic relationships tend not to follow through as well as those who make more modest commitments (Peetz & Kammrath, 2011). The people making these romantic commitments may sincerely mean what they say at the moment, but sometimes it's just the optimistic bias talking.

The Sydney Opera House and Boston's "Big Dig" project, both of which took much more money and time to create than originally planned.

The optimistic bias sounds like a good thing, but it can create big problems. The **planning fallacy** is unjustified confidence that one's own project, unlike similar projects, will proceed as planned (see Kahneman & Tversky, 1979). Thus, the planning fallacy is one specific type of optimistic bias. For example, Buehler, Griffin, and Ross (1994) described how the first stadium with a retractable roof, announced for the Montreal Olympics in 1976, was not completed until 1989—and at a cost greater than the cost of the entire 1976 Olympics. Australia's Sydney Opera House, estimated for completion in 1963 at a cost of $7 million, did not open until 1973 and actually cost $102 million. Boston's 3.5-mile tunnel known as the "Big Dig" was estimated to cost $2.8 billion but may have cost $22 billion—and with questionable structural outcomes. We get inspired by these big ideas and gloss over the details needed to complete them until they start costing us money, time, or other precious resources (see Alter, Oppenheimer, & Zemla, 2010). Like Baumeister's (1989) optimal margin theory of self-deception (described in Chapter 3), a little optimism can be helpful, but too much can be harmful.

The Main Ideas

- Two mental mistakes that are fairly common are (1) errors due to cognitive overload and (2) wishful or "magical" thinking.

- People are generally cognitive misers, meaning we prefer mental shortcuts when possible. Doing the minimal needed amount of thought is called satisficing; the opposite is called maximizing.

- Magical thinking or wishful thinking is imagining other possible outcomes. Downward counterfactuals, for example, are "at least" thoughts that imagine a worse outcome, while upward counterfactuals are "if only" thoughts that imagine a better outcome. The optimistic bias and planning fallacy are other examples of magical thinking.

⚡ CRITICAL THINKING CHALLENGE

- Describe decisions in which it is more adaptive to maximize and other decisions in which it is more adaptive to satisfice.

- Think of examples from your own life that illustrate different types of magical thinking: counterfactual thinking, optimistic bias, and the planning fallacy.

- If tragedy strikes you, do you tend to use more upward counterfactual thinking or downward counterfactual thinking? Which one leads you to feel better about what happened?

Planning fallacy: The unjustified confidence that one's own project, unlike similar projects, will proceed as planned.

FROM WHERE DOES INTUITION COME?

■ LO 4.4: Explain how intuition uses mental accessibility that comes from priming, experience, and heuristics.

Research about intuition demonstrates how science sometimes makes exciting explanations boring. It tickles our vanity, of course, to imagine that our private dreams somehow predict the future or that our hunches are supernatural insights. Prophesy, psychic gifts, and mental telepathy are much more entertaining than what science has come up with. Are scientists just out to spoil the fun?

Well, yes, depending on how you define "fun." Scientists find their fun by forming their beliefs around the **principle of parsimony**, preferring the simplest answer that explains the most evidence. Parsimony also means "cheap"—so you can think of scientists as intellectual bargain hunters who want a great theory without having to pay for it with exotic explanations. Relying on the simplest, evidence-based explanation is also called "Occam's razor" (Wind's favorite) and "the principle of least astonishment" (Tom's favorite).

The science of social cognition explains intuition with an explanation so ordinary that it does not require any dramatic leaps of faith. Intuition comes from **mental accessibility**, the ease with which ideas come to mind. Figure 4.2 describes how three silent sources of intuition (priming, experience, and heuristics) influence what comes most easily to mind. "Mental accessibility" may sound like an ordinary explanation. But intuition grows more mysterious as we follow the trail of evidence deeper into the human brain.

■ FIGURE 4.2 Three frequent sources of intuition: priming, experience, and heuristics.

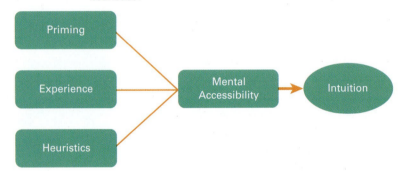

Intuition Relies on Mental Accessibility

For Sgt. Tierney (described at the beginning of this chapter), his life-saving flash of intuition had to penetrate two distinctive barriers: mental availability and mental accessibility (see Tulving & Pearlstone, 1966). First, Sgt. Tierney's brain had to privately reach the conclusion that there was something suspicious about two kindergarten boys locked inside a car on a hot day (**mental availability**—the knowledge is present in your mind). Second, Sgt. Tierney had to be able to access that information (mental accessibility—you can gain access to that knowledge). As patrol leader, Sgt. Tierney had many other competing claims on his attention (Chapman & Johnson, 2002; Epley, 2004; Epley, Boaz, & Van Boven, 2004; Epley & Gilovich, 2001, 2004; Gilbert & Gill, 2000; Shedler & Manis, 1986; Strack & Mussweiler, 1997).

When it works, intuition is astonishing. If you are 20 years old, then a relatively conservative estimate is that you know about 40,000 distinct words derived from more than 11,000 word families—and you will keep on learning new words (Brysbaert, Stevens, Mandera, & Keuleers, 2016). That works out to about 2,100 new words per year or 40 new words every week. Did you consciously learn 40 new words every week, every year, from the day you were born? Of course not. You learned those words (and how to use them) in spectacular bursts during critical periods of brain development (Wasserman, 2007). You acquired most of your knowledge intuitively, through context and deduction, without knowing that you were learning. Your intuitive knowing extends to your listening skills; you can recognize words within just 200 milliseconds

Principle of parsimony: The tendency for individuals to prefer the simplest answer that explains the most evidence.

Mental accessibility: The ease with which an idea comes to mind.

Mental availability: The information already salient in one's mind.

(a fifth of a second) and understand words tumbling out of other people's mouths at a rate of six syllables per second (Aitchison, 2003).

As Figure 4.2 indicates, mental accessibility relies on three major sources. This section of the chapter reviews the first two (priming and experience) and provides a Spotlight on Research Methods feature from a famous priming study. The next section will cover the third source, heuristics, in depth and provide several examples.

Priming Increases Mental Accessibility

If you played a word association game starting with the word *dogs,* you might associate "dogs" with "cats," "barking," or even "pets." The word *pets* is probably associated with "hamsters," "snakes," "goldfish," and perhaps even "taking responsibility" (for feeding and caring for pets). Each word branches off into new sets of words. The entire collection of associations is called a **semantic network**, mental concepts that are connected to one another by common characteristics. **Priming** refers to the initial activation of a concept (such as "dogs") that subsequently flashes across our semantic network that allows particular ideas to come more easily to mind (Cameron, Brown-Iannuzzi, & Payne, 2012). Once one category is primed, other related categories are also primed. The term *priming* means that after initially thinking about something, thinking about it again later will be easier and faster. It's like priming an engine to get it started or priming a wall before you paint it. Priming is preparation for what comes later.

Bargh, Chen, and Burrows (1996) designed an *experiment* using word puzzles to explore the effects of priming. They created three experimental conditions by having college students complete word puzzles featuring (a) words concerned with being rude (e.g., *disturb, intrude, obnoxious*), (b) words concerned with being polite (e.g., *respect, considerate, cordially*), or (c) neutral words (e.g., *normally, send, clears*). Depending on the condition, the concept of politeness or rudeness was primed (or nothing was primed in the neutral *control condition*). The researchers then sent the students on an errand that required them to interrupt two people who were talking and ask them for directions. A higher percentage of participants who had been primed with rude words interrupted the two people talking; a lower percentage of participants primed to be polite interrupted the conversation (and the difference between groups was *statistically significant*).

In a similar experiment, they discovered that people walked more slowly after being primed with words related to aging (e.g., *Florida, gray, careful, bingo*), compared to a neutral *control condition*. The researchers believed that priming words related to aging led to slower walking because it increased mental accessibility to participants' semantic network related to what it means to grow old. Even though the researchers never specifically primed anything about walking or speed, simply priming the mental category of old age led to priming of all the mental constructs related to that category; all of the relevant concepts became more accessible.

There has been considerable controversy over this particular study, however. Other researchers using similar procedures have not been able to replicate the slower movements of students down a hallway after being exposed to words associated with aging (Doyen, Klein, Pichon, & Cleeremans, 2012). In science, others repeating your experiment and getting the same results is more than just a good idea. *Replication* is necessary. Despite the lack of replication, we have chosen to include this second study (the one done in 2012) in our discussion about priming because the researchers did find the effect when *the researchers* expected to see it—in other words, they were priming themselves instead of the participants! Perhaps that's why they named their study *Behavioral Priming: It's All in the Mind, but Whose Mind?*

Semantic network: A collection of mental concepts that are connected by common characteristics.

Priming: Initial activation of a concept within a semantic network that allows related ideas to come more easily to mind.

HOW PRIMING CAN TEST FOR RACISM

Spotlight on Research Methods

Your mental network of related concepts is both personal and social. For example, the word *boxer* could prime "dog," "Muhammad Ali," or even "underwear." Which category jumps to mind first tells us something about your particular semantic network. A famous research study used the idea of priming as the foundation for a creative and intriguing test of racism (Correll, Park, Judd, & Wittenbrink, 2002). They tested the strength of the associations between the concepts of "African American" and "weapons" and "danger."

This research team was inspired by a series of tragedies: police officers who fatally shot innocent suspects. Police officers are in a very difficult situation. They must make split-second decisions about whether a particular person is dangerous or not, and waiting too long can be a deadly error. To determine whether someone is dangerous, they might have to quickly assess what's in someone's hand—is it a gun, a knife, a wallet, or simply a cell phone?

As if playing a video game, participants in the study watched as a bus stop, a convenience store, a park, and other scenes flashed by. One of these scenes included either a White or an African American man holding something in his hand. Participants had to push one computer button to "shoot" the man if he was holding a weapon (such as a knife or gun) and a different button to "not shoot" the man if he was holding something else (such as a wallet or a cell phone). The *hypothesis* was that for at least some of the participants, the concepts of "African American" and "weapons" would have a strong association in their semantic network.

Thus, when an African American person popped up on the screen, priming the concept of "African American"

would also prime "weapons" for people with higher levels of racism. This would lead to those participants mistakenly "shooting" the African American targets, even when they were holding something innocent. And that is exactly what happened when college students participated. They were more likely to "shoot" the African Americans on the screen, compared to the White people on the screen, regardless of what people were actually holding. In this case, priming led to errors based on stereotypes. While priming does increase mental accessibility of concepts, sometimes that mental accessibility takes us into a semantic network of associations that leads to a tragedy.

The good news of this potentially controversial study was that when the researchers tried to *replicate* the findings with actual police officers from Chicago, they didn't find the same results. In fact, the police officers were less likely to make mistakes in either direction; they shot people on the screen holding weapons (regardless of what race those people were) and did not shoot people on the screen holding other things (again, regardless of the race of the people on the screen).

If this is surprising to you, given the number of false shootings that police officers have made that appear in the news, remember that a story about an innocent person being shot is more likely to make the news than when a guilty person is shot. In other words, rare mistakes are going to make the news while hundreds of correct decisions won't. That experimental finding, of course, is no comfort to the families who have suffered such a terrible tragedy. These are heart-breaking stories. The goal of the researchers is not to accuse but to discover (and then prevent) whatever lies behind such tragedies.

The feature above, How Priming Can Test for Racism, presents additional examples of the priming effect.

Experience Improves Mental Accessibility

Experience may be intuition's best teacher. For example, college students' brief, intuitive observations of a teacher (totaling only 30 seconds) at the start of a semester were fairly

Do you get strong impressions of your teachers or professors within minutes of the first day of class?

good predictors of average student ratings of the teacher at the end of the semester (Ambady & Rosenthal, 1993; Babad, Avni-Babad, & Rosenthal, 2004). Why are students so good at sizing up teachers? Well, what have you been doing over the past 15 to 20 years? You have been going to classes with many different teachers. Consequently, you have gotten very good at intuiting in the first few seconds how you will feel about the teacher and the class by the end of the year.

Personal experience also seems to explain why both gay men and lesbians are more likely than heterosexuals to intuitively detect someone's sexual orientation in still photographs and even in 1-second videos—a phenomenon jokingly referred to as "Gaydar" (Ambady, Hallahan, & Conner, 1999). The participants in this study could not say what they saw, but they saw it—because they had seen it many times before. In a similar feat of intuition, African American judges were more accurate than White judges at detecting subtle forms of nonverbal racial bias (Curhan & Pentland, 2007). They, too, could not say what they saw, but they saw it—because they had seen it many times before. Experience had sharpened their intuition.

> A surgeon who had trained many other surgeons across a long career summed up the importance of experience at refining intuition. "Good judgment comes from experience," he reported, "and experience comes from bad judgment."

The Main Ideas

- Intuition is influenced by ordinary events and ideas that are both available and accessible to us.

- The mental accessibility of ideas is influenced by (a) priming our semantic networks, (b) personal experiences, and (c) heuristics.

- Priming refers to how the initial mental activation of a concept makes processing that concept faster and easier. Other, related concepts will also be made accessible through our semantic network.

- Mental accessibility and intuition are also positively correlated with experience.

- The belief that "going with your first choice" (or trusting intuition) when taking a multiple-choice test is not helpful (Lilienfeld, Lynn, Ruscio, & Beyerstein, 2011). Instead, thinking more about a particular problem increases the probability of getting it right. Why do you think that this psychological myth is so popular?

- This section covered one possibility for why police officers could occasionally make the fatal error of shooting innocent people, due to priming and mental associations. If this is the case, how could officer training change this pattern? What kinds of exercises or procedures could prevent this type of error?

- This section discussed several possible pairings within semantic networks (such as certain races being paired with stereotypes or priming rudeness words with the likelihood of interrupting someone). What other interesting research studies could be done using the idea that priming one concept might prime another, at least with certain types of participants? Would experience have an influence on the results?

CAN WE TRUST OUR INTUITION? THE ROLE OF HEURISTICS AND BIASES

LO 4.5: Analyze why we can respect, but not always trust, our intuition.

We've seen that both priming and personal experience help particular ideas come more easily to mind. Now add one more to that list: **Heuristics** are mental shortcuts that make it easier to solve difficult problems. Like the shortcuts that Tom likes to take when driving, sometimes heuristics don't work out and may even make get us lost. In other words, they can lead to mistakes.

Heuristics Facilitate Mental Accessibility

A third-year medical student correctly diagnosed that a young patient's strange symptoms were the result of a skull deformity rather than what everyone else had assumed (some kind of neurochemical brain disorder). The diagnosis had stumped everyone else. Was she (the medical student) an unusually brilliant, magically gifted, intuitive diagnostician? No. Over lunch, she had been leafing through a journal that some previous student had left behind and found an article discussing the effects of particular skull deformities. The article had become mentally accessible to her over lunch, but her casual sharing of the idea after lunch seemed to signal genius to her fellow medical students and professors.

In a stress-free, no-hurry world, there is a purely logical approach to such problem solving. An **algorithm** is a systematic way of searching for an answer that will eventually lead to a solution—if there is one. Remember from the first section of this chapter that we are capable of both quick, intuitive thought and slow, logical thought; using algorithms to solve problems is definitely logic. It is usually a slower but surer way to solve a problem such as what was troubling the patient with the skull deformity. For psychology students looking for answers in journals, digital databases such as PsycINFO now make it more realistic to search through every (available) journal article and conference presentation. But this takes time.

In addition, many everyday problems don't have a comprehensive database that can be accessed with high-speed computers. Consequently, algorithmic approaches to

Heuristic: A mental shortcut that makes it easier for an individual to solve difficult problems by facilitating the mental accessibility of certain ideas. Examples include the anchoring and adjustment heuristic, the availability heuristic, and the representativeness heuristic.

Algorithm: A systematic, logical method of searching for a solution to a problem or question.

everyday problem solving are often impractical. So the human brain, cognitive miser that it is, decides it is better to tolerate a few errors in the name of efficiency. When faced with a problem, our preferred or default approach to specific problems relies on mental shortcuts, particular kinds of heuristics. Algorithms rely on logic; heuristics rely on intuition (even though we may fool ourselves into thinking that we are being logical). Basic research has identified several specific types of common heuristics, but we will introduce you to just three of them: anchoring and adjustment, availability, and representativeness.

The Anchoring and Adjustment Heuristic.

The **anchoring and adjustment heuristic** occurs when we make decisions by starting with an arbitrary number that unduly influences our final solution. The anchoring and adjustment heuristic demonstrates that our intuitive impulse to everyday problem solving is to grab for any answer—even if it comes from an unreliable source. We seem to like just having an answer, even if it isn't a very good one. For example, answer the following question by choosing either (a) or (b) below. Then write down your most precise estimate.

> "On average, how many full-time college students <u>in the entire United States</u> drop out before graduation?"
>
> ___ More than 200 students
>
> or
>
> ___ Fewer than 200 students
>
> Now indicate your own most precise estimate here: _____

When making your own estimate of how many students drop out, you probably fell victim to this heuristic. Why? Because your most honest answer to this question is probably, "I have no idea how many college students drop out before graduating, but it's probably much higher than 200." You may be able to think of 5 or even 10 at your own school, but your knowledge about this issue is probably uncertain. So, being a lazy, cognitive miser, you grab at whatever fragmentary information happens to be available. In this case, we brought to your mind what felt like a hint: 200. It was so low that it wasn't a very helpful hint—but our mentioning it made it mentally accessible. But what if, instead of hearing the number 200, we had hinted at a different number by asking the question like this:

> "On average, how many full-time college students <u>in the entire United States</u> drop out before graduation?"
>
> ___ More than 25 million students
>
> or
>
> ___ Fewer than 25 million students
>
> Now indicate your own most precise estimate here: _____

Again, your most honest answer to this question probably would be, "I have no idea how many college students drop out, but it's probably much lower than 25 million students." In the first question, your estimate would be "anchored" by 200; in the second question, your answer would be anchored by 25 million.

Anchoring and adjustment heuristic: Occurs when an individual makes a decision using information within a problem that unduly influences his or her final answer. The tendency to adjust little when a plausible estimate, or anchor, has been provided, despite not knowing whether the information is reliable.

A boat can only move a certain distance from an anchor—and perhaps our judgments can only move a certain distance from a mental starting point.

The moral of the story here is that when you were asked to "indicate your own most precise estimate," your two estimates would *not* have met in the middle because your thinking was anchored by the different "hints." If the obviously low number of 200 had been suggested to you, then you might estimate as high as 30,000 students per year, or even 200,000. However, if the obviously high number of 25 million had been suggested to you, then you might estimate 2 million students per year or even 500,000 (Kahneman & Frederick, 2005; Mussweiler & Strack, 2001; Nisbett & Wilson, 1977; Trope & Gaunt, 2000; Tversky & Kahneman, 1974). Your estimates would be *anchored* by what was mentally accessible (either 200 or 25 million) and then *adjusted* upward from 200 or downward from 25 million—even though both numbers are arbitrary.

The anchoring and adjustment heuristic is based on the metaphor of a boat in the water. The boat can float or adjust a certain amount as the waves move it around—but the anchor keeps it within a certain general area. For the heuristic, the idea is that the initial "hint" or number provided serves as an anchor for your thought process. Your mind can float above or below the initial starting point, but the anchor will keep your estimates within a certain range. When we have nothing else to go by, we will use almost any information to anchor our mental estimates as long as it comes easily to mind (Cervone & Peake, 1986; Marrow, 2002; Wilson, Houston, Etling, & Brekke, 1996).

People tend to stop adjusting as they approach a more plausible estimate (Epley & Gilovich, 2006). And we seem to be politely reluctant to challenge someone else's crazy estimate—unless it is about some issue that is important to us (Epley, Keysar, Van Boven, & Gilovich, 2004) or one in which we have some expertise (Bruza, Welsh, Navarro, & Begg, 2011). We will generally disregard someone who makes the crazy claim that only four students in the entire United States drop out of college in their first year. However, we are more likely to challenge the person if we just wrote a term paper on that topic and are certain that we know better. The anchoring and adjustment heuristic is another indicator that much of our thinking is guided by the principle of satisficing—being satisfied with a "good enough" answer to a question.

The Availability Heuristic. Fame is another way that particular ideas come more easily to mind (they are more accessible), and it has a funny effect on our social thinking: We inflate the frequency and importance of famous people and events. For example, McKelvie (2000) found that in a memory task for a list of names people had seen earlier, participants overestimated the frequency of famous names compared to nonfamous (and made up) names, probably because they noticed the famous names more.

The mental accessibility of any name, of course, depends on its mental availability in the first place—Napoleon is not famous to you if you have never heard of him. Fame is thus one example of the **availability heuristic**, our tendency to overestimate the frequency or importance of something based on how easily it comes to mind (Tversky & Kahneman, 1973). Researchers pointed out, for example, that we are likely to assess the divorce rate in our community by recalling the number of divorces among our own acquaintances. The effect of those scandalous headlines in

Availability heuristic: The tendency to overestimate the frequency or importance of information based on how easily it comes to mind. Occurs when an individual makes a decision using the most easily available information.

tabloids sold at grocery checkout lines also makes us estimate that Hollywood couples are much more likely to have ugly divorces than they are to live happily ever after, simply because divorces get more attention (and sell more tabloids). Certainly, we notice scandalous divorces more than quiet, happily married couples—so the divorces become more available and more accessible to us. As the Spotlight on Research Methods feature pointed out, mistaken shootings by the police are also more likely to make headlines than justified and correct shootings, so we might think mistaken shootings are more common than they really are—another example of the availability heuristic.

Certain cues tell us whether someone in a store probably works there—when we rely on these cues, we are using the representativeness heuristic.

The availability heuristic influences our social perceptions is subtle ways. People who spend a lot of time on Facebook are more likely to think that their friends are happier than they are themselves and more likely to think that life is unfair (Chou & Edge, 2012). This effect is probably because people are more likely to post positive or even boastful status updates on Facebook than negative or embarrassing updates; thus, we see a constant stream of happy accomplishments from our friends. To sum up, the availability heuristic is another corner-cutting way we cognitive misers think more efficiently but also make mental miscalculations (Dougherty, Gettys, & Ogden, 1999; Nisbett & Ross, 1980; Rothman & Hardin, 1997; Schwarz, 1998; Taylor & Fiske, 1978; Travis, Phillippi, & Tonn, 1989).

The Representativeness Heuristic. We use heuristics to solve many everyday problems and always with the same trade-off between efficiency and errors. For example, when you need a store clerk, you probably would not use the algorithmic method of approaching everyone in the store and saying, "Do you work here?" Instead, you would more likely substitute the easier-to-answer (and much more efficient!) heuristic of looking for someone wearing a uniform or a nametag (Kahneman & Frederick, 2005; Shepperd & Koch, 2005).

Looking for someone dressed like a typical store clerk is an example of a thinking strategy called the **representativeness heuristic**, a way of answering a question by classifying observations according to how closely they resemble the "typical" case. The representative heuristic substitutes an easier question ("What does a store clerk typically wear?") for the laborious algorithmic task of asking every person in the store, "Do you work here?" So we look for someone who "represents" our idea of a stereotypical clerk.

Of course, some shoppers may also be dressed as if they could be store clerks, and some store clerks may appear to be ordinary customers. You have to balance the small risk of making an error against the reward of finding a clerk quickly. Like pushing your way through a "push" door, the representativeness heuristic often works so well that we don't even notice that we are using it. But the example below, adapted from Swinkels (2003), shows how easily our intuition can mislead us when it relies on the representativeness heuristic:

> Janelle is a 24-year-old who takes a bus to work in the daytime, eats easy-to-prepare inexpensive meals, and lives in an apartment next to a college campus.

> Like Janelle, Luisa is also a 24-year-old who takes a bus to work in the daytime, eats easy-to-prepare inexpensive meals, lives in an apartment next to a college campus, and spends a great deal of money on textbooks.

Representativeness heuristic: Occurs when individuals make a decision based on how closely their observations resemble the "typical" case. The tendency to classify observations according to a preexisting, typical case and using that process to come to a conclusion.

The only difference between Janelle (on the left) and Luisa is that Luisa spends a great deal of money on textbooks. Which is more likely to be a college student?

Who is most likely to be a college student?

____ Janelle ____Luisa

Most people, relying on their automatic intuition, will use the representative heuristic to estimate that Luisa is more likely to be a college student because they know that the "typical" college student does, indeed, spend a great deal of money on textbooks. But that conclusion is statistically impossible, a logical fallacy. The additional characteristic (spending money on textbooks) means that the total pool of people who fit the description can only be smaller. In other words, *some* college students don't spend a lot of money on books. Each time we add another criterion to the list, the percentage of people who fill *all* of the criteria gets smaller. So, statistically speaking, Janelle is more likely to be a college student. But notice how difficult it is to stop believing our intuition, even when logic stands in the way.

Parallel Heuristics

Our mental shortcuts are rapid and automatic, and they can operate simultaneously—that is, in parallel. When these mental shortcuts all come up with the same false intuition, they can be extremely persuasive. For example, read the following memories from people who claimed to have observed a live, televised version of the tragic terrorist bus bombing at London's Tavistock Square on July 7, 2005 (from Ost, Granhag, & Udell, 2008, p. 82).

> Participant 9. *Bus had just stopped to let people off when two women got on and a man. He placed the bag by his side, the woman sat down and the doors closed, as the bus left there was the explosion and everyone started to scream while a leg was on the floor.*

> Participant 13. *The event was shown after a brief report. The bus had stopped at a traffic light. There was a bright light and a loud bang and the top of the bus flew off and lots of screaming and then everything seemed still.*

> Participant 24. *Bus moving normally, then explosion, debris everywhere, chaos.*

> Participant 131. *The bus was moving slowly in traffic and then the back of the bus exploded. A lot of debris everywhere and people panicking.*

> Participant 158. *Bus appears to turn into Tavistock Square and people stand to get off and there is a flash and then nothing.*

There is only one problem with these dramatic firsthand accounts: They cannot be true because there were no live broadcasts of this terrible event. Ost and colleagues

The 2005 London bombing was devastating to many people.

(2008) wondered if increased media exposure about this tragedy had somehow evolved into false but sincerely believed memories. So they recruited participants in Great Britain (where media coverage was extensive and repeated) and in Sweden (where there was less overall coverage). They first asked all participants the same question: "How well do you remember the television coverage of the London bombings?" Then, as usually happens in an *experiment,* they *randomly assigned* the participants to one of three conditions by asking them whether they remembered seeing on television (1) the real aftermath of the explosion, (2) a computerized reconstruction of the explosion, or (3) closed-circuit, live television footage of the actual event. The last two conditions simply could not be correct, because they weren't possible; there had never been any computerized reconstruction on television, and there were no closed-circuit television broadcasts of the actual event, only its aftermath.

■ **FIGURE 4.3** Heuristics can produce false memories.

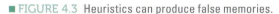

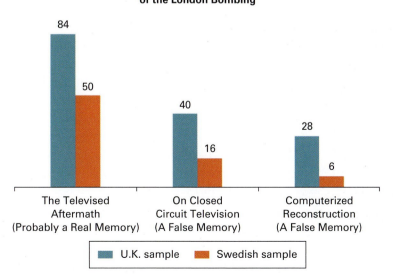

% Reporting How They Saw Television Coverage of the London Bombing

| | 84 | 50 | 40 | 16 | 28 | 6 |

The Televised Aftermath (Probably a Real Memory)   On Closed Circuit Television (A False Memory)   Computerized Reconstruction (A False Memory)

■ U.K. sample   ■ Swedish sample

SOURCE: Ost et al. (2008).

Social Psychology in Action: False Memory Experiment

©SAGE Publications

Nevertheless, Figure 4.3 indicates that a higher percentage of people in the U.K. sample (compared to the Swedish sample) reported seeing both the nonexistent closed-circuit televised event and the nonexistent televised reconstruction (Ost et al., 2008). Increased media exposure had encouraged them to create intuitively appealing but entirely false memories about this tragic event (Fiske, Kenny, & Taylor, 1982; Nisbett & Ross, 1980; Shedler & Manis, 1986; Taylor & Thompson, 1982).

Several different heuristics combined to create social misperceptions about this tragic event. It was a vivid, easy-to-imagine, and famous tragedy (*availability*) that probably *anchored* people's imaginations so often that it began to feel like an authentic memory. Their stories followed what they thought would be typical or *representative* of an exploding bus. When all that social thinking told the same story, it was easy for the U.K. citizens to believe that they really had witnessed this tragedy on television. Their intuitions were wrong.

We Can Respect—but Not Trust—Our Intuitions

Heuristics are mental shortcuts that, as seen in Figure 4.3, sometimes lead to errors. However, it would be just as wrong to conclude that we should *never* trust our intuition as it is to believe that we can *always* trust our intuition. We cannot avoid using our intuition; we need our intuition, and sometimes our intuition is wonderfully insightful. So the intelligent middle ground is to respect but not blindly trust our intuitions.

The Confirmation Bias: A Dangerous Way to Think.
Without realizing it, we often think in terms of the **confirmation bias**, searching for evidence that confirms what we already believe and ignoring evidence that contradicts our beliefs. For example, let's say your intuition is flirting with astrology as a way to describe personality. It seems to describe you and others you know well. As your belief grows a little stronger, you start to "see" more evidence that confirms what you are starting to believe. Your roommate is a Pisces and they are supposed to be moody—and you start to notice how moody your roommate is. However, looking at astrology through the lens of science tells a different story. Dean and Kelly (2003) did not find correlated personalities when they studied 2,100 time-twins (individuals born within minutes of one another), who should have been similar if astrology were accurate.

Perhaps you are thinking, Where's the harm, fun killer? Maybe nothing. However, persistent gamblers pay attention to their wins and explain away their losses (Gilovich, 1983). People who expressed a hypothesis about how a crime occurred early in their review of a police file were more likely to be biased later (O'Brien, 2009). Psychiatrists persisted in a diagnosis that confirmed their original hunch despite contradicting information (Mendel et al., 2011). Decision makers kept believing in nonexistent weapons of mass destruction (WMD) during Operation Iraqi Freedom. There may have been other justifications for what has become America's longest war, but WMD was not one of them (see Johnston, 2005; Straus, Parker, & Bruce, 2011). Nickerson (1998) believes that the confirmation bias is the leading cause of "disputes, altercations, and misunderstandings that occur among individuals, groups, and nations" (p. 175). Confirmation bias can work with *any* belief system.

The Hindsight Bias: A Self-Deceiving Way to Think.
The **hindsight bias** occurs when you believe that you could have predicted an outcome—but only after you know

Confirmation bias: Occurs when individuals only search for evidence that confirms their beliefs while ignoring evidence that contradicts their beliefs.

Hindsight bias: Occurs when individuals believe they could have predicted the outcome of a past event but only after they already know what happened; the false belief that they "knew it all along."

Rick Kern / Contributor / WireImage / Getty Images

As physicist Neil deGrasse Tyson says, "The good thing about science is that it's true whether or not you believe in it."

Hindsight bias: Few people predicted Donald Trump would win the 2016 election for U.S. president, but many people said afterward, "I knew it was going to happen."

what happened. It's the false belief that "I knew it all along." The hindsight bias may be just as subtle and dangerous as the confirmation bias because it creates an illusion of understanding that makes it difficult to learn from the past (Fischhoff, 1975, 2002, 2007).

For example, since we can now "connect the dots" that led to the 9/11 terror attacks, we falsely believe that we should have been able to predict it (see Bernstein, Erdfelder, Meltzoff, Peria, & Loftus, 2011). Authorities conveniently forget about February 26, 1993. A yellow Ryder van was exploded in a failed attempt to tip the North Tower into the South Tower. Despite this attack, everyone was shocked and surprised at the second, successful attack; at the time, people did not predict what was going to happen in the future. The danger of the hindsight bias is that it gives an illusion of understanding.

Negativity bias: The automatic tendency to notice and remember negative information better than positive information.

The Negativity Bias: Bad Is More Memorable Than Good. The **negativity bias** is our automatic tendency to notice and remember negative information better than positive information. For example, unpleasant odors are perceived as more intense and evoke stronger emotional reactions than pleasant odors (Royet, Plailly, Delon-Martin, Kareken, & Segebart, 2003). It's easier and faster for us to find an angry face hidden among happy faces than a happy face hidden among sad faces (Hansen & Hansen, 1988). "Better safe than sorry" seems to be the guiding motto of the negativity bias (Fiedler, Freytag, & Meiser, 2009; Öhman & Mineka, 2001)—it's good for us to pay attention to people in our environment who are angry, to bad smells, and so on.

Are those dark clouds really a tornado heading our way? The negativity bias exists because we may only get to be wrong once about real threats.

The automatic negativity bias can be both good and bad. It's good when it keeps us alive—but it can be exhausting! Figure 4.4, for example, reminds us that if you live in tornado alley within the United States, then you are keenly aware that dark clouds and high winds

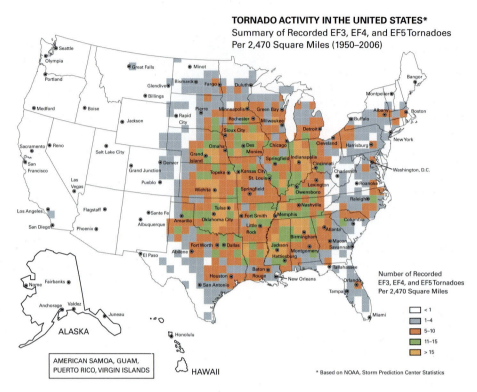

TORNADO ACTIVITY IN THE UNITED STATES*
Summary of Recorded EF3, EF4, and EF5 Tornadoes
Per 2,470 Square Miles (1950–2006)

Number of Recorded
EF3, EF4, and EF5 Tornadoes
Per 2,470 Square Miles

☐	< 1
☐	1–4
☐	5–10
☐	11–15
☐	> 15

* Based on NOAA, Storm Prediction Center Statistics

SOURCE: United States Federal Emergency Management Agency.

sometimes predict devastating tornados. People with a greater negativity bias will be more likely to find shelter and survive. You may only get to be wrong once about a tornado. The "key organizing principle" for managing our negativity bias seems to be to "minimize danger and maximize reward . . . at each point in time" (Williams et al., 2009, p. 804). Or, as social psychologists keep reminding us, our behavior and thought processes depend on the situation.

The Main Ideas

- An algorithm is a systematic, logical approach to problem solving; a heuristic is an intuitive, mental shortcut approach to problem solving. Three examples of heuristics are anchoring and adjustment, availability, and representativeness.

- Heuristics operate automatically and simultaneously (in parallel) as we make decisions and solve problems.

- Three cognitive biases that occur due to faulty intuition are the confirmation bias, the hindsight bias, and the negativity bias.

 CRITICAL THINKING CHALLENGE

- Think of someone you judged negatively the moment you first saw that person. Was your quick, intuitive judgment correct or are the confirmation bias and the hindsight bias influences that conspire for you to ignore evidence that does not support your first impression?

- Try to think of five specific examples of times when a friend gave you a compliment. Now, try to think of five specific examples of a time when someone in school said something mean about you. If the second list is easier than the first list, have you fallen victim to the negativity bias? What are ways to combat the negativity bias?

CHAPTER SUMMARY

How do we think?

Social cognition is the study of how people combine intuition and logic to process social information. These two systems of thinking combine and work together, and our ability to use both is called dual processing. Intuition is emotional, automatic, effortless, implicit, and fast. Logic, on the other hand, is analytical, systematic, effortful, explicit, and slow. Generally, our default is to use intuition, but we can quickly shift into logical thinking when needed. Each system of thought has advantages and disadvantages.

People only have a certain and limited capacity to process information, as well as individual differences in whether people prefer intuition or logical thought in general. People who prefer to rely on logic have a high "need for cognition." Social cognition is also influenced by our culture. For example, "Western" cultures tend to emphasize individuality, whereas "Eastern" or some Asian cultures tend to emphasize collective thinking and values.

How do we remember social information?

We have three types of memory or mental structures that help us organize and interpret social information: schemas, scripts, and stereotypes. Scripts and stereotypes are two more specific types of schemas.

A schema is a memory structure that labels and organizes incoming information. It provides a cognitive structure for us to understand the world. One type of schema, for example, is a script; scripts guide our expectations for common, specific types of events. We have scripts for funerals, weddings, different types of restaurant experiences, and so on. A second type of schema is a stereotype, which is when we assume that everyone from a group different from our own is the same. For example, if you are not from New York, you might have a stereotype that everyone from New York is aggressive. Stereotypes are discussed in depth in Chapter 9.

Why do our brains sometimes make mistakes?

We sometimes make mental mistakes for two reasons. The first is due to information overload; we can't process too much information at any given time. We are also cognitive misers, meaning that most people only think as much as needed (and not more). The general tendency to think to a minimum level is called satisficing; the opposite is called maximizing. There are advantages and disadvantages to each, and different situations may require each.

The second common reason for mental mistakes is called magical thinking, which refers to wishful thinking about alternatives to reality. Downward counterfactual thinking, for example, is when people imagine another outcome that's worse than what really happened as a way to comfort themselves. After a tragedy, people might think, "At least we're still alive." On the other hand, upward counterfactual thinking is when we imagine outcomes better than what really happened. After a tragedy, people might think, "If only we had more warning, we could have saved more people." Upward counterfactual thoughts are not very emotionally comforting, but they can motivate us to change for the better the next time around.

Another form of "magical" thinking is the optimistic bias, which is an unrealistic expectation that things will turn out well. The optimistic bias has been found when people estimate their chances of being in an accident, getting a divorce, and so on. One specific type of optimistic bias is the planning fallacy, which is when people believe a project will go as planned and not need any additional time, money, and so forth to be completed.

From where does intuition come?

While intuitive decisions sometimes seem mysterious or "psychic," the principle of parsimony suggests that intuition comes from mental availability and accessibility. Three things that can increase mental accessibility (or how quickly/easily concepts come to mind) are priming, experience, and heuristics. The first two are discussed in this section of the chapter, while heuristics are covered in the final section.

Priming refers to the initial mental activation of a concept (like "cake") that subsequently makes that concept more likely to come to mind or to be processed more easily. Priming one concept can also, indirectly, prime concepts related to the first one in someone's semantic network (for example, priming "cake" might also prime "ice cream" or "birthdays"). Several studies have shown that priming concepts can lead to interesting results relevant to stereotypes; for example, priming "old" caused people to walk more slowly in one study.

Another variable that is positively correlated to mental accessibility is experience with a subject. For example, African Americans are more accurate at detecting subtle forms of racism compared to White participants.

Can we trust our intuition?

We often rely on intuition because it allows for very efficient problem solving. However, it can lead to several cognitive errors and biases. Fewer errors are made if we use algorithms, which are systematic, logical approaches to solving problems—but algorithms are slow. Faster (but potentially mistaken) approaches include heuristics, which are mental shortcuts we use to solve problems.

The anchoring and adjustment heuristic occurs when we make decisions by starting with an arbitrary number that unduly influences our final solution. The availability heuristic is our tendency to overestimate the frequency of something based on how easily it comes to mind. A third common heuristic is the representativeness heuristic, which occurs when we make guesses based on how closely people resemble the "typical" case of a certain category we have in mind. These heuristics all work in parallel and can be very persuasive when they point toward a common answer.

While intuition doesn't always lead to errors, it does influence our tendency to use biased thought processing. For example, the confirmation bias occurs when we search for evidence that confirms what we already believe (and ignore or forget information that goes against what we believe). The hindsight bias is when we think we "knew something all along," even though we would not have guessed an outcome beforehand. A third example of biased intuition is the negativity bias, which leads us to focus on, notice, and remember negative information more than positive information.

THEORIES IN REVIEW

- Dual processing theory
- Schemas (scripts and stereotypes)
- Counterfactual thinking
- Principle of parsimony
- Heuristics (anchoring and adjustment, availability, representativeness)

CRITICAL THINKING, ANALYSIS, AND APPLICATION

- According to dual processing theory, humans are good at switching back and forth between intuition and logic, as needed. Do you think any other species have this ability? If so, provide specific examples to illustrate your point of view.

- On a scale of 0 to 100, how much balance do you like to have between easy, but frequently mistaken thought and difficult, but accurate thought? If 0 means "super easy but often filled with mistakes" and 100 means "super difficult but always leading to the correct decision," where do you fall on this continuum? What would be the consequences if everyone in the world thought the same way that you have chosen?

- This chapter identified many examples of errors in social cognition thought processes. Choose the three errors, biases, or mistakes that you think are common in your own life and describe them. If you can identify these as frequent errors, does that mean you can change them? Do you want to change them?

- Now that you know more about social cognition, can you use your knowledge of other people's common mental mistakes to get them to do what you want? How could you use knowledge from this chapter to get people to like you, buy a product, vote for you, and so on?

PERSONAL REFLECTION

Even as an older student, two of the most difficult psychological insights for me to accept were that my memories were unreliable and that my intuitions could not always be trusted. It was disturbing to think that *my* memories were not "the whole truth and nothing but the truth." And somewhere along the way, I had absorbed the vague belief that "going with your gut" was usually a good thing. But as I slowly became more comfortable with those twin insights from social cognition, I found them liberating rather than discouraging. No longer did I have to defend my every memory and every decision as "right." It was easier to admit that my hunches about everything from how to avoid a traffic jam to major life decisions could be wrong. I'm not sure that the phrase, "You shall know the truth and the truth shall set you free," was meant for this situation, but that's how I experienced these two helpful insights from the science of social cognition. [TH]

Visit **edge.sagepub.com/heinzen** to help you accomplish your coursework goals in an easy-to-use learning environment.

- **Visual Key Concepts**
- Mobile-friendly **eFlashcards**
- Mobile-friendly practice **quizzes**
- **Video** and **multimedia content**
- EXCLUSIVE! Access to full-text **SAGE journal articles**

$SAGE edge™

PRACTICE AND APPLY WHAT YOU'VE LEARNED

▶ **edge.sagepub.com/heinzen**

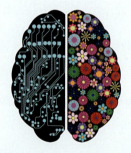

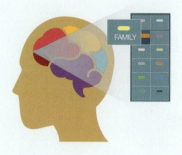

L04.4 **Explain** how **intuition** uses **mental accessibility** that comes from **priming, experience**, and heuristics.

So_p

L04.5 **Analyze** why we can **respect**, but **not always trust, our intuition**.

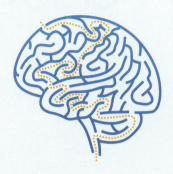

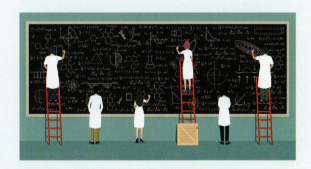

Get a tour of **ALL Visual Key Concepts** and their definitions at **edge.sagepub.com/heinzen**

5 | Person Perception

5.1 Explain how first impressions create social perceptions that can become self-fulfilling prophecies.

5.2 Illustrate how we communicate through facial expressions, body language, and cultural symbols.

5.3 Analyze why we use science-like thinking to infer why people behave as they do.

5.4 Evaluate why we make flawed attributions about one another's behavior.

Can walking through someone's dorm room or bedroom provide you with an accurate impression of that person's personality? One study (Gosling, Ko, Mannarelli, & Morris, 2002) indicated the answer is yes; independent observers used someone else's personal space to predict their personality. Look around your own room. What personality impressions do your clothes, objects, photographs or posters, and the like make on others? Think back to when you were younger. Did you decorate your room with images or objects that had a special significance to you—that reflected who you were at the time? Taking this idea even further, Omri Gillath and colleagues (Gillath, Adams, & Kunkel, 2012) used even *less* information to predict what people might be like—photographs of people's shoes!

When you meet someone new, do you purposely try to make a certain kind of impression with how you dress, whether you smile, and if you have a firm handshake? And what about the flip side? Do you quickly form impressions of other people based on the same criteria? We can learn how your brain accomplishes the impressive feat of quickly forming impressions by answering four core questions about how we impose meaning on social information to understand one another, a process called person perception.

HOW DO WE FORM IMPRESSIONS OF OTHERS?

LO 5.1: Explain how first impressions create social perceptions that can become self-fulfilling prophecies.

A dorm room, pictures of shoes, your public Facebook profile, and online dating services all convey critical, first impressions. We form these impressions automatically, but they can quickly influence how we treat other people, make assumptions about them, and more. That raises a disturbing question: How much of our self is the product of someone else's expectations that have been thrust upon us?

First Impressions, Expectations, and Self-Fulfilling Prophecies

Our perceptions of one another (called **person perceptions**) are based on a network of assumptions about what characteristics go together (Bruner & Tagiuri, 1954; Schneider, 1973). For example, if someone's shoes are neat and polished, then we also may expect self-control, neatness, and organization in other parts of the personality. If someone is wearing hand-painted combat boots, we expect something very different.

Person perceptions: People's perceptions of one another based on initial impressions of their behavior and assumptions concerning what characteristics correspond with that behavior.

First impressions are automatic and may be harmless in many cases. We form impressions of people at parties we'll never see again; here, our perception doesn't have much—if any—effect on the other person. In other cases, however, impressions and person perceptions can have an important influence on how social interactions go. Imagine you're going to interview a job candidate and your coworker told you, "I knew that person 20 years ago, and she wasn't very friendly." Now, when you meet the candidate, your behavior nonverbally communicates your expectation—you don't smile as much, your posture leans away, and so on. The candidate picks up on this and gets nervous, then responds more formally . . . and she isn't particularly friendly. You then think, "I knew it!"

When our expectations about someone else change our behaviors, which then change the other person's behaviors such that they fulfill our expectation, a **self-fulfilling prophecy** has occurred. The candidate's behavior would have been different if you had acted differently, based on a different expectation. Sometimes this phenomenon is called an expectancy effect, because your expectations have come true—but only because you expected them.

Halo Effects. Sometimes, a single piece of information becomes hugely important when we are first forming impressions. In a classic example of this effect, Asch (1946) and Kelley (1950) used words, rather than shoes. They *randomly assigned* students to read identical descriptions of someone who was about to come speak to their class—identical, that is, except for one word: "cold" versus "warm":

> "People who know him consider him to be a rather cold person, industrious, critical, practical, and determined."

Or

> "People who know him consider him to be a rather warm person, industrious, critical, practical, and determined."

Of course, the participants in each group thought that they were all reading the same description. When they listened to and then evaluated the speaker, their first impressions had been manipulated only by those two little words forming the *independent variable*: "cold" versus "warm."

Who could have imagined that those particular four-letter words could be so powerful? "Cold" and "warm" produced what Kelley (1950, p. 435) called **halo effects**, when an entire social perception of a person is constructed around a single central trait (Allport, 1937, 1966; Allport & Vernon, 1933; Cooper, 1981; Dennis, Newstead, & Wright, 1996; Downey & Christensen, 2006; Feely, 2002; Ian, 2007; Kelley, 1950; Remmers, 1934). In a halo effect, a single trait (such as "cold" or "warm") affects our overall person perception, like an aura that encompasses their entire self. It represents a **central trait** that creates a unified impression about the entire person. Participants' evaluation of the speaker—the *dependent variable*—differed according to that one dimension. People who read that the lecturer was "cold" formed an impression of someone who was judgmental and impatient—a generally negative description. People who read that the lecturer was "warm" decided he was a person of character and strength—a generally positive description. For example, the students in this experiment indicated the following:

The lecturer described as "cold":	The lecturer described as "warm":
"is intolerant."	"is unyielding in principle."
"would be angry if you disagree."	"is not easily swayed."

Ask the Experts: Susan Fiske on the Halo Effect

©SAGE Publications

Self-fulfilling prophecy: When an individual's expectations about someone else change his or her behavior, which then changes the other person's behaviors such that they fulfill the first individual's expectations.

Halo effect: When an entire social perception of a person is constructed around a single trait.

Central trait: A major characteristic of an individual's personality that indicates the presence of several associated traits, together creating a unified impression about the entire person.

Both groups heard the same lecturer give the same talk, but their perceptions of the speaker were different. The subtle manipulation created different expectations in each group—and their perceptions matched their expectations. Expectations we hold going into social situations shape what we perceive and experience.

What-Is-Beautiful-Is-Good. Beyond "cold" and "warm," other traits produce halo effects. For some reason, we tend to focus on and imbue these central traits with rich layers of meaning. For example, physical attractiveness creates a strange first-impression halo effect called the **what-is-beautiful-is-good effect** (Dion, Berscheid, & Walster, 1972). Men, women, working professionals, and college students are all similarly influenced by physical beauty.

For example, teachers rate physically attractive children as smarter (Clifford & Walster, 1973). Pretty people get higher starting salaries and more raises at work (Frieze, Olson, & Russell, 1991), and attractive defendants in court are given lighter prison sentences (Gunnell & Ceci, 2010). People with attractive profile photos on Facebook are more likely to get friend requests from strangers (Wang, Moon, Kwon, Evans, & Stefanone, 2010), and physically attractive students are more likely to be given scholarships (Agthe, Spörrle, & Maner, 2010). Presumably, being attractive has little to do with one's intelligence, ability to get work done, or likelihood of committing crimes. Nevertheless, most people perceive attractive individuals as "better" in general and thus give them the benefit of the doubt. Thus, the "what-is-beautiful-is-good" effect is one specific type of halo effect.

Although the beauty bias may have declined somewhat over time (Hosoda, Stone-Romero, & Coats, 2003), the halo surrounding physical beauty is still so bright that it confers the same kind of social status as intelligence, charm, humor, and athletic ability. Beautiful people are therefore given more opportunities to practice their social skills (Feingold, 1992). In this way, the benefits and privileges society gives to beautiful people allow them to have more status, education, and attention; these benefits may result in really making them more interesting or cultured. In short, the "what-is-beautiful-is-good" effect may also be an example of a self-fulfilling prophecy. The accompanying feature, "Self-Fulfilling Prophecies in Hollywood Films," presents additional examples.

It may not elicit much sympathy from the rest of us, but Feingold's (1992) *meta-analysis* (a study that summarizes and statistically combines many individual studies on a particular topic) suggests that physically attractive people do have a few problems that don't plague the rest of us. First, highly attractive people may have difficulty diagnosing the sincerity of any compliments they receive about their skills or abilities (Major, Carrington, & Carnevale, 1984). They may be unclear whether compliments are sincere or whether the person giving the compliment simply wants to manipulate them somehow; this confusion over why someone is treating you in a particular way is called **attributional ambiguity**. Second, despite the "what-is-beautiful-is-good" bias, highly attractive women do not always report having higher self-esteem (Fleming & Courtney, 1984; Marsh & Richards, 1988). And occasionally, being "too" attractive might lead to jealousy and discrimination (e.g., Agthe et al., 2010).

Social Psychology in Action: Beautiful is Good

©SAGE Publications

What-is-beautiful-is-good effect: When physical attractiveness creates a halo effect such that individuals who are beautiful are also perceived to have several other positive characteristics.

Attributional ambiguity: Confusion individuals have concerning the cause of the way others treat them, experienced most often by members of stigmatized groups.

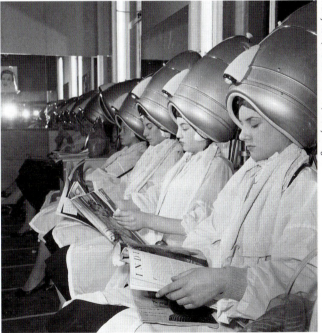

Harry Kerr / Hulton Archive / Getty Images

For decades, or even centuries, women have spent money and time at "beauty parlors." Perhaps they are trying to benefit from the "what-is-beautiful-is-good" effect.

SELF-FULFILLING PROPHECIES IN HOLLYWOOD FILMS

Social Psychology in Popular Culture

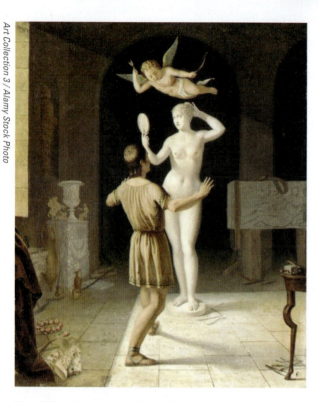

Art Collection 3 / Alamy Stock Photo

This 1890 painting of the Pygmalion myth by Jean Leon Gerome tells the story of how a wish becomes a reality.

Self-fulfilling prophecies are sometimes called the Pygmalion effect. In the Greek myth, the shy sculptor Pygmalion fell in love with his own sculpture of Galatea, the most beautiful woman he could imagine. He asked the goddess Aphrodite to breathe life into her. With the twisted humor characteristic of Greek gods, Aphrodite granted his request but did not allow Galatea to love him back. This story illustrates the idea of wishing something into being. This is the psychological basis for self-fulfilling prophecies, when something comes true because we imagined it already was true.

A more modern example of metaphorically wishing someone into life happened in *My Fair Lady* (Warner & Cukor, 1964), the musical movie version of George Bernard Shaw's play *Pygmalion.* By changing her accent and language, the refined linguistic Professor Higgins transforms Eliza—a screeching street-seller of flowers— into a proper lady (McGovern, 2011). The professor believed that he could turn a street girl into a woman with high-class language and behavior, and thus he made it so.

You can hear echoes of the Pygmalion myth in the Disney version of *Pinocchio* (Disney, Sharpsteen, & Luske, 1940) when a poor toymaker's wish breathes life into a wooden boy. In the 1983 movie *Trading Places* (Russo & Landis, 1983) a Wall Street tycoon bets his friend that he can transform a street hustler into a successful stockbroker. In each story, someone's life was transformed by others' expectations. But are we only the sum of other people's expectations? Are other people's wishes and expectations shaping us, as if we were marble or wooden puppets?

J. K. Rowling set up this same conflict in the Harry Potter novels (Rowling, 1997, 1998, 1999, 2000, 2003, 2005, 2007). In the magical boarding school Hogwarts, students are assigned to a certain "house" within minutes of their arrival. Each house is associated with stereotypes and expectations: Gryffindor is for the brave, Ravenclaw is for the intelligent, Hufflepuff is for the loyal, and Slytherin is for the cunning. Do the students have these central traits before they even hit puberty, or does living in each house create expectations that shape the people they become?

The *Pygmalion* myth lives a vibrant, diverse life in popular culture about wishes and expectations that sometimes create their own reality.

Applications of Self-Fulfilling Prophecies

Sociologist Merton (1948) described a case study of a bank failure to demonstrate how even a false belief can turn into a self-fulfilling prophecy. In 1932, bank manager Cartwright Millingville was feeling justly proud that his bank was flourishing in the midst of the Great Depression. One Wednesday morning, the men from the local steel plants were coming in too soon—payday wasn't until Saturday. But a nasty rumor had gotten started that the bank was insolvent. More and more customers starting withdrawing their money—and by the end of the day, the bank *was* insolvent. Rumor had become reality: a self-fulfilling prophecy. It wouldn't have happened unless people already thought it was true.

Prophecy and Experimenter Bias.

Social psychology research on self-fulfilling prophecies started in the 1960s with the work of Robert Rosenthal. In his first self-fulfilling prophecy experiment, Rosenthal's student-experimenters thought that they were training their lab rats to run a maze. But Rosenthal was really testing whether the student-experimenters' expectations would influence how well the rats could run that maze.

Half of the student-experimenters were led to believe their rats were "maze bright," and the other half believed their rats were "maze dull." In other words, half of the students expected their rats to do really well—and half didn't. In reality, the rats had been randomly assigned to each student. By the end of the study, the rats' maze-running abilities fulfilled whatever their student-experimenters believed about their rats (Rosenthal, 1994; Rosenthal & Fode, 1963). What the student-experimenters *expected* to happen, happened. Somehow, the students had affected the actual results of how well the rats ran the mazes. This might be an important lesson for all researchers; we should be alert for experimenter biases.

Prophecy and Elementary Schoolchildren.

When clinical and social psychologist Robert Rosenthal began corresponding with Lenore Jacobsen, a school principal in San Francisco, the stage was set for one of psychology's most famous—and still controversial—experiments. Rosenthal and Jacobsen (1968) gave students in 18 different classrooms across six different grade levels a test with a fancy (but meaningless) name, the Harvard Test of Inflected Acquisition. They used the so-called test to give teachers *bogus feedback* about students in their classroom.

Let's be blunt: Bogus feedback is lying, but it is a lie with an experimental purpose. Professor Rosenthal and Principal Jacobsen lied to the teachers about 20% of the students. They told the teachers that, according to the Harvard Test of Inflected Acquisition, these 20% of students across six grade levels were *expected* to be "intellectual bloomers" who would "show surprising gains in intellectual competence during the next eight months of school" (Rosenthal, 2002). In reality, the students had been selected completely at random. Figure 5.1 shows us that what the teachers expected to happen did happen for the students in first and second grade (especially for boys' verbal ability and girls' reasoning ability).

Halo Effects and "Intellectual Bloomers."

The label of "intellectual bloomer" created powerful halo effects and self-fulfilling prophecies. You can see from Figure 5.1 that being labeled a "bloomer" led at least some of the children to improve in their intelligence scores—but they improved in other ways as well. Teachers described the children in the experimental group as more likely to succeed, more interesting, more curious, more appealing, better adjusted, less in need of social approval, and even happier. Remember that these students had been chosen completely at random! Like a pebble dropped into a pond, the label of "intellectual bloomer" rippled in many directions.

But wait. Some students who were *not* identified as intellectual bloomers also showed significant gains in IQ. What effect did their *un*expected success have on their teachers? "The more children in the *control group* gained in IQ, the more *un*favorably they were judged by their teachers" (Rosenthal, 1994, p. 179). They had violated

■ FIGURE 5.1 Students as bloomers.

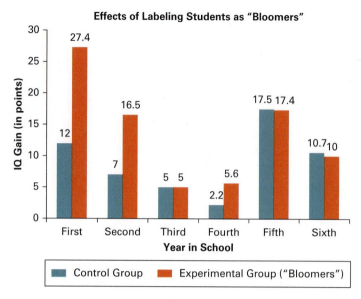

Effects of Labeling Students as "Bloomers"

SOURCE: Rosenthal and Jacobson (1968).

their teachers' expectations—in a good way—but they were still judged unfavorably for their success. It makes you wonder what in the world a kid has to do to shake off a bad reputation. Figure 5.2 shows the steps that occur when a self-fulfilling prophecy affects a student's performance.

Replicating and Refining the Research.

Rosenthal and Jacobsen's (1968) report triggered a controversy, partly because their findings finally gave people someone whom they could blame for all the ills of education: It's the teacher's fault! If those darn elementary school teachers would only believe in their students a little bit more, then all the other sociological, motivational, and family-related problems in education would magically melt away.

For example, if girls aren't doing as well as boys in middle school math classes, it must be because math teachers are simply encouraging boys and ignoring or discouraging girls. In addition, whenever there is an attention-getting finding from the world of research, you can count on the press to exaggerate the conclusions to sell more advertising. More important, chronically skeptical researchers scrutinized how the research was conducted and tried to *replicate* the findings—repeating an experiment is always a scientifically sound endeavor.

Hundreds of studies testing the reality of self-fulfilling prophecies have been conducted since that first dramatic experiment. In 2005, Jussim and Harber published a review of what we have learned about self-fulfilling prophecies since 1968:

1. Self-fulfilling prophecies do occur in the classroom, but they are only one of many influences on student achievement.

2. The effect of a self-fulfilling prophecy declines over time.

3. Self-fulfilling prophecies can be especially influential on students who belong to groups that are already stigmatized (prelabeled in a negative way).

4. It is unclear whether self-fulfilling prophecies tend to do more harm than good. More research is needed.

5. Sometimes, what looks like a self-fulfilling prophecy is an accurate assessment made by a teacher.

In 2002, Rosenthal himself also reviewed the now sophisticated scientific literature that he had helped create almost 40 years earlier. By looking at the *meta-analyses,* Rosenthal confirmed that self-fulfilling prophecies can occur in classroom settings, but

■ FIGURE 5.2 How self-fulfilling prophecies become true in a classroom.

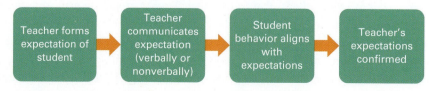

exactly how they play out is complicated. He identified four ways in which teachers unknowingly communicate their expectations to particular students:

1. *Emotional climate,* through nonverbal cues that create a warmer social-emotional environment.

2. *Expectations of effort,* by teaching more material and more difficult material.

3. *Increased opportunities,* by giving students more opportunities to respond, including more time to respond.

4. *Differential feedback,* by giving certain students more individualized feedback that allows them to assess their own progress.

The External Validity of Self-Fulfilling Prophecies.

As you have probably suspected, self-fulfilling prophecies are not limited to bank failures, maze-running lab rats, and teacher-student relationships. The process of a self-fulfilling prophecy appears to have *external validity;* that is, it applies to many situations.

Indeed, the real-world settings for self-fulfilling prophecies are quite varied. Parents, of course, create powerful expectations in their own children. For example, one study (Lamb & Crano, 2014) showed that students whose parents assumed they were using marijuana—even though they were not at the time—were more likely to *actually* use marijuana over the course of the following year. Conversely, students who *were* already using marijuana but whose parents said that they weren't were more likely to stop using over the course of that same year.

At work, managerial expectations covertly influence employee productivity (Eden, 1990); higher expectations from your boss can lead to more productivity and to a better relationship in general (Whiteley, Sy, & Johnson, 2012). In court, judges' expectations can influence the directions they tell a jury in ways that can pave the way for verdicts of guilt or innocence (Blanck, Rosenthal, Hart, & Bernieri, 1990). In nursing homes, a caretaker's positive expectations can reduce depression in the residents (Learman, Avorn, Everitt, & Rosenthal, 1990). And positive illusions about your romantic partner are expectations that can actually help that person rise to your optimistic expectations (Murray, Holmes, & Griffin, 1996a, 1996b).

© istockphoto.com/JBryson

Have you ever had a teacher who expected you to behave well or expected you to behave badly? Did your actual behaviors come to match their expectations?

Application: Expectations About Young Hockey Players. A strange but powerful final example of self-fulfilling prophecies outside of the psychological laboratory comes from the world of athletics (Dubner & Levitt, 2006).

Many people in Canada are, to put it mildly, enthusiastic about hockey. The formal recruiting process for potential players begins with a strictly observed rule that a boy must have turned 10 by January 1 to be recruited. So a boy born in late December who has just turned 10 years old could be playing against boys who turned 10 almost a year earlier. A difference of 11 or 12 months can be significant at this age, when we can expect uneven development and dramatic changes in physical maturity. For early maturing boys, those extra months can represent the difference between a child's relatively frail body and a body maturing into a muscular adolescence. The same trend

■ TABLE 5.1 Birth Dates for Players on the 2007 Canadian Championship Youth Hockey Team, the Medicine Hat Tigers

Name of Player	Date of Birth
Scott Wasden	January 4, 1988
Daine Todd	January 10, 1987
Tyler Swystun	January 15, 1988
Darren Helm	January 21, 1987
Trever Glass	January 22, 1988
Bretton Cameron	January 26, 1989
Jakub Rumpel	January 27, 1987
Mark Isherwood	January 31, 1989
Jordan Bendfield	February 9, 1988
Brennan Bosch	February 14, 1988
Shayne Brown	February 20, 1989
Gord Baldwin	March 1, 1987
Matt Lowry	March 2, 1988
Colton Grant	March 20, 1989
Jordan Hickmott	April 11, 1990
Kevin Undershute	April 12, 1987
Matt Keetley	April 27, 1986
Kris Russell	May 2, 1987
David Schlemko	May 7, 1987
Ryan Holfeld	June 29, 1989
Michael Sauver	August 7, 1987
Chris Stevens	August 20, 1986
Jerrid Sauer	September 12, 1987
Tyler Ennis	October 6, 1989
Derek Dorsett	December 20, 1986

SOURCE: Data from Dubner and Levitt (2006).

Note the birthdays of these champions; 14 are in the first 3 months of the year, while only 2 are in the last 3 months of the year.

was found in Czechoslovakia—a naturally occurring *replication* of the finding across the world. January birthdays have a big advantage in this context, as Table 5.1 and Figure 5.3 both demonstrate.

On the other hand, when coaches and parents confuse physical maturation with "talent," they are applying a label to a child who can turn into a self-fulfilling prophecy. Lots of good things flow toward the "gifted" or "talented": better coaching, more playing time, encouragement, status, and higher levels of competition. So, boys born in January get a double advantage; they have a developmental edge, but they also get more attention and experience higher expectations, which might lead them to try harder to live up to these higher standards. A network of reinforcing experiences improves skills and raises expectations even higher. Meanwhile, both advantaged and disadvantaged children experience the mysterious power of a self-fulfilling prophecy that began with nothing more remarkable than when they were conceived.

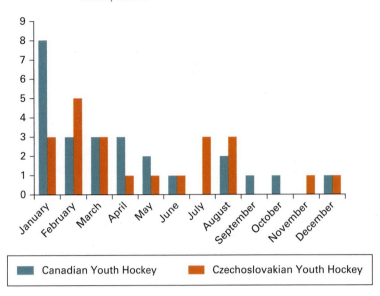

■ FIGURE 5.3 Number of births by month of two championship youth hockey teams.

SOURCE: Data from Dubner and Levitt (2006).

The Main Ideas

- Perceptions of other people are influenced by first impressions. First impressions are sometimes based on a single trait that seems more important than others, such as physical attractiveness; this is called a halo effect.

- Expectations can be communicated in ways that become self-fulfilling prophecies (also called the Pygmalion effect).

- Self-fulfilling prophecies can lead to both positive and negative outcomes; research has replicated these effects across a wide variety of real-world settings, such as with children in classrooms.

⚡ CRITICAL THINKING CHALLENGE

- How certain are you about the validity of your personality impressions? Have you ever changed your mind about someone? What did it take to overcome your first impression?

- Why are "warm vs. cold" and physical attractiveness central traits when we're forming first impressions—what is it about these particular traits that seems so important?

- Think about how self-fulfilling prophecies have affected your own life, in the classroom, on sports teams, in social situations, or in your own goals and dreams for the future. What is one *positive* way that self-fulfilling prophecies may have pushed you toward something greater, and what is one *negative* way that self-fulfilling prophecies may have held you back?

HOW DO WE COMMUNICATE NONVERBALLY?

LO 5.2: Illustrate how we communicate through facial expressions, body language, and cultural symbols.

How did those elementary school teachers communicate their expectations to the students who had or had not been labeled as "intellectual bloomers"? They could have just told them, of course, by saying something like, "Reza, you are going to make great gains in mathematics this year. I am expecting great things from you." But they also would have conveyed their expectations through **nonverbal communications**, the many ways we communicate through body language, tone of voice, and facial expressions. One early research question was whether nonverbal communications were universal across human cultures. Does a frown and squint in the eyes mean the same thing all over the world?

Facial Expressions Across Cultures: The Universality Hypothesis

Some research says yes, nonverbal facial expressions are universal, regardless of culture; this basic idea is now called the **universality hypothesis**. For example, Friedman (1964) noticed that a blind, breastfed baby smiled in response to her mother's voice and even turned her eyes in the mother's direction. The infant could not imitate her mother's loving gaze and smiling face because she could not see her mother. The baby's natural instincts to smile and shift her head toward her mother seemed to support the universality hypothesis. A blind infant appears to have an instinct to smile at its mother.

Paul Ekman and Walter Friesen (1971) created a more specific test of the universality hypothesis. They showed people in various literate cultures photographs of people expressing six basic emotions: fear, disgust, surprise, anger, sadness, and happiness. These facial expressions conveyed the same information across cultures. A fearful face and a happy face, for example, look the same in every culture. Sure, it was still possible that these facial expressions had been learned and communicated across cultures, perhaps through art and travel. But the evidence was building that some core emotions were universal.

Nonverbal communication: The many ways individuals communicate through body language, tone of voice, and facial expressions.

Universality hypothesis: The idea that nonverbal facial expressions are universal, regardless of culture.

These photos show the six "universal" emotions through facial expressions that some research indicates can be understood regardless of culture. Can you identify which face is afraid, disgusted, surprised, angry, sad, and happy?

Cross-Cultural Tests of the Universality Hypothesis. However, time was running out on the most obvious way to test the universality hypothesis: Study people whose lives had not been influenced by other cultures. Fortunately, Ekman and Friesen (1971) were able to study the South Fore people of New Guinea, a geographically isolated, preliterate tribe with no previous contact with Western civilization. They first conveyed to the South Fore people short, emotional stories. Then they asked them to match the story to pictures of Americans portraying various emotions. The South Fore people understood American emotional expressions—more evidence for the universality hypothesis. If you were keeping score in the nature-nurture debate, this would have been a point for nature.

Almost 40 years later, Matsumoto (2009) invented another test of the universality hypothesis. It was a creative idea because it used photographs of emotional expressions at the 2004 judo competition at the Olympic Games and the Paralympic Games (held immediately after the Olympic Games). These contests allowed researchers to compare authentic emotions between (a) athletes who had been born blind (so they could not have learned to smile by seeing other people do it), (b) athletes who were blind but had experienced sight earlier in their lives, and (c) sighted athletes.

The experiment itself was "blind" in another important way to control for expectations that might be communicated nonverbally by the experimenters: Professional photographer Willingham did not know the hypothesis being tested. In fact, it was what experimenters call a *double-blind study* because the athletes being photographed also were unaware of the hypothesis being tested. Recall (from Chapter 2) that single-blind studies occur when participants don't know what experimental condition they are in or what the hypothesis is. Double-blind studies also keep that information from anyone who communicates with the participants, just in case that knowledge could inadvertently influence behavior (another example of a self-fulfilling prophecy).

Willingham photographed athletes at three points in time: (1) immediately after competing, (2) when they received their medals, and (3) when they posed on the podium. Both blind and sighted individuals expressed the full range of emotions in their facial expressions at these critical moments—and everyone who saw Willingham's photographs understood their emotional meanings. Unsighted people who smile when happy provide more evidence signaling that critical emotional expressions are the product of a biological instinct.

Converging Evidence Through Replication. **Converging evidence** occurs when different types of studies from independent researchers using different methods reach the same conclusions; it's one form of *replication.* The converging evidence about the universality hypothesis suggests that we're all (probably) the same in how we express core emotions, no matter what culture we come from. The same universality appears to apply to emotions associated with social interactions such as pride, shame, and embarrassment (Ekman, O'Sullivan, & Matsumoto, 1991; Harrigan & O'Connell, 1996; Keltner & Shiota, 2003). Some studies have questioned parts of the universality hypothesis (e.g., Gendron, Roberson, van der Vyver, & Barrett, 2014; Jack, Garrod, Yu, Caldara, & Schyns, 2012). However, in general, the universality hypothesis has received a lot of statistical support.

Can You Tell When People Are Lying?

How often do people lie? One study asked people to carry small notebooks with them at all times for an entire week. Their task was to record every lie or deception they

Converging evidence: Occurs when different types of studies from independent researchers using different methods reach the same conclusions.

The television series *Lie to Me* (2009–2011) was based on a man who was supposedly the world's leading expert in reading facial expressions, including whether people were telling the truth.

used in social interactions, no matter how big or small (DePaulo, Kashy, Kirkendol, Wyer, & Epstein, 1996). Out of 77 college students and 70 community members (with an age range between 18 and 71 years old), the students reported telling two lies every day and the community members reported one per day. It seems that lies are very common. Does our experience telling lies make us good at detecting them?

Be careful here—you probably are not as good at detecting lies as you would like to believe. Despite the universality of emotional expressions, our faces are still not always easy to read. Imagine, for example, that you have been pulled over by a police officer for driving too fast. You might smile politely at the officer, hoping to avoid a ticket. However, it's a phony smile and an experienced officer probably recognizes it. **Facial leakage** occurs whenever concealed emotions are betrayed by automatic muscle responses (sometimes called "reliable" muscles; Ekman & Friesen, 1974; Ekman & O'Sullivan, 2006).

Micro-Expressions: Duping Delight Versus the Duchenne Smile. Paul Ekman, one of the world's experts on facial expressions, named involuntary flashes of emotional honesty **micro-expressions**. They were first observed by slowing down a film of psychiatric patients lying about whether they were taking their medications (Ekman & Friesen, 1969; Ekman & O'Sullivan, 2006). The researchers even discovered an expression they called **duping delight**, the facial smirk that appears when people think that they have gotten away with a lie (see also Ekman & Frank, 1993).

There is a noticeable difference between a felt smile and a feigned smile. A genuine, felt smile is called a **Duchenne smile** (named for the French neurologist Guillaume Duchenne de Boulogne, who first described it). The authentic, genuine Duchenne smile uses the muscles that surround the eyes to pull up the cheeks, produce crow's feet wrinkles, and slightly lower the eyebrows. The ability to distinguish between genuine and fake smiles may be present even in 10-month-old infants (Fox & Davidson, 1988).

Sometimes, awkward situations elicit emotional dishonesty. For example, in a job interview study, women displayed more false smiles (and did not interview as

Facial leakage: Occurs whenever concealed emotions are betrayed by automatic muscle responses.

Micro-expression: An involuntary flash of emotional honesty.

Duping delight: The facial smirk that appears when people think that they have gotten away with a lie.

Duchenne smile: A genuine, felt smile.

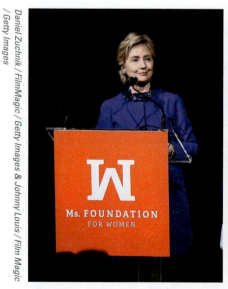

Can you tell if either presidential candidate is smiling sincerely?

well) when the interview included three inappropriate sexually related questions (Woodzicka & LaFrance, 2005). They were trying to be polite in the job interview situation, but their faces automatically conveyed their felt emotions. Similarly, the faked smiles of women hearing sexist jokes leaked more disgust than amusement (LaFrance & Woodzicka, 1998).

While some people believe they are naturally better than others at detecting sincerity (or lack of sincerity), social situations can sometimes affect our ability to do so. For example, one study (Bernstein, Sacco, Brown, Young, & Claypool, 2010) *randomly assigned* participants to write essays about times they had been either socially excluded or socially included. The *independent variable* (the type of essay) condition led to differences in the *dependent variable,* which was whether the essay writers could correctly assess videos of 20 different people smiling at the camera. Half of the people in the videos displayed sincere (Duchenne) smiles, while half displayed fake smiles.

Feeling rejected is a big deal to us. Participants in this study who had been primed to think about being excluded or ostracized (by writing the essay on this topic) were able to tell the different smiles apart and indicated that they would prefer to work with the sincere people. In contrast, participants who had written essays about being socially included had a harder time telling the smiles of others apart. Apparently, even thoughts of temporary social exclusion make us particularly sensitive to cues from others.

With training, experience, situational priming, and slow-motion cameras, we can learn to distinguish between felt and faked facial emotions—but it is not easy. And the fleeting nature of micro-expressions is not the only reason we find it difficult to read people accurately.

Affect Blends and Negative Emotions. Another awkward situation might occur when a friend is engaged to marry someone you think is a very bad match. Your face will display an **affect blend** of contradictory emotions. Your eyes may wrinkle with genuine happiness for your friend, but your mouth may tighten into a forced smile. People are complicated. The everyday reality of affect blends suggests that we should be cautious about our ability to read people accurately.

One of my [Tom's] colleagues has little control over her facial expressions. She will roll her eyes at bureaucratic bunglings, shake her head when bad ideas are being taken seriously, and light up with happiness at her own and her friends' achievements. To some degree, all of our faces "tell" what we are feeling; her face simply talks more freely than others. But we still need to be cautious about our ability to accurately "read" other people's expressions. In addition to the confusion caused by affect blends, we also are more sensitive to negative information than to positive information.

For example, if you have ever seen someone take a swallow of sour milk, then you know that their look of disgust is sending a clear and urgent message: Do NOT drink this milk. On the other hand, the facial expression of someone drinking milk along with a tasty cookie may display some satisfaction, but that positive expression won't be communicated as dramatically as the negative expression. Even when confronted with ambiguous facial expressions, we tend to automatically assume the emotion being expressed is negative instead of positive (Neta & Tong, 2016; Tottenham, Phuong, Flannery, Gabard-Durnam, & Goff, 2013).

It Is Difficult to Lie Well

Both of the authors of this book are terrible liars. I [Tom] remember trying to lie to my aunt on the telephone and she called me on it right away saying, "Come on, now.

Affect blend: When two or more contradictory emotions are shown on different parts of an individual's face, making it difficult to accurately understand his or her expression.

That's not true." She didn't even have to see me! Something in my voice or my story betrayed me. Similarly, people often ask me [Wind] how my day is going, and I usually conform to the socially acceptable, "Fine." But when I'm distracted, tired, or annoyed, people usually just laugh and say something like, "Your 'fine' was not very convincing." You also may have sensed when someone is not being completely honest with you. But are you correct?

One fascinating study used *naturalistic observation* to compare liars and truth tellers in a high-stakes situation: televised footage of real people pleading for the return of missing relatives (ten Brinke & Porter, 2012). Later, half of the people were convicted of killing the person who was missing (based on overwhelming scientific evidence). They had tried to lie, but "failed attempts to simulate sadness and leakage of happiness revealed deceptive pleaders' covert emotions" (p. 469). Liars also used fewer words in their pleas and words that were more tentative, compared to their honest counterparts.

Here are four reasons to be cautious about your ability to detect lies:

1. You're not an expert at discerning micro-expressions. Ekman, O'Sullivan, and Frank (1999) concluded that "most of us would do well to entertain some skepticism about our ability."

2. Affect blends are tricky; you might be picking up only one of several facial emotions, or you might be confusing affect blends with lying.

3. You are more sensitive to negative information than positive information.

4. Even if you do accurately detect a lie, there are many alternative explanations for why someone might lie—for example, they may simply be nervous. Don't leap to judgment; most people are not able to tell a lie from the truth (Porter, ten Brinke, & Wallace, 2012).

One barrier to accurate lie detection is that there are so many different types of lies. Ekman (2006) proposed a continuum of the intention to deceive that would look approximately like that shown in Figure 5.4. Our face is more likely to betray us when lies are consciously intended to deceive. Successful deceptions, on the other hand, are

■ FIGURE 5.4 Continuum of intention to deceive.

1. Denial, Repression, Dissociation (unconscious rejection of reality)

2. Non-Conscious Self-Deceptions, Flawed Self-Assessment (unconscious lying to the self)

3. Positive Illusions, Self-Aggrandizement, Distortions (biased cognitions)

4. Factitious Disorders, Repetition to Belief (e.g., convincing yourself you are sick)

5. White Lies, Social Courtesies, Flattery, False Compliments (socially acceptable deception)

6. Malingering (pretending to be sick for convenience)

7. Deceptions of Kindness (e.g., doctors pretending to care more than they really do)

8. Deliberate High-Stakes Lying, Blatant Whoppers (purposeful lying to control others)

SOURCE: Adapted from Ekman & O'Sullivan (2006).

most likely to occur when individuals believe what they are saying, such as when they honestly don't remember doing something.

Culturemes Communicate Social Impressions

While many studies indicate that facial expressions are understood regardless of culture, other types of nonverbal communication are culture specific. Like inside jokes, cultures are filled with nonverbal messages that outsiders cannot be expected to understand (Angell, 1909; Buchner, 1910; Ekman, 2006; Fridlund, 1994; Izard, 1990; Lindstrom, 2011). For example, religious traditions have symbols of their faith, professional societies and governments adopt official seals, and corporations spend millions of dollars

Adam Jones CC BY-SA 2.0 & CC BY-SA 3.0

The right-facing Nazi swastika (shown on the flags) conveys a different cultural message than the left-facing swastika (shown on the building) on this Buddhist temple in South Korea, where it means energy or good luck.

branding their products into our neural structures (Lindstrom, 2011). Such **culturemes** represent cultural communications that convey widely shared social impressions (Feyereisen, 2006; Poyatos, 2002a, 2002b).

Some cultural symbols change meaning or acceptance over time. For example, the modern German army no longer gives out medals, even for heroism, after the Nazis embedded the now-hated symbol of the right-facing swastika on the once-revered Iron Cross (see Kulish, 2008). However, the swastika represents a very different cultureme to Buddhists and a slightly different cultureme to Hindus. The left-facing swastika has been used for 5,000 years in Hindu art and architecture as a symbol of good fortune. Ramesh Kallidai of the Hindu Forum in Britain pointed out that "just because Hitler misused the symbol . . . does not mean that its peaceful use should be banned any more than Americans should ban crosses because they have been abused by the Ku Klux Klan" (BBC News, 2008). Even a powerful visual symbol such as the swastika only has meaning within a cultural context.

Culture and religion can also change how we interpret certain symbols. For example, modern Christianity includes several symbols that originally meant other things. Have you ever wondered why Easter celebrations include pastel colors, bunnies, and eggs? These symbols have very little to do with the story of Jesus, but they are important parts of any Christian child's experience of the holiday. These symbols were incorporated into Easter when the early Christian church wanted to combine remembering the resurrection that lies at the

Nathan Benn / Corbis Historical / Getty Images

A cross can be a symbol of faith, forgiveness, and charity—or a symbol of racism and hatred.

core of their belief with pagan celebrations of spring, fertility, and birth. See Table 5.2 for additional examples of how culture and religion affect our interpretation of certain symbols (Fontana, 1993).

■ TABLE 5.2 Culturemes and Symbols Vary by Religion and Culture.

Symbol	Modern Christianity	Alternative Interpretation
	Many Christians today see an inverted cross as a symbol of Satanic belief.	Originally, the inverted cross was a Christian symbol of humility. St. Peter requested an inverted cross for his own crucifixion because he saw himself as unworthy of the same death Jesus received.
	A common modern Christian interpretation of the five-pointed star, or pentagram, is again that it represents Satanism or anti-Christianity.	In Judaism, the pentagram can represent the five books of the Torah. For Wiccans, it can symbolize five elements of life (spirit, fire, air, water, and earth).
	A harp can symbolize passage to Heaven for modern Christians, as angels are frequently depicted as playing the instrument.	In ancient Celtic cultures, the god of plenty Daghda played the harp to summon each of the four seasons. It is now a national symbol of Ireland.
	An evergreen tree is one of the most recognized symbols for Christmas celebrations.	Originally used to celebrate the winter solstice in Scandinavian pagan rituals, early Christians combined the holidays and many of the symbols used by the more ancient religion.

The Main Ideas

- The universality hypothesis is that some facial expressions of emotion are recognized in all humans, regardless of culture.

- Facial leakage and micro-expressions betray our genuine feelings, but affect blends make it difficult to read others' faces accurately.

- Culturemes convey shared social impressions whose meanings are immediately understood within a particular culture but not understood by people from other cultures.

⚡ CRITICAL THINKING CHALLENGE

- Find another student in this class and engage in this activity: First, convey different facial expressions and ask your partner to identify them. Next, each person should tell the other three facts—two of which are truths and one of which is a lie. Then, discuss how you decoded your partner's nonverbal signals during each part of the activity. Could your partner tell what you were conveying and which of your "facts" was a lie?

- Think about the culturemes you use in your own life. Do you have tattoos, jewelry, or art in your home that displays symbols? Do others understand these symbols immediately, or is their meaning private? When you see others displaying a cultureme, do you immediately have assumptions about the type of people they might be or what their beliefs are?

HOW DO WE EXPLAIN OTHER PEOPLE'S BEHAVIOR?

LO 5.3: Analyze why we use science-like thinking to infer why people behave as they do.

Understanding one another is hard work (and cultural differences don't make it any easier). Fortunately, the human brain is relentlessly curious; unfortunately, like water bugs skimming the surface, we are often satisfied with superficial explanations. Having *any* explanation sometimes seems to be more important than having an accurate explanation. So what influences how we answer the "why" question about one another's behavior?

Attribution Theory: We Try to Isolate the Cause of Behavior

Attribution theory views people as naïve or amateur scientists who automatically use commonsense explanations to answer the "why" question of events around us (Heider, 1958; Kelley, 1955, 1973; Wegener & Petty, 1998). **Attributions** are how we explain to ourselves why people and events turn out as they do—what was the cause? Imagine you are in a public park and an attractive stranger smiles at you. Why did this happen? Is the person interested in you? Does the person smile at everyone? As you will see, our willingness to be satisfied with superficial attributions sometimes gets us into trouble.

One of our first impulses when we try to answer the "why" question is to quickly scan whatever explanations come most easily to mind. We then choose from among them based on the **principle of noncommon effects** that isolates a causal explanation by looking for a single factor that seems to account for what occurred (see Gilbert & Malone, 1995; Jones & Davis, 1965). Our decision about what's most likely may be based on rumors, stereotypes, or what you prefer to be true—but that's why they were the explanations that most easily came to mind. Our final attribution might also be based on a logical deduction based on the "noncommon" factor involved.

Imagine your friend gets engaged to someone who is mean-spirited, unmotivated, dishonest, and extremely wealthy. You might notice that three of these traits are negative while one is usually considered positive (or, at least, attractive in a potential marriage partner)—so it's easy to make the attribution that your friend is marrying for money. Wealth is the noncommon factor that stands out as different from the others, and it therefore becomes salient as the most probable explanation.

Attribution theory: The idea that individuals attempt to understand the behavior of those around them by forming commonsense explanations for the cause of others' behavior.

Attributions: How individuals explain the causes of others' actions and events.

Principle of noncommon effects: The idea that individuals make attributions by looking for a single factor that seems to account for what occurred based on its degree of difference from the other possible factors.

We Make Internal and External Attributions

Isolating possible causes is a scientific way of thinking. Scientists, however, have to dig deeper than whatever explanations come most easily to mind. As a psychological scientist, you are expected to make attributions based on evidence—and to be especially skeptical of subjective impressions. Isolating causal variables is what psychology students learn to do more formally in classes such as statistics and experimental design.

We tend to divide our attributions into **internal** (within the person, sometimes called dispositional attributions) or **external** (outside of the person, sometimes called situational) explanations. Internal attributions are explanations based on someone's personality or conscious choices—they are in control. External attributions, in contrast, are things outside of one's control, such as the situation, getting sick, the weather, someone else controlling what happens to us, or plain old bad luck.

The Danger of Internal Attributions: Victim Blaming. For example, people who believe that being overweight is due to some kind of internal "failure" like choosing not to exercise or to eat too much are more likely to display prejudice toward this group (King, Shapiro, Hebl, Singletary, & Turner, 2006). Thus, their prejudice toward overweight people is based on an internal attribution, instead of an external attribution (stressful circumstances, genetic predispositions, etc.). In similar ways, prejudice toward those with a physical handicap is higher when observers attribute their handicap to some sort of internal moral failing (Goffman, 1963; Lerner & Miller, 1978).

By the same twisted and unfortunate logic, some observers of rape victims will make internal attributions leading to the false beliefs that they were "asking for it" or somehow deserved to be assaulted (Bargh, 1997; Bargh & Chartrand, 1999; Bargh et al., 1996; Crall & Goodfriend, 2016; Hafer, Begue, Choma, & Dempsey, 2005; Strömwall, Alfredsson, & Landström, 2013). The same pattern is found in victims of domestic violence (Valor-Segura, Exposito, & Moya, 2011). Internal attributions can thus place blame on people when really, an external attribution is the cause.

The Injustice of Believing in a Just World. Why do we tend to blame the victim (Lerner, 1965)? Internal attributions seem cruel when people have already suffered some terrible misfortune. Most of us don't want to be cruel, vicious, judgmental, or unkind, so why do we sometimes think about people with physical disabilities, for example, in an unkind, negative way? The **just world hypothesis** asserts that individuals have a need to believe that they live in a world where people generally get what they deserve (Lerner & Simmons, 1966; see also Anderson, Cooper, & Okamura, 1997; Gilbert & Hixon, 1991; Kleinke & Meyer, 1990; Murray, Spadafore, & McIntosh, 2005). We reveal our belief in a just world when we say things like, "What goes around comes around" or "Karma will catch up with him."

Believing in a just world is associated with negative attitudes toward many things, such as being poor (Furnham & Gunter, 1984), having a disability, the effectiveness of charitable giving (Furnham, 1995), being abused by a relationship partner (Valor-Segura et al., 2011), having AIDS, and being a victim of rape (Furnham, 2003; Strömwall et al., 2013). A strong belief in a just world even leads people to discount scientific facts about global warming (Feinberg & Willer, 2011). Why? The researchers explain that "the potentially dire consequences of global warming threaten deeply held beliefs that the world is just, orderly, and stable" (Feinberg & Willer, 2011, p. 34).

Internal attributions: Explanations for an individual's behavior that are based on factors that are within the person's control, such as an individual's personality or conscious choices.

External attributions: Explanations for an individual's behavior that are based on factors that are outside of the person's control, such as getting sick, the weather, or bad luck.

Just world hypothesis: The idea that individuals have a need to believe that they live in a world where people generally get what they deserve, which can lead to incorrect internal attributions for others' behavior.

MEASURING BELIEF IN A JUST WORLD

Instructions: Next to each item, write how much you disagree or agree with it using this scale:

1	2	3	4	5	6
Strongly disagree					Strongly agree

____ 1. I've found that a person rarely deserves the reputation he or she has.

____ 2. Basically, the world is a just place.

____ 3. People who get "lucky breaks" have usually earned their good fortune.

____ 4. Careful drivers are just as likely to get hurt in traffic accidents as careless ones.

____ 5. It is common occurrence for the guilty person to get off free in American courts.

____ 6. Students almost always receive the grade they deserve in school.

____ 7. People who keep in shape have little chance of suffering a heart attack.

____ 8. The political candidate who sticks up for his or her principles rarely gets elected.

____ 9. It is rare for an innocent person to be wrongly sent to jail.

____ 10. In professional sports, many fouls and infractions never get called by the referee.

____ 11. By and large, people deserve what they get.

____ 12. When parents punish their children, it is almost always for good reasons.

____ 13. Good deeds often go unnoticed and unrewarded.

____ 14. Although evil people may hold political power for a while, in the general course of history good wins out.

____ 15. In almost any business or profession, people who do their job well will rise to the top.

____ 16. American parents tend to overlook the things most to be admired in their children.

____ 17. It is often impossible for a person to receive a fair trial in the USA.

____ 18. People who meet with misfortune have often brought it on themselves.

____ 19. Crime doesn't pay.

____ 20. Many people suffer through absolutely no fault of their own.

Scoring: Before adding the items together, first we have to "reverse score" some of them. So, for only Items 1, 3, 4, 5, 8, 10, 13, 16, 17, and 20, flip the scale. If you wrote a 1, cross it off and write a 6 instead. A 2 becomes a 5, a 3 becomes a 4, a 4 becomes a 3, a 5 becomes a 2, and a 6 becomes a 1.

Then, add up all of your responses. Higher scores mean a stronger belief in a just world; the possible range is 20 to 120.

Source: Rubin and Peplau (1975).

Locus of Control. You can measure your own belief in a just world by taking the scale shown in the "Applying Social Psychology to Your Life" feature above. Scores don't seem to be tied to gender, age, or socioeconomic status, so a wide variety of people can have high or low scores on the measure. People with high scores tend to have an **internal locus of control**, which is the general belief that they are in control of

Internal locus of control: The general belief that an individual is in control of his or her own fate.

Other people's misfortunes can threaten our belief in a just world. When you see victims of misfortune, do you assume they did something to deserve their fate? Are homeless people only homeless because they don't work hard enough or are alcoholics? If you think so, you might believe in a "just world."

External locus of control: The general belief that one's future is up to fate, chance, powerful other people, or some higher power, rather than within that person's own control.

Defensive attribution: Attributions made by individuals to avoid feeling fear about the potential for future negative events.

Terror management theory: The idea that an awareness of our own mortality terrifies individuals, forcing them to cling to comforting beliefs.

Worldview: The way an individual perceives and approaches the world.

their own fate. People with low scores tend to have an **external locus of control**, meaning they believe that one's future is up to fate, chance, powerful other people, or some higher power.

When this scale was originally developed, researchers Rubin and Peplau (1975) found that higher scores were positively correlated with (a) authoritarianism, the belief that society should follow rules about what is "right" and "moral"; (b) uncritical acceptance of authority figures; (c) stronger or more extreme religious faith; and (d) belief that hard work leads to success. They also found that high scores had a negative correlation with activism among college students. Why bother shaking up the status quo if a just world always provides us with the leaders we need?

Believing in a just world leads us to blame victims for their misfortune. After all, they must have done something to deserve their terrible fate. The false belief that bad things can't happen to good people calms our nerves when facing an unpredictable and dangerous world—if we tell ourselves that other people are bad and that we are good, then bad things won't happen to us.

Defensive Attributions: Terror Management Theory. We persist in believing that the world is fair and just because the alternative implies that no one is in charge and that random chaos is forever storming the gates of civilization (see Becker, 1973). In addition, "if others can suffer unjustly, then the individual must admit to the unsettling prospect that he too could suffer unjustly" (Lerner & Miller, 1978, p. 1031). So, making internal attributions about those who are victims of life's many peculiarities is a **defensive attribution**; it makes us feel better and brings us comfort. One explanation for this defensive strategy comes from **terror management theory**, which suggests that an awareness of such injustices, including our unavoidable death, is profoundly disturbing (Pyszczynski et al., 1996; Pyszczynski, Greenberg, & Solomon, 1999; Pyszczynski, Greenberg, Solomon, Arndt, & Schimel, 2004). Terror management theory suggests the following basic psychological ideas:

1. Humans, as a species, are uniquely aware of our own eventual mortality.

2. Thinking about our own unavoidable death is terrifying.

3. When possible, we will distract ourselves from mortality by manufacturing meaning out of our lives, such as through beliefs about cultural values or religions that comfort us.

4. When forced to confront the possibility of death, we will cling to beliefs that help us feel comforted or meaningful. These beliefs are called our **worldviews**.

To manage the terror coming from our own mortality, we come up with psychological acrobatics that calm us down and bring a sense of order back to our lives. Blaming the victim of a crime such as sexual assault or domestic violence, for example, allows us to keep thoughts of our own vulnerability at arm's length. We reason,

"They got what they deserved, even if I can't explain why." When mortality makes us uncomfortable, we restore comfort by embracing views or values that make us feel like the world makes sense or that we matter in it. To learn more, see the Spotlight on Research Methods feature.

Kelley's Covariation Model of Attribution

Sometimes we become amateur Sherlock Holmes detectives, piecing together clues about why something happened. One of the most critical pieces of information that we use in this search for clues is to ask, "What else was also going on with these people or in this situation just prior to the major event?" In scientific terms, we're looking for variables that *covary* or happen in *correlation* with the event. Kelley (1967) proposed a three-step or three-dimensional **covariation model of attribution** that he believed we use automatically when trying to understand why an event occurred.

To understand Kelley's model, imagine that you're in class and your professor starts yelling at another student, Carlos. You will probably immediately wonder, "Why is this happening?" It could be something about the professor, something about Carlos, or something unique about this particular situation. According to Kelley's covariation model, you'll attempt to make an attribution based on these three questions:

- **Consensus:** *Do other people act this way toward the target?* Consensus refers to whether other people act the same way toward the target person in the situation—in this case, that's the student, Carlos. Do other teachers also yell at Carlos? If the answer is yes, then your attribution will lean toward the belief that Carlos probably deserves what he's getting.
- **Consistency:** *Is this how the actor usually behaves?* Consistency refers to the main actor in the situation—in this case, that's the professor—and whether he or she acts this way toward everyone. Does the professor yell at every student? If the answer is yes, then your attribution will lean toward the belief that your professor is the cause of the situation, and Carlos just happens to be the latest innocent victim.
- **Distinctiveness:** *Do the actor and target always act this way together?* Distinctiveness refers to whether the same actor and same target (Carlos and the professor) always act this way when together. If yes, then your attribution will be that it's about both of them. If not, you'll assume there's something unique going on here! Maybe one of them had a particularly bad day.

Even these seemingly logical steps of detective work will not always lead to accurate explanations of why people act the way they do. We blame victims, we look for the easiest explanation (even when it's not always correct), we avoid attributions that make us feel uncomfortable, and we rely on heuristics and stereotypes. And—as we learned in Chapter 4—we cannot always trust our intuition.

Dogs don't seem to wonder why other dogs sniff in certain spots or wag their tails in a particular way. Birds don't seem to ask themselves why other birds build nests in certain locations and in certain styles. But we humans seem to be relentless explainers of one another's behavior, never discouraged by our frequent errors. Perhaps our capacity for wondering why is part of what makes the human species special.

Covariation model of attribution: The idea that individuals make attributions concerning the cause of an event between two people, the actor and the target, by assessing these three dimensions: whether other people typically act that way toward the target (consensus), whether the actor typically behaves that way (distinctiveness), and whether the actor and target always act this way together (consistency).

Consensus: The dimension of Kelly's covariation model of attribution that refers to whether other people tend to act the same way toward the target person in the situation.

Consistency: The dimension of Kelly's covariation model of attribution that refers to whether the actor in the situation tends to act the same way toward everyone.

Distinctiveness: The dimension of Kelly's covariation model of attribution that refers to whether the same actor and same target always act the same way when together.

EXPERIMENTALLY MANIPULATING THOUGHTS OF DEATH

Spotlight on Research Methods

Shutterstock / Syda Productions

Terror management theory suggests that when we can't avoid thinking about our own deaths, we will embrace beliefs that help us feel comfort. Creative researchers have tested this theory by making the idea of death more vivid to some individuals, a manipulation called **mortality salience.**

The *independent variable* in these studies is based on *random assignment* to write a particular kind of essay. In many studies on terror management theory, half of the participants are asked to write down their responses to the disturbing question: "What do you think happens to you as you physically die and once you are physically dead?" In contrast, the rest of the participants are asked to write about what will happen to their bodies when they suffer a severe (but not life-threatening) injury or when

they experience powerful dental pain. While either condition is grim, researchers control for the logical *confounding explanation* by making sure that both conditions are unpleasant physical experiences. That way, any differences in the outcome or *dependent variable* can't be due to thinking about pain or discomfort. They wanted data based only on whether one group of participants had to confront death, while others didn't.

The results of several experiments tell the same general story. Participants who have to write about death—the "mortality salience" condition—assign more blame to people who have experienced something unfortunate compared to those who only had to write about a painful experience (thus, the dependent variable was amount of blame; Hirschberger, 2006). When the prospect of death and disaster is made real to us, belief in a just world leads us to have even *less* compassion for the innocent (Hirschberger, Florian, & Mikuliner, 2005). Similarly, people who write death essays recommend harsher penalties for prostitution, compared to people who write dental pain essays (Jonas et al., 2008).

In another study, Israeli high school students who wrote death essays were more likely to say they were motivated to join the national military than high school students in the control group (Taubman-Ben-Ari & Findler, 2006). When we have to think about our own mortality, we embrace anything that we can believe in, because these worldviews bring us comfort. In essence, we can tell ourselves, "At least my death *means* something."

Mortality salience: When researchers make the idea of death, especially an individual's own unavoidable death, more vivid.

The Main Ideas

- Attribution research explores how we automatically use science-like reasoning to explain why people behave as they do. We try to isolate causal influences.

- We often distinguish between internal attributions (a cause related to the person who did something) and external attributions (a cause related to the situation or environment).

- Our conclusions tend to be biased by factors such as our belief in a just world, which leads us to blame victims for their misfortunes, and conclusions are biased when we are reminded of our own mortality.

- We rely on covariance to reach conclusions, including questions of consensus, consistency, and distinctiveness.

- People who believe in a just world are more likely to blame innocent victims if they believe the person "deserved" what happened. However, people who believe in a just world are also more likely to get upset if they think something unfair happened, such as when a friend gets fired. What variables might account for when people with this belief system decide that the victim of an event "deserved" it or not? How could you test for the influence of those variables in a research study?

- Think about each of the circumstances below. For each, analyze what's happening using the three steps of consensus, consistency, and distinctiveness. As you consider each situation and each step, how does your attribution change based on your conclusions for each step?

  - You see your classmate flirting with someone in the grocery store.
  - Your supervisor at work compliments you and suggests that you might be considered for a raise or promotion.
  - Your friend comes out of a movie theater crying.
  - As your roommate goes through her mail, she gets increasingly upset and frustrated.

WHY DO WE MISJUDGE ONE ANOTHER?

■ LO 5.4: Evaluate why we make flawed attributions about one another's behavior.

Once a faulty understanding takes root in our minds, it becomes like a stubborn weed that we can't seem to get rid of. For example, we sometimes assume that actors who play good, pleasant characters must be nice in real life—and actors who play villains must be terrible people in real life (Tal-Or & Papirman, 2007). In what others ways do our misunderstandings or assumptions lead to errors in social judgment?

Cognitive Errors Accumulate Into Flawed Perceptions

We have identified many persistent types of mental errors in these first few chapters—and there are more to come. For example, it may surprise you to learn that false confessions of crimes are not unusual. But it is not surprising that a jury is persuaded by the vividness of a detailed, videotaped confession.

A confession of guilt gives a jury almost everything their cognitive biases desire. To a juror, a confession makes sense only if the person is guilty (an internal attribution). A confession also means that the jury won't have to work very hard to reach a decision (they can be cognitive misers). In a trial, a videotaped confession also may be the first thing jurors learn from a prosecutor (first impressions). This negative first impression lasts longer in memory than positive information that might come later (the negativity bias). A confession of guilt also makes it easy to judge everything else about the defendant as negative (the halo effect). They notice only evidence that supports what they already believe while disregarding contradictory evidence (the confirmation bias). When all those cognitive errors accumulate, a social perception that is dead wrong can still make perfect sense to jurors—simply because they got started on the wrong foot (Anderson, Lepper, & Ross, 1980).

Julie Andrews usually plays warm, nurturing characters like Mary Poppins (1964) or a singing nun in *The Sound of Music* (Wise & Wise, 1965), while Kevin Spacey is known for playing manipulative antagonists in films such as *Seven* (Kopelson, Carlyle, & Fincher, 1995) or the television show *House of Cards* (Fincher et al., 2013-2017). It is easy to assume their personalities in real life match those they play on the screen.

The Fundamental Attribution Error. One of our most common flawed perceptions is so pervasive in our thinking that even its name says it's a fundamental bias. The **fundamental attribution error** is our tendency to overestimate the influence of personality and underestimate the power of the situation.

At first, we can only guess about why other people do what they do. Imagine you go to dinner and find that your waiter is particularly nice to you. On the way home, however, your bus driver is particularly gruff and cold. Most of us automatically assume that the waiter is a kind and friendly person, while the bus driver is a mean and rude person. We forget to factor the situation into account. The waiter might be pretending to like customers just to increase his tip, while the bus driver might not engage in chitchat with passengers to stay focused.

Attributing behavior to personality (internal or dispositional causes) rather than to situations (external causes) is deeply ingrained in our causal reasoning (Gilbert & Malone, 1995; Heider, 1958; Jones, 1979; Ross, 1977). One of the early experimental demonstrations of the fundamental attribution error involved two groups of students reading the same opinion essay that was highly critical of a political leader. One of the two groups had been told that the author of the essay had *chosen* to express this opinion. The other group had been told that the author had been *required* to express the opinion (Jones & Harris, 1967). Like believing that an actor is a mean person because he played a mean role in a movie, knowing that a writer had been required to express an opinion did not seem to matter. Both groups of participants perceived the author as believing in whatever opinion was expressed.

The fundamental attribution error isn't going away. People who see positive status updates on Facebook assume that other people's good fortunes are due to their personality instead of to passing circumstances (Chou & Edge, 2012). We tend to perceive that members of high-status groups must have earned their membership in some way and

Fundamental attribution error: The tendency to overestimate the influence of personality and underestimate the power of the situation when making attributions about other people's behaviors.

ignore inherited privilege or socioeconomic status (Nier, Bajaj, McLean, & Schwartz, 2013). Teenagers attribute bullying behaviors to the personality of either the bully or the victim rather than situational influences such as peers or the school environment (Thornberg & Knutsen, 2011). And, unfortunately, teachers who use ineffective methods are more likely to attribute student failure to their students than to themselves or their methods (Wieman & Welsh, 2016).

Kurt Lewin, social psychology's pioneer, might have been disappointed that so many of us try to explain why something happened without recognizing the power and perception of the immediate situation.

The Actor-Observer Attribution Bias.

There is some fine print to the fundamental attribution error. The **actor-observer bias** is our tendency to think of personality when explaining other people's behavior but external, situational causes when explaining our own behavior (Nisbett, Caputo, Legant, & Marecek, 1973). In other words, we take the situation into account when thinking about why we make *our own* decisions, but we focus on personality when explaining other people's behavior.

One explanation for this pattern may be that we are the experts about our own lives, and we can see how our own behavior or outcomes change based on the situation. Sometimes we're friendly, sometimes we're mean—and we can see how important situations are in determining these differences. However, when we see other people behaving in a certain way, we don't have the same information. We don't have access to everything that's been happening in their lives leading up to that point. All we have to observe is what's happening right now, so it's easy to focus on the behavior instead of what might have led up to it.

Researchers Gordon and Kaplar (2002) devised a clever way to teach their students about the actor-observer bias. They modified a game called *Scruples* that confronts people with moral dilemmas such as whether to provide an alibi for a friend having an extramarital affair. In the game, people have to say what they would do in a variety of ethical dilemmas with either a "yes," "no," or "depends on the situation" card. People were more likely to endorse "depends on the situation" when the moral dilemma was supposedly happening to them, compared with when the same situation was supposedly happening to someone else. We see how our own behavior "depends on the situation."

Attributions to Explain History.

When people try to explain the events of the Holocaust and World War II, attributions often depend on whether they are German citizens or not. These differences are another example of the actor-observer bias. People born inside Germany (even people born after World War II) sometimes explain what happened based on the situation; they reason things like, "You weren't there—you don't understand what it was like to live under Nazi rule" (Doosje, Branscombe, Spears, & Manstead, 1998). For them, situational causes led to the German people's behavior, not something inherently evil about their culture or the people. But the people born *outside* of Germany sometimes have a different attribution. They might think, "The world was watching you. You knew exactly what you were doing."

The reality of German cruelty to Jews must be vivid to people waiting in line to see the Anne Frank House Museum in Amsterdam, the Netherlands. That's where Doosje and Branscombe (2003) asked both non-Jewish Germans and non-German Jews waiting in the line to rate two simple statements:

- "I think the Germans mistreated the Jews because Germans are aggressive by nature." (A dispositional attribution)
- "It is important to consider the behavior of the Germans towards the Jews in a historical context, rather than judge their acts in isolation." (A situational attribution)

Actor-observer bias: An individual's tendency to think of personality when explaining other people's behavior but external, situational causes when explaining their own behavior.

Now in Amsterdam, people line up every day to visit the Anne Frank House, where she wrote her famous diary while hiding from the Nazi regime.

Shutterstock / 4kclips

■ **FIGURE 5.5** Internal and external attributions for the Holocaust.

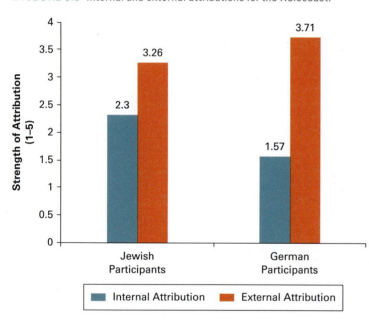

SOURCE: Doosje & Branscombe (2003).

Figure 5.5 describes how the actor-observer bias influenced how they responded. While both groups were more likely to make external attributions compared to internal attributions, there was a *statistically significant* difference between the two groups in this *quasi-experimental study*. The (non-Jewish) Germans waiting in line assigned more responsibility to the "historical context"—to the situation. The (non-German) Jewish people standing in the same line were more likely to assign responsibility to the Germans who were "aggressive by nature"—to the national German personality. Doosje and Branscombe (2003) found that the actor-observer bias was even greater for those with a strong national identity.

Cultural Expectations Affect Attribution Errors

As Table 5.3 demonstrates, even people from different cultures who speak the same language can easily misunderstand one another. When you add cognitive errors to cultural miscommunications, you have the opportunity for profound misperceptions of one another's motives.

Cross-cultural research suggests that the fundamental attribution error may not be quite as fundamental as was once believed. Forgas (1998) found that simply being in a happy mood increases attributions to someone's personality. A bias is not very "fundamental" if it can be modified by a temporary change of mood (see Harvey & McGlynn, 1982; Harvey, Town, & Yarkin, 1981; Reeder, 1982). A more telling argument is that

Phrase	Meaning in American English	Meaning in British English
"Turn it up."	"Increase the volume."	"I don't believe you."
"How did you find the train?"	"How did you locate the train?"	"Did you enjoy the train trip?"
"Are you through?"	"Are you finished?"	"Did you make a phone connection?"
"I knocked her up this morning."	"I got her pregnant this morning."	"I knocked on her door this morning."
"May I have a rubber, please?"	"May I have a condom, please?"	"May I have an eraser, please?"

people in independent, self-reliant cultures are more likely to use dispositional explanations than people in collectivistic, relationship-oriented cultures (Norenzayan & Nisbett, 2000; Sampson, 1988; Smith & Bond, 1993). For example, American Olympic athletes attributed their success to dispositional causes such as working hard, whereas Chinese Olympic athletes were more likely to say their success was due to national support in print and broadcast media stories (Hua & Tan, 2012).

Another comparison of American versus Chinese culture (Morris & Peng, 1994) analyzed how newspapers from each nation explained two very similar mass murders. Gang Lu was a Chinese physics student who had lost an award competition, appealed unsuccessfully, and was not able to find an academic job. He shot his advisor, the person who handled his appeal, fellow students and bystanders, and finally himself. Thomas McIlvane was an American postal worker who lost his job, appealed unsuccessfully, and was unable to find employment. He also shot his supervisor, the person who handled his appeal, coworkers and bystanders, and then himself.

Reporters from both English-language and Chinese-language newspapers sought to explain both of these tragedies. As Table 5.4 demonstrates, the English-language newspaper, the *New York Times,* emphasized personality traits (internal attributions). The Chinese-language newspaper, *World Journal,* emphasized relational and situational explanations (external attributions).

We Make Self-Serving Attributions

We are all part of the problem that makes it difficult to explain why people behave as they do. We are the problem because we tend to engage in a variety of self-serving biases that explain outcomes in ways that advance or protect our personal interests.

■ TABLE 5.4 Newspaper Explanations of Mass Murders

	About Mr. Lu	About Mr. McIlvane
What the Chinese-language newspaper reported	"did not get along with his advisor" "rivalry with slain student" "isolation from Chinese community"	"gunman had been recently fired" "post office supervisor was his enemy" "followed the example of a recent mass slaying in Texas"
What the English-language newspaper reported	"very bad temper" "sinister edge to Mr. Lu's character" "darkly disturbed man" "whatever went wrong was internal"	"man was mentally unstable" "had a short fuse" "had repeatedly threatened violence"

NOTE: When reporting about two crimes involving similar circumstances, a Chinese-language paper seems to emphasize the circumstances, while an English-language newspaper seems to emphasize personality traits.

The False Consensus Bias. For example, the **false consensus effect** is the false assumption that other people share our values, perceptions, and beliefs. We naïvely assume that others see the world just as we do—a familiar idea in psychology (Clement & Krueger, 2002; Hoch, 1987; Holmes, 1968, 1978). This self-serving, biased way of answering the "why" question occurs partly because we tend to believe that whatever comes most easily to mind must be important and occur more frequently: the availability heuristic (Dawes, 1989; Dawes & Mulford, 1996; Nisbett & Kunda, 1985; Sherman, Chassin, Presson, & Agostinelli, 1984).

We all probably prefer to spend time with people who are similar to ourselves. We are more likely to "friend" people on Facebook who agree with most of our beliefs. Consequently, we are exposed to people who agree with us more than to those with a different opinion. It's also comforting to believe that other people agree with us and see our behavior and choices as "normal."

So, it is not surprising that students who admitted to cheating tended to believe that other students also cheated (Katz, Allport, & Jenness, 1931). Similarly, student athletes who use illicit performance-enhancing drugs overestimate how many other athletes do the same thing (Dunn, Thomas, Swift, & Burns, 2012). College men who admit to being perpetrators of sexual assault are significantly more likely to overestimate how many of their friends have done the same thing (Dardis, Murphy, Bill, & Gidycz, 2016). If we experience life in a certain way, then we overestimate the number of people who experience their lives in the same way.

Of course, using our own experience is not an unreasonable way to estimate reality, especially if our private experience is the only evidence we have. But, like first impressions, the false consensus bias persists even when people are later provided with contradictory information. What has been called the **truly false consensus effect** occurs when we believe that others share our beliefs—even after we have objective, statistical information that contradicts that belief (Krueger & Clement, 1994; Krueger & Zeiger, 1993). One student accidentally demonstrated how tightly false consensus had wrapped itself around his thought. With unintended humor, the student declared, "I, like most people, do not generalize from myself to others" (Clement, Sinha, & Krueger, 1997, p. 134).

The False Uniqueness Bias. The **false uniqueness bias** is the belief that we are more unique than others when it comes to socially desirable traits (Furnham & Dowsett, 1993). Do you see yourself in any of these examples? A false sense of uniqueness leads most store clerks to believe that they are tougher than most other store clerks at carding people when they try to buy cigarettes or alcohol (McCall & Nattrass, 2001). Most college students think that they are more constructive and less destructive in their romantic relationships than other college students (Van Lange, Rusbult, Semin-Goossens, Gorts, & Stalpers, 1999). And most high school students think that they are more prosocial and helpful than other students (Iedema & Poppe, 1999; Monin & Norton, 2003).

The false uniqueness bias is sometimes called the **Lake Woebegone effect** in honor of the retired radio humorist Garrison Keillor. Each week he created another story about the ordinary people in a Minnesota town called Lake Woebegone—a pleasant little fantasy town—where "*all* the children are above average." It is easier to believe that we are special when we convince ourselves that our bad traits are common but our good traits are rare (a self-serving bias you learned about in Chapter 3).

©iStockPhoto.com/Dorottya_Mathe

Ninety-nine percent of pet owners think their pet is above average in intelligence. Do you think this is true of your dog, cat, or other pet family member?

The Good and Bad of Bias. The self-serving bias can lead us to comical conclusions. For example, Nier (2004) discovered a self-serving glow of goodness so bright that it even shines on our pets. Almost all (99%) pet owners believe that their pets are above average in intelligence, and 18% of pet owners think that their pets are probably geniuses (Matheny & Miller, 2000). Similarly, 87% of Americans believe that they are likely to go to Heaven, a percentage that is higher than the one that they assigned to Mother Teresa or Oprah Winfrey (Stanglin & Gross, 1997).

However, the self-serving bias can shift from comedy to tragedy (Walther & Bazarova, 2007). Some hospitals maintain a self-serving organizational silence when faced with threats to patient safety (Henriksen & Dayton, 2006). The hospitals never admit blame or take responsibility because they are trying to protect their reputation. In general, it is probably safer to admit our errors, endure the bad publicity, and correct mistakes—if our self-serving impulses allow us to acknowledge those mistakes in the first place. For college students, sometimes admitting that a bad grade *was* due to your own choices can help you improve the next time. Self-serving biases can comfort us in the short term but can be damaging in the long term because we don't admit that we might have had something to do with the failure.

The Main Ideas

- When cognitive errors accumulate, they can lead to faulty social perceptions such as the fundamental attribution bias and the actor-observer bias.

- Cultural expectations make the fundamental attribution bias more likely to occur in independent cultures than in interdependent cultures.

- The false consensus bias occurs when we believe that others perceive the world in the same ways that we perceive the world; the false uniqueness bias occurs when we believe that we are more unique than others when it comes to socially desirable traits.

⚡ CRITICAL THINKING CHALLENGE

- When you share your opinion with others in social settings, such as discussing music or movie preferences with your friends, are you surprised when people disagree with you? If so, do you think this surprise is due to the false consensus error—or are there other possible explanations?

- Consider times in your life when things didn't work out as you would have preferred, such as doing badly on a test or breaking up with a romantic partner. How much of this "failure" was due to your own faults or shortcomings, and how much was due to someone else or the situation? If you think that the majority of the blame lies somewhere else, are you making a self-serving and biased attribution?

How do we form impressions of others?

Person perception is how we form impressions of other people. Sometimes particular traits will become more important than others; for example, how physically attractive people are affects our perception of them in general. When one trait affects how we view someone overall, it's called a halo effect. One specific type of halo effect is the what-is-beautiful-is-good effect, which is when physically attractive people are perceived as better in other ways as well (friendlier, more intelligent, etc.).

Sometimes, our impressions of others lead us to have expectations about their behaviors. When these expectations lead us to change our own behaviors, and our behavior affects the outcome of a social situation such that our expectation comes true, it's called a self-fulfilling prophesy. If you expect people to be unfriendly, and thus you act more coldly toward them, they may respond by being unfriendly—so your expectation has come true. This is also sometimes called the Pygmalion effect (named after a character from a Greek myth).

Self-fulfilling prophecies have been found in a variety of real-world settings. For example, one study found that teachers' expectations of students led those students to actually perform better or worse over time. Similar patterns of results are found in studies of courtrooms, in workplace settings, and even in the world of sports. In short, our expectations of others can shape their behaviors to make our expectations come true.

How do we communicate nonverbally?

Nonverbal communication occurs through body language, tone of voice, facial expressions, and more. Several studies have investigated whether facial expressions, for example, are universal across culture (this is called the universality hypothesis). Some evidence indicates that at least six basic emotions are universally expressed through facial expressions, regardless of culture (fear, anger, disgust, surprise, sadness, and happiness).

Other research has examined facial expressions in terms of whether we can control our face when we are dishonest. Facial leakage occurs when emotions we wish to conceal are expressed through automatic muscle responses; these momentary and involuntary expressions are sometimes called micro-expressions. Research has also explored whether people can tell a genuine (also known as a Duchenne smile) from a fake smile. Decoding facial expressions is more difficult when they show an affect blend, or a combination of emotions.

A different type of nonverbal communication is a cultureme, which is a symbol used to convey meaning within a given culture. Culturemes, unlike facial expressions, are usually not understood by people from other cultures. Examples are religious symbols or government symbols. The meaning of any given symbol can also change over time or be interpreted in very different ways by different cultures.

How do we explain other people's behavior?

When we guess at the cause behind an event or someone else's behavior, we make an attribution. One way we might do this is by looking for a factor that seems to be the best explanation because it stands out from other explanations; this is called the principle of non-common effects. When our attribution is based on something about a person's personality, motivation, or inner values, it's called an internal attribution (sometimes called a dispositional attribution). When our attribution is based on something about the situation or environmental circumstances, it's called an external attribution.

We often make attributions with the general belief that "good things happen to good people" and vice versa; this belief is called belief in a just world. Sometimes, this can lead to blaming innocent victims of misfortune. In general, believing that our fate is in our own hands is referred to as an internal locus of control. An external locus of control is when people believe that our fate is up to something outside of ourselves, such as fate, luck, or a powerful other person or supernatural being. Finally, our decisions and attributions can be biased when we are reminded of our own mortality, something that is studied within terror management theory.

One way that we attempt to make logical attributions about situations is by using Kelley's covariation model of attributions. Here, we ask ourselves three questions about the situation, including (1) consensus, (2) consistency, and (3) distinctiveness. Our answers to these three questions help us understand why something happened or why others acted like they did.

Why do we misjudge one another?

Sometimes when we attempt to understand other people, we make mistakes. A very common mistake—so common that it's called the fundamental attribution error—is when we assume other people's actions are due to their personality and we forget to take the situation or circumstances into effect. While we do this when making attributions about other people, we don't make this mistake when explaining our own behavior. In other words, we can see how our own behaviors change due to different situations. The difference in how we make assumptions about other people's behavior versus our own is called the actor-observer bias. In addition, while people from "independent" cultures tend to make the fundamental attribution error, people from "interdependent" or collectivistic cultures are less likely to do so.

We also tend to make attributions and assumptions about other people that protect our view of the self or our own interests. For example, the false consensus effect is the tendency to think that most other people agree with our personal opinions. The false uniqueness bias, on the other hand, is the perception that our good or positive qualities are fairly rare (and therefore we are special and above average). While these tendencies help us feel good about ourselves, they may prevent us from improving or confronting negative behaviors.

- Self-fulfilling prophecies
- Halo effect

- Universality hypothesis of facial expression
- Attribution theory

- Belief in a just world
- Locus of control
- Terror management theory
- Covariation model of attribution
- Fundamental attribution error

CRITICAL THINKING, ANALYSIS, AND APPLICATION

- Think about the self-fulfilling prophecies that different groups of people have to live with in your culture. For example, different races probably have different stereotypes and expectations about the types of adults they will become. How much of an influence do you think self-fulfilling prophecies have on the opportunities that different groups are given by society? How could educators, politicians, or other leaders use self-fulfilling prophecies to better the human condition?

- Some people are better than others at decoding nonverbal communication cues from others. For example, one symptom that's common in people on the autism spectrum is the lack of ability to understand subtle nonverbal cues such as when tone of voice indicates sarcasm. If you were speaking with someone you knew had trouble understanding nonverbal cues, how would you change your behaviors to communicate in other ways?

- Think of a time when you made an attribution about why someone did something—and it turned out later that you were wrong. What do you think happened to lead you to the wrong conclusion? What variables or aspects of the circumstance, the person, or your own frame of mind affected your ability to make a correct attribution—and can you control for these variables going into the future?

- Consider the way that news media (television, radio, etc.) cover stories about crimes, such as murders or terrorist attacks. Is the tendency for the reporters to assume the crimes occurred because the criminals were bad people—or do they think about other, external or situational explanations, such as oppression, religion, mental illness, and so on?

PERSONAL REFLECTION

My [Tom's] worst job ever was working in a wire-making factory. Sometimes the copper wire speeding through the machine would snap as it was being drawn (or stretched) down to a particular diameter. The wire would whip about dangerously until the machine finally came to a stop. That's when my job began: unclipping the layers of copper wire wrapped tightly around the flywheels while smelly, milky-looking, liquid animal fats (used to lubricate the wire) poured over my green work uniform. After 12 months of this, I had the single best career idea I have ever had: night school.

I didn't recognize it until several years later, but I also learned something important about social perception in that job. When you push a machine beyond its capacity, something has to give—and

our mental machinery works the same way. When asked to process more information than we can handle, our brain starts whipping out cognitive errors that are very difficult to undo. Some of those cognitive errors are assembled into social misperceptions that, like some factory-made products, make it past our mental quality control checkers and into our daily lives. Most of the time, our mental machinery works so well that we don't even notice it is functioning.

But experiments like those we have shared in this chapter reveal that our mental machinery also makes errors. And that terrible job? It didn't get any better, but it became easier for me to put up with it knowing that night school had put me on a path that might lead to something better. [TH]

Evaluate why we make **flawed attributions** about one **another's behavior**.

Get a tour of **ALL Visual Key Concepts** and their definitions at **edge.sagepub.com/heinzen**

6 Attitudes and Persuasion

AP Photo/BOB JORDAN

Core Questions

1. What are attitudes, and do they predict behavior?

2. From where do attitudes come?

3. How are attitudes measured?

4. Why does cognitive dissonance influence attitudes?

5. How do attitudes change?

6. What persuasion techniques are used to change attitudes?

Learning Objectives

6.1 Explain how attitudes are composed of evaluative beliefs that do not reliably predict behavior.

6.2 Evaluate how nature and nurture interact to form particular attitudes.

6.3 Illustrate why attitudes need to be measured both directly and indirectly.

6.4 Explain how cognitive dissonance motivates self-justification and attitude change.

6.5 Analyze two distinct paths to persuasion.

6.6 Apply specific persuasion techniques to attitude or behavior change.

Was it a witch hunt for rumored child sex abusers—or did the employees of a small daycare center really commit these horrible crimes? The gossip was bad enough, especially in a town as small as Edenton, North Carolina. The group of accused daycare workers included Bob and Betsy Kelly, several of their employees at the Little Rascals daycare center, and a friend of Bob's who had never even visited the daycare.

Like rising water in a bad storm, powerful attitudes about child sex abuse swept away critical thinking, lifelong friendships, and even established legal standards. Many people following the case made up their minds right away—and then refused to change even after the moral panic had subsided. They had come to believe that their own friends and neighbors, labeled the Edenton 7 by journalist Lew Powell, must be guilty of gross acts of child sexual abuse.

You may be tempted to think of the people in Edenton as evil or corrupt. But when I [Tom] became interested in this case, I went to Edenton and chatted with several residents, including some of the people involved. They were nice people, normal people. Most of them were courteous, interested, friendly to a stranger—and still confused about what had happened to them and to their little town a quarter of a century earlier. It was not a case for a clinical psychologist; it was and still is a casebook phenomenon for social psychology.

When the legal case against Bob Kelly finally went to trial, it lasted for 8 months. In the end, Kelly was declared guilty of 99 out of 100 charges and sentenced to 12 consecutive life sentences—one for each of the 12 alleged victims represented in court. Like the witch trials of Salem, it appeared that fear and panic had overcome logic. Only a few years later, all 99 convictions were reversed. The attitudes that drove the Little Rascals case into the national spotlight help explain why Gordon Allport (1935) declared that attitudes were social psychology's "most distinctive and indispensable concept."

WHAT ARE ATTITUDES, AND DO THEY PREDICT BEHAVIOR?

LO 6.1: Explain how attitudes are composed of evaluative beliefs that do not reliably predict behavior.

Attitudes are an inner tendency to judge or evaluate something or someone either positively or negatively (see Eagly & Chaiken, 2007). In Edenton, North Carolina, the judgments were negative and became stronger each time the police reported arresting

Attitudes: An inner tendency to judge or evaluate something or someone either positively or negatively.

another daycare worker. The "object" (or target) of these attitudes shifted from hating child sexual abuse in general to demonizing seven people in particular believed to be guilty of that crime. Attitudes are a good example of a psychological construct, an abstract and theoretical idea. Social psychologists have worked hard for decades to operationalize attitudes and invent experiments that allow us to discover how attitudes influence human behavior.

Attitudes Evaluate Something

Attitudes are directed at an **attitude object**, something that you explicitly or implicitly evaluate. It doesn't have to be a person. It could be a political issue, sports team, television series, song, or even an abstract painting or idea (see Petty & Cacioppo, 1996). You may not be aware of them, but beneath the surface of those attitudes are different kinds of beliefs. For example, believing that Santa Claus exists and lives at the North Pole is an **informational belief** about an attitude object (Santa Claus). However, liking Santa Claus because of the perception that he is kind and unusually generous (even toward naughty children) is an **evaluative belief**. Beliefs become attitudes when the attitude object is judged as either positive or negative.

The Model of Dual Attitudes.
During the infamous witch hunt in Salem, Massachusetts, one of the village's previous ministers, Reverend Burroughs, had been accused of witchcraft. As he stood before the gallows, he recited the Lord's Prayer perfectly—something that witches were not supposed to be able to do. Suddenly, the citizens of Salem were "of two minds" about Reverend Burroughs, but only one of them could win out. The Reverend Cotton Mather reminded the crowd that Burroughs had been tried in court and found guilty. They trusted the judgment of their court system and their prestigious Harvard-trained minister who was also the author of a book about witchcraft. Despite their doubts, they hanged their former minister.

We often have **dual attitudes** that represent contrasting beliefs about the same attitude object. An addict will both love and hate whatever drug he or she is addicted to. A teenager might both love his parents yet also feel embarrassed and annoyed by them. A professional actor may love her career for its sublime artistic pleasures yet hate her career because of its instability and frequent rejection. How do we arrive at all these love-hate attitudes toward drugs, family members, our jobs, and everything else in our lives? The **model of dual attitudes** proposes that new attitudes override (rather than replace) old attitudes (Wilson, Lindsey, & Schooler, 2000), meaning a small piece of an opposing attitude might linger. That is why former lovers may fondly remember one another even in the midst of a bitter breakup; the old beliefs and feelings do not magically disappear—they just acquire another complicating layer of beliefs.

Implicit Versus Explicit Attitudes.
Would you eat a chocolate cockroach? Keep chocolate cockroaches in mind as you learn more about dual attitudes.

There are two explanations for why we might develop contradicting attitudes toward the same attitude object. First, attitudes come from three different sources: affect (emotions), behavior, and cognition—and they don't always come to the same conclusions (Smith & Nosek, 2011). For example, we may get a feeling (the affective or emotional component) that we should not trust someone. Nevertheless, we may act (the behavioral component) as if we trust the person because the individual belongs in the mental category of someone—such as a teacher or coach—that we believe (the cognitive or logical component) we can trust.

Attitude object: The object, person, place, or idea an individual explicitly or implicitly evaluates and directs his or her attitude toward.

Informational belief: A fact-based belief that includes no positive or negative judgment.

Evaluative belief: A belief about an object, person, place, or idea that leads to or includes a positive or negative judgment.

Dual attitudes: When an individual holds contrasting positive and negative beliefs about the same attitude object.

Model of dual attitudes: A model for understanding attitudes that proposes that new attitudes override, rather than replace, old attitudes.

Second, we may not even be aware that we have an attitude toward something because we have both implicit and explicit attitudes. **Implicit attitudes** are based on automatic, unconscious beliefs about an attitude object. **Explicit attitudes** are the product of controlled, conscious beliefs about an attitude object. For example, I [Tom] am aware that I love chocolate (an explicit attitude). However, I was relatively unaware how much I dislike bugs with lots of little legs (an implicit attitude) until I visited a specialty chocolate store and saw some chocolate cockroaches that looked very much like the real things. Yech! I definitely had dual attitudes toward eating chocolate cockroaches.

Attitudes Facilitate Decision Making. You, too, might have a dual attitude toward eating chocolate cockroaches. Despite the complexity of our underlying beliefs, we can vote for only one candidate, must either reject or accept a marriage proposal, and can either eat or not eat a chocolate cockroach. (I suppose you could nibble on a chocolate cockroach but somehow that seems even more disgusting.) Attitudes help us make **uni-valenced decisions** that an attitude object is either good or bad—but not both. We don't have to think very hard if we always vote for one political party, plan to say yes to any marriage proposal, or are always willing to try a piece of chocolate, no matter how many little legs it seems to have.

Many people have positive explicit attitudes toward eating chocolate, but when asked to eat a chocolate cockroach, you might have mixed feelings.

Gordon Allport (1935) called attitudes a "predisposition or readiness for response." They are premade judgments that allow us make a quick thumbs-up or thumbs-down heuristic decision (Priester & Petty, 1996). But just like all of the mental shortcuts we've discussed so far, preformed beliefs are risky because we know that we might be wrong (see Ajzen, 1991; Eagly & Chaiken, 1993; Thompson, Zanna, & Griffin, 1995; Wilson et al., 2000). For example, the prosecutors and jury (and many townspeople) in Edenton all arrived at the same uni-valenced decision when thinking about their friends and neighbors involved with the Little Rascals case: guilty.

They were wrong. After years of appeals, almost all of the charges were overturned. But not until after seven daycare workers were arrested and found guilty of over 400 counts of sexual assault, having intercourse in front of children, conspiracy, and other similar charges. There was no physical evidence and Little Rascals had an open-door policy, so parents could pick up their children at any time and for any reason. It was not plausible that the staff could even get away with such outrageous behavior without it being noticed. No one ever noticed because those sexual assaults never occurred.

In a cautionary tale to students thinking of becoming therapists, attitudes also help explain how the psychological therapists made the situation much worse. The therapists had been asked (usually by the police and/or parents) to evaluate the children for signs of sexual abuse. The therapists perceived what they had been primed to believe—that the children would be suffering from symptoms due to their assaults—leading to confirmation bias in their counseling and assessment sessions. They expected to find symptoms of child sex abuse . . . so they did.

However, there were also reasons for healthy skepticism that came from a *naturally occurring quasi-experiment*: Some children also named (by other children) as victims were sent to psychological therapists in another region of North Carolina. These therapists had *not* been told to look for signs of child sex abuse—and those children were never identified as showing any signs of being traumatized or molested.

Implicit attitudes: Attitudes based on automatic, unconscious beliefs about an attitude object.

Explicit attitudes: Attitudes that are the product of controlled, conscious beliefs about an attitude object.

Uni-valenced decision: A decision based on an attitude about an attitude object that is either good or bad but not both.

Bob Kelly, one of the owners of the Little Rascals daycare center. A 1997 story in *The New York Times* compared the case to the Salem witch trials.

Do Attitudes Predict Behavior?

A seemingly obvious hypothesis might be, "Attitudes predict behavior." If you like waffles, you'll order waffles at your favorite breakfast restaurant. If you are politically conservative, you'll vote for the conservative political candidate. And if you're racist, you'll refuse to work with people of color. Right? But when researchers applied the scientific method to test this simple idea, they discovered that the link between attitudes and behaviors wasn't that simple after all.

Converging Evidence About Attitudes and Behavior. Sociologist Richard LaPiere (1934) helped create a crisis in social psychology by questioning the assumption that attitudes always predict behavior, and he did it with data. LaPiere spent 2 years traveling across the United States with a young Chinese student and that student's wife during a period in U.S. history when Chinese people were the object of intense prejudice and discrimination. The travelers stayed in 66 hotels and lodgings and ate in 184 restaurants, but they were refused service only once. Yet, 92% of these same establishments who answered a letter from LaPiere 6 months later declared that they would *not* serve Chinese people.

The *survey following a field study* wasn't a perfect study. They did not ensure that the people answering the survey were the same people who decided to let them into their hotel or restaurant. The Chinese couple both spoke unaccented English, which may have influenced the decision. Nevertheless, the evidence was still convincing: The general attitudes of the people managing all those hotels and restaurants did not appear to predict their behavior.

When tested in *controlled experiments,* LaPiere's surprising findings turned out to be the rule, not the exception (see Dockery & Bedeian, 1989). For example, students' attitudes toward cheating did *not* predict whether or not they actually cheated (Corey, 1937). A positive attitude toward religion did *not* predict church attendance. In 1969, Wicker reviewed the converging evidence about attitude-behavior research and suggested that for psychology research, "It may be desirable to abandon the attitude concept" (p. 29).

Among social psychologists, the pendulum of excitement toward attitude research had swung from being an indispensable concept to abandoning the concept altogether. (Ironically, many social psychologists had now formed a negative attitude about the concept of attitudes.) If attitudes don't predict actual behavior, what are they good

■ TABLE 6.1 Correlations Between Four Attitudes and Increasingly Specific Behaviors

Attitude Object	Correlation With Behavior
1. Attitude toward birth control	.083
2. Attitude toward birth control pills	.323
3. Attitude toward using birth control pills	.525
4. Attitude toward using birth control pills during the next 2 years	.572

SOURCE: Davidson, A. R., & Jaccard, J. J. (1979). Variables that moderate the attitude-behavior relation: Results of a longitudinal survey. *Journal of Personality and Social Psychology, 37*(8), 1364-1376.

for—and why invest all this time studying them? The crisis in social psychology was slowly resolved by something that the psychological therapists in Edenton did not have: unbiased data.

The Specificity Principle. Eventually, more data moved the pendulum to a more realistic assessment of the link between attitudes and behavior. The **specificity principle** proposes that the link between attitudes and behaviors is stronger when the attitude and the behavior are measured at the same level of specificity.

Table 6.1 demonstrates the specificity principle by examining attitudes toward using birth control. There is a very low correlation when you ask people about their *general* attitude toward birth control and their actual use of birth control. But the correlation grows stronger as you ask more specific questions (Davidson & Jaccard, 1979). For example, maybe LaPiere's survey should have asked, "How likely are you to refuse service to a nice-looking Chinese couple accompanied by a professional-looking White man?"

Self-Perception Theory and the Facial Feedback Hypothesis. The old question of which came first, the chicken or the egg, also describes the "attitude-behavior problem." Which came first, the attitude or the behavior? Attitude predicting behavior assumes that the attitude came first—but could it be the other way around?

For social psychologists, the way to resolve such questions is always the same: unbiased data. But, research from different studies has led to a relatively controversial idea called the facial feedback hypothesis. The hypothesis comes from a larger theory called self-perception theory that you learned about in Chapter 3. Recall that self-perception theory states that we infer our own attitude from our own behavior (Bem, 1972; Fazio, 1987; Laird, 1974). In other words, maybe behavior comes first.

Here's a simple test of self-perception theory. Place a pen in your mouth first by holding it with your teeth only (forcing your face into a smile) and then with your lips only (forcing a frown), as you can see in Figure 6.1. Researchers used this same procedure to test the connection between facial expression and a particular emotion (Strack, Martin, & Stepper, 1988). This experiment tested the **facial feedback hypothesis**, that we infer our emotions from what our face is doing (Buck, 1980).

The researchers in this well-known study first created a *cover story* by implying that the study was about helping "physically impaired people who use their mouth to write or use the telephone" (p. 770). You already know that the *independent variable* was asking people to hold a pen in their mouth in ways that created two different conditions: a smile or a frown. The *dependent variable* (the outcome variable that was measured) was how funny the participants rated cartoons they saw while holding pens in their mouths. Results seemed to confirm the facial feedback hypothesis: Participants tricked

Specificity principle: Proposes that the link between attitudes and behaviors is strong when the attitude and the behavior are measured at the same level of specificity.

Facial feedback hypothesis: The idea that individuals infer their own emotions based on the facial expression they are making.

■ FIGURE 6.1 Try holding a pen or pencil in your mouth as shown in the photos, which forces your face into a frown or smile. Do you feel happier when you are smiling?

into smiling rated the cartoons as funnier than participants who were tricked into frowning. Thus, the behavior (facial expression) came first and the attitude (whether the cartoons were funny) followed.

These interesting results have been cited in over 1,000 other studies and have been supported in several similar experiments (e.g., Soussignan, 2002). However, the facial feedback hypothesis has many critics. If your facial expression can affect your own attitude at all, it's unclear how long these feelings last (Labroo, Mukhopadhyay, & Dong, 2014; Schnall & Laird, 2003). In addition, a team of researchers from 17 separate psychology laboratories in eight different countries attempted to *replicate* the findings from the original study—and found almost zero evidence in favor of the hypothesis (Wagenmakers et al., 2016). The jury appears to still be out on the strength, validity, and reliability of this interesting but controversial hypothesis.

Self-Affirmation Theory. In addition to the specificity principle and self-perception theory, the attitude-behavior problem forced social psychologists into a third insight: Some attitudes are nothing more than impression management, a way of strategically trying to manipulate or influence how others perceive us (see Chapter 3; Steele, 1988). You may be able to relate to this if you've ever pretended to agree with a friend or share an attitude with a boss. Thus, sometimes expressed attitudes do not predict behavior because they are merely temporary or disingenuous beliefs designed to manage the impressions we make on others (Gordon, 1996; Higgins, Judge, & Ferris, 2003; Jones & Pittman, 1982; Yukl & Tracey, 1992).

Long-term impression management often has a different audience: yourself. According to **self-affirmation theory**, we try to impress ourselves to preserve our sense of worth and integrity (Sherman & Cohen, 2002). In other words, we focus our thoughts on attitudes that make us feel good about ourselves. In several experiments, participants who have just been reminded of attitudes or values they hold that are viewed positively in society (the "self-affirmed" condition) exhibit less stress (Creswell et al., 2005) and are better at problem solving (Creswell, Dutcher, Klein, Harris, & Levine, 2013), and women show higher satisfaction with their body types (Buccianeri & Corning, 2012).

Self-affirmation theory: The idea that individuals try to impress themselves to preserve their sense of worth and integrity; they focus their thoughts and attitudes on what makes them feel good about themselves.

Attitudes and the Theory of Planned Behavior

Whether attitudes really predict behavior started to make more sense when Ajzen and Fishbein (1980; see also Fishbein & Cappella, 2006) proposed the **theory of planned behavior**. The theory slowed the wildly swinging pendulum about the utility of attitudes by putting them in their proper place. This theory suggests that attitudes are only one of three categories of belief—attitudes, subjective norms, and perceived control—that together predict behavioral intentions. These intentions, in turn, predict behavior (see Figure 6.2). In short, attitudes are just one of three categories of reasons that predict how we will behave.

Subjective Norms and Perceived Control.

Armed with these several new insights, social psychologists discovered that specific intentions predicted specific behaviors such as underage drinking (Lac, Crano, Berger, & Alvaro, 2013), leaving abusive partners (Edwards, Gidycz, & Murphy, 2015), committing digital piracy (Yoon, 2011), and academic cheating by college students (DeVries & Ajzen, 1971). For example, you may have a negative *attitude* toward cheating but be more likely to cheat if you perceive that cheating is the *subjective social norm* ("everyone else is cheating—so I might as well do it too") and if you think that you can get away with it (*perceived control*). The theory of planned behavior helped restore the importance of attitudes as a powerful—but now qualified—predictor of behavior.

For example, the American problem with obesity has not, it appears, arrived in Durango, Colorado, where people have a very positive attitude toward fitness. But attitudes are not the only reason for a town full of healthy-looking people. In Durango, fitness is also the social norm, and it is fairly easy to control your fitness when opportunities for healthy recreation beckon around every corner and from every beautiful mountaintop. In the right setting, even someone with a relatively negative attitude about healthy living and eating might become fit if that person thinks (a) everyone else has a healthy lifestyle (subjective norms) and (b) it's easy to get fit in a town full of outdoor activities and organic grocery stores (perceived control).

Perceived control has a rich history in psychological research (Rotter, 1954, 1990). Adler (1930) described control of our environment as "an intrinsic necessity of life itself" (p. 398). Bettelheim (1943) linked at least a minimal sense of control as critical to surviving a concentration camp. Seligman (1975) connected learned helplessness (the perceived loss of control) to clinical depression. Langer and Rodin demonstrated that feeling in control helped residents of a nursing home live longer, more active lives (see Langer & Rodin, 1976; Rodin & Langer, 1977a, 1977b; Ubbiali et al., 2008). Others have linked loss of control to increased rates of disease and death (Schmale & Iker, 1966).

Three Predictors Are Better Than One.

One fascinating example of how the theory of planned behavior can explain outcomes in the "real world" comes from the Vietnam War. A Department of Defense study (Robins, 1974, 1993) quantified

Ask the Experts: Christian Klöckner on the Theory of Planned Behavior

©SAGE Publications

■ FIGURE 6.2 Three factors predict our intentions and, thus, our behaviors.

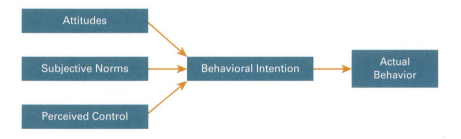

Theory of planned behavior: The idea that attitudes are only one of three categories of belief—attitudes, subjective norms, and perceived control—that together predict behavioral intentions, which then predict behavior.

During war, soldiers sometimes use drugs for recreation or to avoid facing the reality of their current situation.

what returning veterans had been telling people about their experience in Vietnam: Drug use by U.S. soldiers was rampant. Forty-five percent of Army enlisted men had tried narcotics, 34% had used heroin, and 38% had used opium. Over 90% had used alcohol and almost 80% had used marijuana. In short, a large proportion of the American army in Vietnam was stoned—and not just occasionally. One in five soldiers reported that they were addicted to narcotics.

However, the army was also surprised that relatively few returning veterans relapsed into drug use when they got home: only 5% after 1 year and only 12% after 3 years (Blomqvist, 2007). Had the soldiers' favorable attitude toward narcotic use magically changed when they got on the airplane home? The theory of planned behavior explains that attitudes are only one piece of the puzzle when it comes to predicting drug addiction. The soldiers' attitude toward narcotic use probably didn't change very much when they came home. Opium still provided a welcome escape; heroin still felt good; the soldiers' bodies were accustomed to having the drugs. What changed?

For one thing, the social norms in Vietnam encouraged use of narcotics—but that changed when the soldiers got home—even during the infamous "hippie era" of the 1960s and early 1970s. Veterans were no longer living with people using narcotics every day. In addition, perceived control was low. In Vietnam, the cost of addiction to a pure version of opium or heroin was only about $6.00 per day, so getting stoned was easy, cheap, and convenient. But it was more difficult for veterans to get stoned when they got back home. Subjective social norms and inconvenience appeared to be more influential than attitudes when it came to predicting drug use.

So—do attitudes predict behavior? Attitudes are important for predicting what people will do, just not quite as important as was first believed.

The Main Ideas

- There are many types of attitudes, but they always evaluate some attitude object and come from affect (emotions), cognition (beliefs), and behaviors.

- Attitudes help us make rapid, uni-valenced decisions about attitude objects.

- The discovery that attitudes do not reliably predict behavior led to three insights: (a) the specificity principle, (b) behavior sometimes leads to attitudes, and (c) attitudes sometimes reflect impression management tactics and strategies.

- The theory of planned behavior clarified that our behavioral intentions are influenced by attitudes, subjective norms, and perceived control.

⚡ CRITICAL THINKING CHALLENGE

- Name three attitude objects (a person, a place, and an idea) about which you have some version of a dual attitude, such as a love-hate attitude toward a person who both attracts and repels you. Specify what makes these attitudes dual attitudes.

- Think about deceiving your friends, family, or boss by pretending to agree with them when really you don't. What is the balance between simply appearing to be agreeable or trying to avoid a nasty fight and being authentic and honest? In what situations is impression management acceptable versus unacceptable?

- Which of the following is the best predictor of your intention to donate your organs when you die: attitude, subjective norms, or perceived control? Have you indicated on your driver's license that you are an organ donor? If not, why not?

FROM WHERE DO ATTITUDES COME?

LO 6.2: Evaluate how nature and nurture interact to form particular attitudes.

Here's a question that can keep you busy for the rest of your life: Does your behavior come from nature (your inherited biology, genes, hormones, etc.) or from nurture (the social environment, how you were raised, and your life experiences)? As we discussed in Chapter 1, the familiar phrase "the nature-nurture debate" is unfortunate because it suggests that any behavior or attitude can be traced back either to its biological/genetic source ("nature") *or* to its social/environmental source ("nurture").

But the sources of behavior and of attitudes are seldom just nature or just nurture. For example, if you root for a sports team, why do you root for that particular team? We are unlikely ever to find a gene, set of genes, or even a gene trigger that exclusively explains the fan enthusiasm displayed by people living in Wisconsin for their Green Bay Packers football team. We might find an inherited genetic predisposition to support and protect one's own group in general. But if a Green Bay Packers fan had lived only in Chicago, he or she probably would have rooted for the Chicago Bears to beat the Green Bay Packers. Both nature and nurture are at work in the formation of attitudes that we carry around with us every day.

Nature and Nurture Interact: Twin Studies

One way that nature and nurture interact is through **assortative mating**, the process by which organisms that are similar tend to mate with each other. Even though we have the saying "opposites attract," for the most part, it's actually similarity that brings people together. For example, imagine that many years ago, a young couple, both in their 20s, fell in love after meeting in the bleachers at Wrigley Field while rooting for the Chicago Cubs baseball team.

In terms of nature, they were biologically at an age when they were prepared to meet and mate with somebody. In terms of nurture, they also have a lot in common. They live in the Chicago area, buy cheap tickets, and have maintained loyalty for a team that, until 2016, played the role of "loveable losers." Assortative mating brings people together, but it's difficult to tell how much influence biology (nature) versus the environment (nurture) has on the blossoming

Our tendency to adorn ourselves and publicly display group membership is probably a product of both genetic instinct (nature) and social conformity and norms (nurture).

Children often show a natural tendency to model the behaviors of their parents, which is one example of social learning theory.

new relationship. Fortunately, there is a way to estimate how much of attitudes is due to nature and nurture.

Twin studies, in which sets of twins can be compared to each other, can help quantify the interacting influences of nature and nurture on attitude formation. For example, Klump, McGue, and Iacono (2003) compared eating attitudes between 11-year-old twins and 17-year-old twins. They found that, among the younger children, the genetic influence on eating disorders was 0%. However, among the adolescents, the genetic influence on eating disorders jumped to 54%. In this case, the genetic influence on food intake appeared to be activated during puberty, possibly due to changes in the hormone estradiol (Butera, Wojcik, & Clough, 2010; Klump, Keel, Sisk, & Burt, 2010). The interacting variable was stage of development.

Attitudes toward different attitude objects (romance, religion, food, and politics) all tell the same general story about nature and nurture: There is a whole lot of interacting going on! The influence of nature and nurture may vary with different attitude objects. It seems that while many of our attitudes are influenced by our life circumstances, at least some of them are strongly influenced by our biological destiny. For example, Kandler, Bleidorn, and Riemann (2012) used twin studies to explore **political orientation**, an attitude that would appear to lean heavily toward the nurture side of the debate. But they also found that personality dispositions shaped by our genetic inheritance influence political attitudes. Once again, there's a whole lot of interacting goin' on.

Attitudes Come From Experience

"Don't make me turn this car around!"

Many parents report the odd experience of saying things to their children that sound almost exactly in word and tone what their parents once said to them. Even when this disturbing event occurs, we aren't sure whether our replication of what our parents said is nature (our parents certainly contributed their genes) or nurture (we may have learned how to be a parent from observing them). Most of psychology has focused on the nurture side of the debate, and we can offer insight into how "nurture" or experience leads to attitudes from three separate lines of research: social learning (learning by observing others), classical conditioning (learning by experiencing associations), and operant conditioning (learning from experiencing consequences).

Social Learning Theory. **Social learning theory** proposes that we learn attitudes by observing and imitating others (Bandura, 1977; Perry & Bussey, 1979). One research team (Morgan, Movius, & Cody, 2009), for example, found that people showed more positive attitudes toward organ donation after viewing four television shows featuring characters in need of organ transplants: *CSI: NY, Numb3rs, House,* and *Grey's Anatomy.* Furthermore, the effect was more pronounced if the viewers had become emotionally involved in the storyline.

Another study about social learning showed that college students studying engineering became increasingly negative toward female engineers after more exposure to the field—and this was true of both male and female engineering students (Yoshida, Peach, Zanna, & Spencer, 2012). Exposure to attitudes around us can influence what we think. Social learning also might help explain the increasing acceptance of marijuana

Assortative mating: The process by which organisms that are similar tend to mate with each other, meaning an individual is more likely to mate with someone who shares his or her features and interests (see *similarity-attraction hypothesis*).

Political orientation: An attitude held by an individual concerning matters of politics and government often characterized by the possession of liberal or conservative ideas.

Social learning theory: A model for understanding social behavior that proposes that we learn attitudes by observing and imitating others.

Fast food and soda companies are well known for commercials in which models and actresses consume their products in "sexy" ways. The companies hope you'll transfer any positive feelings toward the models to their product—an example of classical conditioning.

as a recreational drug over the past 30 years in the United States. Likewise, social learning theory predicts that the increased acceptance of same-sex marriage and the rights of transgender individuals should increase with greater acceptance and as people increasingly grow up in a world where these issues are not considered taboo.

Classical Conditioning.

Attitudes are also acquired when we learn to associate one thing in the environment with another due to personal experience, a process called **classical conditioning**. Advertisers have long known, for example, that humor enhances a consumer's attitude both to the advertisement and to the brands shown (Chung & Zhao, 2003; Gelb & Zinkhan, 1986; Lee & Mason, 1999). Once the reward network in the brain has us laughing, or at least amused, positive associations can take place—sometimes below the level of our awareness (Strick, van Baaren, Holland, & van Knippenberg, 2009). In other words, we might feel positive and happy about a product not because of the product itself but because we have learned an association between that product and happiness due to exposure to commercials.

You've probably also heard the famous phrase, "Sex sells," but does exposure to certain body types in advertising lead to attitudes other than a strange attraction to the product? At least one study says yes. Researchers *randomly assigned* some women to complete a computer task in which they were led to associate very thin models with the words "false, phony, artificial, sham, and bogus" and "normal"-sized models with the words "natural, true, genuine, authentic, and sincere" (Martijn et al., 2013, p. 435). Compared to women in a *control group* who didn't receive the training, women who had the classical conditioning training found the very thin models to be less ideal and were more satisfied with their own bodies.

Operant Conditioning.

Operant conditioning is the process of learning to predict outcomes of given behaviors based on the outcomes we've experienced for those same behaviors in the past. If a certain behavior is rewarded, you'll be more likely to do it again; if that behavior is punished, you'll be less likely to repeat it—because you assume the same consequence might occur.

Classical conditioning: A process that occurs when individuals learn to associate one thing in their environment with another due to personal experience.

Operant conditioning: A process that occurs when individuals learn to predict the outcomes of given behaviors based on the outcomes they've experienced for those same behaviors in the past.

If people laugh at your jokes, for example, then you are more likely to use humor and eventually develop a self-attitude that you are a good joke-teller. If you get compliments on your luxuriant hair, you'll have a positive attitude toward your shampoo brand. Adolescents have a more positive attitude toward drinking alcohol when they believe drinking is rewarded by popularity and more party invitations (Goldstein, Wall, Wekerle, & Krank, 2013). Attitudes learned from operant conditioning—because they have led to rewards in the past—are particularly strong and persistent over time (Davies, 1982; Guenther & Alicke, 2008; Slusher & Anderson, 1989).

Applying Attitude Acquisition to Real Life. These three principles of learning are fairly easy to understand. However, applying them to the complicated situations that make up our daily lives is more difficult. For example, in one of his last letters home (published in the book *Last Letters Home*) before he became one of the American casualties of the war in Iraq, 29-year-old Captain Joshua Byers (2004) described one of his

> soldiers calming down a little girl (probably 2 or 3 years old)—cute as a button + crying her head off—as you can imagine. We get one candy per a week (on average) . . . and he was giving her his candy bar, feeding it to her a piece at a time until she stopped crying. He did that just moments after being shot at and shooting men in this girl's house, probably her Dad and brothers/cousins. It really touched me. (p. 34)

Fear of soldiers would certainly be one of the attitudes classically conditioned by bullets whizzing through this little girl's home—a natural fear of bullets and death would come to be associated with anyone in a soldier's uniform. Now this brave soldier was trying to recondition her with operant conditioning; if she learns that approaching soldiers is rewarded with kindness and chocolate, her attitude might change. This more positive attitude would be stronger if she could use social learning by observing other children having positive interactions with soldiers. The battle for hearts and minds is not an easy one to win, especially when contradictory forms of conditioning are taking place.

The Main Ideas

- Attitudes come from both nature and nurture interacting together; twin studies can help us understand this interaction more precisely.

- On the nurture (or experience) side, we acquire specific attitudes through social learning, classical conditioning, and operant conditioning.

- Applying the principles of learning in the real world is more complex than what we can isolate in a laboratory setting.

⚡ CRITICAL THINKING CHALLENGE

- Select any two of the following attitude objects and describe how both nature and nurture might influence its development, maintenance, and strength: binge drinking, studying statistics, flying in an airplane, participating in extreme sports, and sexual promiscuity.

- Identify a product that you feel either positively or negatively toward not because of the product itself but because of an association you have with it. The association might be due to a commercial, a memory you have of using the product, and so on. Explain how classical conditioning led to your attitude toward the product.

- Operant conditioning predicts that some of your attitudes exist because you have been rewarded for having them or have been punished for not having them. Can you identify any examples of this from your own life? Further, can you identify a time when your attitude has changed due to social consequences or pressure from others?

HOW ARE ATTITUDES MEASURED?

LO 6.3: Illustrate why attitudes need to be measured both directly and indirectly.

Brenda Ambrose's child attended the Little Rascals daycare center in Edenton, North Carolina—but Brenda herself also worked there. She told *FRONTLINE,* "I still lie awake at night thinking how could they have done it with me in the room right across the hall?" Nevertheless, she sent her son to therapy and became convinced that he must have been molested. At the same time, Brenda was also aware of the town's pervasive paranoia as her long-time friends and neighbors developed negative attitudes without any regard for the evidence. Like the confused citizens of Salem who murdered their minister, Brenda had complicated, contradictory dual attitudes toward the supposed scandal at Little Rascals.

To measure such attitudes accurately, we must recognize the rich complexity of the beliefs that support those attitudes. There are two general strategies for measuring attitudes. A direct approach is needed when measuring explicit attitudes; an indirect approach is appropriate when measuring implicit attitudes.

Direct Measures of Explicit Attitudes

Do you always tell the truth (the whole truth and nothing but the truth)? Probably not. But that is the assumption when we present people with many scales intended to measure attitudes. The direct approach to measuring explicit attitudes looks deceptively easy and can be described as, "Just ask."

In psychology research, this approach often comes in the form of *self-report* measures, or surveys people take in which they simply answer questions about their beliefs. Most of the chapters in this book feature self-report measures so you can score yourself on one of the variables discussed in that section. This works fine if people are both (a) able and (b) willing to tell us the truth, the whole truth, and nothing but the truth about what they believe—but as we discussed in Chapter 2, that's a big "if." And even when people are able and willing to self-report all their beliefs, it is still an enormous amount of work to measure those attitudes.

Social Desirability and the Bogus Pipeline. The simple-sounding "just ask" approach to measuring attitudes requires a lot of work. Even when you use a *valid* and *reliable* scale, self-report measures can still have a problem, summed up by one of our students after she asked some of her friends to participate in a survey. "They're lying," she reported bluntly to the class. "I know these people, and they were just trying make themselves look good." We will keep running into this *social desirability bias* (described earlier in Chapter 2) because it is one of the main difficulties when studying human behavior.

In an effort to circumvent social desirability, psychologists sometimes use a **bogus pipeline**, a fake lie detector machine. We tell people, or at least give them the impression, that we can use some device as a metaphorical pipeline to the truth about what they believe. In plainer language, we lie to them about our ability to detect when they

Bogus pipeline: A fake lie detector machine used to circumvent social desirability bias.

are lying to scare them into telling us the truth. A bogus pipeline could be a large, impressive-looking machine with lots of dials and electrical cords. However, it doesn't matter what a bogus pipeline actually looks like as long as people believe that we (the researchers) can tell if they are lying.

The bogus pipeline does seem to scare some people into telling the truth some of the time. For example, it seemed to work—on average—with some child molesters because they told different stories when they were *randomly assigned* to a fake lie detector condition rather than to a straightforward questionnaire (Gannon, Keown, & Polaschek, 2007). However, the bogus pipeline did not seem to work in a study comparing what people told researchers about their use of alcohol and marijuana (Aguinis, Pierce, & Quigley, 1995). In another study, being hooked up to a bogus pipeline had more of an effect when college students were asked about romantic cheating than when they were asked about academic cheating (Fisher & Brunell, 2014). Consequently, researchers have looked for additional ways to capture what is going on beneath the surface of our attitudes.

Indirect Measures of Implicit Attitudes

For social psychologists, the indirect approach to measuring attitudes seems to be particularly useful under two circumstances. The first is when people might not want to admit to their true attitudes. The second is when we are trying to assess beliefs that participants can't articulate or are not aware of—in other words, implicit attitudes. For example, you may never have realized you felt a certain way about a group of people until you started to feel nervous and awkward around them.

The Implicit Associations Test (IAT).

Probably the most famous—and controversial—indirect measure of implicit attitudes is the Implicit Associations Test (IAT). You may recall first learning about the IAT in Chapter 3. The "Applying Social Psychology to Your Life" feature tells you how to experience the IAT for yourself. Greenwald et al. (2002) used reaction times to measure our automatic, unconscious associations that we may have acquired earlier in our lives through, for example, exposure to prejudiced messages in our culture (Bargh & Williams, 2006; Thaler & Sunstein, 2008). If we were asked directly, then we might not *explicitly* endorse or agree with any those prejudiced assumptions, but they still are part of our private network of mental associations.

For example, in the early history of television, portrayals of African Americans were almost exclusively negative or demeaning. For the children growing up with those images, the messages may have led to subtle but persistent mental associations between African Americans and negative stereotypes. The IAT is a way to measure whether those associations exist in a given person and how strong they are. For example, do any particular ethnic groups come *immediately* to mind as you read each list in Table 6.2?

■ TABLE 6.2 Associations Toward Ethnic Groups

Ethnic Group 1	Ethnic Group 2
criminal	responsible
lazy	industrious
unemployed	hard-working
dangerous	reliable
untrustworthy	trustworthy

SOURCE: Goodfriend (2012).

Want to experience the IAT for yourself? Just follow these instructions:

1. Go to the IAT website: https://implicit.harvard.edu/implicit/

2. On the left side of the screen ("social attitudes"), make sure the little flag matches your situation, and then click the orange "go" box.

3. Read the disclaimer, then click "I wish to proceed" at the bottom of the page.

4. Choose any test that is of interest to you (you'll see several choices)! Follow the links and instructions you are given to complete the test. Note that after you are done, you'll get to compare your score to the thousands of other people who have taken the same test you did.

How does the IAT test measure the strength of these associations when we're not even aware that we have them? Participants sitting in front of a computer screen are asked to complete sorting tasks. In the first task, they see pictures of people from different ethnicities and simply sort them by pressing one key for Category 1 (such as "African American") and a different key for Category 2 (such as "Asian American"). Next, they are given words to sort that are from the first list above (generally "bad" words) or from the second list (generally "good" words).

Here's where the IAT starts to do its work. In the next task, participants see all of the faces and words again, one at a time, but in a random order (it might be face, face, word, face, word, word). The genius of the IAT is that the sorting tasks will be paired together—participants are asked to press the "a" key on a computer for *either* African American faces or bad words and to press the "l" key for *either* Asian faces or good words. Then, they have to do the entire task again but with the keys mixed up: Now, press the "a" key for *either* Asian faces or bad words, and press the "l" key for *either* African American or good words.

Scores on the IAT are calculated based on how quickly people associate certain words (such as "criminal") with certain images (such as the faces of people from different ethnic backgrounds). If the participants have an implicit attitude that African Americans are more likely to have the negative traits on the list, then this "association" will come out with faster response times. Over thousands of participants, results from the IAT show that most people show at least small signs of unconscious stereotypes—even when they don't explicitly agree with these stereotypes.

The IAT has been criticized because rapid mental associations do not necessarily predict actual prejudiced behavior (Blanton et al., 2009). In addition, several studies have questioned whether implicit associations lead to any meaningful outcomes beyond the difference of a few milliseconds on a strange computer task. That said, many social psychologists believe the IAT captures something important about our automatic beliefs, even if it's just measuring someone's exposure to cultural prejudices. The IAT is only one of several indirect ways of measuring implicit attitudes (Jordan, Spencer, & Zanna, 2005; Sheldon, King, Houser-Marko, Osbaldiston, & Gunz, 2007).

The Main Ideas

- There are two general strategies for measuring attitudes: a direct approach (for explicit attitudes) and an indirect approach (for implicit attitudes).

- The bogus pipeline is a measurement technique that tries to circumvent the problem of the social desirability bias for self-report measures by pretending to be a lie detector.

- The Implicit Association Test (IAT) is one way to measure implicit attitudes; it measures the strength of evaluative associations through reaction times on a computer task.

Social Psychology in Action:
Festinger's Cognitive
Dissonance Study

©SAGE Publications

⚡ CRITICAL THINKING CHALLENGE

- Think of your least favorite fast-food restaurant and create a short, five-item self-report attitude scale that directly measures explicit attitudes toward that particular fast-food restaurant. You might try writing statements that people can either agree or disagree with. Now think about why you do—and do not—trust the results of your scale.

- Think of two reasons to *not* trust the results of an IAT. Now go one step further: How would *you* go about measuring attitudes toward something that people were reluctant to talk about? In other words, what would be a better way to measure implicit attitudes?

AN INGENIOUS METHOD TO CREATE COGNITIVE DISSONANCE

Spotlight on Research Methods

Leon Festinger's classic and famous study on cognitive dissonance used a creative and clever methodology (Festinger & Carlsmith, 1959). College students were asked to complete an extremely boring task for several minutes: turning knobs over and over. Then, the experimenter asked them for a favor: Would they mind telling the next participant (who was actually a *confederate,* a researcher pretending to be a participant) that the task was super exciting and fun? Participants were told they would be paid for telling the lie, but here's where the experimental manipulation came in (the *independent variable*): Half were given $1 for telling the lie; the other half were given $20. After the participant had lied, they were then asked to report their true feelings about the task. How much fun was it really to turn those knobs?

Most people don't like to think of themselves as liars. When we're offered $20 for a simple lie that doesn't seem to do much harm, though, we can easily tell ourselves that

we're willing to lie for $20; we have *sufficient justification.* Here, we're not particularly motivated to believe in our own lie; dissonance is very low. However, consider the mind-set of people who were only paid $1 to tell a lie. A dollar isn't much—so if you're willing to tell a lie for only $1, what kind of person are you? Most of us wouldn't want to believe that we're willing to lie to an innocent stranger for a measly $1, an idea that Festinger and Carlsmith (1959) called *insufficient justification.*

Lying for just $1 creates cognitive dissonance. We've already told the lie, so how can we avoid even more anxiety and discomfort at this violation of our self-concept? The simple solution is to tell ourselves that hey, it's not a lie . . . turning those knobs was actually kind of fun after all! Festinger and Carlsmith found that the participants in the $1 condition were more likely to convince themselves that the boring task really was enjoyable. Their higher levels of cognitive dissonance led to attitude change.

HOW DOES COGNITIVE DISSONANCE INFLUENCE ATTITUDES?

■■■ LO 6.4: Explain how cognitive dissonance motivates self-justification and attitude change.

How do terrorists sleep peacefully at night? And how do the Somali soldiers who assaulted women, buried them up to their necks, and then stoned them to death for refusing to marry them (Gettleman, 2011) eat breakfast the next morning without self-loathing? Is it the same mental-emotional process that an office worker uses to bring home an "extra" thumb drive or that students use to cheat only "lightly" on a test? In short, how do we justify actions we know are unethical?

Self-justification is the desire to explain one's actions in a way that preserves or enhances a positive view of the self. And the engine of self-justification that leads us to change our attitudes—not always for the better—is **cognitive dissonance**, a state of psychological discomfort that occurs when we try to maintain conflicting beliefs and behaviors (Festinger, 1957; Tavris & Aronson, 2007). Festinger's research methodology to create and measure cognitive dissonance in participants is one of the most famous studies in social psychology; to learn the details, see the Spotlight on Research Methods feature.

Cognitive Dissonance Motivates Attitude Change

When Festinger introduced the theory of cognitive dissonance, he framed his theory around a curious historical question: What did believers in religious cults do when their prophecies failed to come true? Festinger (1957) was fascinated by the idea that many followers in doomsday cults often become *more* committed when their leaders' prophecies fail.

Logically, that doesn't make sense, but history shows that it's happened over and over again. Prominent examples of failed prophecies of Jesus' return occurred in Turkey (in the second century), Germany (in 1533), among some Jewish believers (in 1648), and in the United States (in 1844). Each time, when Jesus failed to appear, at least some portion of the prophecy believers became more, not less, committed to their groups (Nichol, 1944).

Believers in alien cults display the same pattern. One group of believers expected an alien named Sananda to save them from a world-ending flood by sending flying saucers (Festinger, Riecken, & Schachter, 1956/2008). The cult's leader, Mrs. Keech, named December 21, 1954, as the doomsday date. Members of this group performed strange rituals as they prepared for Sananda's return. Some lost their jobs and huddled together as they waited. One member noted, "I've cut every tie, I've burned every bridge . . . I can't afford to doubt" (p. 170).

December 21 came . . . and went. There were no floods, flying saucers, or aliens. The cult's leader, however, claimed that she then received a message from Sananda that the little group's sturdy faith had saved the world! The believers started calling reporters to share

Self-justification: The desire to explain one's actions in a way that preserves or enhances a positive view of the self.

Cognitive dissonance: A state of psychological discomfort that occurs when an individual tries to maintain conflicting beliefs and behaviors.

Marian Keech (a.k.a. Dorothy Martin) led a group who believed aliens would save them from a world-ending flood on December 21, 1954.

The Watergate scandal, which occurred during President Nixon's time in office, is often used an example of how group dynamics lead to poor decisions.

the good news. When the original prophecy failed, the believers could have resolved their cognitive dissonance by changing their attitudes to disbelief and leaving the group—and some did. But they also could resolve their dissonance by *increasing* their faith in the cult's beliefs. Some chose the latter option—possibly to avoid the dissonance (and embarrassment?) of having to admit they were wrong.

Some researchers have suggested that cognitive dissonance has influenced the course of human history. Tavris and Aronson (2007) perceived cognitive dissonance at work in President Lyndon Johnson's stubborn justification for continuing to commit American troops to Vietnam, to President Richard Nixon's desperate justifications for the Watergate affair, and to President George W. Bush's ever-shifting justifications for invading Iraq after failing to discover weapons of mass destruction. These researchers (Tavris & Aronson, 2007) concluded that self-justification leads to "foolish beliefs, bad decisions, and hurtful acts." They even identified the distinctive language marker (the passive voice) that public officials use to admit fault without taking blame: "Mistakes were made" with the silent implication "but not by me."

For example, during the Watergate hearings, it became painfully obvious that President Nixon was guilty of lying, obstructing justice, deceiving Congress, and trying to bribe his way out of trouble. President Nixon eventually resigned from office but never admitted to his guilt. During the scandal, people who had voted for Nixon persevered with their positive beliefs about Nixon while people who had voted for his opponent, George McGovern, became more negative in their beliefs about Nixon (Carretta & Moreland, 1982; see Reston, 2007). Their previous support for Nixon made people experience cognitive dissonance when their candidate didn't do well, so justification kicked in and they defended their beliefs even more.

Beware of the Rationalization Trap

Cherry-picking data occurs when people select only the data that support what they want to believe and ignore contradicting data. That's why Festinger turned from historical data to controlled laboratory settings such as the famous lie-telling experiment in the Spotlight on Research feature. On the other hand, the little lies that researchers get participants to tell in a laboratory are not as consequential as hanging people for witchcraft, sending innocent daycare workers to jail, or miscalculating the date of the apocalypse. But self-justifications don't begin as big lies. We get seduced by telling ourselves little lies that grow bigger with more elaborate justifications.

Vohra and Singh (2005) refer to this as a "mental trap," but Pratkanis and Aronson (2001) are blunter and call the same idea a **rationalization trap**—progressively larger self-justifications that lead to harmful, stupid, and immoral outcomes. Rationalizing might explain why American soldiers who actually killed Iraqis during that conflict were more likely to believe the war was beneficial to *both* countries, compared to soldiers who didn't have to kill people (Wayne et al., 2011).

Cherry-picking data: Occurs when people select only the data that support what they want to believe and ignore contradicting data.

Rationalization trap: Progressively larger self-justifications that lead to harmful, stupid, and immoral outcomes.

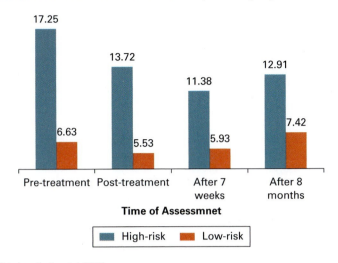

■ FIGURE 6.3 Bulimia scores before and after experiencing cognitive dissonance.

SOURCE: Data from Becker et al. (2008).

You might be tempted to think that cognitive dissonance is a bad thing—but it can lead people to change their attitudes in positive ways. For example, public health researchers videotaped teenagers giving advice to other teenagers about how to increase their fruit and vegetable intake. The teenagers who gave that advice ended up improving both their own diets and their self-concepts (Wilson et al., 2002). Likewise, some sorority sisters experienced dissonance when they were required to publicly speak out against the thin ideal of female appearance. They reduced their bulimic behaviors. Moreover, Figure 6.3 shows us that for high-risk participants, cognitive dissonance continued to reduce their bulimia-related behaviors 8 months later (Becker, Bull, Schaumberg, Cauble, & Franco, 2008).

Individual, Situational, and Cultural Differences in Dissonance

Some of the people in Mrs. Keech's alien doomsday group abandoned her when her prophecies failed; others stayed on. There are individual differences in how much dissonance we can stand before we abandon a treasured belief (Stone & Cooper, 2001).

Some researchers try to explain such differences by emphasizing the emotions involved in dissonance (Guild, Strickland, & Barefoot, 1977). Extroverts can tolerate more dissonance than introverts (Matz, Hofstedt, & Wood, 2008), as do people with more symptoms of being a psychopath (Murray, Wood, & Lilienfeld, 2012). Situations also matter; we're more likely to experience dissonance when we're worried about being perceived as a hypocrite (Aronson, 1999) or when our self-concept is threatened (Steele, 1988).

Festinger also anticipated that culture influences dissonance, and subsequent research has supported his hunch. Mealy, Stephan, and Urrutia (2007) compared attitudes toward six different types of lies among Euro-American and Ecuadorian college students. Overall, Euro-Americans rated lying as more acceptable than Ecuadorians, but people in both cultures rated lying to an out-group as more acceptable than lying to their in-group. Culture also influenced dissonance when Kitayama and colleagues found that *in*dependent-minded Americans experienced dissonance when their personal sense of competency was threatened. By contrast, *inter*dependent-minded Asians experienced more dissonance when they were threatened with group rejection (Kitayama, Snibbe, Markus, & Suzuki, 2004).

These cultural differences in dissonance reflect how different cultures conceive of the self. The ideal (individually oriented) self in a Western culture is very different from the ideal (group-oriented) self in an East Asian culture (Hoshino-Browne et al., 2005; Markus & Kitayama, 1991; Triandis, 1989, 1996). They both experience dissonance that motivates them to change their attitudes, but what they experience as dissonant varies from one culture to the next.

The Main Ideas

- Cognitive dissonance (incompatible thoughts, feelings, and behaviors) creates a discomfort that motivates us to change our attitudes, often through self-justification.

- Experimental tests of cognitive dissonance use research to explain patterns Festinger identified in historical examples of failed prophecies.

- Cognitive dissonance can be applied in ways that lead to positive therapeutic outcomes.

- Individual and group differences in cognitive dissonance suggest that the degree of dissonance we experience depends, in part, on cultural differences in how we conceive of the self.

 CRITICAL THINKING CHALLENGE

- Identify three fictional villains who use self-justification to resolve cognitive dissonance they may feel regarding their evil deeds. In other words, how do these three villains avoid feeling guilty about their actions (and avoid feeling badly about themselves) by justifying what they do?

- Discuss why historical evidence is not sufficient to establish a scientific principle. Why are controlled studies needed for social psychological theory and conclusions?

- Which would be more upsetting: being rejected by a graduate school that accepted three of your friends or being told that you had failed to qualify for graduate school because your standardized test scores were too low? What does your answer suggest about your cultural values of independence versus interdependence?

HOW DO ATTITUDES CHANGE?

LO 6.5: Analyze two distinct paths to persuasion.

Changing attitudes isn't easy. There were many points in the Little Rascals daycare case when the prosecutors, the townspeople, and even the jury could have changed their minds due to the lack of physical evidence and the sheer implausibility of the charges. What techniques might psychology have suggested to help change the jurors' and judges' minds?

There Are Two Paths to Persuasion

There is something both ordinary and ominous about the science of deliberately changing other people's attitudes. Think of all the ordinary people who would be out of work if they didn't believe they could change other people's attitudes. There would be no more politicians, preachers, or prostitutes—they are all in the persuasion business. The advertising industry would also disappear. Professors would stop harping about critical thinking, and it would be pointless trying to impress a potential romantic partner about how wonderful you are. To be an ordinary, successful, social animal, we humans must be able to persuade and be persuaded.

Inoculation Against Persuasion. But there is also something ominous about the science of persuasion: We can manipulate people to behave in ways that benefit us but may harm them or society. So, how do we (a) change one another's beliefs and (b) resist being changed? Building up resistance to attempts at persuading us is called **attitude inoculation.**

McGuire (1964) identified several ways to inoculate people to resist messages attempting to persuade them: People can (a) think of examples from their own lives that contradict the message; (b) read counterarguments provided to them, to get them started down the path of resistance; and (c) generate their own counterarguments. The strategic goal in inoculation against persuasion is to get people to psychologically "own" their counterarguments (Lewan & Stotland, 1961). As you read through this next section, notice how studies of persuasion attempts are often balanced with studies about how to resist persuasion.

The Elaboration Likelihood Model (ELM) and the Heuristic-Systematic Model (HSM). The next ideas describe two ways we can be persuaded to change our minds. One is direct; the other sort of sneaks up on you.

Advertisers use both approaches—and so do lovers, religious evangelists, people selling steak knives, and professors. The direct approach says, "Think! Here are seven reasons to buy Brand X toothpaste: (1) It will make your teeth brighter. (2) You'll have fewer cavities. (3) . . . ." The indirect approach is more like a magician using indirection: You see a commercial in which two lonely people start using Brand X toothpaste. As their teeth brighten, so does their romantic interest in one another. Brand X is never mentioned in the dialogue, but the logo is embedded in the visual story. The advertiser is using emotions and beautiful people to sell you on the product.

The **elaboration likelihood model (ELM)** proposes these same two routes or paths to persuasion: a direct, explicit, "central" route (which requires "elaboration" or deliberate thinking about the logic behind arguments) and an indirect, implicit, "peripheral" route (that sort of sneaks up on you based on other aspects of the message, like emotional appeals). The main difference is the amount of effort needed to process the persuasive message (Petty & Cacioppo, 1986; see Monroe & Read, 2008). A similar model, the **heuristic-systematic model (HSM)** (Chaiken, 1980; Chen & Chaiken, 1999), uses slightly different language but proposes the same two distinct paths to persuasion: a direct, systematic path to persuasion and an indirect, heuristic path to persuasion (see Petty & Wegener, 1998).

Both persuasion models make the same prediction: If we have high motivation and the ability to think logically, then we'll be persuaded by direct, logical arguments. If we have low motivation or ability, then we're more likely to be persuaded by indirect, heuristic cues toward one opinion or another. Professional persuaders don't care which method they use; they only want to use the one that works.

Applying the Persuasion Model to the Courtroom. Imagine you're on the jury for the Little Rascals case about accusations of child sex abuse at a daycare. Two lawyers are trying to persuade you to see their side of the story. Some of your fellow jurors will rely on logical reasoning and physical evidence and be open to complicated explanations for motive and opportunity. These types of arguments follow the direct,

Attitude inoculation: The process of building up resistance to attempts at persuasion.

Elaboration likelihood model (ELM): A model for understanding how an individual can be persuaded that proposes that there are two paths to persuasion: a direct, explicit, "central" route that requires deliberate, logical thinking and an indirect, implicit, "peripheral" route that relies on emotional appeals (see *heuristic-systematic model*).

Heuristic-systematic model (HSM): A model for understanding how an individual can be persuaded, which proposes that there are two paths to persuasion: a direct, systematic path and an indirect, heuristic path (see *elaboration likelihood model*).

Social Psychology in Popular Culture

Everett Collection, Inc. / Alamy Stock Photo & Everett Collection, Inc. / Alamy Stock Photo

In the comedic *My Cousin Vinny* (Launer et al., 1992) a rookie lawyer named Vinny from New York has to defend his younger cousin in a small-town Southern court. Vinny doesn't fit into the culture at all and thus can't use a peripheral approach. His accent, New York personality, and leather outfits don't send heuristic messages of credibility to the jury; in fact, they seem to annoy everyone in the town. Thus, Vinny is forced to go through every piece of evidence in the trial one by one, using logic and science (the central route to persuasion) to show how his cousin can't be guilty after all.

In the drama *A Time to Kill* (based on the 1989 novel by John Grisham; Milchan, Grisham, Nathanson, & Lowry, 1996), an African American man is tried for the revenge murder of a White man who abused and killed his young daughter. This time, the defendant's lawyer knows that his client is guilty—there's even a confession—but he wants the jury to see things from the defendant's perspective. Instead of arguing with facts and logic, the lawyer uses the peripheral route to persuasion. He attempts to highlight his legal credibility and appeals to the jurors' empathy and emotions as he describes the grisly death of the defendant's daughter.

Both methods can be effective. But the most effective approach depends on the actual evidence, the situation, the jury, and the skill of the attorney.

Central path: A type of persuasion in which appeals are direct, elaborate, and systematic; requires close attention and careful evaluation of alternatives by the individual being persuaded.

Peripheral path: A type of persuasion in which appeals are indirect, implicit, and emotion based; requires little effort by the individual being persuaded, leading to quick and easy conclusions.

---

elaborate, systematic, or **central path** to persuasion. They require the audience to both pay attention and understand the arguments. Theoretically, this kind of careful evaluation of reasonable doubt lies at the heart of the American judicial system.

However, the lawyers for the prosecution will probably add other indirect methods of persuasion. Innocent children should never be victimized! It is our responsibility as adults to protect our children. They will use emotional appeals based on fear of the suspect and empathy toward the victims. They may try to impress the jury by wearing expensive suits—and it doesn't hurt if the lawyers are good looking. This type of evidence follows the (indirect) **peripheral path** to persuasion. Whereas the central path requires paying close attention and systematically evaluating the strengths and weaknesses of the various alternatives, the peripheral path uses mental shortcuts (heuristics) to reach a conclusion quickly and easily. Read more about persuasion in the accompanying Social Psychology in Popular Culture feature.

Applying the Persuasion Model to Retail Sales. How do you judge the quality of a purchase when you are in a hurry? Cialdini (2001) described how the peripheral, heuristic route to persuasion worked when a retail storeowner was having difficulty selling turquoise jewelry to well-to-do vacationers. She had directed an employee to reprice the items at half off, but the employee misunderstood the message and doubled the price. The surprising thing was that the tourists quickly bought out the previously

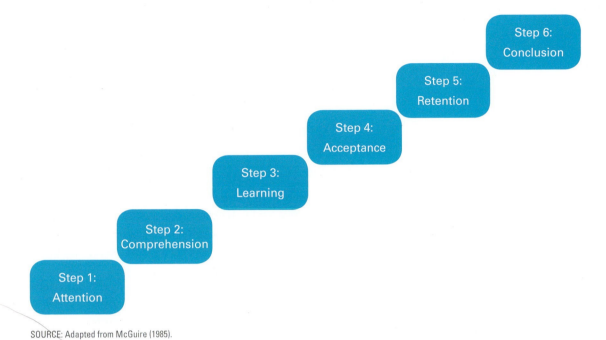

SOURCE: Adapted from McGuire (1985).

difficult-to-sell jewelry at the much higher price. Why? The tourists were probably using a heuristic that simplified their decision making to "More expensive = Better quality" or "You get what you pay for." They quickly determined the jewelry was valuable and therefore had to have it.

Explaining Celebrity Endorsements: The Communication-Persuasion Matrix.

Are famous people effective persuaders for products they don't know anything about (Gakhal & Senior, 2008)? The **communication-persuasion matrix** (McGuire, 1985) helps answer this simple but troubling question about the persuasion process by laying out six steps to persuasion.

Figure 6.4 indicates that famous people get us started by capturing our attention at Step 1. After all, you have to get past Step 1 before you can get to Steps 2, 3, and onward. If we were already interested in the product, then we wouldn't need Step 1, the celebrity endorsement; we could use the central route to decide whether to buy it (Kim & Na, 2007; Lee & Thorson, 2008). But, if we weren't already thinking about the product, the celebrity might capture our attention. In this way, celebrities endorsing products involves peripheral persuasion (Pieters, Warlop, & Wedel, 2002).

Four Elements of Persuasion: The Message-Learning Approach

Carl Hovland tried to be as simple as possible when he created the **message-learning approach** to explain the persuasion process. His approach, represented in Figure 6.5, reasoned that there were four elements to the persuasion process: the source, the message, the recipient, and the context (Hovland, Janis, & Kelley, 1953). An easy way to remember these elements is that they all answer the same general question: "Who (the source) did what (the message) to whom (the recipient) and how (the context)"? Each variable can change our attitudes, and for people to be persuaded, they need to pay attention, understand the message, and yield to it.

Communication-persuasion matrix: A model for understanding persuasion that proposes that there are six steps in the persuasion process—attention, comprehension, learning, acceptance, retention, and conclusion—which build on each other due to exposure to the four elements of persuasion—the source, the message, the recipient, and the context—resulting in attitude change.

Message-learning approach: The idea that there are four elements to the persuasion process: the source (who is doing the persuading), the message (the persuasive information), the recipient (who they are persuading), and the context (how they are persuading).

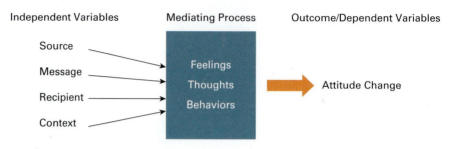

SOURCE: Petty & Wegener (1998).

Source Variables.

Source variables answer the "who" part of Hovland's question, "Who did what to whom, and how?" What kinds of lawyers, politicians, salespeople, and new friends are going to be the most persuasive? Research on source variables has focused on three characteristics of the person who made the message more or less persuasive:

- *Credibility:* Sources are considered more credible (and thus more persuasive) when they present a message that seems *un*popular (Eagly, Wood, & Chaiken, 1978) or when they seem impartial. For example, political ads are more persuasive when they come from unknown interest groups than from the candidates themselves (Weber, Dunaway, & Johnson, 2012). Credibility is also stronger when the source seems to argue against its own self-interest (such as if your college professors led a campaign to reduce their salaries). Expertise also matters; feminine topics are more credible when presented by a woman, and masculine topics are more credible when presented by a man (Levenson, Burford, Bonno, & Davis, 1975). Anything that contributes to credibility is likely to be persuasive.
- *Attractiveness:* You already know about the what-is-beautiful-is-good effect; physical beauty seems to induce a kind of stupor that leads people to believe a communication (Chaiken, 1980; Puckett, Petty, Cacioppo, & Fisher, 1983). For example, Praxmarer (2011) found that physical attractiveness increased perceived trustworthiness and expertise among more than 800 young professionals and university students who reacted to television commercials about a food supplement. But she offered a cautionary note: She did not study *extremely* attractive people. Some people are so gorgeous that their beauty elicits jealousy.
- *Social power:* We're more motivated to pay attention to people who have power over us (such as our boss; Raven, 1958). Similarly, we're more persuaded by messages coming from a majority in our community (we presume the majority opinion is probably right), unless we really care about the issue. In that case, we're especially likely to pay attention to messages coming from the minority, especially when we tend to agree with this minority opinion (Baker & Petty, 1994).

Message Variables.

Message variables are the "what" elements of the question, "Who did what to whom and how?" There seem to be two main factors here:

- *Personal importance:* Lawyers' courtroom arguments will become important if you're emotionally tied to the case, if you personally care about this type of crime, and so on. We put in more effort when processing persuasive messages when we think the issue is important (Johnson & Eagly, 1989) or personally relevant (Petty, Cacioppo, & Haugtvedt, 1992; Sherif, Sherif, & Nebergall, 1965; Zimbardo, 1960).

Source variables:
Characteristics of individuals that make their message more or less persuasive, including their level of credibility, their attractiveness, and their social power.

Message variables:
Characteristics of a message that can make it more or less persuasive, including whether the listener personally cares about the topic and how the message is presented.

- *Framing:* How the message is presented also matters. For example, one study investigated pregnant women's attitudes toward getting flu vaccinations (Marsh, Malik, Shapiro, Omer, & Frew, 2014). Women were more likely to indicate they wanted a flu vaccination if they received messages about benefits to their child than about benefits to themselves and if the message focused on positives aspects of taking the vaccine (such as better infant health) versus negative aspects of *not* taking it (such as low birth weight).

Recipient Variables. The "to whom" elements of the "Who did what to whom and how" question are the **recipient variables**: the audience, or the people receiving the message. Some recipient variables that matter are as follows:

- *Attitude strength:* Strong attitudes are stable, are cognitively accessible, and influence other, related beliefs (Krosnick & Petty, 1995). It's easy to understand why strong attitudes will be harder to change than weak ones; we're going to cling to beliefs that we've had for a long time or are important to our self-concept.
- *Intelligence:* Intelligence and education influence how your attitude can be changed. Better-educated people are more likely to understand scientific evidence, for example, and thus able to focus on central messages instead of peripheral messages (Petty & Wegener, 1998; Rhodes & Wood, 1992).
- *Personality:* Personality influences how we perceive arguments. The trait "openness to experience" describes people willing to consider new perspectives; not surprisingly, people high in openness are more persuadable due to their "open" minds (Gerber, Huber, Doherty, Dowling, & Panagopoulos, 2013).
- *Self-esteem:* Self-esteem has similar effects as intelligence. People with high self-esteem have the confidence to look deeply into a message, analyze it, and come to a reasoned conclusion. Note, however, that both intelligence and high self-esteem can have a drawback: People can become stubborn in their opinions, believing their opinion is superior (Perloff & Brock, 1980). People with low self-esteem can be persuadable if they judge others as more qualified to make decisions.
- *Need for cognition:* Finally, need for cognition describes people who regularly engage in cognitive activity, as described in Chapter 4 (see Cacioppo & Petty, 1982). Do you enjoy intellectually demanding reading and crossword puzzles more than watching bland, predictable television shows? If so, then you are probably high in the need for cognition and more likely to respond to the central path to persuasion. People low in the need for cognition tend to be cognitive misers likely to take mental shortcuts (Cacioppo, Petty, Feinstein, & Jarvis, 1996). Which lawyer looks more successful? I'll side with that one.

Context Variables. Finally, **context variables** are the "how" part of the "Who did what to whom and how" question. They include the following:

- *Distraction:* Imagine a lawyer trying to persuade you when all you can think about is how much catch-up work you'll have at your job when the trial is over. Any distraction makes you less influenced by the message, because it forces you to switch from the central path to the peripheral path (Festinger & Maccoby, 1964; Insko, Turnbull, & Yandell, 1974; Kiesler & Mathog, 1968).
- *Forewarning:* If you're specifically trying *not* to be persuaded by a message, knowing that the arguments are coming up can help you prepare for them. Imagine learning that your college is considering a required comprehensive exam that you must take to graduate. Petty and Cacioppo (1979) found that

Recipient variables: Characteristics of the people receiving a persuasive message that make them more or less likely to be persuaded, such as their attitude strength, intelligence, personality, self-esteem, and need for cognition.

Context variables: Characteristics concerning how a persuasive message is delivered that can make it more or less persuasive, including distraction, forewarning, and repetition.

knowing about this potential change in advance enabled students to generate counterarguments (see also Cialdini, Levy, Herman, Kozlowski, & Petty, 1976; Leippe & Elkin, 1987; Tetlock, 1992). Forewarned is forearmed, as the old saying goes, and a head's up about a coming change leads to greater resistance to persuasion attempts.

- *Repetition:* Plain old repetition is also persuasive. It is also an easy-to-understand persuasion technique, which is probably why politicians try to get their names plastered on every billboard, TV commercial, and lawn sign they can (Gorn & Goldberg, 1980). If the lawyers say that the suspect is guilty 50 times, it's more likely to sink in than if they only say it 5 times. Some advertiser is celebrating every time a musical jingle gets stuck in your head. You're doing their repetition work for them.

The Main Ideas

- Studies of the persuasion process include how to inoculate individuals from being persuaded (in other words, how people can resist persuasion).

- Two ways (paths) influence us to change our attitudes: an attention-demanding central path and a heuristically guided peripheral path.

- People with high ability and motivation will be more persuaded by the central path; low ability and/or motivation will lead people to the peripheral path.

- There are four basic elements of a potentially persuasive communication: source, content, recipient, and context.

⚡ CRITICAL THINKING CHALLENGE

- The heuristic-systematic model (HSM) and the elaboration likelihood model (ELM) both propose two paths to persuasion. In what ways does this fit with the dual process for social thinking (logic vs. intuition) that you learned about in Chapter 4?

- Search YouTube for popular commercials. For each product, describe whether the company is using the central route to persuade you (such as telling you how the product will improve your life) or the peripheral route (such as using attractive celebrities, fear, or humor).

- Think about a situation in which you want to persuade your college professor to do something for you, such as give you an extension on an assignment. Identify at least one way you could improve your chances using the information you learned about source, message, recipient, and context.

WHAT PERSUASION TECHNIQUES ARE USED TO CHANGE ATTITUDES?

LO 6.6: Apply specific persuasion techniques to attitude or behavior change.

You already know about the two paths to persuasion (central route vs. the peripheral route). But there are also specific techniques that companies, politicians, and social persuaders use to gain your compliance. Knowing what these persuasion attempts look like can help inoculate you against their effectiveness. When you recognize them, you can wake up and say, "Aha! I can see what's going on here." Or, on the other hand, you can always use them yourself to persuade others.

Commitment and Consistency

Commitment and consistency go hand in hand because most of us want to present ourselves as logical, reliable, and "good" people, both to others and to ourselves. For example, if we made a promise (especially a public one), we would be embarrassed if we didn't keep it. If we said that we would volunteer on Sunday for a charity event, it would look bad (and we probably would feel bad) if we didn't show up. In the world of persuasion, it doesn't matter if you are really consistent—you only have to appear to be consistent. Our preference for commitment and consistency leads us to be persuaded by two specific persuasion techniques.

The Lowball Technique. Cialdini (2007) describes a technique he observed in salespeople at a car dealership. The dealership would offer a fantastic deal, such as zero percent financing. Potential buyers would visit based on the offer and while there would engage in "ownership" behaviors such as test driving the car and discussing the car's benefits. Once the customer decided to purchase the car, however, the salesperson would suddenly discover a problem with the original incentive, such as the customer's low credit score. While some potential buyers would then leave, a surprising number bought the car anyway! Of course, the "scam" is that no one actually gets to cash in on the amazing offer.

The **lowball technique** keeps buyers moving toward a decision even though the original incentive has been removed due to the terms of the agreement being changed. Cialdini (2007) explains this strange decision as being caused by commitment and consistency. Customers have cognitively and emotionally committed to the purchase. It would be inconsistent to not purchase a product they want—even when the terms have changed.

Foot-in-the-Door. The **foot-in-the-door** technique occurs when agreeing to a small, initial request makes us more likely to later agree to a much larger request. Charities often begin with asking you for a very small commitment, such as simply providing your email address or signing a petition. They might then follow this with progressively larger requests such as asking for donations of time or money. If you agreed to the first request, you must support this charity and believe in what it does— right? Failing to then agree to a later request may cause dissonance if you see your actions as inconsistent.

The name for this persuasion technique is a metaphor harking back to the old-fashioned door-to-door salesman, who might stick his foot in your door to avoid getting it shut in his face. If he can just get you to agree to a brief conversation about his fantastic product, you might then agree to invite him in. If you invite him in, then you might watch his demonstration and even purchase his product. The longer you continue on the path, the more likely you are to keep going because your behavior indicates that you must be interested.

Perhaps the most famous scientific study of the foot-in-the-door technique comes from residential California in the 1960s (Freedman & Fraser, 1966). Psychologists posing as volunteers walked around neighborhoods asking homeowners if they would be willing to display a small (3-inch square) sticker reading, "Be a Safe Driver." Almost everyone agreed to this tiny request. After all, isn't everyone in favor of safe driving? But Phase 2 of the study was the central test: When those same homeowners were approached 2 weeks later and asked if they would agree to a huge, ugly billboard in their yard reading "Drive Carefully," would they say yes this time?

Freedman and Fraser (1966) found that if the request to display a billboard in the yard was the *first* thing they asked people, almost everyone refused. However, when they

Lowball technique: A persuasion technique where an incentive is offered at the beginning of a deal, such as a low price, but then is later removed due to the terms of the agreement being changed. Despite the change, cognitive and emotional commitment to the item from the original deal often leads to acceptance of the new, less attractive deal.

Foot-in-the-door: A persuasion technique that occurs when agreeing to a small, initial request makes an individual more likely to later agree to a much larger request.

specifically went to the homes of people who had first agreed to post the tiny sticker 2 weeks earlier, fully 76% of these residents agreed to the billboard request. The researchers concluded that people who agreed to the initial, small request viewed themselves as agreeable, civic-minded citizens who cared about safe driving in their neighborhood. So refusing a request on the same issue later would be inconsistent with their view of themselves. Commitment and consistency led them to agree to actions that most other people saw as unreasonable.

The Norm of Reciprocity

Other techniques come from social norms. One is the **norm of reciprocity**, which directs us to respond in kind to courtesies and concessions from others: You scratch my back; I scratch yours. We expect a fair exchange, and we feel guilty if we're the ones to break this social norm. Two specific persuasion techniques make use of the norm of reciprocity.

Door-in-the-Face. The **door-in-the-face** technique occurs when compliance is gained by first making a large request (usually refused) and then following it with a smaller request. It's the opposite of foot-in-the-door, which starts small and gets progressively bigger due to commitment and consistency. Door-in-the-face starts big and then gets smaller—but the trick to this technique is that the eventual small request is what the asker wanted all along.

Imagine you want your friend to help you move a heavy chair. To get her to help, you might start by asking her if she is willing to *buy* you a new chair! She will probably (and reasonably) say no. You could then ask her to help you move all of the furniture in your apartment—and she might well say no again. But now, if you say, "Are you at least willing to help me move this one chair?" she is more likely to agree. You compromised—so she'll feel pressure to compromise as well, and you get what you wanted all along. (We don't recommend this manipulation as a way to gain or keep friends.)

Cialdini and his research team first asked students to volunteer to chaperone a group of juvenile delinquents on a field trip to a zoo; 83% refused. But that was only the baseline comparison rate. Their rate of acceptance *tripled* when they first asked students to do something much more demanding: to spend 2 hours per week for at least 2 years as counselors to juvenile delinquents (Cialdini et al., 1975). The field trip now seemed like small potatoes, by comparison. Asking for something big first—and then being turned down (a metaphorical door slammed in your face)—makes it easier to engage the norm of reciprocity and gain compliance with a second, relatively smaller request.

Not-So-Free Samples. Free is never free. The norm of reciprocity makes people more likely to fork over some money if they first have been given a small "gift." In addition to sampling the product, we feel guilty about getting something for nothing, especially when it comes from a smiling and friendly person. Charities use this technique when they send "free" stickers with your name and address printed on them in their mailed requests for donations. In many large, tourist cities, homeless people offer travelers help with direc-

Norm of reciprocity: The idea that individuals respond in kind to courtesies and concessions from others.

Door-in-the-face: A persuasion technique that occurs when compliance is gained by first making a large request, which is usually refused, and then following it with a smaller request, which is usually accepted.

Harvey Silver / Corbis Historical / Getty Images

Hare Krishnas made thousands of dollars by giving away flowers—then asking people for donations to their cause.

tions, then ask for spare change. Survey companies will sometimes include a crisp $1 bill when they mail out their surveys, hoping people will feel guilty if they take the dollar without returning the survey.

In the 1970s, the religious sect known as Hare Krishnas received thousands of dollars of donations from strangers they approached on the street or in airports, simply because the Krishnas first handed out "free" books and flowers. Surprised people accepted the flowers, and when the Krishnas then asked for a donation to their cause, people gave—because the norm of reciprocity would make them feel guilty otherwise. These persuasion techniques work. Whether you use these techniques ethically is another matter.

The Main Ideas

- Our preference for commitment and consistency in our thoughts and actions leads to persuasion from the "foot-in-the-door" and lowballing techniques.

- The social norm of reciprocity underlies the "door-in-the-face" technique and why we feel compelled to agree to requests after receiving a "free" gift.

⚡ CRITICAL THINKING CHALLENGE

- Consider the four specific persuasion techniques covered in this section and try to think of times when they have affected your own life. Now, think of something you want from someone else and how you might use each technique to get that person to agree to your request.

- Spend a few minutes watching a television station that sells products or simply watching ads between shows. Can you identify the techniques from this section in the programming? What other techniques can you identify now that you are considering the persuasion attempts from a social psychology perspective?

- Imagine that you want to convince the professor of this class to offer you an extra credit assignment. How might you use all four of the techniques in this section to persuade him or her to do so?

CHAPTER SUMMARY

What are attitudes, and do they predict behavior?

Attitudes are an inner tendency to evaluate something (an attitude "object") either positively or negatively. We can have dual attitudes (mixed); sometimes this occurs because attitudes can be made up of both explicit beliefs (conscious, controlled beliefs) and implicit beliefs (unconscious, automatic beliefs). But, they can also help us make uni-valenced decisions (not mixed).

The question of whether attitudes actually predict behavior was debated by social psychologists for several decades. Early research indicated that surprisingly, people's behaviors did not seem to match with attitudes they publicly expressed. However, studies over the years have refined our ideas. For example, the specificity principle notes that attitudes and behaviors will match when both are measured at the same level of specificity. If you want to know whether someone will cheat on

a math exam, you should measure his or her attitude toward cheating on a math exam—and not toward cheating or dishonesty in general.

Some research suggested that perhaps behaviors come first, then attitudes; this was tested in the facial feedback hypothesis. Researchers originally found that forcing people into facial expressions of smiles led to people thinking that cartoons were funnier, compared to people forced into facial expressions of frowns. However, some replications of this study have failed to find any effects. People might also not behave according to their expressed attitudes if they have pretended to have an attitude for some social reason (such as impressing a boss).

Finally, the theory of planned behavior suggests that attitudes are only one of three predictors for actual intentions and behavior. To really predict behavior, we must also know what subjective social norms are about the behavior and someone's level of perceived control over the behavior. Only when all three variables can be measured will prediction of behavior be reliable.

From where do attitudes come?

The origin of attitudes is one context in which the "nature versus nurture" question can be applied. To understand the potential influence of "nature," studies of identical twins can be useful. If identical twins have closely aligned attitudes, it's possible that these attitudes were at least partially formed due to biological influence.

However, attitudes are also certainly influenced by our experiences. Three lines of research provide insight into how experience can shape attitudes. First, we form our attitudes by observing others in our environment and by imitating them; this is called social learning. Second, we form attitudes because certain attitude objects have been associated with positive things (such as sexual attraction or happy memories) while other attitudes objects have been associated with negative things (such as fear or pain); this is called classical conditioning. Third and finally, we can form attitudes because certain behaviors have led to rewards or punishments in the past; this is called operant conditioning.

How are attitudes measured?

Attitudes can generally be measured through two approaches. The first approach is direct measures of explicit attitudes; the most common form of direct measurement is self-report scales. However, due to social desirability, people may not be entirely honest in this type of scale. One way to avoid social desirability biases in responses is to use a "bogus pipeline," or a fake lie detector test.

A second way to measure attitudes is indirect; this can be used to measure implicit attitudes (or attitudes that may be on a hidden, unconscious level where the participant isn't even aware of them). The most famous example of this method is the IAT, or Implicit Association Test, which uses a computer to measure reaction times. People are asked to complete sorting tasks with pairs of items; if people are faster at responding to certain pairs, then they may have implicit attitudes that those two attitude objects go together. However, the IAT is controversial because some social psychologists question (a) whether results are actually associated with any relevant behaviors and (b) whether results measure individual prejudice or simply someone's awareness of prejudice in their culture of origin.

Why does cognitive dissonance influence attitudes?

Self-justification is the desire to explain our actions in a way that maintains a positive view of the self. One way that self-justification can drive attitude change is when we experience cognitive dissonance, which is anxiety or discomfort that occurs when we have to confront contradictory beliefs and/or behaviors. For example, most people want to think of themselves as honest. When research participants in a famous study by Festinger told a lie, people who were paid $20 for the lie weren't uncomfortable—they had sufficient justification to know why they did it. However, participants who were only paid $1 did experience dissonance because they didn't want to think of themselves as people who would become liars so easily. Thus, the people in the $1 condition were more likely to change their attitude such that they were no longer "lying."

Research on cognitive dissonance was inspired by historical examples of people in doomsday cults who ironically became more committed to the cult when their prophesies didn't come true. One way this strange commitment seems to occur is through a rationalization trap, which is when progressively larger self-justifications lead to very bad outcomes. However, other research on cognitive dissonance shows that it can lead to positive outcomes as well, such as healthier eating behaviors.

There are individual differences in how much dissonance someone can tolerate. For example, extroverts and people with symptoms of psychopathy can tolerate more dissonance than others. Culture also seems to influence how and why people experience cognitive dissonance. People from independent cultures may experience more dissonance when their sense of competency is threatened; people from interdependent cultures may experience more dissonance when their social acceptance is threatened.

How do attitudes change?

Attitude "inoculation" occurs when we build up a resistance to persuasion. However, when our attitudes do change, it's likely to be through one of two "routes." Both the elaboration likelihood model and the heuristic-systematic model suggest that we can be persuaded through a central or systematic route, which is based on logical arguments, or through a peripheral or heuristic route, which is based on shortcut cues such as attractive models or emotional appeals.

Attempts to persuade us will also be more or less influential based on four elements: (1) source variables (such as credibility or attractiveness), (2) message variables (such as personal importance or message framing), (3) recipient variables (such as our personality or self-esteem), and (4) context variables (such as whether we're distracted or if the message is repeated multiple times).

What persuasion techniques are used to change attitudes?

Four specific persuasion techniques were covered in this section, coming from two general ideas. The first general idea is commitment and consistency, meaning that people like to think of themselves as reliable and consistent. The lowball technique comes from this idea because it's when someone sticks with a decision (such as to buy a product) even when the original reason to buy it has been taken away. This occurs because people convince themselves they want the product anyway. The foot-in-the-door technique happens when people who agree to an initial, small request then become more likely to agree to a larger request because their first action indicates commitment to a cause or product.

The second general idea is the social norm of reciprocity, the idea that we should respond to "favors" from others by returning a favor. The door-in-the-face technique occurs when someone asks a large favor of us that they assume we'll turn down; when they follow this with a request for something smaller, we're more likely to say yes than if they didn't ask us for the larger favor first. We are persuaded to do the second request because we feel that they have compromised, so we should as well. Finally, "free" samples are often used as a way to get people to feel that they "owe" you something, so people who have received a small gift (even without asking for it) are more likely to then comply with requests.

THEORIES IN REVIEW

- Model of dual attitudes
- Facial feedback hypothesis
- Self-affirmation theory
- Theory of planned behavior
- Social learning theory
- Classical conditioning

- Operant conditioning
- Cognitive dissonance
- Elaboration likelihood model
- Heuristic-systematic model
- Message-learning approach to persuasion
- Norm of reciprocity

CRITICAL THINKING, ANALYSIS, AND APPLICATION

- First, identify a personal attitude you have about (a) a particular politician, (b) a musical group you either love or hate, and (c) a social controversy of your choice (capital punishment, abortion, civil rights, etc.). For each of these three attitudes, try to identify (a) how you formed this attitude—the source of your opinion—and (b) whether your attitude seems to predict actual behavior.

- Almost every chapter in this book includes a self-report scale in which you answer questions about an attitude or opinion you have. As you take these scales, are you always completely honest? If not, why not? Do you find yourself potentially being dishonest because you want others to have a certain impression of you—or is it possible that you are even being dishonest with yourself?

- Think about two specific times that you changed your mind after someone tried to persuade you. One incident should be a time when you were persuaded through the "central route," and one should be a time when you were persuaded through the "peripheral" route. Identify differences in how you were persuaded and whether the two different routes led to any discrepancies in the outcomes (e.g., different emotions about your changed opinion, differences in how long the change lasted).

- Is it ethical to use the persuasion techniques such as lowballing, foot-in-the-door, and door-in-the-face? Does the answer depend on what you are trying to get someone to do—such as vote for a politician versus live a healthier lifestyle? Defend your answer.

PERSONAL REFLECTIONS

As professors, we worry about our many students who want to become therapists but don't understand the need for critical thinking. Many want to become child therapists, similar to the child therapists in Edenton, North Carolina, who inadvertently helped send seven innocent people to jail and prison. The therapists and social workers were probably hard-working, sincere, compassionate individuals. But they had not learned the practical skepticism that comes with courses in statistics, and they were insensitive to the dangers of confounding variables learned from courses in experimental design. It takes more than being a nice, decent person to be an effective therapist—you also have to have the ability to think critically, objectively, and scientifically. If you become a therapist, real lives are depending on your ability to be an authentic critical thinker. [TH and WG]

Visit **edge.sagepub.com/heinzen** to help you accomplish your coursework goals in an easy-to-use learning environment.

- **Visual Key Concepts**
- Mobile-friendly **eFlashcards**
- Mobile-friendly practice **quizzes**
- **Video** and **multimedia content**
- EXCLUSIVE! Access to full-text **SAGE journal articles**

$SAGE edge™

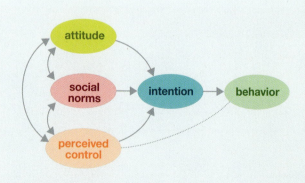

LO6.5 Analyze two distinct paths to persuasion.

LO6.6 Apply specific persuasion techniques to attitude or behavior change.

Get a tour of **ALL Visual Key Concepts** and their definitions at **edge.sagepub.com/heinzen**

7 Social Influence: Conformity, Social Roles, and Obedience

Core Questions

1. What types of social influence exist?
2. Why and when do we choose to conform?
3. How do social roles change our behavior?
4. What can we learn from Milgram's experiments on authority?

Learning Objectives

7.1 Compare and contrast implicit versus explicit social influence.

7.2 Differentiate between informational and normative social pressures to conform.

7.3 Analyze how social roles lead us to conform to situational expectations.

7.4 Explain the person, procedures, and competing interpretations behind the Milgram experiments on authority.

You are not alone if you recall middle school and high school as hard chapters in your life. It is a time when social influence applies constant peer pressure (Brown, 1982) and popularity depends on knowing and conforming to unwritten rules. Fortunately, as we grow older, our possible social roles expand well beyond the boundaries of high school stereotypes around sports, geekdom, or the arts.

But social roles still influence us; adults at social gatherings tend to ask, "What do you do for a living?" to identify individuals and begin to form impressions. While sometimes we can feel the pressure of too many or conflicting social roles (e.g., for women, Arthur & Lee, 2008), our deeper commitments to certain roles (as parent, employee, lover, or friend) are a form of social influence that stabilizes society—we gradually become the gears that keep societies up and running.

There can be dangers as we negotiate our way into new social roles, especially when those social roles require obedience to an authority. Conforming and obeying authorities appear to be wired into the human experience because they keep society functioning. However, they also are associated with the dark side of social influence.

The most disturbing, early observations about social influence were connected to World War I and then again to World War II and the Holocaust. A common defense for the mass torture and murder of Jews, Communists, homosexuals, the disabled, and others was simply, "I was just following orders" and "I didn't do anything unique; everyone else did the same thing." A century of basic research in social psychology has significantly increased our understanding of social influence, but there is still much more to be discovered.

WHAT TYPES OF SOCIAL INFLUENCE EXIST?

LO 7.1: Compare and contrast implicit versus explicit social influence.

Social influence describes how our thoughts, feelings, and behaviors respond to our social world, including our tendencies to conform to others, follow social rules, and obey authority figures. Social influence takes two basic forms: implicit expectations and explicit expectations. **Implicit expectations** are unspoken rules. Like the unwritten laws of middle school, implicit expectations are enforced by group norms. For example, no

Social influence: How an individual's thoughts, feelings, and behaviors respond to their social world, including tendencies to conform to others, follow social rules, and obey authority figures.

Implicit expectations: Unspoken rules enforced by group norms that influence an individual's behavior.

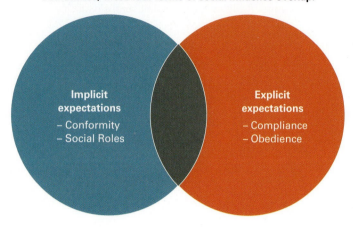

Implicit expectations (conformity and social roles) plus explicit expectations (compliance and obedience). Sometimes, these four forms of social influence overlap.

Conformity: A type of implicit social influence where individuals voluntarily change their behavior to imitate the behavior of others.

Social roles: A type of implicit social influence regarding how certain people are supposed to look and behave.

Explicit expectations: Clearly and formally stated expectations for social behavior.

Compliance: A type of explicit social influence where an individual behaves in response to a direct or indirect request.

Obedience: A type of explicit social influence where individuals behave in a particular way because someone of higher status ordered them to do so.

one has to tell you that you will likely be expected to dress differently at formal religious events compared to attending a retro grunge rock concert.

Implicit expectations can be further subdivided into two types. The first is **conformity**, which occurs when you voluntarily change your behavior to imitate the behavior of your peers. Twenty-five years from now, you will probably look at a current picture of yourself and wonder how you could have made such terrible fashion choices way back when. At the time, you were probably wearing what everyone else was wearing.

A second form of implicit social influence comes from **social roles**, or expectations from a group about how certain people are supposed to look and behave. We share stereotypes about how elementary school teachers, rock musicians, clergy, and presidential candidates publicly engage with others. These expectations are implicit because while everyone knows the "rules," they aren't necessarily written down or formalized.

Unlike implicit expectations, **explicit expectations** are clearly and formally stated—not at all subtle. There are also two forms of explicit expectations: compliance and obedience. **Compliance** occurs when you behave in response to a direct or indirect request. When healthy graduate students asked people on a New York City subway to give up their seat, about two thirds of the subway riders complied (Milgram & Sabini, 1983)—just because someone asked. With compliance, there isn't necessarily any threat of punishment for not doing the behavior—it is a request, not a demand.

In contrast, **obedience** occurs when you behave in a particular way because someone of higher status has ordered you to do so. It might be your boss at work, a parent, or a professor at school; in any case, the expectation is stated clearly and often accompanied by some kind of social punishment if you fail to obey. In general, obedience can be considered a more extreme version of compliance.

arastiralim.net

August Landmesser defied social pressures to give the Nazi salute, probably because he had fallen in love with a Jewish woman, Irma Eckler. He was banned from the Nazi party after he and Eckler became engaged, and they were later denied a marriage license. If you want to learn more, several websites describe his quiet heroism in fighting against social pressures—and its tragic consequences.

Social Norms and the Herd Mentality

Are you more of an independent thinker or a conformist? Our impulse to conform begins much earlier in life than you might imagine. Infants will imitate others when they are only 2 to 3 weeks old (Meltzoff & Moore, 1977, 1989). Growing infants will automatically clap when others clap; as small children, they will whisper back when others whisper to them, and a little later they will imitate one another's eating habits (Johnston, 2002).

As we grow, we absorb these behaviors as **social norms** (also called **group norms**)—rules that indicate how people are expected to behave in particular social situations. There is an implied payoff for conforming to social norms for humans, as well as many other species. It increases our odds of meeting, mating, and protecting our offspring until they reach their own reproductive maturity (Buss & Kenrick, 1998). Put another way, however, the reverse is also true: If we fail to meet social norms, our chances of being accepted by the group decrease—and our stubborn independence reduces our chances of finding a life partner.

But that's only part of the story behind group norms. Group norms can also create a **herd mentality** (the tendency to blindly follow the direction your group is moving toward). Suddenly you may find yourself proclaiming strange and dangerous beliefs. "Going along to get along" can also lead to authoritarian leaders, and a herd mentality can make small conflicts mushroom into dangerous confrontations. For example, prior to World War I, both sides recruited many thousands of enthusiastic volunteers. Both sides were certain that the conflict would be short and glorious. This war wasn't short and it wasn't glorious. The herd mentality helped recruit and then destroy almost an entire generation.

In a herd of animals, each has to move in the same direction or they might get trampled. Can this be a metaphor for human tendencies to conform?

> " I don't want to belong to any club that will accept people like me as a member. "
>
> —Groucho Marx (1967)

Conforming Is Contagious

Conforming is contagious. For example, it can be awkward to attend your first holiday meal with new in-laws if no one tells you that Grandpa always sits in a particular chair or that the holiday meal, announced for 2 p.m., is never served until 4:30. Your new family members do not have to say anything to communicate their group norms, however. Instead, you observe that at 2 p.m., the dining room table isn't set, the cooking is just getting started, the teenagers are just getting out of bed, and no one else seems surprised that the meal is so "late."

However, to their way of thinking—your new family's social norm—the meal is right on time. "Dinner is at 2 p.m." really means, "Come on over sometime in the afternoon; we'll start cooking." Your social network (new relatives) will guide you to conform according to the cultural expectations that your new spouse probably forgot to mention (see Gulati & Puranam, 2009). The social norms practiced by your new relatives provide specific but implicit guidance about how you are expected to behave.

Social Contagion. One of social psychology's simplest yet strangest experiments demonstrates the importance of group size in **social contagion**, the spontaneous

Social norms: Rules that indicate how people are expected to behave in particular social situations, which, in combination with attitudes and perceived control, often predict intended behavior.

Group norms: See *social norms*.

Herd mentality: The tendency to blindly follow the direction your group is moving toward; when group norms encourage individuals to conform to those around them, especially when it comes to their beliefs.

Social contagion: The spontaneous distribution of ideas, attitudes, and behaviors among larger groups of people.

distribution of ideas, attitudes, and behaviors among larger groups of people. One person on a busy New York City street stopped on the sidewalk and stared up at a sixth-floor window of a building (Milgram, Bickman, & Berkowitz, 1969). That's all it took to start a small social contagion. Make no mistake: There was nothing special in the window—just some distant, difficult-to-see people looking back at them.

After only 60 seconds, the first person stopped staring and moved on. After pauses long enough to allow new sets of participants to enter the scene, groups of 1, 2, 3, 5, 10, or 15 *confederates* (members of the research team pretending to be among the participants) stopped and repeated the procedure while researchers discreetly made a movie of the crowds that formed and dissolved. They discovered that the bigger the initial crowd, the more compelling it was for other people to join it.

Here's the apparent take-home message from this odd experiment: The mere existence of the crowd justified conforming to it. Perhaps people felt pressure to fit in; perhaps they wanted to find out what was so interesting to everyone else. It was a reasonable assumption by the passersby that there must be something up in that window worth looking at. Either way, the experiment demonstrated something that might not be unique to the streets of New York City. When more people engage in a particular behavior, others will feel more pressure to follow along.

Mass Psychogenic Illness. About 15 minutes after arriving at Warren County High School in Tennessee, a teacher noticed a "gasoline-like" smell in her classroom. She was about to trigger a disturbing form of social contagion called **mass psychogenic illness**, socially contagious physical symptoms with no physical cause. The high school teacher soon developed a headache, nausea, shortness of breath, and dizziness. The school was evacuated, and 80 students and 19 staff members went to the emergency room, resulting in 38 hospitalizations (Jones et al., 2000).

The school reopened 5 days later, but the "epidemic" was not over; 71 more people went to the emergency room even though extensive testing could find no physical cause or evidence of toxic compounds. Researchers eventually noticed that the strange symptoms were communicated through "line of sight." Simply seeing someone whom you believed was ill could trigger hyperventilation. Rashes, none of which suggested exposure to a toxic substance, appeared to be caused by scratching. Despite being caused by purely psychological factors relating to social conformity, the Tennessee "outbreak" involved

- 18,000 person-days of lost labor
- 178 emergency room visits
- Eight ambulance trips
- About $100,000 in direct medical expenses (in 1998 dollars)
- Thousands of dollars for laboratory tests and field studies
- 12 government agencies
- Eight laboratories
- Seven consulting groups
- Many private consultations

Mass psychogenic illness: A form of social contagion where physical symptoms of an illness appear within a cohesive social group, although the illness appears to have no physical cause.

The Tanganyikan Laughter Epidemic. Social contagion also explains why television laugh tracks are effective: We tend to mimic one another when we hear laughter (Provine, 1992) and then conclude that we must find something funny about the situation (Neumann & Strack, 2000). An extreme version of this form of social contagion was the "Tanganyikan Laughter Epidemic." Three girls attending a small, missionary-run boarding school in what is now Tanzania started laughing. Strangely, the laughter quickly spread to the other students and was accompanied by fainting, a rash, unexplained pain, and occasional screaming. The teachers never "caught" the laughing disease, but when it eventually affected 95 of the 159 students, the school had to be closed.

Things got worse, but only if you consider more laughter a bad thing. When the students went home, other people in their towns starting laughing and the phenomenon eventually spread to thousands of people in the region. After 18 months, it all stopped, but only after a total of 14 schools had to be shut down and 1,000 people experienced the "symptoms" (Provine, 1996). No medical reason could be found for what had happened. The laughing epidemic suggests that a wide variety of social expectations—even laughter—can be distributed through social contagion.

Laughing in Tanganyika (now Tanzania)

The Main Ideas

- Social influence can be either implicit (including conformity and behaving according to a social role) or explicit (including compliance and obedience).

- Informal social norms (also called group norms) are communicated through a process called social contagion and can lead to a herd mentality.

- One extreme form of social contagion or conformity is mass psychogenic illness.

⚡ CRITICAL THINKING CHALLENGE

- Identify which form of social influence is most likely at work in the following situations: (a) Being robbed at gunpoint, (b) buying a home that you cannot afford, and (c) wearing a costume to a Halloween party even though it makes you uncomfortable.

- Think of two examples when conformity to group norms helps the group but harms the individual. Now, think of two examples of the opposite—when conformity helps the individual but leads to problems for the group.

- How might social contagion be related to driving habits such as speeding, running yellow lights, or rapid lane switching? How could you accurately (and safely) measure whether your hypothesis is supported?

WHY AND WHEN DO WE CHOOSE TO CONFORM?

LO 7.2: Differentiate between informational and normative social pressures to conform.

Imagine going to an unfamiliar religious ceremony with a friend. A little nervous, you start looking around to see how other people are acting. If they take off their shoes, you will probably do the same. If they kneel or sit or stand, again, it's likely that you will follow along. Most of us perform these actions because we both (1) are uncertain about what the correct behavior is and (2) have anxiety about fitting in. These two concerns help explain that the **theory of informational and normative influence** describes two ways that social norms cause conformity: informational conformity and normative conformity (Deutsch & Gerard, 1955, 1972).

Informational Social Influence

This time, imagine you're in a history class and the professor asks if you remember the capital city of Switzerland. Your first thought is "Geneva," but someone else in the class speaks first and answers, "Bern." You then notice that several other students nod and seem to agree. Most people in this situation would start to doubt themselves—was I wrong? What's the correct answer? Would you pull out your phone and double check? The frequency of searching for quick information through phone web browsers highlights how often we are *un*certain about everyday information.

Muzafer Sherif (1936) wanted to find out how informational *un*certainty influences people in situations when we can't check somewhere for the answer. His studies pioneered research on **informational social influence**, voluntarily conforming to group standards when we are uncertain about the correct answer or behavior. To study this idea scientifically, Sherif took advantage of a strange optical illusion. The **auto-kinetic effect** occurs when we perceive a stationary object as moving due to natural, intermittent movements of our own eyes (called saccades). In other words, it's an optical illusion. To learn how Sherif studied this phenomenon using the scientific method, see the Spotlight on Research Methods feature.

Why We're Tempted by Informational Social Influence

Our lives are filled with uncertainty. Many non-Europeans are unsure what the capital cities are for that continent. Many of us are still uncertain about which fork to use in a fancy restaurant or how much to tip the bathroom attendant. Even when we have the luxury of high-speed digital connections and a reliable information source, we still often have to rely on conformity to cope with an uncertain social world.

Public and Private Conformity. Admitting to uncertainty can be disturbing, but it doesn't have to be. Instead, it can be helpful to understand the connection between conformity and the uncertainty that we experience in the absence of cultural hints or social norms. Under conditions of uncertainty, we tend to grab at *anything*, any tidbit of information that tells us how to behave. For example, a set of experiments that also used the auto-kinetic effect (described in Spotlight on Research Methods feature) demonstrated a distinction between public and private conformity. Participants came back to Sherif's lab, day after day, to experience the auto-kinetic effect repeatedly and make their estimates of how far the dot of light had moved.

As the days went by, the participants' conformity increased—even when they were tested alone in the room and no immediate peer pressure was involved. Both **public conformity** (conforming thoughts or behaviors shared with others) and **private conformity** (conforming thoughts or behaviors kept to oneself, not shared or observed by others) increased over time, based on the artificial group norm first announced—sometimes days earlier—by the original confederate. The participants weren't simply providing answers to fit in; they had honestly become convinced that the light was moving a certain amount

Theory of informational and normative influence: The idea that there are two ways that social norms cause conformity (see *informational social influence* and *normative social influence*).

Informational social influence: When individuals voluntarily conform to group standards because they are uncertain about the correct answer or behavior.

Auto-kinetic effect: An optical illusion that occurs when an individual perceives a stationary object as moving due to natural, intermittent movements of the eyes.

Public conformity: Conforming thoughts or behaviors shared with others; these actions may not be genuinely endorsed (see *private conformity*).

Private conformity: Conforming thoughts or behaviors that are kept to oneself and are felt genuinely by the individual (see *public conformity*).

SHERIF AND THE AUTO-KINETIC EFFECT

To study the auto-kinetic effect, Sherif created a *controlled experiment* by first placing participants in a darkened room and then having them look at a dot of light (Sherif, 1935, 1936). Sure enough, the dot of light seemed to dance about in the darkness. Individual people in the *control group* of the experiment—who were tested by themselves without others to influence them—estimated that the light had moved an average of 4 inches; this estimate became the baseline for later comparisons. Of course, the reality was that the dot of light had not moved at all. In the control group, people simply gave their best guess.

Next, Sherif arranged for a *confederate* in the *experimental group* to provide a fake estimate of how far the light had moved. Sherif told the confederate to estimate that the light had moved about 15 inches. The confederate did this out loud, so that others in the room could hear the estimate. Soon, everyone else was conforming around the

confederate's estimate of 15 inches. And when the confederate in a third experimental group started with an estimate of only 2 inches, estimates from the real participants conformed around this much smaller number.

Remember that the idea behind control groups and experimental groups is to provide meaningful comparisons by keeping everything the same except for the variable of interest (the *independent variable*). In this experiment, the *only* thing that changed was the confederate's declaration of how far the dot of light had moved—and the experiment tested how that initial number caused participants' answers to change for their own estimates (the *dependent variable*). Why did the experimental group participants conform around 15 inches and 2 inches? Social psychologists say the answer is informational social influence that occurs when we are uncertain about what is correct.

even though the only influences were the group norms. When we publicly conform, we might secretly acknowledge that we're just pretending to go along with the group—but private conformity means that we've really become convinced.

Generational Influence on Conformity. Several years later, two researchers at Northwestern University followed the thread of Sherif's auto-kinetic experiments to an additional discovery. This study (Jacobs & Campbell, 1961) demonstrated a **generational influence**, a cultural belief or norm that transcends the replacement of people. Thinking of a generation as the replacement of persons rather than as generations based on birth, life, and death within a family gave Jacobs and Campbell a way to study generational transfer without having to wait for 40 or 50 years.

The initial confederate in Sherif's auto-kinetic experiment had declared that the dot of light had moved about 15 inches; now Jacobs and Campbell (1961) did the same thing in their study. Notice that they started out this new study with a *replication* of an old study—and found the same effect as previous researchers. But the added twist to their new study occurred after everyone in the group had provided an estimate of how much the light moved. That's when a *new* participant replaced the "eldest" member of the group: one generation. The original confederate, the person who had started the "tradition," was no longer in the room! Nevertheless, when a fresh new round of estimates began, the entire group conformed around what the now-departed confederate had declared: the social norm of 15 inches.

As actual participants were replaced by new "generations" of people, the "eldest" members (people who had been present for more trials or "rounds" of the study) always

Generational influence: A cultural belief or norm that transcends the replacement of people; when individuals continue to conform even when the originator of the behavior is no longer present.

gave their estimates first and the "newest" gave their estimates last. It usually required five to eight "generations" of new participants until the average estimate merged with the baseline estimate from the control group. Three conclusions emerged from these auto-kinetic experiments: (a) uncertainty promoted conformity, (b) conformity increased over time, and (c) conformity endured—across five to eight generations—even when the origin of the "tradition" was based on nothing but one person's incorrect statement about how much a light had moved when it really hadn't moved at all.

Traditions vary all over the world for socially normed events such as weddings. How did these traditions start? Why are they passed down from one generation to the next?

- - - - - - - - - - - - - - - - - - -

Descriptive norm: What an individual perceives to be the behavior of most people in a specific situation; what most people do, or what is commonly done.

Injunctive norm: What an individual perceives to be the socially acceptable behavior in a specific situation; what is socially sanctioned, or what society says people are supposed to do.

Normative social influence: When individuals publicly conform to gain social acceptance and avoid rejection.

- - - - - - - - - - - - - - - - - - -

Normative Social Influence

There are two types of norms. **Descriptive norms** refer to what is commonly done, that is, what most people do. **Injunctive norms** refer to what is socially sanctioned, that is, what society says people are *supposed* to do. The distinction between the two types of norms is apparent when you think about littering. You're not supposed to litter (the injunctive norm), but in certain areas, littering is so common that many people will do it anyway, partly because everyone else is littering (the descriptive norm; see Cialdini, Kallgren, & Reno, 1991). It's not easy to resist the power of social norms. We may privately disagree with the group's decision or behaviors, but we still give in to the publicly expressed social norms. See one way of measuring someone's tendency to conform in the Applying Social Psychology to Your Life feature.

Uncertainty encourages conformity, especially when we feel social pressure to be "correct"; this motivation is the basis for informational social influence. But what if there is no uncertainty—what if we are fairly sure of our answer? Solomon Asch explored this question by asking people to provide an answer as obvious as what you can see in Figure 7.2: "Which line on the right matches the length of the line on the left?"

Asch was one of several energetic social psychologists trying to make sense of what had happened to humanity during World War II. He wrote a textbook that discussed how propaganda could be used in education either to promote (a) "independent thinking and self-reliance" or (b) the kind of conformity created by the Nazis to "indoctrinate blind obedience to state and church" (Asch, 1952, p. 620).

Unlike informational social influence, Asch's famous experiments explored **normative social influence**, which occurs when we publicly conform, often to gain social acceptance and avoid rejection. Thus, normative social influence is more likely to lead us to pretend to agree with a group because we want to fit in—our conformity is public but not necessarily private (we don't actually become convinced that the group's direction is correct). When Asch started his studies, he believed that few people would ever answer anything other than Line B, the clearly correct answer (see Bond & Smith, 1996; Cialdini & Trost, 1998; Friend et al., 1990). Asch (1952, 1956) was about to be surprised by the results of his own experiments.

■ **FIGURE 7.2** Can you tell which line on the right matches the one on the left?

Target line

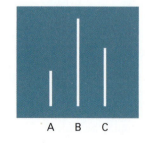

A B C

SOURCE: Adapted from Asch (1952).

MEASURING CONFORMITY

Instructions: Please use the following scale to indicate the degree of your agreement or disagreement with each of the statements below. Record your numerical answer to each statement in the space provided preceding the statement. Try to describe yourself accurately and generally (that is, the way you are actually in most situations—not the way you would hope to be).

−4	−3	−2	−1	0	+1	+2	+3	+4
Very strong disagreement				Neither agree nor disagree				Very strong agreement

_____ 1. I often rely on, and act upon, the advice of others.

_____ 2. I would be the last one to change my opinion in a heated argument on a controversial topic.

_____ 3. Generally, I'd rather give in and go along for the sake of peace than struggle to have my way.

_____ 4. I tend to follow family tradition in making political decisions.

_____ 5. Basically, my friends are the ones who decide what we do together.

_____ 6. A charismatic and eloquent speaker can easily influence and change my ideas.

_____ 7. I am more independent than conforming in my ways.

_____ 8. If someone is very persuasive, I tend to change my opinion and go along with them.

_____ 9. I don't give in to others easily.

_____ 10. I tend to rely on others when I have to make an important decision quickly.

_____ 11. I prefer to make my own way in life rather than find a group I can follow.

Scoring: First, reverse-score Items 2, 7, 9, and 11. For this scale, all you have to do is cross off the plus or minus in front of what you wrote and change it to the other sign (so, for example, a −3 becomes a +3). Zeros stay the same. Then, add up all of the numbers to get your composite score, which should be between −44 and +44. Higher numbers mean more of a tendency to conform to others.

Source: Mehrabian and Stefl (1995).

Fitting in Beats Being Right

Asch assembled groups of seven to nine participants for what appeared to be an exceptionally boring study. In successive trials, the group members were to compare the length of a single vertical line with the length of three other vertical lines of varying lengths—one of which was clearly a match for the first line (see Figure 7.2 again). Participants announced their answers aloud according to the order in which they were seated. For the first two trials, everyone was in perfect agreement.

But the experiment very quickly went from boring to disturbing when, on the third trial, unanimous opinion agreed about the *wrong* line! In fact, most of the participants in the study were actually *confederates* in the experiment. Only one person in the group was not in on the *deception*: the real participant in the experiment—and he was almost the last one to voice his opinion.

Asch's conformity experiments. (Photo reproduced with permission. © 1955 *Scientific American*, a division of Nature America, Inc. All rights reserved.)

Asch's research model, or *research paradigm,* was in place: He had created a repeatable set of procedures to collect data. His simple line judgment task thrust naive participants into a situation in which they would have to choose conforming to group pressure or the certain evidence of their eyes. In control studies with no confederates, participants had provided the correct answer 98% of the time.

Asch arranged for the confederates in the experimental condition to give the wrong answers more than 50% of the time, placing the participant in what Roger Brown (1965) called "an epistemological nightmare" (p. 671) that occurs when our lifelong way of knowing suddenly appears to be invalid. The face of the participant (the man in the middle) in the photograph above suggests what that nightmare must feel like as "deeply rooted assumptions—of mutually shared perceptions and expectations—are decisively shattered" (Friend, Rafferty, & Bramel, 1990, p. 42). Social pressure to conform was so powerful that in about 37% of their answers, the participants gave in and said the wrong answer—and 75% of the participants conformed to the wrong answer at least once (Asch, 1951).

To help explain why participants behaved as they did, Asch combined both *quantitative data* (results in numerical form, such as scores on self-report measures or the percentage of people who act in a certain way) and *qualitative data* (results in subjective forms such as the content of essays or interviews) from follow-up interviews (Asch, 1955). Some of those who resisted the pressures to conform reported a sense of obligation to simply tell the truth as they saw it. Surprisingly, among those who did conform, a few people did seem to have done so due to informational social influence. These participants genuinely started to question their sensation and perception abilities. A few other participants stated that they went along with the others because they didn't want to mess up Asch's data, a motivation called the "*good subject bias,*" one form of social desirability.

However, others clearly stated that they knew the answer they had provided was wrong. Why did they say it? Because they felt the peer pressure of fitting in with the group: normative social influence. For example, one participant noted, "I was standing out [like] a sore thumb . . . I didn't want particularly to make a fool of myself . . . I felt I was definitely right [but] they might think I was peculiar" (Asch, 1956, p. 416). This participant privately knew the answer was wrong, but group pressure made him publicly give in.

Many other psychologists started using Asch's research paradigm. In a 1996 publication, Bond and Smith reviewed 133 such studies conducted over four decades and from 17 different countries. One interesting conclusion was that conformity in the United States has declined since the early 1950s. However, the 1996 review also found that conformity increased when

(a) the size of the majority increased,

(b) the stimuli being used to test conformity were more ambiguous (the lines were more similar to each other),

(c) the majority group only included members of one's social ingroup, and

(d) the proportion of women participants increased.

Why might the presence of others in your social in-group increase conformity? One explanation is that the risk of rejection is much greater. And for women, they

CONFORMITY IN
MEAN GIRLS AND *THE DUFF*

Social Psychology in Popular Culture

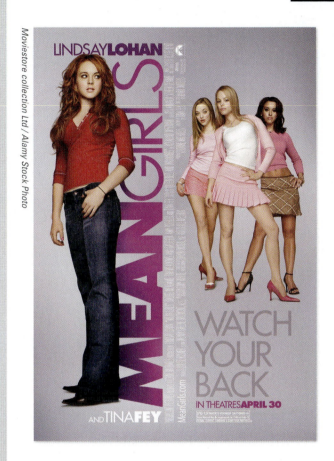

Moviestore collection Ltd / Alamy Stock Photo

In *Mean Girls,* the main character, Cady, has to learn how to gain friends quickly as she moves to the United States after being raised in Africa by her scientist parents. She quickly learns that the high school is made up of social cliques such as "Asian nerds," "band geeks," and "varsity jocks." The group of girls in the most popular social group are called "the plastics" by the other groups, because they look like real-life Barbie dolls. The plastics decide to include Cady, but only if she follows certain rules, including the following:

- on Wednesdays you have to wear pink,
- you can't wear a tank-top 2 days in a row,
- you can only put your hair in a ponytail once a week, and
- jeans or track pants are only allowed on Fridays.

Cady is torn between following the conformity rules so she can be accepted versus defying the rules, because she sees them as arbitrary, superficial, and—as the name of the movie conveys—mean. Eventually, she becomes so caught up in the social expectations of her world that she becomes the leader of the plastics, embodying everything she originally tried to scorn.

In *The DUFF,* protagonist Bianca finds out that she is her social group's "Designated Ugly, Fat Friend" and decides to embark on a training journey of how to be more popular to avoid this label. Still, she uses her own labels for others in her world, such as "the nice one" and "man whore." Both movies have several funny parts, often due to social commentary regarding how arbitrary, but often cruel, the world of conformity can be for young people trying to find their identity and place in their social worlds.

Perhaps for many of us, the pressure to conform reached a peak in middle school and high school. Unsure of their identity, teenagers may feel anxiety about fitting into their increasingly complicated social worlds. This pressure and anxiety are highlighted in the comedies *Mean Girls* (2004) and *The DUFF* (2015). In both, a theoretically less attractive girl is thrown into the world of stereotypes and social pressure as she tries to get the attention of a boy.

may have been more socialized to conform, to "be nice" and "not make trouble." Asch started this research paradigm in the 1950s, and the review summarizing all those subsequent experiments was published in the mid-1990s. Social roles for men and women were sharply defined in the 1950s, but the American culture in general and the cultural expectations for women and men both changed dramatically during those intervening years. That's why the next section explores how culture influences conformity.

Cultural Values and Conformity

What would you have done if you had been a participant in Asch's study? Twenty-four percent of Asch's participants didn't conform on a single trial—not even once (Asch, 1957)! Were these people brave rebels who had so much self-confidence they didn't care if they fit in? At least some research indicates that cultural values—rather than personal courage—may be the most potent force influencing social conformity (Triandis, 1989).

Conformity, Culture, and Eating. Chandra (1973) found high rates of conformity in a replication of the line judgment experiment (about 58%) done in Fiji. The participants in those studies were primary school teachers and teachers-in-training. Fiji is a culture in which social conformity is highly valued. Amir (1984) found approximately the same rates of conformity in a replication done in Kuwait that Asch found in the United States. If culture can change the likelihood of people saying the wrong answer—even when they know it's wrong—can it affect other types of conformity as well?

An interesting example emerged when Berry (1967) compared the Temne people from Sierra Leone (on the west coast of Africa) with Inuits (formerly sometimes called Eskimos) from Baffin Island (in the northernmost section of Canada). Berry discovered that the Temne people demonstrated a strong tendency to go along with the group norm while the Inuits almost entirely disregarded group pressure. Berry came to believe that how a culture accumulates food contributes to these wide cultural differences in conformity.

Does this food accumulation hypothesis sound like a far-fetched explanation for conformity patterns? If so, perhaps you never have been personally threatened by hunger or belonged to a group threatened with hardship (or even starvation) if a crop fails. The Temne are mostly rice farmers who can harvest only one crop per year, so they accumulate a great deal of food at one time and raise their children to be obedient, dependable, and cooperative. They have to be: Conforming contributes to their survival. A Temne participant in the line judgment experiment said, "When Temne people choose a thing, we must all agree with the decision—that is what we call cooperation."

The Inuits of Baffin Island, on the other hand, have no vegetation. Surviving for these people requires independent, adventurous individuals who can fish and hunt independently, rugged individualists who can take care of themselves in harsh conditions. They are lenient with their children, encourage independence, and value self-reliance. When the Inuits from Baffin Island participated in the line judgment experiment, they would usually say nothing at all but "would often display a quiet, knowing smile" as they pointed toward the correct line (Berry, 1967, p. 17).

Berry's experiments are important because the Temne and Inuits are profoundly different cultures. However, this same pattern of cultural differences shows up in less dramatic comparisons. What people in the individualistic-inclined culture in the United States criticize as "conformity" is highly valued in collectivist cultures as "social sensitivity." In a collectivist culture, embarrassing someone by pointing out their errors is not perceived as bravely speaking your mind—it is considered rude. To collectivist-inclined cultures, conforming isn't caving in; it is a virtuous social courtesy that puts the group's needs before your own (Markus & Kitayama, 1994).

Ironic Conformity: Hippies and Goth. For many people in the United States, conformity was viewed as a good thing in the 1950s. But attitudes toward conformity changed during the latter half of the 20th century, especially as college students began to question authority during the Vietnam War. Social conflict promoted independent thinking, and conformity was viewed as "selling out" (see Larsen, 1974, 1982, 1990; Perrin & Spencer, 1981).

The "hippie" era in the United States during the late 1960s and early 1970s was a time when young people attempted to question the status quo and be non-conformists. Does this make it ironic that so many of them generally dressed and acted the same as each other?

However, social pressures to conform are subtle as well as powerful. In the midst of the social turmoil of the 1960s, Birney, Burdick, and Teevan (1969) suggested that the cultural revolution of the 1960s was itself an exercise in ironic conformity. It seemed as if everybody was buying bell-bottomed pants, wearing peace medallions, marching against the war in Vietnam, and smoking pot. Nonconforming had become the thing to do; all the "nonconformists" started to look and act the same. It is, of course, an ironic observation about 1960s "hippies." They were more likely to be cultural rebels if their culture communicated that it was okay to be a rebel.

More recently, young people have chosen other ways to "rebel" as "nonconformists"; for example, some people choose to embrace "Goth" culture by dressing in black and wearing specific types of jewelry. Again, however, while the people participating in this subculture highly value nonconformity, the unwritten rules of how to fit in ironically mean that many "Goth" youths all look alike, profess to enjoying the same types of music, and so on.

The Main Ideas

- Informational social influence occurs when we conform in order to be correct; it leads to both private and public changes.

- Normative social influence occurs when we conform in order to gain acceptance and avoid rejection; it leads to public changes but private disagreement.

- Cultures vary in the degree to which they value conformity.

⚡ CRITICAL THINKING CHALLENGE

- How do you think you would have behaved in the Asch line judgment experiment? Name something you do (or do not do) simply because it imitates how others behave.

- How has your cultural upbringing influenced whether you think of conformity as a good thing or a bad thing? Is nonconformity a way to break up the status quo and to live authentically—or is it simply being selfish and valuing your own needs more than the group's needs?

- We discussed how culture can influence whether and when people conform. What other variables might predict higher or lower conformity? For example, are there personality traits, childhood experiences, or other ideas that increase or decrease conformity? Do these variables predict rates of informational conformity (desire to be correct), normative conformity (desire to fit in), or both?

HOW DO SOCIAL ROLES CHANGE OUR BEHAVIOR?

LO 7.3: Analyze how social roles lead us to conform to situational expectations.

Ask the Experts: Craig Parks on the Stanford Prison Study

©SAGE Publications

One of our students provided an informal definition of social roles to a student she was tutoring. A social role is "knowing what to do when you wake up in the morning." It's a pretty good definition. It hints at how just having a social role helps resolve personal uncertainties by supporting a sense of self. Social roles tell us how to act (think, feel, and behave) in a variety of situations. The studies in this section explore the surprising power of social roles. They demonstrate how profoundly the mere suggestion of a social role can influence our behavior—especially under conditions of uncertainty.

Social roles are a bigger idea than you might imagine. To Kurt Lewin (1948, pp. 43–45), whose Jewish mother disappeared during the Holocaust, social roles helped explain what happened within Germany in the 1930s and 1940s. Hitler had persuaded the Germans there was one unacceptable social role—"decadent inefficient lawlessness," which referred to Jewish people, homosexuals, the disabled, Communists, and so on—and one acceptable role (following his autocratic, fascist lead).

These disturbing dynamics are not uniquely German or limited to the 1930s and 1940s (see Morrock, 2010); genocide continues to this day—and today we can't deny that we know about it (see Pinker, 2011). The disappearing sense of self and individuality has to be replaced by something else, and the famous Stanford prison study investigated how quickly the self can disappear into a social role.

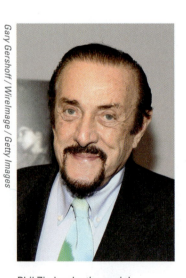

Gary Gershoff / WireImage / Getty Images

Phil Zimbardo, the social psychologist behind the Stanford prison study—perhaps the most controversial study ever done on the influence of social roles on behavior.

The Setup for the Stanford Prison Study

The prison wasn't real—but it felt that way to the participants in this controversial demonstration of the power of social roles. The "prison hole" for bad prisoners was a 2 × 2 × 7–foot closet used for solitary confinement. There were a few small rooms for cells that were just big enough to hold a single cot, but not much more. The rooms were located along a 35-foot-long basement hallway of the Stanford University psychology building in California.

It felt like a real prison even though the participants were all volunteers and Stanford students. They had been told that they couldn't leave, but no one physically restrained them. They all knew that it was only an experiment. Any participant could have walked out of the experiment any time he chose. But psychologically, it started to feel like a real prison when neighbors watched as the young men who had volunteered for the experiment were handcuffed and taken away in squad cars. The experiment had officially begun (see Zimbardo, 1973).

The simulated prison experiment tested whether social roles and situational pressures could overwhelm someone's personality (Haney, Banks, & Zimbardo, 1973). The participants had been screened in advance. The only people allowed in the study were normal, healthy, well-adjusted young men. The next step used *random assignment* to groups; each participant would, purely by chance, be assigned to play the social role of either a prisoner or a guard (thus, assignment of social role was the *independent variable*).

Random assignment to social roles means that the two groups of men started out as equivalent. Therefore, anything that happened later was probably *not* the result of naturally aggressive people becoming guards or all the dependent personalities becoming prisoners. Random assignment to groups was the only thing that determined whether a participant would be a prisoner or a guard. How people acted within each role was the *dependent variable.*

The researchers used clothing and similar symbols to prime participants into their social roles. They wore mock uniforms and symbolic ankle chains. Numbers replaced names. The guards wore official-looking uniforms and carried symbols of their pretend authority. However, unlike the "prisoners," the guards got to go home at night. In the privacy of their homes, the guards could think over what had happened during the day and why they were doing it.

Unfortunately, that extra time away from the basement in the Stanford Psychology Department did not stop the dangerous psychological process of **deindividuation**. This loss of individuality occurs when self-awareness is replaced by a social role or a group identity—the individual disappears into a social role. Deindividuation led to cruelty in the Stanford prison study. When participants put on a uniform and were given implicit permission to enact certain behaviors, the resulting feeling of anonymity or a substitute identity led them to do things they wouldn't normally consider doing.

In this case, cruelty quickly evolved as a control technique among the people randomly assigned to play the role of guards. For example, the guards forced one prisoner to simulate a sexual act. They placed a second uncooperative prisoner in the isolation hole and then instructed the other prisoners to pound on the door to this tiny closet and loudly criticize their fellow prisoner. Imagine what it was like to be alone in that dark closet while others pounded on the door and blamed you for their problems.

No one had to teach the guards how to act or what the expectations of their social role were; they figured out the mechanics of cruelty and control all by themselves. The prisoners, for their part, also embraced their social roles and identified themselves by their assigned prison numbers rather than by their names. They adopted stereotypical prison roles such as "the rebel" and "the conformist." No one had to instruct them either; the prisoners submerged their own personalities into their randomly assigned social role. Deindividuation had occurred.

Anonymity, Deindividuation, and Disinhibition

Once in their social role of prison guard, the Stanford students randomly assigned to that condition began acting in ways they probably wouldn't have in other circumstances. Why can situations have such a powerful effect on behavior?

In a simple but telling *field study* using *naturalistic observation,* Diener and colleagues (Diener, Fraser, Beaman, & Kelem, 1976) explored the process of deindividuation; they tested more than 1,300 children approaching 27 different homes in Seattle during Halloween. Researchers hid while trick-or-treaters were given the opportunity to steal candy and money from a home they visited. They found that children were more

Deindividuation: A psychological process that occurs when self-awareness is replaced by a social role or group identity, resulting in the loss of individuality.

likely to steal when (1) they were in a group (and thus might not be individually held responsible), and (2) they had not been asked for their names by the person greeting them at the door. Of course, being in a Halloween costume probably also helped provide a sense of anonymity. Without *random assignment* and a *control group* of children not in costume, this conclusion can only be speculation. Nevertheless, the evidence points to a provocative conclusion: Anonymity encourages deindividuation.

On its face, that may not sound surprising. It is a bit more interesting to recognize that decreasing self-awareness can lead to deindividuation. And it starts to become provocative as you understand that, as we saw in the Stanford prison study, the effect of deindividuation is to disinhibit (or loosen) customary social restraints (see Diener, 1979; Prentice-Dunn & Rogers, 1982). For example, students are less likely to cheat in a room with a mirror facing them, as a reminder of their identity (Vallacher & Solodky, 1979). These findings suggest that one possible path to social disinhibition looks like the chain of outcomes shown in Figure 7.3.

■ FIGURE 7.3 A possible path to social disinhibition.

The simple observation that anonymity encourages deindividuation gains more importance when you consider social media. The Internet provides many more opportunities for the kind of anonymity that decreases self-awareness and leads to deindividuation. "Trolling" online, for example, allows people to anonymously write unpopular and offensive beliefs without fear of having it reflect badly on themselves (Bargh & McKenna, 2004; Steinfeldt et al., 2010). Anonymous comments left on blogs allow people to state offensive things when no one can trace the comments back to their author. People are more willing to lie in an email than with pen and paper (Naquin, Kurtzberg, & Belkin, 2010); it seems that simply using a computer helps people feel less personally tied to their actions—something to think about in an age when job applicants, tax returns, and bureaucratic reports are submitted electronically.

But hold on! Is social disinhibition always a bad thing? A temporarily disappearing self might feel like a vacation to some people. For example, do you necessarily start harming others when you cut loose at a concert, yell at the television in the privacy of your home, or loudly complain about a referee within the safety of a crowd of fans at a football or hockey game? Deindividuation on the Internet is not necessarily a bad thing, either. The anonymity of the Internet allows users to practice social skills and experiment with "new behaviors and beliefs without fear of being judged" (Barnett & Coulson, 2010, p. 171; see Sutton-Smith, 1998). This use of the Internet can promote self-discovery and healthy exploration. Anonymity can have both socially positive as well as socially negative consequences.

Clothing Can Facilitate Particular Social Roles

The prisoners and the guards in the Stanford prison study wore uniforms that identified their social roles. The guard role was authoritative. They had the same military-like uniforms, whistles, and symbols of authority. The prisoner role was submissive; they wore smocks with ID numbers and other degrading symbols. No matter which social role a participant was randomly assigned, his clothing seemed to help him merge his former self into his new role. Like members of the Ku Klux Klan (KKK) who wear face-hiding hoods, their "costumes" appeared to release people from what Festinger and colleagues (Festinger, Pepitone, & Newcomb, 1952) called "inner restraints."

Clothes That Prime Positive and Negative Social Roles. What about good social roles? Johnson and Downing (1979) wondered more specifically whether clothing could prime both antisocial behavior and prosocial behavior. They compared groups who saw a photograph of someone dressed either in a nurses' uniform (priming the stereotype of a prosocial, caring person) or a Klan-like uniform (priming antisocial, aggressive stereotypes). In the experiment, the people in both groups were further subdivided into another two groups: individuated (with a large nametag) or relatively deindividuated (no nametag, a *control group*).

The *experimental design* for this study is represented in Table 7.1. It is called a *2 × 2 factorial design* because there are two *independent variables* (type of uniform and the presence or absence of a nametag) and two levels of each variable. If the study had included people wearing some third type of uniform, say that of a soldier, then it would have been known as a *2 × 3 factorial design*.

All participants in the Johnson and Downing (1979) study were then allowed to make decisions about whether to increase or decrease the amount of electric shock experienced by another person (the *dependent variable*). Figure 7.4 shows the results

■ TABLE 7.1 The Experimental Design for Johnson and Downing (1979)

	KKK Uniform (Negative Stereotype)	Nurse Uniform (Positive Stereotype)
Large nametag (individuated)	Condition 1	Condition 2
No nametag (deindividuated)	Condition 3	Condition 4

■ FIGURE 7.4 Type of clothing and deindividuation.

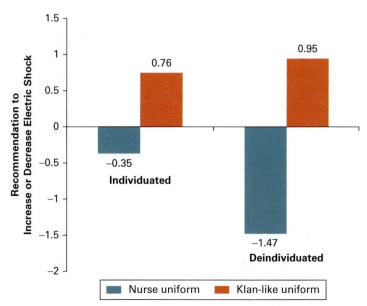

of this experiment. Compared to the individuated group, participants who were deindividuated (did not have a nametag—were more anonymous) showed less inhibition for both *pro*social and *anti*social behaviors. Their recommendations for electric shock levels were more extreme in both directions. In other words, deindividuated people seemed to let themselves take on whatever identity was suggested by the clothing: Nurse uniforms led to kinder behaviors; KKK uniforms led to more aggressive behaviors. The study suggests that anonymity/deindividuation disinhibits—both positively and negatively.

Anonymity That Encourages Intimacy.

When Gergen, Gergen, and Barton (1973) investigated deindividuation by putting people in a dark room, they noticed that participants did not become more aggressive. Instead, they became, well, more affectionate. The 18- to 25-year-olds were mostly college students who were told that they had volunteered for an experiment about the environment. The researchers admitted into the room only six or seven people at a time, male and female. Participants were asked to remove their shoes, empty their pockets, and bring nothing else into the room with them. The room was about 10 × 12 feet with padded walls and completely dark except for a small red light over the door.

The comparison group for this study received the same instructions—but the lights were on. In other words, the *independent variable* was the lighting conditions: lights on (not anonymous) or lights off (anonymous). They assessed the effects of anonymity in three ways (the *dependent variables*): They (1) tape recorded the conversations to see if people's conversation topics changed, (2) used infrared cameras to track their movements in the room, and (3) asked them to write down their impressions at the end of the experiment. Judge for yourself whether the instructions from the experimenter accidentally encouraged participants to behave in a particular way:

> You will be left in the chamber for no more than an hour with some other people. There are no rules . . . as to what you should do together. At the end of the time period you will each be escorted from the room alone, and will subsequently depart from the experimental site alone. There will be no opportunity to meet the other participants.

The anonymity of darkness led to more touching and caressing compared to the lighted room. About 90% of the participants in the darkened room "touched each other on purpose, while almost none of the light-room subjects did." Almost 50% in the dark room hugged another person and about 80% reported feeling sexual excitement. One female participant wrote that after initial tension and nervousness, "The darkness no longer bothered me." By the end of the hour, the group "sat closely together, touching, feeling a sense of friendship and loss as a group member left. I left with a feeling that it had been fun and nice. I felt I had made some friends. In fact, I missed them."

One male wrote that he "felt joy over the possibility of not having to look at people in clichéd ways. Enjoyed feeling of a self-awareness surrounded by a rich environment." Touching and caressing just because it is dark still suggests disinhibition. The participants didn't start caressing strangers in the lighted room. An important variation in this experiment occurred when participants were told that they would meet one another at the end of the experiment. In that condition, participants "were less likely to explore . . . more likely to feel bored, less likely to introduce themselves, less likely to hug . . . and more likely to feel panicky." Intimacy declined. Knowing that you're anonymous and that you'll never meet people again leads us to do behaviors we might normally censor in ourselves.

The Self Behind the Mask. In the previous experiment, anonymity through darkness encouraged a temporary intimacy. However, this next experiment demonstrates negative behavior associated with anonymity through wearing a mask. In the United States, several regions created antimask laws due to crimes being committed by people wearing Ku Klux Klan hoods. More recently, laws have been passed banning people from wearing "Guy Fawkes" masks in public (named after a famous British political protestor) because the online hacking group known as "Anonymous" has chosen this image as their icon.

AFP / Getty Images

Criminals sometimes wear masks. Certainly, one reason to do this is to protect your identity so you're not caught. However, masks also make the wearers feel anonymous, which may empower them to enact behaviors they wouldn't do if their identities were known. Here you can see people wearing a "Guy Fawkes" mask, made famous in the movie *V for Vendetta* (2005) and now associated with the online hacking group called "Anonymous."

Some of the studies described so far have included only male participants. To test the possibility of a gender difference, Zimbardo (1970) allowed one group of women to become deindividuated by wearing hoods and loose-fitting clothing. The comparison group wore their own clothes and large nametags. When given the opportunity to deliver an electric shock, the *de*individuated group of women held the lever down twice as long, even "as their victims twisted and moaned right before them" (see Zimbardo, 2007, p. 300). That experiment did not support popularly assumed gender differences that men tend to be more aggressive and that women tend to be "nice." When relatively anonymous, these women didn't hesitate to painfully shock a victim.

In another experiment by Lightdale and Prentice (1994), women were just as willing as men to "let go" of their inhibitions and harm others, but only in the deindividuation condition. Given the right circumstances, such as anonymity, women become just as nasty and aggressive as men. Perhaps most of the time, women and men seem more different than they really are, simply because they are both conforming to stereotypical social roles.

The Main Ideas

- Social roles can become more important than individual personality when predicting behaviors in given situations. The famous Stanford prison study explored social roles and deindividuation by randomly assigning students to pretend to be either a prisoner or a guard.

- Deindividuation occurs when people's inhibitions are lowered due to perceived anonymity.

- Variables such as clothing or darkness can predict increases or decreases in feelings of deindividuation.

- Imagine you were given an opportunity to be a participant in a study like the Stanford prison study. Would you do it, knowing in advance that you wouldn't be able to choose between being assigned the prisoner or guard roles?

- Consider the ethical implications of studies like the Asch conformity study and the Stanford prison study. After the studies were done and the participants were debriefed (told the true purpose of the study), the people had to live with their choices—some of which were not particularly positive. Should studies like this be allowed, given the potential risks to the participants? Would you want to be confronted with the knowledge that you are capable of negative behaviors, given the right circumstances?

WHAT CAN WE LEARN FROM MILGRAM'S EXPERIMENTS ON AUTHORITY?

LO 7.4: Explain the person, procedures, and competing interpretations behind the Milgram experiments on authority.

So far, this chapter has gone in depth to help you understand implicit forms of social influence, focusing on conformity and social roles. What about explicit forms of social influence? When we change our behavior due to explicit influence, we do something because of either compliance (agreeing to someone's request) or obedience (following an order). The scientific study of obedience led to perhaps the most controversial social psychology studies ever done (Griggs & Whitehead, 2015). Many students in psychology know the basics of what happened in Milgram's labs—but not many know the details. We will describe several of the studies as we consider some of the intended and unintended lessons we can learn from Stanley Milgram's studies about social influence created by obedience to an authority.

The Man Behind the Controversy: Stanley Milgram

The genius of psychological science is that it (gradually) provides small answers to big questions. Asking questions, and using experiments to answer them, was the normal way to live for Stanley Milgram (1933–1984). Milgram was the child of hard-working immigrant parents. They lived in the South Bronx section of New York City, a place Milgram described as "not a neighborhood of patsies" (see Blass, 2004, pp. 5–16). Milgram and Zimbardo attended the same high school, knew one another, and pursued similar research interests in social psychology.

To the young Milgram, conducting experiments "was as natural as breathing. I tried to understand how everything worked." Milgram was still an adolescent in the aftermath of World War II. The world was struggling to accept a brutal insight into human nature: Hitler and Stalin had lots of help. The level of human slaughter required bricklayers, plumbers, middle management, engineers, social coordination, and even creativity to murder so many people so quickly (Cropley, Cropley, Kaufman, & Runco, 2010; Heinzen, 1995). Like Asch and Zimbardo, Milgram (1974) wanted to know why people "who are in everyday life responsible and decent" (p. 125) became knowing contributors to mass murder. So Milgram designed an *experimental paradigm* that established procedures simulating the phenomenon he was interested in—the

Social Psychology in Action:
Milgram's Obedience Study

©SAGE Publications

psychology of ordinary people behaving in extraordinarily harmful ways, because they were obeying an authority figure.

The Historical Context

By now, you understand that there is much more to social psychology than exploring the dark underbelly of human cruelty and mass murder. But we can't deny the historical context of war that eventually led to Milgram's studies. The World War I German foot soldier Kurt Lewin got us started by trying to explain social influences on his fellow soldiers in the trenches. In the 1930s, before World War II commanded our attention, Sherif created the autokinetic experiments to study how social influences lead to conformity under conditions of uncertainty. Asch created the line judgment studies that explored conformity when everyone knew what was happening, and Zimbardo explored the power of how a social role and uniform lead to deindividuation and cruelty. Milgram's studies add one more possible explanation: the power of obedience.

The Study's Procedure

The basic question Milgram wanted to answer was, "How far will someone go when obeying an authority figure until they refuse to continue?" Milgram had two goals in mind when he designed these experiments: (1) use simple procedures because "complicated procedures only get in the way" (Milgram, 1974, p. 14), and (2) aim for *experimental realism* by designing situations that are realistic, approximate the variables of interest, and are consequential to participants. Make them matter.

To begin, Milgram placed an announcement in the New Haven, Connecticut, newspaper: "Persons Needed for a Study of Memory." It was a *cover story*, a choice to use strategic *deception* that camouflaged the true nature of the experiment to capture authentic responses to the situation Milgram had created. They would be paid $4 (an amount with much more buying power at that time) if they agreed to be part of an experiment about memory. When they arrived at prestigious Yale University, they were told that the study was about how receiving a punishment after a mistake might motivate someone to learn more effectively.

When they arrived, the participants met a *confederate* who pretended to be just another person off the street, and the experimenter then pretended to randomly assign one of them to the role of "Teacher" (this role always went to the actual participant) and one to the role of "Learner" (always the confederate). The job of the Teacher was to read word pairs out loud (such as "fast/car" or "white/bird") to the Learner. The Learner's

■ FIGURE 7.5 Levels of electric shock in Milgram's famous obedience studies.

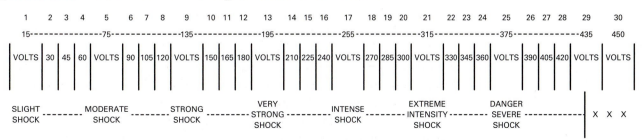

SOURCE: © 1974 by Stanley Milgram; by permission of Alexandra Milgram.

job was to memorize the word pairs and then take a memory test. The Teacher was to respond to any memory failures by delivering gradually increasing levels of electric shock—15 volts more with each failure—as the punishment. The electric shocks were another *deception;* the shock machine wasn't actually hooked up to the confederate, so he never really got shocked. But the participant didn't know that. The *dependent variable* was simple: How far up the electric shock scale shown in Figure 7.5 would they go?

Milgram anticipated that as the sessions progressed, at least some of the participants would show doubt and ask for advice about whether to continue. So, he set up four verbal prods to use whenever a Teacher expressed reluctance to continue:

Prod 1: "Please continue" or "Please go on."

Prod 2: "The experiment requires that you continue."

Prod 3: "It is absolutely essential that you continue."

Prod 4: "You have no other choice, you *must* go on."

When he first tested his procedures on Yale college students, Milgram was surprised to discover that they raced past posted warnings on the machine such as "DANGER SEVERE SHOCK," until they reached the maximum shock level of 450 volts. While some of them did ask the experimenter whether they should keep going, he found that after the four verbal prods were given, most of the participants continued to deliver increasing levels of shock. In this first experiment, 26 out of 40 Yale students (65%) shocked to the maximum.

In his book about the study, Milgram (1974) notes with surprise, "In the absence of protests from the learner, virtually every subject in the pilot study, once commanded, went blithely to the end of the board" (p. 22). Milgram thought maybe the participants didn't realize what was supposed to be happening . . . so he ramped up the procedure for his own *replication.* What happens when the Teacher starts to hear the Learner scream with pain?

Milgram's Replications

Milgram set up the entire experiment again, but this time he wrote a script for the Learner to follow if the participant kept going to each level of shock shown in Table 7.2 (Milgram, 1974, pp. 56–57).

Did hearing the Learner scream and note that he had heart problems stop the participants from obeying the authority figure in the room? Again, surprisingly, most of them just kept going: This time, 65% of the participants went all the way to 450 volts.

Milgram replicated his study a full *18* times, trying to understand the psychology behind what was happening. Most of the participants really did seem willing to cause pain—and maybe even death!—to a stranger they just met, who had done nothing to deserve this fate, simply because they were being ordered to do so. When Milgram ran the procedure with women as participants, the result was exactly the same: 65% obeyed all the way.

Across these many replications, sometimes the number of people who obeyed did fluctuate based on the experimental conditions. For example, obedience went down when the participant had to sit in the same room as the Learner (only 40% went all the way to 450 volts). It went down even more when the participant had to force the Learner's hand onto the electric plate in order to receive the shock: only 30%. And when there were two additional confederates pretending to be administering shocks who protested at the orders and said they wouldn't continue, obedience from the participant

Level of Shock	Response
75 volts	Ugh!
90 volts	Ugh!
105 volts	Ugh! [Louder]
120 volts	Ugh! Hey, this really hurts.
135 volts	Ugh!!
150 volts	Ugh!!! Experimenter! That's all. Get me out of here. I told you I had heart trouble. My heart's starting to bother me now. Get me out of here, please. My heart's starting to bother me. I refuse to go on. Let me out.
165 volts	Ugh! Let me out! [Shouting]
180 volts	Ugh! I can't stand the pain. Let me out of here! [Shouting]
195 volts	Ugh! Let me out of here. Let me out of here. My heart's bothering me. Let me out of here! You have no right to keep me here! Let me out! Let me out of here! Let me out! Let me out of here! My heart's bothering me. Let me out! Let me out!
210 volts	Ugh!! Experimenter! Get me out of here. I've had enough. I won't be in the experiment any more.
225 volts	Ugh!
240 volts	Ugh!
255 volts	Ugh! Get me out of here.
270 volts	[Agonized scream.] Let me out of here. Let me out of here. Let me out of here. Let me out. Do you hear? Let me out of here.
285 volts	[Agonized scream.]
300 volts	[Agonized scream.] I absolutely refuse to answer any more. Get me out of here. You can't hold me here. Get me out. Get me out of here.
315 volts	[Intensely agonized scream.] I told you I refuse to answer. I'm no longer part of this experiment.
330 volts	[Intense and prolonged agonized scream.] Let me out of here. Let me out of here. My heart's bothering me. Let me out, I tell you. [Hysterically.] Let me out of here. Let me out of here. You have no right to hold me here. Let me out! Let me out! Let me out of here! Let me out! Let me out!
345–450 volts	[Silence]

SOURCE: Milgram (1963).

© Stanley Milgram

Obedience to authority declined to 30% when the participant had to physically hold the victim or "Learner" down to receive painful shocks.

went down to only 10% going all the way to 450 volts. Note, of course, that there were still 10% of people who were willing to keep going.

The Path to Disobedience

While it's chilling that most of the participants appeared willing to obey an authority when ordered to cause pain to someone else, it's important to keep in mind that at least some of the participants refused to obey. Why? Moral values come to mind, of course, but the series of studies following Milgram's initial paradigm show that many other variables are at play. Milgram outlined five stages along the path to disobedience (see Figure 7.6).

When trying to understand why some people disobeyed, Milgram understood that, "at first, we are inclined to say that they do so because it is immoral to shock the victim" (Milgram, 1974, p. 153). But according to the results, an authority perceived

■ FIGURE 7.6 The path to disobedience.

Milgram identified five steps along the path to disobedience

as legitimate (e.g., from a prestigious place like Yale) can overrule personal moral standards (Kelman & Hamilton, 1989). However, moral and religious convictions can also encourage *dis*obedience to authority (Skitka, Bauman, & Lytle, 2009). So, moral values *can* influence obedience to authority but, on average during these experiments, situations and social expectations appeared to overwhelm moral values.

Three specific participants illustrate reactions to disobedience. One man, a professor of religion, stopped at 150 volts. When the experimenter told him, "You must go on," he responded, "If this were Russia maybe, but not in America" (Milgram, 1974, p. 48). A second man, an industrial engineer, stopped at 255 volts. When the experimenter said, "It is absolutely essential that you continue. . . . You have no other choice," this man said,

> I *do* have a choice. Why don't have I have choice? I came here on my own free will. I thought I could help in a research project. But if I have to hurt somebody to do that, or if I was in his place, too, I wouldn't stay there. I can't continue. I'm very sorry. I think I've gone too far already, probably. (p. 51)

Finally, one of the women who participated in the study was an immigrant from Germany. She had been witness to what obedience to an authority could do as her country tried to recover from World War I and fell onto the path leading to the Holocaust. She was raised in a culture of Nazi propaganda and participated in the Hitler youth program. When she stopped at 210 volts and was asked why she refused to continue, her answer was, "Perhaps we have seen too much pain" (p. 85).

Ethical Considerations

Thanks to the popularity of Milgram's grainy black-and-white film of what happened, the obedience studies have become "part of our society's shared intellectual legacy"

(Ross & Nisbett, 1991, p. 55). However, Milgram's studies prompted negative reactions by many within psychology, primarily over the ethics of his experiments (Baumrind, 1964; Mixon, 1972). In his own defense (also controversial), Milgram asserted that his procedures did not violate any of the research norms of that time period, and his procedures had been preapproved by the National Science Foundation (NSF).

In fact, Milgram's NSF grant application included a special section about ethical responsibility to the participants (see Blass, 2004). Milgram also reported that he debriefed participants after the experiment and kept in touch with them long after the experiment had ended. That assertion is also controversial in light of recent evidence.

The American Psychological Association's ethical guidelines for research with human participants are part of the legacy of Milgram's experiments. There are two practical lessons from these studies. First, use your *institutional review board* (IRB) to protect your study participants (and yourself). They will review the ethics of your procedures *before* you start conducting an experiment. Second, use Morling's (2015) ethical decision-making matrix to help you evaluate risk as you make ethical decisions. Table 7.3 can help you evaluate the trade-off between the risks and rewards of conducting a particular research project.

Australian journalist Gina Perry deserves significant credit for the 4 years she spent reexamining the archives from this most famous of psychological experiments (Brannigan, 2013). She listened to 140 audio recordings of the original experiments, to hours of debriefings with participants, and to experts and family members of the actors, and she read the mountains of documentation. Her conclusions fundamentally challenge how scholars have interpreted (and presented) Stanley Milgram and his experiment. Brannigan (2013) identified many categories of criticism from this investigation, including

■ **TABLE 7.3** Morling's (2015) Ethical Decision-Making Matrix. Milgram's obedience experiments involved high risk and high reward. Does the potential reward mean that the risk is worthwhile?

	Low Risk	High Risk
Low reward		
High reward		The Milgram Obedience Experiments

SOURCE: Adapted from Morling (2011).

(1) minimizing or hiding the degree of trauma experience by many participants,

(2) providing deliberately misleading reports about those traumas,

(3) not reporting participants' skepticism about the various deceptions,

(4) misrepresenting how the prods were used,

(5) failing to debrief most participants,

(6) cherry-picking data, and

(7) creating a pseudo-documentary film that whitewashed all these shortcomings.

These are serious charges, and we must keep in mind that Milgram's death means that he cannot explain, modify, or rebut those assertions. However, the archives indicate that, in contrast to what he reported, Milgram did not debrief all participants and minimized negative consequences when he knew about them (see I. A. M. Nicholson, 2011, 2015; I. R. Nicholson, 2011; Perry, 2013). For example, one participant indicated that he had lost his job "due to an emotional outburst during a discussion about the experiment . . . another reported that he had suffered a mild heart attack . . . implying that the extreme stress of the study was at least partially responsible" (Brannigan, Nicholson, & Cherry, 2015, p. 554).

Beyond Obedience:
Sacrificing for a Higher Cause

The most radical new interpretation of the Milgram shock experiments comes from Haslam, Reicher, and Birney (2015)—and from Milgram's own notes. Their review of participants' comments about their experience in these famous experiments led them to propose that participants were more than just obedient—they were engaged followers, proud to commit their time to the noble cause of science.

Haslam, S. A., Reicher, S. D., Millard, K., & McDonald, R. (2015). 'Happy to have been of service': The Yale archive as a window into the engaged followership of participants in Milgram's 'obedience' experiments. British Journal of Social Psychology, 54(1), 55-83.

Sacrificing for a "Noble" Cause. Think of a modern terrorist who, for the sake of a higher cause, sacrifices his or her life in a suicide mission. While each person is unique and some are coerced, there also are volunteers willing and even eager to die for their cause. At one level of understanding, the suicide bomber is not so different from a man in the Milgram studies who could not hide his nervous laughter as he went through the levels on the shock machine. He tried to explain that, despite his conflicted emotions, he continued to deliver shocks because, "in the interest of science, one goes through with it" (Milgram, 1974, p. 54).

The suicide bomber and the conflicted participant in Milgram's study sacrificed for a higher, "noble" cause—something bigger than themselves. Of course, whether the cause is "noble" is subjective and will be seen in a very different light by the other side, especially the victims. Milgram's own notes also express initial ambivalence about whether he is observing obedience or cooperation with a cause. Table 7.4 (from the Yale archives of the study) organizes sample quotations of what the participants had to say about their experience according to their level of engagement (see Haslam, Reicher, Millard, and McDonald, 2015, p. 72).

■ TABLE 7.4 Participants' Experience in Milgram's Study

Level (1–7)	Description	Example Illustrative Comments	# of People	%
7	Very highly engaged	*I feel I have contributed in some small way toward the development of man and his attitudes towards others. I would be glad to participate in other studies. I thoroughly enjoyed participating in the program and hope I will be called on again.*	33	23.6
6	Highly engaged	*The experiment was very interesting and worthwhile. I think that studies of this kind are very helpful and should continue.*	27	19.3
5	Moderately engaged	*Any study with an aim, if properly conducted, can do no harm and might be of some value.*	34	24.3
4	Neither	*It is good to know that you would not permit me to give the learner the actual shocks under the condition of this experiment.*	33	23.6
3	Moderately disengaged	*It was only after speaking to you on the phone that I concluded the experiment had been prearranged and in all truthfulness somewhat silly. I would suggest that more experiments are conducted but that they be conducted on the more serious side.*	8	5.7
2	Highly disengaged	*You might be interested to know that my opinion of Yale is quite low because of this experiment. Kindly furnish me with the name & address so that I can satisfy my own thought about this experiment.*	5	3.6
1	Very highly disengaged	*[no comments]*	0	0
	Total		140	

SOURCE: Adapted from the Yale University Library.

Historical Evidence. One of the most famous Nazi officers was Adolf Eichmann, one of the main organizers and supervisors of the concentration campus. Within that organization, Eichmann was a man with both influence and initiative. Late in the war, after it was clear that the Nazis were fighting a losing cause, senior military leaders tried to assassinate Hitler. Nevertheless, Eichmann pressed forward with loyalty to the cause. He organized an extraordinary 144 transports to Auschwitz for approximately 440,000 Hungarians in just 2 months. And he did so with such a strong sense of higher purpose that he defied orders from his Nazi superiors to cut back until the direction of the war effort was more settled.

Grobman and colleagues (Grobman, Landes, & Milton, 1983) report a speech by Himmler given to SS officers exterminating Jews at Poznan, in Poland:

> Most of you know what it is like to see 100 corpses lie side by side, or 500 or 1,000. To have stood fast through all this and . . . at the same time to have remained a decent person. . . . This is an unwritten and never-to-be-written page of glory in our history . . . we have carried out this most difficult of tasks in a spirit of love for our people. (pp. 454–455)

In their own minds, they weren't really murderers and certainly not evil. Instead, they were special people who nobly suffered for the good of others (according to them), doing the unpleasant but necessary work needed to make the world a better place.

This represents a new way to understand Milgram's experiments. If it holds up, then it has far-reaching implications—and not just for our understanding of the past. Understanding how viciousness is experienced as virtue can help us understand not just interpersonal cruelty but also how terrorists privately make sense of and rationalize mass murder.

Two Interpretations of Milgram—and of the Holocaust. During the grant review process, Milgram's obedience studies had been criticized for not having a guiding theory. One reviewer noted that it was "clear that Dr. Milgram neither has nor plans to have an elaborate a priori theory" (see Blass, 2004, p. 71). We don't know if Milgram disagreed with that assessment, but by the time Milgram (1974) issued the book summarizing these experiments, that theoretical framework was firmly in place.

Universal History Archive/Universal Images Group/Getty Images

Daily workers at the Auschwitz World War II concentration camp take a break. Their capacity for happiness suggests that they were engaged and willing participants in the mass murder of at least 1.1 million people at Auschwitz.

Milgram (1974) began with the assumption that "some system of authority is a requirement for all communal living" (p. 3). Then he reasoned that "a potential for obedience is the prerequisite of such social organization . . . because organization has enormous survival value for any species." By the end of the obedience studies, Milgram concluded that "we are born with a potential for obedience" (p. 126). In other words, Milgram believed we could all display this kind of behavior, given the right circumstances.

So we now have two interpretations of what happened in the Milgram shock experiments: (1) obedience to authority and (2) engaged followers who believe in a cause. The first explanation recognizes that in every society, some authority will have to decide that all cars will drive either on the right-hand or the left-hand side of the road and that the stop signs will be painted red. People who agree to obey that authority will have a better chance of surviving, getting along with each other, and feeling secure that people in power have the ability to keep the world in running order.

The second interpretation is in some ways scarier. Participants in the Milgram studies were proud to have made a contribution to science, to a higher cause. Other causes perceived to be noble may also lead people to justify behaviors that will be perceived as immoral from an outsider's point of view. Stanley Milgram and his data from the shock experiments are still speaking—and psychologists are still debating why so many participants continued to shock innocent people up to the maximum of 450 volts. Despite its many flaws, that's still one powerful, provocative experiment.

The Main Ideas

- Milgram's obedience to authority experiments demonstrate how many people will follow orders from an authority, even when it means engaging in behaviors they might consider immoral.

- The obedience experiments used simple procedures and included a series of replications with different variations.

- Some participants disobeyed; the path to disobedience begins by expressing inner doubts.

- Two possible interpretations of Milgram's results are (1) people have an inner tendency to obey authority figures, and (2) people will sometimes justify "immoral" behavior if they believe in a cause they perceive as noble.

⚡ CRITICAL THINKING CHALLENGE

- If you felt that all ethical concerns had been met, then what comparison conditions would you like to add to the Milgram obedience experiments?

- Did Milgram's qualitative observations add significant insights into what happened during the obedience experiments?

- Think back to the Nazi guards in concentration camps during World War II. What kinds of psychological processes did they have when ordered to enact atrocities? Can you think of other historical examples of times or events that illustrate obedience to authority despite it leading to immoral behaviors?

CHAPTER SUMMARY

What types of social influence exist?

Social influence occurs when our thoughts, feelings, and/or behaviors are influenced by other people. Social influence can take two basic forms. Implicit social influence occurs when we follow subtle, unwritten rules communicated nonverbally. One example of implicit social influence is conformity, when we voluntarily change our behavior to follow what others are doing. Another example comes from social roles, our expectations about how certain people are supposed to look or behave (such as police officers vs. librarians). The second basic form of social influence is explicit, which occurs when we follow obvious, direct requests from others (called compliance) or orders from others (called obedience).

Social norms are rules about how people should behave in certain situations, which often lead to conformity. Extreme conformity can lead to a herd mentality, or the tendency to follow the direction of a group without question. In general, conformity seems to be contagious; we feel more pressure to conform when the group is larger. This can sometimes even lead to a phenomenon called mass psychogenic illness, which is when psychological conformity leads to people experiencing physical symptoms of illness when there is no physical cause.

Why and when do we choose to conform?

Informational conformity or social influence occurs when people change their behavior because they want to be correct. Here, people follow along with what others are doing because they believe the behavior is right; thus, conformity is both public and private (meaning we agree with what we are doing). This type of conformity is more likely to occur when we are unsure what the "correct" answer is. Classic research on informational public conformity was started by Sherif when he studied the auto-kinetic effect, an optical illusion in which people's guesses about how much a stationary light moved were influenced by other people's answers. This effect has been shown to occur over "generations" of participants.

On the other hand, normative social influence occurs when we go along with group behaviors in order to fit in or be accepted. Here, our public behavior might not reflect private conformity (we secretly know that what we're doing isn't "correct"). The most famous example of normative conformity is a series of studies by Asch in which participants provided what was clearly the wrong answer to a perception task after confederates had provided a wrong answer. Participants indicated that they went along with the wrong answer because they didn't want to seem strange or not fit in (75% of participants went along with the incorrect group answer at least once). There are individual differences in how likely people are to conform, based on variables such as cultural values.

How do social roles change our behavior?

Social roles guide us in how to think, feel, and act in a variety of situations, like characters in a play. The most famous social psychology study of social roles is the Stanford prison study created by Zimbardo; he turned the basement of the Stanford psychology building into a fake prison, then randomly assigned students to play either the role of prisoner or guard. The students quickly seemed to lose their individual identities and simply played the part, or they went along with their assigned social role.

One factor that increases our conformity to a social role is called deindividuation, which is when we feel more anonymous due to things like wearing a uniform, wearing a mask, or being in the dark. While deindividuation has been tied to several negative social behaviors, such as cruelty or criminal actions, it has also been tied to positive social behaviors, such as kindness.

What can we learn from Milgram's experiments on authority?

Milgram conducted a series of studies regarding whether people are willing to deliver potentially painful and dangerous electric shocks to someone else, simply because they were ordered to do so. In all of his studies, the person supposedly receiving the shocks was a confederate and no shocks were actually delivered (although the participants didn't know this). Approximately two thirds of the participants in Milgram's initial conditions went to the maximum shock level available, which they thought might even have killed the other person. Milgram continued with a series of replications of the study with slight changes; for example, when he replicated the study with women participants, about two thirds of them also showed obedience.

Some participants did disobey, and Milgram suggested that the path to disobedience starts with inner doubts, then progresses through public dissent, threat, and finally to disobeying the authority figure. While Milgram defended the ethics of his study, recent examination of the original study materials questions some of his ethical claims. Finally, recent reinterpretations of his findings note that there are two possible explanations for the findings. The first is Milgram's explanation—that most of us have the capacity to follow orders from an authority, given the right circumstances. An alternative interpretation is that the people involved continued because they believed in the "cause," which was scientific knowledge in this setting. Either explanation might apply to why Nazi guards did terrible deeds during World War II when obeying orders from a leader.

THEORIES IN REVIEW

- Social contagion
- Theory of informational and normative influence
- Social roles

- Deindividuation
- Obedience

CRITICAL THINKING, ANALYSIS, AND APPLICATION

- Identify two times in world history when someone stood up against a group (they exhibited nonconformity) and helped change a negative group decision or movement. Then, identify two times in world history where conforming to the values or needs of the larger group helped a community make a good or progressive decision, even if some people in the group disagreed.

- As times change, social roles change as well. For example, the social roles expected of "stereotypical" men and women have changed over the past 100 years. What are positive aspects of this change—and are there any negative aspects of this change?

- This chapter discussed several famous studies that some people consider unethical. Do you think an unethical study is more likely to become famous compared to an ethical one? Why or why not? Provide examples as evidence of your answer.

- The theories and phenomena in this chapter (conformity, social roles, compliance, and obedience) were presented as possible social psychological explanations for the Holocaust (or, at least, contributing factors). What other theories that you've learned about in this book so far might also be included as possible explanations for what happened?

PERSONAL REFLECTION

I was the only girl in a family with four children. While my three brothers all played video games, mowed the lawn, and went on Boy Scout camping trips, my mother wanted me to be her little princess. She put me in old-fashioned, pink, frilly dresses; taught me how to bake pies; and paid for me to take ballet lessons. Through all of this, I felt torn. On one hand, I wanted to fit in with the other girls, have friends, be popular, and obey my mother—which meant acting "like a girl." On the other hand, I hated all of it. I wanted to play soccer, do karate, and smear my face with mud. This resulted in paradoxical situations. I attended ballet lessons, for instance, but changed into my ballet shoes after arriving in combat boots and was teased for wearing a black unitard instead of a pink one. I learned very early the price of nonconformity as I didn't get invited to birthday parties or sleepovers. Even though it took me a long time to gain the self-confidence to be myself despite enormous peer pressure in school and the clear preferences of my mother, eventually I realized that I could only be happy by being authentic—even if it meant also being a bit lonely. Fortunately, I eventually found other people who both accepted me despite being "weird" and who were, in their own ways, also strange. Now, in addition to teaching psychology, I'm a professor of gender studies. Choosing independence can be hard, but being true to yourself is almost always the best path. [WG]

Visit **edge.sagepub.com/heinzen** to help you accomplish your coursework goals in an easy-to-use learning environment.

- **Visual Key Concepts**
- Mobile-friendly **eFlashcards**
- Mobile-friendly practice **quizzes**
- **Video** and **multimedia content**
- EXCLUSIVE! Access to full-text **SAGE journal articles**

⑤SAGE edge™

LO7.1 **Compare** and **contrast** **implicit versus explicit** social influence.

LO7.2 **Differentiate** between **informational** and **normative social pressures** to conform.

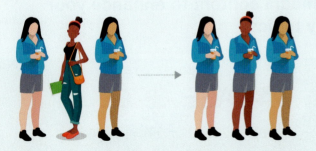

L07.3 **Analyze** how **social roles** lead us to **conform** to **situational expectations**.

L07.4 **Explain** the person, procedures, and competing interpretations behind the **Milgram experiments** on **authority**.

8 Group Processes

Core Questions

1. Why are groups so important to us?

2. Why are we more committed to certain groups?

3. How do groups help and hinder individual effort?

4. How do individuals influence groups?

5. What increases group creativity?

Learning Objectives

8.1 Explain how groups provide social and practical benefits to individuals.

8.2 Identify ways that groups gain and maintain their authority over individuals.

8.3 Analyze how groups can both help and hinder individual efforts.

8.4 Analyze how leadership succeeds or fails, how group decisions turn risky or safe, and how a minority can influence the majority.

8.5 Evaluate what circumstances help and hurt group creativity.

Thirteen people painted the Sistine Chapel, but we credit the achievement to just one person (Michelangelo). The first computer software was written when six women were given a stack of wiring diagrams and instructed to "figure out how the machine works and then figure out how to program it" (Isaacson, 2014, pp. 97–98). The enduringly popular show *Saturday Night Live* (Michaels et al., 1975–) employs many writers and comedic actors who work together to come up with new skits every week. These examples all demonstrate the creative potential of groups.

Groups can also go bad, however, and sometimes there is only a faint line between creating and destroying. Even though the Beatles enjoyed fantastic fame and success as a popular band, they eventually broke up under emotional circumstances. In many cities all over the world, groups such as gangs or the mafia form to better engage in criminal behavior. And sometimes, groups that lose the ability to disagree with each other and therefore fail to engage in critical thinking can make disastrous decisions. This chapter explores both the creative and the destructive potential of groups by asking and answering five core questions.

WHY ARE GROUPS SO IMPORTANT TO US?

LO 8.1: Explain how groups provide social and practical benefits to individuals.

Groups occur when two or more individuals interact with one another or are joined together by a common fate. When you think back to high school, you can probably remember how students spontaneously sorted themselves into different groups. Some groups were based on popularity (the "cool," rich, and/or beautiful kids), and others depended on common interests (in band, athletics, theater, social rebels, etc.). Some of those group memberships—and friendships—were the product of chance events such as classroom seating assignment (see Vallacher, Coleman, Nowak, & Bui-Wrzosinska, 2010) yet still endured for a lifetime.

Groups are important to us because they provide evolutionary advantages, such as sharing of food and shelter in times of scarcity. Perhaps because of their importance for our survival, humans have an instinct to flock together and form alliances, even in

Group: When two or more individuals interact with one another or are joined together by a common fate.

Ask the Experts: Craig Parks on Group Dynamics

©SAGE Publications

The Lewis and Clark Expedition across the newly formed United States (1804 to 1806) required individuals to band together into a cohesive group, at least in part to help their survival on the dangerous journey. Here is a depiction of the group, guided by Sacajawea.

Group cohesiveness: The degree to which members of a group feel connected to one another.

Functional distance: The tendency for people who are in close proximity due to the geographic and architectural design of an environment to be more likely to develop a cohesive group, such as a friendship or a romantic relationship.

modern computer games with strangers (Belz, Pyritz, & Boos, 2013). Cohesive groups that share more of their resources enjoy many advantages. They allow individuals and subgroups to specialize, define social roles, develop an identity, share critical information, and provide a safer environment for everyone.

For example, the 33 members of the U.S. Lewis and Clark Expedition (from 1804 to 1806) became a temporary family that divided up chores and together both suffered and celebrated the consequences of their good and bad decisions (see Kameda & Tindale, 2006). They survived extraordinary hardships, in part, because of **group cohesiveness**, the degree to which members of a group feel connected to one another (see Dion, 2000).

In modern times, group cohesiveness can be seen in a wide variety of settings ranging from certain types of workers in a company (such as the marketing department or the sales force) through majors in a college (psychology, biology, etc.) to fans of given sports teams. We can better understand our impulse to form groups by exploring four benefits of belonging to groups: (1) cohesiveness that supplies social support, (2) a sense of identity, (3) safety and security, and (4) meaningful information.

Groups Provide Social Support

Group cohesiveness can be a wonderful experience, but it is difficult to identify the ingredients that create a great volleyball team, innovative work group, or effective volunteer organization. Fortunately, two famous *field studies* in housing projects studied group cohesiveness in its natural setting. They both were case studies that closely examined everyday life in two very different kinds of housing projects. Both studies discovered a similar pattern: Group cohesiveness emerged from "apparently minor features of design" (Festinger, Schacter, & Back, 1950, p. 13). In other words, architectural features of the physical setup of the buildings influenced group cohesiveness. Group cohesiveness, in turn, influenced the social support experienced by the people living in the housing projects.

The Westgate Housing Projects at MIT. The first housing project was built at the end of World War II when the Massachusetts Institute of Technology (MIT) created housing complexes (Westgate and Westgate West) to accommodate returning soldiers and their families going to college on the GI Bill (Festinger et al., 1950). Festinger recognized that this first *case study* was also a *naturalistic experiment* because they had meaningful comparison groups that were not manipulated by an experimenter. For example, assignment to particular housing units was not perfectly random, as would be the case in a controlled experiment. Three other experiment-like controls were that the apartments were somewhat isolated geographically from the rest of the area, the apartments were all similar in style and space, and the residents shared similar backgrounds and ambitions.

The research team discovered that the friendships and group cohesiveness that evolved in this isolated setting could be predicted, not by personality but by **functional distance**, or the physical constraints such as geography or architecture. Here, functional distance was how close an apartment was to stairwells or to mailboxes—places the other residents had to be. Residents of each building formed friendships with people they saw and interacted with more, simply because those people happened to live in an apartment that was physically located in a spot with a lot of social traffic. (For more on the Westgate study, see Chapter 12.)

Living in the same building encourages group cohesiveness. A group of mothers in this Chicago housing project are keeping an eye on one another's children.

A finer-grained reinterpretation of this famous study brought attention to "the physical circumstances of having to care for very young children" (Cherry, 1995, p. 76). This gendered understanding of the Westgate study is significant because most of the interviewees were new mothers who had to budget carefully and care for children in a setting with strangers. In the Westgate housing project, cohesive friendships emerged for two overlapping reasons: (1) the nuances of where people lived and (2) the need for new mothers, far from their families, to find meaningful social support. Both were situational factors that influenced the formation of friendships.

The Housing Projects at the Robert Taylor Homes. At first glance, you might expect the results of the field study at the Robert Taylor Homes in Chicago to produce different insights. Instead of MIT engineering students, this field study was a *case study* of a Chicago drug gang operating out of a notorious city housing project. The critical data were gathered when graduate student Venkatesh (2008) became a *participant observer* who was allowed to follow a gang leader's daily activities for an extended period of time. He reported his observations in the book *Gang Leader for a Day*.

Venkatesh also discovered that friendships and group cohesiveness were influenced by functional distance and physical features of the dilapidated housing development. Venkatesh's reports contradicted the television stereotype of macho drug dealers wearing expensive jewelry, listening to music while being pampered by beautiful women. Instead, most drug dealers lived with their mothers and worked long hours for low pay, often in terrible weather, and at high personal risk. So, why didn't they just quit? Many did, especially as they got older. But the gang was also a cohesive group that satisfied deeper survival needs for friendship, money, and social support.

The fine-grained details that emerged from Venkatesh's (2008) observations demonstrated how cohesive groups of mothers squeezed the most benefits out of their meager resources. One apartment might have working plumbing, another a working stove, and a third a television, or heat, or air conditioning. Among them, they had approximately one working apartment, so they shared their resources and shifted their daily activities as required. What looks careless and unkempt to an outsider is sometimes creative coping by the insider. For example, Venkatesh discovered that sometimes mothers would allow people to urinate in the stairwells immediately outside their apartments because the terrible odor kept the drug dealers, prostitutes, and gang members from hanging out near their doors—and their children.

Both case studies demonstrated how functional distance and physical characteristics influenced the impulse to form cohesive groups. The mothers in the Robert Taylor Homes worked together to keep their children safe, just as the wives of postwar MIT engineering students formed cohesive groups to take better care of one another and their children. In both cases, groups provided social/emotional support and practical social support (such as heat or shelter) that made it a little easier to get to tomorrow.

Groups Provide a Sense of Identity

In addition to cohesiveness and the resulting social support, groups can also provide a **sense of individual identity** (Tajfel & Turner, 1986), an impression of how we uniquely fit into a larger group. On a larger scale, participating in groups can help us figure out what career path best matches our ambitions. We look into the social mirror of our groups, make social comparisons, and conclude, "I'm good at this, but not so good at that" (see Chapter 3; Berry et al., 2000). Like a sports team needing to fill different playing positions, each person contributes something different—but everyone is needed for maximum group success.

For example, how does a musician know if he or she is any good at making music? The musicians in the 36 rock and roll bands and 4 country bands in O'Conner and Dyce's (1993) study used social comparisons to learn about their own musical ability. The members of these bar bands had been playing together for an average of 1.7 years when the researchers asked them to assess musical ability by (a) rating their own musical ability (self-appraisal), (b) rating each other's musical abilities (other-appraisal), and then (c) rating how they thought the other musicians would rate them (reflected appraisal).

The research team found that self-appraisals conformed most closely with reflected appraisals. In other words, how the musicians thought about themselves most closely matched how they believed other musicians would rate them. Thinking about what their fellow musicians thought of them was a way of spying on their own musical abilities. All those impressions come together in the context of each person's standing relative to the other members of the group. In this way, being in a group helps us define our own talents and purpose in a larger social world.

Groups Make Us Feel Safe

When you feel threatened in some way, do you gravitate to be with some group of people? Schachter (1959) demonstrated that a third benefit of belonging to groups is feeling safe when threatened. The experiment tested the *hypothesis* that "misery loves company" by threatening study participants with the possibility of electric shock. Sure enough, the threatened people clustered together.

But that observation wasn't the end of the research story. Two years later, Sarnoff and Zimbardo (1961) conducted an experiment that first *replicated* the Schachter study. But the researchers then used an experimental manipulation that made people feel anxious instead of afraid—and they found that anxious people did *not* tend to cluster with other anxious people. What's going on here? Do anxious people want to be left alone? Actually, they don't. Firestone, Kaplan, and Russell (1973) found that anxiety still leads to a desire to be with others. But unlike fear, anxiety makes us want to be surrounded by people who are *not* anxious.

It seems that both fear and anxiety motivate us to affiliate with others, but when we're afraid, we like to be with people who feel the same way; this could help us bond together against a common enemy. In contrast, when we're anxious, we like to be with

Sense of individual identity: How individuals perceive themselves to uniquely fit into a larger group. Such social comparisons and group role development contribute to individuals' self-concept.

people who are *not* anxious because they can calm us down. Both motivations appear to be driven by the need to feel safe and secure—a major benefit of belonging to a group. In short, misery does love company, but the kind of company we crave depends on the kind of misery we are experiencing.

Groups Provide Meaningful Information

Testing whether misery loves company revealed a fourth benefit from belonging to a group: Groups provide cognitive clarity by supplying meaningful information. For example, what kind of roommate (A or B) would you want if you were waiting to receive heart surgery? Roommate A is about to go in for heart surgery. Roommate B just came back. Roommate A can empathize with your anxiety, but Roommate B can provide meaningful information about your upcoming experience and can also be comforting (if the surgery went well).

Two studies (Kulik & Mahler, 1989; Kulik, Mahler, & Moore, 1996) found that presurgery coronary bypass patients preferred roommates already recovering from surgery (Roommate B). In that situation, information was more important than empathy. But there is still more to the story: What about patients with no roommate at all? Patients with information-rich roommates (roommates who had already gone through the surgery) were also less anxious, began walking sooner after their heart surgeries, and were discharged sooner from the hospital compared with patients who had single rooms in the hospital (no roommates). Apparently, any companion in the midst of misery is better than no companion at all.

The Main Ideas

- Individuals are instinctively motivated to form groups because they provide several survival advantages, including both social/emotional and practical support when needed.

- Groups can also provide a sense of individual identity when we use social comparisons.

- Groups make us feel safe and secure, and our motivation to be in a group increases when we experience fear or anxiety.

- Another advantage of groups is that other members can provide meaningful information about future possible outcomes.

⚡ CRITICAL THINKING CHALLENGE

- Think of times in your recent life when you felt afraid or threatened, then think of times when you felt anxious. Did your social patterns match the research described in this section?

- Identify two famous groups from history that originally were separate but eventually came together to form a single, larger group as a way to fight a common enemy. If they were successful, did the original groups re-form or did the new group stay together afterward?

- List three groups to which you have belonged at some point in your life, and for each, identify what your specific role was in the group (e.g., tenor in the school choir, goalkeeper on the soccer team, psychology major at your school). Consider what psychological or situational variables made you want to focus on the group's welfare or success versus your own, individual welfare or success. Turn your thoughts into a hypothesis and create a research procedure to test your hypothesis.

WHY ARE WE MORE COMMITTED TO CERTAIN GROUPS?

LO 8.2: Identify ways that groups gain and maintain their authority over individuals.

It doesn't take much to start a garage band. You only need another musician, instruments, and a place to play. However, if you want to become a member of certain fraternities or sororities, then you may have to endure some humiliating public rituals. If you want to rise within a political party, then you may have to volunteer your time knocking on doors or passing out pamphlets. If you want to join the Navy SEALS, then you have to endure extremely rigorous intellectual and physical tests. This raises an interesting question: Are we more committed to groups that are harder to get into? In general, why do we feel more committed to some groups over others?

Social Psychology in Action:
Group Initiations

©SAGE Publications

Difficult-to-Get-Into Groups Are More Appealing: The Initiation Effect

We are, indeed, usually more committed to groups that are difficult to get into. Recall the heuristic, "If it's expensive, it must be good quality." With groups, a parallel thought might be, "If membership is exclusive, it must be a wonderful group." Groups where anyone can come and go as they please aren't elite and don't give us the feeling of being special. Thus, if a group requires some kind of initiation or annual dues, or if it only gains new members through invitation instead of application, becoming a member seems to impart a feeling of honor or prestige. The harder it is to join, the more we want to join. Cognitive dissonance helps explain this finding, and a classic study establishing this trend is described in the "Spotlight on Research Methods" feature.

Some groups are more prestigious and elite—and harder to get into. The Freemasons, for example, started in the 14th century. Members hold various ranks based on their service to the organization. Several famous political leaders and celebrities have belonged to the Freemasons, including George Washington, Jesse Jackson, Buzz Aldrin, John Wayne, Sir Arthur Conan Doyle, Charles Lindbergh, and the musicians Beethoven, Bach, and Mozart. Women are not allowed to join traditional lodges in the Freemasons.

Keystone-France / Gamma-Keystone / Getty Images

Recall that cognitive dissonance (see Chapter 6) predicts that when we have thoughts and behaviors that don't align, we'll feel uncomfortable and will adjust accordingly. Once people have gone through embarrassing, effortful, or expensive efforts to gain membership in a group, it would create cognitive dissonance if they believed those efforts were a waste of time. So, instead, we simply convince ourselves that the group is wonderful! This example of cognitive acrobatics is called **effort justification**, or sometimes the **initiation effect**. Just as cult members didn't want to admit they were wrong when they gave up jobs and friends due to expectations of an apocalypse that never came, groups can ironically increase commitment of their members if they make membership difficult.

We Get Caught in the Escalation Trap: The Hazing Effect

Have you ever worked on a class paper or project for hours and hours, realized it's not really that great and you'd like to switch topics, but you continued forward just because you didn't want to start over? We sometimes do this even if we know that starting over would lead to a better result. The **escalation trap**, sometimes called the **sunken cost fallacy**, can get all of us: We increase our commitment to a failing situation to justify previous investments of time, effort, or resources.

Poor poker players fall into this trap when they refuse to fold a losing hand and instead escalate their bets (especially on the last hand of the night). Car owners may keep throwing good money into a bad car because they have already spent so much money repairing it. Sometimes, even romantic partners will continue a harmful relationship simply because they already have invested so much in the relationship (Goodfriend & Agnew, 2008; Rusbult, 1980). Haslam et al. (2006) argue that we foolishly "stick to our guns" to preserve our social identity—our sense of self (see also Seibert & Goltz, 2001).

Hazing is like a trip wire into the escalation trap. **Hazing** occurs whenever members of a group establish arbitrary rituals for new members that may cause physical or emotional harm. Few university fraternities and sororities still perpetuate dangerous hazing activities, which is a good thing. One research team (Keating et al., 2005) happened to be collecting data about hazing when a student died during a ritual requiring him to drink large quantities of water through a funnel.

Campus hazing rituals have been less popular—and officially banned by several universities—for many years now. However, Finkel (2000) described Greek organizations that required pledges to swallow nausea-inducing drinks, be branded with cigarettes, and submit to sexual assaults. Even more recently, the sports network ESPN has conducted several investigations of hazing in athletic teams. According to ESPN, 40 young men on high school teams were subjected to sodomy sexual assault by different teammates across the country who claimed their actions were just "hazing" (Barr, Malbran, Berko, Lockett, & Kostura, 2012).

We shouldn't pick on fraternities, sororities, and sports teams, because hazing occurs throughout society. The *generalizability,* or social ubiquity, of hazing was documented when Winslow (1999) described how the Canadian Air Force employed rituals of binge drinking, demeaning tasks, and painful activities. The generalizability of hazing was demonstrated again when Gleick (1997) described "blood pinning" rituals among U.S. Marine paratroopers. Soldiers reworked medals in uniforms so that when another soldier hits them, the pin pierces the skin until it bleeds. Even college marching bands can resort to hazing in the form of public humiliation and degradation (Silveira & Hudson, 2015).

Effort justification: The tendency for individuals to convince themselves that a group they belong to is wonderful if they have gone through embarrassing, difficult, or expensive efforts to gain membership in the group.

Initiation effect: See *effort justification.*

Escalation trap: When individuals increase their commitment to a failing situation to justify previous investments of time, effort, or resources.

Sunken cost fallacy: See *escalation trap.*

Hazing: Whenever members of a group establish arbitrary rituals for new members that may cause physical or emotional harm, which can be a type of escalation trap for aspiring members (see *effort justification*).

For the online story by ESPN on high school hazing that escalated to sexual assault from one teammate to another, check out http://www.espn.com/espn/feature/story/_/id/17507010/otl-investigation-trend-sodomy-hazing.

GROUP INITIATIONS FOSTER GROUP COMMITMENT

Spotlight on Research Methods

Aronson and Mills (1959) wanted to see if people would become more committed to groups if they were required to go through an initiation ritual, similar to many social groups in the "real" world (such as fraternities and sororities). They tested this hypothesis using an ingenious and now famous research study with college women. The participants thought they were trying to join a small discussion group about sex—a topic that was socially taboo back in 1959 when the study was done, especially for a proper college lady. While talking about sex might seem titillating, Aronson and Mills purposely designed the actual conversation to be downright dull and boring. So how did they get some of the participants to say the group was exciting and interesting?

Using *random assignment to groups,* the experiment started by placing participants into groups with different initiation experiences. Participants in the *control condition,* the lowest or easiest level, only had to state that they were willing to discuss sexually oriented material to join the group. In one *experimental group* (the mild embarrassment condition), participants read some mildly sexual passages out loud that included the words *prostitute, virgin,* and *petting*—again, fairly embarrassing for the deeply conservative 1950s. However, in the severe embarrassment condition, participants read (out loud) vivid descriptions of explicit sexual activity—essentially, they had to read pornography aloud to the researchers.

After each woman completed her level of "initiation," she was allowed to "eavesdrop" on a conversation the discussion group was having. The *dependent variable* was each woman's attitude toward the group—was it interesting, and did they like the group? Figure 8.1 shows you the results. The women who experienced the most severe initiation (reading pornography aloud) gave the most positive attitude ratings to the very dull discussion group (and to the people in the group). The women in the "porn" condition justified their embarrassing efforts to join by telling themselves that it was all worthwhile to join such an exciting group—even though the group was perceived as pretty boring by everyone else.

■ FIGURE 8.1 The effect of severity of initiation on attitude toward the group.

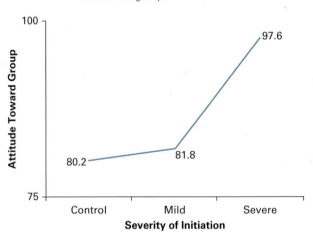

Many graduate students earning master's or doctorate degrees complain about the intimidating and harsh oral defenses they have to give of their research projects—but when those same people become professors, they may continue the tradition for the next generation of scholars. Hazing rituals occur across cultures and begin early in life (Martini, 1994). Why is hazing such an intimate part of social living?

Initiation Rituals Strengthen the Group's Authority

Cognitive dissonance offers one explanation for why hazing increases commitment to the group: We don't want to feel foolish at "wasted" efforts for a group that's not worthwhile. However, there are other psychological explanations.

Initiation rituals such as hazing also strengthen a particular group's authority over the individual being hazed. Keating et al. (2005), for example, pointed out that different kinds of groups require different kinds of initiation rituals. Hazing rituals in fraternities and sororities tend to include high levels of social deviance and embarrassment, whereas athletic and military groups require more physical challenges and pain endurance. The end result is that each initiation ritual affirms the social hierarchy, values, and goals of that particular group.

Maltreatment Effects. Why do people put up with hazing? One answer is **maltreatment effects**, which happen when hazing elicits social dependency that promotes allegiance to the group (Keating et al., 2005). By the end of the process, the abused person starts to connect with or even love the people who hurt him or her.

One explanatory model (Keating et al., 2005) is based on attachment theory (see Chapter 12 for more on this theory; Bowlby, 1982), which generally predicts that people are comforted by having a secure "home base" in other people, such as parents. The attachment explanation described in Figure 8.2 proposes a five-step model:

Greek societies on college and university campuses are famous for including "hazing" rituals that can involve public humiliation or pain, such as being hit with paddles like the ones shown here. But while most fraternities and sororities have done away with harsh initiation rituals, this tendency can be found in a variety of groups throughout all levels of society.

- Step 1: Maltreatment creates confusion, especially when delivered by friends or family members.
- Step 2: Confusion creates uncertainty about our value or place in a social world.
- Step 3: Uncertainty leads to emotional vulnerability.
- Step 4: Vulnerability creates a dependency on the people who hold such power over you; you need their acceptance.
- Step 5: Dependency creates gratitude when your needs are met. For example, a stale piece of bread and a cup of water can feel like a deep kindness when you are starving, even when it comes from the enemy that is starving you.

Stockholm Syndrome. This process shown in Figure 8.2, sometimes called the **Stockholm syndrome**, occurs when hostages develop affection for their captors (West, 1993). The name came from a 1973 bank robbery in Stockholm, Sweden, in which four hostages resisted being rescued. Even after they were rescued, the former hostages defended the robbers and refused to testify against them in court. According to the FBI, about 8% of hostages end up agreeing with their captors' demands or feeling friendship or romantic attraction to their captors (Sundaram, 2013).

A similar effect occurred in 1974 when newspaper heiress Patty Hearst was kidnapped by the Symbionese Liberation Army (SLA) and then joined their cause (Hearst & Moscow, 1988). The SLA robbed several corporate banks in San Francisco, and Hearst was famously caught on camera holding a gun and actively participating. She also denounced her rich and famous family. After she was arrested, she claimed the Stockholm syndrome as her defense in court. She was convicted and sent to prison for 7 years, but President Bill Clinton eventually pardoned her.

■ FIGURE 8.2 The maltreatment effect model.

Maltreatment 〉 Uncertainty 〉 Vulnerability 〉 Dependency 〉 Gratitude

SOURCE: Keating et al. (2005).

Maltreatment effects: When hazing elicits social dependency that promotes allegiance to the group.

Stockholm syndrome: When hostages develop affection for their captors.

Patty Hearst was famously kidnapped but then appeared to join the cause of her kidnappers. What would motivate her to become allies with a group that treated her badly?

More recently, British reporter Yvonne Ridley was kidnapped by the Taliban in 2001. After being held prisoner for 11 days, Ridley was released—and she proceeded to convert to Islam, praise the Taliban's practices, and denounce "Western" values. Unlike Hearst, Ridley refused the idea of Stockholm syndrome and claimed that her experience had simply awakened her understanding of a better lifestyle (Adorjan, Christensen, Kelly, & Pawluch, 2012). For both Hearst and Ridley, did brainwashing occur? If someone treats you badly, do you eventually see the world from their point of view? At least some psychological evidence points to an answer of yes, especially if you depend on their kindness and generosity for your survival.

The Stockholm syndrome appears to be at work when abused spouses and children do not immediately leave their abusers (Boulette & Andersen, 1986; Dutton & Painter, 1993). The "cycle of abuse" theory (Walker, 1979) within adult abusive relationships posits that these relationships go through a tension-building phase and then a violent phase, but afterward, they also include a phase of reconciliation, attention, and apology. Victims of abuse may be so reinforced by the final stages that they come to believe their abuser really has their best interests at heart—they come to affiliate with their captor.

Fear of Being Ostracized

Popular music suggests the social importance of rejection; think of all the songs on the radio about romantic heartache. Experiencing rejection can trigger deep-seated fears (see Sloman, 2000). Consequently, group norms become powerful influences because of **rejection sensitivity**, the fear of social rejection and ostracism (see Downey & Feldman, 1996).

At a more practical level, fear of rejection may be powerful in part due to the potential loss of all the advantages groups give us (see Baumeister & Leary, 1995). All social animals likely developed rejection sensitivity because social exclusion threatens our survival (Gruter & Masters, 1986; Van Beest & Williams, 2006; Williams, 2002). Like jabs from a four-pronged pitchfork, rejection threatens our

1. need to belong by separating us from our group,

2. self-esteem because it implies that we are unlikeable,

3. need for control because we cannot influence the decision, and

4. sense of existence, both metaphorically and in reality.

Rejection sensitivity: The fear of social rejection and ostracism.

One experiment increased social conformity by having participants *watch someone else* being ridiculed because, "His acne was so bad as a teenager we used to call him 'pizza face.'" Merely observing someone else being ridiculed produced increased

MEASURING REJECTION SENSITIVITY

How sensitive are you to social rejection or ostracism? Instructions: Consider each situation below and rate how concerned you would be in each one, using this scale:

1	2	3	4	5	6
Very unconcerned					Very concerned

_____ 1. You ask your parents or another family member for a loan to help you through a difficult financial time. How concerned or anxious would you be over whether or not your family would want to help you?

_____ 2. You approach a close friend to talk after doing or saying something that seriously upset him or her. How concerned or anxious would you be over whether or not your friend would want to talk with you?

_____ 3. You bring up the issue of sexual protection with your significant other and tell him or her how important you think it is. How concerned or anxious would you be over his or her reaction?

_____ 4. You ask your supervisor for help with a problem you have been having at work. How concerned or anxious would you be over whether or not the person would want to help you?

_____ 5. After a bitter argument, you call or approach your significant other because you want to make up. How concerned or anxious would you be over whether or not your significant other would want to make up with you?

_____ 6. You ask your parents or other family members to come to an occasion important to you. How concerned or anxious would you be over whether or not they would want to come?

_____ 7. At a party, you notice someone on the other side of the room that you'd like to get to know, and you approach him or her to start a conversation. How concerned or anxious would you be over whether or not the person would want to talk with you?

_____ 8. Lately you've been noticing some distance between yourself and your significant other, and you ask him or her if there is something wrong. How concerned or anxious would you be over whether or not he or she still loves you and wants to be with you?

_____ 9. You call a friend when there is something on your mind that you feel you really need to talk about. How concerned or anxious would you be over whether or not your friend would want to listen?

Scoring: Add all of your responses; higher scores indicate a greater level of rejection sensitivity.

Source: Modified from Downey and Feldman (1996); original scale includes likelihood ratings for each situation and scores are found by multiplying a reverse score for concern with likelihood for each item (then all items are averaged).

social conformity in observers (Janes & Olson, 2000). We want to be accepted, and we're willing to be flexible in our behaviors to ensure that acceptance, sometimes through conformity.

Rejection hurts. One study scanned participants' brains when they were suddenly excluded from a computer game of virtual ball-tossing. The social pain of being excluded occurred in the same part of the brain (the dorsal anterior cingulate cortex) that registers our physical pain (Eisenberger, Lieberman, & Williams, 2003). In other words, the social pain of this mild form of virtual rejection was experienced as a real neurological event. Ouch.

We're so sensitive to rejection that participants in experiments experience painful rejection even when

- social exclusion comes from members of an outgroup (Eisenberger & Lieberman, 2005), including groups that the participants strongly *dislike,* such as the Ku Klux Klan (Gonsalkorale & Williams, 2007);
- rejection is caused by a "technical problem" (Eisenberger & Lieberman, 2005) that's not even perceived as the participant's fault or as personal;
- ostracism comes from a computer instead of from another person (Zadro, Williams, & Richardson, 2004); and
- being ostracized leads to a financial reward (Van Beest & Williams, 2006).

These irrational reactions signal that the self perceives rejection as an existential threat. Of course, some people can take rejection better than others. To see how you might fall on this continuum, check out the self-report scale in the Applying Social Psychology to Your Life feature on the previous page.

Optimal Distinctiveness Theory: Being Special Matters

How do we balance our need for attention and independence with our need to belong to a group? Brewer (1991) suggested a solution called **optimal distinctiveness theory**. Her original paper was called "The Social Self: On Being the Same and Different at the Same Time" (p. 475). Optimal distinctiveness is the idea that we can simultaneously achieve the advantages of being seen as a unique and important individual *and* of being in a group by being an identifiable member of a small and elite group. In this way, we're not "too" distinct (which might mean social isolation or stigma) or "too" anonymous (losing our individuality). We want a level of distinctiveness that's right in the middle.

Mohd Samsul Mohd Said / Getty Images Sport / Getty Images

Optimal distinctiveness theory: The idea that individuals can simultaneously achieve the advantages of being seen as a unique and important individual and of being in a group by being an identifiable member of a small and elite group.

In 2017, the Malaysian gymnastics team won the gold medal at the Southeast Asia Games. Each player is recognized for her individual skills, but the entire team was needed to win.

Small, elite groups provide all the advantages of groups in general (social support, a sense of identity, information, and safety). In addition, their elite status provides prestige and pride (and more commitment to the group, as we saw with hazing). At the same time, elite groups are small enough that we still maintain our individuality and sense of importance. Like each player on a world-class sports team, each individual is identifiable and needed—but the entire team is needed to reach success.

The Main Ideas

- People tend to become more committed to groups when membership requires difficult initiation due to a process called effort justification.

- Effort justification is probably due to a combination of cognitive dissonance and the escalation trap.

- When people grow to like and agree with their captors or abusers, it's called the Stockholm syndrome.

- Some people are particularly attuned to the possibility of being socially isolated or ostracized, a variable called rejection sensitivity.

- Optimal distinctiveness theory predicts that people will want to balance individual needs with group needs; one way to do this is to have a unique position within a small, elite group.

⚡ CRITICAL THINKING CHALLENGE

- List four groups you have purposely joined in the past 5 years. For each, consider (a) what kind of requirements the group had for membership, if any at all, and (b) how much you enjoyed being a member of the group or felt committed to it. Does your pattern of data match the ideas in this chapter? If not, what other variables might have an influence on perceptions of group membership?

- Consider a group in which you have a leadership position. Based on the ideas in this section of the chapter, what activities could you ask group members to do that would result in increasing their commitment to the group? Can you ask them to do these activities in an ethical way?

- Do you think different personality or situational variables affect the likelihood someone is to feel the Stockholm syndrome? Try to identify two personality and two situational variables that might come into play.

HOW DO GROUPS HELP AND HINDER INDIVIDUAL EFFORT?

LO 8.3: Analyze how groups can both help and hinder individual efforts.

You've probably heard the phrase, "Two heads are better than one," implying that a group can achieve more than an individual. But you've also heard the opposite idea, "Too many cooks spoil the broth." The second phrase implies that groups can cause disagreement and havoc, leading to a bad outcome. Can both be true? There is a two-sided mystery about how and why our behavior changes in group settings.

Do group efforts always lead to better outcomes?

The Presence of Others Can Help Performance: Social Facilitation

Four small observations about athletic performance suggest how easily we are influenced by the presence of others. First: When bowlers roll a strike, they probably won't smile about that achievement until they turn and face their friends (Kraut & Johnson, 1979). Second: Joggers ran faster when a woman was seated facing them than when her back was turned (Worringham & Messick, 1983). Third: Michaels and colleagues (Michaels, Blommel, Brocato, Linkous, & Rowe, 1982) discovered that *more* skillful pool players sank an even higher percentage of shots when others were watching; *less* skillful players sank a lower percentage of shots when others were watching. The fourth observation is not exactly an athletic performance, although the participants in the annual Coney Island hot dog eating competition might disagree. Figure 8.3 shows that we generally eat more in the presence of others (see de Castro, 2000).

However, we don't *always* eat more in the presence of others, and the number of people at the table seems to make a difference. Our food consumption levels off when there are four to six people at the table—and then it takes a big jump. Those four observations stimulate questions on **social facilitation**, improved effort and individual performance in the presence of others. What's going on here?

The pressure of World Series Game 6 appeared to improve Reggie Jackson's performance in 1977. After ending the previous game with a walk-off home run, Jackson walked on four pitches in his first at bat. But then he hit the first pitch of three consecutive at-bats with a home run off three different pitchers. Social psychologists might say that his hitting that day was helped by social facilitation.

The Competitive Instinct: Triplett's Bicycle Racing Experiments. Triplett conducted one of the earliest experiments in social and sports psychology, probably because he was a bicycle-racing enthusiast (Vaughan & Guerin, 1997). Triplett (1898) observed that racing times were faster when racing against one another than when racing alone, against the clock. So he proposed a testable *hypothesis:* "the bodily presence of another rider is a stimulus to the racer in arousing the competitive instinct" (p. 516). If people work harder when other people are around, then it would be one example of social facilitation.

As a racing enthusiast, it is not surprising that Triplett looked to a "competitive instinct" to provide a psychological explanation for the effect he observed. But Allport (1920) extended Triplett's observations to noncompetitive mental tasks and coined the term *social facilitation* because it proposes that the mere presence of others enhances performance—even without the sense of competition.

Triplett and Allport had different explanations, but they were making a similar observation: Humans (and other animals) tend to perform better or faster in the presence of others (see Bond & Titus, 1983; Zajonc, Heingartner, & Herman, 1969). The "others" don't even really have to be there; people only have to believe or

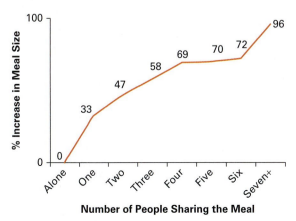

Coney Island hot dog eating competition.

imagine that they are there. For example, this effect happens even when participants are using virtual reality and the other people are simply computer avatars (Anderson-Hanley, Snyder, Nimon, & Arciero, 2011). In the presence of a group, people give more money to charity (Izuma, Saito, & Sadato, 2010), and airport security staff speed up when doing simple tasks (Yu & Wu, 2015). However, social facilitation only occurs when we are doing simple or well-practiced tasks.

When Facilitation Fails.
As often happens in science, researchers bumped into some unexpected plot twists that—later on—made perfect sense. The particular plot twists in this research story involved some weird but still interesting experiments, such as measuring how long it takes men to begin to urinate and how fast cockroaches can find their way to a dark corner when other cockroaches are watching. The plot twist was that sometimes "performance" got better, but at other times it got worse.

In one memorable and ethically questionable study (see Koocher, 1977; Middlemist, Knowles, & Matter, 1976, 1977), a research team hung signs in a men's restroom reading, "Don't use; washing urinal" to force male participants into one of three experimental situations in which they (1) stood alone, (2) were separated from another man by one urinal, or (3) stood right next to another man. (If you want a peek into the world of "Dude Rules" regarding restroom etiquette, then search the Internet for "The Urinal Game.") We will spare you all the details of how the research team made their observations, but it involved a pilot test of listening to people urinate, an observer hiding in a stall, an upside-down periscope hiding in a stack of books, and a stopwatch.

The data in Figure 8.4 show us that the presence of another person approaching the personal space of someone else did *not* facilitate the individual's "performance" at the urinal. In fact, the closer someone else was to a participant, the longer it took him to, well, get going. So even though this was an unusual *field experiment,* it suggested that the body does react physiologically to the presence of others. Other researchers made similar observations without resorting to questionable ethical procedures (see Bond & Titus, 1983; Zajonc, 1965; Zajonc & Sales, 1966).

Social facilitation: When individuals exhibit improved effort and individual performance in the presence of others.

■ FIGURE 8.3 How much do you eat in the presence of others?

% Increase in Meal Size

Data points: Alone 0, One 33, Two 47, Three 58, Four 69, Five 70, Six 72, Seven+ 96

Number of People Sharing the Meal

SOURCE: de Castro (2000).

Have you ever attended an exercise class, such as a spin class for bicycling? If so, your efforts and exertion probably were increased compared to when you exercise alone, due to social facilitation.

For example, four decades before the public restroom experiment, Pessin (1933) found that college students were worse at memorizing made-up words (nonsense syllables) in front of spectators. And while the airport security study cited above found that security agents sped up their simple tasks when other people were watching, they actually slowed down for complicated tasks when they knew they were being watched (Yu & Wu, 2015). Researchers kept confronting the same confusing plot twist: Groups seemed to be helping in some situations but hurting in others. More research was needed to clarify how groups influence individuals either to choke or to achieve.

The Cockroach Experiments. **Comparative social psychology** is an approach to studying human social behavior by comparing it with nonhuman animals. In this case, Zajonc et al. (1969) constructed something like enclosed cockroach sports luxury boxes at a cockroach stadium that allowed cockroaches to see (and be seen) by other cockroaches. So now experimenters could observe (and time) cockroaches as they responded to a noxious blast of light (cockroaches don't like light).

In simple mazes like the one shown in Figure 8.5, cockroaches run faster when other cockroaches are present. However, in complex mazes (that require turns), cockroaches slow down compared to their time when other cockroaches are present. Notice that the cockroaches were behaving like the pool players described earlier (Michaels et al., 1982). In that study, four researchers stood around the pool table, closely following the action—like the cockroach audience observing the action from their luxury boxes. The skilled players got better and the unskilled players got worse. The same pattern happened with the airport security staff: Easy tasks got faster, but complicated tasks slowed down when they were being watched (Yu & Wu, 2015). Zajonc (1965) reconciled the two

Comparative social psychology: Species-level comparisons of social behavior usually used to determine the uniqueness of human behavior.

■ FIGURE 8.4 Onset and persistence of urination.

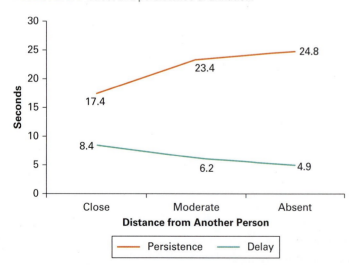

SOURCE: Middlemist, Knowles, and Matter (1976, 1977).

sets of contradictory experimental findings about social facilitation with a more precise conclusion: Social facilitation occurs when the presence of others improves the performance of easy tasks—but the presence of others inhibits the performance of difficult tasks. When you're being watched, easy things get easier and harder things get harder. Figure 8.6 expresses the chain of events that leads either to superior or inferior performance by both cockroaches and humans.

Evaluation Apprehension Versus Mere Presence.

One explanation for social facilitation is the **evaluation apprehension hypothesis** (Henchy & Glass, 1968). This explanation says that our anxiety about being judged by others is what causes physiological arousal and consequential changes in behavior, and that's why we can improve on simple/easy tasks, but we flounder on difficult or new tasks (Geen, 1989). We worry about being judged if we do badly, so performance goes up because of our need to be accepted and liked.

Cottrell and colleagues (Cottrell, Wack, Sekerak, & Rittle, 1968) tested this idea by having other people present, but blindfolded, so that participants knew that they could not be evaluated. The people were "present"—but they couldn't observe and judge you by your appearance. The results were similar to those joggers who did not run any faster in the presence of an observer whose back was turned. Our fear of being evaluated goes down when the other people in the room can't see us.

However, other social psychologists have disagreed that evaluation anxiety is at the core of social facilitation. They believe in the **mere presence hypothesis**, which argues that simply having other people in the room—even if they aren't watching you—will increase your physiological arousal and that this arousal will help performance on easy tasks and hinder performance on difficult tasks, as shown in Figure 8.6. This debate still occurs among some researchers (see, e.g., Bond & Titus, 1983; Le Hénaff, Michinov, Le Bohec, & Delaval, 2015; Mesagno, Harvey, & Janelle, 2012). Do you find one hypothesis more convincing than the other?

The Presence of Others Can Hinder Performance: Social Loafing

Social facilitation is when the presence of others helps performance—but the section you just read already showed that other people can hurt performance on difficult, complicated, or new tasks. But there's another way that being in a group can make performance go down—and this time, the person doing the action does worse on purpose.

■ FIGURE 8.5 (A) A simple "cockroach maze." Light (which cockroaches don't like) is shined on the starting point, which makes cockroaches search for the darkness of the goal. (B) When other cockroaches are added in "audience boxes," a cockroach in the maze runs faster in a simple maze but runs more slowly in a complex maze (compared to when alone).

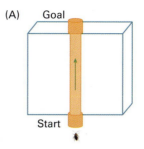
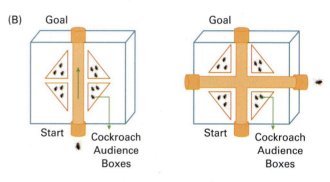

SOURCE: Zajonc, Heingartner, & Herman (1969).

■ FIGURE 8.6 Social facilitation.

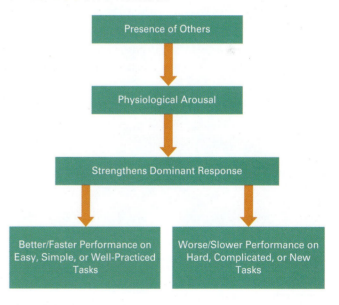

If you've ever been in a group project and one of the group members doesn't contribute—but still wants to share in a good evaluation or grade—then you know what it feels like to have a social loafer around.

Evaluation apprehension hypothesis: The idea that individuals' anxiety about being judged by others is what causes physiological arousal and consequential changes in behavior, accounting for the tendency to improve on simple tasks in the presence of others, but flounder on difficult or new tasks.

In *Star Trek: The Wrath of Khan* (1982), the alien Mr. Spock says, "Logic clearly dictates that the needs of the many outweigh the needs of the few." If you agree with Spock, then you are probably less likely to be a social loafer.

Social loafing occurs when people working in a group reduce their individual level of effort (see Jackson & Williams, 1985; Sanna, 1992). If you're the "loafer" or slacker, you get to coast on the efforts of others. But if you're not the loafer, you have to work even harder to accomplish the work expected of two (or more!) people, which feels unfair as well as frustrating. This is why so many students hate group projects—they are afraid they'll have to work even harder to make up for the loafing of others.

Free Riders: Ringelmann's Oxen Experiments.

The animal model wasn't cockroaches this time; it was oxen—which gives practical meaning to the phrase that expresses whether someone is "pulling his or her weight" in a group project. The French agricultural engineer Ringelmann (1913) was interested in social loafing (although he didn't use that phrase) as it related to using farm labor more efficiently.

Ringelmann's (1913) experiments demonstrated that both individual people and oxen would pull less hard on a rope when working together than when working alone. Ringelmann also found that the larger the group size, the lower the individual effort (see Kravitz & Martin, 1986). Today, we refer to social loafers as **free riders** or, more informally, as "slackers"—people who gain more benefits from the group than they contribute to the group.

These social loafing effects have also been *replicated* in experiments involving rope pulling (Ingham, Levinger, Graves, & Peckham, 1974), evaluation of poems and editorials (Petty, Harkins, Williams, & Latane, 1977), pumping air (Kerr & Bruun, 1981), and how loud cheerleaders yell (Hardy & Latane, 1988). More recently, psychologists have seen social loafing in professional handball players (Hoigaard et al., 2010) and in hotel employees (Luo, Qu, & Marnburg, 2013). Even more worrisome is when people decide not to get vaccines, thinking, "If everyone else gets a vaccine, then I don't need one" (Betsch, Bohm, & Korn, 2013). When it comes to public health, there's a dangerous side to social loafing.

Not Everyone Loafs: Situational, Personality, and Cultural Effects.

But do those experiments really indicate how *you* (or even most people) are likely to behave? Field experiments can provide an answer because they test the *external validity* of an experiment, whether the findings apply to (or *generalize* to) other people and other real-world situations.

Karau and Williams's (1993) meta-analysis of 78 social loafing studies indicated that you are *not* likely to be a social loafer when

1. You are doing something difficult.

2. Your contributions can be identified as coming from you.

3. You believe that what you are doing is valuable.

4. You are working with people you know.

Social loafing also goes down when self-identity with the group goes up. In the early days of *Saturday Night Live,* some of the writers worked extremely hard while others spent more time hanging out with the band—socially loafing (Forsyth, 2010). But as the show caught on and gained more viewers and critical acclaim, the loafing writers began to identify with the show, were proud to be identified with it, wanted to be part of its success, and started pulling their weight.

In addition, several personality variables have been linked to the likelihood of social loafing. For example, people high in **conscientiousness** are less likely to loaf (Schippers, 2014); conscientiousness is a personality trait that includes a striving for achievement, attention to detail, and a sense of responsibility. People are also less likely to be social loafers if they are high in **agreeableness**, meaning they are willing to be flexible, to cooperate, and to try to please other people (Schippers, 2014).

Karau and Williams's (1993) meta-analysis found that social loafing does occur across cultures but to a *lesser* degree among women and among people from Eastern cultures (they studied people from China, Japan, and Taiwan). Collectivist values are less likely to allow social loafing because their cultures frequently emphasize the good of the group over the good of any given individual. Social loafing is also less likely among individuals who have a high "**Protestant work ethic**" (Smrt & Karau, 2011). They value discipline, honoring commitments, and doing a good job in any setting. A simple and short scale has been developed to measure individual differences in tendencies to be a social loafer, which you can take in the Applying Social Psychology to Your Life feature.

Process Loss Versus Coordination Loss.

Not everyone loafs—and it's also possible that at least some people who reduce their effort aren't doing it on purpose. One study (Hardy & Latane, 1988) found that cheerleaders yelled louder when they thought they were alone, compared to when they knew they were in a group. But the leaks in their energy and cheerleading efforts weren't deliberate—they didn't actually cheer more quietly on purpose. So how did their reduced effort happen accidentally? Steiner (1972) identified two general explanations for the loss of productivity when working in groups: process loss and coordination loss. **Process loss** is a reduction of effort in group settings that comes from a lack of motivation. Social loafing is a big contributor to process loss.

Mere presence hypothesis: The idea that being in the presence of others, even if they aren't watching, will increase an individual's physiological arousal, and this arousal will help performance on easy tasks and hinder performance on difficult tasks.

Social loafing: When people working in a group reduce their individual level of effort.

Free riders: People who gain more benefits from the group than they contribute to the group; social loafers or "slackers."

Conscientiousness: A personality trait that includes striving for achievement, attention to detail, and a sense of responsibility; people high in this trait are also less likely to be social loafers.

Agreeableness: A personality trait that includes the willingness to be flexible, to cooperate, and to try to please other people; people high in this trait are also less likely to be social loafers.

Protestant work ethic: A set of personality traits that includes valuing discipline, honoring commitments, and doing a good job in any setting; people high in this trait are also less likely to be social loafers.

Process loss: The reduction of effort—and thus productivity—in group settings that comes from a lack of motivation, often due to social loafing.

Applying Social Psychology to Your Life

Instructions: How much do you agree with each statement below? Respond to each using this scale:

1	2	3	4	5
Strongly disagree				Strongly agree

____ 1. In a team, I am indispensable.

____ 2. In a team, I will try as hard as I can.

____ 3. In a team, I will contribute less than I should.

____ 4. In a team, I will actively participate in the discussion and contribute ideas.

____ 5. In a team, it is okay even if I do not do my share.

____ 6. In a team, it does not matter whether or not I try my best.

____ 7. In a team, given my abilities, I will do the best I can.

Scoring: First, reverse-score what you wrote for Items 1, 2, 4, and 7. This means that if you wrote a 1, it becomes a 5, a 2 becomes a 4, a 3 stays the same, a 4 becomes a 2, and a 5 becomes a 1. Then, add up your answers; higher scores mean you are more likely to be a social loafer.

Source: Ying, Li, Jiang, Peng, and Lin (2014).

The second type of loss is **coordination loss**, which occurs when lack of cooperation and communication weakens the group's effectiveness. Coordinating a group may be as simple as getting people to say, "1-2-3 Lift!" so that everyone understands exactly when to put forth their maximum effort. Ancient sailors would sing rhythmic songs to coordinate their rowing, and marching bands began as a way to help armies stay coordinated. Most people have probably observed the captain of a cheerleading team yell, "Ready? OK!" as a signal for every cheerleader to begin at exactly the same time. These efforts are all attempts from a group to avoid coordination loss.

Diffusion of Responsibility. Social loafing also *in*creases when there is **diffusion of responsibility**, that is, when each individual feels less responsible for the outcome, when they think, "I don't need to take care of it . . . someone else will." Social psychologists were inspired to investigate diffusion of responsibility under unfortunate circumstances: a grisly sexual assault and murder.

In 1964, a woman named Kitty Genovese was stabbed, assaulted, and murdered in Queens, New York. At the time, the *New York Times* published a story stating that the murder took place just outside her apartment building and that at least 37 of her neighbors heard and saw the attack—but not a single one called the police. While later reports questioned whether this was actually true, the story inspired the idea that if witnesses didn't call, it wasn't because they didn't care. Instead, they all may have believed that one of the other neighbors probably already called . . . so they didn't need to. (For more on the Kitty Genovese story and how it inspired research on when people will and will not help others, see Chapter 10.)

Coordination loss: When a lack of cooperation and communication weakens a group's effectiveness, leading to a loss of productivity.

Diffusion of responsibility: When an individual feels less responsible for an outcome due to the presence of others.

Among college students, diffusion of responsibility is more likely when the project is big or involves many students—and less likely when students get to grade one another (see Aggarwal & O'Brien, 2008). Among full-time workers, one study (Liden, Wayne, Jaworski, & Bennett, 2004) found that diffusion of responsibility was more likely when employees (a) did not believe that others were likely to notice their lowered effort, (b) noticed other people's lowered efforts, and (c) perceived unfairness within the organization. Diffusion of responsibility appears to kick in when listeners of public radio (such as NPR) refuse to make a financial contribution to support the station. They can easily think, "Thousands of other people will send in money . . . so they don't need my $10."

Chip Somodevilla / Getty Images News / Getty Images

Do you ever listen to National Public Radio or watch public television? If you do but do not contribute to their fundraisers, then what are you quietly telling yourself about why you don't need to contribute?

The Main Ideas

- Social facilitation occurs when individuals work harder in the presence of others.

- Social facilitation may be caused by the mere presence of other people affecting our physiological response and/or our anxiety about being evaluated.

- Being around other people will typically make easy or well-practiced tasks go faster, but hard or new tasks will slow down.

- Social loafing occurs when people working in a group reduce their individual level of effort.

- There is variability in social loafing based on personality traits, situational circumstances, and cultural influence.

- Group output might also suffer from coordination loss and from diffusion of responsibility.

⚡ CRITICAL THINKING CHALLENGE

- Think of specific times when you've had to work in a group at school, at work, or even socially. Identify people in the group who seemed to work harder versus people who seemed to work less. What differences can you identify in the two different responses, and do the ideas in this section align with your experiences? If not, what other variables should be studied by social psychologists to fully understand social facilitation versus social loafing?

- Imagine that you are in charge of a group filled with a bunch of social loafers. What could you do to motivate them to work harder?

- Many people say they care about the ecosystem and would theoretically be in favor of recycling programs, better rules about car emissions, and additional research on how we can combat global climate change. However, on an individual level, many people still drive gas-guzzling cars, don't recycle, and so on. Can diffusion of responsibility explain these individual decisions? If so, what could be done to make people feel more personal responsibility so that they change their behaviors?

ABC Photo Archives / Disney ABC Television Group / Getty Images

D.C. Comics offers a superhero group that had enjoyed enduring popularity: The Justice League of America (JLA). First appearing in 1960 in "The Brave and the Bold" Comic #28, the JLA includes powerhouse heroes like Superman and Batman, as well as Wonder Woman (although when the JLA first started, she was unfortunately relegated to the sexist role of "secretary").

This band of superheroes is always, inevitably, successful. What makes the Justice League of America such a successful group? To start, to join the Justice League, you have to go through a *difficult initiation*. Aronson and Mills's famous study on group initiations was done in 1959—and the JLA appeared only 1 year later. Coincidence? Probably. But it's still fun to know that in "Justice

League of America" #9, readers see the origin story of the group, including a harsh test of membership. Individual superheroes all work against an alien attack and a dangerous meteor headed for Earth. After realizing they can only accomplish success through a group effort, they form the official league. It was tough to join, making them even more committed.

Second, the JLA members would never suffer from *social loafing* or *diffusion of responsibility*. In part, this is because they are so committed to the group and because many of them are high in conscientiousness. The team also benefits from the fact that each member has individual superpowers, forcing individual action when needed (if you need speed, call on the Flash; if you need to talk to a fish, Aquaman is ready).

Finally, the group is certainly small, elite, and prestigious, and each member is famous and admired for his or her own special role. This means that being a member of the Justice League is a perfect opportunity for *optimal distinctiveness*. Each superhero can remain individually valued but also gain the benefits of being in a respected and supportive community. Remember: If you end up with superpowers, use them for good, not evil.

For a more detailed analysis of group dynamics in the Justice League of America, see the book The Psychology of Superheroes: An Unauthorized Exploration *and read the chapter "The Social Psychology of the Justice League of America" by Goodfriend (2008).*

HOW DO INDIVIDUALS INFLUENCE GROUPS?

LO 8.4: Analyze how leadership succeeds or fails, how group decisions turn risky or safe, and how a minority can influence the majority.

The previous section discussed how being in a group environment can affect individuals—but what about the other way around? How can individuals affect the group?

In 1974, Bangladeshi economics professor Muhammad Yunus discovered that a group of local women who were working as basket weavers were borrowing money to pay for materials at an interest rate so high that they never really made any profit (Yunus, 2007). They were hardworking, but they were perpetually impoverished, uneducated, and stuck in a male-centric culture that provided them almost no opportunity. So, Yunus took a small chance: He lent 42 women a total of approximately $30. He was creating what came to be called "micro-loans" with a social mission.

The women repaid the loans, supported one another as a group, began to make more profit, and then reinvested their money in themselves and their businesses. They soon began pulling themselves—and their families—up and out of poverty. In 1983, Yunus started Grameen Bank, founded on the practice of trust and group solidarity. The bank has enjoyed an extraordinary record of success with its small business loans: 94% of its borrowers are women, over 98% of loans are repaid, and the bank collected an average of $1.5 million in *weekly* installments that it keeps reinvesting in poor people with ambition (Yunus, 2007).

In 2006, Yunus was awarded the Nobel Peace Prize, and in 2009 President Barack Obama awarded him the Presidential Medal of Freedom. Yes, groups affect individuals—but the success of Grameen Bank demonstrates that individuals can also have a profound influence on groups.

Muhammad Yunus, an individual who had an important impact on a group, starting with 42 women in Bangladesh.

The Most Effective Leader Depends on the Situation

Group dynamics are the social roles, hierarchies, communication styles, and culture that naturally form when groups interact. Some people will emerge as leaders, while others prefer to stand back. The leaders may choose very different styles—and these choices will have an influence over how the group members perform and feel.

Contingency Theory of Leadership. The **contingency theory of leadership** aligns with Lewin's early equation that viewed behavior as the product of both the person's individual personality and his or her environment or social situation: Different situations call for different kinds of leaders. A business that is about to go bankrupt may require a leader with a forceful personality; a business that is growing smoothly may require a leader with a lighter touch. Young parents leading a family with four children under the age of 11 probably will need a different leadership style than the 35-year-old parents of just one child. The situation matters and so do the personalities—just as Lewin predicted.

Applying the Contingency Theory of Leadership. Lewin was particularly interested in the effects that different kinds of leaders had on their groups. He had just witnessed what happened in Nazi Germany when an autocratic leader gained power, so Lewin (1948) compared three leadership styles: autocratic, democratic, and laissez-faire (and he concluded that a democratic style was best). He also produced an early film record of an experiment that documented the different effects of these leadership styles on children. His methods were imperfect and may have been interpreted in a slightly biased manner, but his studies have largely stood the test of time (Taylor, 1998). Leaders have a profound influence on the groups that they lead—for better and for worse.

Fiedler (1967, 1996) also developed a contingency approach to leadership. Fiedler spent more than 45 years studying leadership, often in branches of the military: ROTC, infantry squad leaders, Coast Guard officers, and army and navy

Group dynamics: The social roles, hierarchies, communication styles, and culture that naturally form when groups interact.

Contingency theory of leadership: The idea that there is no one best leadership style; different types of people, environments, and situations call for different kinds of leaders.

When is a transformational leader likely to be most effective?

personnel. He observed people making real decisions that had real consequences. Fiedler's experiments persuaded him that a leader's effectiveness depended "on how well the leader's personality, abilities, and behaviors match the situation in which the leader operates."

Types of Leaders. Thus, Fiedler did not believe in a single "leader" personality trait. Instead, he identified leaders who tended to be more effective in different types of situations. For example, a **task leader** focuses on completing assignments. By contrast, a **social leader** is focused on the people involved and invests time in building teamwork, facilitating interactions, and providing support. In an emergency, you probably want a task leader—you don't want the person in charge to stop and ask how you're feeling about everything. But when cooperative teamwork is required, you probably want a social leader who knows about and cares for each member of the group. The best type of leader is contingent on the situation.

A variation on the contingency view of leadership defines **transactional leaders** as those who use rewards and punishments to motivate group members. Transactional leaders can be useful when an organization or government wants to maintain the status quo. On the other hand, **transformational leaders** use inspiration and group cohesiveness to motivate group members (see Nye, 2008) and are useful for challenging established rules or procedures. Research (e.g., Bass, 1998) supports the idea that transformational leadership can influence society toward positive change. For example, Pittinsky (2010) identified Martin Luther King Jr. and Nelson Mandela (shown in the photo at left) as two classic historical examples of transformative leaders. Muhammed Yunus (who gave poor women small loans for their businesses) represents another transformational leader who influenced many people.

Individuals Can Influence Group Decision Making

Have you been asked to serve on a jury yet? You probably will be. Even though it will definitely interrupt your life, it is one of the many citizen responsibilities in a democracy. Plus, as a student of psychology, you will find it fascinating to observe the court system, participate in the selection process, and engage in group decision making. Does one person try to bully everyone else into an agreement? If the jury is allowed to decide on things like monetary damages, how do they reach a final number? Can one person really influence the final outcome if everyone else disagrees? Three lines of research have explored how an individual can influence group decision making: group polarization, groupthink, and minority influence.

Group Polarization and the Risky Shift. Group polarization research started out with a slightly different name and only looked at change in one direction. **Risky shift** is the tendency of groups to make riskier or more daring decisions than the average of individuals (Stoner, 1968; Wallach & Kogan, 1965). This tendency went against folk wisdom that groups will always lead to moderate or level-headed decisions. Instead, if the individual members of a group are leaning toward moderate risk at the outset, discussion will eventually lead to a much more extreme decision than they started with.

Task leader: A type of leader who focuses on completing assignments, achieving goals, and meeting deadlines.

Social leader: A type of leader who focuses on the people involved and invests time in building teamwork, facilitating interactions, and providing support.

Transactional leader: A type of leader who uses rewards and punishments to motivate group members; these leaders help to maintain the status quo.

Transformational leader: A type of leader who uses inspiration and group cohesiveness to motivate group members; these leaders are useful for challenging established rules or procedures.

Risky shift: The tendency of groups to make riskier or more daring decisions than the average of individuals (see *group polarization*).

In the classic film *12 Angry Men* (1957; remade in 1997), a lone juror tries to convince the rest of the group to change their verdict. Can one person really have that much influence over a group? How do groups come to final decisions?

Stoner (1961) discovered this when he asked participants to consider this scenario:

Mr. A, an electrical engineer, who is married and has one child, has been working for a large electronics corporation since graduating from college 5 years ago. His job is stable with a modest income but little chance of increasing. He's offered a job at a different, new company with a highly uncertain future. The new job would pay more to start and offers the possibility of shares in the company. What is the lowest probability you consider worthwhile for Mr. A to take the new job?

Participants each provided an independent answer, then joined a group to discuss and come up with a new, final answer. After the discussion, answers shifted toward being more willing to accept risk. Do group discussions always lead to riskier decisions?

Later research clarified that the shift can also move in the other direction—toward a less risky position. So, the more precise description is that **group polarization** occurs when a group makes more extreme decisions than the average of individual decisions. The shift, then, can be either riskier or more conservative. The direction of the shift depends on which direction most individuals were headed in *before* they got together as a group (Moscovici & Zavalloni, 1969). It seems that we can question our own, individual decision but that exposure to a group of other people who start with general agreement can "fuel the fires" and make people feel more assured and confident.

For example, in one early study, moderately pro-feminist women became more feminist following a group discussion (Myers, 1975). Several more recent studies have shown that if you lean toward one political candidate or party, exposure to others who also favor that person or party will eventually lead your opinion to become much stronger and more extreme (e.g., Iyengar & Westwood, 2015; Keating, Van Boven, & Judd, 2016; Stroud, 2010). Have you observed this during

Group polarization: When a group makes more extreme decisions than the average of individual decisions, toward either a more or less risky position.

CNN is known for being a liberal news network, while Fox News is known for being conservative. If you tend to watch only one of these networks, or your Facebook friends tend to post only one kind of message, or you mostly talk with people who share your views, then your opinions gradually will become more extreme: group polarization.

major elections, in which people tend to become more extreme as they surround themselves with like-minded others?

Daniel Isenberg (1986) identified two explanations for *why* group decision making becomes more extreme: social comparisons (a normative influence) and persuasive arguments (an informational influence). Social comparisons encourage us to push one another in the socially approved direction until we find ourselves advocating for an extreme perspective that is far from where we started. Normative influences push us to agree with our friends—and to keep on agreeing even as decisions become more extreme.

The second explanation for group extremism focuses on persuasive arguments. Any group we join is probably inclined toward a viewpoint we agree with—that's why we joined it in the first place. So, conservatives tune in to radio shows that reinforce their conservative viewpoint while liberals associate with programs that present the other side. Both sides hear more and better arguments in the same direction (and are not exposed to counterarguments) and thus become increasingly persuaded toward that perspective.

Groupthink. George Orwell's frightening dystopian novel *1984* (written in 1948) introduced several new phrases to the English language, notably "Big Brother," "doublethink," and "thoughtcrime." They were all about how the suppression of ideas can lead to brainwashed, ignorant masses. In 1972, psychologist Janis introduced another memorable term, **groupthink**, which describes the tendency for people in groups to minimize conflict by thinking alike and publicly agreeing with each other.

In general, people don't like to be disagreeable troublemakers or the only ones holding a contrary opinion—so they sometimes stay silent. But if all the contrary

■ **TABLE 8.1** Tragic U.S. Events Attributed to Groupthink

Event	Historical Context
Attack on Pearl Harbor	1941: During the F. D. Roosevelt administration, groups analyzing intelligence data dismissed evidence about a possible attack on U.S. ships at Pearl Harbor.
The failed invasion of Cuba: Bay of Pigs	1961: Three months into the Kennedy administration, White House planners miscalculated Cuban resistance and underfunded the military effort.
Escalation of the war in Vietnam	1965–1968: During the Johnson administration, the president and his cabinet escalated U.S. troop commitments to Vietnam from 16,000 to 537,000 with an average of about 1,200 U.S. fatalities each month.
The Watergate cover-up	1972–1974: During the Nixon administration, the president and his staff covered up their involvement in illegal "dirty tricks" during the 1972 reelection campaign.
Destruction of the space shuttle *Challenger*	1986: A group of NASA officials ignored specific warnings not to launch the space shuttle because O-rings separating rocket boosters were less resilient in cold temperatures.
9/11 terror attacks	2001: Groups analyzing intelligence data dismissed evidence suggesting that an attack was imminent.
Destruction of the space shuttle *Columbia*	2003: A group of NASA officials decided to ignore suggestions to look more closely at damage during launch to the heat-shielding tiles.
The U.S. invasion of Iraq	2003: The George W. Bush administration decided to invade Iraq to remove the threat of weapons of mass destruction that never existed.
Penn State sex scandal	2014: Coaches and professionals from the Penn State football team ignored concerns that Jerry Sandusky was sexually abusing children on campus.

opinions remain silent, then no one realizes the size of the doubt members have. This self-silencing can lead to groupthink. Table 8.1 describes some of the actual U.S. historical events—and tragedies—that Janis and others have identified as influenced by groupthink. This list suggests that one thing we learn from history is that we don't learn from history—we repeat our mistakes.

Here is an odd feature of what it is like to be part of a group likely to make disastrous decisions: You *like* being part of the group. You come together, quietly tell each other how smart, moral, and wonderful you all are, and then make decisions that affect other people's lives, confident that you really are well informed—even though you are not. Janis identified three general conditions under which groupthink is most likely to occur:

- *High group cohesiveness.* Group members who feel connected to one another are less likely to criticize themselves.
- *Strong, directive leadership.* A group structure with a strong, directive leader will tend to isolate the group from alternative opinions and discourage disagreement.
- *Stressful situations.* A crisis requires groups to make fast decisions based on incomplete information; this can promote the illusion that there is a clear consensus of opinion.

Groupthink: The tendency for people in groups to minimize conflict by thinking alike and publicly agreeing with each other, especially in groups with high group cohesiveness, strong and directive leadership, and a stressful situation to resolve.

The symptoms of groupthink seem obvious in retrospect, but they are subtle when groupthink is seducing you into a terrible decision. How can groups avoid making this mistake? They can look for the symptoms of groupthink and purposely try to avoid them. See Table 8.2 for a list of symptoms and matching example statements.

■ TABLE 8.2 Groupthink Symptoms and Example Statements

Symptom	Statement
Overestimating the expertise of the group and its leader.	"We really are the best people for this job; our leader is wiser than other leaders."
Becoming close-minded toward alternative opinions.	"Other people's ideas may have some merit, but our insights are special."
Using someone as a "mindguard" to pressure dissenters to conform.	"How can I shut that person up? Doesn't he know that his comments are bringing everyone else down?"
Self-censoring by not voicing disagreements or concerns.	"My contrary idea probably isn't right anyway."
Perceiving a unity of opinion that does not really exist.	"We must be right; no one has spoken up about a disagreement."
Limiting the range of alternative decisions.	"We don't have to consider some of these stranger ideas."
Being reluctant to question your objectives or reconsider dismissed alternatives.	"We already made up our minds about that. Let's not go over it again."
Focusing on positive outcomes while minimizing risk assessment.	"This is going to work great! I just know it is!"
Limiting the amount of incoming, potentially contradictory information.	"We've heard enough. It's time to make a decision."
Failing to consider contingency plans in case things don't succeed.	"What will happen if it doesn't work? It doesn't matter. It *has* to work."

Just as getting the right diagnosis of a disease makes it easier to cure the disease, Janis's articulation of the problem of groupthink makes it easier to suggest cures for groupthink. Beyond being on the lookout for the symptoms and statements in Table 8.2, the following solutions seem obvious in light of the description of the problem:

- Consult with outsiders who disagree or who have different information.
- Criticize your own ideas.
- Replace the "mindguard" with a "devil's advocate" whose job is to *dis*agree and find fault with group decisions, even if they personally agree.

Janis departed from social psychology's customary ways of developing knowledge by analyzing historical events and *case studies* rather than conducting controlled experiments. The tendency to rely on historical events outside the lab as evidence of groupthink has continued. For example, psychologists suspect groupthink when journalists report the same stories without independently checking facts (Matusitz & Breen, 2012). This kind of groupthink has influenced reporting about radical terrorist groups (Tsintsadze-Maass & Maass, 2014), the torture that occurred at Abu Ghraib (Post & Panis, 2011), and several U.S. presidential decisions made post-9/11 (Kennedy, 2013).

The Spiral of Silence and Pluralistic Ignorance.
Have you ever felt afraid to voice an opinion in a group?

Groupthink is thought to produce what has been described as a **spiral of silence**, which occurs when fear of rejection leads people to keep silent about a private opinion, misperceive the louder opinion as a majority opinion, and therefore become even less likely to express their private opinion (Noelle-Neumann, 1993; see Figure 8.7). People tend to feel more anxious when they are part of a group whose opinions they do not share (see Morrison & Miller, 2008). This anxiety and the desire to be accepted results in the gradually increasing reluctance to express a minority opinion (Bassili, 2003): a spiral of silence.

Part of what keeps people with a minority opinion silent is **pluralistic ignorance**, the false impression that others do not share your private perspective. In one of many empirical studies testing pluralistic ignorance, students on a large Midwestern university campus falsely believed that their personal reservations about using alcohol were not shared by others (Suls & Green, 2003). For example, students believed that not drinking made them social deviants. Essentially, people changed their behavior because they thought—incorrectly—that their opinion was unique and that others all felt differently. Pluralistic ignorance sucks us deeper down into the spiral of silence. It seems that for many of the problematic group phenomena covered here, a brave person willing to speak his or her mind would be extremely helpful.

Spiral of silence: When fear of rejection leads people to keep silent about a private opinion, misperceive the louder opinion as a majority opinion, and therefore become even less likely to express their private opinion.

Pluralistic ignorance: When a majority of individuals in a group get the false impression that others do not share their private perspective, making them less likely to express their opinion.

■ FIGURE 8.7 Spiral of silence.

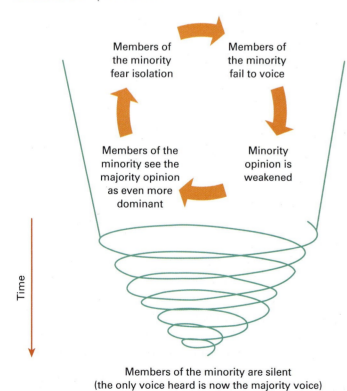

Members of the minority fear isolation

Members of the minority fail to voice

Members of the minority see the majority opinion as even more dominant

Minority opinion is weakened

Time

Members of the minority are silent (the only voice heard is now the majority voice)

SOURCE: Noelle-Neumann (1974).

The Main Ideas

- Contingency leadership is the idea that different kinds of leaders are useful for different kinds of situations; four leadership styles are task, social, transactional, and transformational.

- Group decisions tend to be more extreme than individual decisions, a general tendency called group polarization.

- Groupthink is the tendency for people in groups to minimize conflict by publicly agreeing with each other, even when it leads to bad decisions. Groupthink can be caused by pluralistic ignorance, which contributes to the spiral of silence.

⚡ CRITICAL THINKING CHALLENGE

- Identify your own leadership tendencies and analyze whether your leadership style changes depending on the situation (reinforcing the idea of contingency leadership). Then, think about the type of leadership you prefer in others. Why do you seem to thrive under that particular style of leadership?

- Imagine your college, social group, religious community, or any other important personal group is going to vote on a new leader—and there are several strong candidates. What policies or procedures could you suggest to the group to help each member avoid group polarization from occurring?

- Think of either additional historical examples you think came from groupthink or examples of groupthink leading to bad decisions in your own life. Looking back now, what could have happened to stop the groupthink from occurring? Can you apply this lesson to future group decisions?

WHAT INCREASES GROUP CREATIVITY?

LO 8.5: Evaluate what circumstances help and hurt group creativity.

One of the "big questions" in Chapter 1 was, "What are the benefits and drawbacks of living in groups?" You now know that the answer is complicated and that it depends on the situation *and* the people involved. Groups can lead to a lot of really bad decisions—but in other cases groups can lead to creative and groundbreaking innovation.

The Wisdom of Crowds and Crowdsourcing

Video game developers, marketing professionals, social entrepreneurs, the creators of Wikipedia, and other types of social problem solvers have stumbled onto an important source of group creativity that psychologists call the **wisdom of crowds** (Surowiecki, 2005). The same idea is known as "crowdsourcing" by digital innovators. Both ideas refer to the same thing, which is using the collective insights of many people to test, develop, and refine new ideas, products, and services.

The best modern example of the wisdom of crowds is probably the website Wikipedia. Originally, the site was meant to complement online encyclopedias written and maintained by experts for each entry, but the idea of Wikipedia was always that any person from the public could contribute information and edit the site.

Wisdom of crowds: Using the collective insights of many people to test, develop, and refine new ideas, products, and services; also called "crowdsourcing."

WIKIPEDIA
The Free Encyclopedia

Main page
Contents
Featured content
Current events
Random article
Donate to Wikipedia
Wikipedia store

Interaction

Article | Talk

History of Wikipedia

From Wikipedia, the free encyclopedia

Wikipedia formally began with its launch on 15 January 2001, two days after the do Sanger. Its technological and conceptual underpinnings predate this; the earliest k made by Rick Gates in 1993,[3] but the concept of a free-as-in-freedom online enc proposed by Richard Stallman in December 2000.[5]

Crucially, Stallman's concept specifically included the idea that no central organiza stark contrast to contemporary digital encyclopedias such as Microsoft Encarta, Er which was Wikipedia's direct predecessor. In 2001, the license for Nupedia was cha

A screenshot of the Wikipedia page that discusses the history of Wikipedia—a website completely based on the wisdom of crowds.

Wikipedia is now among the top 10 visited websites (in terms of daily users), and it increases by about 800 new articles every day. (What's the source for this information? Wikipedia.org, of course.)

Brainstorming Can Help

Like a smooth-running surgical team or a well-rehearsed symphony orchestra, some groups require intense cooperation and creativity. One of the first scientific efforts to understand group creativity occurred after advertising executive Osborn (1957) created procedures for **brainstorming,** a group approach to problem solving that emphasizes nonevaluative creative thinking. Osborn's methods were simple: Generate lots of ideas, encourage wild ideas, don't judge any idea, and modify or expand other people's ideas. In other words, no sneering or snickering was allowed when people said weird things— it was time to suspend judgment and let your creativity flow!

Brainstorming: A group approach to problem solving that emphasizes nonevaluative creative thinking where members generate lots of ideas, encourage wild ideas, don't judge any idea, and actively modify or expand other people's ideas.

Inspiring Creativity. The extravagant promise, or at least hope, of brainstorming was that ideas would collide in ways that sparked imaginations and fueled creativity. Early research results mostly supported Osborn's idea. Brainstorming increased both the quantity and quality of ideas, and even more so if individuals had already been trained in brainstorming techniques (see Parnes & Meadow, 1959). But the research path soon started taking the kind of twists and turns that meant we were in for another complicated series of studies that ended at the destination of "it depends" (see Diehl & Strobe, 1987; Weldon, Blair, & Huebsch, 2000).

When Brainstorming Doesn't Work. Despite all the hope and hype, brainstorming did not get a lot of support when Dunnette, Campbell, and Jaastad (1963) tested it among research scientists and advertising personnel employed by the Minnesota Mining and Manufacturing Company. The sum of creative ideas produced by *individuals* brainstorming was greater than that of people brainstorming in groups. It was the opposite of what was supposed to happen. Why wasn't brainstorming working as well as advertised?

One explanation for the mixed results of brainstorming is diffusion of responsibility (Mullen, Johnson, & Salas, 1991; Paulus, Nakui, Putnam, & Brown, 2006).

One of the keys to successful brainstorming is that everyone maintains a supportive and positive attitude.

© istockphoto.com/fstop123

Use a facilitator to remind everyone of the rules of brainstorming and keep their attention focused on the task.
Encourage people to take an "incubation break," a rest period following intense effort to solve a problem.
Begin brainstorming with "brainwriting," an approach that generates ideas by having group members independently write down their ideas on paper and then sharing them with the group.
Embed independent diversity of viewpoints when selecting members of the group.

SOURCE: Dugosh et al. (2000).

Another explanation is evaluation apprehension: Even though brainstorming groups aren't supposed to judge any ideas, people can still be afraid that their contributions will be seen as silly, so they just don't say them out loud. The fear of evaluation is especially salient to people with social anxiety. In a *quasi-experiment,* Comacho and Paulus (1995) found that groups of four people who had tested high in social anxiety were less productive than groups of four people who were all low in social anxiety. While online brainstorming groups seem to generate more ideas than face-to-face groups (Connolly, Routhieaux, & Schneider, 1993), self-censoring due to social anxiety remains a problem even in these settings.

Guidelines for Successful Brainstorming. While some research showed that brainstorming didn't work, other research simply noted criteria for when it can work. Dugosh and colleagues (Dugosh, Paulus, Roland, & Yang, 2000) suggested four practical guidelines, shown in Table 8.3.

More modern research has shown several specific examples of successful brainstorming. One study found that women who engaged in creative problem solving got higher scores in the experimental brainstorming group compared to a control group (Al-khatib, 2012). Patients with cancer who worked with counselors to brainstorm ways to talk with their families about their condition indicated appreciation for the sessions (de Geus et al., 2016). Middle school children who brainstormed were judged to be more creative than a control group (George & Basavarajappa, 2016).

There are many more examples published just in the past few years. And again highlighting that certain conditions make brainstorming more effective, a series of three studies showed that alternating between individual and group idea generation sessions produced more creative solutions to problems than either working alone all the time or working in a group all the time (Korde & Paulus, 2017). Brainstorming can be an effective strategy for creative problem solving, especially under ideal conditions.

The Main Ideas

- The "wisdom of crowds" and "crowdsourcing" both refer to the same idea: using the collective insights of many people to test, develop, and refine new ideas, products, and services.

- Brainstorming is a group approach to problem solving that emphasizes nonevaluative creative thinking.

- Brainstorming outcomes can be hurt by diffusion of responsibility and by evaluation apprehension, especially when members of the group have social anxiety.

- Brainstorming outcomes can be helped by procedural rules such as reminding members not to judge ideas, taking breaks, asking for individual generation of ideas first, and encouraging diversity in the group.

- Despite Wikipedia's popularity, the site has received criticism for the ability of anyone to edit content. What are the advantages and disadvantages of this aspect of the website?

- In an earlier section of the chapter, you read about leadership styles. List different leadership styles, and for each, describe whether this style would be helpful or harmful in guiding group brainstorming (and why).

- Four ways to increase successful brainstorming were offered in Table 8.3. What's missing from this table, based on your experience or your understanding of social psychological principles? What other concepts from the book so far could be applied to research studies on brainstorming that you hypothesize would help or hurt the process or outcome?

CHAPTER SUMMARY

Why are groups so important to us?

Groups occur when two or more people interact with each other or share a common experience or fate. We have a natural instinct to form groups because they offer several advantages. One advantage is that they provide social support. Two studies of friendships and group cohesion within residential housing areas showed that people bonded when they had more interaction with each other and when they could work together for pragmatic resources (such as safety needs).

Second, groups also help us form an individual identity by providing social comparisons and giving us a specific role in a group. Third, groups can offer emotional support when we are feeling afraid or anxious; research shows that either emotion leads us to affiliate with other people. Finally, groups can provide meaningful information; when other people can share information such as how they experienced a certain event, we can be more confident in predicting that event for ourselves.

Why are we more committed to certain groups?

We are more committed to groups that are difficult to join; this is called the initiation effect. The same phenomenon is also sometimes called effort justification, because perhaps we decide that we like a group simply to justify the effort we've put into joining it to avoid feeling foolish—this could be one example of cognitive dissonance. We also sometimes increase our commitment to a failing situation or bad decision to justify the investment of time or resources we've already put in; this is called an escalation trap (or sometimes called the sunken cost fallacy).

One example of how real-life groups use the initiation effect is through hazing. Fraternities, sororities, and sports teams are known for the negative and harmful side effects of hazing, but they likely are aware that difficult or humiliating initiation rituals both increase members' commitment to the group and increase the group's authority.

Specifically, when hostages develop affection for their captors, it's called the Stockholm syndrome.

We are also particularly sensitive to social rejection and ostracism. Optimal distinctiveness theory suggests that we will particularly value small, elite groups because they balance our needs to (a) affiliate with a group but also (b) to feel unique and special.

How do groups help and hinder individual effort?

Social facilitation occurs when our performance on simple, easy, or well-practiced tasks goes up in the presence of other people (compared to when we're alone). Originally, the explanation for this tendency was a competitive instinct, but facilitation occurs even when we're not directly competing with others. There are now two major hypotheses that explain the effect. One is evaluation apprehension; this idea is that our fear of being judged by others makes our performance improve. However, the mere presence hypothesis is the idea that simply having other people around us increases our physiology and that this helps performance for easy tasks—but it hurts performance for difficult tasks. Some research supports each hypothesis.

How do individuals influence groups?

The contingency theory of leadership is the idea that different leadership styles will be needed depending on the given situation. Task leaders focus on completing assignments. Social leaders focus on the people involved and their well-being. Transactional leaders use rewards and punishments to motivate their group, while transformational leaders use inspiration and group cohesiveness to motivate group members and are useful for challenging established rules or procedures.

Sometimes, discussions in groups make people's initial opinions change; if someone were leaning toward one decision, talking with people who also leaned toward that decision would likely make everyone in the group more confident regarding their decision. This tendency is called group polarization: when a group makes more extreme decisions than the average of the individual decisions.

Finally, sometimes groups make bad choices because people with minority opinions (in other words, people who disagree with the group's decision) fail to speak up. Groupthink is the tendency for people in groups to minimize conflict by publicly agreeing with each other. This phenomenon has been applied to several case studies throughout history to explain why a group of people made a bad decision. Groupthink is more likely in highly cohesive groups with strong leaders under stressful situations.

What increases group creativity?

Both the wisdom of crowds and crowdsourcing refer to the idea that groups can provide collective insight to test, develop, and refine ideas and products. When groups are asked to generate creative solutions, one well-known technique is brainstorming. Brainstorming asks members of a group to both generate new ideas and to be nonevaluative of other people's ideas. While some research has shown that brainstorming is not particularly effective, other studies have established that it can be effective under the right circumstances.

THEORIES IN REVIEW

- Optimal distinctiveness theory
- Social facilitation
- Social loafing
- Contingency theory of leadership

- Group polarization
- Groupthink
- The wisdom of crowds
- Brainstorming

CRITICAL THINKING, ANALYSIS, AND APPLICATION

- Groups offer many benefits, as described in the first section of this book. However, a previous chapter described how groups can also offer the opportunity for anonymity and deindividuation, which can sometimes lead to negative behavior (e.g., online trolling or crime). Do the advantages that groups offer society outweigh the disadvantages? Provide specific examples to support your answer.

- Some social psychologists still debate whether social facilitation is due to evaluation apprehension or the mere presence of others (which increases our physiological arousal). Which hypothesis is more convincing to you, personally, and why? How would you design a research study to help resolve this debate?

- This chapter introduced four specific leadership styles (task, social, transactional, and transformational). Identify one famous person who is an example of each style listed here, and provide examples of why you think this person matches that style.

- Positive outcomes from group settings include social facilitation and increased creativity (due to brainstorming). Negative outcomes include social loafing, diffusion of responsibility, group polarization, and groupthink. What are practical things that a group leader can do to influence group dynamics such that the positives of groups increase and the negatives of groups decrease?

PERSONAL REFLECTIONS

There are practical benefits to initiation rituals. I once worked in a factory that sent new employees to a distant warehouse to bring back a "skyhook"—a nonexistent tool. The employee learns that the skyhook has been sent to another department, and then to another and another until he (this seemed to be a male ritual) figures out that he is getting the run-around. But there are practical benefits to "skyhooking" new employees. The employee learns his or her way around a large factory, other employees learn that there is a new employee, and they all get to observe him in an awkward situation—potentially valuable information if you are going to work together on large, dangerous punch presses and high-speed machinery. [TH]

Due to my perfectionist personality, I always hated group work precisely because I didn't trust others not to be social loafers. I usually just ended up doing all the work myself. However, last year I volunteered to be part of a group of women faculty who decided to write a play over the course of a year. The group was led by one of my university's theater professors, and her style of leadership was very relaxed and easygoing. I frequently got frustrated when I perceived that time was being "wasted" or when we didn't have an agenda for meetings. Over the year, however, I realized that my way of doing things wasn't the only right way—and we did end up writing and performing a play that won a creativity award. Different styles of leadership really can work if we learn to relax and trust each other. [WG]

PRACTICE AND APPLY WHAT YOU'VE LEARNED

► **edge.sagepub.com/heinzen**

LO8.4 **Analyze** how **leadership succeeds** or **fails**, how **group decisions turn risky** or **safe**, and how a **minority can influence** the **majority**.

LO8.5 **Evaluate** what **circumstances help** and **hurt group creativity**.

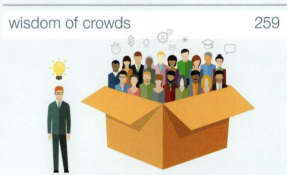

9 Stereotyping, Prejudice, and Discrimination

Core Questions

1. Why do we stereotype?
2. How do stereotypes turn into prejudices?
3. Is prejudice a personality problem?
4. Has prejudice decreased over time?
5. How can we reduce stereotyping, prejudice, and discrimination?

Learning Objectives

9.1 Explain several ideas regarding why we tend to categorize and label people.

9.2 Analyze how categorizing leads to prejudice.

9.3 Describe how prejudice emerges from the interaction between personality and situation.

9.4 Analyze how forms of prejudice and discrimination have changed over time.

9.5 Apply methods of prejudice reduction to real-world settings.

Frank Roque from Mesa, Arizona, was working at a Boeing aircraft plant when he learned about the terror attacks of September 11, 2001. He told coworkers and then a waitress at an Applebee's restaurant that he wanted to shoot some "towel heads." Four days later, he fired five shots at Balbir Singh Sodhi (pictured here), killing him instantly as he was planting flowers (one report said that he was arranging American flags) outside his gas station. That murder was called the "First 9/11 Backlash Fatality" (2011).

Sodhi was 49 years old, the father of two daughters, and from India—a country that had nothing to do with 9/11. He was also one of 20 million Sikhs, the fifth largest religion in the world, whose men typically wear a beard and a turban. The Sikh turban looks very different from the traditional Arab headscarf. And a Sikh American business owner from India looks very different from the 9/11 terrorists. Most of those men were ostensibly Muslim and came from Saudi Arabia.

The hijackers were not wearing headscarves when they boarded the planes on September 11, 2001. Even if Sodhi had been from the Middle East and had been wearing a different kind of headgear, these facts would have nothing to do with the type of person he was. He had been targeted by Roque based only on stereotypes and fear. Roque objected to being arrested: "I'm a patriot and American. I'm American. I'm a damn American. . . . How can you arrest me and let the terrorists run wild?" (*State of Arizona v. Frank Silva Roque,* 2006).

The Pluralism Project at Harvard University (2013) documented many similar cases of post-9/11 violence against Asians, Jews, and Sikhs. In addition, Human Rights Watch (2002) reported that the FBI recorded a 17-fold increase in anti-Muslim crimes nationwide during 2001 (even though 9/11 occurred near the end of the calendar year). Many in the United States were gripped by fear—imprisoned by stereotypes and prejudice.

WHY DO WE STEREOTYPE?

LO 9.1: Explain several ideas regarding why we tend to categorize and label people.

Prejudice has been a salient topic in the United States around each presidential election of the past two decades. People discussed whether the country was ready for its first president of color (Barack Obama, who won) or its first female president (Hillary Clinton, who lost). After each election, crimes that victimized traditionally oppressed groups based on race, sex, gender, sexual orientation, and religion were on everyone's minds. For example, several news outlets reported spikes in anti-Semitism (prejudice against Jewish people) and crimes against Muslims in the few months after President Trump was elected. For victims of these crimes, stereotypes, prejudice, and discrimination are not things of the past.

Frank Roque's decision to murder Balbir Singh Sodhi was based on a **stereotype**, a belief that all members of a group have the same characteristics. Stereotypes describe group members in terms of their perceived physical characteristics, personality traits, behaviors (such as foods they eat), and so on. Stereotypes are closely linked to **prejudices**, emotion-centered judgments or evaluations about people based on their perceived membership in a particular group. Finally, both stereotyping and prejudice are connected to **discrimination**, unfair behaviors toward a particular group or members of a group.

Each of these terms (stereotyping, prejudice, and discrimination) is sometimes used to describe the combined effects of all three. But when we use the words more precisely, stereotyping usually refers to how we think (the cognitive component), prejudice refers to our feelings (the affective component), and discrimination refers to our actions (the behavioral component); see Table 9.1. In the case of Frank Roque, they became the same deadly psychological cocktail that likely guided the 9/11 terrorists in the first place.

Imagine that you wanted to put a stop to the kind of stereotyping, prejudice, and discrimination that led to Balbir Singh Sodhi's death. It would make sense to simply stop the chain reaction at the beginning—stop using stereotypes. That's a pretty good idea, but it faces one major obstacle: Using stereotypes seems to be a basic human instinct. Every recorded culture in every time period in the history of the world has included some form of stereotypes. Why are the presence of group categories and labels so pervasive throughout human history?

Let's discuss three explanations from social psychology regarding why stereotypes exist: (1) categorizing people into groups is a human instinct that benefits survival, (2) spending time with similar others is comforting and validating, and (3) our culture reinforces stereotypes and teaches them to the next generation.

Stereotypes Are Efficient but Biased: Adaptive Categorization

Adaptive categorization is the first explanation for the existence of stereotypes. This perspective argues that the instinct to group and label other people and things in the environment arose because it was a benefit to survival.

Stereotypes Help Us to Be Cognitive Misers. Lazy thinkers! Cognitive misers! Whatever we call it, we inherited the basic human tendency to simplify the world. Each day we're overloaded with information, so our automatic mental spam filter operates on what Allport (1979, p. 173) called "the principle of least effort." We stereotype because we are cognitive misers who adopt mental shortcuts whenever possible (see Chapter 4).

Stereotype: A type of oversimplified and overgeneralized schema that occurs when an individual assumes that everyone in a certain group has the same traits.

Prejudice: Emotion-centered judgments or evaluations about people based on their perceived membership in a particular group.

Discrimination: Unfair behaviors toward a particular group or members of a group based on a stereotype or prejudice.

Adaptive categorization: The idea that the instinct to group and label other people and things in the environment arose because it was a benefit to survival.

■ **TABLE 9.1** Making Distinctions Among Stereotypes, Prejudice, and Discrimination

Term	Component	Example	Example	Example
Stereotype	Beliefs (cognitive)	Belief that men wearing any kind of headscarf are Muslim	Belief that women are emotional	Belief that gay people are stylish
Prejudice	Feelings (affective)	Negative emotions toward Muslims; judgment that they are all "terrorists"	Negative judgment that women make for bad leaders	Positive judgment of gay people and their fashion sense
Discrimination	Actions (behavioral)	Refusing to board an airplane with anyone perceived to be Muslim	Not voting for female political candidates	Choosing a gay man as your hairdresser

Across cultures and time, stereotypes have simplified our lives by relying on the most obvious external characteristics, such as skin color, age, sex, or clothing that suggests social class. These traits are the first thing we can learn about a stranger when meeting him or her—we don't even need to speak to see these cues and start forming a stereotype about what type of person stands before us. Thus, we can make very fast decisions—efficient, split-second, cognitively lazy decisions.

These split-second cues for impression formation (and use of stereotypes) are automatic reactions. We know that because *brain imaging studies* suggest that racial stereotypes trigger automatic reactions to perceived dangers—even when those dangers do not exist. For example, White participants were shown facial images of both Black people and White people, and the two groups of images were further subdivided by how long the image flashed on a screen: 30 milliseconds (3/100 of a second) or 525 milliseconds (a little more than half a second). Thus, the *independent variables* are (a) race of the facial images and (b) how long the images appeared on the screen.

This 2 × 2 **factorial design**—meaning a study that combines more than one *independent variable*—creates opportunities to make *meaningful comparison groups*. Thirty milliseconds is a very brief exposure, but we know that the participants perceived *something* during that flash of time because their fear response (the *dependent variable*, shown by neural activity in the amygdala) was significantly greater for Black faces than for White faces (Cunningham et al., 2004). These participants apparently had an automatic, emotional reaction to the Black faces.

While this finding may be depressing, there is a good side to this research story. The comparison group of participants saw those same Black and White faces for 525 milliseconds (about half a second). That was still very fast, but now there was more activation among the complex neural pathways in the prefrontal cortex and the anterior cingulate—the thinking, logical parts of the brain.

In other words, for the 30-millisecond condition, different faces caused different levels of fear—but when given just a tiny bit more time, logic could take over. While we may not be able to escape our instinctive drives to categorize and label other people, it takes only half a second of logical and effortful thought to start restraining those automatic impulses. Perhaps this difference is part of why implicit and explicit measures of stereotypes and attitudes in general differ (see Chapter 9).

The Minimal Group Paradigm.
You already know that groups provide a variety of benefits to their members (see Chapter 8). Group membership provides personal access to resources, emotional comfort, physical safety, recreation, potential mating partners, and . . . well, lots of stuff that make our lives easier to manage and enjoy.

Groups mean so much to us that our basic tendency is to align ourselves with others and then to protect that community. Merely insulting someone's group is experienced as a personal insult. Our **ingroups** are groups in which we are members, such as our race, nationality, sex, sexual orientation, and so on. Our ingroups also include chosen groups, such as the college or university we attend and groups based on activities like the choir or tennis team. In contrast, **outgroups** are any groups in which we are not members—everybody else!

The human instinct to protect members of our ingroups is so strong that we even protect groups that we belong to purely by chance. Tajfel (1970) studied this tendency

Feije Riemersma / Alamy Stock Photo

Just by looking at this person, what stereotypes might pop into your head? You already know she is old, female, and Native American, so assumptions about her personality, behaviors, and so on can begin to form immediately.

Factorial design: A type of experiment in which two or more independent variables are used for each participant. The combination of independent variables creates several layers of experimental condition.

Ingroup: Any group in which an individual is a member; these groups can be based on chosen or nonchosen characteristics such as race, nationality, sex, sexual orientation, club membership, favorite sports team, or where an individual went to college.

Outgroup: Any group in which an individual is not a member.

in what he called the **minimal group paradigm**, an experimental method to create groups based on meaningless categories to study intergroup dynamics. Tajfel suspected that we will show ingroup favoritism and outgroup negativity even when group formation had no meaning.

To create these "minimal" groups, Tajfel showed some English schoolboys (14 to 15 years old) very brief images of dots and asked the boys to estimate how many dots they had seen. The catch was that the boys were given *bogus feedback* about their answers. In this case, the boys were told that they were either "overestimators" or "underestimators" of how many dots they had seen. It was a ridiculous, fictional, randomly assigned label that only had meaning if the boys believed it. He then gave the boys the opportunity to either be fair or to discriminate against the other group by assigning points that represented real money to each group.

Tajfel found that the boys who had been told that they were "overestimators" took away points from the "underestimators"—and the "underestimators" also took away points from the "overestimators." Simple group membership had led to promoting the ingroup and denigrating the outgroup—that's all it took for stereotypes, prejudice, and discrimination to kick in. There was *nothing* special about the boys' ability to estimate the number of dots (even if it had been a real ability), and it certainly wasn't justification to start taking away resources from the "others."

But to make sure, Tajfel *replicated* the experiment by using a slightly different but equally ridiculous criterion. This time he led two groups of schoolboys to believe (once again, using bogus feedback) that they preferred the abstract paintings of either artist Paul Klee or Wassily Kandinsky. It happened again: ingroup favoritism and outgroup bias. How low was the bar needed to create this kind of prejudice? In a third experiment, group prejudice emerged once again even when participants *could observe* that assignment to a group was based on chance—pulling a lottery ticket out of a can. Participants *still* rewarded other members of their new ingroup at the expense of the perceived outgroup (Billig & Tajfel, 1973; Tajfel, Billig, Bundy, & Flament, 1971).

The minimal groups experiments tell us how easily we can form an "us versus them" mentality, even when group divisions are random and meaningless.

Minimal group paradigm: An experimental method to create groups based on meaningless categories to study intergroup dynamics.

Do you prefer the painting on the left, by Klee, or the one on the right, by Kandinsky? Do you think you deserve more money, land, or food than people who disagree with you?

The justifications we devise to eventually treat people differently (discrimination) seem to be excuses for something far more fundamental about the human impulse to survive. We protect people we perceive to be "us"—and believe that "we" somehow deserve more than "they" do.

Ingroups Are Comforting and Validating: Social Identity Theory

Take another mental trip back to high school, this time to the cafeteria. The groups were not based only on friendships. The people in lunch groups were connected by other social ties such as playing in the band, on a sports team, or being in theater. Our grouping tendencies became the theme of a controversial book written by social psychologist Beverly Tatum (1997) called *Why Are All the Black Kids Sitting Together in the Cafeteria?*

You may have heard the phrase, "Birds of a feather flock together." We like spending time with people who are similar to ourselves, and that tendency reinforces stereotypes. When other people share experiences, agree with our opinions, and tell us that we're right, we feel comforted and validated. Our identities blend a personal identity (including our individual traits and what makes us unique) with a social identity (the parts of our "self" that include our group memberships). **Social identity theory** (Tajfel & Turner, 1979) is the idea that we have an automatic tendency to categorize each other and to form "us versus them" groups that validate our perceptions of ourselves in flattering and useful ways.

Everett Collection Inc / Alamy Stock Photo

Beverly Tatum is the author of *Why Are All the Black Kids Sitting Together in the Cafeteria*? Social psychology tries to explain the common trend of people to gather together with others who are similar to themselves.

If we spend time only with our own ingroups, there are two consequences that lead directly down the path to stereotypes. The first outcome is **ingroup heterogeneity**. This term refers to the idea that it's easy for us to see the wonderful, wide diversity within our ingroups because we get to know each member as a unique individual. Think about people who go to your college and how different they are from each other! You can probably see how any stereotypes about students at your college are silly generalizations, which may lead you to resent those stereotypes.

The other outcome of spending time only with our ingroups is **outgroup homogeneity**, which is the perception that all the members of a particular outgroup are exactly the same. When you don't know anyone in the outgroup personally and don't spend any time learning about them, all you have to go on is a stereotype. You might have heard that students at the University of California at Berkeley are politically correct, tree-hugging hippies. If you meet someone from UC Berkeley and don't have any other information about him or her, then you might fall back on that stereotype.

Social identity theory: Psychological theory that proposes that our self-concept is composed of two parts: a personal identity that is based on personal characteristics and a social identity that is based on social role characteristics.

Ingroup heterogeneity: The tendency for individuals to see wide diversity within their ingroups.

Outgroup homogeneity: The perception that all members of a particular outgroup are identical to each other.

An individual feather is easily pushed off—but a huge pile of them can hurt. The same may be true for individual incidents of stereotypes, prejudice, and discrimination—and a lifetime of small incidents can feel like a ton of feathers.

Culture: A collection of shared beliefs, customs, attitudes, values, social norms, and intellectual pursuits that distinguishes one group of people from another.

The popular show *2 Broke Girls* features a "poor" girl who is sassy with street smarts and a "rich" girl who is stylish and condescending. Even when the characters show some change and depth, they still reinforce basic stereotypes.

Culture Reinforces Stereotypes: The Power of Privilege

How do all of these stereotypical ideas get into our heads in the first place? Where do all those specific images, beliefs, assumption, expectations, stereotypes, and prejudices come from? Who decided which groupings matter and why certain stereotypes go with certain groups?

Culture, a collection of shared beliefs, strengthens stereotypes because culture is "like a fish's understanding of the notion of water" (see Whitley & Kite, 2010, p. 6). We don't even notice our culture is there because it's simply part of our existence—we might never question it until someone takes us out of our metaphorical water. For example, Sue (2003) used a *qualitative methodology* to ask White people in the United States—part of the dominant culture—"What does it mean to be White?" Common responses were, "Is this a trick question?" "I've never thought about it," and "I don't know what you are talking about."

A feature of any culture is that members of the dominant group have the privilege of being oblivious to the fact that they have power. Some people of color may worry about being pulled over by the police for being "suspicious" drivers—but White people can drive without ever being afraid of race-biased law enforcement. Bandages, clothing, and makeup that comes in "nude" coloring often match White skin. White people don't have to worry about housing discrimination. And so on. In general, the social benefits of being White in White-centric societies is called **White privilege**.

Privilege comes in other forms as well, based on which group has social power. Women might worry about not being paid the same amount as men in the same job—but men don't have to think about the wage disparity. Gay spouses might worry about putting pictures of each other on their desk at work—but heterosexual spouses don't even think about it. These subtle, persistent parts of privilege accumulate into an experience for the oppressed that Caplan (1994) describes as "lifting a ton of feathers." Each one is seemingly light, but put together they can be crushing.

Intergenerational Transmission: Social Learning Theory. Once a stereotype has made its way into a culture, it gets passed along to the next generation. **Social learning theory** is the idea that individuals observe what others do and copy them, especially when those behaviors lead to success or rewards (Bandura, 1986). Cultures reward stereotypes in subtle ways every day, and thus perceptions of different groups are transmitted from one generation to the next. **Social agents** are the ones sending the messages about cultural beliefs and expectations. They can be parents, the media, or any source that transmits information to others.

For example, when researchers examined the portrayal of Arabs in more than 900 Hollywood movies, they found that Arabs were consistently stereotyped as uncivilized, savage, religious fanatics (Shaheen, 2003). In television and news coverage of athletes, the focus on female athletes is often how physically attractive they are, whereas the focus on male athletes is their skill (Messner, 1988). Television shows frequently endorse stereotypical gender roles, as well as stereotypes of the wealthy and the poor (Newman, 2007).

Stereotypes as Self-Fulfilling Prophecies: Social Role Theory.

Another way that culture passes stereotypes from one generation to the next is by teaching young people what is socially acceptable behavior for different groups. **Social role theory** is the idea that stereotypes form when we observe the roles that different kinds of people occupy in the world and we then reinforce those roles by assuming the people occupying them are well suited to the roles (Eagly, 1987; Eagly, Wood, & Diekman, 2000).

For example, for centuries, men were generally in charge of providing resources to their families, such as food and shelter. Women, on the other hand, were expected to stay at home and take care of children. This split in duties probably resulted from the physical reality that women give birth and that men tend to be physically stronger—but that basic biological divide led to unfounded generalizations. Many cultures assigned women *all* caretaking and nurturing roles with the assumption that women must be suited for these roles by biological "design."

Social role theory notes that when this stereotype arises, the culture accordingly shifts the lessons it sends to little boys and little girls, training them for the roles they are expected to fill later in life. Thus, boys will be rewarded for independence and competitiveness while girls will be rewarded for kindness and gentleness. This leads to a self-fulfilling prophecy that many men and women find hard to overcome as adults.

Toys are frequently marketed toward boys versus girls—and they often send messages about what each sex should be learning and practicing for adulthood.

Gender stereotypes may be the most pervasive social stereotype—and therefore the most difficult to overcome. When the Mattell toy company released its "Teen-Talk Barbie," the doll was programmed to say stereotypically feminine phrases such as, "Do you have a crush on anyone?" "I will always be there to help you," and most famously, "Math class is tough!" The challenge to raise awareness of gender stereotypes inspired some social activists to form the Barbie Liberation Organization (BLO). BLO members purchased talking Barbies and GI Joes and performed "corrective surgery" on their voice chips before sneaking the dolls—in their original packaging—back onto the store shelves. Now the surgically modified Barbie declared in a gravelly voice, "Gung Ho!" "Cobra! Attack!" and "Dead men tell no tales." And GI Joe was eagerly asking, "Do you want to go shopping?"—and bemoaning the fact that math class was so hard.

If you think that dolls don't have any kind of influence about how children perceive the world around them, check out the "Spotlight on Research Methods" feature, which summarizes a study done with dolls that made it all the way to the U.S. Supreme Court.

White privilege: The cultural benefits of being White in White-centric societies.

Social learning theory: A model for understanding social behavior that proposes that we learn attitudes by observing and imitating others.

Social agents: Individuals who send messages about cultural beliefs and expectations that help transmit ideas from one generation to the next; social agents include any source that transmits information, such as parents and the media (see *social learning theory*).

Becoming Our Own Worst Enemy: Stereotype Threat.

It's frustrating enough when other people stereotype us just because of our group memberships, many of which are unavoidable and unchosen. However, sometimes stereotypes can be at least somewhat true, a concept acknowledged by the **kernel of truth theory**. Some people wearing glasses really are smart, some rich people really are condescending, and so on. Sometimes, though, these truths result from the fact that our culture has shaped us to fill particular roles that become self-fulfilling prophecies.

DOLLS, PREJUDICE, SCHOOLS, AND THE SUPREME COURT

In 1954, the Supreme Court made what was possibly the most consequential constitutional decision of the 20th century: *Brown v. Board of Education,* which led to racial desegregation of schools. One of the ways the justices came to their conclusion was by considering research from psychology (Benjamin & Crouse, 2002). The Court concluded that "to separate [African American children] from others of similar age and qualifications . . . may affect their hearts and minds in a way unlikely ever to be undone."

The pivotal research cited by the Court, now known as the "doll studies," was first conceived by Mamie Phipps Clark as part of her master's degree. She and her husband Kenneth Clark were the first two African Americans to earn doctorates from Columbia University (see Johnson & Pettigrew, 2005). In their experiments, the Clarks provided African American children with dolls that were identical except that one doll was white-skinned and the other was brown-skinned (Whitman, 1993). It was a *within-subjects design* because the same children saw both a white-skinned doll and a brown-skinned doll. Then they asked the children a series of questions about which doll they preferred: "Give me the doll that you like to play with," ". . . you like best," ". . . is a nice doll," ". . . looks bad," ". . . is a nice color"—and, finally, ". . . is most like you?"

Some 90% of these 3- to 7-year-olds accurately indicated they were like the brown-skinned doll—but about two thirds preferred the white doll. In examining their results, the researchers compared the responses of children attending segregated schools in Washington, D.C., and those of children attending racially integrated schools in New York. Comparing these two preexisting groups made their research a *quasi-experimental design.* The preference for the white doll—indicating a negative prejudice toward their own race—was much more pronounced in the children from segregated schools. Culture had taught them self-hatred, and they transferred those feelings to the dolls.

Some of the children's reactions were disturbing. One girl who had described the brown doll as "ugly" and "dirty" burst into tears; others refused to continue the experiment; some giggled self-consciously; one little boy tried to escape his dilemma by insisting that he had a suntan. The fact that this internalized racism was greater for children from segregated schools was a pivotal piece of information in the Court's decision that segregation led to negative outcomes.

The American Psychological Association (APA) was disturbingly quiet in the aftermath of *Brown v. Board of Education* (see Benjamin & Crouse, 2002). In 1970, Kenneth Clark was elected president of the APA and in 1994 was honored for his lifetime contributions. In his acceptance speech, he admitted that "thirty years after *Brown,* I must accept the fact that my wife left this earth despondent at seeing that damage to children is being knowingly and silently accepted by a nation that claims to be democratic" (from Benjamin & Crouse, 2002, p. 48).

Social role theory: The idea that stereotypes form when individuals observe the roles that different kinds of people occupy in the world and then reinforce those roles by assuming the people occupying them are well suited to the roles.

Kernel of truth theory: The idea that stereotypes can be at least somewhat based on truth, even though they contain other fictitious elements, may be exaggerated, and/or are out of date.

Stereotype threat occurs when an individual feels at risk for confirming a negative stereotype about his or her group (see Lee & Ottati, 1995; Steele & Aronson, 1995; Wheeler & Petty, 2001). The anxiety we feel about living up to a negative stereotype leads us to be distracted and self-conscious—and this anxiety and distraction can make the stereotype come true. For example, most White people are aware of the stereotype that White people are bad dancers. When they hit the dance floor, they might be so worried about looking foolish that they don't relax—and this makes them dance badly. Stereotype has led to a self-fulfilling prophecy. While being a bad dancer isn't particularly harmful, at other times stereotype threat can lead to long-term, serious damage—and it is another reason why cultural influence makes stereotypes difficult to eliminate.

Steele (1997) pointed out that a girl in a math class dominated by boys and a Black student in an all-White classroom face similar problems. Materially, everything could be the same: textbook, teacher, and even how the teacher treats everyone. But there is "a threat in the air"—stereotype threat—that creates a more distracting classroom experience. The girl might feel pressure because she knows she is not expected to do as well as the boys, and the Black student might feel the same with respect to the White students.

That extra layer of worry means that for a woman to continue in math, for example, she "might have to buck the low expectations of teachers, family, and societal gender roles" (p. 613). The irony here is that the added anxiety of trying *not* to live up to stereotypes about poor performance becomes a distraction. The distraction, in turn, can lead to poor performance—exactly what the threatened individuals are trying to avoid. They have inadvertently fulfilled the stereotypes.

There is a glimmer of hope. Spencer, Steele, and Quinn (1999) found that it's possible to remove stereotype threat, equalizing the math performance of different groups. How did they do it? They simply told participants at the beginning of the study that the test they were about to take had never shown different results from different groups. In other words, if people believe that the test is really about individual ability, they no longer worry about being a token representative of their group—and they can focus on achievement. In this particular study, that was all it took for women to perform just as well as men in advanced mathematics.

The Main Ideas

- Stereotypes are beliefs about members of a group, prejudice is evaluations of the group, and discrimination is unfair behaviors toward someone based on his or her group membership.

- Adaptive categorization is the idea that the instinct to group and label other people and things in the environment arose because it was a benefit to survival. Our instinctive tendency to prefer ingroups over outgroups can be seen even in groups that are arbitrary and meaningless.

- Social identity theory notes that we categorize each other into ingroups and outgroups because it is comforting and validating, but this leads to outcomes such as outgroup homogeneity.

- Social learning theory notes that people will learn stereotypes by observing others and repeating what they see, especially when others are rewarded for their behavior.

- Cultures pass stereotypes from one generation to the next through media messages and self-fulfilling prophecies.

⚡ CRITICAL THINKING CHALLENGE

- Examples of stereotypes, prejudice, and discrimination often focus on either race or sex. What other important categories or group labels and assumptions about groups affect your own life?

- Stereotypes of men often show them sacrificing themselves for women and children. Discuss how this tendency could have developed due to evolutionary instinct or advantage (nature)—or whether it could only have developed due to culture (nurture).

- Identify three specific ways that growing up in a certain culture led you to learn stereotypes about different groups. Looking back on these messages now, can you identify any negative influences they had on your perceptions or behaviors?

- Have you ever experienced stereotype threat, when you were afraid of confirming a negative stereotype about one of your ingroups? Was it distracting? How did you respond?

Stereotype threat: When an individual feels at risk for confirming a negative stereotype about his or her group; this anxiety can be distracting and can ironically cause the stereotype to come true as a type of self-fulfilling prophecy.

HOW DO STEREOTYPES TURN INTO PREJUDICES?

■■■ LO 9.2: Analyze how categorizing leads to prejudice.

Let's review: (1) We categorize. It seems to be a basic instinct. (2) We prefer to live in groups. It's safer and more comfortable. (3) Cultures teach the next generation how to think about one group versus another. But those three characteristics don't make us prejudiced—or do they?

Simply having beliefs—or stereotypes—about certain groups of people might not be so bad. Describing women as nurturing, gay men as fashionable, or scientists as smart is what social psychology calls a **positive stereotype**—beliefs about groups that are in a favorable direction or valence (Siy & Cheryan, 2016). So how could positive stereotypes be bad? They are basically compliments, right?

Even though they are called "positive" stereotypes, social psychologists generally agree that while the *content* of these beliefs is "positive," the *outcome* is still negative. Stereotypes still put unfair expectations on people. If group members don't live up to these roles, they can be judged particularly harshly. Sometimes the "compliments" are just condescending. And frequently, stereotypes will morph into evaluations, judgments, and feelings about groups that are very damaging: Stereotypes become prejudices. Four major theories explain the subtle shift from belief-based stereotypes into emotional prejudices: conflict over limited resources, frustration, the need for high self-esteem, and emotional reactions.

We Compete Over Limited Resources: Realistic Conflict Theory

If you want something that someone else has, can you justify why you really deserve it more than he or she does? That simple question is the root of **realistic conflict theory**, which proposes that prejudice results from the justifications we create to determine that our ingroup should receive an unfair amount of limited resources (Sherif, 1966a; Sherif & Sherif, 1969).

Realistic conflict theory can explain why some Canadian landlords didn't want to rent their apartments to certain types of people in the late 1980s. In this study, the authors (Hilton, Potvin, & Sachdev, 1989) asked landlords in Greater Montreal two simple questions: (1) How willing are you to rent to people of a particular ethnic background (such as those in Figure 9.1)? (2) How might renting to that group affect the value of your rental properties?

The context of this study matters: At the time, apartments in Montreal were scarce, and landlords wanted to maximize the value of what they owned. All of the landlords were French-Quebecers (the ingroup), and only 15% had previously rented to non-French-Quebecers (the outgroups). The landlords wanted to protect the scarce resource they had by keeping its value high, so they justified prejudice against outgroups by perceiving that renting to them would decrease the value of their property. They were potentially making an excuse—a justification—for their prejudice when they told themselves it wasn't personal; it was business.

Realistic conflict theory can become extremely dangerous when played out on a national scale. Colonizers of almost every nation and time period have justified taking land from the natives because the people who already lived there were "savages," practiced the wrong religion, or needed to be "civilized." If people can convince themselves

Positive stereotype: Overgeneralized or oversimplified beliefs about a group that are in a favorable direction or valence; positive stereotypes still lead to negative outcomes.

Realistic conflict theory: The idea that prejudice results from the justifications we create to determine that our ingroup should receive an unfair amount of limited resources.

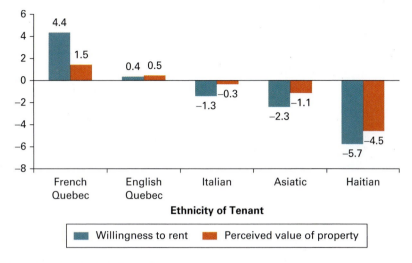

■ FIGURE 9.1 Economic prejudice by landlords in Montreal.

SOURCE: Data from Hilton, Potvin, & Sachdev (1989).

that they "deserve" the resource more by judging the outgroup negatively, then they don't feel as guilty about taking it.

More recent studies have shown the link between desire for a limited resource and prejudice. For example, prejudice toward immigrants increases when people believe that the economy is bad and that jobs may be limited (Filindra & Pearson-Merkowitz, 2013). In another study, prejudice against Asian Americans increased when participants were led to think about economic threats (Butz & Yogeeswaran, 2011). The results of this study went further: Thinking about economic threat increased their prejudice only toward Asian Americans—a group perceived as potentially taking higher-paying and higher-status jobs. Thinking about economic threats did not increase prejudice toward African Americans (who are associated with a different kind of threat). Prejudice seems to be targeted toward groups perceived as threats to getting or keeping the resources we decide we want. Conflict over those resources inspires prejudice as a way to justify simply taking what we decide we "deserve."

Frustration Leads to Aggression: Scapegoat Theory

Most of us don't like to admit it when we make mistakes. It's much easier to blame other people for our problems. When this tendency reaches beyond the individual and surfaces in groups, it's called **scapegoat theory**, or the idea that prejudice is the result of one group blaming another innocent group for its problems (Allport, 1954; Joly, 2016). The most famous example is one we've already discussed in depth: the Nazi party blaming Jews, gypsies, Communists, homosexuals, and many other groups for their nation's poor economy after World War I. Hitler characterized these groups as greedy, dirty, and diseased and managed to convince millions of people that all their problems would go away if these groups were eliminated.

One of the explanations for why humans have the tendency to blame others for our problems is called **frustration-aggression theory** (Dollard, Miller, Doob, Mowrer, & Sears, 1939; Hogg, 2016). This theory proposes that when things aren't going our way, due to poor economic conditions, important failures, or humiliating losses, we become

Scapegoat theory: The idea that prejudice is the result of one group blaming another innocent group for its problems (see *frustration-aggression theory*).

Frustration-aggression theory: The idea that individuals' frustration builds a physical and psychological tension that they feel must be let out, frequently in the form of aggression toward "weaker" targets.

One reason prejudice exists is because we like to blame other people for our problems, a tendency called scapegoating.

frustrated. That frustration builds a physical and psychological tension that we feel must be let out, and frequently the outlet is aggression. When we do aggress, we'll choose targets who are weaker than us (so they can't put up much of a fight) and who can somehow be tied to our problem (so we can justify the prejudice and aggression). We displace the blame and aggress toward our imagined enemy, and we develop prejudice as a way to justify that action.

Unfortunately, anti-Semitism due to frustration doesn't seem to be going away. As recently as 2010, a study showed that citizens of Poland and Ukraine displayed higher discrimination against Jewish people under conditions of economic deprivation (Bilewicz & Krzeminski, 2010). Kressel (2012) has documented how socially and economically frustrated people are encouraged in their anti-Semitism. Newspapers publish poems praising Hitler, children are encouraged to use Jews as scapegoats, and anti-Jewish advocates use the same language and justifications as the Nazis.

Economic frustration was also transformed into aggression after the American Civil War. Many Whites were financially devastated when slaves were freed. Between 1882 and 1930, patterns of violence against African Americans showed that anti-Black prejudice increased when the economy was troubled. For example, during that time period, the price of cotton and the number of lynchings of Black men by White men was *negatively correlated* between –0.6 and –0.7 (quite a high correlation!); as the price of cotton went down, the number of lynchings went up (Hovland & Sears, 1940). As the price of cotton declined and Whites became frustrated over their financial situation, they blamed the former slaves and aggressed against them with shameful murders.

Maintaining Positive Self-Esteem: Applying Social Identity Theory

Maintaining positive self-esteem is important to most of us. And our self-esteem is tied to the groups that we belong to (as predicted by social identity theory; see Chapter 3). So, prejudice against particular groups provides a mental and emotional shortcut that allows us to maintain a positive view of our self and our ingroups.

For example, sports fans (and people who have to live with crazy sports fans) will remember the idea of Basking In Reflected Glory (or BIRGing) discussed in Chapter 3. People will make their group membership salient, or obvious, when the group (their favorite team) is publicly succeeding or is viewed positively. If your college or university hits the news for some fabulous achievement, you might be more likely to wear your school sweatshirt when you go out for drinks. Being part of a successful group makes us feel successful, too—even if we had nothing to do with that success. BIRGing is evidence in support of social identity theory, because we use our group membership to boost our public image and private self-esteem when it benefits us.

When Frank Roque bragged that he was going to kill some "towel-heads," he probably was imagining himself as a hero-to-be. We can't know that for sure, of course, but two findings support the idea that the battle for self-esteem influences our prejudices. First, adolescent bullies tend to have high self-esteem (Johnson & Lewis, 1999; Simon, Nail, Swindle, Bihm, & Joshi, 2017; Tsaousis, 2016). Perhaps these bullies perceive that their victims "deserve what they get" (prejudiced evaluations). Second, when people with high self-esteem sense a threat to their self-concept, they can protect their positive self-image by putting others down (Crocker & Luhtanen, 1990; Crocker & Major, 2003; Crocker, Thompson, McGraw, & Ingerman, 1987; Fein & Spencer, 1997; Spencer, Fein, Wolfe, Fong, & Dunn, 1998). Prejudice may serve at least some people as an immature way to maintain self-esteem; if I call you names, I feel better.

We React With Emotions: The Stereotype Content Model

While stereotypes are cognitive beliefs, prejudice is emotion based. Our evaluations and judgments of outgroups are not logical; they are based on irrational reactions toward others. The Jewish stereotype is one of shrewd wealth—and the emotions that trigger anti-Jewish prejudice are envy and a fear of losing resources. The stereotype of African Americans is one of criminals and sexual predators—and the emotions that trigger anti-Black prejudice are often fears of being physically harmed. In contrast, our ingroups usually trigger pleasant emotions such as comfort and happiness. Different groups, then, trigger different emotional profiles (Cottrell & Neuberg, 2005).

Fiske, Cuddy, Glick, and Xu (2002) wondered about how we construct our emotional profiles—and the kinds of prejudices that they lead to. Their **stereotype content model** proposed two categories of judgment: warmth and competence. What is so special about warmth and competence? Groups that do not compete with us pose no threat, so it's easy to like them—to perceive them as warm. Groups that are high in status have resources, so it's easy to admire them—to perceive them as competent. Table 9.2 names and describes the four possible combinations, identifies the corresponding emotional responses, and suggests representative groups in current U.S. culture. Note that Table 9.2 is from the perspective of the group currently in power.

Stereotype content model: The idea that two categories of judgment, warmth and competence, interact to form four different types of prejudice: paternalistic prejudice (high warmth, low competence), admiration prejudice (high warmth, high competence), contemptuous prejudice (low warmth, low competence), and envious prejudice (low warmth, high competence).

■ TABLE 9.2 The Stereotype Content Model

	Low in Competence	High in Competence
High in warmth	*Paternalistic prejudice* toward people who are low in status and do not compete with the ingroup. Our emotional responses include pity and sympathy. Examples elderly people, people with disabilities, and housewives.	*Admiration prejudice* for people who have high status and do not compete with the ingroup. Our emotional responses include pride and admiration. Examples: Our ingroups or allies.
Low in warmth	*Contemptuous prejudice* toward people with low status who compete with the ingroup. Our emotional responses include contempt, disgust, anger, and resentment. Examples: Welfare recipients and very poor people.	*Envious prejudice* toward people with high status who compete with the ingroup. Our emotional responses include envy and jealousy. Examples: Asians, Jews, rich people, and feminists.

SOURCE: Fiske et al. (2002).

The Main Ideas

- Realistic conflict theory proposes that prejudice results from the justification we create to determine that our ingroup deserves limited resources.

- Scapegoat theory is the idea that prejudice is the result of one group blaming another innocent group for its problems. Frustration-aggression theory notes that scapegoating is a likely result when people feel the frustration of poor circumstances and take that frustration out by aggressing against an innocent victim.

- Social identity theory notes that prejudice can also result from the desire to maintain self-esteem; one way to keep esteem high is by perceiving that our ingroups are better than our outgroups.

- The stereotype content model is the notion that different forms of prejudice develop when we perceive groups to be high or low in warmth and competence.

⚡ CRITICAL THINKING CHALLENGE

- Think of three examples of a "positive" stereotype and explain why these beliefs, while seemingly complimentary, lead to negative effects for members of the relevant groups.

- Identify two historical events that may have been caused, at least in part, by realistic conflict over limited resources (such as land, jobs, oil, gold, etc.) and how this conflict led to prejudice between the parties involved.

- List five groups that were not included in Table 9.2 describing the stereotype content model. Then, try to identify which of the four categories each group would fall into, and explain why.

IS PREJUDICE A PERSONALITY PROBLEM?

LO 9.3: Describe how prejudice emerges from the interaction between personality and situation.

Do you remember Kurt Lewin's famous equation to predict behavior? He said that behavior is a function of both the individual and the social situation. The theories described in the previous section explain why stereotypes and prejudice exist based on historical or environmental influences. But what about the other predictor in Lewin's equation? Can prejudice be considered a personality trait, just like competitiveness, extraversion, or any other individual characteristic?

Social psychology's **interactionist perspective** focuses on the joint effects of personality and situation. Many researchers have suggested personality traits that either directly or indirectly relate to an individual's personal tendency to be more or less prejudiced toward outgroups. Theoretically, someone with a prejudiced personality will have a general tendency to dislike any outgroups and members of those outgroups, across the board. Three constructs that may be tied to overall prejudice are authoritarianism, social dominance orientation, and religiosity.

Interactionist perspective: The idea that personality and situation jointly affect an individual's social behavior.

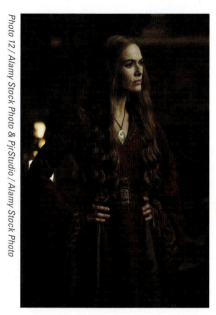

Some people may have "prejudiced personalities"; they tend to dislike any outgroup. Cersei Lannister from *Game of Thrones* finds anyone except her older brother and children to be a threat. Cartman from *South Park* explicitly believes anyone not like himself is not as good. Both individuals routinely denigrate and oppress anyone who is unlike themselves.

The Authoritarian Personality

"Kiss up" and "kick down" is the shorthand description of the authoritarian personality. It was the first and most influential attempt after World War II to define and measure a prejudiced personality that would eagerly join the Nazi party and believe its propaganda. Adorno, Frenkel-Brunswik, Levinson, and Sanford (1950) suggested that the **authoritarian personality** generalizes prejudices across many different groups using a structure of authority and order as a foundation. The authoritarian personality includes three major behavioral tendencies: (1) submitting to authority (when that authority is perceived as legitimate), (2) disciplining those who defy authority, and (3) conforming to conventional beliefs.

The most popular scale now to measure authoritarian personality was first developed by Altemeyer in 1981 and updated in 1994; you can see several of the items in the "Applying Social Psychology to Your Life" feature. Note that the scale has received criticism for two reasons. First, some of the items include more than one idea. For example, one item is, "Homosexuals and feminists should be praised for being brave enough to defy traditional family values" (this item is *reverse-scored*). When a scale item includes more than one basic idea, people have difficulty knowing how to respond if they agree with one of the ideas but not the other. Such an item is called a **double-barreled item.**

A second criticism of the scale is that it is the "Right-Wing Authoritarianism Scale." In short, it implies that people with an authoritarian personality are only found on the "right-wing" side of the political spectrum (Altemeyer, 1990; Ray, 1990). Some people have argued that this assumes that conservative people are prejudiced but that left-wing or liberal people are not—an implication that is justifiably offensive to conservatives.

That said, high scores on this scale have been found to be *correlated* with a wide variety of group prejudices, just as the concept of a "prejudiced personality" would predict. People with high scores tend to have prejudice against African Americans (Rowatt & Franklin, 2004), feminists (Duncan, Peterson, & Winter, 1997), gay people (Cramer, Miller, Amacker, & Burks, 2013; Crawford, Brandt, Inbar, & Mallinas, 2016), overweight people (Crandall, 1994), immigrants (Duckitt & Sibley, 2010),

Authoritarian personality: A personality characterized by three major behavioral tendencies: submission to authority, discipline toward those who defy authority, and the tendency to conform to conventional beliefs.

Double-barreled item: A scale item that includes more than one basic idea, making it difficult for individuals to know how to respond if they agree with one of the ideas but not the other.

and more. High scores are also correlated with support for racial profiling by police (Saunders, Kelly, Cohen, & Guarino, 2016) and with "restrictions on civil liberties and violations of human rights as part of the War on Terror" (Swami et al., 2012, p. 444).

Social Dominance Orientation

Like the authoritarian personality, a **social dominance orientation** or SDO (Pratto, Sidanius, Stallworth, & Malle, 1994), refers to a general tendency to exhibit outgroup prejudice. SDO is a preference for social hierarchies and a clear understanding of which groups do and don't possess power. Of course, most people high in SDO want their own ingroups to hold the most social power; hierarchies aren't as much fun when you're at the bottom of the pile. Preference for strict hierarchies also means that people high in SDO are against social equality or giving people at the bottom "extra" resources they might need to move up the social ladder. In short, high-SDO people send the message that groups on the bottom should "stay in their place."

Again, you can see items from the SDO scale in the "Applying Social Psychology to Your Life" feature. Research shows that people high in SDO are more likely to make a variety of unethical decisions such as polluting the environment, exploiting workers in a less developed country, or marketing a profitable but harmful drug (Son Hing, Bobocel, Zanna, & McBride, 2007). Other studies show that SDO scores are *positively correlated* with a variety of social prejudices (although a *true experiment* is needed to verify any causal relationship; Kteily, Sidanius, & Levin, 2011). Interestingly, one study found that people high in SDO resent it when African Americans claim to be victims of discrimination, but those same people support Whites who claim discrimination (Unzeuta, Everly, & Gutierrez, 2014). This particular pattern shows a clear preference for helping groups that are already privileged.

Social dominance orientation: Individuals with a tendency to exhibit outgroup prejudice due to a desire for social hierarchy and power within a situation.

Religiosity: The degree to which one is religious and why.

Religiosity

Prejudice against certain religions is an important part of history. Anti-Semitism has existed for 5,000 years, including everything from enslavement of Jewish people in ancient Egypt to the use of phrases like, "I Jewed him down" when referring to shrewd bargaining for a good price. Prejudice against Catholics was a main tenet of the early Ku Klux Klan. Today in the United States, prejudice against Muslims is an important concern. But what about the flip side of this coin: Does being religious lead to perpetrating prejudice as well?

While religion isn't a personality trait in the same way that authoritarianism or SDO might be, it's still an interesting individual difference to consider. Most psychological research on this question hasn't focused much on whether particular types of religion are prejudiced. Instead, it has studied **religiosity**, or the degree to which one is religious and why. It seems ironic to ask if being more religious is *positively correlated* with being more prejudiced, considering that most major religions teach tolerance and forgiveness—but research indicates that this association is a complicated one.

Do you think of religion as associated with love and tolerance—or with judgment and self-righteousness?

In an early review of 38 studies on the topic, Batson, Schoenrade, and Ventis (1993) showed that higher religious involvement was correlated with several forms of prejudice. In fact, these authors concluded that "religion is not associated with increased love and acceptance but with increased intolerance, prejudice, and bigotry" (p. 302). If you are religious, though, you might be reading this and feeling a bit offended. Isn't it prejudiced to say that religious people are prejudiced? The answer seems to be that it depends on *why* people are religious.

People with **intrinsic religiosity** have a sincere belief in their faith's teachings and attempt to apply those principles to everyday behaviors. If their religion does indeed teach tolerance, these people should have low levels of general prejudice, and that seems to be the case (Batson et al., 1993). An alternative motivation is **extrinsic religiosity**, which is being religious because of social or practical rewards. Someone might be religious because it offers community acceptance, provides business networking opportunities, or looks good in a political election, for example. Studies show that being higher in extrinsic religiosity is *correlated* with various forms of prejudice, such as racism (Herek, 1987) and homophobia (Lough, 2006). After finding that extrinsic religiosity was associated with prejudice and dogmatic thinking but not associated with helping others, Donahue (1985) noted that extrinsic religiosity is "the sort of religion that gives religion a bad name" (p. 416).

Two additional forms of religiosity have been suggested by social psychologists (sample items to measure all four forms of religiosity can again be found in the "Applying Social Psychology to Your Life" feature). **Fundamentalism** is a form of religiosity in which people believe their chosen faith is the only true faith, that religious texts should be taken literally, and that forces of evil are active and present all around us. Fundamentalism can be found in most, if not all, major religions (Armstrong, 2000), and it is *positively correlated* with several types of prejudice (Spilka, Hood, Hunsberger, & Gorsuch, 2003).

On perhaps the opposite side of the spectrum is a form of religiosity called **religion as quest**, in which people view religion from a philosophical and spiritual stance. Here, asking questions is more important than finding answers; skepticism and doubt are welcomed. Quest-oriented people tend to have consistently low levels of prejudice (Batson, Coke, Jasnoski, & Hanson, 1978; Hunsberger, 1995; McFarland, 1989).

Intrinsic religiosity: When individuals hold sincere belief in their faith's teachings and attempt to apply those principles to everyday behaviors.

Extrinsic religiosity: When an individual is religious because of social or practical rewards.

Fundamentalism: A form of religiosity in which people believe their chosen faith is the only true faith, that religious texts should be taken literally, and that that forces of evil are active and present all around them.

Religion as quest: A form of religiosity in which people view religion from a philosophical and spiritual stance, involving skepticism, doubt, and exploration.

Mark Reinstein / Corbis News / Getty Images

The Westboro Baptist Church is well known for its racist and homophobic demonstrations. Many other Christians do not want to be associated with members of this group due to their prejudice.

MEASURING "PREJUDICED" PERSONALITY TRAITS

Applying Social Psychology to Your Life

Below you'll see several statements that are example items from scales that some people believe measure aspects of a "prejudiced personality." After you take the scale, see the scoring instructions to know which items measure which traits. Rate how much you agree or disagree with each statement using this scale:

1	2	3	4	5	6	7
Disagree strongly			Neutral			Agree strongly

____ 1. Our country desperately needs a mighty leader who will do what has to be done to destroy the radical new ways and sinfulness that are ruining us.

____ 2. The only way our country can get through the crisis ahead is to get back to our traditional values, put some tough leaders in power, and silence the troublemakers spreading bad ideas.

____ 3. Our country will be destroyed someday if we do not end the perversions eating away at our moral fiber and moral beliefs.

____ 4. What our country needs is more discipline, with everyone following our leaders in unity.

____ 5. God's laws about abortion, pornography, and marriage must be strictly followed before it is too late, and those who break them must be strongly punished.

____ 6. Some groups of people are simply inferior to other groups.

____ 7. In getting what you want, it is sometimes necessary to use force against other groups.

____ 8. It's OK if some groups have more of a chance in life than others.

____ 9. It's probably a good thing that certain groups are at the top and other groups are at the bottom.

____ 10. Inferior groups should stay in their place.

____ 11. It is important to me to spend periods of time in private religious thoughts and meditation.

____ 12. I try hard to carry my religion over into all my other dealings in life.

____ 13. Religion is especially important to me because it answers questions about the meaning of life.

____ 14. The church is most important as a place to formulate good social relationships.

____ 15. I pray chiefly because I have been taught to pray.

____ 16. Occasionally, I find it necessary to compromise my religious beliefs in order to protect my social and economic well-being.

____ 17. God has given mankind a complete, unfailing guide to happiness and salvation, which must be totally followed.

____ 18. The long-established traditions in religion show the best way to honor and serve God and should never be compromised.

____ 19. Whenever science and sacred scripture conflict, science must be wrong.

____ 20. As I grow and change, I expect my religion to grow and change.

____ 21. It might be said that I value my religious doubts and uncertainties.

____ 22. Questions are far more central to my religious experience than are answers.

Instructions: These items are just examples from the original, longer scales. Note that the original scales had different answering scales; these have been modified for simplicity to all use the same scale. For each set of items below, add up your responses (higher scores indicate stronger beliefs in favor of that concept).

Authoritarianism: Add Items 1 to 5

Social dominance orientation: Add Items 6 to 10

Intrinsic religiosity: Add Items 11, 12, and 13

Extrinsic religiosity: Add Items 14, 15, and 16

Fundamentalism: Add Items 17, 18, and 19

Religion as quest: Add Items 20, 21, and 22

The Main Ideas

- The interactionist perspective studies the joint effects of personality and situations on human social behavior.

- People high in authoritarianism generalize their prejudices across many different groups using a structure of authority and order.

- People high in social dominance orientation prefer for society to be structured in hierarchies, with some groups on top in terms of power. They do not believe in equal opportunity for all.

- Religiosity measures the degree to which a person is religious and the person's motivation for participation in religion. There are four types of religiosity: intrinsic, extrinsic, fundamentalist, and religion as quest. Extrinsic and fundamentalist are more associated with a variety of prejudices, compared with intrinsic and quest.

⚡ CRITICAL THINKING CHALLENGE

- Are there people in your life who seem to have high or low amounts of prejudice toward outgroups in general, supporting the idea of a "prejudiced personality"? If not, can you think of other television/film characters or even celebrities who appear to have high or low levels of a prejudiced personality?

- What do you think causes someone to have high or low levels of a prejudiced personality? Is it something biological, something about the person's early childhood experiences, or some other factor or factors?

- What other personality traits do you think are related to either consistently high or consistently low levels of prejudice toward outgroups?

HAS PREJUDICE DECREASED OVER TIME?

▮ LO 9.4: Analyze how forms of prejudice and discrimination have changed over time.

Sudden social change can leave people worried and confused, especially if they think the change is harmful. To some people, the legal acceptance of same-sex marriage came relatively quickly—but to others, very slowly. But same-sex marriage is now legal throughout the United States and in more than 20 countries around the world. The acceptance of women in the workforce shows a similar pattern. In 2012, 75% of White women who had just graduated from high school enrolled in college, compared with 62% of White men with diplomas (Lopez & Gonzalez-Barrera, 2014). Between 2012 and 2016, seven small but prestigious liberal arts colleges chose African American presidents (Education Advisory Board, 2016). Are these statistics evidence that prejudice has decreased and that discrimination is a thing of the past? Most social psychologists would feel obliged by the data to say no. Prejudice and discrimination still exist; they have simply become more subtle and surreptitious, as you'll see in the following sections.

Bettmann / Bettmann / Getty Images

Explicit prejudice like that displayed on this sign is much less likely to be seen today. Does that mean prejudice has decreased—or simply that it has changed to more subtle forms?

Old-Fashioned Prejudice

Being explicitly or overtly prejudiced toward certain groups is less socially acceptable today than it was in the past. Many groups are legally protected, and most people would react strongly to public racism, sexism, or prejudice toward people with disabilities. These forms of obvious, overt prejudice, which are considered inappropriate by most social standards today, are sometimes called **old-fashioned prejudice**. Forcing people of a specified race to drink only from a certain water fountain, for example, would be unthinkable in modern public buildings. In the United States, the civil rights movement of the 1960s made many of these old-fashioned beliefs salient, and it was clear that they would not be considered acceptable or "politically correct" anymore.

However, some prejudices are more accepted than others. For example, many media representations of overweight people are negative or contemptuous. Some states have passed laws that business owners can refuse to provide services to potential customers whose practices do not align with the owners' religious beliefs. A baker, for example, could refuse to make a wedding cake for a gay couple in such a state. Interestingly, one explanation of why particular forms of prejudice are more or less socially acceptable posits that prejudice toward groups that people choose to join (such as political parties) is more acceptable than prejudice toward groups that people do not belong to by choice (such as people with disabilities; Crandall & Eshleman, 2003). Thus, people who believe that being overweight or gay is a choice—and not due to biological factors—feel more justified in their prejudiced attitudes.

Some people argue that because old-fashioned prejudice appears to have decreased, this implies that prejudice in general is a thing of the past. For example, when the "Black Lives Matter" campaign become popular in 2015 and 2016, many argued that the United States offers equal opportunity to people of all races, so the campaign was actually "reverse racism." Similarly, after Donald Trump was elected president, hundreds of thousands of women marched in demonstrations the day after the inauguration in a protest of what they perceived to be sexist policies endorsed by Trump; others argued that sexism is no longer a problem and that the women had nothing to complain about. Within social psychology, the study of prejudice is still going strong—and most social psychologists would argue that while old-fashioned prejudice may have decreased, other more subtle forms have simply taken its place.

Modern-Symbolic Prejudice

One form of prejudice thought to exist today is called **modern-symbolic prejudice** (McConahay, 1983, 1986). People with this form of prejudice like to think of themselves as valuing equality and respect for all people, but they simultaneously oppose social change that would allow equality to occur. This ambivalence results in a resentment of minority groups and other historically oppressed groups when they ask for attention or additional resources. Sears and Henry (2005) summarized the beliefs within modern-symbolic prejudice as follows:

- Most forms of prejudice and discrimination no longer exist or are rare.
- Any remaining group differences in socioeconomic outcomes or class are the result of some groups' lack of motivation to work hard.
- Because those groups are unwilling to work toward goals, their continuing anger or claims of discrimination are not justified.

Old-fashioned prejudice: Obvious, overt prejudice that is considered inappropriate by most social standards today, such as forcing people of a specified race to drink only from a certain water fountain.

Modern-symbolic prejudice: A form of prejudice where individuals think of themselves as valuing equality and respect for all people while they simultaneously oppose social change that would allow equality to occur.

- Rather than committing to more effort, those groups seek special favors.
- Relative to the historical majority or group that used to be in power (such as White men), minorities have been getting more than they deserve due to these special favors.

In short, this form of prejudice blames groups without power for being powerless. They are in that situation due to their own lack of effort. Because people high in modern-symbolic beliefs perceive that prejudice is no longer a problem, they resent anything that appears to "favor" minorities, such as affirmative action policies and scholarships for people of color. In their view, such policies are no longer necessary and represent "reverse" discrimination.

An example of modern-symbolic prejudice is the "men's rights movement," which includes several official and nonofficial groups of men who believe that feminism has caused a shift such that women now have more power than men. For example, they say that child custody decisions generally favor mothers, that women are not required to register for the military draft, and that women are less likely to be convicted of crimes. While some of these statistics may be true, others argue that there are even more examples of continued oppression of women and that men's rights movements are simply a reaction against loss of power and privilege.

Benevolent + Hostile = Ambivalent Prejudice

Benevolent prejudice is the perception that members of certain groups have positive qualities that should be praised and valued. So far, this doesn't sound so bad, right? One problem with benevolent prejudice, though, is that when group members fails to live up to these unfair standards, they will be judged particularly harshly. Another problem is that the stereotype of what people in that group "should" be still restricts opportunities for the group. Finally, some of the values inherent in benevolent prejudice may be condescending and paternalistic toward the relevant outgroup.

The focus of research on benevolent prejudice has been on benevolent sexism, first suggested by Glick and Fiske (1996, 2001). Consider the types of "positive" stereotypes many people have of women: They are gentle, pretty, kind, polite, and pure. People with high levels of benevolent sexism believe that most women possess these qualities—and that women *should* possess these qualities. Women who fit this model are then especially liked and praised.

The backlash comes when some women do not fit this stereotype—and they are then judged particularly harshly, an attitude called **hostile sexism**. In one study,

Benevolent prejudice: The perception that members of certain groups have positive qualities that should be praised and valued; benevolent prejudice can be condescending and paternalistic toward the outgroup, which results in unfair standards, harsh judgment, and restricted opportunities.

Hostile sexism: When an individual exhibits overtly aggressive behavior toward or dispenses harsh judgment toward women who do not fit prescribed gender stereotypes.

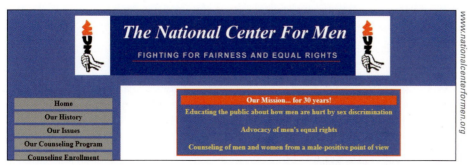

www.nationalcenterformen.org

This screenshot of the homepage for the National Center for Men shows an example of one group in the "men's rights" movement.

While the "Madonna/whore complex" refers to the New Testament Madonna (the Virgin Mary), enduring pop star Madonna has played on this concept to help her achieve fame.

Ask the Experts: Susan Fiske on Ambivalent Sexism Theory

©SAGE Publications

- - - - - - - - - - - - - - - - -

Ambivalent sexism: A combination of hostile and benevolent sexism that occurs when an individual views "good" women from a benevolent perspective but is hostile to women who fail to meet these standards.

- - - - - - - - - - - - - - - - -

employers with high levels of hostile sexism gave women poor evaluations if those women didn't fit sexist expectations at work; those same employers did not respond well to female applicants for jobs traditionally held by men (Masser & Abrams, 2004). Men who are high in hostile sexism are more accepting of both sexual harassment (Begany & Milburn, 2002; Russell & Trigg, 2004) and domestic violence toward women (Glick, Sakalli-Ugurlu, Ferreira, & de Souza, 2002), and they are more likely to blame rape victims for what happened (Viki & Abrams, 2002).

The idea that women are either virtuous angels or sinful devils has been called the "virgin/whore false dichotomy" or the "Madonna/whore complex" (in which "Madonna" refers to the Christian Virgin Mary). When people view "good" women from a benevolent perspective but are hostile to women who fail to meet these standards, they are showing **ambivalent sexism**. In the 2016 U.S. presidential election, scores on a measure of ambivalent sexism were found to be significantly strong predictors of whether people intended to vote for Hillary Clinton (Blair, 2016).

The Main Ideas

- Old-fashioned prejudice is obvious, overt prejudice that would generally be considered inappropriate by today's standards. While this form of prejudice has decreased, many social psychologists believe it has been replaced by other forms of prejudice.

- Modern-symbolic prejudice is a form that denies that inequality still exists. This belief translates into resentment when minority groups ask for attention or resources. Benefits given to these groups are viewed as "reverse" prejudice.

- Ambivalent prejudice is made up of two aspects. The first is benevolent prejudice, which is the belief that members of some groups possess positive qualities that should be protected. Hostile prejudice occurs when members of those stereotyped groups do not fulfill expectations and are thus judged particularly harshly.

⚡ CRITICAL THINKING CHALLENGE

- Modern-symbolic and ambivalent prejudice are only two forms of current, more subtle prejudice that social psychologists have suggested are still present. Can you think of other examples of thoughts, feelings, or behaviors that you would consider "modern" forms of stereotypes, prejudice, or discrimination?

- Imagine that you have a White friend who tells you she's frustrated that there are no college scholarships specifically reserved for White people. Can you explain her views using one or more of the concepts covered in this section?

- This section specifically covered benevolent sexism, but there are other forms of benevolent prejudice, such as benevolent racism, heterosexism, and so on. List three examples of "benevolent" stereotypes or prejudiced statements you've seen or heard.

HOW CAN WE REDUCE STEREOTYPING, PREJUDICE, AND DISCRIMINATION?

█████ **LO 9.5:** Apply methods of prejudice reduction to real-world settings.

So far, this chapter may have been a bit depressing. Stereotypes are a basic human instinct that we may not be able to avoid. Prejudice hasn't gone away; it's just become sneakier. Discrimination can be seen all around us. Fortunately, social psychologists have devoted decades of study toward finding solutions to these problems. How might we reduce stereotypes, prejudice, and discrimination?

"It required years of labor and billions of dollars to gain the secret of the atom. It will take a still greater investment to gain the secrets of man's irrational nature. "

—*Gordon Allport (1954),* The Nature of Prejudice

An Early Hope: The Contact Hypothesis and Robbers Cave

When Allport (1954) formalized the study of prejudice in his classic book *The Nature of Prejudice,* he summarized the problem with the following conversation:

"See that man over there?"

"Yes."

"Well, I hate him."

"But you don't know him."

"That's why I hate him."

To Allport, that brief exchange also pointed toward a potential solution: If you hate people because you don't know them, then the solution is to get to know them. Allport's (1954, p. 281) **contact hypothesis** proposes that prejudice may be reduced by increasing contact—or exposure—to outgroups. Recall from earlier in this chapter that one of the reasons why stereotypes form is because we're more comfortable interacting with similar others.

Amir (1976) summarized the spirit of the contact hypothesis:

Interaction between people changes their beliefs and feelings toward each other. . . . Thus, if only one had the opportunity to communicate with others and appreciate their way of life, understanding and reduction of prejudice would follow. (p. 245)

Could stereotypes and prejudice be reduced if we made ourselves get out of our comfort zones by spending time with others who are different from us? One of the early tests of the contact hypothesis became one of the most famous studies ever done on prejudice, and it has an intriguing name: the Robbers Cave Study. Muzafer Sherif and his team (Sherif, 1956) wanted to study how prejudice forms between two newly created groups and whether the contact hypothesis can help to erase this prejudice. To do this, they carefully selected several 11-year-old boys and invited them to a 3-week summer camp held in Robbers Cave State Park in Oklahoma.

Sherif wanted to experimentally manipulate the prejudices formed, so he made sure that the boys coming to the camp were all as identical to each other as possible. His goal was to eliminate *confounding variables* such as preexisting ingroup prejudices based on factors such as religion, social class, or race. The boys had no idea they were about

Social Psychology in Action:
Blue Eyes, Brown Eyes

©SAGE Publications

Contact hypothesis: The idea that increasing contact or exposure may reduce prejudice if the groups' members perceive themselves to be of equal status, group members interact on an individual level, authority figures appear to be supportive, and the groups have common goals.

Boys at Sherif's famous Robbers Cave study, playing baseball.

to become participants in a study; they thought they were simply going to a regular summer camp for boys. They did not know each other, and they were split into two equivalent groups not by *random assignment* but by *matched pairs,* ensuring that each group had parallel characteristics.

The camp counselors were *participant observers* trained not to influence the boys' behavior (unless they were in danger). Safely tucked away in separate campsites, each group of boys initially believed that they were the only group camping at Robbers Cave. No one told the boys that they should name their groups, but one group became the Rattlers and the other became the Eagles. By the end of the first week, the boys were proud of who *they* had become, but their cabins were far enough apart that the groups still did not know that the other group even existed.

During the second week of camp, the counselors arranged for the two groups to discover one another at the baseball field. The members of each group clustered close together and eyed the other group with apparent suspicion. The two groups soon started competing over everything: baseball, tug-of-war, tent pitching, and other typical camp activities—all with minimal adult supervision. The competitions led to accusations of cheating. During a tug-of-war, one group sat down and dug in their heels so that they could neither lose nor win. Prejudiced feelings oozed out of such situations: The two groups started calling each other bad names. One made a flag that put down the other group. A stolen pair of pants was dragged through the dirt, cabins were raided, and accusations of bad character ("stinkers" and "sneaks") filled the air.

By the end of their second week, these two groups of boys—who had every demographic reason to become friends—were at war with one another. They marked their territories, sent spies to gather information about enemy movements, and conducted more cabin raids. The camp counselors only intervened when the boys prepared for a major battle by building stockpiles of rocks and escalating their weaponry: swinging socks filled with rocks. They were one incident away from serious, life-threatening violence. Could the contact hypothesis now make this prejudice go away?

Sherif first attempted to bring the boys together during meals. It didn't work; the two groups battled with each other to be first in line, and the losing team tried to save face by yelling "Ladies first!" at the winners. When an Eagle bumped into a Rattler, the Rattler would make a display of brushing "the dirt" off his clothes (p. 418). Similar conflicts continued in other settings, such as trying to watch a movie together. Sherif was not surprised; he hadn't really expected this kind of contact to help. In fact, it seemed to have only made the prejudice stronger. What could he try next?

Sherif's Solution: Superordinate Goals

Not even Allport would have been surprised by Sherif's findings at that point in the Robbers Cave Study. Allport recognized that not all forms of contact would be positive; he specified that interaction between two hostile groups would, in fact, only lead to decreased prejudice if four criteria were met:

- The groups had to have equal status (one group couldn't have more power than the other).
- Group members had to be able to get to know each other on an individual level (not just as anonymous members of the "other" group).
- Any authority figures in the situation had to support the groups' positive change.
- The groups had to work together, cooperatively, on a common goal.

Sherif's next step in the Robbers Cave Study was to make sure all of these criteria were met, and he focused in particular on the final criterion. Prejudice had spontaneously occurred in a context of *competition* between the two groups. Could cooperation be the answer to that same prejudice going away? Sherif and the camp counselors brought the boys back from the brink of violence by creating situations that promoted individual contact and cooperative tasks that made it difficult for stereotypes and prejudice to survive. Sherif called these tasks **superordinate goals**—objectives that neither group could achieve without the other's cooperation. To move forward, "us versus them" had to become "we."

For example, the camp counselors went to the large holding tank that supplied water to the camp and turned it off. Then they sent teams of boys to survey different parts of the line for a leak. Only a few of the Eagles voluntarily worked with a Rattler. But when they discovered that the valve had been turned off at the source, they turned it back on and cheered their victory—as a group. When a vehicle supposedly got stuck in the mud, first one group and then the other tried to push it out. But the driver discreetly kept his foot on the brake until both groups of boys got out and pushed together. When the boys wanted to rent a movie, they could only afford it by pooling their money together.

By the end of the third week, they were all friends and appeared to have enjoyed a wonderful 3 weeks of summer camp. Cooperation and superordinate goals had saved the day and made the boys appreciate each other. For a fictional story that highlights some of the same features in this famous research study, see the "Social Psychology in Popular Culture" feature that discusses the movie *Remember the Titans*.

Applying Superordinate Goals: Jigsaw Classrooms

Allport's criteria for successful intergroup contact and Sherif's demonstration of their power have been inspirational in a variety of contexts. For example, if we could reduce prejudice in children, perhaps the next generation could solve some of our enduring intergroup problems. This is exactly what was attempted when Aronson and his colleagues invented an elementary school technique called the **jigsaw classroom.**

In a jigsaw classroom, the students are first put into small "expert groups." These groups all learn about some aspect of the day's lesson. If the lesson is about Eleanor Roosevelt, for example, one expert group learns about her early life, one group learns about her activism in the civil rights movement, and so on. Then, the expert groups are broken up and new groups are formed—the "jigsaw" groups. Each of these groups has

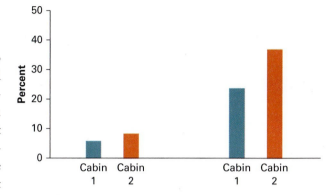

■ FIGURE 9.2 During conflict between the two groups in the Robbers Cave experiment, there were few friendships between cabins (left). After cooperation toward common goals had restored good feelings, the percentage of boys reporting friendships across cabins rose significantly (right).

SOURCE: Sherif (1956).

Superordinate goals: Objectives that cannot be achieved without the cooperation of an outgroup; superordinate goals often result in overcoming personal differences for a shared reward and therefore can reduce prejudice.

Jigsaw classroom: A technique used by teachers where students are first divided into "expert groups" that learn a certain set of information and then are mixed such that the second set of teams, the "jigsaw groups," each include one member from the expert groups. Jigsaw requires that the members rely on each other to learn the material.

PREJUDICE REDUCTION IN *REMEMBER THE TITANS*

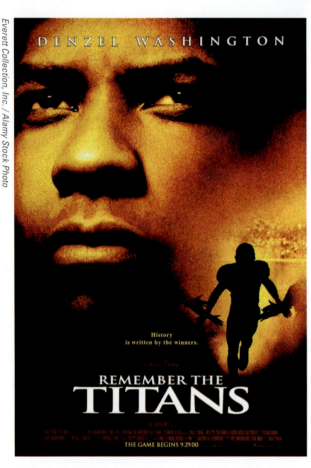

Everett Collection, Inc. / Alamy Stock Photo

The popular movie *Remember the Titans* (Bruckheimer, Oman, & Yakin, 2000) is based on a true story of two high school football teams—one White and one Black—who are forced to combine after desegregation in a largely racist 1971 Virginia. While the movie has a typical Disney happy ending in which the Titans overcome racism and prejudice, it also features all four of Allport's criteria for successful intergroup contact:

1. Equal-status groups: The new head coach (played by Denzel Washington) explicitly tells the players that no one will get a particular team position due to race—every position is based on individual talent, attitude, and effort. This immediately puts them all at an equal starting point.

2. Group members must interact on an individual level: Before the season starts, their coach takes them on a training retreat. While there, all White players must share a bedroom with a Black player. In addition, each player must learn personal details about the lives of players of a different race. This forces them to see the diversity within the outgroup and thus eliminates outgroup homogeneity.

3. Authority figures must be supportive: A clear theme in the movie is the coach's explicit attempts to overcome racism both in the players and in the other coaches working with him. In this way, he serves as a positive role model.

4. Finally, common goals: The team members must obviously become a cooperative unit to win games and, eventually, the championship. They all have the same superordinate goal, and it can only be accomplished if they respect and protect each other.

In addition to simply being an enjoyable, humorous, and poignant film, *Remember the Titans* just happens to follow almost an exact outline for the criteria Allport suggested were necessary for positive ingroup contact to reduce prejudice.

one representative from each of the expert groups. The key here is that the students have to teach each other what they learned earlier in their expert groups—the "expert" in each jigsaw group is the only one who knows that particular set of facts. To succeed in the class, they must rely on each other, respect each other's knowledge, be patient with each other, and so forth. It no longer matters what race or religion another student is—prejudices go away as the jigsaw groups work cooperatively toward a superordinate goal.

■ **FIGURE 9.3** In a jigsaw classroom, first teams are "expert groups" that all learn a certain set of information. Then, groups are mixed up such that the second set of teams, the "jigsaw groups," each includes one member from the expert groups. Each jigsaw group must then rely on the other members of the team to teach them the needed material.

(a) Expert Groups

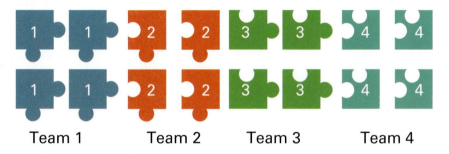

Team 1   Team 2   Team 3   Team 4

(b) Jigsaw Groups

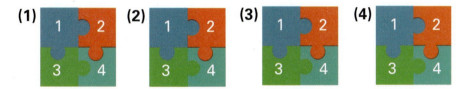

Try This at Home: Forming Friendships

It has become fashionable to mock efforts to bring warring parties together diplomatically as a tree-hugging, soft-hearted, unrealistic effort to impose friendship and understanding. A sneering tone of voice typically makes fun of the idea of "holding hands and singing Kumbaya." However, a handshake between enemies helped end the violence in Ireland after 30 years of bloody conflict. Telling one another's stories helped South Africa make a difficult transition away from Apartheid. Perhaps Frank Roque would not have murdered Balbir Singh Sodhi if they previously had enjoyed a pleasant conversation at Sodhi's gas station. Perhaps the terrorists would have been less likely to board those planes if they had previously formed friendships with a few people in the United States.

Is this soft-hearted, or is there any scientific support for the value of friendship as a way to reduce prejudice? So far, all of the techniques for reducing stereotypes, prejudice, and discrimination have required some kind of external intervention, such as working together toward a common goal. But is friendship with people you automatically dislike something that you can do as an individual?

Friendship is powerful—and risky. Binder et al. (2009) reported how **friendship contacts**—individual, positive, personal interactions—reduced prejudice among students. This impressive study involved people from 33 different schools and three different countries (Belgium, England, and Germany). The most common minority groups in the Belgian sample were from African countries, especially Morocco. But there were also students from Southern Europe and from Turkey. In the German sample, most minority group members were people of Turkish descent. In the English sample, most minority group members were Bangladeshi, Afro-Caribbean, or African. Despite this diversity, simple friendships led to less prejudice almost across the board.

Friendship contacts: Individual, positive, personal interactions that reduce prejudice.

Friendship contacts reduced prejudice, but the fine print in this study was even more revealing in two ways. First, the *quality* of those ingroup and outgroup contacts was more important than the *quantity* of contact. A friendship can become intensely influential if it is deeply meaningful, even if you only see your friend once every year or even less. Second, friendship contact reduced the prejudice of the majority group member more than it did for the minority group member. Perhaps the friend with a life of privilege has a bit more to learn, a bit more to realize, a bit more empathy to gain. The bottom line was that quality friendships reduced prejudice (over a relatively long-term, *longitudinal* 6-month study) among people from extremely different backgrounds. All people, at any time, can choose to apply this lesson to their own life circumstances if they so choose.

The Main Ideas

- The contact hypothesis is the idea that prejudice will be reduced with more exposure to members of outgroups. Allport noted that in order for this to be successful, certain criteria must be met regarding the type of contact.

- Sherif's famous Robbers Cave Study involved boys in a summer camp setting. The experimenters created prejudice between groups through competitive contexts, then reduced prejudice through cooperative contexts and superordinate goals.

- Jigsaw classrooms use the idea of superordinate goals to reduce prejudice in elementary schools.

- Personal friendships have also been shown to reduce outgroup prejudice.

⚡ CRITICAL THINKING CHALLENGE

- Many students in our social psychology courses over the years have complained that Sherif only used generally equivalent White, male, preteens in his study. What would your hypotheses be if we were able to replicate this study using a different type of participant, such as all girls, all poor children, or all adults? What might happen if the participants were not selected to be similar to each other but were allowed to come from different outgroups?

- Try to be honest in identifying prejudiced attitudes you hold right now. What groups make you uncomfortable or seem to live in a way you don't approve of? Would you be comfortable in purposely seeking out members of those groups to learn more about them as an attempt to reduce this prejudice? If not, why not?

- What variables affect how meaningful a friendship becomes? Is it possible for you to ethically manipulate these variables to become closer to certain people in your life?

CHAPTER SUMMARY

Why do we stereotype?

Stereotypes are beliefs about members of a group; prejudices are judgments or evaluations of members of a group, and discrimination is behavior toward people because of their group membership. There are several theories regarding why humans seem to have a basic tendency to engage in these social phenomena. One idea is that we tend to label people as quickly as possible because we are cognitive misers and that these labels serve as efficient (but biased) heuristics; this theory is called adaptive categorization. The idea is that fast, efficient decisions generally helped people survive. Our tendency to favor our own group (and to disadvantage other groups) is so strong it happens within arbitrary, meaningless groups. A series of studies on this tendency made use of meaningless groups and is called the minimal group paradigm.

Another idea for why humans stereotype is because ingroups (groups in which we are a member) are validating and comforting. Social identity theory is the idea that we automatically categorize people into "us" versus "them" in ways that flatter our self-concept. Finally, culture reinforces stereotypes over generations through social learning theory, the idea that we observe and imitate others in our social world (such as parents, peers, and ideas we see in media images). Sometimes cultural stereotypes become self-fulfilling prophecies, an idea explored by social role theory. This tendency also occurs within stereotype threat, which is when anxiety about fulfilling a negative stereotype causes distraction, and that distraction leads to us performing badly on a task (thus fulfilling the stereotype).

How do stereotypes turn into prejudices?

Four major theories explain the subtle shift from belief-based stereotypes into emotional prejudices: conflict over limited resources, frustration, the need for high self-esteem, and emotional reactions. The first relevant theory is realistic conflict theory, which suggests that we form prejudices to justify taking resources from another group. For example, colonizers who wish to take land from a native group may justify the action by believing the natives are "savages."

The second theory is that prejudice is used to blame other people for problems; this is called scapegoat theory. Research and historical examples show that we are most likely to aggress against a chosen scapegoat when we are frustrated due to economic failure; this idea is called frustration-aggression theory (in other words, we're most likely to become aggressive toward someone we blame when we are frustrated).

Third, we use prejudice to feel good about our social ingroups by believing that outgroups are not as good; this is social identity theory. Finally, the stereotype content model suggests that we have four different kinds of prejudice depending on whether we view a particular outgroup as high or low in warmth and competence.

Is prejudice a personality problem?

People with a "prejudiced personality" have higher prejudice toward outgroups of all kinds. Three constructs that may be tied to overall prejudice are authoritarianism, social dominance orientation, and religiosity. Authoritarian personalities prefer to submit to authorities (when they are perceived as legitimate), discipline those who defy authority, and conform to conventional beliefs. Higher scores in authoritarianism are positively correlated with prejudice of various types—but the most common measurement of authoritarianism has been criticized.

A similar idea is social dominance orientation, which is a personality trait associated with people who have a preference for structured social hierarchies, with some groups on the top with power and other groups on the bottom (without power). Again, high scores in social dominance orientation are positively correlated with a variety of outgroup prejudices.

Finally, research has investigated a link between prejudice and religiosity, which is the degree to which someone is religious and why (and is not simply what religion they believe). There are four types of religiosity: intrinsic, extrinsic, fundamentalist, and religion as quest. Extrinsic and fundamentalist are more associated with a variety of prejudices, compared with intrinsic and quest.

Has prejudice decreased over time?

While "old-fashioned" or explicit, overt prejudice has decreased over time due to it being less socially acceptable, social psychologists argue that other forms of prejudice have simply taken its place. One current form of prejudice is modern-symbolic. People high in modern-symbolic prejudice deny that prejudice is still a problem and thus perceive any attempts to recognize oppression of minorities or to help them with resources as "reverse" discrimination.

Another current form of prejudice is benevolent prejudice, which is ostensibly positive beliefs, but these beliefs still have a negative effect on the relevant group. The "positive" stereotypes endorsed in benevolent prejudice are limiting and sometimes condescending. In addition, any members of the group who do not fit these "ideals" are judged particularly harshly, which is called hostile prejudice. The combination of benevolent and hostile prejudice is ambivalent prejudice—here, members of the group are seen as belonging to either the "good" category (which matches stereotype) or the "bad" category (which defies the stereotypes). An example is women who "should" be gentle and kind (benevolent prejudice), and women who do not appear to have these traits are judged harshly (hostile prejudice).

How can we reduce harmful stereotyping, prejudice, and discrimination?

An early idea in social psychology regarding how to reduce prejudice was the contact hypothesis, the idea that more interaction with outgroup members would reduce prejudice. A famous study done by Sherif called the Robbers Cave Study tested this hypothesis. Sherif brought similar boys to a summer camp that was secretly run by psychologists and divided them into two groups. He caused the groups to be prejudiced toward each other after a series of sports events. When he tried to bring them together peacefully (the contact hypothesis), simply having them spend time together did not work. Sherif eventually did reduce prejudice between the groups by forcing them to work together on what he called superordinate goals.

One application of the superordinate goal research is a classroom technique called the jigsaw classroom. Here, students must depend upon each other to fully learn any given lesson and achieve a good grade. Some research has shown that jigsaw classrooms can decrease prejudice among students. This research also highlights the finding that cross-group friendships can increase respect and liking for people in outgroups.

THEORIES IN REVIEW

- Adaptive categorization
- Minimal group paradigm
- Social identity theory
- Social learning theory

- Social role theory
- Stereotype threat
- Realistic conflict theory
- Scapegoat theory

- Frustration-aggression theory
- Stereotype content model
- Authoritarian personality
- Social dominance orientation
- Religiosity
- Modern-symbolic prejudice
- Benevolent prejudice
- Hostile prejudice
- Ambivalent prejudice
- Contact hypothesis

CRITICAL THINKING, ANALYSIS, AND APPLICATION

- We typically think of stereotypes, prejudice, and discrimination as positive thoughts, judgments, and behaviors (respectively) toward people due to group membership. What are examples of "positive" stereotypes (meaning complimentary thoughts), "positive" prejudice (meaning warm or favorable judgments), and "positive" discrimination (meaning behaviors that benefit group members, e.g., voting for certain candidates, hiring certain types of people, dating certain types of people based on their group membership)?

- Consider again Table 9.2, which shows the stereotype content model. Can you identify any stereotypes or prejudices toward groups that have changed categories over time? Why did this change occur—and do you think it led to positive or negative outcomes for the group in question?

- Identify three fictional characters you believe exemplify concepts from this chapter. Write a paragraph about each that explains who the character is and examples of how their thoughts or actions display one of the ideas in the chapter (similar to the pop culture features you've read in each chapter of the book).

- Sherif's famous study showed that working together on superordinate goals helped reduce prejudice between two groups of boys. Other examples throughout history have shown that warring groups can put aside animosity if they suddenly have to bond together against a common or shared enemy. Does this mean that the best hope of eliminating human prejudice is an outside threat, such as an alien attack or zombie uprising?

PERSONAL REFLECTIONS

I was a little boy in the early days of the civil rights movement when our family stopped at a motel to spend the night. My mother sent me to the manager's office to ask for more towels. I spotted a young Black kid about my age and for some reason assumed that he worked there. I asked him for some towels, but I must have done it in some insulting way using the word *boy*—a word my parents never would have used in that way. I remember all this because my mother overheard me and got so angry with me that she made me go find him and apologize. I mostly remembering bursting into tears of embarrassment at having to apologize to someone my own age—and not being very clear about what it was that I had done that was so wrong. Over the years, I have wondered what became of that kid. Does he even remember a crying little White kid sputtering out an apology? Or was it just one of thousands of everyday insults that accumulated into a ton of feathers that he had to endure across his life? I am sorry; I hope he found a way to be forgiving. [TH]

We often use little phrases or words without knowing their true meaning. I remember in college I met a friend's fiancée for the first time. We were sitting down for a "get to know you meal," making small talk, and I made an offhand remark about how I hoped this restaurant would be good because another, similar one had "gypped" me in the past. Immediately, my friend's fiancée looked extremely hurt and angry. She stared at me for a few moments and then asked, "Do you realize that I come from a Gypsy family?" All I could do was blink and apologize. Until that day, I never realized that the word *gypped* referred to the stereotype of gypsies being thieves—I had used the phrase without knowing what it meant. I felt terrible. Since that day, I have not only stopped using the phrase but have felt the need to point it out to others who might be making the same ignorant mistake. Sometimes our culture teaches us lessons we'd rather not learn. [WG]

THEY are the problem and yet they're protesting!

LO9.4 **Analyze** how forms of **prejudice** and **discrimination** have **changed over time**.

GOLF CLUB
NO WOMEN ALLOWED

we need to **reduce pay of all men** to make it equal to women's pay

that's like a punishment for being male—**that's NOT going to happen**

EQUALITY FOR ALL

LO9.5 **Apply** methods of **prejudice reduction** to **real-world settings**.

Get a tour of **ALL Visual Key Concepts** and their definitions at **edge.sagepub.com/heinzen**

10 Helping and Prosocial Behavior

Core Questions

1. What motivates people to help others, in general?

2. Why do some people help more than others?

3. What circumstances make helping more or less likely?

Learning Objectives

10.1 Explain several general motives for why helping behaviors occur.

10.2 Analyze individual differences regarding why some people are more likely to help.

10.3 Apply psychological concepts regarding what situational variables lead to more or less helping in different settings.

Mark and Scott Kelly are identical twin astronauts who have devoted their lives to space exploration. In 2012, Scott volunteered to spend a year in space so that scientists could study long-term damages to his body due to space travel—and his twin Mark served as the Earth-bound control condition participant. Both astronauts have sacrificed time with their families and physical health so that other people can learn from their experiences.

"The White Helmets" is a nickname for the Syria Civil Defense organization, a nongovernmental, non-profit group whose members tried to save lives of civilians in Aleppo, Syria, affected by the war there. According to Raed Al Saleh, the head of the White Helmets, these volunteers had saved over 60,000 lives by 2016—but more than 140 of the White Helmets died while trying to help others. The group was nominated for a Nobel Peace Prize and states that they try to live by the Koran's words, "To save a life is to save all of humanity."

Malala Yousafzai won the Nobel Peace Prize in 2014. At the age of 12, she stood up to the Taliban in Pakistan when she wrote a blog arguing that all women have a basic right to education. She has been the victim of several assassination attempts and threats, but she refuses to stop advocating for other girls around the world.

What motivates these people—and all of the other self-sacrificing heroes throughout history—to help others?

The White Helmets, Syria

Malala Yousafzai

WHAT MOTIVATES PEOPLE TO HELP OTHERS, IN GENERAL?

LO 10.1: Explain several general motives for why helping behaviors occur.

Have you ever donated blood? Spent a weekend volunteering for Habitat for Humanity? Given money to a charity? Held the door for someone holding a heavy package? If so, you've tried to help someone in need. **Prosocial behavior** is a general term for helping others, either on an individual level (like helping someone who's lost) or on a group level (like donating to a charity). Helping others is perhaps one of the best parts of a social network, and we've all probably experienced the joy of feeling that we've made a positive difference in the world.

However, the social psychology of helping is complicated, just like all of the topics covered in this book. One debate that might never go away is over exactly *why* people help others. Some people believe that it's possible for us to exhibit **altruism** (sometimes called **pure altruism**), that is, to help others purely out of selfless concern for their well-being (Batson, 1990, 1998). Purely altruistic acts are motivated *only* by the desire to help—and nothing is expected in return. However, slightly more cynical (or more realistic, depending on your view) people argue that pure altruism is a myth. They argue that prosocial behaviors really stem from **egoistic altruism**, or helping behaviors done in exchange for some kind of personal benefit.

You might protest at this point, thinking, "But I do help others, expecting nothing in return!" Certainly, when we help a stranger, we might never expect to see that person again. When we give to charity, we are sacrificing those financial resources and things we might enjoy buying for ourselves. But when you engage in prosocial behaviors, do you feel like a better person? Are you happier and more fulfilled? If so—isn't that a reward? If you don't help, you might feel guilty or sad—and so, could helping be a selfish way to avoid those negative emotions? These indirect or emotional rewards of helping are part of egoistic altruism.

Social psychology has studied the motivations behind helping and prosocial behaviors in general in an attempt to answer these questions scientifically. So far, the field has offered four major explanations for why we engage in prosocial behaviors: evolutionary benefits to the larger group, social norms, avoiding negative emotions, and empathy (see Table 10.1). Let's talk about each idea.

The Evolutionary Perspective: Prosocial Behaviors Help Our Groups Survive

Life is a little easier if you have good neighbors. It doesn't matter whether they lived on the next farm three miles down the road or in the opposite apartment only three steps across the hall. For all social animals, there are evolutionary advantages to being a good neighbor. Among our ancient ancestors, these daily prosocial exchanges probably began over food. If you had killed more meat than you could consume before it got rotten, then you would probably trade away your extra meat for someone else's excess fruit, grain, or other resource. It's also possible that at some point, you might have given extra resources to someone in the group without immediately expecting something in return.

Ask the Experts: Catherine Borshuk on Altruism

©SAGE Publications

Prosocial behavior: Any action performed to help others, either on an individual level or a group level.

Altruism: Helping others purely out of selfless concern for their well-being.

Pure altruism: See *altruism*.

Egoistic altruism: Helping others in exchange for some kind of personal benefit.

■ TABLE 10.1 Four Explanations for Prosocial or Helping Behaviors

Theory	Motivation for Helping	Type of Altruism
Evolutionary perspective	To help our group survive and to have more opportunities to mate	Egoistic
Social norms	To fit into our group's expectations of social behavior	Egoistic
Negative state relief	To avoid feeling sadness or guilt	Egoistic
Empathy-altruism	To help someone in need	Pure

Social exchange refers to the evolution of prosocial trading of resources that strengthens the group. Cosmides and Tooby (1992) describe social exchange between humans as "universal and highly elaborated across all human cultures" (p. 164). We exchange favors with neighbors, exchange money for electronic devices, and even exchange promises when negotiating complex treaties between nations. The advantages of sharing food probably led to other prosocial exchanges such as cooperative hunting, mutual defense, communal childcare, and so on.

Over many generations, the trait of altruism would be naturally selected as one of the constellation of characteristics that made it so advantageous to live in cooperative groups. Selfish loners would be more likely to starve to death, be eaten by prey, or at least be less attractive as sexual and relationship partners. Their genes would slowly be washed out of the gene pool. In contrast, helpful, cooperative, generous altruists would survive by becoming skilled at group living. They would attract strong sexual and relationship partners. Their genes would slowly come to dominate the gene pool (see Nesse, 2001; Van Vugt & Van Lange, 2006). In this view, then, prosocial behaviors offer two advantages: (1) they help individuals survive by promoting opportunities to reproduce and thus pass on one's genes, and (2) and they help the group survive in times of need (by spreading food around, etc.).

Kinship Selection.

We described the advantages of being a good neighbor, but you are probably more likely to loan money to a family member than to your neighbor. **Kinship selection** refers to the evolutionary urge to favor those with closer genetic relatedness. In his best-known book, *On the Origin of Species,* Darwin (1859, p. 238) pointed out that cattle breeders wanted cattle with "flesh and fat well marbled" together. But when they found such an animal, farmers couldn't breed the animal—because they had already slaughtered it. Darwin noted that cattle breeders did the next best thing: They bred the dead animal's closest living relatives. Darwin realized that these English cattle (and dog) breeders understood the principle now called **inclusive fitness**, the probability that our genetic heritage will be preserved in the offspring of relatives.

Another naturalist named William Hamilton proposed a mathematical equation for when prosocial behaviors are most likely to occur. According to **Hamilton's Inequality**, prosocial behavior will emerge whenever $(r \times b) > c$. That is, helping happens when r (the genetic relatedness of the person who needs help) multiplied by b (the benefits of helping) is greater than c (the cost of helping). What we might call altruism is really just our genes struggling to survive—and defaulting to our closest relatives when our own welfare is not in danger.

Inclusive fitness also appears to shape helping behavior among humans. Essock-Vitale and McGuire (1985) interviewed 300 randomly selected White, middle-class Los Angeles women about patterns of helping between kin (family members) and nonkin. They discovered that the women were more likely to help (a) those who were more closely related and (b) those with high reproductive potential.

Burnstein, Crandall, and Kitayama (1994) found a similar pattern when they presented undergraduates with life-or-death moral dilemmas. The students consistently recommended more help for close kin and for younger people. They even recommended more help for premenopausal rather than postmenopausal women. Human decision making seems to include an intuitive sense of inclusive

Social exchange theory: See *interdependence theory*.

Kinship selection: The evolutionary urge to favor those with closer genetic relatedness.

Inclusive fitness: The probability that our genetic heritage will be preserved in the offspring of relatives.

Hamilton's inequality: A formula for understanding when prosocial behavior will emerge that can be written as $(r \times b) > c$, where r is the genetic relatedness of the person who needs help, b is the benefit of helping, and c is the cost of helping.

sjbooks / Alamy Stock Photo

Dawkins's (1976) book *The Selfish Gene* discusses the genetic benefits of helping others—but only if the people you help are related to you and thus share your genes.

fitness, due to the egoistic altruism motive of helping pass on our genes—even if that has to happen indirectly through our blood relatives.

Reciprocal Altruism. While helping is more likely within the family, we certainly help nonrelatives as well. Evolutionary motives for helping, such as keeping one's group alive or getting more opportunities to reproduce, represent egoistic altruism (helping others for long-term personal benefits). In addition, within most groups where people see each other frequently, prosocial behaviors may occur due to **reciprocal altruism**, or the expectation that our helpfulness now will be returned in the future.

We humans are not alone when it comes to trading favors. Many other social animals also evolved reciprocal altruism (Van Vugt & Van Lange, 2006). Vampire bats, for example, famously feast on blood, usually from large mammals such as wild pigs, cows, and horses (but rarely from humans). They need a lot of blood. Vampire bats will drink about half their body weight during an uninterrupted feeding—so much that they sometimes have difficulty taking flight. DeNault and McFarlane (1995) discovered why vampire bats are so bloodthirsty. A vampire bat will die if it goes more than 48 to 72 hours without a blood meal. They also found that both male and female vampire bats will, in an apparent act of altruism, regurgitate some of their blood meal and share it with starving neighbors. But the story of vampire bat altruism is even more sophisticated.

> **Reciprocal altruism:** Altruistic behavior that occurs because individuals expect that their helpfulness now will be returned in the future.

Vampire bats are selective in their sharing of blood. When Wilkinson (1984) studied vampire bats in Costa Rica, he discovered that they were more likely to donate blood to those bats with the greatest need for a meal. Furthermore, their altruistic food sharing was not limited to their immediate kin. Frequent roost-mates were more likely to be the beneficiaries. And the evidence suggests that vampire bats are able to identify, remember, and *not* help those vampire bats that had *not* donated blood to other starving bats. Essentially, "cheaters can be detected and excluded from the system" (Wilkinson, 1990, p. 82). Helping can directly lead to increasing your own survival in times of need—a very adaptive pattern of behavior.

Inclusive fitness and reciprocal altruism take the "nature" side of the nature versus nurture debate when viewed from the evolutionary psychology lens. What about the nurture side?

© CanStockPhoto.com/kentoh

It may surprise you that vampire bats are a species with a highly evolved system of helping each other, through a system called reciprocal altruism.

Prosocial Social Norms Increase Helping

Astronaut Scott Kelly still isn't directly helping his brother Mark by going through health-threatening experiments in space. Putting his life at risk isn't going to help either one of them. So, there must be other explanations for prosocial behaviors than just protecting our genes. One alternative explanation is that helping behaviors result from a group's social norms. Taking risks is what astronauts do—it's their social norm.

Recall from Chapter 7 that social norms are unwritten rules about how members of a group are expected to act. Some of these norms are specifically about helping. You already know about one norm, called reciprocity (the expectation that favors will be returned later). There are other relevant social norms, but the psychological forces that promote prosocial behaviors don't easily yield their secrets to researchers.

The Difficulty of Studying Prosocial Behavior. Think about why it might be difficult to get our scientific arms around helping behavior. *Random assignment to groups* is almost always the best way to conduct an experiment. Random assignment means that each group is likely to start out as equal at the beginning of the experiment. Starting out equal creates a fair test, similar to marathon runners using the same starting point to see who runs the fastest. If the groups really are equal in every way except the *independent variable*, then any differences in the *dependent variable* (what you measure as the outcome) must be caused by the different experimental conditions.

But social psychologists can't go around randomly assigning people to be in a life-threatening emergency as part of a comparison group for an experiment! Preventing such abuses is why organizations have *institutional review boards (IRBs)* that screen the ethics of research projects before they are allowed to go forward. Bierhoff, Klein, and Kramp (1991/2006) got around this problem by creating equivalent groups through a **post hoc matched groups design**. They started by identifying people who had provided first aid after a traffic accident that happened naturally; that became Group 1. Then they created a meaningful comparison group—Group 2—by (a) matching the people in Group 1 with others who were similar in sex, age, and socioeconomic status and (b) including only people in Group 2 who had witnessed an accident and *not* helped. It wasn't as good as using random assignment, but it was a lot more ethical.

The comparison between these two groups indicated that people in Group 1— those who had helped—were more empathetic. No surprise there (we'll discuss empathy later). But they dug even deeper and found that the Group 1 helpers also believed in two social norms: (1) a just world and (2) social responsibility.

Helping and Belief in a Just World. Many people say that they offer help because they want to "pay it forward" or because "what goes around comes around." But do we all eventually get what we deserve? Is goodness always rewarded and evil punished? Remember from Chapter 5 that belief in a just world is the idea that the world is a fair place in which good things happen to good people—and bad things happen to bad people (Lerner, 1980).

One of the most famous cases in the history of the civil rights movement demonstrates the connection between prosocial behavior and belief in a just world. In 1943, a Montgomery, Alabama, bus driver named James Blake ordered a Black passenger named Rosa Parks to get off his bus and then reenter through the rear door (the standard policy for Black passengers at the time). She complied, but while she was off the bus and heading toward the rear door, he simply drove away.

More than a decade later, on December 1, 1955, Blake was once again the driver when bus No. 2857 stopped to pick up a passenger, a White man. Blake ordered a Black woman to give up her seat—and it was the same woman he had left waiting on the side of the road 12 years earlier. This time, Parks refused to obey, leading to her arrest. Parks's defiance made her into one of the heroines of the civil rights movement. This type of blatant discrimination did not fit into many people's beliefs that the world should be just and fair.

What followed was a yearlong bus boycott; if people of color were not to be treated fairly, then they wouldn't ride at all. The success of the boycott depended on hundreds of people making many small but critically important altruistic sacrifices; help from everyone was needed to benefit the group. Instead of riding a bus, people had to get up earlier and endure long walks to work, shop, and so forth—and enough people had to do it for the bus company to suffer from the lack of passengers.

In the long run, people in the boycott would be helping themselves (they would get better treatment on the bus), but in the short term, they had to make sacrifices

Post hoc matched groups design: A research design used when random assignment is not feasible. The experimenter (a) first identifies an experimental group, (b) then creates a control group with matching characteristics (sex, age, etc.).

Civil rights icon Rosa Parks participated in a movement to end racial discrimination that did not align with belief in a just world. This photo shows her riding the bus on the day Montgomery, Alabama, ended its racist policies.

Are you more likely to give money to a homeless person who doesn't appear to "deserve" being homeless? If so, the dual norms of a just world and social responsibility may have affected your behavior.

for the good of the group. For many, the motivation was that racist laws were not just or fair. These people were willing to help the entire group of oppressed people of color by sacrificing their own comfort and convenience because they believed in a just world.

Helping and the Social Responsibility Norm. Parks and the other participants in the civil rights movement certainly believed that everyone should be treated equally—it's only fair. However, a second social norm was also at play: the **social responsibility norm**. This norm is the idea that each individual has a duty to improve the world by helping those in need. If you are on an elevator with someone who is unable to push a button for the floor he needs (maybe his arms are full of boxes), it's a social expectation that you should ask him what floor he wants and push the button for him.

The social responsibility norm can be tricky, though. Have you ever held the door open for someone, only to find yourself standing there holding the door for many more? How long are you expected to stay there, potentially making yourself late or separated from your friends who already went inside? You might have experienced a similar problem in a city with homeless people asking for spare change . . . you can't give away all of your money or help every homeless person you see!

The social responsibility norm must be strong enough to "compel people to provide aid" but sensitive enough to help only "those who deserve help" (Simmons & Lerner, 1968, p. 224). This may be where the social responsibility norm overlaps with the just world norm. For example, some homeless people make signs reading "homeless vet" or "God bless you," hoping that you will be more likely to help them if you believe they don't "deserve" to be homeless.

We Help to Avoid Negative Emotions: Negative State Relief

Abraham Lincoln may have understood egoistic altruism. After a companion praised him for rescuing some baby pigs from drowning, Lincoln said that his behavior was "the very essence of selfishness." When his companion asked him why, he replied, "I should have had no peace of mind all day had I gone on and left that suffering old sow worrying over those pigs. I did it to get peace of mind" (Sharp, 1928, cited in Batson, Bolen, Cross, & Neuringer-Benefiel, 1986). While this story may be more folklore than fact, Lincoln's hypothetical words indicate an awareness that helping can really be selfish, done to simply avoid feeling sad or guilty later.

The **negative state relief model** of helping posits that seeing another person in need causes us emotional distress and that helping decreases those negative emotions (Dovidio & Penner, 2001; Schaller & Cialdini, 1990). This model supports the "egoistic" or selfish aspect of helping; behaviors that may appear to be pure altruism are really done for selfish reasons. Research on this idea has found that simply being in a negative mood doesn't seem to increase helping behaviors (Forgas, 1998; Habashi, Graziano, & Hoover, 2016), but sadness and guilt do seem to increase compliance when someone directly *requests* help.

CAPTAIN AMERICA: A PARAGON OF PROSOCIAL ACTION

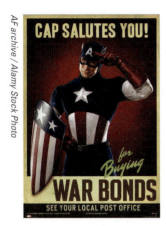

AF archive / Alamy Stock Photo

In the world of comic book superheroes, Captain America is one of the most pure of heart. Consistently ethical, loyal, and the epitome of patriotism, he also encapsulates the idea of pure altruism, or willingness to sacrifice himself to help others with no expectation of reward.

This altruism is highlighted in an early scene from *Captain America: The First Avenger* (Feige & Johnston, 2011), in which the military is attempting to decide which new recruit they will choose for their experimental program to create a super-soldier. The military officers argue with the scientists regarding which traits are most important, and they seem to settle on "guts" and heroism. To test the candidates, one of the officers throws a dummy grenade at the group of soldiers. While most of the men immediately run for cover, Steve Rogers jumps onto the grenade in an attempt to save everyone else. This ultimate altruism and self-sacrifice is what distinguishes him from the crowd and ultimately leads to him becoming Captain America.

An example of this phenomenon was found in a study of college students (McMillen & Austin, 1971). To start, the researchers had to experimentally manipulate participant emotions. They asked students to complete a multiple-choice exam in exchange for extra credit, and each participant was given information about the correct answers from a confederate when the researcher was out of the room. When the researcher returned and asked the participants if they had any knowledge of the study or the test, some participants said "no"—a harmless little white lie, right?

However, the next part of the study showed that people who told the lie might have felt at least a little guilty. All of the participants were then asked if they would help the researchers by volunteering to score some of the tests. Participants who had *not* lied earlier in the study helped for an average of about 2 minutes. In contrast, people who had lied to the researcher stayed for over an hour—an average of 63 minutes!

We can infer that the people who lied may have felt guilty and volunteered to help as a way to relieve that negative emotion (and potentially a negative view of themselves as bad people). The negative state relief model includes the idea that we help when we see other people suffering because not helping would make us feel bad, and we want to avoid that feeling. But it also suggests that when we're in a bad mood for other reasons, helping can help improve our mood—so we might seek out helping situations purely to improve our own emotional state (Dietrich & Berkowitz, 1997; Fultz, Schaller, & Cialdini, 1988).

We Help Because We Care: The Empathy-Altruism Hypothesis

So far, you might think that social psychology is a pretty cynical science—all of the theories above conclude that people only help for selfish, egoistic reasons, because we want

Social responsibility norm: The idea that each individual has a duty to improve the world by helping those in need.

Negative state relief model: The idea that seeing another person in need causes individuals emotional distress, and helping decreases those negative emotions (see *egoistic altruism*).

to comply with social norms, or because we want to avoid feeling guilt or sadness. If so, you'll be relieved to know that the final theory suggests that sometimes, people help others simply out of the goodness of their hearts.

Consider the case of two women on a commuter train in Portland who were being harassed because they appeared to be Muslim (Dobuzinskis, 2017). Their harasser was angrily yelling racial and religious slurs. Three men who saw the harassment occurring intervened—and all of them were stabbed by the harasser. Two of the men who bravely tried to help the women died due to the stabbing. All three people who stepped in risked physical danger for a complete stranger. The accompanying feature, "Social Psychology in Popular Culture," discusses the altruism of the comic book superhero, Captain America, to highlight a well-known fictional example of risking one's own life to help others. But knowing that there are real-life heroes like these men can be even more inspiring.

The **empathy-altruism hypothesis** proposes that feelings of compassion create a purely altruistic motivation to help (see Batson, 1991, 1998; Toi & Batson, 1982). While Batson, the major proponent of this hypothesis, doesn't deny that all of the egoistic reasons for helping *also* exist, he argues that pure altruism is, indeed, possible. Batson's foundational idea is that when we see people who need help, we empathize with them; we put ourselves in their shoes and feel compassion.

However, simply feeling empathy is not enough to predict helping—in this model, feeling empathy is necessary but not sufficient. To follow our compassion with actual prosocial behaviors, we must also:

- be capable of helping (e.g., we may not offer to help a friend with calculus homework if we don't understand the subject),
- perceive that our help will actually benefit the person (e.g., we might not waste our time simply *pretending* to help), and
- perceive that our help will be more beneficial than someone else's help (e.g., we might not volunteer to lead a group if someone else is available who has more experience or expertise).

Thus, the empathy-altruism hypothesis suggests that pure altruism is *possible,* under the right circumstances. A classic study by Batson and his team (Batson, Duncan, Ackerman, Buckley, & Birch, 1981) asked women participants to listen while another young woman received painful electric shocks (as you might have suspected, no one actually got shocked in the study; the shocks were just the *cover story* and an example of experimental *deception* that the IRB allowed because it was necessary for the study to work). Participants also heard the woman explain that due to a childhood accident, she was particularly sensitive to shocks.

When the experimenter asked each participant if she was willing to take the other woman's place, most of them agreed. This happened even though the participants thought their own part of study was done and they could go home (that is, they could easily escape from the situation). It is also interesting to note that participants were especially likely to volunteer to take the shocks if they believed that the other woman was very similar to themselves in attitudes and interests, which presumably helped the participants empathize with her.

Participants in the study thus volunteered to experience painful shocks, for no compensation, for a woman who was a stranger. While other researchers have argued that this prosocial choice may have, again, been due to things like avoiding feelings of guilt later (Schaller & Cialdini, 1988), it is hard to believe that empathy for the woman played no role in their decision to help. The people at the start of this chapter, such as the twin

Empathy-altruism hypothesis: The idea that feelings of empathy and compassion create a purely altruistic motivation to help.

astronauts, the White Helmets, and Malala Yousafzai, all made significant sacrifices to help others. It may be that they did this simply because they want to help other people, despite the relatively high cost to their own lives—which would be pure altruism.

The Main Ideas

- Prosocial behavior is behavior designed to help others. Two theoretical reasons for helping are (1) pure altruism, or helping simply to benefit another person, or (2) egoistic altruism, helping because it somehow benefits the self.

- According to the evolutionary perspective, prosocial behaviors evolved because they help one's group survive and because people who helped more received greater opportunities for reproduction. Helping may also increase survival if it is reciprocated by others in the future.

- Two social norms for prosocial behavior are belief in a just world (the idea that everyone should be treated fairly) and social responsibility (the idea that each individual has a duty to help the group).

- While the negative state relief model suggests that people help others to avoid unpleasant emotions such as sadness or guilt, the empathy-altruism hypothesis suggests that pure altruism is possible.

⚡ CRITICAL THINKING CHALLENGE

- Consider the debate regarding whether true altruism is possible or whether all prosocial behaviors somehow benefit the person who helped (an egoistic altruism perspective). Do you, personally, think that pure altruism is possible? If so, can you identify any specific instances of pure altruism from your own life experiences?

- One implicit idea behind social norms for prosocial behavior is that if you do not engage in these norms, people in your social groups may judge you negatively or punish you in some social way (e.g., ostracize you from the group). Have you ever experienced this? Have you ever failed to help someone and then perceived that other people were perceiving you negatively—or have you made this judgment about someone else?

- Consider the three examples of helping behavior from the opening of this chapter. For each example, which theories or ideas from the first section of the chapter best explain that individual's choice to help? Can you apply these ideas to those specific examples?

WHY DO SOME PEOPLE HELP MORE THAN OTHERS?

LO 10.2: Analyze individual differences regarding why some people are more likely to help.

The theories you just learned explain general helping behaviors—but you know from life experience that some people are more likely to help than others. Think again about Malala Yousafzai, the young Pakistani girl who stood up to the Taliban and risked her life (several times) to help girls everywhere have access to an education. There are millions of other young girls in similar situations. What motivates some people to help, while others simply walk on by? Let's consider personality, religious norms, gender, and culture.

A Prosocial Personality

Is there a "helping" personality trait? If so, people high in this trait would be more likely to help a variety of different people in a variety of situations, compared to people low in the trait. Several different versions of a prosocial personality have been explored by social psychologists.

On one hand, for example, some research has found that people are more likely to help if they have a high need for approval or acceptance from others (Deutsch & Lamberti, 1986). Helping is also more likely to come from people who are high in empathy, as the empathy-altruism hypothesis would predict (Krueger, Hicks, & McGue, 2001). On the other hand, prosocial behaviors are *negatively correlated* with a trait called **Machiavellianism**, meaning the more Machiavellian someone is, the less likely he or she is to help another person. Named after the 15th-century Italian philosopher Niccolo Machiavelli, this trait describes people who are manipulative, distrustful of others, and egocentric.

One of the most popular general personality theories in psychology, the **Big 5 Model**, suggests that across cultures, five fundamental personality traits differentiate between people and predict behaviors (see McCrae & Costa, 1987; Mooradian, Davis, & Matzler, 2011). To learn what the five traits are—and how they might be related to prosocial behaviors—see the "Spotlight on Research Methods" feature. In addition, you can rate your own prosocial tendencies by scoring yourself on two related personality traits in the "Applying Social Psychology to Your Life" feature.

Religious Norms Promote Obligations and Options

Most major world religions have norms that support prosocial behavior. For example, giving a percentage of your wealth to the poor is one of the five pillars of Islam. There is a similar obligation within Judaism, called Tzedakah, which emphasizes that giving is a matter of justice rather than generosity. Hinduism promotes Yajna, a term that suggests that sacrificing for others is a way of behaving in harmony with universal laws. The words of Jesus advise extreme altruism: "Love your enemies, and do good to those who hate you" and "Sell your possessions and give to the poor." All these religious ideals influence altruistic behavior. However, the role of religious norms in prosocial behavior is more subtle than obedience to those commandments.

Intrinsic Versus Quest Religiosity. Batson and Gray (1981) discovered that *why* you are religious influences *how* you are religious. Recall from Chapter 9 that people high in intrinsic religiosity attempt to internalize their faith's teachings and live according to them. In contrast, quest religiosity uses religion as a way to question, doubt, and reexamine values and beliefs. In other words, it might not matter what religion you belong to—but what matters is what motivates your religious belief.

In the Batson and Gray (1981) experiment, 60 religiously oriented women were confronted with someone in emotional distress. Those who were oriented toward intrinsic religiosity offered their help whether or not it was welcome; they were responding to their own internal need to be helpful (a more egoistic response). However, those oriented toward religion as a quest offered help only if the person wanted help; they were responding to the expressed needs of the victim (a more altruistic response). This pattern has been replicated by others (e.g., Hansen, Vandenberg, & Patterson, 1995). In other words, why you are religious influences how you provide prosocial behavior based on religious motives.

Machiavellianism: A personality trait that describes people who are manipulative, distrustful of others, and egocentric.

Big 5 Model: A model of personality that posits that five fundamental personality traits differentiate between people and predict behaviors: openness to experience, conscientiousness, extraversion, agreeableness, and neuroticism.

PERSONALITY AND PROSOCIAL BEHAVIOR

"The search for the prosocial personality has been long and controversial" (Habashi et al., 2016, p. 1177). This is the first sentence in an article devoted to studying whether different personality traits really can be linked to helping others. Habashi and her colleagues started with the most popular general theory on personality, which most researchers call the Big 5 Model of Personality (McCrae & Costa, 1987; Mooradian et al., 2011). According to this model, five culturally universal personality traits predict behavior fairly reliably:

- **Openness to experience:** enjoyment of adventure, new experiences, independence, curiosity
- **Conscientiousness:** attention to detail, responsibility, self-discipline, high achievers
- **Extraversion:** highly social, energetic, assertive, spontaneous
- **Agreeableness:** cooperative, peacemakers, compassionate toward others
- **Neuroticism:** anxious, prone to stress, more likely to be depressed and socially insecure

When you consider these five traits, which would you hypothesize is most likely to be associated with more prosocial behaviors?

The research team asked college students at Purdue University to come to a session under the *cover story* that they would be reviewing a new program for the university's radio station. The broadcast was an interview with a senior student, "Katie," at Purdue who had lost both parents and a younger sibling in a car accident; she was now left with no financial resources and no family support, and she was struggling to graduate while caring for her remaining younger siblings. The participants didn't know that "Katie" was not a real person.

All of the participants completed self-report scales of the "Big 5" personality traits. The major outcome of the study was measured when the participants were given the opportunity to help Katie. The participants wrote down how many hours they would volunteer to help her personally, how many hours they would work on trying to get others to help, and how much money they would donate. They also rated how much personal distress they felt when thinking about Katie's story. Each of these variables was *correlated* with each of the "Big 5" personality traits; the results are shown in Table 10.2. Remember that correlations can range from −1.0 to +1.0, and numbers closer to 1 in either direction mean that the two variables are more closely associated with each other.

As you can see, only agreeableness was significantly correlated (shown in bold in the table), with people being more likely to donate their time and money to a person in need. Being higher in openness to experience, conscientiousness, or extraversion had no relationship with prosocial behaviors in this study. Interestingly, people who were high in either agreeableness or neuroticism were likely to say that Katie's story caused them personal distress—but only those high in agreeableness followed that up by expressing a willingness to help.

■ TABLE 10.2 Statistically Significant Correlations

	Openness to Experience	Conscientiousness	Extraversion	Agreeableness	Neuroticism
# Hours willing to volunteer	+.03	+.09	+.11	**+.17**	+.03
# Hours willing to get others to help	+.13	+.12	+.06	**+.20**	+.13
Amount of money willing to donate	+.07	+.12	+.13	**+.15**	+.07
Personal distress	+.03	−.03	−.05	**+.18**	**+.19**

SOURCE: Data from McCrae & Costa (1987) & Mooradian et al. (2011).

MEASURING PROSOCIAL PERSONALITY TRAITS

Applying Social Psychology to Your Life

In the Spotlight on Research Methods feature, you read about a study (Habashi et al., 2016) showing that two personality traits are positively correlated with feelings of personal distress on hearing about someone in need of help: agreeableness and neuroticism. However, only people high in agreeableness actually offered to help.

Researchers in that study assessed participants' personality traits using one of the most popular measures of the "Big 5" traits (John & Srivastava, 1999). The items shown here are from the same scale, but we have included only items meant to measure agreeableness and neuroticism (not the other three traits in the model).

Instructions: Next to each item, write a number indicating whether the word or phrase describes how you see yourself, using this scale:

1	2	3	4	5
Strongly disagree		Neutral		Strongly agree

I see myself as someone who . . .

_____ 1. tends to find fault with others.

_____ 2. is depressed, blue.

_____ 3. is helpful and unselfish with others.

_____ 4. is relaxed, handles stress well.

_____ 5. starts quarrels with others.

_____ 6. can be tense.

_____ 7. has a forgiving nature.

_____ 8. worries a lot.

_____ 9. is generally trusting.

_____ 10. is emotionally stable, not easily upset.

_____ 11. can be cold and aloof.

_____ 12. can be moody.

_____ 13. is considerate and kind to almost everyone.

_____ 14. remains calm in tense situations.

_____ 15. is sometimes rude to others.

_____ 16. gets nervous easily.

_____ 17. likes to cooperate with others.

Scoring: First, reverse-score Items 1, 4, 5, 10, 11, 14, and 15. This means that if you wrote a 1 it becomes a 5, a 2 becomes a 4, a 3 stays the same, a 4 becomes a 2, and a 5 becomes a 1.

Then, add up your scores for the odd-numbered items; this is your score for agreeableness. It can range from 9 to 45. Next, add up your scores for the even-numbered items; this is your score for neuroticism. It can range from 8 to 40. According to Habashi et al. (2016), higher numbers in either trait predict more emotional distress when you see someone else in need, but only higher numbers in agreeableness predict that you will actually help others consistently.

Source: John and Srivastava (1999).

When Religion Isn't Enough: The Good Samaritan Experiment. In the Christian Bible, there's a story called "The Good Samaritan." A traveler is stripped, beaten, and left to die next to a road. Two religious men, a priest and a Levite, both pass by and fail to help the man. Finally, a man from Samaria (considered unworthy by the priest and the Levite) stops and helps the traveler. This parable was used in a creative way by social psychologists to test the strength of prosocial religious motives.

In 1973, Darley and Batson staged what is now known as "The Good Samaritan" *field experiment*. Their study pitted the power of religious norms against the power of an immediate situation. The participants were 40 students at the Princeton Theological Seminary who all passed the same needy person in an alley: a man slumped in a doorway who coughed and groaned as the students passed by. As you may already have guessed, the man was really a *confederate* of the research team.

These ministers-in-training didn't know it, but before they walked past the man in need, each had already had been assigned to different groups based on two different independent variables. The first *independent variable* divided students into two groups. One group prepared a brief talk about careers for ministers; the other group prepared a brief talk about the Good Samaritan story. The researchers wanted to know if thinking about this story—which is specifically about stopping to help people in need—would make the students more likely to, well, help someone in need. After preparing their speeches, all of the participants were told to go to another building to record their talks—a short walk designed to take them directly past the groaning man in the alley.

The second *independent variable* further subdivided the students into three groups based on an urgency manipulation. One group was told, "They were expecting you a few minutes ago . . . the assistant should be waiting for you, so you'd better hurry." The instructions were more moderate for a second group: "The assistant is ready for you, so please go right over." A third group—the *control group*—had no reason to rush: "It'll be a few minutes before they're ready, but you might as well head on over." Table 10.3 lays out the setup of this interesting *2 X 3 factorial design*.

The results of this famous study might surprise you (see Figure 10.1). First, across all six conditions, only about 40% of the seminary students stopped to help the groaning man. Perhaps even more interestingly, preparing a speech explicitly about the need to help (the Good Samaritan story) did not have a *statistically significant* effect on whether people helped. What did matter was whether the participants were in a hurry. If they were feeling rushed, then they were much less likely to stop to offer help.

In fact, Darley and Batson (1973) observed that "on several occasions, a seminary student going to give his talk on the parable of the Good Samaritan literally stepped over the victim as he hurried on his way" (p. 107). It seems that religious social norms or religiosity can make some people more likely to help but only if they don't have other things to do.

Perceiving and assessing our own moral behavior is brimming with opportunities to deceive ourselves, and Batson suggests that we often want to *appear* to be making moral decisions while actually avoiding inconvenience by doing as little as possible. Thus, **moral hypocrisy** is the motivation to appear moral while avoiding the costs of behaving morally (Batson, Kobrynowicz, Dinerstein, Kampf, & Wilson, 1997; Batson,

■ **TABLE 10.3** The Six Conditions in Darley and Batson's (1973) "Good Samaritan" Study

	Independent Variable 1: Talk Topic	
	Careers in the Ministry	**The Good Samaritan**
Independent Variable 2: Urgency		
High urgency	1	4
Moderate urgency	2	5
Low urgency (control)	3	6

SOURCE: Darley & Batson (1973).

Moral hypocrisy: Occurs when individuals desire to appear moral while avoiding the costs of behaving morally.

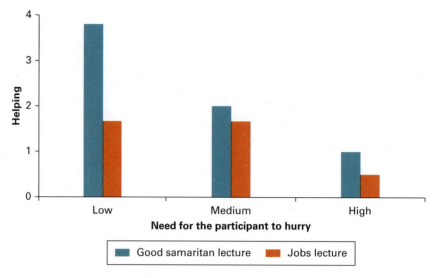

■ **FIGURE 10.1** Do religious motivations increase helping behavior? The results from Darley and Batson's (1973) "Good Samaritan" study.

SOURCE: Darley & Batson (1973).

Thompson, & Chen, 2002). Prosocial behavior—and especially pure altruism—is much more likely to come from people who are high in **moral integrity** instead, the motivation to actually live up to one's own standards of morality and ethics.

Gender and Communal Behaviors

Who helps more—men or women? Many gender differences in helping patterns persist cross-culturally. For example, women across cultures tend to behave with greater social and ethical sensitivity, a higher degree of nurturance, and less combativeness than men (Kamat & Kanekar, 1990; Miranda & Kanekar, 1993). While many cultures include social norms around caring for aging parents, this obligation often falls to women more than men in terms of everyday tangible support (Lee, Spitze, & Logan, 2003; Silverstein, Gans, & Yang, 2006). What makes men and women act differently in prosocial situations?

Gender Socialization: Agency and Communion. Just as different countries have different cultures with different social norms (see the next section for more), men and women also have different social expectations. **Gender socialization** establishes the expected patterns of behavior deemed appropriate for men and women (see Bakan, 1966; Eagly, 2009) by rewarding each sex for doing what is considered "appropriate." This includes how—and when—to be helpful.

One key dimension of gender socialization is **agency**, the stereotypically male-oriented pattern of behavior that emphasizes being masterful, assertive, competitive, and dominant (see Spence & Buckner, 2000). In contrast, **communion** is a stereotypically female-oriented pattern of behavior that emphasizes being friendly, unselfish, other-oriented, and emotionally expressive. Agency and communion describe a pattern of gender differences that is common across cultures (Kite, Deaux, & Haines, 2007), and while agency promotes the self, communion emphasizes the good of the group and being kind to others. Several researchers have suggested that girls are raised to have higher moral reasoning and empathy than boys, which leads to more helping and prosocial behaviors (see Eisenberg, Fabes, & Shea, 1989; Kumru, Carlo, Mestre, & Samper, 2012).

Moral integrity: Occurs when individuals are motivated to live up to their own standards of morality and ethics, resulting in an increase in altruistic behavior.

Gender socialization: The expected patterns of behavior deemed appropriate for men and women by rewarding each sex for doing what is considered socially acceptable.

Agency: A stereotypically male-oriented pattern of behavior that emphasizes being masterful, assertive, competitive, and dominant.

Communion: A stereotypically female-orientated pattern of behavior that emphasizes being friendly, unselfish, other oriented, and emotionally expressive.

One way the difference between agency and communion translates into behavior is through career choices, including the "helping" professions. Eagly (2009) drew on the U.S. Bureau of Labor statistics to identify the different prosocial occupations deemed appropriate for men and for women. Women are a minority within prosocial professions that stereotypically require initiative and physical strength, such as firefighters (only 5% are women), police officers (15%), and soldiers (14%). By contrast, women are a significant majority within professions that stereotypically require cooperation and nurturing such as preschool and kindergarten teachers (98%), social workers (79%), and registered nurses (92%; U.S. Bureau of Labor Statistics, 2009).

In other words, both men and women help; gender norms simply train them toward different prosocial paths. A study in Polynesia found that girls engage in more prosocial behavior than boys, but they hypothesized it is because girls are required to engage in cooperative housework for the good of the family, while boys are allowed to be more independent (Graves & Graves, 1985). We train children to be helpful—but how this is defined appears to differ based on whether we're training boys or girls.

Eagly's (2009) review concluded that "men tend to extend heroic help in dangerous emergencies" (p. 649), intervene in accidents to help strangers, are chivalrous to help women, and are more likely to serve their nation in war. Women may be less inclined to stop to offer help to someone on the side of the road, for example, due to fears of assault. But in a 2010 survey of over 200,000 students first entering college, 62% of men and 75% of women said that helping others is either "very important" or "essential" (Pryor, Hurtado, DeAngelo, Blake, & Tran, 2010).

Changing Patterns of Gender Socialization. Over the past 50 years, there have been profound changes in gender expectations across many cultures. Warfare, for example, relies more on technology than brute strength, and that has opened opportunities for and acceptance of women in the military. These changes may affect gendered helping behaviors.

Changing gender roles were examined in depth by Diekman across a series of studies. In her first publication on the topic (Diekman & Eagly, 2000), her findings showed that both men and women perceive that over time, women are remaining fairly stable in their high levels of communion and are simultaneously increasing in

As time progresses, traditional ideas of how and when women versus men help others may change.

their levels of agency. In a series of follow-up studies (Diekman & Goodfriend, 2006), she found that both men and women are relatively accepting of these changes. Both expect women to increasingly possess *both* traditionally "feminine" and traditionally "masculine" characteristics.

Interestingly, women in these studies (Diekman & Goodfriend, 2006) expressed displeasure that men were not equally changing to increase in their perceived levels of communion. Recall that the traditionally feminine traits—communion—refer to helping and prosocial qualities such as being friendly, unselfish, other-oriented, and cooperative. Agentic traits are relatively selfish and self-promoting. Some of the women in these studies noted that men need to make more efforts to be nurturing, care for children, and generally help family dynamics in personal ways. When it comes to helping at home, at least, dynamic gender roles are promoting a more equal distribution of tasks. Similarly, Jackson (2006) anticipates a gradual weakening of sex differences in prosocial behavior as time goes by.

Cross-Cultural Differences in Helping

Two of the "big questions" in this book are "nature versus nurture" and "how much are thoughts and behaviors influenced by culture?" Culture is one way that nurture influences our general behavioral tendencies, and prosocial behavior is no exception. Several studies have investigated how cultural norms and values influence the likelihood of people to engage in helping behaviors.

In general, studies have shown that collectivistic cultures lead to more prosocial behaviors than individualistic cultures (Barrett et al., 2004; Bontempo, Lobel, & Triandis, 1990)—but individuals in collectivistic cultures are especially likely to help people in their own group (Kemmelmeier, Jambor, & Letner, 2006). One review of studies examining 21 different nations showed that cultures focused on the good of your own group were less likely to help strangers but potentially more likely to help family members, an interesting mix of the "nature versus nurture" question regarding prosocial behaviors (Chen, Kim, Mojaverian, & Morling, 2012).

Some recent research has focused on helping in children and adolescents in different cultures. For example, one study focused on 5th- through 10th-grade students and their **prosocial moral reasoning**, or ability to analyze moral dilemmas in which two or more people's needs conflict with each other and where formal rules of what to do are absent (Carlo, Koller, Eisenberg, Da Silva, & Frohlich, 1996). These researchers hypothesized that prosocial moral reasoning might be influenced by cultural values and norms and therefore conducted a *quasi-experimental* study comparing children from two different cultures. They gave U.S. and Brazilian participants seven dilemmas such as this one:

> One day Mary was going to a friend's party. On the way, she saw a girl who had fallen down and hurt her leg. The girl asked Mary to go to the girl's house and get her parents so the parents could come and take her to a doctor. But if Mary did run and get the girl's parents, Mary would be late to the party and miss the fun and social activities with her friends. (p. 233)

After each dilemma, the children indicated what the main character should do and why. Results show that the U.S. children got higher internalized moral reasoning scores, on average, than Brazilian children—a finding that was a *replication* of other

Prosocial moral reasoning: An individual's ability to analyze moral dilemmas in which two or more people's needs conflict with each other and where formal rules are absent.

studies (e.g., Hutz, De Conti, & Vargas, 1994). The researchers suggested this difference may be due to the emphasis on critical thinking in U.S. school systems.

However, they also point out that patterns of response *regardless* of culture in the children indicated that individual participants with self-focused concerns about maximizing one's one pleasure were *negatively correlated* with helpfulness, whereas other-oriented, communal concerns were *positively correlated* with generosity and prosocial moral reasoning (Carlo et al., 1996).

Another *quasi-experimental* study compared German and Indian 19-month-old toddlers in their prosocial behavior (Kärtner, Keller, & Chaudhary, 2010). Here, researchers played with the toddlers and pretended that a teddy bear's arm broke off. Prosocial behavior from the toddlers was measured by whether they tried to comfort the researcher (by hugging, kissing, etc.) or offered a new toy to replace the bear. In both samples, about 30% of the toddlers showed prosocial behavior—the two different cultures did not show *statistically significant* results.

However, the researchers suggested that there were different motives driving helping behaviors, based on culture. When the toddlers' mothers were compared to each other across the two cultures, mothers from India emphasized relational social norms (such as obedience and helping) more than mothers from Germany. This different emphasis seemed to motivate the Indian children to help due to situational cues, while the German children seemed motivated by empathy. Thus, this study emphasized that while objective helping behaviors may look the same from the outside, motives for helping may change based on culture (Kärtner et al., 2010); they note, "there may be culture-specific developmental paths to prosocial behavior" (p. 913).

A final example of research on cross-cultural differences and similarities compared adolescents from Spain and Turkey (Kumru et al., 2012). Spain and Turkey were chosen because both are quickly moving from agricultural, patriarchal, and traditional cultures to modern and more egalitarian cultures—but Spain has moved along this continuum more quickly. As the researchers expected, the Spanish adolescents displayed higher levels of prosocial moral reasoning and prosocial behavior. Again, they suggest this may be due to different emphases in the school systems, with Spanish schools emphasizing abstract and deductive reasoning. They also noted, however, that motives for helping might change based on culture. Their data indicated that in Spanish culture, helping seemed to be motivated by gaining the approval of others. If this is true, the helping is egoistic and not truly altruistic.

The Main Ideas

- Prosocial behavior is associated with certain personality traits. Specifically, Machiavellianism (a trait associated with cynicism and manipulation of others) is negatively correlated with helping, while agreeableness (a trait associated with cooperation and empathy) is positively correlated with helping.

- While some research shows that certain types of religiosity are associated with prosocial behaviors, other studies find that situational demands (such as whether people are in a hurry) are more predictive of who is most likely to help.

- Culture encourages men to be more agentic (independent and competitive) and women to be more communal (concerned with caring for others), but both traits are associated with helping in different settings. Research has also investigated whether national culture affects the likelihood of helping and motives behind helping.

- Research in this section noted that some personality traits are associated with more prosocial behavior (such as agreeableness and being high in empathy) while others are linked to less prosocial behavior (such as Machiavellianism). If you wanted to design school activities for children that would promote agreeableness and decrease Machiavellianism, what kinds of activities would you create? What would you suggest parents could do to encourage agreeableness and discourage Machiavellianism in their children at home?

- What hypotheses do you have about whether religious people are more likely to have moral integrity versus moral hypocrisy? Can you think of people in your life who display one tendency or the other—and can you see patterns in the two types of people? Do you think one path over the other is based on life experiences, related personality traits, forms of religion, or other variables? Can you think of a way to scientifically test your hypotheses?

- Do you agree with Diekman's research participants that women are changing over time to be high in both communion and agency? And do you agree that men seem to be staying high in agency but seem not to be changing much in their levels of communion? Explain your view and provide at least two examples.

- What aspects of your national culture or particular subcultures either encourage or discourage helping of others? Does your culture encourage helping some kinds of people, or helping in some situations, more than others?

New York Daily News Archive / New York Daily News / Getty Images

Kitty Genovese, who was murdered in 1964.

WHAT CIRCUMSTANCES MAKE HELPING MORE OR LESS LIKELY?

LO 10.3: Apply psychological concepts regarding what situational variables lead to more or less helping in different settings.

The scientific study of what situations make people more or less likely to help was inspired by a grisly murder. In Queens, New York, in 1964, a young bartender named Kitty Genovese arrived home to her apartment complex around 3:00 a.m. A man chased her across the parking lot with a hunting knife and stabbed her twice. When she screamed for help, the man ran away . . . but he came back a few minutes later, stabbed her several more times, sexually assaulted her, and stole $49. He then left her in the hallway, bleeding. Overall, the attacks took place over half an hour, and Genovese died about an hour later.

Unfortunately, murders take place every day. Why was this one so special? Two weeks after Genovese's death, the *New York Times* ran a story that made her famous. The headline of the story was, "37 Who Saw Murder Didn't Call the Police" (Gansberg, 1964). According to the story, 37 people in Genovese's apartment complex either heard her screams for help or saw the attack happening, but not a single one called the police. The story claimed that one neighbor actually turned up his radio to avoid the annoying noise of

Social Psychology in Popular Culture

New York Daily News Archive / New York Daily News / Getty Images

The murder of Kitty Genovese—and the headlines about how many people witnessed it without helping or even calling the police—are infamous. Even though later investigations questioned whether it was really true that 37 people failed to help, the Genovese story has inspired not only social psychology research but also two films. Both were released in 2016; the first is called *37* (Grasten et al., 2016) and the second is called *The Witness* (Solomon, Genovese, Jacobson, & Valva, 2016).

37 is a fictional version of the famous murder in which the characters represent the types of people who might have lived in Genovese's apartment building. The film suggests a wide variety of reasons why people might not have helped. Characters experience all of the following situations (and more) that lead them to not help:

- Interpreting her cries for help as a radio program
- Not hearing the noise due to family arguments
- Mental illness leading to incorrect attributions that the cries were hallucinations
- The belief that the noises were simply children playing a prank
- Concern that the police might ask uncomfortable questions about the neighbors' personal lives

In a review of the film for the *New York Times* (2016), critic Andy Webster comments about the final scenes, "Pressure builds in a protracted sequence of sputtering lobby lights, leaky fixtures, dying dowagers, the assault itself and the hysteria of [a] young girl. Implicit is the idea that the murder embodied a neighborhood's moral decay."

The second film, *The Witness,* was the result of Genovese's brother Bill, who was only 12 years old at the time of her murder. He was able to speak with some of the former friends of his sister and with people still living in the neighborhood, as well as with his extended family. The film raises some of the same doubts as the film *37* about the accuracy of the original report. But it also explores the effect of so much public and research attention on the remaining family members.

What really happened that night is still controversial. But it is gratifying to see that the searching questions raised by this case study and the subsequent films continue to provoke deep conversations about social responsibility.

the attack. Several people used the story as an example of society's increasing apathy and callousness toward victims—a lack of prosocial behavior when it's needed most—especially in big cities like New York.

While the story about Genovese's uncaring neighbors was sensational, it was also wrong (Manning, Levine, & Collins, 2007). Later investigations showed that several people did call the police. One neighbor yelled at the attacker to leave her alone. Interviews with the rest of the neighbors revealed that while they admitted they had heard something, they had no idea it was a murder; they simply thought it was a couple arguing or a group of drunk friends. You can read more about the Kitty Genovese story in the accompanying "Social Psychology in Popular Culture" feature.

Even if the details weren't accurate, several social psychologists heard about the case and were inspired to scientifically study helping. Some people focused on general motives to help, personality traits, or culture, which you read about earlier in this chapter. Others, however, noted that regardless of family bonds, personality, culture, or any of the other variables discussed so far in this chapter, situational circumstances seem to make almost everyone more or less likely to help.

More People = Less Helping

When is helping most likely? An obvious answer might be the more people, the better! If 100 people see someone faint suddenly, aren't the chances of the person getting help 100 times better than if only one person is there to witness the problem? It turns out that the answer is no. Why not?

The Urban Overload Hypothesis.

Earlier, we discussed the social responsibility norm that everyone should help others. But we also pointed out that if you tried to help every homeless person you saw in a big city, you would quickly be out of money. There would still be hundreds of homeless people needing help—and one of them now might be you. Often, people from a rural area who visit a big city for the first time feel that the city-dwellers seem harsh, callous, and unfriendly . . . but there are psychological reasons for their behavior.

One explanation is the **urban overload hypothesis**, which points out that people in cities avoid social interactions with strangers simply because they are overwhelmed by the number of people they encounter each day (Milgram, 1970). On the way to work, someone from a city may pass hundreds of others on the street, in the subway, or in public parks. They don't have time to smile and say hi to everyone, much less help every tourist with a map and a confused look or every homeless person they see. Even highly agreeable and empathetic people would be exhausted.

Many studies have supported the urban overload hypothesis, which provides for more information about cultural differences—but this time the cultural comparison is urban versus rural cultures. For example, when researchers pretended to be bleeding and yelping in pain, about half of people in small towns stopped to help, compared with only 15% of people in large cities (Amato, 1983). Growing up in a small town and learning "small town values" doesn't seem to matter much, either; in a review of 35 studies, prosocial behavior occurred more in rural areas than in urban areas, regardless of where the witnesses grew up as children (Steblay, 1987).

Diffusion of Responsibility: The Bystander Effect.

In the years shortly after Kitty Genovese's murder, Latané and Darley didn't think that urban overload was enough to explain why crowds of people who witness emergencies fail to help. They suggested that another explanation could easily be applicable: diffusion of responsibility (Darley & Latané, 1968; Latané & Darley, 1970). Remember from Chapter 8 that diffusion of responsibility occurs when

Urban overload hypothesis: The idea that people in cities avoid social interactions with strangers simply because they are overwhelmed by the number of people they encounter each day.

REUTERS/Juan Medina

The bystander effect is the ironic tendency for people to receive less help when more people are there to witness the problem.

each person in a group feels less accountable to take action because there are other people who can do something.

Diffusion of responsibility directly explains why, ironically, you're more likely to be helped with fewer people around. Latané and Darley suggested, for example, that if Genovese's neighbors did hear the emergency and didn't do anything about it, they could easily have simply thought, "Someone else must have already called the police." It's not that people didn't care; they just assumed their help might not be needed because others might help. The finding that the likelihood of being helped in an emergency is *negatively correlated* with the number of people who witness that emergency is now known as the **bystander effect** (Darley & Latané, 1968; Latané & Darley, 1970).

The bystander effect has been found in a wide variety of settings. For example, one study showed that managers who know of fraud occurring in their organizations are more likely to report it when they alone have the relevant information (Brink, Eller, & Gan, 2015). Another study found the bystander effect in witnesses to theft (van Bommel, van Prooijen, Elffers, & Van Lange, 2014). Similarly, the number of witnesses to cyberbullying has been shown to have a negative correlation with each witness's sense of responsibility and intention to intervene (Obermaier, Fawzi, & Koch, 2016). Other research has found that less helping behavior occurs when people play multiplayer video games than when they play single-player games, both during game play and afterward (Stenico & Greitemeyer, 2015).

Social Psychology in Action: Bystander Effect

However, there seem to be boundaries around the bystander effect. For example, diffusion of responsibility seems to decrease when the specific situation requires help from multiple people instead of just one (Greitemeyer & Mügge, 2013, 2015). In addition, witnesses of a staged bike theft were more likely to stop the thief when he or she looked dangerous only when other witnesses were present; in this case, the participants may have felt that the presence of other people made it safer to confront a dangerous-looking criminal (Fischer & Greitemeyer, 2013). People are also more likely to help (despite other witnesses being present) if they know a security camera is filming them (van Bommel et al., 2014).

Finally, in a *field study* conducted in bars throughout Amsterdam, researchers purposely dropped items to see who would help pick them up. Results showed that the size of the bar's crowd had no influence on helping (a lack of the traditional bystander effect). However, the amount of alcohol consumed before the help was needed did influence how quickly help was offered: Drunker people helped faster (van Bommel, van Prooijen, Elffers, & Van Lange, 2016).

We Help People We Like (and Who Are Similar to Us)

You're probably not shocked by this news: We're more likely to help people we like. Obviously, you'll be more inclined to make sacrifices for people who are friends or family. The more interesting news might be that we're also more likely to help people we *assume* we would like, even when they are complete strangers. How do we decide how likeable we think they might be? One answer is that we assume we'd like people who are similar to ourselves.

You already know that we tend to spend time with our ingroups, which leads to stereotypes about outgroups (see Chapter 9). It follows that we're also more likely to help people we think are members of our ingroups (Dovidio & Morris, 1975). An early study done in 1970 on a Midwestern university campus showed this tendency with a very simple procedure. *Confederates* of the study dressed in either conservative or "hip/

Bystander effect: A phenomenon in which the likelihood of being helped in an emergency is negatively correlated with the number of people who witness that emergency.

counterculture" clothes (remember, this was the time of hippies!) and walked around campus asking other students for some spare change to make a phone call. When the confederate asked for help from someone wearing the same type of clothes, about two thirds of them helped, compared with less than half when they approached someone dressed differently (Emswiller, Deaux, & Willits, 1971).

Anyone familiar with international soccer ("football" to everyone except people living in the United States) knows that team loyalty and rivalries are extremely important—but are they so important they might mean you don't help someone who favors a different team? In 2005, a research group (Levine, Prosser, Evans, & Reicher, 2005) tested this question with participants who were fans of the Manchester United team in England. Each participant seemingly happened upon a person (a *confederate* of the researchers) who was jogging along but then slipped and appeared to be hurt. The jogger was wearing a jersey that was either (1) a blank, generic sports jersey; (2) one supporting Manchester United; or (3) one supporting Liverpool, which is Manchester United's rival team.

The results can be seen in Table 10.4 in the "Study 1" rows. The confederate was much more likely to be helped if he was wearing a shirt indicating at least one similarity to the participant. In this case, only one participant failed to help a fellow fan of the team. In contrast, people wearing a plain jersey or a rival team's jersey were helped by only about one third of the participants.

But a closer look at Table 10.4 shows that there was a second study—and this time, helping behaviors for the confederate wearing a Liverpool jersey showed the opposite effect! How did the researchers get the Manchester United fans to help someone supposedly supporting their rival team? This time, before the participants came across the hurt jogger, they filled out a survey focusing on how all soccer fans have good qualities and on what all these fans have in common, regardless of team alliance. While Study 1 participants might have thought of a Liverpool fan as a rival, Study 2 participants were primed to think about how similar *all* soccer fans are to each other—and this perception of similarity switched their behavior toward helping.

Latané and Darley's Five-Step Model of Helping

What can we conclude about when people are most likely to help? To examine that question, let's return to the work of Latané and Darley. These two researchers conducted a long series of creative and informative studies about when people will (or won't) help in emergencies. As a result, they were able to create a five-step model predicting the specific circumstances that lead to prosocial engagement. A summary of their model

■ TABLE 10.4 Team Loyalty of Manchester United Fans

	Type of Jersey		
	Manchester United	Plain	Liverpool
Study 1 Not helped Helped	1 12	8 4	7 3
Study 2 Not helped Helped	2 8	7 2	3 7

SOURCE: Levine et al. (2005). Copyright by SAGE Publishing.

(Latané & Darley, 1970) is shown in Figure 10.2.

People are more likely to help if the answer is "yes" to each of the following five questions:

Step 1: Notice the Event.
Of course, to help, you must first realize that help is needed. People might fail to help simply because they were distracted or weren't paying attention, especially if they were in a hurry (which might be one explanation for the findings of the "Good Samaritan" study described earlier).

Step 2: Interpret the Event as an Emergency.
When Kitty Genovese's neighbors heard noises at 3:00 a.m. outside their apartment complex, they probably didn't immediately assume someone was being attacked. Instead, some reported that they simply thought it was a romantic couple having a fight or drunk friends returning from a night on the town. We're only able to help when we interpret the situation as one in which help is needed.

One reason we might *not* interpret an emergency as what it really is could be pluralistic ignorance. In Chapter 8, we reviewed pluralistic ignorance as a reason not to speak up with a minority opinion in a group—you think you're the only person who thinks that way. In situations that might be interpreted as emergencies, we often look around to see if other people are reacting the same way we are. If they don't appear to be worried, we tell ourselves that everything must be okay after all.

Latané and Darley (1970) demonstrated this when they put participants in a room to complete a survey—then slowly filled the room with smoke. When participants were alone in the room, 75% of them quickly got up to report what was happening. But when three participants were in the room—real participants, not confederates—only 38% of the three-person groups had someone report the smoke within the first 6 minutes of the procedure. In over half of the groups, all three participants sat quietly, even when the smoke was so thick they couldn't see what they were writing on their surveys. Apparently, these participants felt that if the other two people didn't think there was a problem, then they didn't want to look like a fool or a troublemaker.

Step 3: Take Responsibility.
We already know that prosocial behaviors like helping will increase when people feel responsible. This is more likely to be the case when they are alone and no diffusion of responsibility can take place. It also seems to be the case when they feel compelled to help others who are, at least on the surface, similar to them and therefore potentially a member of their ingroup. Emergency training (such as CPR classes) often emphasizes increasing responsibility by instructing people to point to a single person in the room and say, "You! Call 911!" Due to diffusion of responsibility, this will lead to much faster responding than simply yelling, "Someone call 911!"

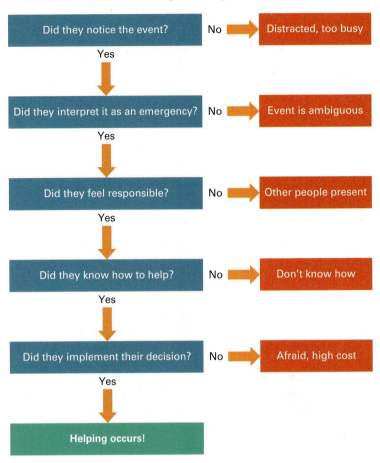

■ FIGURE 10.2 Latané and Darley's five-step model of helping.

SOURCE: Latané & Darley (1970).

Step 4: Knowing How to Help. Even if we know an emergency is happening and we want to help, we might not be able to do so. Perhaps someone is trapped under something so heavy, we can't lift it; perhaps someone needs a car mechanic and we've never learned those particular skills. Even the most empathetic, agreeable person won't be able to help in every situation.

Step 5: Implementing the Decision to Help. Finally, we must decide to actually engage in a helping behavior. We might choose not to do this if we perceive that the costs outweigh the potential benefits. For example, earlier we noted that women may hesitate to help a stranded motorist on a rural road due to fears of being assaulted. When I [Wind] was in high school, a rumor circulated that if you saw another car at night without its headlights on, you shouldn't flash your own lights to help the other driver. Why not? I was told that certain "dangerous gangs" had decided to drive without lights on purpose and murder the first person who flashed at them. (This was unlikely in the middle of Iowa in the 1980s, but it was troubling enough to keep me from helping by flashing my lights.)

Sometimes, these fears may be justified. Ted Bundy, the famous serial killer, used to pretend to be injured until a young woman offered to help—and then he would choose her to be his next victim (Byrne & Pease, 2003). Intervening can cost lives—just as the White Helmets introduced at the beginning of this chapter can tell you from personal experience. When they decide to help victims of a war by purposely going into an area with terrorists, bombs, and guns, they implement their decision knowing the risk might be high. Of course, first responders, such as police, firefighters, and EMTs, risk their lives every day to help others in emergencies.

The Main Ideas

- Ironically, helping is less likely when more people are present. This effect can be due to urban overload or to diffusion of responsibility.

- We are more likely to help people we like and people who are (or appear to be) similar to ourselves.

- Latané and Darley proposed that helping will only occur when five steps are all in place. To help, a person must notice the situation, interpret it as an emergency, feel responsible, know how to help, and implement the decision.

⚡ CRITICAL THINKING CHALLENGE

- Imagine that you find yourself in a big city, in need of help. Explain four specific ways that you could increase the chances of getting the help you need, based on concepts from this chapter.

- Do you think that the "five steps" toward helping outlined in this section are comprehensive? In other words, what steps might be missing from this model? When you are considering whether to help someone else, are there other circumstances or decisions that you make beyond the five identified here?

- This chapter discussed (1) general helping motives, (2) how different kinds of people are more likely to help than others, and (3) situational circumstances that lead to more or less helping. Consider all three factors and determine how important you think each one is, relative to the others, in terms of how much it influences helping. If you had 100 "points" that you could assign to these three factors, with more points indicating a stronger influence, how would you distribute those points?

What motivates people to help others, in general?

Prosocial behavior is the general term for helping others. Social psychology differentiates between pure altruism, which is helping purely out of selfless concerns, versus egoistic altruism, which is helping that leads to some kind of personal benefit. There are four major theoretical explanations for why people engage in prosocial behaviors; the first three are all considered egoistic explanations, while only the last idea is considered a pure altruistic explanation.

The first theoretical explanation for helping is that prosocial behaviors evolved as a way for individuals to promote their own genes in future generations. Kinship selection shows that helping goes up with people who share more of our genes, such as immediate family members. However, we also help people in our community when prosocial behaviors strengthen the entire group. This kind of exchange system has been shown in several species.

Social norms also promote helping; two examples are belief in a just world and the social responsibility norm, or the idea that each individual has a duty to improve the world by helping those in need. The third explanation for egoistic helping is called the negative state relief model. This model suggests that we help to avoid feeling guilt or other negative emotions we might experience if we fail to help.

The true altruism explanation for helping is encompassed in the final explanation, called the empathy-altruism hypothesis. Here, research shows that we can help due to purely empathetic or compassionate motives if we (1) feel empathy, (2) are capable of helping, (3) perceive that our help will actually benefit the other person, and (4) perceive that we are the best person who can help at that moment.

Why do some people help more than others?

This section of the book considered four variables that might have an influence on whether individuals are more or less likely to display prosocial, helping behaviors. The first variable was personality. Several traits have been linked to prosocial behaviors; Machiavellianism is negatively correlated to helping, while agreeableness is positively correlated to helping.

A second variable is religious norms. People motivated by intrinsic religiosity seem to help due to personal needs (egoistic helping), while people motivated by religion as quest seem to help out of empathy to the victim (altruistic helping). A classic study called the "Good Samaritan experiment" showed that priming religion and helping did not seem to have a significant effect on helping in participants but that manipulating the situation in terms of urgency did. Participants who were in a hurry due to feeling urgency on another task were less likely to help someone in need.

Gender has also been examined in terms of prosocial behaviors. Stereotypically masculine traits, called agentic traits, are more self-focused such as being competitive or aggressive. In contrast, stereotypically feminine traits, called communal traits, are more prosocial such as being nurturing and kind to others. Several studies have shown that girls and women are more likely to help than men, but the situation also matters; men are more likely to help when physical strength is needed or when physical danger is a potential outcome of helping. Research shows that over time, however, these gender differences are decreasing.

Finally, research on national culture has also explored differences in helping behaviors. Several studies show that while objective likelihood of helping may not differ across cultures, motives behind that helping may change. For example, people in collectivistic cultures are more likely to help family members, but they are less likely to help strangers.

What circumstances make helping more or less likely?

A famous case study of people supposedly not helping is the Kitty Genovese story, in which a young woman was stabbed to death outside her apartment complex in New York. Newspaper stories reported that up to 37 people heard her cries for help and failed to help. While more recent reports have questioned the validity of these claims, Genovese's case inspired several years of research on situational effects and how circumstances might make helping behaviors more or less likely.

One well-replicated finding is that ironically, we are less likely to be helped when there are multiple people present. One explanation for this finding in big cities is the urban overload hypothesis, which points out that people in cities avoid strangers simply because they are overwhelmed with the number of people they encounter every day. It would be impossible to help every homeless person in a city, for example. Another explanation is diffusion of responsibility. If multiple people can see that someone is in need of help, each person's personal feeling of responsibility will go down. They can think, "I don't need to help because all of these other people can do it." The decrease in helping with an increase in witnesses to an emergency is sometimes called the bystander effect.

Other research shows that we are more likely to help when we like the person who needs it or when we simply perceive that they are similar to us (and therefore we might be more likely to like them). However, our perceptions of whether others are members of our ingroups (and therefore similar to us) can be manipulated, such as pointing out that they are fans of a different sports team (manipulation of differences) versus pointing out that both people are sports fans in general (manipulation of similarity).

Finally, Latané and Darley created a five-step model to explain the process that needs to occur in order for people to help. They suggest that for anyone to help in a given situation, that person must (1) notice the event, (2) interpret the event as an emergency, (3) take responsibility, (4) know how to help, and (5) implement the decision to help.

- Reciprocal altruism
- Kinship selection

- Hamilton's inequality
- Social responsibility norm

- Negative state relief model
- Empathy-altruism hypothesis
- Big 5 model of personality
- Religious norms and religiosity

- Gender socialization
- Urban overload hypothesis
- Bystander effect
- Latané and Darley model of prosocial engagement

CRITICAL THINKING, ANALYSIS, AND APPLICATION

Identify three specific examples of people making significant sacrifices to help others (at least one of your examples should be nonfiction). For each example, analyze the person's motives for helping based on the four theoretical explanations from the first section of this chapter (promoting our own genes, social norms, avoiding negative emotions, and pure altruism).

- Think about the different circumstances in which people are more likely to help—and tie each into one of the helping motives. Are these circumstances going to lead to egoistic or altruistic helping behaviors?

- Levine et al. (2005) showed that priming people to think about how all soccer fans are good people led participants to help fans of a rival team. How could this simple procedure be used in the real world, to motivate individuals to help those in need such as refugees from other countries?

- As technology advances and travel to other parts of the world becomes easier, do you think that views of other countries and cultures will change as well? How will these advances in technology influence the likelihood of helping people from other cultures? For example, will citizens of other countries still be considered part of an outgroup, or will the emphasis on being a "global citizen" change how we view others and whether we're likely to help them?

PERSONAL REFLECTION

Just like in a movie, one time I was on an airplane about to take off when a flight attendant used the speaker system to ask, "Is there a doctor on the airplane? If so, please push your call button now. Another passenger needs your help." In this situation, I immediately thought of Latané and Darley's five-step model for emergencies. Step 1 was a yes; everyone on the plane noticed the situation after the announcement. Step 2 was also a yes; we all interpreted the situation as an emergency—we knew the flight attendant wouldn't have worried us over something small. For me personally, Steps 3 and 4 were more problematic. I would have been happy to take responsibility to help (Step 3) because I assumed there weren't very many doctors on the flight; it was a fairly small airplane. However, Step 4 is what really got me. While I was, technically, a doctor, I knew of course that the flight attendant wanted a medical doctor, not someone with a PhD in psychology. I knew that in this situation, I didn't know *how* to help—so I sat quietly and did nothing. Fortunately, there was a medical doctor on the plane who quickly assessed the passenger who needed help. It turned out that the passenger had simply passed out from being extremely drunk—so drunk that his heart had slowed to a very low rate. Luckily, there was someone else on the plane who could answer "yes" to all five steps toward helping. [WG]

Visit **edge.sagepub.com/heinzen** to help you accomplish your coursework goals in an easy-to-use learning environment.

- **Visual Key Concepts**
- Mobile-friendly **eFlashcards**
- Mobile-friendly practice **quizzes**
- **Video** and **multimedia content**
- EXCLUSIVE! Access to full-text **SAGE journal articles**

$SAGE edge™

PRACTICE AND APPLY WHAT YOU'VE LEARNED

▶ edge.sagepub.com/heinzen

HEAD TO THE STUDY SITE WHERE YOU'LL FIND

- **Visual Key Concepts to make core material more memorable**

- **eFlashcards to strengthen your understanding of key terms**

- **Practice quizzes to test your comprehension of key concepts**

- **Videos and multimedia content to enhance your exploration of key topics**

Apply psychological concepts regarding what situational variables **lead to more or less helping** in **different settings**.

urban overload hypothesis   322

bystander effect   323

Get a tour of **ALL Visual Key Concepts** and their definitions at **edge.sagepub.com/heinzen**

11 Aggression

1. What does it mean to be "aggressive"?

2. Is aggression explained by biological instincts?

3. Is aggression explained by cultural influences?

4. Is aggression explained by situational influences?

5. How can we manage or reduce aggression?

11.1 To explain typologies that define and organize different forms of aggression and apply them to aggression in humans over time.

11.2 To analyze biological and evolutionary explanations for aggression.

11.3 To analyze cultural explanations for aggression.

11.4 To analyze situational explanations for aggression.

11.5 To compare and contrast ideas for decreasing aggression in social situations.

Humans have become efficient killers.

At the Battle of Gettysburg in 1863, it required 3 days to kill approximately 8,000 Union and Confederate soldiers; the deaths occurred in hand-to-hand combat or from gun blasts at close range. On the first day of the Battle of the Somme in 1916, it required only 1 day to kill approximately 19,000 British soldiers; most died from machine guns positioned about 200 hundred yards (185 m) away. Near the end of World War II in 1945, it required less than 1 second to vaporize approximately 75,000 Japanese soldiers and civilians; the *Enola Gay* was flying approximately 5 miles above the Earth when it dropped the atomic bomb named *Little Boy* on the city of Hiroshima (see Figure 11.1).

The stakes could not be any higher as we turn to social psychology for explanations and answers to the frequency, intensity, and duration of human aggression. The short-term tactics and weapons used by ancient warriors versus modern-day humans may differ—and aggression happens every day outside of war zones. But the underlying psychology of aggression appears to be the same. Social psychological explanations unite with other disciplines to provide insight into the origins of aggression and how to manage our own aggressive impulses. Understanding aggression can help us decrease harmful—and too often deadly—conflicts.

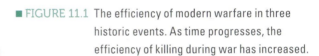

■ FIGURE 11.1 The efficiency of modern warfare in three historic events. As time progresses, the efficiency of killing during war has increased.

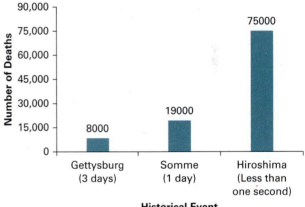

WHAT DOES IT MEAN TO BE "AGGRESSIVE"?

LO 11.1: To explain typologies that define and organize different forms of aggression and apply them to aggression in humans over time.

Aggression is behavior intended to harm others who do not wish to be harmed. Our focus on the *intention to harm* allows us to include nonviolent forms of aggression such as backstabbing office politics (Neuman & Baron, 2011) and the interpersonal aggression portrayed in acts like bullying. Social psychologists generally do not

Aggression: Behavior intended to harm others who do not wish to be harmed.

Aggression can be hard to define. Is it aggression when two boxers hit each other, even though both have consented to the activity and neither really wishes to cause permanent damage?

consider it aggression to honestly earn or win a promotion, a mating partner, or sporting contest; in those contexts, confidence and competition are expected. But we do consider it aggression to take credit for someone else's efforts, gossip about a romantic rival, or use unnecessary roughness to defeat an opponent during an athletic competition.

Deciding exactly what kind of behaviors qualify as aggression can be subjective. Consider these examples and analyze whether you think they are aggression:

- A group of people who feel oppressed by the government holds a protest.
- A woman who doesn't like rabbits in her yard shoots them.
- A relationship partner who is annoyed that the other person never does the dishes decides to purposely leave dirty dishes all over as a "signal."
- One roommate steals from another.
- A group of people who disagree with their government's policies forms a militia and begins fighting using guerilla tactics, hoping to cause a revolution.
- A sports fan paints his or her face and loudly yells at both teams during a match or game.
- An employee who doesn't like his boss secretly hides dead fish in the ceiling to cause a terrible smell.

There are so many forms of aggression, and they can be so hard to specifically define that our first step is to organize them into categories. That helps us discover what, if anything, these different types of aggression have in common.

Typologies Help Define Aggression

We harm one another in so many different ways that we need to use **typologies** just to organize the complex list into categories. Typologies are categorical systems that help us think more clearly about complex but related events. The first typology is descriptive; the second is motivational. The third discusses a specific form of aggression and divides it into categories.

A Descriptive Typology. Table 11.1 presents a descriptive typology (adapted from Buss, 1961, p. 8) that helps us understand how (but not why) people become aggressive. The typology subdivides aggression according to three categories: (1) physical or verbal,

Typologies: Categorical systems that help individuals think more clearly about complex but related events.

■ TABLE 11.1 Buss's Typology of Eight Different Forms of Aggression

| | Direct | | Indirect | |
	Active	Passive	Active	Passive
Physical aggression	Hitting, stabbing, beating, etc.	Positioning your car to prevent someone else from changing lanes	Cheating in a competition or hiring a "hitman"	Refusing to stop the bleeding of an enemy soldier
Verbal aggression	Putdowns and insults	Giving someone the silent treatment to punish that person	Spreading mean rumors or negative gossip	Failing to defend someone who you know is being accused unfairly

SOURCE: Adapted from Buss (1971).

(2) direct or indirect, and (3) active or passive. It will help your understanding to create examples from your own life that fit into each category.

Real-life aggression often blurs the lines between the categories. For example, I [Tom] witnessed a nursery school conflict when one child, denied a toy by the other, called him "a big poopie-head!" and then ran to his friends to giggle with them over how clever he had been. The name-calling was direct, active, verbal aggression. Getting other children to join in the putdowns was also active and verbal, but it was more indirect because he used others to make the first child feel bad. The descriptive typology helps us understand *how* humans are aggressive.

A Motivational Typology. Another typology focuses on what motivates aggression. **Hostile/reactive aggression** is an emotion-based reaction to perceived threats. In contrast, **instrumental/proactive aggression** is a thoughtful or reason-based decision to harm others to gain resources such as territory, money, self-esteem, or social status (see Berkowitz, 1989; Dodge, Lochman, Bates, & Pettit, 1997; Feshbach, 1964).

Bushman and Anderson (2001) think of hostile and instrumental aggression as a continuum anchored at one end by our brain's automatic impulses (hostile aggression) and at the other by reasoned, purposeful responses (instrumental aggression). For example, you may go into an automatic rage when you first learn of your lover's infidelity. However, those emotions can mature into a calculated plot to win back your lover, harm your rival, or regain your self-esteem. A motivational typology helps us understand *why* people are aggressive (see more in the next section of this chapter).

Microaggressions. A relatively new—and somewhat controversial—conceptualization of aggression has been one that includes **microaggressions**, which have been defined as brief and "everyday" types of "verbal, behavioral, and environmental indignities . . . that communicate hostile, derogatory, or negative slights and insults" (Sue, 2010, p. 5). Often microaggressions are said to be motivated by prejudice that the aggressor may have on either an explicit or implicit level (racism, homophobia, transphobia, etc.).

Microaggressions are thus considered examples of subtle or covert prejudice and discrimination by some researchers (Wang, Leu, & Shoda, 2011). Examples might be asking an Asian American if he or she were born in the United States, holding more tightly to a purse when a person of color gets in an elevator, or telling women in college that they might not be suited for majors in the sciences, math, or technology.

Like the typologies you've already seen in this chapter, a typology of three forms of microaggressions was developed by Sue and his colleagues (Sue, 2010; Sue et al., 2007):

- Microinsults: Rude statements that demean someone's heritage (e.g., asking Latinx students if they are legal citizens; refusing to sit next to someone wearing a headscarf on an airplane)
- Microassaults: Overt behaviors meant to psychologically harm someone (e.g., calling someone by a racial slur; spray-painting hate symbols such as a swastika on their property)
- Microinvalidations: Statements or behaviors that invalidate the target's feelings on an individual or group level (e.g., telling a person of color that you don't "see color"; telling a transgender person that he or she needs therapy)

The Persistence of Aggression Over Time

If you were hoping that psychology might somehow cure the human impulse to be aggressive, then you are going to be disappointed. That's not likely to be a winning

Hostile/reactive aggression: An impulsive, emotion-based reaction to perceived threats.

Instrumental/proactive aggression: A thoughtful, reason-based decision to harm others in order to gain resources such as territory, money, self-esteem, or social status.

Microaggressions: Statements or behaviors that subtly insult a marginalized group by expressing an aggressor's prejudice and discrimination, with or without their conscious intent to do so. Microaggressions include microinsults, microassaults, and microinvalidations.

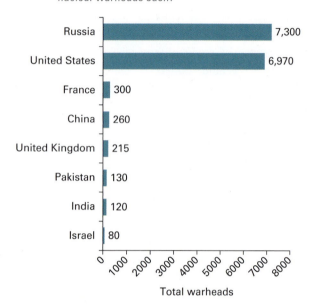

SOURCE: Created using data from Chuck (2016).

strategy because aggression has always been a part of the human story—and that's not to change any time soon. Archeologists, for example, have found large collections of stone axe heads at sites occupied by our ancestors. It seems likely that primitive people stockpiled these axe heads to use as weapons (Clarkson, 2010). Evolutionary psychology asserts that we inherited their primal anxieties—and still stockpile weapons. This instinctive anxiety may explain why Russia and the United States continue to maintain nuclear arsenals when just one nuclear device is more than enough to make your point (see Figure 11.2).

In 1991, two hikers stumbled over more evidence that aggression has always been part of the human story. They were hiking in the Italian Alps when they made "one of the most sensational archeological discoveries ever" (Baroni & Orombelli, 1996). They found an almost perfectly preserved 5,300-year-old skeleton of a man who came to be known as the "Iceman." He died with a dagger in his right hand, the preserved blood of two other people on his body, a bow and quiver with 14 arrows by his side—and a 1-inch arrowhead that had entered through his back (see Buss, 2005). Buss and Duntley (2006) also described the discovery of 59 skeletons in an Egyptian cemetery, estimated to be 12,000 to 14,000 years old. Almost half the skeletons had embedded stone projectiles and other features indicating violent deaths, particularly of the male victims. Human-to-human aggression stretches as far back in time as our historical indicators allow us to see.

The persistence of aggression over millennia is also vividly reported in books that many revere as holy. The Bible, for example, is full of violent commandments to sacrifice, knife, stone, and burn people. These "histories" recommend or warn about plucking out eyes and cutting off various body parts (see, e.g., Genesis 22, Deuteronomy 22, and Matthew 5). Buss (2005) asks us to consider the strange instructions in Judges 21:11 as one example: "You shall utterly destroy every male, and every woman that has lain with a man." The soldiers' reward for such violence is in the next verse; they rounded up "400 young virgins" and brought them back to their camp.

The Escalation of Aggression: Stages of Provocation

Let's face it. We humans are stuck living with our primal but increasingly destructive aggressive tendencies. So, is there anything we can do to at least keep them in check? One promising approach is to first recognize and then prevent the **escalation of aggression effect**, an upward spiral of increasingly aggressive exchanges from which the antagonists are seemingly unable to free themselves (Goldstein, Davis, & Herman, 1975). For example, based on film footage, Russell (2008) observed that fights between sports fans often have "exceedingly trivial beginnings . . . a stare, or perhaps a gesture" (p. 19). Zillmann's (1994) three **stages of provocation model** (see Table 11.2)

Escalation of aggression effect: The tendency for aggression between individuals to spiral into increasingly more aggressive exchanges from which the antagonists are seemingly unable to free themselves.

Stages of provocation model: A model for understanding aggression within which an individual's thoughts, feelings, and behaviors collectively contribute to the escalation of aggression in three stages.

	Stage 1	Stage 2	Stage 3
Cognitive	Irritated, but capable of good judgment	Angry thoughts and less empathic	Biased conclusions, no empathy, with illusions of power
Emotional arousal	Low to moderate	Moderate to high	Extremely high
Behavioral	Cautiously assertive with self-control	Strongly assertive, unyielding, hostile	Impulsive, explosive, and irresponsible

SOURCE: Adapted from Zilmann (1994).

describes how thoughts (cognition), feelings, and behaviors collectively contribute to the escalation of aggression.

In Stage 1, provocation doesn't lead to particularly aggressive responses. Our cognitive response is annoyance. In Stage 2, we experience angrier thoughts and become mildly physiologically and emotionally aroused. Perhaps our heart beats a bit faster with mild anger. We may become more assertive in our verbal interaction. By Stage 3, our thoughts are clouded by biased perceptions and overreactions. Our physiological and emotional response is to feel the surge of adrenaline and rage. Our behavioral response in Stage 3 is one of explosive physical or verbal attack with the intention to harm the person who "started it" or "deserves to be taught a lesson" (convenient things we can tell ourselves to justify our aggression).

Notice the escalation of aggression in the Robber's Cave experiment (Sherif, Harvey, White, Hood, & Sherif, 1961) described in Chapter 9. In just 2 weeks, two groups of 11-year-old boys escalated from competition in baseball and tug-of-war to marked territories, mud-smeared faces, stockpiles of stones, and potentially lethal weapons (rocks in socks). But in the third week of summer camp, a few strategic interventions based on superordinate goals deescalated the aggression. The boys all returned home with, apparently, mostly happy memories of their summer camp experience.

The Big Picture of Worldwide Aggression

Here's a surprise. There has been a persistent, long-term decline in worldwide violence. Do you find that hard to believe? Our impressions of the present are biased by the vividness of instant communications, high-resolution digital photos, and the ability to see modern conflicts on live television. This chapter even primed the idea of increasing violence with how we started (such as the escalation shown in Figure 11.1).

However, Pinker's (2011) book *The Better Angels of Our Nature: Why Violence Has Declined* offers hope. His research into worldwide violence rates argues that, over time, humans have become more intelligent—and with increased intelligence comes a decreased need for violent aggression (see Figure 11.3). So, although we have become far more *efficient* at killing one another, our *actual* killing of one another through homicides, genocide, wars, terrorism, and the like has been decreasing.

Think about aggression at a personal level: Do you tend to have aggressive responses to others? One way to answer this question is to complete the scale in the Applying Social Psychology to Your Life feature. The next few sections of this chapter discuss different explanations for why we are aggressive—but the final section discusses how we might continue to manage and decrease violent behaviors.

Ask the Experts: Anthony Ellis on Violence and Society

©SAGE Publications

MEASURING AGGRESSIVE TENDENCIES

Applying Social Psychology to Your Life

Instructions: Do you tend to be a more aggressive person, in general? Next to each item, write a number indicating whether the item describes how you see yourself, using this scale:

1	2	3	4	5
Extremely uncharacteristic of me				Extremely characteristic of me

____ 1. Once in a while I can't control the urge to strike another person.

____ 2. Given enough provocation, I may hit another person.

____ 3. If somebody hits me, I hit back.

____ 4. I get into fights a little more than the average person.

____ 5. If I have to resort to violence to protect my rights, I will.

____ 6. There are people who pushed me so far that we came to blows.

____ 7. I can think of no good reason for ever hitting a person.

____ 8. I have threatened people I know.

____ 9. I have become so mad that I have broken things.

____ 10. I tell my friends openly when I disagree with them.

____ 11. I often find myself disagreeing with people.

____ 12. When people annoy me, I may tell them what I think of them.

____ 13. I can't help getting into arguments when people disagree with me.

____ 14. My friends say that I'm somewhat argumentative.

____ 15. I flare up quickly but get over it quickly.

____ 16. When frustrated, I let my irritation show.

____ 17. I sometimes feel like a powder keg ready to explode.

____ 18. I'm an even-tempered person.

____ 19. Some of my friends think I'm a hothead.

____ 20. Sometimes I fly off the handle for no good reason.

____ 21. I have trouble controlling my temper.

____ 22. I am sometimes eaten up with jealousy.

____ 23. At times I feel I have gotten a raw deal out of life.

____ 24. Other people always seem to get the breaks.

____ 25. I wonder why sometimes I feel so bitter about things.

____ 26. I know that "friends" talk about me behind my back.

____ 27. I am suspicious of overly friendly strangers.

____ 28. I sometimes feel that people are laughing at me behind my back.

____ 29. When people are especially nice, I wonder what they want.

Scoring: First, reverse-score Items 7 and 18.

Then, add up your scores for the subscales here:

- Physical Aggression: Items 1–9 (possible range is 9–45)
- Verbal Aggression: Items 10–14 (possible range is 5–25)
- Anger: Items 15–21 (possible range is 7–35)
- Hostility: Items 22–29 (possible range is 8–40)

Higher numbers indicate more aggressive tendencies in each category.

Source: Buss, A. H., & Perry, M. (1992). The aggression questionnaire. *Journal of Personality and Social Psychology, 63*(3), 452-459.

Homicide rates in five Western European regions, 1300–2010. Homicides have dramatically decreased around the world over the past several centuries. Are humans becoming less aggressive as technology and education increase?

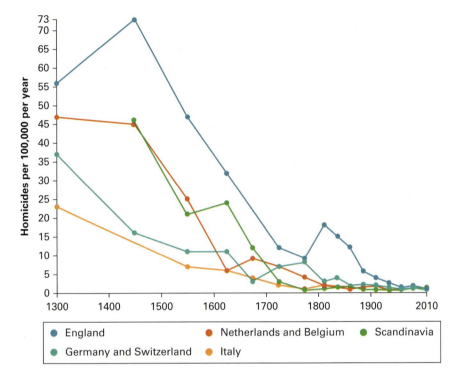

SOURCE: Roser (2017). CC-SA-4.0.

Author and psychologist Steven Pinker is well known for his hypotheses regarding the ebb and flow of violence within societies over time.

The Main Ideas

- Aggression can be defined and categorized using typologies. One typology (Buss) breaks it down into (1) physical or verbal, (2) direct or indirect, and (3) active or passive aggression. Another distinguishes between hostile/reactive aggression (an emotion-based reaction to perceived threats) and instrumental/proactive aggression (a thought-based plan to harm others to gain resources).

- Microaggressions can also be categorized as insults, assaults, or invalidations.

(Continued)

- The escalation of aggression effect is an upward spiral of increasingly aggressive thoughts and/or actions; it can be broken into three stages that progress toward more extreme reactions.

- While humans have become more efficient in killing over time, historical data indicate that interpersonal human aggression has decreased overall in the past several centuries; this may be due to increased intelligence.

⚡ CRITICAL THINKING

- Educators are increasingly concerned about cyberbullying in children. Cyberbullying occurs when aggression takes place through social media (such as mean messages posted to Facebook), email, Snapchat, or other online venues. When you consider this type of aggression, which category in Buss's typology would you say applies, and why?

- Many proponents of gun ownership in the United States believe that stockpiling guns (or other weapons) is the only way to ensure their personal safety in case of attack. Do you agree or disagree with their view, and why? Does simply owning an "arsenal" of weapons count as a form of aggression? Explain your answer.

- In Pinker's book, he argues that in humans, aggression is negatively correlated with intelligence, education, and reasoned thought. Based on your own knowledge of history, do you agree or disagree, and why? Also consider this question on an individual level—do you see this trend in certain individual people?

IS AGGRESSION EXPLAINED BY BIOLOGICAL INSTINCTS?

LO 11.2: To analyze biological and evolutionary explanations for aggression.

Some of our favorite animals appear to display instinctive aggression; even little dogs like Chihuahuas will automatically bark and bare their teeth at strangers. Have they been abused (a "nurture" explanation) or are these dogs instinctively aggressive (a "nature" explanation)? Part of evolutionary psychology's explanation for human aggression is simple: genetic determinism. It's an automatic behavior; the Chihuahua has to bark.

Genetic Determinism

Notice how basketball player Charles Barkley reacted when a local man named Jorge Lugo tossed some ice cubes at him in a bar (see Griskevicius et al., 2009). Barkley could have reasoned, "The guy's a jerk. It's just water. Walk away." It appears, however, that Barkley's automatic, instinctive response got to his behavior before his reasoning powers could slow him down: Barkley tossed Lugo through a plate glass window. On the other hand, did Barkley even have a choice? Was he

Dog breeds like pit bulls are known for aggression, but do they deserve this reputation?

overwhelmed by impulses that he could not control? **Genetic determinism** proposes that a gene's influence alone determines behavioral outcomes—a biological fate.

Genetic determinism is a compelling force. Monarch butterflies, for example, are genetically directed to fly to the same place in Mexico that their ancestors occupied. It takes four (short) generations to complete the annual journey, but each generation somehow knows where to go and what to do next. In humans, genetic determinism compels some people to have brown eyes, go bald in their 30s, or have Down syndrome.

But did genetic determinism compel Barkley to throw Lugo through a window? For Barkley's bar fight, walking away would have (a) insulted his sense of male honor and (b) required *publicly* backing down. Perhaps he reasoned that to avoid future conflict, he had to take care of this threat now. Barkley later reached an out-of-court settlement and paid a fine. A light sentence for a wealthy person, but society didn't let him off the hook entirely.

Another part of evolutionary psychology's approach to aggression has an equally simple explanation: It works. People who automatically respond with aggression tend to gain resources that improve their reproductive opportunities. As we have observed in previous chapters, boiling human behavior down to either genes (nature) or environment (nurture) is too simplistic. Barkley's story, for example, is more complicated than genetic determinism.

Status and Mating Motives

Griskevicius's research team (Griskevicius et al., 2009) discovered that for most men, status and mating motives increase direct (face-to-face) aggression—but only when they know that other men are watching. For women, status and mating motives increase *in*direct aggression (social exclusion). They found the same pattern (see Figure 11.4) when they asked male and female college students about the frequency and types of aggression over their entire lives: Men favored direct aggression; women favored indirect aggression. Both men and women seem to benefit when aggression raises their social status in ways that create better opportunities for mating.

The "be the biggest bully" strategy makes some evolutionary sense in a bar fight, but what about more "polite" company? Well, this is embarrassing to reveal in a psychology textbook, but bullying can occur even in psychology graduate programs (see Yamada, Cappadocia, & Pepler, 2014). Some professors' drive for status, recognition, and money lead them to abuse their graduate students. (Ask your psychology professor for stories—most of us have them.) We like to think of academic institutions as places of teamwork and scholarly collaboration—and that's what many graduate students get to experience. But even professors motivated to understand human behavior can ironically become examples of the worst kinds of the very behavior they are studying. Sometimes, relatively polite expressions by professors are forms of aggression that can lead to the rewards of higher status. In short, aggression and bullying seem to occur in a very wide variety of social situations and settings, perhaps because they lead to higher status, more resources, and better survival and reproduction rates.

Tossing people through windows is a form of direct, physical aggression. Bullying graduate students is a form of either direct or

Genghis Khan (1167–1227), the famous historical empire builder, stated, "The greatest pleasure is to vanquish your enemies, to chase them before you, to rob them of their wealth, to see their near and dear bathed in tears, to ride their horses and sleep on the white bellies of their wives and daughters."

Genetic determinism: The idea that genetic influence alone determines behavioral outcomes.

■ FIGURE 11.4 Lifetime number of aggressive acts recalled. Men slightly favor direct aggression; women prefer indirect aggression.

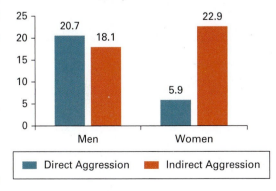

SOURCE: Griskevicius et al. (2009).

indirect verbal aggression, depending on the specific circumstances. Both are intended to harm someone else to gain status, possibly to prevent future aggression.

Biological Mechanisms of Aggression

The goal of aggression, according to evolutionary theory, is not to just win but to survive and reproduce. That's the strategy that worked for our ancestors, so our bodies inherited biological mechanisms that select for whatever strategy is most likely to be effective in a given situation.

Responding to Threat. There are at least four biological responses to threat (see Table 11.3). The first is the "fight" alternative of the "fight or flight" response (Taylor & Gonzaga, 2006). A threat triggers a rush of adrenaline that prepares us for high-energy action: fighting or fleeing. A third, nonaggressive survival strategy also evolved: freezing until enemies or predators pass them by. Taylor's (2002) book *The Tending Instinct* frames the scientific argument for a fourth survival strategy: "tend and befriend."

A "tend and befriend" reaction is a common instinct among social animals such as honeybees, squirrel monkeys, and prairie voles (see pp. 91–92). In human societies, it is an impulse sometimes favored by women who are more likely, for example, to form book clubs or create events around food, conversation, and mutual support. The Mundurucu women of Brazil, for example, travel in groups for mutual protection (Murphy & Murphy, 1974). And when women in the Wape area in Papua, New Guinea, hear the sounds of an escalating domestic argument, they have been known to "descend upon the house and stand around it until the woman joins them outside" (Mitchell, 1990, p. 148). Women who form bonds with other women are more likely to survive and then pass those bonding "instincts" to the next generation.

A Low Resting Heart Rate. While not found in most parenting advice books, one surprisingly reliable way to predict extreme adolescent antisocial and aggressive behavior is by measuring the child's resting heart rate (Patrick & Verona, 2007). Wadsworth (1976) studied 1,800 British schoolboys and found that a low resting heart rate at age 11 was a fairly strong predictor of delinquency at age 21. Subsequent *meta-analyses* have confirmed this counterintuitive effect (Ortiz & Raine, 2004). You might think that a low heart rate would mean that someone is not very excitable and therefore prone to be peaceful. That makes sense, but it doesn't fit with the story the data tell—and the data always win out in the end. Instead, outward calm seems to be correlated to aggression.

Here are two possible explanations. First, perhaps children with a low resting heart rate are "less sensitive to the negative consequences of their behavior" and are therefore less likely to develop a moral conscience. In other words, perhaps people with a low heart rate are less responsive to their environment—which might make them less empathetic toward others. Second, these children also might be more sensation seeking—they're bored, so they use aggression to create their own excitement (Patrick & Verona, 2007, p. 114). A lower moral conscience and lack of impulse control are symptoms of antisocial personality disorder, the mental illness associated with serial killers and people who torture animals. Notice the scary details in a study with perpetrators of domestic violence in the Spotlight on Research Methods feature.

The Role of Alcohol in Aggression. It's not surprising that Charles Barkley was in a bar when he threw Jorge Lugo through the window. More than any other

Animals—including humans—appear to have four biological responses to threat: fight, flight, freeze, and tend and befriend. The phrase "deer caught in the headlights" emphasizes the "freeze" option—probably not the best option for this particular deer.

Kelly Shannon Kelly / Alamy Stock Photo

Spotlight on Research Methods

The connection between people's resting heart rates and violent tendencies was found by accident when Jacobson and Gottman (1998) studied perpetrators of domestic violence. They recruited participants in the Seattle, Washington, area by posting fliers asking for people to participate in a study on relationship conflict—and both couple members had to attend the sessions. Imagine being part of this strange study.

They first selected couples who admitted to domestic violence—including some cases of severe abuse. All of the couples were heterosexual, and the man was the primary abuser. (This is not always the case; see Johnson, 1995; Leone, Johnson, & Cohan, 2007.) Then they asked the couple to get into an argument! During the conflict, the researchers observed the men's physiological arousal through heart rate monitors and galvanic skin response (sweaty palms). Their *hypothesis* was that as the argument got more heated, the men's physiological arousal would also go up—they predicted a *positive correlation*.

Results confirmed the hypothesis for most of the men; about 80% of them showed this pattern. Jacobson and Gottman call these men the "pit bulls," because their increasing anger and aggression were obvious. They would yell, their faces would become red, and their

The pit bull may appear more aggressive, but the cobra is calmly waiting to strike with a deadly attack.

posture leaned forward and clearly expressed anger. The surprise, however, was that about 20% of men showed the opposite pattern: a *negative correlation*. For these abusers, as conflicts with their wives or girlfriends progressed, their physiological responses got calmer and more peaceful.

Here's the scary part: The calmer, lower-heart-rate men were the most abusive. Jacobson and Gottman labeled these men "cobras," because they sat back calmly, waiting to strike. Their calm demeanor masked more extreme violent tendencies, a pattern also found in psychopaths and people with antisocial personality disorder. Wives of "cobras" were less successful in leaving their abusive partners, compared to pit bulls. Perhaps they understood how scary their partners could become.

---

illicit drug, alcohol is implicated in aggressive behavior (Kretschmar & Flannery, 2007). After throwing him through the window, the *Washington Post* ("Barkley Is Arrested," 1997) reported that Barkley said, "You got what you deserve. You don't respect me. I hope you're hurt."

Alcohol affects GABA, the brain's main inhibitory neurotransmitter. After a few drinks, things that normally seem to be a bad idea suddenly might not seem so bad—such as a bar fight. The **alcohol disinhibition hypothesis** proposes that alcohol interferes with the brain's ability to suppress violent behavior by lowering anxiety and harming our ability to accurately assess a situation. However, disinhibition is not the only way that alcohol influences aggression.

In one study, intoxicated people had more trouble seeing their romantic partner's point of view about a conflict (MacDonald, Zanna, & Holmes, 2000). Violence is more likely when your soggy brain can't resolve even minor disagreements.

■ TABLE 11.3 Four Instinctual Responses to Threat

Fight
Flight
Freeze
Tend and befriend

Alcohol disinhibition hypothesis: The idea that alcohol interferes with the brain's ability to suppress violent behavior by lowering anxiety and harming an individual's ability to accurately assess a situation.

The stereotype of a bar fight may come from the tendency of people to be more aggressive after consuming alcohol.

Among 1,401 women surveyed in a family practice clinic, 20% reported currently experiencing some type of intimate partner violence, most often physical or sexual violence, and substance abuse was the strongest predictor of that violence (Coker, Smith, McKeown, & King, 2000). More optimistically, aggression is less likely among recovering alcoholics (Murphy & O'Farrell, 1996).

The Influence of Testosterone on Aggression.

The connection between testosterone and physical aggression is stronger among nonhuman animals than among humans. In an early (1939) testosterone study, low-ranking hens were administered testosterone and then began crowing—and acting—like roosters. In fact, the social order of the entire flock began to change (Allee, Collias, & Lutherman, 1939).

Since then, two meta-analyses of the many studies about testosterone and aggression have found a strong, *positive correlation* in nonhuman animals and a smaller (but still positive) correlation in humans (Archer, Birring, & Wu, 1998; Book, Starzyk, & Quinsey, 2001; Knickmeyer & Baron-Cohen, 2006). A third meta-analysis by Archer (2004) focused on gender differences in real-world settings and with a more cross-cultural sample. He found that early in their lives, boys tend to be more physically aggressive than girls, but aggression peaked in both men and women when they were in their 20s (when testosterone is at its highest point).

One study (Chance, Brown, Dabbs, & Casey, 2000) found higher-than-average levels of testosterone among a psychiatric group of older boys with disruptive behavior (ages 9–11). Testosterone levels among female inmates in a maximum-security state prison also were related to aggressive dominance—and both aggression and testosterone declined as inmates got older. There may also be a cycle in which testosterone increases aggression, but anger increases testosterone; this pattern was shown in a *pretest-posttest experimental design* in which participants were made angry by the procedure (Peterson & Harmon-Jones, 2012).

For ethical reasons, we can't use a true *experiment with random assignment* to study the connection between testosterone and sex differences in humans. However, the increasing number of transgender individuals receiving hormone treatments (both male-to-female and female-to-male) creates some interesting research opportunities. A Dutch research team measured the aggression, sexual motivation, and other cognitive abilities of both groups (Van Goozen, Cohen-Kettenis, Gooren, Frijda, & Van De Poll, 1995). Increases in testosterone were *positively correlated* with increased aggressive inclinations, likelihood of becoming sexually aroused, and some spatial abilities—a pattern that reversed among people suppressing testosterone.

The Main Ideas

- An evolutionary psychological view of aggression argues that aggressive tendencies continue because they are adaptive; they help our genes survive into the next generation by leading to more resources, social status, and access to sexual partners.

- Several other biological factors (beyond genes) have also been linked to aggression, including heart rate, alcohol, and testosterone.

⚡ CRITICAL THINKING

- Do you agree with Freud when he said that the two basic human instincts are to love and to hate (in other words, be aggressive) or to create and destroy? Are there other instincts he did not include in his theory? What examples from human history or from your own life do you have to support your opinion, either way?

- In Chapter 10, we discussed prosocial and helping behaviors. How could evolutionary psychology explain the two opposite tendencies to both help others and to hurt others? Can both be simultaneously supported by a "survival of the fittest" perspective?

- If ethics were not a concern, what experimental study would you design to text causal effects of biological influences on aggression? Identify the independent variable and dependent variable, and operationalize each by explaining your procedure.

IS AGGRESSION EXPLAINED BY CULTURAL INFLUENCES?

LO 11.3: To analyze cultural explanations for aggression.

Consider the following examples of how culture might encourage aggression:

- In countries where soccer (known outside of the United States as football) is popular—such as England—a culture of "football hooliganism" is well known for aggressive, unruly, unpredictable, destructive behavior. In cases where rivalries between team fans have become extreme, fighting has caused deaths of fans, police, and innocent bystanders after riot police attempted to break things up using body armor, tear gas, dogs, water cannons, and armored vehicles (Podnar, 2007; Wainwright, 2015).

- The Yanomamö tribe of South America is known for being a particularly violent group in a "state of chronic warfare" with other local tribes (Chagnon, 1983). They sing songs about killing and how they "hunger for flesh" (p. 183).

- American educator and documentarian Jackson Katz is well known for his programs regarding how U.S. culture includes a "crisis of masculinity" that leads young boys to be aggressive, misogynistic, and homophobic; statistics and examples are highlighted in his popular film *Tough Guise* (Jhally, Ericsson, & Talreja, 1999).

REUTERS/Pawel Kopczynski

In England, concerns about the aggression of "football hooligans" are frequently discussed in media outlets.

Culture can help explain why certain groups may be more aggressive than others. While previous chapters have frequently discussed cultural differences in terms of national trends (such as comparing the cultures of Germany and India), this section explores how aggressive tendencies are affected by other types of cultural forces: cultures of honor, gender roles, and sports-related violence.

Cultures of Honor

How insulted would you be if somebody bumped into you and called you an "asshole"?

That happened to some students in an experiment at the University of Michigan, but they didn't know they were in an experiment (Cohen, Nisbett, Bowdle, & Schwartz, 1996). The men who had been deliberately bumped came from the northern or southern regions of the United States. After being bumped and called a name, the men from the south were more likely to:

(a) think their masculine reputation had been threatened,

(b) be emotionally upset (measured by their cortisol levels),

(c) become physiologically primed for aggression, and

(d) engage in more aggressive and dominant behaviors.

The researchers believed these different reactions could be traced to a **culture of honor** that perceives an insult as a threat to one's reputation for masculine courage that must be restored through dominance and aggression—similar to Charles Barkley tossing an annoying bar patron through a plate glass window. One study (Saucier et al., 2016) explored the different values supported in a culture of honor; see Table 11.4.

Other studies have confirmed that many people from the southern United States display a "culture of honor" mentality. For example, just 2 weeks after the 9/11 attacks, students from a southwestern university (University of Oklahoma) desired the deaths of the terrorists responsible for the 9/11 attacks more than their northern counterparts (Pennsylvania State University). This is despite the fact that Penn State is not far from where Flight 93 crashed in Shanksville, Pennsylvania (Barnes, Brown, & Osterman, 2012). As you probably suspected, cultures of honor are not caused merely by geography.

Sociologist Venkatesh (1997) also found a culture of honor in densely populated (northern) Chicago housing projects that police seldom patrolled. In another part of the world, two studies found that people from honor cultures in Turkey were more likely to show aggressive intentions after being insulted, compared to Dutch participants (van Osch, Breugelmans, Zeelenberg, & Bölük, 2013). Within Latinx samples, participants who endorsed culture of honor values were also more likely to accept relationship violence and more approving of the violent perpetrator (Dietrich & Schuett, 2013). In one study of Brazilian inmates, most of the men convicted of murder said that their motivation for the homicide was "honor" (Souza, Roazzi, & Souza, 2011). Beyond nationality, men who believe in the values within a culture of honor are more likely to find insulting

Culture of honor: A culture where individuals, especially men, tend to perceive insults as a threat to their reputation for masculine courage, pride, and virtue that must be restored through dominance and aggression. Following an insult, individuals from a culture of honor are more likely to feel threatened, be emotionally upset, become physiologically primed for aggression, and engage in aggressive or dominant behaviors.

■ TABLE 11.4 Values in a Culture of Honor

Masculine courage (e.g., men should be able to take pain)
Pride in manhood (e.g., men should be independent)
Socialization (e.g., men with honor stand up to bullies)
Virtue (e.g., fighting is admirable if done out of honor)
Protection (e.g., men should protect women)
Provocation/insult (e.g., men should not accept insults)
Family and community bonds (e.g., family is a man's first priority)

SOURCE: Saucier et al. (2016).

MEASURING BELIEF IN A CULTURE OF HONOR

Applying Social Psychology to Your Life

Instructions: Consider each statement and mark your level of agreement using this scale:

1	2	3	4	5	6	7
Disagree very strongly						Agree very strongly

_____ 1. It is very important for a man to act bravely.

_____ 2. A man should not be afraid to fight.

_____ 3. It is important for a man to be able to take pain.

_____ 4. It is important for a man to be more masculine than other men.

_____ 5. A man should be embarrassed if someone calls him a wimp.

_____ 6. A man should be expected to fight for himself.

_____ 7. If a man does not defend his wife, he is not a very strong man.

_____ 8. If your son got into a fight, you would be proud that he stood up for himself.

_____ 9. As a child, you were taught that boys should defend girls.

_____ 10. You would praise a man who reacted aggressively to an insult.

_____ 11. Physical aggression is always admirable and acceptable.

_____ 12. Physical violence is the most honorable way to defend yourself.

_____ 13. A man should stand up for a female who is in his family or is a close friend.

_____ 14. It is a male's responsibility to protect his family.

_____ 15. If a man's wife is insulted, his manhood is insulted.

_____ 16. If a man is insulted, his manhood is insulted.

_____ 17. It is important for a man to be loyal to his family.

_____ 18. A man's family should be his number one priority.

_____ 19. It is important to interact with other members of your community.

_____ 20. It is a man's responsibility to respect his family.

Scoring: Add up your answers to get your total score, which can range from 20 to 140 (higher numbers mean more endorsement of the values in a culture of honor).

Note that the original scale includes more items and has subscales for each aspect of the culture of honor (e.g., masculine courage, pride in manhood).

Source: Saucier et al. (2016).

slurs offensive and to say they would respond with physical aggression—especially when masculinity was offended (Saucier, Till, Miller, O'Dea, & Andres, 2015).

You can see how "culture of honor" values are defined and measured—and you can score yourself on this scale—by referring to the Applying Social Psychology to Your Life feature. At least in cultures of honor, aggression is tied to how men define their social roles and expectations. The next section discusses how gender roles influence aggression on a larger scale.

Gender Roles and Aggression

Archer (2006) correlated female empowerment in different cultures with how frequently women were victimized by aggression. These *archival data* all told a similar story. As gender equality and individualism increased, female victimization decreased: a *negative correlation*. Less female victimization is good news, and Archer's findings produced even more nuanced insights into *how* culture influences aggression. Cultures that valued individualism (more than collectivism) experienced less female victimization, along with slightly more *male* victimization.

That last part might surprise you—why would more individualistic cultures have slightly more male victimization? Are some liberated women "getting even"? Archer also found that sexist attitudes and approval of wife beating increased women's victimization (no surprise there) but were *not* associated with *general* levels of violent crime. In some cultures, apparently beating your wife was okay—but being aggressive in general was not. Carefully defined gender roles within particular cultures influenced how aggression was expressed.

The link between gender and culture is complicated; Sweden is an interesting case study. The employment rate of women in Sweden is the highest in the European Union. In addition, women in Sweden gain more education, have higher salaries, and are more likely to be board members of companies than the average woman in Europe ("The Current Situation," 2013). At the same time, Sweden is the rape capital of Europe ("Case Closed," 2010); there are 46 reports of rape for every 100,000 Swedish citizens. This is twice the rate in the United Kingdom and four times the rate of Germany and France. Some people believe that women's relative equality in Swedish culture creates a "backlash" when some men are threatened and feel the need to aggress toward them as a way of regaining power. If this is true, it is a truly terrible response to increased equality between the sexes.

Sports Culture

Many sports, such as auto racing, boxing, American football, and soccer, require participants to risk serious injury. More and more attention is going toward the possibility of athletes receiving multiple extremely dangerous concussions; the most concussions occur in football, hockey, and women's soccer.

For example, Figure 11.5 displays the average number of head impacts per practice and per game experienced by one youth team (ages 7–14) practicing and playing American football. Head impacts, of course, can lead to concussions. Figure 11.6 reports the number of medically diagnosed concussions per 1,000 athletic exposures (AEs; 1 AE = one practice or game). In the absence of medical personnel capable of making a diagnosis at each practice and game, these data are probably severe underestimates of the actual incidence rate of concussions experienced.

There are now more rules about what to do and how to treat a player who may have suffered a concussion. But sports-related aggression extends far beyond the rules that regulate those competitions. Russell (2008) has taken a social psychological look into the larger world of sports-related aggression. It's not a pretty picture.

Perpetrators and Targets. There are many positive benefits to participating in athletic activities (Findlay & Coplan, 2008). There are

■ FIGURE 11.5 Head impacts per 1,000 AEs per practice and game on a youth football team.

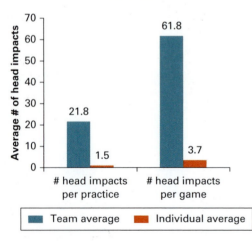

SOURCE: Wong et al. (2014).

even potential benefits to fans when they closely identify with a team (Wann, 2006). These benefits will continue to be pursued given centuries of enthusiastic, cross-cultural participation in athletic activities. But athletic competition can also create a dangerous subculture of aggression. Athletes, their support staff, their coaches, and their fans have all displayed purposeful aggression.

For example, prior to the 1994 Olympics, figure skater Tonya Harding apparently escalated her aggression from competition on the ice to aggression in a hallway by arranging for her former husband to cripple her rival, Nancy Kerrigan's, legs with a telescopic baton. Mike Tyson bit off 1 inch of Evander Holyfield's right ear during a boxing match. In France, Christophe Fauviau confessed to spiking the water bottles of 27 of his daughter's tennis opponents—one defeated rival died after falling asleep while driving. In Brisbane, Australia, a 19-year-old female referee officiating a 13-and-under rugby competition was chased into the dressing room by angry parents. Tennis star Monica Seles was stabbed in the back during a match by a fan of her rival Steffi Graf. Coaches, parents, players, and fans need to understand how easily sports passions can escalate into overt hostility.

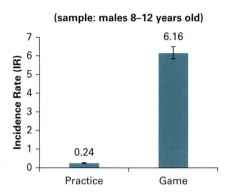

■ FIGURE 11.6 Number of medically diagnosed concussions per 1,000 AEs.

SOURCE: Kontos et al. (2013).

The Color Black: A Cultural Cue for Aggressive Behavior.

Frank and Gilovich (1988) pointed out that the color black conveys a deeply negative cultural bias. For example, the Great Depression began on "Black Thursday," and it is a bad thing to be "blackballed," "blacklisted," or "blackmailed." Baseball suffered through a "dark" chapter when a betting scandal "blackened" baseball's reputation in the infamous "Black Sox" affair. We even eat white angel food cake and black devil's food cake.

These observations led Frank and Gilovich (1988) to analyze 17 years of penalty records in the National Football League and the National Hockey League (another *archival study*). They focused their attention on teams that wore black uniforms or switched to black uniforms. Both experimental and archival studies found consistently high rankings in penalties for teams switching to black uniforms or already wearing black uniforms. We see black uniforms and then expect violence.

Does this black effect in sports come from culture, or is there something intrinsically evil about the color black? Some might argue that modern culture's connection between the color and perceptions of aggression are tied to racism against African Americans. But priests, Hassidic Jews, and stereotypical New York actors or spoken word poets don't seem to behave more aggressively because of their black clothing. The meaning of black on a priest conveys a different social meaning than black on a member of the Hell's Angels motorcycle club—so black does not seem to be intrinsically evil or aggression making. Instead, it appears that cues in the environment, such as black football uniforms, take on particular cultural meanings within particular contexts.

Unfortunately, cultural perceptions of blackness have important and tragic effects when they are applied to people on a racial level—and these effects are especially sad when they affect children. In an article titled "The Essence of Innocence: Consequences of Dehumanizing Black Children" (Goff, Jackson, Di Leone, Culotta, & DiTomasso, 2014), a series of four studies showed that Black children are **dehumanized** more than White children, meaning they are cognitively perceived as lacking positive human

Dehumanize: When an individual cognitively perceives another individual as lacking positive human qualities but as retaining negative, animalistic qualities.

Indiana University basketball coach Bobby Knight was famous for his rage and abusive behavior toward players and referees. He was nicknamed "The General" for his harsh tactics and combative manner with the press and referees.

qualities but as retaining negative, animalistic qualities such as aggression. If a Black child is compared to an objectively equal White child, the Black child will be perceived as (1) less innocent, (2) older, (3) more responsible for his or her actions, and (4) more appropriate targets of police violence.

Sports Can Be a Humanizing Influence. As you probably suspected, the influence of sports on aggression depends on many factors. In World War I, trench soldiers were deliberately kept occupied with "football for the men and rugby and cricket for the officers" because military planners did not want to "allow soldiers too much opportunity to act and think as individuals" (Ellis, 1976, p. 142). In this case, sports competition had been co-opted by top military planners to keep levels of aggression (and obedience) high.

On the other hand, the widespread Christmas Truce of 1914 was a bottom-up expression of mutual goodwill. It was initiated, maintained, and expanded by individuals in the trenches—without permission from high command. One of its highlights was a game of soccer between the Lancashire Fusiliers and a Saxon unit (reportedly won by the Lancashire team 3–2). The effect of playing soccer against their enemy was sobering. Ellis (1976, p. 172) observed that "many soldiers were surprised to find that their enemy seemed quite human." An officer from the London Rifle Brigade described their enemy as, "Jolly good sorts . . . I now have a very different opinion of the Germans."

In this case, sports competition had supplied a humanizing framework for peace between combatants; soccer was used as a substitute for fighting and as a good-natured way to simply take a day off from the hard work of killing one another. Indeed, the true definition of "good sportsmanship" is an expectation of honoring and respecting your sports rival—the traditional, idealistic view of the international Olympics. As has so often been the case with predicting social behavior, understanding how sports culture and aggression combine is as fascinating as it is complicated.

The Main Ideas

- One explanation for aggression is cultural influence. For example, a culture of honor endorses aggression from men as a reaction to perceived insult or threat to their masculinity.

- Gender roles also influence perpetration of aggression, with aggressive behaviors more expected of (and accepted in) men compared to women.

- Sports culture also sometimes endorses aggression, and being a fan of sports can lead some individuals to aggressive actions. However, sports can also be used as a relatively peaceful way to interact with groups from other cultures.

⚡ CRITICAL THINKING

- Consider the values included in a culture of honor. For each, do you agree or disagree (e.g., that family should be a man's first priority)? Can these values be endorsed *without* leading to aggression? Does defending one's "honor" always require physical aggression? Why or why not?

- Some very popular movies and books feature aggressive female protagonists (Black Widow from *The Avengers*, Katniss Everdeen from *The Hunger Games*, etc.). How do audiences seem to react when a woman expresses the same amount of violent behaviors as a man? Is it more culturally acceptable, or less? Why?

- Reflect on how popular sports are in modern culture. Do you think sporting events encourage aggression and violence, or do they maintain respectful competition through endorsement of rules and regulations? How might sports culture focus more on peaceful, but still exciting, play and competition between athletes and teams?

IS AGGRESSION EXPLAINED BY SITUATIONAL INFLUENCES?

LO 11. 4: To analyze situational explanations for aggression.

You may not think of yourself as a particularly angry, violent, or aggressive person. On the other hand, all of us have a temper, and all of us might do things we might later regret. So far we've discussed whether aggression is a biological instinct or drive that helps us survive, and we've talked about cultural differences in whether aggression is perceived as acceptable—or even honorable. But a discussion of what drives aggression wouldn't be complete without considering how certain situations or environments bring aggression out, even from the most peaceful or calm individuals. This might be due to a nationalistic call to war, modeling aggression in violent television or video games, or cues in our environment.

Aggression in Times of War

At the start of the Great War of 1914–1918 (what later was known as World War I), millions of young men enthusiastically joined their armies for what both sides believed would be a short and glorious war. Their friends were going, the young women were prerolling bandages to heal any future wounds, and parents, teachers, aunts, and uncles all were encouraging them with stirring words and patriotic songs. Great crowds gathered to send their young men off to war with cheers, tears, and confidence that they would be back very soon. The great writer Rudyard Kipling pleaded poetically for the nation to prepare for war. Even the energetic movement to grant women the right to vote—so close to victory—was swept aside by war fever. People who were normally pacifists got caught up in the swell of war that was perceived as patriotic aggression.

Both sides were in the grip of war hysteria. If you were 16 to 22 years old, would you be able to resist all that public support for aggression? Mass social psychology made killing and risking being killed a courageous necessity in service of a nobler cause (see Hochschild, 2011). Thousands of young men and women observed all the enthusiasm and volunteered. They could not know that thousands of them were about to fall into the most innovative, numerically staggering, global aggression that humans had ever experienced.

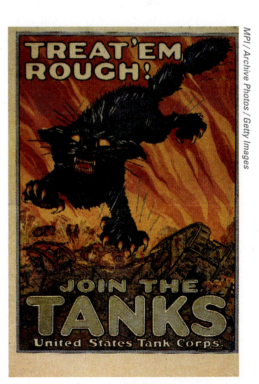

MPI / Archive Photos / Getty Images

Propaganda posters from World War I emphasize the "patriotic duty" to become aggressive to fight the enemy during war.

Modeling Aggression

If we're lucky, we'll only be exposed to war by watching it on a movie or television screen. But does even this level of exposure affect aggression? Psychology students know better than most people that *correlation does not imply causation*. For example, even if there is a correlation between watching violence on television and behaving violently, we can't say that watching violent TV *caused* more violent behavior. Maybe enjoying violent acts makes people want to watch more violence on TV, so the causation is flipped. Maybe being home alone (without parents) gives children more opportunities to do both (watch adult programming and get into trouble), so there's a third variable involved. Establishing causality requires *experiments* with things like *control groups, random assignment to condition*, and so on. Luckily for science, someone rose to that challenge: Albert Bandura.

Bandura's Bobo Doll Studies. Understanding the possible effects of viewing violence became more urgent during the 1950s and 1960s as television sets invaded people's homes and absorbed their time. Bandura and his research team (Bandura, Ross, & Ross, 1961) devised a laboratory experiment that supplied 4-year-old children from the Stanford University daycare center with a large, bouncy doll. It had a drawing of a clown named Bobo on it, and it was weighted at the bottom so that children could punch it as many times as they liked, and it would always return to an upright position. This series of studies is now known as the "Bobo doll studies."

Over several studies, different children watched various role models—adults first and then children on television—as they modeled aggression by punching and hitting the Bobo doll, saying things like "Sock him," "Hit him down," "Kick him," beating it with a mallet, and throwing it in the air. Of course, there was a nonaggressive *control group* in each study, where the models displayed no aggressive behaviors at all.

Study 1: Imitating Adults. In an initial study, one experimental group of little boys and girls watched an adult beat up the Bobo doll. Results showed that both boys and girls were more likely to copy the aggressive behavior they saw in adults—especially when the adult role model was the same sex as themselves.

Study 2: Imitating Adults on Television. Two years later, they found that aggressive models on television produced the same effects (Bandura, Ross, & Ross, 1963a). The children were more likely to imitate aggression when the aggressive TV model was rewarded with things like candy and were less likely to imitate when the model had been punished.

Study 3: Imitating Children on Television. A third study (Bandura, Ross, & Ross, 1963b) clarified *why* children imitated other children on television by watching a conflict between two boys: Rocky and Johnny. Rocky strikes Johnny with a rubber ball, kicks a plastic doll, shoots darts at Johnny's cars and plastic farm animals, stumbles over Johnny's toys, sits on Johnny, tries to spank him, hits him with a baton, lassos him with a hula hoop, and pulls him to a far corner of the room!

In one experimental condition, the film ends with Johnny seated in a corner while Rocky triumphantly plays with all the toys. Then Rocky helps himself to snacks and happily rides a rocking horse singing, "Hi ho, hi ho, it's off to play I go." Rocky disappears off screen carrying a big bag of loot while an announcer declares Rocky the victor. It's the same film in the comparison condition, but with a different ending. When Johnny tries to spank Rocky, Johnny turns the tables and thrashes Rocky. This time it is Rocky who flees to the corner while Johnny collects toys in his sack and walks triumphantly away. An announcer comments on Rocky's punishment.

Once again, the boys who saw Rocky being rewarded for his aggression displayed the highest levels of aggression. However, the girls who saw Rocky triumph did not imitate him. Their overall level of aggression was similar to those who had seen Johnny turn the tables and beat up Rocky. For these children, gender identification was an important component of role modeling aggression.]

Insights From Qualitative Interviews. At the end of the final study mentioned above, the children were asked who they most wanted to be like: Rocky or Johnny?

The famous Bobo doll, used by Bandura in his series of studies regarding what situations will lead to children displaying aggressive tendencies.

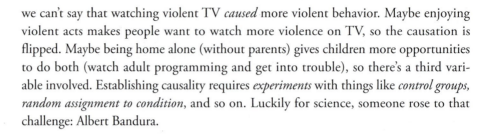

In the condition where Rocky the bully was rewarded for his aggression, he won big in the eyes of 4-year-olds (see Figure 11.7). They said:

"Rocky is harsh, I be harsh like he was."

"Rough and bossy."

"Mean."

"He whack people."

"He come and snatched Johnny's toys. Get a lot of toys."

"Rocky beat Johnny and chase him and get all the good toys."

"No one would ever get the toys from Rocky."

"He was a fighter. He got all good toys."

They observed—and learned—that aggression was rewarded.

One little girl even asked for a sack like the one Rocky used to haul away his loot! The children rationalized their support for Rocky by blaming Johnny for being weak. For Johnny, they said:

"He was a cry baby. Didn't know how to make Rocky mind."

"If he'd shared right in the beginning, Rocky might have played nice. He didn't share."

Johnny, the victim, was described as "sulky," "selfish," "mean," and "sort of dumb."

The take-home message was clear to these 4-year-olds, and they were quick to blame the victim: Aggression works.

Media Cues. Aggression has always been part of television. First viewed in 1903, *The Great Train Robbery* (Porter, 1903; available on YouTube) was the very first moving picture to tell a story. Only 10 minutes long, the silent film begins when a stationmaster

Social Psychology in Action: Bandura's Bobo Doll Experiment

©SAGE Publications

■ FIGURE 11.7 Who do you want to be like?

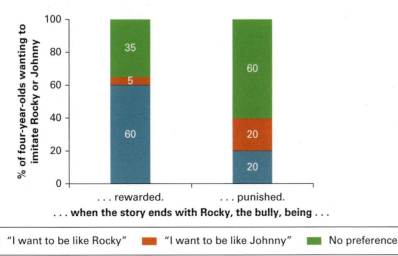

SOURCE: Data from Bandura, Ross, & Ross (1963b).

The final shot of *The Great Train Robbery* (1903).

is beaten unconscious and then tied up by a gang who secretly board the train. They exchange five shots with a guard before killing him, exploding a safe, and taking the loot. (The actor playing the dead guard wiggles around until he gets his arm in a more comfortable position, but he is *supposed* to be dead.)

The film shows approximately one act of violence per minute and a gunshot for every 12 seconds during history's first storytelling film. The audience was thrilled during the final scene, when the bad guy looked directly at the camera and fired his gun repeatedly until he ran out of bullets.

Violent Television. Following in Bandura's footsteps, many other researchers have examined the connection between exposure to violence and tendencies to act violently. One example is highlighted in the Social Psychology in Popular Culture feature; this study analyzed interpersonal violence in the 90 top-grossing teen films of the 1980s, 1990s, and 2000s.

Another study *randomly assigned* children to watch either movies showing professional wrestling (not sports wresting) or movies of Christian gospel musicals (thus, film type was the *independent variable*). Then children got to play with inflated balloons, and behaviors were coded for aggression (the *dependent variable*). Children who watched wrestling were significantly more likely to play violently, and this was true for both boys and girls (Mbaeze, Ukwandu, & Ndubuisi, 2011). A *longitudinal field study* demonstrated that children's exposure to violence in the media early in a school year predicted more verbally aggressive, relationally aggressive, and physically aggressive behavior, as well as less prosocial behavior later in the school year (Gentile, Coyne, & Walsh, 2011). While not all of the studies done on the link between exposure to violent media and aggressive behavior are experimental in design, enough research has supported this hypothesis to make it hard to doubt that watching violent TV influences children's aggression.

Violent Video Games. In one of the notorious events connecting video games with violence, Eric Harris and Dylan Klebold assaulted their own Colorado classmates with a variety of firearms, killing 13, wounding 23, and then committing suicide. The two boys were more than just fans of the video game *Doom*. In a video class project, they also dressed in trench coats, carried guns, and "killed" student athletes. Did playing violent video games influence their behavior?

A *longitudinal* study followed students across all 4 years of high school; results showed that sustained play of violent video games led to increasing aggression during that time—and that playing nonviolent video games did not (Willoughby, Adachi, & Good, 2012). However, the details of how people play video games seem to be important. Three separate studies have shown that aggression goes up when the game is played on a big-screen TV and with a gun-shaped controller to shoot avatars (Hollingdale & Greitemeyer, 2013; Kim & Sundar, 2013; McGloin, Farrar, & Fishlock, 2015). There are dozens of additional studies showing these patterns.

Many people believe the debate is over: Violent video games are contributing—across several cultures—to the problem of social violence (Anderson et al., 2010; Huesmann, 2010). But the story changes—a little—when you look at outcomes that co-occur with increased aggression. For example, Jin and Li (2017) found that playing video games as a team was associated with more prosocial behavior and cooperation—in

To complete her master's degree at Brigham Young University in 2011, Halie Foell Stout completed a content analysis of the 90 most profitable teen movies produced in Hollywood from 1980 to 2009. She focused on how each movie portrayed aggression between the characters that was specifically intended to affect social relationships and/or social status. This aggression included three forms:

- Direct—such as exclusion from a social group or bullying
- Indirect—such as gossiping, spreading rumors, or lying to the person's love interest
- Nonverbal—such as ignoring, rolling eyes, and dirty looks

Overall, she found that 85 of the 90 teen movies included some form of relational aggression, with girls being portrayed as the aggressor more often than boys—and that this gender trend became stronger over time.

Results also showed that girls most often used indirect relational aggression. The four movies with the highest amount of aggression were the following:

#1: *Mean Girls* (Michaels & Waters, 2004; 59 acts of aggression)

#2: *The Mighty Ducks* (Avnet, Kerner, & Herek, 1992; 30 acts)

#3: *My Bodyguard* (Simon, Devlin, & Bill, 1980; 21 acts)

#4: *Just One of the Guys* (Fogelson & Gottlieb, 1985; 20 acts)

Note, while Stout identified five movies with no acts of relational aggression, even these films showed *some* form of aggression (e.g., *Transformers* [Murphy et al., 2007] and *Red Dawn* [1984 version; Beckerman, Feitschans, & Milius, 1984] both have war-like battle scenes). Is it possible to make a Hollywood movie without *any* form of aggression? Maybe—but it might not make a profit.

---

both violent and neutral video games. The problem is not video games; it is the content, context, and style of play of a particular game.

On the positive side, playing video games is contributing to education in many creative ways. For example, video games have contributed to our understanding of artificial intelligence (Lake, Ullman, Tenenbaum, & Gershman, 2016) and more effective ways to teach (Epstein, Noel, Finnegan, & Watkins, 2016). This may be because the principles of good game design parallel established learning principles of psychological science (see Heinzen et al., 2015). Video games are powerful tools that can have both negative and positive consequences—depending on the environmental cues delivered by particular games.

A Cognitive Explanation for Environmental Cues

Black uniforms, hot temperatures, loud noises, unpleasant odors, ozone levels, crowding, and pain are all associated with negative feelings that lead to increased aggression (see Anderson, 1989; Anderson et al., 2010; Berkowitz, Cochran, & Embree, 1981; Griffit & Veitch, 1971; Rotton, Frey, Barry, Milligan, & Fitzpatrick, 1979). Why do such different environmental cues have similar effects? Social cognition proposes a relatively simple answer: Environmental cues activate (or prime) preexisting mental and emotional connections. Any kind of unpleasant experience in the environment activates brain connections that trigger the impulse either to escape (flee) or to attack (fight).

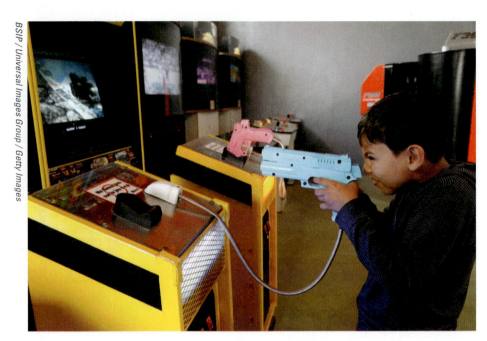

Many modern video games highlight extremely aggressive situations.

Cognitive neoassociation analysis combines the emotions we feel while frustrated (anger, fear) with higher-order thought processes regarding goals (Berkowitz, 1983, 1988). When we're frustrated, it's because we perceive that we might not attain goals we've set for ourselves. Our aggression is an attempt to regain what we feel like we're losing. Further, our decision whether to fight or to flee is often based on logical thought—we only fight if we calculate that our chances of winning are pretty good. In short, an aggressive response can be triggered by particular environmental cues and our perception of the situation.

Weapons Priming. Nice theory. But does it explain real behavior? Berkowitz and Le Page (1967) created three experimental conditions by placing on a table (a) badminton rackets, (b) a rifle and a revolver, or (c) nothing at all (the *control condition*). The group of participants who had been primed by seeing weapons on the table later demonstrated higher levels of aggression. The **weapons effect** occurs when the presence of weapons primes aggressive thoughts, feelings, and behaviors. Here, aggression was increased due to cues in the environment that led participants to cognitively interpret things in a certain direction (when they saw guns on the table).

Weapons are the most obvious environmental cue to behave aggressively. A *field study* version of this experiment *operationalized* (or measured) aggression by counting whether drivers honked their horns at a pickup truck that did not move for 12 seconds after the light had turned green (Turner, Layton, & Simons, 1975). There was more honking when the pickup truck had a rifle in the back and a bumper sticker reading "VENGEANCE," compared to no rifle and a bumper sticker reading "FRIEND."

Cognitive Associations With Alcohol. Simply seeing a picture of a martini glass, a bottle of vodka, or a glass of beer primes people to connect thoughts of alcohol to a network of associated ideas—and alcohol seems to be associated with aggression. That probably explains why Bartholow and Heinz (2006) found that images of alcohol could trigger aggression even when no alcohol had been drunk. Another

Cognitive neoassociation analysis: A theory that predicts aggression is based on both negative emotional reactions and cognitive, logical interpretations of our environment.

Weapons effect: The tendency for the presence of weapons to prime aggressive thoughts, feelings, and behaviors.

study showed participants subliminal images of alcohol and found that these individuals later showed more aggression toward the experimenter than people who saw neutral subliminal messages (Subra, Muller, Bègue, Bushman, & Delmas, 2010). Thus, you don't have to actually drink alcohol to be aggressive—just being around it (even on a subliminal level!) appears to prime aggression.

Heat. I [Tom] was teaching psychology in a maximum-security prison one summer when I received a call not to come in for the next class: There had been a riot. I didn't need to know any psychological literature to guess why it had happened. Although set in a wooded area, those trees did not provide any shade to the prisoners or guards behind the barbed wire fences. The prison buildings were constructed entirely out of brick, concrete, and steel. The place held heat like an oven so 24/7 there was no relief from the summer heat. And heat can make people violent.

Heat and violence are positively correlated—what explains this trend?

Anderson (1987) examined *archival data* that connected heat to increases in violent crimes; murder rates, rape, assault, robbery, burglary, larceny-theft, and stealing cars all went up with higher temperatures. Extreme heat appears to be a situation connected to aggression. When it's hot outside, more baseball pitchers hit the batter with the ball (Larrick, Timmerman, Carton, & Abrevaya, 2011), more children in daycares cry and hit each other (Ciucci et al., 2011), people feel more negatively toward immigrants (Cohen & Krueger, 2016), and more violent crimes occur (Gamble & Hess, 2012).

As usual, these *correlations* have problems related to reaching causal conclusions. For example, the heat may also simply mean that more people are outside in group arenas (compared to in the middle of winter or during a thunderstorm). Thus, there may be more opportunities for riots, fights, conflicts, and so on. But, considering the research reviewed in this section, it's probably best to think twice before you bring your loaded guns to a crowded gun show inside a small, dark whisky bar in the middle of August.

The Main Ideas

- Situations can increase aggression; for example, during times of war, more people may approve of military aggression than in times of peace.

- Aggression can also be increased when it is observed in models. Bandura's famous "Bobo doll studies" showed that children are more likely to copy aggression they've observed if the model is similar to themselves and if the model was rewarded for the aggressive acts.

- Several studies have shown links between exposure to aggression in the media (e.g., television and video games) and the likelihood of expressing violence.

- Cognitive neoassociation analysis predicts that aggression is based on both emotional reactions and cognitive interpretations of our environment. Situational cues that appear to be cognitively associated with aggression are weapons, alcohol, and heat.

⚡ CRITICAL THINKING

- Bandura's series of research studies with Bobo dolls is now classic—but most of these studies were done in the 1960s. If we were to replicate the research today, would the results change? Why or why not?

- Do the studies regarding exposure to aggression on television or in video games lead you to question your own exposure to violence in the media? If you are a parent, or will become one in the future, what do these studies mean about how you might regulate your child's usage of media?

- Why do humans seem to enjoy observing violence in things like horror movies? What does this tendency imply about our inner psychology?

HOW CAN WE MANAGE OR REDUCE AGGRESSION?

■■ LO 11.5: To compare and contrast ideas for decreasing aggression in social situations.

In Chapter 9, you learned that frustration-aggression theory predicts that we'll become violent when we experience frustration. You also now know that aggression may be a basic psychological or biological instinct, that some cultures promote violence, and that certain situations bring out violence more than others. With all of these frustrations, environmental cues, and complex motivations for aggression, why isn't the world even more aggressive than it already is? What are we doing—and what can we do—to manage or decrease aggression? Social psychology has studied many possible answers. Let's start with what *doesn't* work and then talk about what does.

Tempting but Bad Ideas: Catharsis and Revenge

Have you ever been tempted to stick an enemy's picture on a dartboard or punching bag, as a way to vent your frustration and anger? We see many variations on this scene in movies and may even have tried out a few in real life. It stems from the **catharsis hypothesis**, the idea that engaging in aggressive behavior will reduce it overall. Theoretically, it's like letting a bit of steam release from a pressure cooker—getting it out now means that it won't explode later. Catharsis advises you not to repress your feelings (Lee, 1993). But is that theory correct, or partially correct, or even misleading? Is catharsis really a good way to reduce aggression? Research says no.

Testing the Catharsis Hypothesis. One of the early classic studies testing catharsis (Hornberger, 1959) angered participants by having a confederate insult them. Half the participants were then randomly assigned to a "catharsis" condition where they would work out their anger by hitting nails with a hammer for 10 minutes; the control group had no catharsis opportunity. Contrary to the hypothesis, individuals allowed to "vent their anger" through hammering were significantly more hostile toward the confederate afterward.

Another more recent study confirmed that catharsis can easily backfire. Bushman (2002) asked participants to write an essay, which was then insulted by a *confederate* (the confederate put a handwritten note on the top of the paper reading, "This is one of the worst essays I have read!"). Some participants were then allowed to punch a punching bag as hard and as long as they wanted—and were specifically instructed to

Catharsis hypothesis: The idea that purposefully engaging in aggressive behavior releases built-up aggression, reducing aggressive thoughts and behaviors overall.

think about the confederate while they did the punching! This time, participants in the control condition were asked to sit quietly for 2 minutes (thus, punching versus sitting quietly were the two levels of the *independent variable*). Finally, the participants were allowed the chance to "get revenge" on the confederate by making the other person listen to very loud, annoying blasts of sound. How aggressive they were with these loud, annoying sounds was the *dependent variable*.

As you've probably already predicted, the "catharsis" participants were significantly more aggressive compared to the control participants. Punching a bag and thinking about how angry they were didn't release aggression; instead, their aggression got stronger. Bushman (2002) suggested that cognitive neoassociation theory could explain these results. Their emotions were negative, and when this mixed with the cognitive environmental cues of punching, aggression just went up. Catharsis backfired.

Releasing some steam from a pressure cooker helps it not explode, but is this a good metaphor for reducing aggression by letting a little bit of it out?

Catharsis is a popular theory. It is also a dangerous theory. One study found that websites designed to let users write angry rants actually led to worse moods (Martin, Coyier, VanSistine, & Schroeder, 2013). Another showed that "venting" anger by complaining to a third party resulted in even more anger (Parlamis, Allred, & Block, 2010). And while many people argue that violent video games help them relieve pent-up frustration by allowing a safe outlet for their feelings, results show that playing violent games only makes things worse (Bushman & Whitaker, 2010). With few exceptions, study after study tells the same story: Catharsis doesn't work.

But here's a stubborn observation. It *feels* like catharsis is doing something good. Shouting when frustrated *feels* good, and so does getting even with an enemy. Should people abandon their clear intuition just because some crazy social psychologists tell you that they can't replicate your intuition in a laboratory? Do *controlled experiments* tell us more about ourselves than our own intuitions? Try to maintain what you learned about intuition in Chapter 4 as you read about the psychology of revenge.

Revenge Is Sweet, but Only Briefly. Revenge promises the cathartic satisfaction of restoring your sense of fairness by "getting even." Carlsmith, Wilson, and Gilbert (2008) quoted from a blog by a parent whose child had died when Virginia Tech student Seung Hui Cho massacred 32 people before killing himself. The parent wrote, "I don't think there would be anything temporary about the satisfaction I would feel in being permitted to execute the person who killed my child."

Will punching a bag or pillow really relieve stress and anger? Most research indicates it will only make it worse.

Cho's suicide denied this grieving parent the opportunity for cathartic satisfaction. However, predicting our own emotions while grieving is like forecasting rain next month because it is raining right now (Carlsmith et al., 2008). Punishing others only keeps the unhappiness alive for ourselves. We don't get "past it" or "get it out of our system"—we merely maintain our own misery.

You might be frowning at the book in disagreement because in your experience, revenge and other forms of catharsis do, in fact, feel good. That feeling is real, but that feeling is also temporary. It often leads to being even more aggressive later (Bushman, Baumeister, & Phillips, 2001; Bushman, Baumeister, & Stack, 1999; Guerin, 2001; Verona & Sullivan, 2008). Think about it from a social psychological perspective that recognizes that there is another real person at the receiving end of your aggression. Revenge encourages us to tell off our boss, send that nasty email, create a bit of mean gossip, even physically harm someone, or talk trash about someone on Facebook. While these actions may feel wonderful for a brief time, we don't really get anger or frustration "out of our system." And now you have made someone else feel as bad about you as you do about them. Instead of get-it-out-of-your-system aggression, we seem to lubricate our system with ideas and ruminations. As cognitive neoassociation analysis predicts, expressing our aggression empowers us to be more, not less, aggressive.

It's tricky because catharsis really does feel good. It feels so good that you'd like to do it again . . . and again. If catharsis and revenge don't work to decrease aggression, what does?

Hope for the Future: Cultures of Peace and Modeling Forgiveness

Let's end the chapter with a more optimistic tone by focusing on two ideas that show promise in terms of decreasing aggression. The first—establishing a culture of peace—might work on a big-picture scale for entire groups or communities. The second—modeling forgiveness—can be used on a small-picture scale by individuals at any time under almost any circumstances.

Creating Cultures of Peace. Just as there are cultures of relative aggression (such as a "culture of honor"), there are also cultures of relative peace. Bonta (1997) identified 25 relatively peaceful societies, 7 of which are described in Table 11.5. They range across continents and varied geographies, from the Arctic to Tahiti. They vary in how they obtain food, how much they interact with the outside world, and the degree of aggression in their communal stories about themselves. Their only commonality is that each society evolved its own distinctive ways to reduce conflict. Perhaps other, more aggressive cultures could study these and learn alternative conflict management solutions.

Modeling Forgiveness. In Bandura's famous Bobo doll studies, we saw that people will model what they see; if they see aggression, they are more likely to be aggressive. However, another view of the results is that children who saw adults playing in non-aggressive ways were less likely to be aggressive. Children were also less likely to copy aggressive behavior if they had seen that behavior be punished. One potential conclusion from these results is that we could model peacemaking and forgiveness.

This idea has been tested across several different studies, and it shows promise. For example, in one study (Baron, 1972), college students were first introduced to three other students who were supposed to be additional participants but were really *confederates* of the research team. One of the confederates started insulting everyone while the study was getting started (e.g., telling them that they were stupid and would not have the maturity needed to complete the study). The *cover story* told to the participant about the procedure was similar to the story told to the people from the famous Milgram studies (see Chapter 7): that one person would receive (phony) shocks (the "learner") if

Society	Location and Type of Society	Conflict Management Techniques
Balinese (Belo, 1935; Howe, 1989)	Agricultural and commercial on the Indonesian island of Bali	Use self-control to suppress conflicts, usually successfully
Birhor (Adhikary, 1984a, 1984b; Bhattacharyya, 1953)	Nomadic hunters, gatherers, and traders in the forests of central India	Rarely fight, do not commit crimes, and have harmonious relations with neighboring Hindu villagers
Chewong (Howell, 1984)	Agricultural communities in the mountains on the Malay Peninsula	Have no mythology of violence or words for quarreling, fighting, aggression, or warfare
Hutterites (Bennett, 1967; Deets, 1931; Van den Berghe & Peter, 1988)	Communal farmers on the central plains of the United States and Canada (unlike Amish, they use modern farming equipment)	Believe that their Anabaptist faith promotes resolving conflicts without open disagreement
Inuit (Briggs, 1994)	Fishing and hunting communities in northern Alaska, Canada, Greenland	Fear interpersonal aggression, perhaps because murder had been frequent in some Inuit societies
Piaroa (Overing, 1986, 1989)	Native Americans of Venezuela formerly living in forest villages	Are appalled by aggression and treat disease as a sorcery attack from another village deserving a counterattack using sorcery
Tahitians (Levy, 1973, 1978)	Fishing and farming in the Society Islands of Tahiti	Behave with a gentleness that does not increase during festivals, although alcohol occasionally contributes to hitting within a family

they did not learn word-pairs correctly. The other three participants would take turns giving the "learner" shocks in the role of "teachers." Each could choose a level of shock from 1 to 10.

The insulting, obnoxious confederate always volunteered to be the learner. The *independent variable* of the study was whether the first "teacher" to deliver shocks—who was always one of the confederates—demonstrated aggression and revenge by sending high-level shocks or demonstrated forgiveness and reason by sending low-level shocks. As you have probably already guessed, the *dependent variable* was the amount of shock aggression then chosen by the true participant.

Results showed that when the participants saw the first "teacher" give low-level shocks, they chose significantly lower levels of shock themselves (Baron, 1972). Thus, modeling can increase aggression, but it can also increase peacemaking, helping, and forgiveness, a pattern supported by many other studies as well (e.g., Crowder & Goodfriend, 2012; Donnerstein & Donnerstein, 1976; Vidyasagar & Mishra, 1993). Perhaps there is something to Alexander Pope's famous quotation, "To err is human; to forgive, divine." There is also an emerging science of forgiveness that you can read about in the applied social psychology mini-chapter at the end of this book.

The Main Ideas

- The catharsis hypothesis is the idea that engaging in aggressive behavior will reduce it overall; however, several studies have not supported this hypothesis. In addition, studies show that getting revenge leads to short-term satisfaction but only increases aggression in the long term.

- Cultures can influence aggression in a positive or negative way; just as some cultures promote violence, other cultures discourage it and find alternative ways to solve problems.

- Modeling peacemaking and forgiveness has also successfully decreased aggression in observers.

 CRITICAL THINKING

- Think about catharsis or revenge on an international scale. Can you identify historical events that occurred due to one culture seeking "revenge" or "justice" for a past transgression? Did this response lead to positive or negative outcomes?

- Analyze the culture of your own school, family, or local community. Do these cultures encourage or discourage violence as a response to others? Identify three specific examples to support your view.

- Considering research showing that modeling forgiveness helps others choose to forgive, what could parents or teachers do to explicitly decrease aggressive tendencies in children? Discuss two specific scenarios that apply what you've learned from this section.

CHAPTER SUMMARY

What does it mean to be "aggressive"?

Aggression is behavior intended to harm others who do not wish to be harmed. There are many ways to categorize different forms of aggression. A descriptive typology can identify how people become aggressive, such as differentiating between (1) physical versus verbal aggression, (2) direct versus indirect aggression, and (3) active versus passive aggression. A motivational typology can instead identify why people are aggressive; here, we can distinguish between hostile/reactive aggression and instrumental/proactive aggression. Finally, recent ideas on microaggressions (more subtle, "everyday" forms of aggression such as racist statements) can take on the forms of micro-insult, microassault, and microinvalidation.

Evidence from several other academic disciplines, such as archeology or religion, indicates that humans have a long history of aggressive impulses and behaviors. The escalation of aggression effect indicates that aggression often starts because of a small issue, but increasingly aggressive exchanges progress quickly. The stages of provocation model establishes three progressively aggressive responses to conflict. That said, some people argue that in general, human aggressive tendencies have gone down over time, potentially due to increases in intelligence and reasoned thought.

Is aggression explained by biological instincts?

One explanation for aggression in humans (and other species) is that aggression leads to survival and reproductive advantages, and thus aggressive instincts are passed down through genetic generations. Genetic determinism is the idea that our behaviors are determined only by our genes. But, other research from an evolutionary perspective points out that aggression leads to advantages in status and mating opportunities as well.

Other biological drivers of aggression have also been explored. One could be how we respond to threat; the release of adrenaline

might lead to a "fight" response, for example. Perhaps surprisingly, low resting heart rates have been linked to higher chances of aggression. Increased alcohol and testosterone are both positively correlated with aggressive tendencies.

Is aggression explained by cultural influences?

Subcultures all over the world can encourage or discourage violence and aggression. For example, a "culture of honor" in the U.S. South appears to encourage men to consider insults as a threat to their masculinity and as deserving of a violent reaction. Along the same lines, gendered culture seems to encourage men to be more aggressive in general, compared to women. Finally, sports culture seems to encourage violence in certain contexts. Some research shows that when teams wear black uniforms, they are perceived as more threatening or aggressive. Some coaches may model aggressive behaviors to their teams. However, there are interesting examples of how sports can be used as a substitute for violence and how people who engage in sports can come to see their "rivals" in more positive ways, if the culture allows it.

Is aggression explained by situational influences?

Even generally nonaggressive people can become aggressive under the right circumstances. One example is seen when a nation or culture encourages aggression due to "patriotic" needs during war. Social psychology has explored how people might model aggression they see in the media; the most famous series of studies on this topic is the Bandura "Bobo doll studies." Here, children were more likely to be aggressive when they saw aggression being modeled and rewarded on television. Other research has explored this modeling effect in television, movies, and video games.

Aspects of our environment also might serve as cognitive cues; in other words, aspects of the circumstances might prime aggression or aggressive thoughts. Aggression seems to increase when (1) weapons are present, (2) images of alcohol are present, (3) and the temperature is hotter.

How can we manage or reduce aggression?

The catharsis hypothesis is the idea that engaging in aggressive behavior will reduce it, like venting or "letting off steam" to avoid an explosion. While catharsis may feel good and seem to work on an intuitive level, research shows that expressing aggression and anger only increases it. Catharsis can feel good in the short term, but it increases aggression in the long term. Instead of expressing anger, cultures can model forgiveness and peace in the same ways that cultures can encourage aggression. Some research on various cultures around the world indicates that cultures with established conflict management techniques can decrease aggression. In addition, if modeling can increase aggression in television, movies, and video games, perhaps these media could be used to model forgiveness as well.

THEORIES IN REVIEW

- Descriptive typology of aggression
- Motivational typology of aggression
- Microaggression
- Escalation of aggression effect
- Stages of provocation model
- Genetic determinism

- Alcohol disinhibition hypothesis
- Culture of honor
- Dehumanization
- Cognitive neoassociation analysis
- Weapons effect
- Catharsis hypothesis

CRITICAL THINKING, ANALYSIS, AND APPLICATION

- Table 11.1 presented a descriptive typology (Buss, 1961) of eight forms of aggression. Think of an example of each type. Then, rank-order your examples in terms of how harmful they are to (1) the target of the aggression, (2) the individual who is aggressing, and (3) society in general.

- Pinker (2011) suggested that aggression is negatively correlated with intelligence, education, and reasoned thought. Archer (2004) found that aggression peaked in both men and women when they were in their 20s (when testosterone is at its highest point). How do these two findings go together—or not?

- This chapter covered ideas regarding how aggression is influenced by biological factors, cultural factors, and situational factors. Which potential causes of violence did you find the most convincing, and why? Analyze your opinion on which of these three general categories is most influential in predicting aggression and violence.

- The final section of this chapter is, "How Can We Manage or Reduce Aggression?" Does the answer depend on what caused aggression in the first place? For example, if aggression is more caused by biological factors than cultural or situational factors, will it be harder to decrease aggression in general? Discuss.

PERSONAL REFLECTIONS

I never thought I would get in a bar fight. Most of my academic life has been devoted to the prevention of interpersonal violence; logically, I know that violence isn't a good solution to problems. But one night I found myself in a pool hall with a friend. A man harassed us most of the evening, calling us sexist and offensive names. Then he started touching my friend, a woman who was too polite to say anything. I got angry. I yelled at him. He didn't back down and instead started swearing at me and getting in my personal space. I don't know why I did it—but I punched him right in the chest. He was so drunk that he fell down easily. As I saw what was happening almost from a weird, third-party view, I realized I had made a mistake. I told my friend to grab her stuff and we ran out of the bar. I don't even know his name. I've carried that memory for years, feeling strangely justified in my actions but guilty at the same time. I could tell myself that my aggression was really just self-defense, but is that just a convenient excuse? [WG]

My wife and I have been living together for so long that we could assign numbers to our various disagreements, glare at each other, and just say, "Argument 42!" But recently we started up an argument that felt and sounded like some of our worst moments. Catharsis sure wasn't working for us because things only got worse: escalating aggression. Eventually, my wife then called me a series of unprintable names and I suddenly remembered how I had seen a friend (observational learning) defuse an argument with his wife (at a much earlier stage). So I modeled what he had done. When my wife "explained" in more detail why I was such a "XX$%^@#$," I really wanted to go one more round. But after she called me a "XX$%^@#$," I imitated my friend and said, "Well, I'm glad we have that settled." We were both so startled that we started laughing at our own foolishness. There wasn't going to be a winner of this argument. It was a case of whoever has the last word loses. But a small "I don't have to win" joke helped end it. We had settled down and reestablished ourselves in cognitive networks with much more pleasant associations. It was a small victory for something bigger than both of us. [TH]

LO11.1 **Explain typologies** that **define** and **organize** different forms of **aggression** and **apply** them to **aggression in humans over time**.

LO11.2 **Analyze biological** and **evolutionary explanations** for **aggression**.

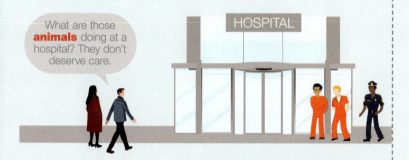

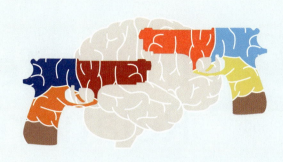

12 Intimate Relationships

Core Questions

1. What causes attraction?
2. What makes us physically attractive?
3. Do we have a relationship personality?
4. How do we decide to commit?
5. Do men and women act differently and, if so, why?

Learning Objectives

12.1 Explain how similarity, mere exposure, and physiological arousal contribute to initial attraction.

12.2 Analyze why some physical features are considered "attractive" across cultures.

12.3 Compare and contrast different "attachment styles" and what this means in relationships.

12.4 Define satisfaction, alternatives, and investments in relationships and apply each concept to how it predicts commitment.

12.5 Analyze why attraction, jealousy, and promiscuity differ between men and women in relationships.

Two of Hollywood's biggest stars, Brad Pitt and Jennifer Aniston, appeared to have a fairytale marriage. In 2000, the year of their marriage, Pitt was named "Sexiest Man Alive" by *People Magazine*, and Aniston was considered by many to be "America's Sweetheart." Movie fans all over the world were shocked when only a few years later, they announced a messy divorce in the midst of a huge scandal. Pitt admitted that he had fallen in love with one of Hollywood's "bad girls," Angelina Jolie, during the filming of their movie *Mr. & Mrs. Smith* (Goldsman, Milchan, Foster, & Liman, 2005).

In 2005, Pitt and Aniston's divorce was finalized while he and Jolie had already begun living together. Pitt and Jolie created a family with six children (some biological, some adopted), got married, and appeared to be forgiven by the world. Eventually, they married. Unfortunately for everyone involved, only 2 years after this second marriage, in 2016, Jolie filed for divorce. Some stories claimed Pitt had another affair with a movie costar; others said they simply couldn't agree on how to raise their children. What happened inside this love triangle? Love, sex, and romantic relationships intrigue us because they are such an important part of our personal experience. What does science have to say about matters of the heart?

Ask the Experts: Shelly Gable on Close Relationships

©SAGE Publications

WHAT CAUSES ATTRACTION?

▇▇ LO 12.1: To understand how and why similarity, mere exposure, and physiological arousal contribute to initial attraction.

Even if you come from a culture that does not allow dating, you have probably experienced the mystery of being attracted to someone. Was the attraction purely physical or was there more to it? You'll have to wait (or skip ahead to the next section) to learn about physical attraction. For now, we will explore three non-sexy-sounding (but actually exciting), *reliable* predictors of attraction: (1) similarity, (2) mere exposure, and (3) physiological arousal.

Similarity

You may have heard the phrase, "Opposites attract." It's a popular plot device in the movies to have the innocent rich girl fall for the street-smart bad boy (or vice versa).

Is it true that opposites attract? Or are we attracted to people similar to ourselves?

But social psychology tells us that the phrase "birds of a feather flock together" is a more accurate description of how real people connect with one another. This general idea, called the **similarity-attraction hypothesis**, predicts that people tend to form relationships with others who have the same attitudes, values, interests, and demographics as themselves (Morry, 2005, 2007). This is true for both friendships and romantic relationships—and within romantic relationships, the same idea is called **assortative mating.**

Now, conduct a mental survey of your friends' relationships or even—if you know—what brought your parents together. They were probably about the same age, came from families with similar incomes, and may have been the same race, ethnicity, or religion. For example, the U.S. Census tracks all kinds of patterns in the population every 10 years. They reported that the number of interracial marriages increased from 2000 to 2010, but only from a very small 7% to the slightly less small 10% (U.S. Census Bureau, 2010). The vast majority of us marry people who look and sound similar to ourselves.

Demographic variables such as age, social class, political leanings, and race or ethnicity may be important. But many of us want to date someone who can share our interests and dreams as well as understand our perspective on the world. When a date wants to see the same movie, play the same video game, or go to a party with the same people, planning an evening becomes easy. Planning an entire life together also becomes easier and more meaningful when two partners can agree on important issues such as whether to have children and how many, whether to spend money on a nicer apartment or on exotic vacations, and whether children should have any religious training. Similarities decrease arguments between couples.

What's behind this tendency to be attracted to someone similar to ourselves? Morry (2005, 2007) asserts that similarity matters because it validates our worldview. People with similar beliefs make us more comfortable with our opinions and affirm that we are logical, smart human beings. In 2015, *The New York Times* published data showing that people from certain regions of the United States were more or less likely to be married by the age of 26 (Leonhardt & Quealy, 2015). People from Utah are particularly likely to marry early, while people from New York City, southern Florida, and northern Alaska are less likely. How might the similarity hypothesis explain these trends?

Similarity-attraction hypothesis: The idea that people tend to form relationships, romantic and otherwise, with others who have the same attitudes, values, interests, and demographics as themselves (see *assortative mating*).

Assortative mating: The process by which organisms that are similar tend to mate with each other, meaning an individual is more likely to mate with someone who shares his or her features and interests (see *similarity-attraction hypothesis*).

Your hometown might affect whether you're married by the age of 26, according to *The New York Times* (Leonhardt & Quealy, 2015).

Of course, people are attracted to and have relationships with others who are different, and these relationships offer some benefits. For example, an individual who has a weakness in such areas as verbal communication can improve this skill if his or her partner is strong in it (Gruber-Baldini, Schaie, & Willis, 1995). Baxter and West (2003) also tested couples to see how they perceived any differences between them. They found that most couples can see the differences between the two people involved—and couple members who perceive these differences as an opportunity to learn from each other viewed this lack of similarity as a positive instead of as a negative.

Mere Exposure and Proximity

So, we tend to be attracted to people . . . like us!

That's not a major revelation, but notice that attitudes, interests, values, and so forth are all internal, personal characteristics. That means that those important predictors are, by definition, invisible. You can't see an attitude—but you can observe whether someone's face seems to smile or sneer when you mention a certain politician, controversial social issue, and so on. (Whether we interpret those looks accurately is another question.)

In addition to internal predictors, a variety of external factors also influence attraction. One of the most famous is called **mere exposure**, or the tendency to like things and people more, the more we are exposed to them. Sometimes this is called the **proximity effect** or the **propinquity effect** when it refers to exposure due to people being in the same physical area as yourself (such as people who live in your dorm room or neighborhood or people you see frequently in classes or at work). In general, the more we know people and the more we're around them, the more we like them (Goodfriend, 2009).

Think about one of your favorite current singers or bands. The first time you hear a new song on the radio, you might think, "This song is OK, but not nearly as good as their previous tracks." Then you hear the song again a few times and start humming along, without even realizing you're doing it. A few more musical exposures later and you could be downloading your new ringtone. You love it!

The mere exposure effect predicts that as we become more familiar with an object or person, our liking for that stimulus increases (Festinger et al., 1950; Monahan, Murphy, & Zajonc, 2000; Van Horn et al., 1997). (Note that this is true only when our original impression was fairly neutral; if we originally hated something, we might just grow to hate it even more.) The mere exposure effect explains why we prefer photos of ourselves that have been reversed instead of actual, original photos—because we're used to looking at ourselves in a mirror. Photos are backward from how we usually see our faces, so they seem "off" without most people realizing why (Mita, Dermer, & Knight, 1977).

The Westgate Housing Study. But does repeated exposure, by itself, really influence attraction between humans? A classic study from early social psychology tested this hypothesis in a creative way. You might remember hearing about this study in Chapter 8. Festinger and two of his colleagues (Festinger et al., 1950) investigated a small community named the Westgate Housing Project on the campus of the Massachusetts Institute of Technology (MIT). They wanted to know what would happen when strangers (here, MIT students) would be randomly thrown together in apartment buildings—in other words, the students would have a very close proximity to each other. Each apartment building included 10 single-family units, with five apartments on each of two floors. Although they were strangers, the residents of

Mere exposure: The tendency for individuals to prefer familiar objects and individuals, especially as exposure to them increases.

Proximity effect: The tendency for individuals to like people who are in close geographic proximity to themselves, due to the mere exposure effect (see *mere exposure*).

Propinquity effect: See *proximity effect.*

Schematic diagram of a Westgate West Building. A typical apartment in the Westgate Housing Project (Festinger et al., 1950). You can see staircases going up to the second floor that start near Apartments 1 and 5. When people in the buildings were asked to rate their neighbors, people in Apartments 1 and 5 were liked the most, while people in Apartments 6 and 10 were liked the least.

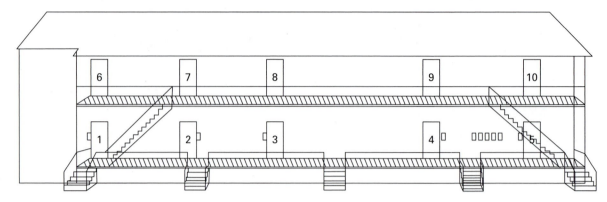

Westgate were similar to each other in terms of background, interests, stage of life, and life goals.

Festinger pointed out that there were two kinds of exposure in these apartments: (1) **physical distance** from one apartment to another—how many steps you'd have to take to get there—and (2) **functional distance**. Functional distance refers to the fact that, because of the buildings' design, some apartments were more likely to be passed by than others. The occupants of these apartments were more likely to be seen by other occupants. If two people see each other often, they are more likely to get to know each other and become friends (Festinger et al., 1950).

Exposure Leads to Liking. Festinger asked people in Westgate to choose the three people in the entire complex whom they were most likely to see socially (in other words, their friends). They listed residents with closer physical and functional proximity to themselves. By looking at Figure 12.1, you can see why people in Apartments 1 and 5 were liked the most. These apartments were at the bottom of staircases leading to the second floor, so all of the residents who lived on the second floor would have to pass those doors (Festinger et al., 1950).

People in Apartments 6 and 10 were usually liked the least, perhaps because the location of their apartments isolated them from their neighbors. Others felt that they didn't really know them. Importantly, this pattern was found across multiple buildings in the complex. That is important because the observations were *replicated*. Observing the same pattern suggested that the results weren't due to particularly nice people who happened to live in Apartments 1 and 5 (or mean jerks in Apartments 6 and 10). The researchers concluded that when all else was equal, mere exposure led to more liking (Festinger et al., 1950).

The mere exposure effect for interpersonal attraction has been replicated in many other ways, in both *controlled laboratory experiments* (e.g., Reis, Maniaci, Caprariello, Eastwick, & Finkel, 2011) and in *field studies*. Those replications came from *multiple research methods* used by independent researchers. They all told the same research story, so we naturally have more confidence in their findings. For example, one field study found that friends who lived in the same room or same town were more likely to remain close than friends who lived apart (Batool & Malik, 2010). Two studies found that cross-ethnic friendships were more likely between adolescents if they lived in the same neighborhood (Echols & Graham, 2013; Kruse, Smith, van Tubergen, & Maas, 2016).

Physical distance: A moderator of exposure dictated by the physical distance between two places (for example, the number of steps an individual would have to take to get from one apartment to another).

Functional distance: The tendency for people who are in close proximity due to the geographic and architectural design of an environment to be more likely to develop a cohesive group, such as a friendship or a romantic relationship.

MISATTRIBUTION OF AROUSAL IN THE SHAKY BRIDGE STUDY

© istockphoto.com/AlanMBarr & © istock photo.com/sasar

Would walking across these two bridges cause you different levels of anxiety and physiological arousal? Research indicates that some people might misinterpret that kind of arousal as attraction to other people who happen to be nearby.

How accurate are you at interpreting physical signals from your body? A famous research study explored this question and the fascinating phenomenon called misattribution of arousal, which happens when people make mistakes about the cause of physiological excitement they are experiencing.

Dutton and Aron (1974) asked a physically attractive female experimenter to spend time waiting in a park, then approach men who might be willing to complete a survey for a study. She told the men that the survey was investigating whether scenic settings had an effect on creativity and that after they completed it, she would be happy to answer additional questions. To emphasize her willingness to see more of each man, she wrote her phone number on a piece of paper and handed it to the men while smiling.

Remember that this experiment was meant to study *misattribution*. The key to how it worked was that the pretty young experimenter approached the men in two different park locations, making this a *quasi-experimental design*. The locations became the *independent variable*. But it's not a true experiment because the locations weren't *randomly assigned* to the different men. Still, Dutton and Aron predicted that one of the locations would lead to more physiological arousal—and thus more attraction to the woman—than the other. Attraction to her therefore became the *dependent variable*.

The locations were near two different bridges. The first bridge, considered the *control group* bridge, was sturdy and made of solid wood. It was wide, had high handrails, and the drop was only 10 feet. The second bridge, however,

was a 450-foot suspension bridge made of individual wooden boards strapped together with cables. To cross it, participants had to walk over a 250-foot canyon full of sharp and scary rocks; the bridge also had the tendency to "shake" and sway in the wind. Imagine what it would be like to cross this shaky bridge. In most participants, it would produce anxiety and fear—which in turn produce physiological changes such as increased heart rate, faster breathing, sweat, and nausea. Sound familiar?

The pretty female experimenter would wait for a young man who was by himself to cross one of the bridges and then would approach him. Next, he would complete the survey and walk away with the woman's phone number. The research team measured how many of these men called the experimenter later and asked her on a date, their way of measuring or *operationalizing* his level of attraction. You can probably predict what happened. Of the men who had crossed the shaky, arousing bridge, 50% called the experimenter, while only 12.5% of the men from the stable bridge called, a difference that was *statistically significant*.

The scientific question to ask is, What accounted for this large difference? Misattribution of arousal suggests that the men who had just crossed the shaky bridge were physiologically aroused due to fear and anxiety caused by the bridge itself. However, when they interacted with a pretty woman immediately after crossing, they may have misinterpreted that physiological arousal as sexual interest. My heart is beating, I'm sweaty . . . I guess I find this woman sexy! Not as many men from the stable bridge called because they didn't feel as physiologically aroused.

Social Psychology in Popular Culture

Moviestore collection Ltd / Alamy Stock Photo

In the popular movie series *The Hunger Games* (Collins, 2008, 2009, 2010), Katniss Everdeen is torn between love for two men. Why does she ultimately choose one over the other? If similarity were the focus of the film, she would probably choose Gale. Gale is very similar to Katniss; they both put protecting family first, they hunt together, and they stand up against the evil government together. But Gale doesn't capture her heart in the same way that Peeta, the other man, does.

Why does Katniss fall for Peeta instead? Peeta has many positive qualities (such as altruism and loyalty), but misattribution of arousal may also play a large part. Katniss and Peeta are constantly thrown together in a series of highly dangerous situations, both fighting for their lives. In a long-term and consistent state of physiological arousal, they are trying to survive multiple attempts to murder them. Being around Peeta in the midst of this chaos might lead Katniss to perceive more attraction to him than she would have felt in calmer conditions; perhaps she interprets her beating heart as caused by love instead of the adrenaline of survival.

Think about how this might affect your own romantic interests. As you get to know certain classmates or peers at work, do you find yourself more likely to become friends or even to start dating? It's likely that Brad Pitt and Angelina Jolie never would have become a couple if they hadn't gotten to know each other while filming *Mr. & Mrs. Smith* (2005). Mere exposure can have powerful effects over time.

Physiological Arousal and Misattribution

Sexual attraction. It's certainly a common part of the package of interpersonal attraction. Think back to the last time you were around someone you found extremely attractive. Your mind was probably racing with excitement—but so was your body. Did your heart beat faster? Did your breathing become short and fast? Maybe you were sweating or had a feeling of vague nausea. When we're sexually attracted to another person, we experience physiological arousal, the third predictor of attraction.

Usually we know exactly why we're experiencing this sort of physiological arousal. But is it possible for us to make an incorrect assumption about why we're sweaty and out of breath? If something in our immediate environment is producing these same reactions, then we might misinterpret physiological reactions as attraction—when we're simply reacting to the environment. In other words, we might make a **misattribution of arousal**. Some researchers call this the **excitation transfer effect** because we tend to transfer our excitement over the situation to excitement about the other person. To learn more about a famous study that tested this effect, see the Spotlight on Research Methods feature.

Misattribution of arousal: The tendency for individuals to misattribute physiological reactions to environmental stimuli as attraction (see *excitation transfer effect*).

Excitation transfer effect: The tendency for individuals to transfer their excitement over a situation to excitement about another person (see *misattribution of arousal*).

The Main Ideas

- Three variables that social psychology says contribute to attraction are similarity, mere exposure, and physiological arousal.

- Two people are more likely to become attracted to each other when they are similar in demographic ways (such as age, race, and social class), common interests, and basic values.

- Increased exposure typically leads to increased liking, a phenomenon called mere exposure. When this happens to people due to being near each other more frequently, it's called the proximity effect.

- Attraction is linked to physiological changes such as increased heart rate, breathing, and sweating. However, these same physiological changes can occur for other reasons and be incorrectly misinterpreted as attraction. This tendency is called misattribution of arousal.

CRITICAL THINKING CHALLENGE

- The research reviewed above suggests that similarity, mere exposure, and physiological arousal all contribute to attraction. Of these three variables, which do you think is the most important in predicting whether you'll want to date someone? Do you think that the answer is the same for everyone?

- In general, more exposure to an object or person means more liking. However, this is usually only true if the initial response to the object or person is neutral. More exposure to someone we don't like can lead to even more dislike. Think of someone you know who doesn't seem to like you. What might you be able to do to get that person to like you more, based on the other variables in this section of the chapter?

- Many social psychologists have applied the phenomenon of misattribution of arousal when giving advice to couples on a first date. Based on Dutton and Aron's research, if you want your date to be attracted to you, what kind of activities should you plan? What are other, alternative explanations for why men on the "shaky" bridge were more likely to call the female experimenter, compared to men on the stable bridge, and how could you set up a study to test for those explanations?

WHAT MAKES US PHYSICALLY ATTRACTIVE?

LO 12.2: Analyze why some physical features are considered "attractive" across cultures.

Have you experienced an immediate spark of sexual attraction toward some stranger? There were no words, no information, just their appearance. What was it about the other person's physical features that hijacked your attention? You already know about the "what-is-beautiful-is-good" effect (see Chapter 5), in which physically attractive people are perceived as having several other positive qualities as well.

There are certainly individual differences regarding what different people find attractive in others. You might be attracted to someone with dark coloring or very pale skin, short or long hair, muscular features, or delicate hands. Despite these individual variations in what we consider our "type," certain physical characteristics seem to be universally appealing to everyone, regardless of age, ethnicity, or culture. Certain celebrities, such as Brad Pitt, Jennifer Aniston, and Angelina Jolie, are considered attractive

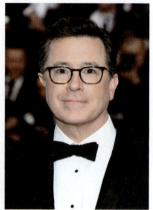

& Dia Dipasupil/ Getty Images Entertainment / Getty images

Denzel Washington is known for being a great actor, but researchers also point out how symmetrical his face is. Do you find him more attractive than Stephen Colbert, who has often been teased for having one ear that seems to hang lower and stick out farther than the other? Did you notice that feature before we pointed it out to you?

by almost everyone who sees them. What explains these cross-cultural similarities in perceived beauty?

Buss is probably the most famous modern social psychologist studying how evolutionary theory applies to human dating and mating. He has published dozens of books and articles about this topic (e.g., Buss, 1985, 1989, 1994). His reasoning goes like this: If researchers can identify certain physical characteristics or traits that are universally considered attractive—regardless of one's upbringing or culture—then these traits probably come from ancient, inherited instincts. Moreover, we experience all these attraction impulses on an unconscious level; we don't even know why we like someone or something.

Despite our lack of awareness, preferences for certain physical traits have endured over time and across dozens of different countries. What are the traits that seem to be almost universally appealing or beautiful? Psychologists have discovered three interesting patterns of appeal, regardless of culture. As we go through each one, think about whether you and the people around you have these traits. In other words, based on these three criteria, would the people around you be considered universally "hot" or not?

Symmetry

Have you ever noticed a person whose facial features are not symmetrical? Perhaps one eye is bigger than the other, there's a scar on one cheek, or one ear sticks out farther than the other. Do you think this factor affects how attractive you perceive the person to be?

Several research studies indicate we experience **bilateral symmetry** as attractive. An object, face, or body is bilaterally symmetrical when the left half perfectly matches the right half. For example, one study found the amount of symmetry in male college students to be significantly—and positively—correlated with ratings of how attractive their faces were (Gangestad, Thornhill, & Yeo, 1994). The effect was much stronger for men than women in this study.

When men and women rated photographs of the "opposite" sex (see below for a discussion of how this phrase may encourage a false dichotomy of sex), bilateral symmetry of the faces was again positively correlated with how attractive the faces

Bilateral symmetry: When the two halves of an object, face, or body perfectly match. Faces with bilateral symmetry are often deemed more attractive than those without bilateral symmetry.

were perceived to be (Grammer & Thornhill, 1994). Perhaps most interestingly, a third study (Thornhill & Gangestad, 1994) measured men's and women's body and facial symmetry by comparing their left-side and right-side feet, ankles, hands, wrists, elbows, and ears. Results showed that for both sexes, greater symmetry was associated with a higher number of sex partners. For men, symmetry was correlated with having sex at an earlier age. The same trend was true for women but was not strong enough to be *statistically significant*.

Why is bilateral symmetry attractive? From an evolutionary perspective, symmetry may be an easy-to-see indicator of genetic quality—a heuristic cue that helps us make fast (but often unfair) judgments about others. If your potential mate is asymmetrical, perhaps he or she has a genetic disorder that could be passed on to any offspring. That explanation may not apply to humans (especially not humans who don't plan to reproduce with their mate), but in other species, asymmetry has been linked to developmental instability. For example, in scorpion flies, lopsided individuals are more likely to have negative reactions to environmental pollution and to carry disease ("Biology of Beauty," 1996). Honeybees also prefer to pollinate symmetrical flowers (Wignall, Heiling, Cheng, & Herberstein, 2006).

We may not realize that we're attracted to symmetry. But symmetry may be an instinct at work when we find ourselves mysteriously attracted to someone. Note the quirky finding that in one study, sober individuals were good at detecting asymmetry in faces and found them less attractive. Drunk people, however, couldn't even tell when faces were asymmetrical (Halsey, Huber, Bufton, & Little, 2010). Perhaps this explains why drinking seems to make people find others suddenly more attractive.

Symmetry is linked to within-species attraction for several animals—including humans.

"Average" Faces

Being "just average" doesn't sound that great in terms of your physical attractiveness, but in this case, being average might be a good thing. Just as symmetrical faces and bodies might be heuristic cues to genetic health, so might **composite or average faces**, faces that do not include any unusual or strange features.

Researchers have investigated this hypothesis by having participants rate the attractiveness of many different faces. Included in this lineup is one computer-generated face that is the composite or "average" of all the other faces (Perrett, May, & Yoshikawa, 1994). When this is done, the computer-generated "average" face is typically rated as the most beautiful or attractive, compared to the individual faces of actual people (Langlois & Roggman, 1990; Langlois, Roggman, & Musselman, 1994).

Check out the computer-generated faces in Figure 12.2; these were created by Langlois for her research lab (you can visit her website to learn more). As you can see, the face on the far left is a composite of 2 individual photos, while the photo on the far right is made up of 32 individual photos. Langlois finds that people tend to rate the 32-face average as more attractive than the 2-face average (Langlois & Roggman, 1990; Langlois et al., 1994). In addition, the averaged faces are rated as more attractive than any of the individual faces used to make them, as long as the averaged face is a computer-generated composite of at least 16 faces.

But here's our usual question: Why? Why are "averaged" faces rated as more attractive? Here are three possibilities. First, it could be a **procedural artifact**, a finding that results from *how* we conducted the experiment. For example, it could be an *order effect*

Composite face: See *average face*.

Average face: A computer-generated composite face created by combining several individual faces, so that it does not contain any unusual or strange features. Average faces are often perceived as more attractive than individual faces.

Procedural artifact: A finding that results from how a researcher conducted the experiment, rather than introduction of the independent variable.

Shutterstock / Sergey Sonvar Nik

■ FIGURE 12.2 Averaged Caucasian female faces. Computer-generated averaged faces are perceived as more attractive than the individual faces on which they are based, and more faces usually means more perceived attractiveness. See this website to learn more: http://homepage.psy.utexas.edu/HomePage/Group/LangloisLAB/averagenessbeauty.html

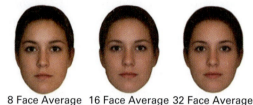

2 Face Average   4 Face Average   8 Face Average   16 Face Average   32 Face Average

SOURCE: The University of Texas at Austin, Department of Psychology.

because seeing an "averaged" face *after* seeing so many similar faces engages the mere exposure effect. (This would only be true for *within-participants designs*.) Second, we may experience "averaged" faces as comforting because they fit our cultural expectations. We are attracted to our social norms and dislike those who are "different." Third, averaged faces are symmetrical cues to genetic health. Small variations that might indicate genetic abnormalities—which could be passed on to potential offspring—disappear as faces are averaged and become more symmetric.

However, you may be questioning the "average" face results because of the commonly held belief that people with "exotic" features are particularly attractive. The "exotic" effect—which in some ways opposes the "average" effect—can also be explained in two ways. First, sometimes models who are people of color are dehumanized and made into animalistic images, which further objectifies and sexualizes them (compared to most models). For example, you might notice that people of color in magazines are more likely to be wearing animal prints, such as a leopard-skin bikini. Second, "exotic" features often highlight specific secondary sex characteristics that are hypermasculine or feminine, such as square jaws and pronounced eyebrows in men and large lips, large eyes, and high cheekbones in women. These particular features are also considered attractive because they signal culturally gendered messages of what is traditional "beauty."

For two interesting insights into views of what is found attractive in nontraditional samples of participants, consider the following studies. First, Scull (2013) spent 18 months observing and interviewing male strippers. Results here found that the men purposely highlighted their traditionally masculine features to attract customers. A second article (Moscowitz, Turrubiates, Lozano, & Hajek, 2013) reviewed two studies on gay men who self-identified as "Bears," a slang term for men in the gay community who are physically large and have a lot of body hair. The Bears in these studies reported having lower self-esteem than non-Bears, and the researchers speculated it was because while they have some hypermasculine physical features, they do not fit into culturally normative and stereotypic views of gay men being physically fit and stylish.

Waist-to-Hips and Waist-to-Shoulders Ratios

Waist-to-hips ratio: The ratio comparing the circumference of the waist to the circumference of the hips, which often plays a role in determining female body attractiveness.

Which of the bodies shown in Figure 12.3 do you think is the most attractive? These bodies differ in an important variable called **waist-to-hips ratio**, which is the ratio comparing the circumference of the waist to the circumference of the hips. If, for example, your waist measured 30 inches and your hips measured 40 inches, then your waist-to-hips ratio would be 3 to 4, or 0.75.

Several studies have shown that across cultures, the most desirable waist-to-hips ratio for women is about 0.7 (Singh, 1993a, 1993b; Singh & Randall, 2007). When men are asked to judge the attractiveness of line drawings of women, such as the one in Figure 12.3, the women with a ratio of 0.7 were rated healthier, more youthful, and to have a higher reproductive capacity (LaForge & Goodfriend, 2012). Interestingly, famous beauties Marilyn Monroe, Sophia Loren, and Kate Moss all had, at least at one point in their popular careers as actresses and models, a 0.7 waist-to-hips ratio.

What about preferences for men's bodies? For them, too, a certain ratio matters. However, for men's bodies, it's the **waist-to-shoulders ratio**, or the ratio comparing the circumference of the waist to the circumference of the shoulders. Again, perhaps surprisingly, the number for the ratio is about the same: between 0.70 and 0.75. That is, for men, the waist should be 70% of the circumference of the shoulders; this is the ratio women find most attractive (Braun & Bryan, 2006; Dixson, Halliwell, East, Wignarajah, & Anderson, 2003) and the ratio gay men find most attractive in other men (LaForge & Goodfriend, 2012).

Does an evolutionary, survival-of-the-fittest explanation fit what you experience as attractive? According to this perspective, heterosexual men are attracted to women with large hips because they suggest a healthy gateway for babies; the small waist indicates aerobic health. So, the most attractive women will be those who are physically fit and thus more likely to survive childbirth and the following year of raising an infant. Heterosexual women are attracted to men with a small waist because it also indicates aerobic fitness; broad, strong shoulders indicate physical strength. This strength would certainly be an advantage for any physical tasks and might be important when a pregnant woman or a child needs protection.

It's important to remember that these preferences typically exist on an unconscious level. According to the evolutionary perspective—which is criticized by many in the field of psychology—they are the legacies of what benefited our ancestors in terms of genetic and reproductive fitness. Thus, while some of these motivations may seem out of date—and potentially sexist—the evolutionary perspective explores variables such as mating and attractiveness from a genetic and biological perspective. Social psychology asserts that *both* nature (our biological impulses) and nurture (cultural preferences) are hard at work creating the physical combination that appears most attractive to each person.

■ FIGURE 12.3 Which body type do you find the most sexually attractive? Research indicates that "C" is the most popular answer.

A   B   C   D

SOURCE: Singh (1993).

The Main Ideas

- The evolutionary perspective predicts that some attraction preferences will be universal or cross-cultural, due to their benefits to us as a species. Note that there are criticisms of this perspective, however.

- Three traits that are considered attractive, regardless of culture, are bilateral symmetry, composites or "averages," and specific waist-to-hips or waist-to-shoulders ratios.

- While we may judge people with these traits as more attractive, we may not realize why; these traits may be appealing on an unconscious level.

Waist-to-shoulders ratio:
The ratio comparing the circumference of the waist to the circumference of the shoulders, which often plays a role in determining male body attractiveness.

- Now that you know about traits that are considered "universally" attractive, are there things you would consider changing about your own appearance or dress that might highlight your own features or disguise things about yourself that go against these desirable traits?

- Recall that studies on bilateral symmetry found that symmetry was significantly correlated with having sex at an earlier age for men but not so much for women. What might explain this difference? What other psychological variables might affect women's age of first sexual encounter?

- Identify three celebrities, then analyze each person for his or her facial symmetry, "average"-ness, and waist-to-hips or waist-to-shoulders ratios as well as you can from photographs. Are the people you see good examples of these three ideas? When you notice someone who doesn't fit these criteria, do you see him or her as less attractive?

DO WE HAVE A RELATIONSHIP PERSONALITY?

LO 12.3: Compare and contrast different "attachment styles" and what this means in relationships.

Relationships produce predictable patterns of behavior, and a few questions will help you recognize some of them. For example, if your relationship partner had to go on a weeklong trip that involved attending lots of parties with attractive people, would you trust that your partner would be faithful? Would you feel jealous if he or she were emotionally—but not physically—intimate with someone else? How often would you want to communicate, and how much would you miss your partner?

The predictable ways in which you react to such questions can be considered your **relationship personality**, behavior patterns that describe your habitual interpersonal dynamics with others. Some people are inherently trusting, while others tend to be jealous. One theory (Clark & Mills, 1979) differentiates between people who have an "exchange" orientation (one in which people expect direct reciprocity—if we watched your favorite movie last week, then it's my turn this week) versus a "communal" orientation (one in which people don't keep explicit track of things); for more on this theory, see the section on forgiveness within marriage in the mini-chapter on forgiveness.

When it comes to forming and maintaining our intimate relationships with family, lovers, and friends, the most-studied theory in social psychology is called attachment theory.

Relationship personality: Behavior patterns that describe an individual's habitual interpersonal dynamic with others.

© istockphoto.com/eli_asenova

Attachment theory suggests that the relationship infants have with their primary caregiver (such as their mother) will serve as a template for all future relationships.

The History of Attachment Theory

The story of attachment theory begins in London, World War II, during "The Blitz." Nightly bombing raids devastated buildings while citizens huddled underground. Parents had only one fear greater than their own death: the death of their children.

To keep the city's young ones safe, the British government evacuated the children to the countryside. After the war, the families who survived were reunited.

Physically, the children were fine. However, an unforeseen side effect had occurred. Some of the children had been separated from their parents at a crucial time in their development, and as young adults they displayed a variety of psychological problems. Many of these adolescents were unable to form strong, loving ties with other people. Attachment theory evolved as psychological researchers tried to explain this pattern of behavior (Berscheid & Regan, 2005; Bowlby, 1958, 1988; Hazan & Shaver, 1987). Since then, thousands of research studies have explored how different attachment orientations (or relationship personalities) affect relationship behaviors, decisions, and interactions between couple members.

Attachment theory focuses on how our familial environment during the formative years (especially infancy) affects our ability to begin and maintain normal, adult relationships—including romantic relationships. The rest of this section discusses the connections between childhood attachment and adult attachment, as well as different attachment "styles" or personalities identified by researchers.

The Strange Situation

British psychologist John Bowlby, inspired by those troubled London children, proposed that our very first relationship in life becomes a model for our future relationships. As infants, our first relationship is with our primary caregiver, typically the mother or father. (In the 1940s and 1950s, it was almost always the mother.) Bowlby believed that if this infant-mother relationship was happy and healthy, then the child would learn to trust others and to grow up to have healthy relationships with others. That meant, of course, that unhealthy first relationships would predict trouble later (Bowlby, 1958).

Bowlby and one of his students, Mary Ainsworth, observed infants and mothers sitting in a room that was filled with new, interesting toys for the infant to explore. Then, a series of exchanges would occur in which an experimenter would enter the room, the mother would leave, and the infant would be left alone with the experimenter (Ainsworth, 1979). Eventually, the mother returned.

This experimental paradigm is called the **strange situation**, which refers to a room that offers child participants a novel environment to explore. In this case, "strange" simply means new and not "weird." Experimenters observed the children at each of these stages: in the room with their mother before she left, with a stranger (another experimenter), and when they were reunited with their mother. Would the child cry and be upset when the mother left? Would he or she play happily with the toys? Was the child's reaction to the temporary absence of the mother predictable, based on how the mother treated the child beforehand? Once the mother returned, how did the infant react to being reunited?

Ainsworth's (1979) research identified three patterns in how the children responded when put in a new environment (the strange situation). First, children with supportive parents who provided a secure "home base" would be a little upset when their mothers left. But they would quickly start to explore the toys and other distractions in the room. They seemed confident that their mothers would quickly come back if needed. A second group of children couldn't handle their mothers' departure. These children were immediately upset and continued to cry constantly, apparently unsure whether Mom would return at all. Finally, a third pattern emerged: infants who seemed diffident, almost uncaring that their mothers had left. These children would explore the room but did not display much confidence or happiness.

Social Psychology in Action:
Strange Situation

©SAGE Publications

- - - - - - - - - - - - - - - - - - - -

Attachment theory: A framework for understanding relationships that focuses on how an individual's familial environment during the formative years affects his or her ability to begin and maintain normal, adult relationships.

Strange situation: Refers to either the experimental paradigm in which a mother and child are observed in a room as the mother leaves and returns or to the room itself in which this occurs.

- - - - - - - - - - - - - - - - - - - -

AP Photo/David Goldman

A typical "strange situation" room, in which infants are observed as their primary caregiver leaves and returns. How will the infant react?

Researchers came to treat these different personalities and reactions as three distinct "attachment styles" (Berscheid & Regan, 2005; Hazan & Shaver, 1987). Table 12.1 summarizes some of the basic differences among these three styles, and the next section explores them in more depth.

Three Attachment Styles

The first style is the **secure attachment** style. This style, produced by consistently supportive parents, translates into healthy, trusting adult relationships. Secure individuals go into relationships assuming that other people are trustworthy and sincere. They also have relatively high self-esteem and believe they deserve to be treated well. Secure people don't get overly jealous or anxious when their partners are absent, and their relationships tend to be long term and happy.

The second style is **anxious/ambivalent attachment**. This attachment style, produced by inconsistent parents, translates into high levels of jealousy and low self-esteem. Anxious/ambivalent children had parents who were sometimes loving and supportive but sometimes not. Their early life experiences taught them that other people are unpredictable. Their lack of security means that they will get jealous easily, will want to maintain a high frequency of contact with their partner, and will have nagging self-doubts about whether they are worthy of being loved.

Secure attachment: A type of attachment style produced by consistently supportive parents, which translates into healthy, trusting, long-term adult relationships. Individuals with a secure attachment style tend to have relatively high self-esteem and aren't overly jealous or anxious.

Anxious/ambivalent attachment: A type of attachment style produced by inconsistent parents, which translates into high levels of jealousy and low self-esteem within adult relationships. Individuals with an anxious/ambivalent attachment style tend to have turbulent relationships.

■ TABLE 12.1 Three Distinct Attachment Styles

Attachment Style	Parents Were...	Level of Anxiety When Parent Leaves	Explore the Strange Situation Room?	Level of Adult Self-Esteem	Tendency to Be Jealous of Romantic Partners
Secure	Consistently good	Moderate	Yes	High	Low
Anxious/ambivalent	Inconsistent	High	No	Low	High
Avoidant/fearful	Consistently bad	Low	Yes	Low	Low

Finally, the third style is **avoidant/fearful attachment**. This attachment style, produced by consistently unsupportive parents, translates into a general lack of trust and isolating behaviors. Children whose parents were absent, abusive, or cruel learned to shut off their trust in others and their desire for close relationships. Thus, as adults, people with an avoidant/fearful attachment style will often become isolated loners, afraid to try forming relationships that they believe will ultimately disappoint them. Their adult romantic relationships, if they have any, may consist of a series of one-night stands.

Advances in Attachment Research

Attachment theory has become one of the most popular frameworks for research on adult romantic relationships. Many of the published studies explore whether different styles are associated with later relationship outcomes and, if so, whether those connections were predicted by the theory. Just in the past 10 years, over 4,000 studies have been published on the topic (based on a search for the term *attachment theory* in the online PsycINFO database). When a search on the database is narrowed down to articles that focus on how attachment styles affect life for college students, there are still well over 500 studies available.

Here are some of the most interesting findings about your peers:

- Students with a secure style are more likely to send regular texts to a partner, whereas avoidant/fearful students are more likely to send "sext" messages (texts with sexual content or illicit photos; Drouin & Landgraff, 2012).
- Anxious/ambivalent people are more likely to jealously check on their partner's Facebook messages (Marshall, Bejanyan, Di Castro, & Lee, 2013).
- Secure people are less likely to accept violence or abuse in their relationships (McDermott & Lopez, 2013) and are more likely to display emotional sensitivity and social skills (Dereli & Karakuş, 2011).
- In gay couples, anxious/ambivalent men are less likely to require a partner to use a condom during sex (Starks, Castro, Castiblanco, & Millar, 2016).

Attachment style predicts a network of relationship expectations and behaviors. For further insight into how attachment styles are measured in research, see the Applying Social Psychology to Your Life feature. Read more about attachment theory and *Harry Potter* in the Social Psychology in Popular Culture feature.

A New Model: Four Styles Instead of Three

Science is always changing as new evidence becomes available, and some recent research about attachment styles proposes four attachment styles instead of three. This new model is organized around two different explanations (or attributions) that people often use when a relationship doesn't go well. Will you decide that the problem is you—meaning you are not worthy of being loved—or that the problem is the other person—meaning that others are not trustworthy to be there when needed? These two attributional explanations result in the matrix shown in Figure 12.4. As you can see, the matrix outlines four attachment styles: secure, dismissing, preoccupied, and fearful.

In this case, the researchers (Bartholomew & Horowitz, 1991) proposed that there are two major variables at play within attachment: (1) view of self (positive or negative) and (2) view of others (positive or negative). A positive view of self is like high self-esteem; it means you feel worthy of being loved and believe you would make a good relationship partner. A positive view of others means that you find other people trustworthy in general and seek out healthy relationships.

Avoidant/fearful attachment:
A type of attachment style produced by consistently unsupportive parents, which translates into a general lack of trust and isolating behaviors within adult relationships. Individuals with an avoidant/fearful attachment style tend to isolate themselves from consistent relationships.

MEASURING YOUR ATTACHMENT STYLE

Applying Social Psychology to Your Life

A good way to understand the different styles of attachment is to see how research psychologists measure them. One of the most popular is a scale called "Experiences in Close Relationships" (Brennan, Clark, & Shaver, 1998; updated by Wei, Russell, Mallinckrodt, & Vogel, 2007). Some of the items have been modified slightly to make them easier for you to score.

Instructions: As you read each statement, write a number next to the item to indicate how much you agree with it, using this scale:

1	2	3	4	5	6	7
Strongly disagree			Neutral			Strongly agree

Anxiety Items

_____ 1. I worry that romantic partners won't care about me as much as I care about them.

_____ 2. My desire to be close sometimes scares people away.

_____ 3. I need a lot of reassurance that I am loved by my partner.

_____ 4. I find that my partner(s) don't want to get as close as I would like.

_____ 5. I get frustrated when romantic partners are not available when I need them.

_____ 6. I often worry about being abandoned.

Avoidance Items

_____ 7. I want to get close to my partner, but I keep pulling back.

_____ 8. I am nervous when partners get too close to me.

_____ 9. I try to avoid getting too close to my partner.

_____ 10. I don't usually discuss my problems and concerns with my partner.

_____ 11. I do not turn to my partner in times of need.

_____ 12. I do not rely on my partner for things like comfort and reassurance.

Scoring: The more you *disagree* with these sentences, the more "Secure" you are. In other words, if you agree with Items 1 to 6, you would be classified as "Anxious/Ambivalent." If you agree with Items 7 to 12, you would be classified as "Avoidant/Fearful." If you don't really agree with any of the items, or your total score for each section is a low number, you are "Secure" and are more likely to have happy, healthy relationships.

■ FIGURE 12.4 An updated, four-category model of attachment.

		View of self	
		Positive	Negative
View of others	Positive	**Secure** (Comfortable with intimacy)	**Preoccupied** (anxious and jealous)
	Negative	**Dismissing** (narcissistic, avoids long-term intimacy)	**Fearful** (avoids social connections in general)

SOURCE: Modified from Bartholomew and Horowitz (1991).

ATTACHMENT THEORY IN *HARRY POTTER*

Social Psychology in Popular Culture

Pictorial Press Ltd / Alamy Stock Photo

One of the best-selling book and movie franchises in history is the *Harry Potter* series (Rowling, 1997, 1998, 1999, 2000, 2003, 2005, 2007), following the lives of several young wizards who fight evil. Luckily for social psychology, the three main characters demonstrate the three major attachment styles first proposed by attachment theory (Bowlby, 1958, 1988).

Hermione Granger is a perfect example of the secure attachment style. Born of parents who are supportive without being suffocating, people with a secure attachment style are confident, feel free to express their emotions, and are happy to trust others. Although we don't see Hermione's parents much in the series, readers learn that they trust their daughter and are completely supportive but also show concern when she's in danger. Hermione thus projects this style onto her own teenage experiments in love. When Ron Weasley repeatedly shows that he's too scared to ask her out, she promptly moves on to someone else (Viktor Krum). She's jealous when Ron starts dating a fellow classmate, but Hermione waits patiently for him to realize that she's a better choice. In short, her self-esteem and her trust in both others and herself show that she's secure, which is considered the healthiest attachment style.

Her object of affection, Ron Weasley, is certainly not secure—he's what we call anxious/ambivalent. The hallmark of parents who produce anxious/ambivalent children is inconsistency. The Weasleys certainly love their seven children, but they are either screaming at them with magical messages or simply distracted and thus basically absent. This leads to children who are unsure of where they stand in relationships, always yearning for love but never confident that they'll actually get it. Ron shows this attachment style in his desire for Hermione and in his doubt that she'll return the interest. Instead, he dates "safe" girls who are less challenging. Ron's relationship personality becomes one of jealousy, clinginess, and, above all, insecurity.

Finally, Harry Potter displays what can be argued as the least healthy attachment style: avoidant/fearful. Harry's birth parents were certainly loving, but he never really knew them. His adoptive parents were cruel and abusive. This leads to Harry's fearful style. He pushes everyone else away, never believing relationships will bring him any comfort. Harry prefers to do everything by himself, something he proves each and every time he has to face a challenge. In relationships, he avoids admitting that he likes anyone, and when he can no longer deny it, his response is to do nothing. For both of his main love interests, he sits back and waits for them to make the first move.

When the researchers tested their model with college students, they found the following patterns or attachment styles (Bartholomew & Horowitz, 1991):

- *Secure* people were most likely to have high levels of intimacy in both romantic relationships and friendships; they also showed self-confidence, warmth, and balance in their relationships. This style matches the one from the earlier model with only three styles.
- *Dismissing* people showed the highest levels of self-confidence but also showed very low levels of emotional expressiveness, empathy, and warmth toward others. They were less likely to rely on others in times of need and were less likely to share personal information with other people.
- *Preoccupied* people were the opposite of dismissing in almost every variable; they showed particularly low self-confidence but particularly high levels of personal self-disclosure, emotional expressiveness (such as frequent crying), and excessive caregiving behaviors.
- Finally, *fearful* people were very low on self-disclosures, intimacy, level of relationship involvement, reliance on others, and self-confidence. In general, they did not put much effort into relationships or expect others to do so.

Importantly for attachment theory, this study also showed moderate correlations between the participants' attachment both to family members and to peers. Consistent findings that describe multiple populations are demonstrating *external validity* through high levels of *generalizability*. Bowlby originally hypothesized that attachment styles would be consistent across relationships—and these data (Bartholomew & Horowitz, 1991) support that hypothesis.

The Main Ideas

- Attachment theory suggests that the way your parents treated you during your early childhood affects your self-esteem and trust in adult, romantic relationships.
- Research using a laboratory model called the "strange situation" identified three distinct attachment "styles": secure, anxious/ambivalent, and avoidant/fearful.
- Secure people have generally healthy self-esteem and trust in others, both in childhood and in later, adult romantic relationships. Anxious/ambivalent people have low self-esteem and high jealousy. Finally, avoidant/fearful people have low trust in others and often avoid relationships, expecting them to end in disappointment.
- A new model of attachment suggests four styles instead of three and seems to be supported by research studies.

⚡ CRITICAL THINKING CHALLENGE

- John Bowlby is famous for saying that the attachment style you form as a young child will follow you "from the cradle to the grave," meaning it will be difficult to change over your lifetime. Do you agree or disagree with this belief? Is it possible that happy, secure children can become anxious or avoidant due to negative experiences in young adulthood, such as an abusive relationship? Alternatively, can people who had challenging childhoods heal these emotional wounds by finding loving, supportive adult relationship partners?
- Think again about the measurement scale in this section. When you think about the relationships you see around you, such as in your friends and family

members, try to guess how each of these people might complete the scale. Does attachment theory explain their patterns of relationship behavior? Do you recommend rewording any of the items?

- This chapter highlighted three characters from *Harry Potter* who display some aspects of the three main attachment styles. The next time you watch a favorite television show or movie, or read a book or play, try to analyze the main characters' attachment styles. Do their current relationship choices reflect their early childhoods, as the theory suggests?

- Do you prefer the three-category model attachment styles or the four-category model? Why?

HOW DO WE DECIDE TO COMMIT?

LO 12.4: Define satisfaction, alternatives, and investments in relationships and apply each concept to how it predicts commitment.

Many psychologists (and individuals!) would like to be able to predict whether a given relationship will last over time. For example, would psychologists have been able to predict that Brad Pitt was going to break up with Jennifer Aniston and date Angelina Jolie instead? How did you (or will you) decide whether to stay committed to someone or to end the relationship?

"Nontraditional" Relationship Options

Predicting relationship commitment and, thus, relationship duration or longevity is the focus of the next big theory we'll cover. However, let's take a brief tangent to consider nontraditional options in relationships. There are many choices for how people interact; what makes one person happy may not work for everyone. Here are four alternatives to the traditional view of relationships in most "Western" cultures.

Arranged Marriages. For some cultures, such as China and India, the "traditional" approach to relationships is an **arranged marriage**, in which the couple members' families decide on the marriage for pragmatic reasons, such as a good match in terms of socioeconomic status or because the two families have land next to each other (for a review of research on arranged marriages, see Merali, 2012). While people from outside of these cultures often view arranged marriages as lacking in romance, people within the cultures often see them as more sacramental (Bhopal, 1999) and more "traditional" from their perspective. Research on satisfaction in these marriages finds inconsistent results (e.g., Blood, 1967; Madathil & Benshoff, 2008).

Hooking Up. Many people prefer to stay single and to have several one-time sexual interactions called **hookups** or "one-night stands." When two people hook up, they typically are more interested in sexual pleasure than in getting to know each other on a personal, psychological level (Paul & Hayes, 2002). Variability in hookups is quite large; for example, one study found a self-reported range in college student hookups between 0 and 65 in a single year (Paul, McManus, & Hayes, 2000).

Note, however, that there seem to be gender differences in how hooking up occurs and how people feel about it afterward. One study (Campbell, 2008) found that men are significantly more likely to report enjoying the encounters afterward, compared to women, and another study implies that at least some heterosexual women hook up because they perceive sexual coercion from their dates (Katz & Wigderson, 2012).

Friends With Benefits. While hookups occur with several different people, another choice some people make is to have casual sex repeatedly with the same person over

Arranged marriage: A marriage that was decided on by the couple members' families for pragmatic reasons, such as a good match in terms of socioeconomic status.

Hookup: One-time sexual interactions that are typically focused on sexual pleasure rather than fostering personal, psychological bonds.

time—but the relationship remains at friendship status instead of being considered an official "relationship." This option, referred to as **friends with benefits**, seems to be quite popular with modern college students; approximately half report having at least one friend with benefits while in college (Bisson & Levine, 2009). Again, there appear to be interesting gender differences; men report their primary motivation to have a friend with benefits is regular access to sex, while women report their primary motivation is an emotional connection with someone (Lehmiller, VanderDrift, & Kelly, 2011).

Polyamorous Relationships. Many people believe it is possible to have multiple committed relationships at once, an idea generally known as **polyamory**. There are several types, including **polyandry** (one man with multiple female partners) and **polygyny** (one woman with multiple male partners). It's not typically group sex—it's more like taking turns among several individuals. Polyamory isn't cheating because everyone involved knows about the other people and is happy with the arrangement. When the people involved are legally married, this arrangement is called **polygamy**. It's also possible to have a relationship with other couples where individuals have sexual encounters with anyone in the group. Polyamory is defined in different ways by different people, but the common understanding is that "exclusivity of both an intimate and sexual nature is not a necessary precursor to love and commitment" (Lehmiller, 2014, p. 214).

Interdependence Theory (Social Exchange Theory)

While there are certainly options for the type of relationship you may want, "happily ever after" in a monogamous couple is appealing to many. But commitment can be hard work, and sometimes relationships struggle to survive. What keeps people together?

Thibaut and Kelley (1959) created **interdependence theory**, a model of romantic relationships that suggests relationship stability is predicted by commitment. In turn, commitment is predicted by two other variables: (1) satisfaction and (2) alternatives. Sometimes called **social exchange theory**, interdependence theory starts with the basic premise that once you enter into a relationship with another person, you are no longer an independent entity. Now, your happiness or unhappiness is, at least to some degree, *interdependent* with that of the other person. If your partner gets fired or promoted, that affects you. If you come home in a bad mood, that affects your partner.

Now that the couple members are interdependent, the question becomes, How long will they continue the relationship? As we've already mentioned, according to interdependence theory, this decision is based on each person's level of **commitment**, an individual's decision to stay in a romantic relationship for the long term. High commitment equals high relationship stability and predicts that the relationship will last over time. Low commitment, of course, means that the relationship will probably end relatively soon. Thibaut and Kelley argued that if you wanted to guess whether any given couple will still be together in a year, you could make a very good guess if you knew two things: the couple members' level of satisfaction and their alternatives.

Satisfaction. Are you satisfied with your relationship? Your most honest answer is probably, "sometimes

AP Photo/Ken McKay/ITV/REX/Shutterstock

Friends with benefits: A type of relationship where an individual has casual sex repeatedly with the same person over time, remaining friends with that person instead of starting an official romantic relationship.

Polyamory: When individuals have multiple committed relationships at once.

Polyandry: A type of polyamorous relationship in which one man has multiple female partners.

Polygyny: A type of polyamorous relationship in which one woman has multiple male partners.

Polygamy: When the individuals in a polyamorous relationship are legally married.

Interdependence theory: A model for understanding romantic relationships that suggests that relationship stability is predicted by commitment, which is, in turn, predicted by a combination of satisfaction within the relationship and the potential for quality alterative relationships.

Social exchange theory: See *interdependence theory.*

Commitment: An individual's decision to stay in a romantic relationship for the long term.

yes, sometimes no, sometimes sort of." The first variable in predicting commitment is **satisfaction**, which the theory defines as an individual's perception of whether a relationship is better or worse than average. When you think about your own relationships, how did you decide whether they were satisfactory? Interdependence theory suggests that we take two mental steps to make this determination.

The first step is to think about the rewards versus costs. Rewards might be things like companionship, support for our ideas, someone to help us overcome difficulties, physical or sexual satisfaction, financial support, and much more. Costs might be things like sacrifices you make to be with each other, time away from friends, money spent on the relationship, and the like. Interdependence theory argues that when we're in a relationship, we make a mental list of the good things (rewards) and bad things (costs) we get out of the relationship and create a ratio, such as "three good things for every one bad thing." The resultant ratio is called our **current outcomes.**

The second step in determining satisfaction is to compare our current outcomes (the ratio of good to bad) to a mental **comparison level**, which is our abstract idea of what an "average" relationship's good-to-bad ratio might be. We each create our own comparison level based on all the relationships we've previously seen. These can include our parents' relationship, friends' relationships, our own past experiences, or even relationships we see on television or in movies. For example, perhaps you think that an "average" relationship has five rewards or good things for every one cost or bad thing. Thus, your comparison level ratio is 5:1.

To determine whether our own, current relationship is satisfactory, we calculate the difference between our current outcomes to this comparison ratio. If your current relationship's ratio is 3:1, even though that's more reward than cost, you might still be unsatisfied because you believe that an average healthy relationship should have a ratio of at least 5:1. In short, the degree of satisfaction we have is based on the distance between our current outcomes ratio and the comparison level ratio. More satisfaction means more commitment, which means the relationship is more likely to last over time. Satisfaction and commitment are also tied to having more positive illusions about one's current partner (Goodfriend et al., 2017).

You might be thinking, "No one sits around and does math to decide whether they're satisfied with their partner." And you're probably right. We think about these steps on a more fluid, abstract, or subjective level, like a running list of "pros" and "cons" we keep in our heads. While the exact numbers might not be identified by people, the general idea of weighing good and bad aspects probably occurs pretty often. The *positive correlation* between satisfaction and commitment has been supported in several research studies, including a *meta-analysis* that reviewed 52 individual tests of the connection (Le & Agnew, 2003).

Alternatives. Satisfaction seems like an obvious predictor of relationship commitment. The second predictor may be slightly less obvious: Do you have a lot of other options?

Thinking about this question doesn't necessarily mean you have an alternative romantic partner already waiting in the wings, like a Plan B—but it could. More precisely, **alternatives** suggests that we calculate the number and quality of the other relationship options we would have if we ended a current romantic relationship. Thibaut and Kelley believed that even when you're in a relatively happy relationship, it's a basic human tendency to always be looking around for other options, just in case.

Interdependence theory states that we'll also compare our current relationship and our outcomes ratio to a mental idea called the **comparison level for alternatives**, which is the next-best relationship scenario you think you could be in, if you ended your current

Satisfaction: An individual's perception of whether a romantic relationship is better or worse than average.

Current outcomes: An individual's perception of the total combined positive and negative outcomes of a relationship, which can be represented as a ratio of rewards to costs.

Comparison level: Individuals' abstract idea concerning what an "average" relationship's ratio of rewards to costs might be based on relationships the individuals have previously seen, including their own past relationships, the relationships of their parents and their friends, or relationships seen in the media.

Alternatives: The actual number and quality of other relationship options individuals would have if they ended their current romantic relationship.

Comparison level for alternatives: The perceived next-best relationship people could have if they ended their current relationship.

relationship. Our alternatives include all of the other people who might want to date us if we suddenly became single. Importantly, another alternative is to not be in any relationship at all; being single might be the best option for some people.

The more alternatives we have or the better quality they are, the less committed we will be to the current partner and relationship. Thus, alternatives and commitment are *negatively correlated:* As the number and quality of alternatives go up, commitment goes down (Le & Agnew, 2003). The association also goes the other way; if we are highly committed to a current partner, we tend to downgrade possible alternatives, telling ourselves that they aren't so great and thus avoiding temptation (Rusbult & Buunk, 1993). This cognitive bias is called **derogation of alternatives** (Johnson & Rusbult, 1989; Simpson, Gangestad, & Lerma, 1990).

These two variables, satisfaction and alternatives, can predict whether two people will stay together. The theory proposes that you need information about both concepts to really make a good prediction. Two people who are dating could realize that the relationship is not particularly rewarding (low satisfaction); however, if both people believe this relationship is their best option (low alternatives), they will stay despite their doubts. On the other hand, two people could have a relationship that seems perfectly happy (high satisfaction), but if an even better option comes along (high alternatives), one of them might leave.

Perhaps this explains why Brad Pitt left his marriage with Jennifer Aniston to pursue Angelina Jolie. He might have been satisfied with Aniston but perceived that Jolie was an even better alternative. Satisfaction and alternatives are good predictors of whether a relationship will last over time (e.g., Le & Agnew 2003; Rusbult, Martz, & Agnew, 1998).

Investments. Social scientists, as usual, kept looking for the best answer to the question at hand. Interdependence theory only included satisfaction and alternatives to predict commitment. However, some people criticized the model as being incomplete. Can you think of any couples who don't seem particularly happy (low satisfaction) and could probably do better elsewhere (high alternatives) but for some reason still stay together? Maybe we need one more piece to this puzzle.

The third variable that many social psychologists believe is needed to make a full prediction of relationship commitment was added by Rusbult (1980). It is **investments**, or the amount of time, energy, and resources put into a relationship that would be lost if the relationship were to end. Rusbult and many other psychologists have found that investments are equally useful in trying to understand why people choose to maintain or end a given relationship. A statistical model that includes all three predictors of commitment (satisfaction, alternatives, and investments) is called the **investment model** (see Figure 12.5).

Even if a relationship has low satisfaction and high alternatives, which interdependence theory would predict should make the relationship end, the investment model argues that the couple members might decide to stay together if they have a high level of investments. If two people have been together for years and years, share a car and a mortgage together, have children together, have made sacrifices for each other, and simply know each other better than anyone else in the world, all of this time and effort might make one hesitant to leave.

If you left a relationship after all of that, you'd have to start from scratch. You'd also have to sort out all kinds of messy details, such as child custody, a complicated friendship network with mutual friends, and other aspects of life that become

Derogation of alternatives: The tendency for individuals who are highly committed to a current partner to downgrade possible alternatives, thus avoiding temptation.

Investments: The amount of time, energy, and resources put into a relationship that would be lost if the relationship were to end.

Investment model: A statistical model for understanding romantic relationships that includes all three predictors of commitment: satisfaction, alternatives, and investments.

Interdependence theory suggested that the stability of any relationship can be predicted by commitment and that commitment is predicted by satisfaction with the relationship (a positive correlation) and available alternatives to the relationship (a negative correlation). The investment model includes everything from interdependence theory but adds a third predictor of commitment called investments (which are also positively correlated with commitment).

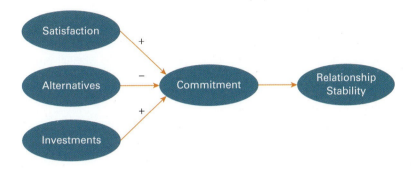

SOURCE: Data from Rusbult (1980).

tied up with one's relationship. Recent research has shown that even future plans made with a partner that haven't happened yet can keep people in a relationship (Goodfriend & Agnew, 2008). Sometimes the prospect of starting over with a new person is simply too daunting, and we decide to take the "easy" way out by simply keeping the status quo. High investments can even keep people in abusive, unhealthy relationships (Rusbult & Martz, 1995).

In another *meta-analysis* including data collected from 37,761 participants and 137 studies over 33 years, satisfaction, perceived alternatives, and investments did predict relationship breakup (Le, Dove, Agnew, Korn, & Mutso, 2010). While it might not seem particularly romantic to think of love in these mathematical terms, the model shown in Figure 12.5 does appear to have predictive power concerning relationship decisions.

The Main Ideas

- Interdependence theory attempts to predict the stability or longevity of any given romantic relationship by predicting commitment using two key variables: satisfaction and alternatives.

- Satisfaction is determined by the difference between one's current outcomes (ratio of rewards versus costs) and one's comparison level, or what someone thinks an average relationship is like. If one's current outcomes are higher than average, satisfaction is high and, thus, commitment is high.

- Alternatives are other relationship options besides one's current relationship (dating others or being single). If alternatives are tempting, commitment to the current relationship will be low.

- The investment model states that a third variable, investments, is also needed to predict relationship commitment and stability. Investments are determined by the amount of time, effort, sacrifices, and so on that have been put into a relationship. The more invested a couple member is, the more committed he or she will be.

⚡ CRITICAL THINKING CHALLENGE

- When you consider the three variables that predict commitment (satisfaction, alternatives, and investments), which one do you think is the most important to you, personally, when you are making relationship decisions? Has one of these weighed more heavily than others in past relationships? Do you think the importance of each variable will change as you grow older and go through different phases of life?

- Do you think any variables are missing from the model shown in Figure 12.5? What other important aspects of a relationship or life do you consider when making relationship decisions? For example, some researchers have suggested that a fourth variable might be whether your friends and family support the relationship (more support is predicted to equal high commitment; Etcheverry & Agnew, 2004). Can you think of additional variables that could be added to the model?

- One criticism of the model shown in Figure 12.5 is that it's very logical and mathematical, like an algebraic equation to explain love. Do you think people really make decisions like this, with lists of pros and cons in our heads? Or, do we more often "go with our gut" and follow our hearts, even if our logical minds tell us we're making a mistake?

DO MEN AND WOMEN ACT DIFFERENTLY AND, IF SO, WHY?

LO 12.5: Analyze why attraction, jealousy, and promiscuity differ between men and women in relationships.

Gender and sexual orientation are not necessarily simple ideas. Many researchers argue that there are more than two sexes, for example (e.g., Harper, 2007), and that referring to men and women as "opposite sexes" encourages belief in a false dichotomy. There are several "intersex" conditions, for example, in which people may not identify with either traditional label because they have ambiguous genitals, less common chromosomal combinations (e.g., XXY instead of XX or XY), or less common testosterone reactivity. Perhaps only using the simple categories of "men" and "women" excludes people who don't feel comfortable with either of these labels, and individuals who transition from one sex to another may not want to use a label for their sex or gender at all (preferring a term such as genderqueer, for example).

Similarly, categorizing sexual orientation as only "heterosexual" or "homosexual" excludes several other possibilities, such as asexuality. Again, traditional labels also reinforce false dichotomies when perhaps a continuum approach is more useful than a categorical approach. The label *bisexual* indicates there are only two possibilities—and this is why many people now prefer the term *pansexual*. **Pansexual** orientation acknowledges intersex and transgender people and notes that sexual attraction is based on an individual, regardless of traditional labels. Encouraging a continuum perspective instead of a categorical perspective, Kinsey and colleagues (Kinsey, Pomeroy, & Martin, 1948) suggested that sexual orientation could range from two extreme poles (see Figure 12.6), with most people being somewhere in the middle.

Still, most research has focused on differences between men and women in traditional, heterosexual relationships because (1) most people self-identify as fitting into these categories and (2) it's simply easier to conduct research on heterosexual couples, because there are more of them available and they are not concerned with being

Pansexual: Sexual attraction based on individuals' personal characteristics, regardless of their sex, gender, or gender identity.

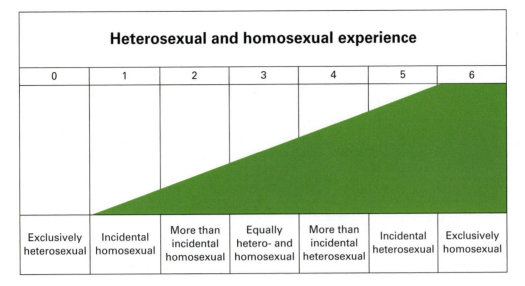

Heterosexual and homosexual experience						
0	1	2	3	4	5	6
Exclusively heterosexual	Incidental homosexual	More than incidental homosexual	Equally hetero- and homosexual	More than incidental heterosexual	Incidental heterosexual	Exclusively homosexual

stigmatized or stereotyped (a privilege of being the group with more social power). Patterns from this sample show consistent and cross-cultural differences in relationship choices between men and women. The final section of this chapter is going to examine three patterns that appear to be different in men and women within relationships, and we'll discuss possibilities regarding why these differences emerge. These patterns involve attraction, jealousy, and promiscuity.

Sex Differences in Attraction

Men and women seem to want different things in a potential partner—and these differences in what we find attractive seem to be true across most cultures (Buss, 2016). As usual, there are two general explanations for consistent differences: nature and nurture. Here are four examples related to how nature explains physical attraction:

When actress Demi Moore married the much younger Ashton Kutcher, many people expressed surprise. Why do most cultures accept men dating younger women but not vice versa?

(1) Earlier in the chapter, we noted that many men are physically attracted to women with a small waist and larger hips, while women want a man with a small waist and wide shoulders. This anatomical difference suggests reproductive potential.

(2) You may also have noticed age differences. In most countries, an older man dating a younger woman is not unusual, but the other way around is. Age differences in reproductive capability explain this difference; younger women are more fertile.

(3) There also are differences in what men and women find most appealing. Many men focus on a woman's physical looks while women seem to care more about whether men have money and other resources. Biological differences in the time required to fulfill separate reproductive and nurturing roles allow men and women to adopt different strategies for getting their genes into the next generation. Men can choose a "quantity" strategy in looking for mates; women are required to emphasize a "quality" strategy.

J. Vespa / WireImage / Getty Images

(4) Finally, many women insist on higher standards when it comes to intelligence and job prestige in potential partners, while men are more willing to accept less intelligent partners simply because they are good looking (Miller & Perlman, 2009). Different reproductive roles require different strategies in the mating game.

The forces (such as culture) that nurture gender differences in attraction often exaggerate the preexisting biological differences. As a result, men and women in any culture are raised with different gender stereotypes and expectations. In the United States, men are expected to be aggressive and competitive, whereas women are expected to be emotional and nurturing (Diekman & Eagly, 2000). If men are trained by their culture to value women for their looks, and women are trained to value men for their money, then it only makes sense that we would see these patterns. The way we raise our children and expect things from potential dates may change the interaction patterns men and women have, especially as they are first getting to know each other through early dating. For example, men often are expected to pay for dinner, movie tickets, and so forth. Thus, differences may be due to culture instead of biological instincts.

Sex Differences in Jealousy

Jealousy can be a powerful emotion, but do you think men and women are jealous for different reasons? Buss and colleagues (Buss, Larsen, Westen, & Semmelroth, 1992) asked participants in a study to consider the following two scenarios and to identify which one of the situations would make them more jealous:

Please think of a serious committed romantic relationship that you have had in the past, that you currently have, or that you would like to have. Imagine that you discover that the person with whom you've been seriously involved became interested in someone else.

What would distress or upset you more (please pick only one):

A. Imagining your partner forming a deep emotional attachment to that person.

B. Imagining your partner enjoying passionate sexual intercourse with that other person.

A full 83% of the women said that emotional infidelity would upset them more (Option A), and 60% of the men in this study said that the sexual infidelity (Option B) would upset them more. This basic result has been replicated in other studies (Brase, Adair, & Monk, 2014; Tagler, 2010). Why does this particular gender difference exist?

Evolutionary theory explains these findings by saying that women don't like it when men love other people because then he might give gifts and resources to them. If Brad Pitt falls in love with Angelina Jolie, he might start to give all of his time and money and gifts to her, instead of to Jennifer Aniston—and this means fewer resources left for Aniston and any potential children she could have. On the other hand, evolutionary theory says that men will be particularly jealous when female partners engage in sexual infidelity for an entirely different reason.

When a child is born, men have a problem called **paternity uncertainty**, doubt about whether a child is genetically theirs. Even if two people are married and supposedly

Paternity uncertainty: Anxiety experienced by men due to doubt about whether a child is genetically theirs.

monogamous, a father could be raising a child that is not genetically his own if his wife had an affair. Note that there's no such thing as "maternity uncertainty"; a woman who is pregnant is 100% sure that the child is genetically her own (unless, of course, surrogacy or in vitro fertilization was involved). Because of paternity uncertainty, this theory makes the prediction that men should be more jealous than women of potential sexual infidelity, which is what this study found.

Again, however, an alternative explanation can be found in cultural expectations of men versus women. In many cultures, it is more socially acceptable for men to be sexually promiscuous than it is for women. Women are trained to be communal, meaning focused on others, putting relationships first, and being nurturing and kind. Thus, women may be more hurt by emotional cheating than by sexual cheating. On the other hand, cultural expectations guide women to be relatively "chaste" and loyal due to benevolent sexism. Consequently, men may be particularly offended if their wives and girlfriends cheat on them sexually, simply because it is so culturally surprising.

As usual, the best explanation relies on how nature and nurture interact in each situation.

Sex Differences in Promiscuity

Who has (or wants to have) more sex—men or women?

Evolutionary theory (nature) and cultural explanations (nurture) offer different perspectives regarding gender differences in **promiscuity**, how many casual sexual partners one has. The stereotype of a heterosexual date in many cultures is that the man will pressure the woman to engage in sexual behaviors. The woman, on the other hand, may demand (or at least expect) some kind of show of commitment before granting sexual favors; she might want him to declare his love, propose marriage . . . or at least go on three dates to show his interest. But does this stereotype reflect reality?

Gender differences in promiscuity were tested in a famous study conducted on a large college campus (Clark & Hatfield, 1989). A social psychology class trained five college women and four college men as *confederates* for the study. (Before the research began, their physical attractiveness was judged to range from slightly unattractive to moderately attractive—but it turned out that their attractiveness didn't affect the results.) All student experimenters were around 22 years old, and they walked around their own college campus looking for people of the "opposite" sex who were sitting by themselves.

When an opportunity arose, the experimenters approached another person and gave this little speech: "I have been noticing you around campus. I find you to be very attractive." The experimenters then followed up with one of three *randomly assigned* questions: (1) "Would you go out with me tonight?" (2) "Would you come over to my apartment tonight?" or (3) "Would you go to bed with me tonight?" No matter what the innocent other person said, the experimenters were instructed to then explain that this was all part of a psychology experiment.

How would you respond? The percentages in Table 12.2 indicate how many people in each condition said "yes" to the request from the male and female experimenters.

When women in college were approached, about half were willing to go on a date, but only a few agreed to go back to a man's apartment, and not a single woman agreed to go to bed with any of the men. The pattern for men in college was much higher and trended in the opposite direction. About half agreed to a date, almost two thirds agreed to go back to a woman's apartment, and fully three quarters of the men agreed to have casual sex!

Promiscuity: The number of casual sexual partners one has.

■ **TABLE 12.2** How Many People Said "Yes" to Three Different Questions From Potential Dates

	Type of Question		
	Date	Apartment	Sex
Female participants	56%	6%	0%
Male participants	50%	69%	75%

SOURCE: Clark and Hatfield (1989).

An Evolutionary Explanation. Evolutionary theory argues that the main reason for men being more promiscuous is because of a gender difference in **parental investment**, the amount of time, effort, and physical resources needed for an individual to produce genetic offspring. The woman clearly has the higher parental investment. After all, from a biological perspective, men only need to contribute some sperm and their job is done. Women must contribute an egg, carry the fetus for 9 months, survive childbirth, and provide milk for a baby until it is able to fend for itself.

Men's relatively low parental investment makes it easy for them to have many partners. In fact, becoming monogamous limits their number of potential children. The male impulse for casual sex (according to this perspective) also provides a genetic advantage as diverse genetic combinations inherit different evolutionary advantages and disadvantages. For example, some offspring may be prone to genetic disorders carried by a particular mother. Having children with a lot of different women thus increases a man's overall genetic strength in the next generation.

However, women's high level of parental investment means that their best strategy is to require a commitment from a potential sexual partner before taking a chance at reproduction. If a woman becomes pregnant, it's quite a commitment to that single child. Thus, women are predicted to be much less promiscuous than men. Women should seek commitment and monogamy from male partners, so that if they do get pregnant, they will have someone to provide financial and emotional support for her and the child.

A Cultural Explanation. Again, however, there is a cultural explanation for the same pattern of results. Many cultures are more accepting of men having more sexual partners and having sex earlier in life, compared to the expectations of women's sexual behaviors. In "Western" cultures, slang terms for men with a lot of sexual experience are generally positive, like "stud," while terms for women are generally negative, like "slut." These double standards indicate that women will be judged much more harshly for exactly the same behaviors; thus, some women may not agree to casual sex simply because they don't want to be judged for it (Conley, Ziegler, Moors, & Karathanasis, 2012).

Clark and Hatfield (1989) themselves point out three possible explanations for their own findings: (1) parental investment, (2) sexual double standards based on culture, and (3) women's concern about safety and sexual assault, making them more cautious to agree to any of the three scenarios with a stranger. Note that more recent research has also questioned the hypothesis that men are more promiscuous; two studies point out that these differences seem to disappear when statistical analyses are done differently or when a "bogus pipeline" methodology (see Chapter 6) is used to encourage more honest responding from participants (Alexander & Fisher, 2003; Pedersen, Miller, Putcha-Bhagavatula, & Yang, 2002; for a full discussion of alternative views, see Conley, Moors, Matsick, Ziegler, & Valentine, 2011).

Promiscuity does not wipe out patterns of sexual preferences. For example, many men prefer younger female partners, and this preference increases the older

Parental investment: The amount of time, effort, and physical resources needed for an individual to produce and raise genetic offspring.

the man is—but women's preference for men who are slightly older than themselves remains stable over life (Grøntvedt & Kennair, 2013). Men consistently value looks in a partner more than women do, but women are more demanding of partners in most other ways, including things like social status (Li et al., 2013; Schwarz & Hassebrauck, 2012). In a study of over 500 college students, another study found that most men are more comfortable with different sexual behaviors, compared to women, and that men overestimate women's comfort with these behaviors (Reiber & Garcia, 2010).

REUTERS/Mike Segar

Same-Sex Relationships

As stated above, the majority of research on close relationships is done on heterosexual couples. However, there are millions of same-sex couples in the world. Social psy-

Some research shows that gay and lesbian couples have a lot in common with heterosexual couples, but more research is needed on same-sex attraction and relationship dynamics.

chological research with these participants has been increasing as more cultures accept same-sex couples. Many studies have found that the patterns identified in this chapter for heterosexual couples also apply to same-sex couples. However, there appear to be a few differences.

For example, Lehmiller (2010) discovered that heterosexual men are more likely to feel committed to a relationship based on tangible investments such as jointly shared objects, but gay men care more about intangible investments such as sacrifices to be together (see Goodfriend & Agnew, 2008). While similarity was reviewed earlier as a predictor of attraction, this tendency appears to be stronger in heterosexual couples. One study (Kurdek & Schmitt, 1987) found that income and education were *significantly positively correlated* for heterosexual couples living together but not for gay or lesbian couples. Similarity also appears to differ more in other ways; about 21% of married gay and lesbian couples are interracial (compared to about 10% of married heterosexual couples; U.S. Census Bureau, 2010).

There are many possible explanations for these differences. One alternative is that gay and lesbian subcultures emphasize different values and social norms. Another possibility is that fewer gay and lesbian individuals exist in any given town or city, making it harder for them to find happy relationships due to simply having fewer options. In short, gay men and lesbians suffer from a smaller **field of eligibles**—a smaller pool of potential dates and mates. Relationship outcomes may also be different in gay and lesbian couples due to homophobia from others. Same-sex couples may not experience the same freedoms due to prejudice and discrimination, and being forced to live "in the closet" may produce stress and challenges that heterosexual couples can blissfully avoid.

That said, many studies show that gay couples and heterosexual couples have a lot in common. Sutphin (2010) applied interdependence theory to gay couples. Couple members with more financial resources usually did fewer household tasks, perhaps indicating more power in the relationship (a typical "masculine" role). For both couple members, satisfaction and commitment went up with being happy about the division of labor in the relationship and with being appreciated for contributions to the home. Relationship violence appears to be a problem in all types of couples, regardless of sexual orientation (e.g., Cruz, 2003; West, 1998). And finally, just as we saw before with the jealousy research, lesbians are more upset with emotional infidelity and gay men are more upset over sexual infidelity

Field of eligibles: The potential dates and mates available for an individual not in a committed romantic relationship, based on that individual's criteria for a romantic partner.

in partners—and paternity uncertainty doesn't work as an explanation this time (Frederick & Fales, 2014).

As we discussed at the beginning of this chapter, love relationships are complicated. They can bring out the best, most wonderful feelings of our lives, and they can cause the deepest, most painful heartaches. While poems, films, novels, and plays may all try to capture the nature of love, social psychology studies it from a scientific perspective. Can scientific methodologies like *control groups, random assignment, hypotheses,* and *theories* really get to the heart of attraction, jealousy, commitment, and sex? Perhaps not—but they sure seem to be getting close. And social psychology will continue to invent new methods, create new data, and provoke new thinking about this fundamental element that is necessary for life itself.

The Main Ideas

- Research has identified different patterns of attraction, jealousy, and promiscuity between men and women in relationships.

- The evolutionary perspective explains these differences based on different biological needs and challenges to successful reproduction. However, the same patterns can also be explained by cultural expectations and stereotypes applied to men versus women.

- Many studies show similarities between heterosexual and gay/lesbian relationships, but more research is needed.

⚡ CRITICAL THINKING CHALLENGE

- With more and more advances in birth control, concerns about pregnancy resulting from sexual encounters are decreased. Do you think that these changes have affected the way modern men and women approach potential sexual mates and encounters? Do you think future generations will continue to see any changes?

- Evolutionary theory assumes that behaviors that lead to successful genetic reproduction will be rewarded and thus kept in the gene pool. How can we explain people who choose not to have children or people who choose to adopt children who are not genetically related to themselves? What about people who choose to live as permanent singles, never committing to a monogamous or exclusive relationship?

- This chapter ended by talking about just a few studies regarding same-sex couples. What other kinds of similarities or differences do you think social psychology research has found when studying gay/lesbian or bisexual relationships, compared to heterosexual relationships? What about polyamorous relationships?

CHAPTER SUMMARY

What causes attraction?

Three psychological variables have been studied regarding why we are attracted to some people more than others. The first is similarity; the similarity-attraction hypothesis predicts that people form relationships with others who have the same attitudes, interests, and demographics as themselves (such as age or socioeconomic status). One reason for this may be that similar others validate us and make us feel comfortable.

A second predictor of liking is mere exposure; we tend to like objects and people more after repeated exposure. When liking increases because of exposure based on physical proximity (such as living near each other or seeing each other frequently at work), this is called the proximity effect. The proximity effect and mere exposure were tested in the famous Westgate Housing study, which found that within apartment buildings, people who lived in apartments that had a lot of social exposure (due to being next to the stairs or mailboxes) were more liked than people who lived in more isolated locations.

A third psychological variable involved in attraction is misattribution of arousal, sometimes known as excitation transfer. The idea is that we are sometimes physiologically aroused due to our environment (such as being scared by something) and that we can misinterpret that arousal as sexual attraction to someone who happens to be nearby. This hypothesis was tested in the well-known "shaky bridge" study, in which men who had just crossed a fear-inducing bridge were more likely to show interest in a female confederate, compared to men who had just crossed a low, stable bridge.

What makes us physically attractive?

Research has attempted to find patterns of what humans seem to find physically attractive, regardless of culture; three variables have been identified. First, bilateral symmetry in faces (the right half mirrors the left half) appears to be attractive. People with symmetric faces are perceived as more attractive and seem to have more sexual opportunities. Second, computer-generated "average" faces are rated as more attractive than individual faces. It is possible that "average" faces indicate more genetic fitness, from an evolutionary perspective.

Third, body type seems to matter. Across cultures, people seem to prefer women who have a 0.7 waist-to-hips ratio, meaning the circumference of their waist is 70% of the circumference of their hips. This may be attractive because it highlights aerobic fitness and/or the ability to have children. In men, a waist-to-shoulders ratio of between 0.7 and 0.75 is perceived as attractive; men with broad shoulders but smaller waists are preferred by many.

Do we have a relationship personality?

One of the most popular theories in psychology to explain relationships is attachment theory, which suggests that our first relationships (in infancy) create a model or template for our relationships throughout life. Research with infants and their mothers established three distinct attachment styles: (1) secure, in which parents were consistently supportive and adult relationships are healthy and trusting; (2) anxious/ambivalent, in which parents were inconsistent and adult relationships are full of jealousy and low trust; and (3) avoidant/fearful, in which parents were consistently abusive or absent and adult relationships are avoided.

Attachment theory has a lot of research support, including interesting findings in college student participants. One popular modern take on attachment theory is that there may be four attachment styles instead of three. The four-model approach splits styles based on a positive or negative view of the self and a positive or negative view of others.

How do we decide to commit?

While monogamous, two-person relationships based on love are considered "traditional" in most Western societies, there are many other types of relationship. Examples of other options are arranged marriages, hooking up, friends with benefits, and polyamory. That said, a popular theory called interdependence theory attempts to predict whether any given relationship will last over time. The theory notes that to make this prediction, two variables are involved: (1) satisfaction, or how one perceives the positives and negatives of this particular relationship, and (2) alternatives, or other relationships that one could be in if this relationship ended. Satisfaction is positively correlated with commitment, while alternatives are negatively correlated.

A third variable was added several years later: investments, or the amount of time, resources, sacrifices, and so on that have been put into the relationship. Investments are positively correlated with commitment. When all three variables are included in a statistical model to predict commitment and relationship longevity, it's called the investment model. Several studies have found statistical support for this model's ability to predict relationship outcomes over time.

Do men and women act differently and, if so, why?

Recent ideas suggest that categorizing people into "men versus women" or "heterosexual versus homosexual" promotes false dichotomies and that perhaps sex, gender, and relationships should be viewed from a continuum approach instead. However, most research on relationships uses heterosexual men and women, and this research has found some relatively stable differences based on sex, regardless of culture.

First, men and women seem to be attracted to different things in mates. Men often prefer physically attractive, younger women while women seem to be attracted to men who have access to resources. Men also appear to more commonly become jealous over sexual infidelity, while women appear to be more jealous over emotional infidelity. Finally, men often display patterns of higher rates of promiscuity compared to women. These differences can be explained both from an evolutionary perspective and from the perspective of understanding different norms and expectations for men and women.

Finally, more research is needed on same-sex relationships. While some studies find interesting differences between gay/lesbian relationships and heterosexual relationships, other studies find that there are commonalities in all monogamous relationships, regardless of sexual orientation.

THEORIES IN REVIEW

- Similarity-attraction hypothesis
- Mere exposure
- Proximity effect (propinquity effect)

- Misattribution of arousal (excitation transfer)
- Bilateral symmetry and attraction
- "Average" faces and attraction

- Attachment theory
- Interdependence theory (social exchange theory)
- Investment model
- Kinsey continuum of sexual orientation
- Paternity uncertainty

CRITICAL THINKING, ANALYSIS, AND APPLICATION

- Some people believe in "love at first sight" or "soulmates." Others believe that marriage is an outdated concept and that humans aren't meant to commit to only one other person for life. What is your opinion on this debate, and what scientific evidence can you use to support your view?

- Some critics of the evolutionary perspective argue that many of the hypotheses are "post hoc," meaning they are only created *after* a trend has already been identified. To be a truly useful perspective, evolutionary psychology should create new, testable hypotheses. Can you identify any additional physical traits that should be correlated with physical attractiveness, based on genetic or reproductive health? How would you design a study to test this hypothesis?

- Attachment theory was originally developed in the 1940s and 1950s. As types of family become more diverse, how might early childhood experiences be affected, which might influence later relationships? For example, if a child grows up in a home with multiple mothers and fathers, a stepfamily, multiple generations living in the same home, and so on, would this affect attachment style?

- When you consider your own patterns of relationships or the patterns you observe in the world around you, what do you think is missing from the theories and ideas covered in this chapter? What variables associated with attraction, interaction styles, or gender differences need further attention in research, and how would you design studies to do so?

PERSONAL REFLECTION

For most of my career in social psychology, intimate relationships have been the focus of my research. I've studied different kinds of investment, abuse and relationship violence, sexual stereotypes and expectations, and more. In my personal life, I've experienced some of the worst parts of love; I've experienced heterosexism and homophobia due to self-identifying as pansexual, uneven power dynamics, and being cheated on. But I've also experienced the best parts, including loving support, generosity, and a sense of humor to make me see things from a happier perspective. Studying love isn't easy—but maybe that's why it's so fun to try. Social psychology offers the challenge and opportunity to explain interpersonal dynamics from a scientific view . . . and it offers exciting new hypotheses around every corner. Both Tom and I encourage every reader of this book to consider the wonders that studying social psychology can bring to your understanding of the world and to your chance to make that world better. [WG]

Visit **edge.sagepub.com/heinzen** to help you accomplish your coursework goals in an easy-to-use learning environment.

- **Visual Key Concepts**
- Mobile-friendly **eFlashcards**
- Mobile-friendly practice **quizzes**
- **Video** and **multimedia content**
- EXCLUSIVE! Access to full-text **SAGE journal articles**

⑤SAGE edge™

PRACTICE AND APPLY WHAT YOU'VE LEARNED

▶ **edge.sagepub.com/heinzen**

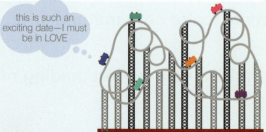

94.7 FM

when I first heard this song I hated it, but now I'm really starting to like it.

this is such an exciting date—I must be in LOVE

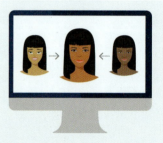

secure   **avoidant**   **anxious/ambinvalent**

Get a tour of **ALL Visual Key Concepts** and their definitions at **edge.sagepub.com/heinzen**

Social Psychology and a Sustainable Environment

Core Questions

Learning Objectives

1. What are environmental threshold effects, and why are they important?

2. What happens when environmental thresholds are exceeded?

1. Articulate how social psychologists can respond to the unique threat posed by multiple threshold effects.

2. Describe how noise and crowding are influenced by subjective perceptions and corresponding roles for social psychologists.

For years, 11 million pounds of trash filled Versova Beach off the coast of India. That was until one man named Afroz Shah—a young lawyer and activist—decided to clean it up (Arora, 2017). He began by simply walking along the beach with a neighbor and some trash bags. In an interview with CNN he said, "I'm going to come on the field and do something. I have to protect my environment and it requires ground action."

Soon over 1,000 volunteers had joined Shah, including local politicians, Bollywood actors and actresses, and children. It took almost 2 years, but eventually the beach became a pristine and impressive tourist spot and was labeled the "world's largest beach clean-up project" by the United Nations (Arora, 2017). After the beach was finished, Shah wasn't done; he and other volunteers continued their environmentalism work by cleaning over 50 public toilets near the beach. He now plans to plant 5,000 coconut trees along the shoreline as well, to restore the beach to its former glory.

What motivates people like Shah to care about the environment—and how do pollution, noise, toxins, crowding, and other negative problems in our world affect us?

One of the beautiful things about social psychology is that many of the theories and principles can be applied to a wide range of possible applied topics. An increasingly vital example is to create a **sustainable environment**, a world that allows living things (including humans) to adapt and survive. Just surviving, however, is a very low bar. That's why creating a sustainable environment is part of a larger set of opportunities for psychology students related to **environmental psychology**, the interplay between individuals and their surroundings.

Sustainable environment:
A state in which the resources of the world are not overtaxed, allowing living things, including humans, to adapt and survive now and in the future.

Environmental psychology:
The psychological study of the interplay between individuals and their surroundings, including natural environments, structural and architectural design, and social settings.

WHAT ARE THRESHOLD EFFECTS, AND WHY ARE THEY IMPORTANT?

LO 1: Articulate how social psychologists can respond to the unique threat posed by multiple threshold effects.

The *Titanic* was doomed after an iceberg scraped holes into 6 of its 16 watertight compartments on the starboard (right) side of the ship. The ship was believed to be unsinkable, thanks to modern (at the time) technology. Due to the ship designer's overconfidence, not enough life rafts were provided. The *Titanic* might have survived one or two compromised compartments—but not six. The human error of overconfidence sunk the *Titanic*.

We are not the first to apply the metaphor of the doomed *Titanic* to environmental crises (Sandler &

F.G.O. Stuart (1823-1943)

The *Titanic* can be used as a metaphor for modern environmental crises.

Studlar, 1999). The compromised compartments of the ship can be compared to aspects of the environment that are in desperate need of help. In this application mini-chapter, we will discuss social psychological responses to a few compromised areas—and if they are not repaired quickly, we'll be in trouble.

Defining Threshold Effects

Many of Earth's "compartments" have exceeded what Rockström et al. (2009, p. 472) call **thresholds**, the unpredictable ways in which Earth's subsystems react when subjected to excessive pressures and the limits the Earth can take:

> Many subsystems of Earth react in a nonlinear, often abrupt, way, and are particularly sensitive around threshold levels of certain key variables. If these thresholds are crossed, then important subsystems, such as a monsoon system, could shift into a new state, often with deleterious or potentially even disastrous consequences for humans.

The consequences of going past the Earth's capacity for pollution, overcrowding, or other concerns are called **threshold effects**. The monsoon subsystem, for example, provides humans with predictable periods of rain. Plants and animals, as well as entire ecosystems and cultures, rely on the predictability of the monsoons to sustain life. A changing monsoon system threatens many millions of lives—and that is only one of many critical subsystems. Table A.1 describes where we were about a decade ago in terms of how much we have exceeded just three estimated threshold levels.

Working from left to right, the column called "Preindustrial Value" is what Earth was experiencing before the Industrial Revolution. The next column, "Proposed Threshold," is the point at which Earth entered the estimated danger zone of unpredictability. That unpredictability is magnified when more than one over-the-threshold subsystem has entered its danger zone. The far right and final column, "Current Status," reports where we are now. Focus on the bottom row as an example. Before the Industrial Revolution, the average number of species that went extinct each year was zero. The current status is that we are losing an estimated 121 unique, never-to-be-seen-again species *each year*. The estimated threshold for species loss is just 35 species per year. Each year, dozens of species enter the danger zone and never come back.

On the *Titanic*, 6 of the 16 compartments were flooded. The massive ship sank in just 2 hours. We will focus on the consequences to humans who have exceeded the thresholds in two areas that have interested social psychologists: noise and crowding. They each appear to have threshold levels that threaten to overwhelm the Earth's carrying capacity. Before we cover those two specific problems, let's consider how social

Threshold: A point that must be exceeded for a certain effect or consequence to occur.

Threshold effects: Consequences that occur as a result of exceeding a certain limit. In the case of environmental psychology, consequences of going past the Earth's capacity for pollution, overcrowding, or other concerns.

■ TABLE A.1 Earth-Systems Processes

Earth-Systems Processes	Parameters	Preindustrial Value	Proposed Threshold	Current Status
Climate Change 1	Atmospheric carbon dioxide concentration (parts per million)	280	350	387
Climate Change 2	Change in radiative forcing (watts per meter squared)	.01–1	10	>100
Rate of biodiversity loss	Extinction rate (number of species per million, per year)	0	35	121

psychologists or environmental activists can follow the example of Afroz Shah and work on behalf of our only environment.

Responding to Threshold Effects

Imagine a slow-motion version of the sinking *Titanic* that magically allows the passengers and crew to move at full speed to try to save themselves by saving their ship. Social psychologists have three important roles to play by (a) learning enough about the scientific process to evaluate scientific claims; (b) helping environmentalists design, collect, and analyze data regarding the extent of damage and prioritize what needs fixing; and (c) persuading others that science has value so that the problems are stopped.

The Carolina parakeet, now extinct due to climate change.

Evaluating Scientific Claims. Every undergraduate psychology student has been reminded (probably in every class) that evaluating scientific claims involves assessing reliability and validity. You know that one isolated scientific claim, even from a respected, peer-reviewed journal, should be accepted with caution. However, if many independent scientists, from many different labs, using a variety of research methods, keep coming up with the same conclusions, then the findings are more likely to be both reliable and valid.

There have been many surveys of the threshold effects due to climate change. Parmesan (2006) summarized the evidence that is now already more than a decade old:

> These observed changes are heavily biased in the directions predicted from global warming and have been linked to local or regional climate change through correlations between climate and biological variation, field and laboratory experiments, and physiological research. (p. 637)

In this case, Parmesan emphasized that the evidence for global warming comes from different independent sources: biological variations, field, lab, and physiological studies. Parmesan groups her *Titanic*-like compartments into marine, freshwater, and terrestrial animals, which includes, well, everything. But the most affected species were animals that had "restricted ranges"—those that could not escape. These "polar and mountaintop species . . . have been the first groups in which entire species have gone extinct due to recent climate change" (p. 637). For example, the range restriction for the Carolina parakeet was limited to forest edges and river bottoms where it could find the foods it had adapted to eat. Called the most colorful bird in North America, the last Carolina parakeet was killed in Okeechobee County, Florida, after losing its native habitat to logging, farming, and the destruction of wetlands.

Collecting and Analyzing Data. Modern research methods are, well, really cool. We are much better now at collecting data automatically, for example, from tracking devices worn by threatened species. However, someone has to develop the skills to analyze those data, to map the data, and to communicate the data to the right audiences. Social psychologists develop expertise in data skills that, if applied to the environment, can help save species.

It's not just birds, of course. The evidence for threshold effects includes the deterioration of beautiful "tropical coral reefs and amphibians." So, if you love the ocean, then start saving the ocean. The fundamental relations within the ecosystem that have endured for millions of years are also changing. The unpredictability of climate change is why some refer to it as "global weirding" rather than to "global warming." A relatively sophisticated understanding of statistical analysis is needed for scientists to understand changing local and global patterns and to be able to communicate these patterns to the general population.

Persuading Others of the Value of Science. Social persuasion is an opportunity for social psychologists to strut their stuff! The topic of persuasion has come up in many forms throughout this (and every other) social psychology textbook. Remember these four approaches to persuasion from earlier:

- The theory of planned behavior (see pages 169–170)
- The elaboration likelihood model and heuristic-systematic model (see pages 183 and 408)
- Specific persuasion techniques, such as foot-in-the-door (see pages 189–190)
- Logical, systematic thinking versus automatic, intuitive thinking (see pages 94–95)

Think again about each of these broad approaches to persuasion, and consider how each could be applied to (a) convincing others that scientific studies, data, and trends should be considered when choices are made on both the individual and national level and (b) convincing others that protecting the environment is an urgent and worthwhile cause. For example, how could you apply social norms and perceived control? How could you increase people's understanding and motivation to consider logical arguments? What specific persuasion techniques could be used to change people's behaviors? And how could you use both logic and intuition, emotion, or heuristics to convince people?

VCG / Visual China Group / Getty Images

© istockphoto.com/

A fifth approach to persuasion—and one you haven't seen yet in this book—comes from the theory of game design (see Heinzen et al., 2015), promoted by the Volkswagen Corporation as "fun theory." It's not a complicated idea, and it is closely tied to a discussion in the next section about careers as a user experience specialist. In the photo shown here, Volkswagen made the task of walking up steps fun by reengineering the steps as piano keys (which both light up and make noise as people walk on them). In this way, people are encouraged to exercise and avoid the electricity-burning escalator. They know it works because they collected *naturalistic observations;* someone unobtrusively counted how many people used the stairs versus the escalator before and after installing the piano stairs.

Volkswagen made it fun to pick up litter in a park and dispose of it by triggering a sound with every piece of trash tossed into the container. The cartoony sound was like something falling a long distance before it crashed into the bottom of a distant canyon. People were reportedly looking for more litter to throw in the trash bin when these containers were installed; thus, the company encouraged environmentalism in a "fun" way.

408 SOCIAL PSYCHOLOGY

Beyond practicing your critical thinking skills and having a discussion in class about how to use the persuasion theories and techniques above to promote environmentalism, what else could you do to get involved? Here are two ideas. First, in a society that encourages open debate, you can seek an internship (including online distance internships) at one of the several advertising agencies that have the mission, talent, and financial resources to influence public policy about climate change. You already know much more about the art of persuasion than most people.

Second, turn yourself into an applied game designer and use your own creativity and skills in research design and statistics to come as close as you can to replicating the trash can intervention described here. As a social psychologist, you will want to measure and report both successes and failures. That will allow the rest of us to learn from your experience, and it will allow all of us to refine our community interventions to increase simple environmentalism in many areas.

The Main Ideas

- Environmental psychology is the study of the interplay between individuals and their surroundings. It includes focusing on the consequences of going past the Earth's capacity for pollution, overcrowding, or other concerns, which is called a threshold effect.

- Social psychologists can help environmentalists in many ways, including three important roles to play by (a) evaluating scientific claims made by others, (b) collecting and analyzing relevant data, and (c) persuading the general population to believe trends in the data and become active in preventing further damage.

⚡ CRITICAL THINKING CHALLENGE

- Imagine that your class decides to create a campaign focused on promoting healthy living and recycling on your campus. Identify three specific ways you could do this using the theories and ideas about persuasion listed above (theory of planned behavior, elaboration likelihood model, etc.).

- Spend time going to three websites for charities such as Habitat for Humanity, the Susan G. Komen Foundation for breast cancer awareness, and so on. Analyze how the websites are designed to persuade people to contribute time or money, and tie these efforts into one specific theory or concept you've learned in this class.

WHAT HAPPENS WHEN ENVIRONMENTAL THRESHOLDS ARE EXCEEDED?

LO 2: Describe how noise and crowding are influenced by subjective perceptions and corresponding roles for social psychologists.

To get a sense of what happens when we exceed the threshold for human functioning, let's examine how we respond to extreme cases of noise and crowding. In both cases, our perception of the problem influences the experienced severity of the problem; the ability to adapt is one of our strengths as a species. However, our ability to adapt to stressors may also mask the severity of the problem on a global level, preventing us from being motivated to solve problems.

Noise

Noise is unwanted and annoying sounds—and that means that your perception influences how you experience sounds. If you look forward to the sound of your neighbor's daughter learning to play the trombone, then it's not noise to you. But if you find her trombone playing disruptive and aggravating, then it qualifies as noise. There are both auditory (physiological) and nonauditory (psychological) responses to noise. We focus on excessive noise because it may not come to mind as quickly as littering, smoke pollution, or chemical spills and because it's a problem often rooted in social interactions.

PTSD and the Sounds of War. Three features make noise stressful: volume, unpredictability, and perceived lack of control. You can see all three at work in Ellis's (1976, pp. 62–63) accounts of an intense bombardment of World War I soldiers:

> Twenty to thirty shells would be landing in a company sector every minute. . . . Suddenly the barrage would lift and then, five minutes later, start up again. As the evening wore on the intervals would get shorter and shorter and the almost continuous noise grow to a crescendo.

You can see the effects of extreme volume, unpredictability, and lack of control in Captain Greenwell's description of the sounds of battle:

> Modern warfare . . . reduces men to shivering beasts. There isn't a man who can withstand shellfire of the modern kind without getting the blues. . . . [Imagine] on some overhead platform ten thousand carters were tipping loads of pointed steel bricks that burst in the air or on the ground all with a fiendish devastating ear-splitting roar that shook the nerves of the stoutest.

Extreme noise has harmful auditory effects through noise-induced hair cell and nerve damage. It also has nonauditory effects such as sleep deprivation that lead to hypertension, cardiovascular disease, and deficits in cognitive performance (Basner et al., 2014). Lieutenant Chandos recorded that "the sensation . . . is not that of a sound. You feel it in your ears more than hear it, unless it is only about one hundred yards away."

Soldier Henri Barbussed wrote that:

> a diabolical uproar surrounds us . . . a sustained crescendo, an incessant multiplication of the universal frenzy; a hurricane of hoarse and hollow banging . . . where we are buried up to our necks, and the wind of the shells seems to set it heaving and pitching.

It didn't take long for the noise and the accompanying fear to have an effect in this setting of war. Healthy soldiers were quickly transformed into "shell-shocked" damaged humans.

The stress created by the consequences of "shell shock" had lasting effects. The modern clinical term, of course, is *posttraumatic stress disorder* (PTSD). In World War I, its effects often lingered, even in soldiers who appeared to have recovered (Ellis, 1976, p. 63):

It is very nice to be home again. Yet am I at home? One sometimes doubts it. There are occasions when I feel like a visitor amongst strangers whose intentions are kindly, but whose modes of thought I neither altogether understand nor altogether approve.

Soundscapes: From Problem to Solution.

Noise-induced stress affects different animals in different ways. For example, noise pollution increased pollination but decreased seed dispersal of honeybees and birds, indirectly influencing patterns of vegetation (Francis & Barber, 2013). The honeybees may have been driven by the stress of noise pollution to load up on food supplies while birds that normally distribute seeds fled noise-polluted environments and did not return. The effects on humans appear to produce changes in learning capability. Matheson and colleagues (Matheson, Stansfeld, & Haines, 2003, p. 243) found that in both field and lab studies of children, "Chronic aircraft noise exposure impairs reading comprehension and long-term memory and may be associated with raised blood pressure."

Do you have faith that technology will come to the rescue? Some innovative technological solutions to noise pollution are emerging in Paris in the form of crowd-sourced scientific observations. French "citizen-scientists" have been equipped with cell phones capable of monitoring the environment and using those data to draw a noise map of Paris (Maisonneuve, Stevens, Niessen, & Steels, 2009). That's interesting in itself, but now others have produced soundscapes of Paris (search for "soundlandscapes" online). You can hear the welcome, comforting sounds of everyday life in Paris during a walk through a park, waiting in a train station, and even listening to a xylophone player performing in a Metro (subway) station. There's no predicting where human creativity will take you when you start solving social problems.

Crowding

Your experience of the problems of overpopulation and crowding depends on where you live and how much you travel. One of your authors lives in Storm Lake, Iowa. It's pretty quiet there compared to your other author's home in northern New Jersey, just outside of New York City. But both of us have experienced far greater crowding when traveling to places such as China and India, where the problems of crowding and noise often mix. Prior to recent noise regulation efforts, some of the three-wheeled taxis in Mumbai, India, had painted "Please beep" signs (in English) on their rear fenders to help drivers navigate tight traffic by sound. In some parts of India, you're legally required to honk when you pass another vehicle, making noise a constant irritation.

Density Versus Crowding.

Density is an objective numerical calculation of how many people occupy a particular space. **Crowding** is the subjective sense that there are too many people in a given space—in other words, it's when psychological perception comes into play. Fear of overcrowding may have been exaggerated by the popular media, however, perhaps due to a lack of good statistical understanding.

Maybe the most well-known and infamous study about crowding is so disturbing that de Waal, Aureli, and Judge (2000) called it a "nightmarish experiment" (see Calhoun, 1962a, 1962b). Calhoun arranged for an expanding population of rats to be crammed into a room. It produced what he called a "behavioral sink" in which rats soon started killing, sexually assaulting, and eventually cannibalizing each other. The popular press ran with this most dramatic element of the research story. "In no time,

Density: An objective numerical calculation of how many people occupy a particular space, expressed as number of people per quantifiable amount of space.

Crowding: The subjective sense that there are too many people in a given space.

Busy subways in India, Los Angeles, or any other major urban area can be good examples of both noise and crowding.

popularizers were comparing politically motivated street riots to rat packs, inner cities to behavioral sinks, and urban areas to zoos" (de Waal et al., 2000, p. 77).

Consequently, Calhoun is best known for what he did not want to be known for: a dismal view of a human future viciously turning on itself due to overpopulation (see Ramsden & Adams, 2008). In reality, Calhoun simply wanted to explore how we could design space more effectively. A review of these crowding experiments by Ramsden and Adams (2008) concluded that

> through the effective design of space, [Calhoun] attempted to develop more collaborative and intelligent rodent communities, capable of withstanding greater degrees of density. For Calhoun, contrary to many interpretations, population growth was not inherently bad and humanity was not destined to destroy itself. (p. 763)

The reality of crowding effects thus might not be quite as dismal as the popular media would have us believe (see Lawrence, 1974). For example, Pinker (2011) makes a statistical argument that human aggression is declining—even in the face of a densely populated Earth.

Environmental Design.

Can we do a better job designing spaces that are more comfortable for humans? Sommer (1983) says yes; he has advocated for social design that construct spaces designed for people. What? Did you assume that all buildings were built with people in mind? Take a look around your own school or home. Many buildings appear to be built with economics in mind and the assumption that whatever works for me must work for others. That is how we end up with kitchen cabinets, coat hooks, signs, and storage compartments on planes that many people cannot reach and equipment (such as many school desks) made only for right-handed people.

The social psychological coping skills that help make living in a dense society pleasant are similar to those that help us cope with noise. We cope better if we have perceived control over a crowded situation. Control means that we can wait for the next elevator, leave a crowded stadium, or excuse ourselves from a too-tight dance floor. We can

Personal space: The individual boundary around an individual's body that gives that person a sense of control over his or her environment.

find ways to assert our **personal space**, the invisible boundary around our bodies that give us a sense of control over our environment.

A Role for Social Psychologists.

One of the emerging careers related to psychology is a **user experience** specialist, someone who focuses on how consumers engage with and experience their everyday environments (see Tullis & Albert, 2013). This is an example of a specific career within the larger field called **human factors**, an academic discipline devoted to designing products or systems to maximize human interaction with them. Many of the skills you are learning as a psychology student apply to measuring and understanding your environment. And once you start looking at your world through the lens of the user's experience, you start seeing all sorts of problems that can be fixed by better design.

For example, Norman (2013) has pointed out that many award-winning designs of doors are often ambiguous—as you approach, you are made to feel uncertain about whether it is a "push" door or a "pull" door. It may look beautiful in a photograph (hence the awards), but a door should not require instructions (doors like this are now even known as "Norman doors"). Likewise, some stove knobs do not signal which burner they light, and many light switches don't naturally tell us which lights will go on. Buildings are often not designed around the people who will use them.

You can start down the road to a career as a user experience specialist by using the skills that you already have as a psychology student. Conduct a survey of one of the buildings at your school and look for examples of bad design. What is the proportion of

© iStockPhoto.com/Bibica

Products such as this curved keyboard are meant to be used in more productive and comfortable ways by humans.

© istockphoto.com/STRINGERimage

User experience: How consumers engage with and experience their everyday environments. Some psychologists study the user experience to make products that are more consumer-friendly.

Human factors: An academic discipline within psychology devoted to designing products or systems that best cater to human needs.

Without the labels on these doors, it would be impossible to know whether they are meant to be pulled open or pushed open; this is an example of poor design.

male and female restrooms relative to the people who use the space? Do the hallways of your academic buildings have alcoves that encourage quiet conversations or are they straight cinderblock corridors that encourage people to get in and get out immediately? Try giving the same survey to people in different locations. Social psychologists tend to be inventive, clever people, so get started on a career as a user experience specialist. Good design can reduce the feeling of crowding.

Just as we focused on noise as one example of threats from environmental stressors, this section's focus on crowding is an example of the many other threats from overpopulation. Even though humans crowded together generally behave better and more creatively than you might expect, there are other crises related to overpopulation—and they are urgent. A research team in India provides a discouragingly long list of the most urgent crises:

> Overpopulation has resulted in a series of catastrophic consequences by causing increased pressure on existing natural resources. Deforestation, welfare, effect on climate change, decline in biocapacity, urban sprawl, food security, increase in energy demand, and effect on marine ecosystems. (Uniyal, Paliwal, Kaphaliya, & Sharma, 2016, p. 1)

The Earth has many more subsystems than the *Titanic* had watertight compartments. But unlike the *Titanic,* Earth's compartments are interdependent. Failures of one subsystem can cascade through all the others. So how do we cope in the face of such a dismal prognosis? De Waal et al. (2000) document an insight but also deliver a warning. "We have a natural, underappreciated talent to deal with crowding, but crowding combined with scarcity of resources is something else" (p. 81).

The Tragedy of the Commons

There is a social psychological problem at the heart of the sustainability crisis. In the words of the famous Pogo cartoon, "We have met the enemy and he is us." Historically, this is called the **tragedy of the commons**. If every person does what is best for him or her, selfishly, then those actions are against the common good. Thus, what's best for the entire group will be ruined through the collective actions of each individual (see Hardin, 1968). If everyone drives a car that has low gas mileage, and no one recycles, and everyone plays their music loudly, and so on, then even though a single person's carbon footprint is small, the overall effect is tragic.

The tragedy of the commons is a social psychological problem because what benefits the individual often harms society. How can individuals thus become convinced to give up their own immediate needs, to sacrifice their own comfort for the good of the planet or the future? The beach in India demonstrates that what benefited the community also benefited many individuals, eventually. The good of the group does benefit every member of the group, if the members can delay gratification and keep the long-term goal in mind.

The tragedy of the commons is *our* tragedy if we don't prevent it.

Tragedy of the commons: The idea that individuals, in their attempt to benefit themselves, will collectively harm society.

The Main Ideas

- One emerging global problem related to social psychology is increasing noise, which becomes stressful based on volume, unpredictability, and perceived lack of control. At extreme levels, noise can even contribute to posttraumatic stress disorder.

- Crowding is the subjective sense that there are too many people in a given space; this problem can be reduced when buildings and products are designed with human users in mind.

- The "tragedy of the commons" refers to situations when problems occur if individuals only do what is best for them, personally (but these individual actions harm the group). Social psychologists might be able to help people see that short-term sacrifices will provide bigger long-term benefits.

⚡ CRITICAL THINKING CHALLENGE

- Analyze whether noise and crowding are problems for your own local campus or town. If so, what might be done to reduce these problems? If they are not problems, what about your environment has prevented noise and crowding, and how could you apply your situation to other people?

- Can you identify two examples of the "tragedy of the commons" in your school, town, or region? What are examples of actions that are harming the larger group because individuals are choosing to engage in behaviors that are good for them, personally?

Social Psychology of Law and the Courtroom

Core Questions

1. How do psychology and law fit together?
2. What career opportunities unite psychology and law?

Learning Objectives

1. Apply the goals and methods of psychology to law and courtroom situations.
2. Compare and contrast various careers that combine psychology and applied law.

The case of Kelly Michaels demonstrates why reliability and validity show up in every psychology textbook. They deserve to be integrated into your life. Her story also might inspire you to become a forensic psychologist.

"It's like public execution, but you stay alive to go at it again, and again, day after day," Kelly Michaels told Oprah Winfrey in 2003 (you can search for the interview on YouTube). It started when the police knocked on her door as the 23-year-old aspiring actress was getting ready for work at the Wee Care Day Nursery. Her name had been mentioned in a case of child sex abuse. The police took her for questioning and released her after hearing her story. She thought the short nightmare was over. But they came back and accused her of playing the piano nude, "Making poopie cakes with the children, inserting silverware into the children . . . just horrible things."

It became the longest trial in New Jersey history and cost multiple millions of dollars. And it was all an illusion. In the absence of direct physical evidence, the prosecution used anatomically correct dolls as they interviewed preschool-aged children about what had happened and where they had been touched. But here's the catch. Most of the prosecution's interviewers were biased to believe that Kelly Michaels had abused the children. For example, to confirm what they already believed, the detectives asked children leading questions such as, "Where *could* Miss Kelly have touched you?" The detectives had not been psychology majors, or they had forgotten what they had learned, because they did not recognize their own leading questions.

Instead, the detectives believed that they were measuring what they intended to measure when children touched or played with the doll's genitalia. They failed to consider that the children might have played with any unusual feature on a naked doll simply because it was a novelty (see Bruck & Ceci, 2009). After 3 years of legal proceedings and millions of dollars, they still did not understand reliability, validity, or confirmation bias. They sent an innocent Kelly Michaels to prison for 47 years (she served 5 of them, until the decision was overturned).

HOW DO PSYCHOLOGY AND LAW FIT TOGETHER?

LO 1: Apply the goals and methods of psychology to law and courtroom situations.

Forensic psychology is the application of psychological theory to legal processes. This relatively wide subfield applies research and theory from many areas of psychology to a wide variety of contexts. Six categories of application are shown in Table B.1.

Forensic psychology: The application of psychological theory to legal processes, such as suspect interrogations, criminal evidence evaluation, personal evaluation for jury duty or competency, family law, workplace assessment, and policy evaluation.

■ **TABLE B.1** Applications of Forensic Psychology

Area or Context	Examples
Interrogations	Ethics of lying to suspects Confessions Lie detection Torture
Evidence evaluation	Fingerprints DNA Criminal profiling Cognitive errors and bias in police, lawyers, jurors, witnesses, etc.
Person evaluation	Jury selection Eyewitness identification Competency/sanity of defendants Trauma assessment Risk assessment
Family law	Child custody Dispute mediation Sexual abuse Relationship violence
Workplace assessment	Harassment Discrimination Policy compliance
Policy evaluation	Program evaluation Prison sentencing Rehabilitation Death penalty

Bettmann / Bettmann / Getty Images

Anatomically correct dolls such as these are sometimes used in court or therapy settings to help children communicate about possible sexual abuse.

- - - - - - - - - - - - - - - - - - - -

False positive: Occurs when an individual or test says an event or condition is present when it is not.

False negative: Occurs when an individual or test says an event or condition is not present when it is.

- - - - - - - - - - - - - - - - - - - -

Some of these categories fit easily with standard training in psychology. For example, you are probably more prepared than you realize to start down a path of conducting particular kinds of assessments and program evaluation. However, as with many partnerships, the relationship between psychology and the law is sometimes both intimate and contentious. It is intimate because law and psychology seem to be working on the same important social problem: individual and social self-regulation (see Goldstein, 1968). But the relationship between them can become contentious because their professional cultures often are in conflict. Many of the attitudes, training experiences, and professional values of lawyers and psychologists simply will not easily fit together.

Common Goals: Reliability and Validity

The anatomically correct dolls that helped send Kelly Michaels to prison are part of a psychological test. The test is intuitively appealing, but it has two ways of being wrong. In this context, a **false positive** occurs when a therapist decides that a child has been abused when he or she hasn't. A **false negative** occurs when a therapist decides that a child has not been abused when he or she has. In addition, the theoretical orientation of the therapist will lead to different interpretations. Refusing to touch the doll could indicate abuse to a Freudian who interprets not touching as repression or denial. However, playing enthusiastically with the doll could also be interpreted as signs of abuse.

Using anatomically correct dolls to test small children for signs of sexual abuse was popular for many years. But from the very beginning, there were concerns about its reliability and validity (Friedemann & Morgan, 1985). In fact, the California Supreme Court decided that it could not determine if using anatomically correct dolls was a *valid* way to assess child sex abuse. So the court referred the problem back to the scientific community (see Yates & Terr, 1988, p. 254), ruling that "use of the dolls . . . is admissible in court only if it has been accepted as generally reliable in the scientific community."

Psychology and lawyers have similar goals that include gathering evidence that is both reliable and valid. In addition, both want the best for their clients, and both have some interest in promoting social justice. So it seems as if there ought to be some degree of meaningful overlap—and there is. However, the points of contention are also fundamental to each discipline.

Consider a few *archival case studies* from both psychology and law.

Different Philosophies: Advocacy Versus Objectivity

Law generally determines what is right by virtue of precedent, or prior authority; psychology determines what is right by virtue of empirical observations. Law can only react to and process ongoing events; psychology gets to choose what it studies. The practice of law is based on advocacy; the practice of psychology requires objectivity. Consequently, trying to fit psychology into law has often been difficult—and this tension between psychology and law has been present from their first interactions.

Hugo Münsterberg. The relationship between psychology and the law got off to a shaky start. When psychologist Hugo Münsterberg published his book *On the Witness Stand* (1908), he was hoping to influence the legal system to accept evidence from psychology in the same way it accepted evidence from other branches of science. He was unsuccessful. Costanzo and Krauss (2015) described the book's "icy reception from legal scholars" (p. 2). One reviewer gave it a "savagely, satirical critique" for Münsterberg's "exaggerated claims for psychology." Even worse, the book was not well received by fellow psychologists.

Louis Brandeis. The next occurrence was more promising. That probably was because a future Supreme Court justice, Louis Brandeis, understood irrational human psychology better than Hugo Münsterberg understood the law. Brandeis cited social science as he argued in favor of improving wages and limiting the workday to 10 hours. The case of *Muller v. Oregon* (see Woloch, 1996) involved a woman working long hours in a laundry factory. Brandeis argued from a social science perspective that excessive work hours produced negative social consequences such as infant mortality and children harmed by neglect.

The data were more typical of sociology than psychology, but it was a start. In these first two examples, the psychologist (Hugo Münsterberg) was trying to push psychology's big ideas through a very small door of legal acceptance. He was ineffective—maybe even counterproductive. But the lawyer (Louis Brandeis) was trying to pull something relatively small (some social science data) through that same small door. His data were specific and limited. He was much more effective—and his success created opportunities for others.

Mamie Clark and Kenneth Clark. We introduced you to the Clarks in Chapter 1 when we described Mamie Clark's original master's thesis. She originated a series of studies that influenced the 1954 Supreme Court case that ended legal school segregation, *Brown v. Board of Education*. But the consequences of that legal victory demonstrate critical differences in how psychologists and lawyers define success.

The lawyers who prevailed in *Brown v. Board of Education of Topeka* (1954) were happy about their legal victory. But the Clarks were, over time, profoundly disappointed because so little changed. The lives of most of the children that they were trying to empower continued to suffer from institutional and cultural discrimination. A longer view, if they had lived to see it, might have given the Clarks some comfort.

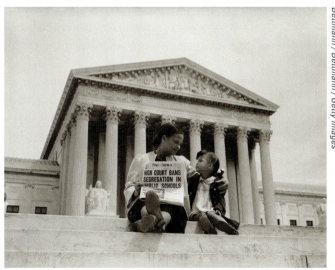

The famous legal case *Brown v. Board of Education of Topeka* (1954) used psychological research as part of its argument to end school segregation.

9 mai 1431. — L'évêque Cauchon menace Jeanne, devant les appareils de supplice, de la mettre à la torture. Jeanne résiste fièrement, déclarant : « Je ne vous dirai rien de plus que la vérité que j'ai déjà dite et si la souffrance me faisait déclarer autre chose, je dirais ensuite que j'y ai été contrainte par force. »

Even though history has shown us repeatedly that confessions under duress, such as torture, are not reliable, it took quite some time for psychological research to provide scientific evidence of this fact.

The Social Psychology of False Confessions

Kelly Michaels, from the chapter's opening, told Oprah Winfrey, "I was absolutely terrified because you were completely defenseless . . . you're being accused, you're being attacked, you can't do anything except say the words, 'I am innocent.'" She probably could have received a shorter sentence if she had been willing to plead guilty. An accused person, whether innocent or guilty, can plead guilty to a lesser crime than the one he or she is charged with and receive a lighter sentence. The alternative is to roll the dice and hope that a jury finds you not guilty.

A Confession Does Not Equal Guilt. It is easy to assume that any confession—even by torture—is an admission of guilt. But there are reasonable alternative explanations. In the United States, many trials involved Black defendants who had confessed—but only after being beaten (Kassin, 1997; Kassin & Wrightsman, 1985; Wrightsman & Kassin, 1993; Wrightsman, Neitzel, & Fortune, 1994). This situation persisted until *Brown v. Mississippi* (1936) started to alter the legal landscape. In that case, the Supreme Court ruled that a trial "is a mere pretense" if a conviction has been "obtained by violence." Jurors tend to accept confessions as authentic even when the confessions (a) have been discredited, (b) are ruled inadmissible, and (c) the judge has instructed jurors to disregard the confession (Kassin & Sukel, 1997; Kassin, Williams, & Saunders, 1990).

There is now a rich psychological research literature about **false confessions**, when people report doing something they didn't really do (see Kassin, 1997, 1998; McCormick, 1992; Wrightsman & Kassin, 1993), and the various psychological reasons why people might admit to doing something they never really did. Costanzo and Krauss (2015, p. 39) organized the literature about false confessions into the four situations summarized in Table B.2.

Instrumental, Coerced Confessions. An **instrumental confession** means that the person has a reason for confessing. A **coerced confession** means that it is forced. In criminal cases, the instrumental, coerced confession is most common. In fact, instrumental,

False confession: A confession given for a crime the accused individual did not commit.

Instrumental confession: A false confession that is given purposefully by the accused individual, even though he or she doesn't believe the confession to be true. An instrumental confession may be coerced, such as to end an interrogation, or voluntary, such as to protect someone else or to gain notoriety.

Coerced confession: A confession that is given as a result of using force, such as torture or prolonged, intense interrogation, on an accused individual. Coerced confessions are not always reliable.

	Coerced (forced)	Voluntary (not forced)
Instrumental (confession for a purpose; confessor does not believe in confession)	Confesses to end the interrogation (e.g., under conditions of torture)	Confesses to protect someone else or to gain notoriety
Authentic (confessor believes confession is the truth)	Confessor gradually comes to believe she or he is guilty	Confessor is delusional or mentally ill

SOURCE: Costanzo & Krauss, 2015.

coerced confessions arguably have become the most contentious issue that the American Psychological Association (APA) has faced in several decades. It's not difficult to understand why people being tortured would confess—they want the torture to stop! And that's why torture is not an effective technique for getting information.

Instrumental, Voluntary Confessions.

Instrumental, voluntary confessions are given for a reason that is typically known only to the person confessing. Costanzo and Krauss (2015) provided several examples of purposeful, voluntary confessions. A parent might "take the fall" to protect a child from harm. Someone seeking notoriety might confess to gain attention. The serial killer Henry Lee Lucas falsely confessed to several murders that he did not commit in an effort to secure his name and reputation as among the elite killers of all time. "Peculiar" was how Costanzo and Krauss summarized many of the motives for these voluntary false confessions.

Authentic, Coerced False Confessions.

In contrast with instrumental confessions, **authentic confessions** occur when people honestly believe they committed the crime in question—even when they didn't. For example, Clifton Lawson admitted to a brutal murder on camera and gave details that could only be known by someone who had been there (Kassin & Wrightsman, 2012). But Lawson had a very low IQ and was anxious; he was simply telling his interrogators what he believed they wanted him to say. And the details of the murder? He had learned them during the long hours sitting in the police station, listening to the officers as they discussed the case. He barely avoided conviction and seemed confused about whether he had actually committed the crime. This confession can be considered coerced because it never would have happened if Lawson had been treated more fairly and with more respect.

Authentic, Voluntary False Confessions.

These cases generally involve someone with mental illness or severe psychological pressure, suffering from a delusion. Someone really believes that he or she committed a crime and confesses to something that he or she did not do. The (unverified) story of Himmler's missing pipe suggests that innocent people being punished may come to believe that they must have done something wrong. The Nazi leader had lost his favorite pipe during a tour of a concentration camp. Six people confessed to stealing it before he discovered it in his own vehicle.

Psychologists and the APA Torture Scandal

Unfortunately, in psychology's recent history, some members of the American Psychological Association secretly promoted instrumental, coerced false confessions. Some of the APA's leadership secretly coordinated with the White House, CIA, and the Department of Defense to create a new ethics policy. It amounted to this: If a health professional were monitoring the interrogation, then it wasn't torture. Psychologists helped them change the rules (secretly) so that they could ignore the existing evidence about coerced confessions and keep on trying to torture meaningful information out of suspects.

Authentic confession: A false confession that is given by accused individuals who honestly believe they committed the crime they have confessed to, even though they didn't. An authentic confession may be coerced, such as if the confessor gradually comes to believe she or he is guilty due to the use of certain interrogation techniques, or voluntary, such as if the confessor is delusional or mentally ill.

We don't have to look far for the powerful situation that pushed their ethics off balance: the terror attacks of September 11, 2001. The situation after 9/11 was panicky and impulsive. A few days after the attack, one of my [Tom's] neighbors said, "I know it's wrong to think this way but I just want to go bomb somebody . . . anybody." It was a bad time to make big decisions. The lessons learned—and still to be learned—are summarized in many articles (see Ackerman, 2015; Richardson & Bellanger, 2016).

The Social Psychology of Eyewitness Testimony

If you are ever a juror on a case with an eyewitness, you need to be extremely cautious.

The problem is that memory is malleable—and that means that it can be manipulated. The **misinformation effect** occurs when exposure to false information or leading questions about an event leads to errors in recall of the original event. Most research on how eyewitnesses fall victim to the misinformation effect is based on the **construction hypothesis**, the idea that memories are not just sitting in our heads, ready to be accessed like computer files. Instead, they are constructed as needed at the time we're asked to use them—and they are subject to bias, stereotypes, probabilities, and wishes (Loftus, 1975; Loftus & Zanni, 1975).

Loftus (1975) demonstrated how easily memories could be pushed around by small influences in how a question was worded. She had participants view a 1-minute film of a multicar accident and then write out a brief description of what they had just witnessed. The crash itself lasted only 4 seconds. The experimenters then asked participants a series of questions about the accident and found that the participants' confidence in their observations was influenced by tiny details. For example, Loftus changed the way the questions were worded.

For example, the survey asked some participants, "Did you see a broken headlight?" and other participants, "Did you see the broken headlight?" The word *the* in the second version is a **presupposition**, wording that assumes something (here, the participants could infer that there was a broken headlight—and if they had been paying attention, they should say "yes" to this question). In reality, there was not a broken headlight—but participants who received the presupposition version of the question were significantly more likely to say "yes."

In other versions of this experiment, Loftus (1975) focused on leading questions by emphasizing that "our concern is not on the effect of the wording of a question on its answer, but rather the answers to other questions asked some time afterward" (p. 562). For example, early on in the survey participants received, Loftus asked people either:

(1) How fast was Car A going when it ran the stop sign?

(2) How fast was Car A going when it turned right?

The critical question was not how fast the car was going but whether or not they believed that they had witnessed seeing a stop sign. Later in the survey, everyone was asked whether they saw a stop sign. Importantly, no stop sign existed in the actual event—but when people had been subtly introduced to the idea of a stop sign in an earlier question, 55% now said yes, they had seen a stop sign. In contrast, only 35% of people who had been asked about the car turning right reported seeing a stop sign. People now remembered false things about what they had witnessed simply because of the process of being asked leading questions.

The most famous version of this experiment was included in a 1974 report by Loftus and Palmer. They showed people a car accident and then asked half of the participants each of these questions:

Misinformation effect: Occurs when exposure to false information or leading questions about an event leads to errors in an individual's ability to recall the original event.

Construction hypothesis: The idea that memories are constructed as needed at the time an individual is asked to use them, making recollection of specific memories subject to bias, stereotypes, probabilities, and wishes.

Presupposition: Wording that assumes a condition in a specific situation is present. When used in a survey or interview, presuppositions can make individuals more likely to suppose that the assumed condition was present.

(1) About how fast were the cars going when they smashed into each other?

(2) About how fast were the cars going when they bumped into each other?

As you would expect, the word *smashed* elicited higher speed estimates. But the more interesting finding was that 1 week later, everyone was asked whether they had witnessed broken glass. Even though there had not been any broken glass, broken glass seemed plausible as a result of a car accident, especially one with "smashing" cars—so people who had received that question a week earlier were now more likely to invent a memory of broken glass.

The participants in these studies had their memories manipulated by researchers asking leading questions—and the "eyewitnesses" had no idea that their memories had been altered. They were probably being honest when they remembered what they thought they saw. Consider the implications of this research on how real-life eyewitnesses might change their memories based on questions they receive from the police, from lawyers, or even from their own family members who ask about what happened. These participants, acting as witnesses, had constructed plausible memories and then convinced themselves that they were telling "the truth, the whole truth, and nothing but the truth." But they were wrong.

Elizabeth Loftus is one of the most famous examples of a psychologist who has devoted a career to conducting research that can apply to courtrooms. Her series of studies investigates how easily memory for events can be manipulated.

The Main Ideas

- Forensic psychology is the application of psychological theory to legal processes. It is most effective when both psychologists and legal representatives (such as lawyers, jurors, etc.) trust reliability and validity.

- Several case studies in the history of law can be used to see how the application of psychology to law evolved over time.

- One example of a modern application of psychology to law is in research on false confessions. For example, a typology by Costanzo and Krauss (2015) identifies four different reasons people might give false confessions.

- Another application of psychology to law is research on eyewitness testimony and the misinformation effect, which occurs when memories are changed based on exposure to postevent incorrect information or leading questions.

⚡ CRITICAL THINKING CHALLENGE

- Why do you think it took a relatively long period of time for lawyers, judges, and juries to make use of psychological research that is relevant to various aspects criminal justice procedures? Alternatively, why did it take psychology so long to devote research to everything psychological that occurs before, during, and after a crime?

- Which of the four reasons to provide a false confession do you think is most common—and which do you think would be most likely to lead to a false confession from you, personally?

- Now that you know about research on the misinformation effect, how confident are you that your own memories are really accurate? Can you identify any specific examples of how your own memories might have been manipulated or changed based on things that happened after the event in question?

WHAT CAREER OPPORTUNITIES UNITE PSYCHOLOGY AND LAW?

LO 2: Compare and contrast various careers that combine psychology and applied law.

Many undergraduate psychology students have a television problem that they don't know about. They suffer from the **CSI effect** (Crime Scene Investigation effect): unrealistic expectations of forensic science that are created by watching fictional television shows (see Cole & Dioso-Villa, 2006; Scanlan, 2015). One colleague joked, with dark humor, "There just aren't enough serial killers to go around" to employ the many students who want to become criminal profilers.

In reality, people who actually do criminal profiling are seldom trained in psychology. Scientific approaches for criminal profiling have not been established or even agreed upon. And the evidence for the accuracy and helpfulness of criminal profiling is so thin that it is seldom admitted in court or considered as expert testimony (see Fulero & Wrightsman, 2008).

The False Television World of Forensic Psychology

Fortunately, we have data about the CSI effect. One study found that regular viewers of crime dramas would probably make slightly better burglars than if they watched other kinds of programs instead! They were more likely to know, for instance, that using gloves and wearing a hat would prevent certain evidence from being left at the crime scene (Vicary & Zaikman, 2017).

Not all television crime dramas are alike, and particular episodes, of course, will feature different content. A comparison of the top three television crime drama franchises included *Law & Order* (1990–2010), *CSI* (2000–2015), and *NCIS* (2003–present; see Hust, Marett, Lei, Ren, & Ran, 2015). The focus of the study was on the degree to which viewers of crime dramas tend to accept myths about rape and their willingness to intervene if they observe sexual assault. When they surveyed 313 first-year college students, they found the following:

(a) Exposure to the *Law & Order* franchise is associated with decreased rape myth acceptance and increased intentions to adhere to expressions of sexual consent and refuse unwanted sexual activity.

(b) The *CSI* franchise is associated with decreased intentions to seek consent and decreased intentions to adhere to expressions of sexual consent.

(c) Exposure to the *NCIS* franchise is associated with decreased intentions to refuse unwanted sexual activity.

CSI effect: The unrealistic expectations of forensic science that are created by watching fictional television.

These are not strong patterns of behavior; this particular aspect of the CSI effect appears to be real but small. But as you make your own career decisions, beware of the CSI effect. It's a reality check if you are considering a career that includes both psychology and the law.

The Real World of Forensic Psychology

So, let's introduce you to the real, non-CSI world of forensic psychology. Costanzo and Krauss (2015) identified everyday working roles enacted by forensic psychologists. They include trial consultants, evaluators, and reformers; we added dispute mediators to the list.

Trial Consultants. **Trial consultants** typically try to influence the outcome of a trial in three ways: (1) by helping to select a sympathetic jury, (2) by developing trial strategies such as persuasion techniques, and (3) by assisting in witness preparation. Kressel (a social psychologist) and Kressel (a lawyer), in their book *Stack and Sway*, describe the variety of skills that psychologists can offer a jury. They explore the costs, the sociology, and the effectiveness of those efforts—and the public's perception of unfairness when only the wealthy can afford the luxury of jury consultants (Kressel & Kressel, 2002).

Jury profiling and juror dynamics are among the most enduring television and movie plot devices (e.g., *Bull* [Attanasio et al., 2016], *Runaway Jury* [Fleder, Kankiewicz, & Milchan, 2003], *Twelve Angry Men* [Fonda, Rose, Donnelly, Lumet, & Friedkin, 1957/1997]). However, it is logically impossible to determine whether jury consultants have been effective, especially considering the fact that jury deliberation is confidential. Psychological jury consultants and researchers will therefore sometimes create mock juries to anticipate how different pieces of evidence might be processed by a real jury.

Understanding the psychological dynamics of a jury is not necessarily reserved for the super-wealthy—but neither is it practical for those with very little money. The more relevant observation is that, on a practical level, very few cases go to trial anyway (Galanter, 2005). Why? Because both sides decide to settle out of court—usually sometime shortly before one or both of the parties spend the last of their money on lawyers.

Dispute Mediation. Remember, almost everyone settles out of court. Jury trials are rare. That has created another industry that appears to be good for psychologists: dispute mediation. Like other areas of overlap between psychology and law, the practitioners are not necessarily lawyers or psychologists—although that training is likely to help. But there are ways to obtain training and sometimes certification in dispute mediation, depending on the nature of the conflict (see Barsky, 2014; Love & Waldman, 2016).

There are as many career opportunities for mediators as there are ways for people to have conflicts with one another. On a large scale, there are dispute mediators between nations to resolve international conflicts (Ascher & Brown, 2014). Many civil disputes involve conflict over land, so particular training in agriculture, forestry, real estate, or boundary disputes may help individuals become better mediators for those circumstances (see Dhiaulhaq, De Bruyn, & Gritten, 2015).

Trial consultant: An individual who tries to influence the outcome of a trial in three ways: (1) by helping to select a sympathetic jury, (2) by developing trial strategies, and (3) by assisting in witness preparation.

Families, however, also get into conflicts that can be solved before siblings or others start taking one another to court (Eisenberg, 2016). A separate skill in divorce mediation can help families take better care of themselves and of children who are unavoidably drawn into the conflict. In those cases, the skills of a family therapist may be more applicable. Judges frequently become advocates for dispute mediation to prevent unproductive lawsuits from clogging up the court system.

Evaluation. As a student, you already participate in the world of evaluation research when you review a product, respond to a survey, or join a focus group. Websites such as RateMyProfessors.com demonstrate the desire for meaningful evaluation research. However, the world of evaluation research is much more sophisticated when people start assessing the consequences of new public policies, such as whether harsh sentencing guidelines for first-time drug offenders are biased against people of color, by age, or in other ways (Spohn, 2014). Every new law needs to be evaluated—or should be, because there are usually real lives or great amounts of money at stake.

Psychology students may not recognize the monetary value of the practical evaluation skills that they already have. Your knowledge of statistics and—more important—the design of experiments is a great advantage. Your scientific training can be put to excellent use in high-paying evaluation departments. You might even want to volunteer or shadow someone at your own university's "institutional research" division to get a sense of how important their work is to the quality of students' experiences.

Reformers. Perhaps the most important role that forensic psychologists have played is to challenge the accepted wisdom of the legal system, including work on vital social issues: false confessions (see Kassin, 2015; Kassin & Kiechel, 1996), eyewitness testimony (Loftus & Palmer, 1996), repressed memories (Loftus & Ketcham, 1996), children's testimony, and the unreliability of anatomically correct dolls (see Ceci & Bruck, 1995). These courageous forensic psychologists often hold up a scientific stop sign that refuses to let dangerous assumptions go forward without being challenged.

These scholars have devoted much of their academic careers to these injustices and have, over time, rescued many innocent lives and restored the dignity of many innocent individuals falsely accused and imprisoned. Social psychologists Kassin, Fiske, Wrightsman, Ceci, and Loftus (and many others) have played important roles in both conducting the basic research related to forensic psychology and to applying it to causes related to social justice.

The case of Kelly Michaels was only one of a large collection of cases of false accusations of child sex abuse in daycare centers. As the media reported one rolling accusation after another, they produced a **moral panic**, the widespread belief that a particular group threatens society (see Downes, Rock, Chinkin, & Gearty, 2013). Social psychologists are often on the front lines of resistance because they are more apt to recognize the signs of a developing moral panic.

The Main Ideas

- The CSI effect creates unrealistic expectations of forensic science, created by watching fictional television. This effect has influence over both real-world forensic scientists and influence over many students' expectations of possible careers.

- Four careers that are possible in forensic psychology are trial consultants, dispute mediators, evaluators, and reformers.

Moral panic: The widespread belief that a particular group of people pose an urgent threat to society, based on accusations of a moral nature.

⚡ CRITICAL THINKING CHALLENGE

- Why does television or movie portrayal of certain types of careers have such influence over people's expectations, when viewers know and acknowledge that the situations are fictional? Can you think of a time when your views or perceptions of a career or certain situation were misguided, and you believe it was due to media influence?

- Which of the four careers in forensic psychology (trial consultants, dispute mediators, evaluators, and reformers) sounds the most appealing to you, personally, and why?

Visit **edge.sagepub.com/heinzen** to help you accomplish your coursework goals in an easy-to-use learning environment.

- Mobile-friendly **eFlashcards**
- **Video** and **multimedia content**
- EXCLUSIVE! Access to full-text **SAGE journal articles**

⑤SAGE edge™

Social Psychology of Stress and Health

Core Questions

1. How do environmental stressors influence health and health care?

2. How can social psychology facilitate adherence to medical advice?

Learning Objectives

1. Explain the techniques and benefits of stress management.

2. Apply persuasion tactics toward increasing adherence to medical advice.

You know what it's like to be sick.

A problem like childhood leukemia is, of course, much more severe than a bad cold. But even a minor illness creates stress that tends to decrease healthy habits such as regular exercise (Oman & King, 2000). Sometimes, it takes only a little push from the environment to get us slipping into a downward spiral of declining health and unhealthy habits. If, as Kurt Lewin predicted, our behaviors—including our health behaviors—are a function of both the individual person and the social environment, then social psychology should be able to help shape people's choices toward better health outcomes.

Psychiatrist George Engel (1977) wrote a landmark article in *Science* suggesting that the model used for medical cases at the time wasn't sufficient. His major criticism was that a model of health and sickness based only on biology neglected to consider how psychological factors and sociological factors come into play. While there are now entire textbooks on the quickly expanding world of health psychology, this application mini-chapter will discuss just two important questions relevant to how social psychology can contribute to our understanding of stress, health, and medical behaviors.

HOW DO ENVIRONMENTAL STRESSORS INFLUENCE HEALTH AND HEALTH CARE?

LO 1: Explain the techniques and benefits of stress management.

Engel's idea that health is the combined product of biological, psychological, and social forces is called the **biopsychosocial model** (see Figure C.1). At the time, it was a significant departure from its predecessor model, which focused only on biological factors. The biopsychosocial model is a comprehensive approach that has been gaining acceptance for more than 40 years (but see also Ghaemi, 2009). In 1977, Engel wrote that

> the dominant model of disease today [in 1977] is biomedical, and it leaves no room within its framework for the social, psychological, and behavioural dimensions of illness. A biopsychosocial model . . . provides a blueprint for research, a framework for teaching, and a design for action in the real world of health care. (p. 135)

The biopsychosocial model makes room for one of the most pervasive influences on our well-being: stress. **Stress** occurs when an individual's assessment of the current environment exceeds his or her coping abilities or resources and therefore threatens his or her well-being (see Lazarus & Folkman, 1984). However, stress is not necessarily a bad thing. The **Yerkes-Dodson law** predicts that moderate amounts of stress are associated with optimal performance (see Belavkin, 2001; Teigen, 1994). The

Biopsychosocial model: The idea that human health is the combined product of biological, psychological, and social forces.

Stress: When individuals' assessment of the current environment exceeds their coping abilities or resources and therefore threatens their well-being.

Yerkes-Dodson law: An empirical relationship between stress and performance that predicts that moderate amounts of stress are associated with optimal performance.

"stress test" in a cardiologist's office helps diagnose heart disease. In the tiny world of microbes, environmental stressors can help initiate beneficial adaptations (Arnold, Jackson, Waterfield, & Mansfield, 2007). However, there is a dark side to the relationship between stress and health.

Hans Selye (1973) was an endocrinologist who proposed a three-stage theory of how organisms respond to stress. His theory, called **general adaptation syndrome**, described how the body reacts to persistent stress in ways that make us vulnerable to

■ FIGURE C.2 Selye's (1973) general adaptation syndrome model suggests that reactions and resistance to stress come in three phases.

General adaptation syndrome: A three-stage theory concerning how organisms respond to stress, which proposes that persistent stress can deplete a body's resources, making an individual vulnerable to disease.

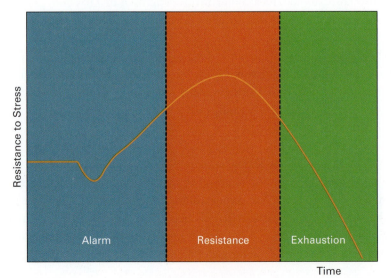

■ TABLE C.1 Hans Selye's General Adaptation Syndrome

Stage	Description
Stage 1. Alarm	The body is briefly stunned but then reacts with preparation for "fight or flight" as the sympathetic nervous system responds to the stressor.
Stage 2. Resistance	The parasympathetic system returns the body toward its normal state, but we remain vigilant.
Stage 3. Exhaustion	If stressors persist beyond the body's capacity, resources are depleted and we become vulnerable to diseases.

SOURCE: Adapted from Selye (1973).

disease. Figure C.2 and Table C.1 suggest the pattern of responses: After an initial alarm phase, the body tries to settle down and readjust if possible. However, we become more vulnerable to diseases if the stressors persist and exhaust our resources.

Stress-Related Health Problems

Flu, sore throats, headaches, and backaches; it's not a happy list. But those are the stress-related illnesses that were found in a study of 75 married couples (DeLongis, Folkman, & Lazarus, 1988). It gets worse. Another team investigated stress during pregnancy and found that stress was associated with earlier births and lower birthweights (Lobel, Cannella, Graham, DeVincent, Schneider, & Meyer, 2008). Stress is among a reliable constellation of variables related to heart disease; these predictors include acute and chronic life stressors, psychological alterations such as anxiety and depression, personality traits such as anger and hostility, reactive behavioral coping strategies, and the absence of social support (Carney & Freedland, 2007).

We may all experience more health-related stress as we age. One of the stress-related risk factors for disease is **ageism**, recurrent experiences with negative stereotypes and discrimination experienced by older individuals due to their age. The theory of **weathering** (often called the "weathering hypothesis"; see Geronimus, 1992) is similar to Selye's general adaptation syndrome. It proposes that the cumulative effects of chronic stressors and high-effort coping predispose individuals to physical deterioration, premature aging, and chronic diseases. There is an ironic twist to ageism for people who spent their working and social lives as part of the dominant culture. Now they too get to experience what it's like to "lift a ton of feathers," the soft but persistent discrimination that other minorities and disenfranchised people have experienced routinely for their entire lives (see Chapter 9 and Carr, Szalacha, Barnett, & Caswell, 2003; Geronimus, 1992).

Posttraumatic Stress Disorder

When stress goes to extremes, it can lead to posttraumatic stress disorder (PTSD). PTSD has its own curious history beginning with what was called in various wars "shell shock," "war trauma," and "battle fatigue." We recommend viewing, even if only for a few minutes, some film clips from World War I (search YouTube for "shell shock"). What you will see is so disturbing that you may not want to watch for very long, but it will help you understand the origins, severity, and devastation associated with PTSD.

The U.S. Department of Veterans Affairs (2017) describes four types of PTSD symptoms, some of which you can see plainly in those early war films:

Ageism: Negative stereotypes and discrimination experienced by older individuals, which often leads to stress.

Weathering: The idea that the cumulative effects of chronic stressors and high-effort coping predispose individuals to physical deterioration, premature aging, and chronic diseases.

1. Reliving the trauma

   a. Nightmares

   b. Flashbacks

   c. Triggers that lead to flashbacks

2. Avoiding situations that remind you of the trauma

   a. Avoiding crowds

   b. Avoiding driving, especially if your trauma involved a vehicle

   c. Keeping busy and avoiding therapy so that you do not have to confront the traumatic experience

3. Negative changes in beliefs and feelings

   a. Avoiding positive, loving relationships

   b. Forgetting parts of the traumatic event

   c. Refusing to talk about the traumatic event

   d. Believing that no one can be trusted in a dangerous world

4. Hyperarousal

   a. Difficulty sleeping

   b. Difficulty concentrating

   c. Deeply startled by loud noises or surprises

   d. Positioning yourself in rooms so that you can keep an eye on everyone

The modern diagnosis of PTSD has expanded well beyond the boundaries of war trauma. It now includes individuals who have experienced varying degrees of trauma from other life events. A brief description of life traumas comes from research by

■ TABLE C.2 Traumatic Event Exposure

Trauma Type	N	%
Physical violence/assault	93	28.9
Sexual violence/assault	66	20.5
Loved one survived a life-threatening accident or illness	62	19.3
Other serious accident	19	5.9
Motor vehicle accident	17	5.3
Natural disaster	16	5.0
Abortion or miscarriage	14	4.3
Other traumatic event not listed	14	4.3
Being stalked	13	4.0
Life-threatening illness	6	1.9
Combat	2	.6

SOURCE: Kubany et al. (2000).

Kubany and colleagues (Kubany, Leisen, Kaplan, & Kelly, 2000). Respondents indicated how often they experienced 22 potentially traumatic events (e.g., physical abuse, sexual assault, natural disaster; see Table C.2); the different types of trauma show that PTSD can come from a wide variety of negative experiences that go well beyond the scope of war.

There is an emotional logic to PTSD that does not make rational sense. For example, in one study, the most enduring PTSD-related symptoms among 157 victims of a violent crime were anger and shame—and shame lasted even longer than anger (Andrews, Brewin, Rose, & Kirk, 2000). They were victims, not perpetrators, yet they somehow experienced a long-lasting shame over something that was done to them (perhaps due to victim-blaming stigmas placed on them by others).

In another study, 56 ambulance service workers first described the most distressing aspects of their work and were then screened for PTSD symptoms. The procedure meant that they were deliberately triggered (or primed) as the researchers probed for symptoms. Of the 56 participants, 21 met the criteria for PTSD and 22 more indicated a need for further screening for psychiatric symptoms—in other words, most of the people in this sample of first responders showed signs of severe stress.

How common is PTSD in the general population? The answer lies in your understanding of the "D" in PTSD. We have all endured something unpleasant, even if it is "only" witnessing a bad traffic accident or one of the experiences in Table C.2. So, we all have some measure of PTS—but most of us can still get through our days without having to experience flashbacks or other symptoms. For those who are suffering from more severe traumas and/or more severe posttrauma symptoms, however, PTSD is a serious problem.

■ TABLE C.3 The Holmes-Rahe Life Stress Inventory

The Social Readjustment Rating Scale INSTRUCTIONS: Mark down the point value of each of these life events that has happened to you during the previous year. Total these associated points.	
Life Event	**Mean Value**
1. Death of spouse	100
2. Divorce	73
3. Marital separation from mate	65
4. Detention in jail or other institution	63
5. Death of a close family member	63
6. Major personal injury or illness	53
7. Marriage	50
8. Being fired at work	47
9. Marital reconciliation with mate	45
10. Retirement from work	45
11. Major change in the health or behavior of a family member	44
12. Pregnancy	40
13. Sexual Difficulties	39

(Continued)

Life Event	Mean Value
14. Gaining a new family member (i.e.. birth, adoption, older adult moving in, etc.)	39
15. Major business readjustment	39
16. Major change in financial state (i.e., a lot worse or better off than usual)	38
17. Death of a close friend	37
18. Changing to a different line of work	36
19. Major change in the number of arguments w/spouse (i.e., either a lot more or a lot less than usual regarding child rearing, personal habits, etc.)	35
20. Taking on a mortgage (for home, business, etc.)	31
21. Foreclosure on a mortgage or loan	30
22. Major change in responsibilities at work (i.e., promotion, demotion, etc.)	29
23. Son or daughter leaving home (marriage, attending college, joined military)	29
24. In-law troubles	29
25. Outstanding personal achievement	28
26. Spouse beginning or ceasing work outside the home	26
27. Beginning or ceasing formal schooling	26
28. Major change in living condition (new home, remodeling, deterioration of neighborhood or home, etc.)	25
29. Revision of personal habits (dress manners, associations, quitting smoking)	24
30. Trouble with the boss	23
31. Major changes in working hours or conditions	20
32. Changes in residence	20
33. Changing to a new school	20
34. Major change in usual type and/or amount of recreation	19
35. Major change in church activity (i.e., a lot more or less than usual)	19
36. Major change in social activities (clubs, movies, visiting, etc.)	18
37. Taking on a loan (car, tv, freezer, etc.)	17
38. Major change in sleeping habits (a lot more or less than usual)	16
39. Major change in number of family get-togethers	15
40. Major change in eating habits (a lot more or less food intake, or very different meal hours or surroundings)	15
41. Vacation	13
42. Major holidays	12
43. Minor violations of the law (traffic tickets, jaywalking, disturbing the peace, etc.)	11

Now, add up all the points you have to find your score.

150 pts or less means a relatively low amount of life change and a low susceptibility to stress-induced health breakdown.

150 to 300 pts implies about a 50% chance of a major health breakdown in the next 2 years.

300 pts or more raises the odds to about 80%, according to the Holmes-Rahe statistical prediction model.

SOURCE: Holmes & Rahe (1967).

Measuring Stress

Creation of stress ratings scales began with the now-famous Holmes and Rahe (1967) Social Readjusment Rating Scale (SRRS). The SRRS (and similar checklists) measured stress by counting events that participants had experienced within 3 years (or some other time frame). As you can see in Table C.3, these events could be negative (a death in the family) or positive (an outstanding achievement). Negative stressors are called **distress**, while positive events are called **eustress**. Even positive events, such as a wedding or a promotion at work, cause stress due to the required changes, pressure to succeed, and so on.

Managing Stress

Holmes and Rahe's (1967) stress scale helped get the research community started on stress research. Later researchers created additional stress scales for specific purposes, populations, cultures, and situations. For example, Boals and Schuler (2017) are working to help establish the scientific foundation for positive psychology by developing a revised version of a posttraumatic growth scale. The possibility of growth by successfully coping with stress is one of positive psychology's contributions to stress management. (There is more about positive psychology in another mini-chapter.) The rest of this section examines different variables and approaches to managing stress. Which seems like it would work best for you?

The Mindfulness Approach to Stress Management. **Mindfulness** is a meditative focus on the present. For the past several years, it has been receiving more attention from experimental researchers, usually as a therapeutic technique. For example, a review of the effectiveness of mindfulness on managing chronic lower back pain suggests that there is a modest benefit to the practice of mindfulness (see Hilton et al., 2016). However, some studies indicate that cognitive-behavioral techniques for stress reduction appear to be more effective, at least when the goal is to reduce work-related stress (van der Klink, Blonk, Schene, & Dijk, 2001).

Still, mindfulness-based stress reduction programs using meditation appear to offer some health benefits (Grossman, Niemann, Schmidt, & Walach, 2004). For example, mindfulness meditation interventions appeared to produce significant benefits for medical students experiencing the stress of their medical education (Shapiro, Schwartz, & Bonner, 1998). Mindfulness also seems to be effective as a stress management approach for generally healthy people (Chiesa & Serretti, 2009).

Social Support. **Social support** is the degree to which you are embedded in a network of people who can provide various kinds of assistance, if needed. There are different kinds of social support, but one succinct definition is whether you have someone you know you can call on if you need $100 right away. Money would be considered "tangible" support.

Uchino (2004) and others have articulated three other types of social support (see Table C.4).

The link between social support and better health is well established—but the psychological mechanisms that make that connection work are not well understood (Uchino, Bowen, Carlisle, & Birmingham, 2012). One explanation is the **buffering hypothesis** (see Farmer & Sundberg, 2010) that social support provides critical resources needed to overcome environmental stressors. People experiencing stress probably don't care about the psychological mechanisms anyway. They only know that their

Distress: Stress due to negative stressors, such as a death in an individual's family.

Eustress: Stress due to positive events, such as a wedding or a promotion at work.

Mindfulness: A meditative focus on the present that is often used to lessen stress.

Social support: The degree to which an individual is embedded in a network of people who can provide various kinds of assistance, if needed.

Buffering hypothesis: The idea that social support provides critical resources needed to overcome environmental stressors.

■ **TABLE C.4** Four Types of Social Support, According to Uchino (2004)

Types of Social Support	Definition and Example
Emotional support . . .	provides warmth and nurturing through empathy and expressions of concern.
Tangible (or instrumental) support . . .	provides material needs such as loaning someone money or a car.
Informational support . . .	provides problem-solving information or advice such as the best way to travel to a foreign country.
Companionship (or belonging) support . . .	provides a sense of belonging by engaging in shared activities.

lives are a little better off, more manageable, and more secure when they have particular kinds of social support.

Personality Types: Promoting Health and Preventing Heart Disease.
You may have noticed that certain people react calmly and appropriately in the face of particular environmental stressors. Others react to minor stressors with dramatic responses. Two personality types that cope effectively with stress are hardiness and resiliency. The **hardy personality** is resistant to stress-related diseases because their thinking style keeps their physiology calm (Allred & Smith, 1989). The **resilient personality** copes positively with adversity (Skodol, 2010) and bounces back from defeats. Both of these personality types are similar in that they deal with stress effectively, but they differ slightly in their approach (hardy individuals keep physiologically calm, while resilient individuals keep psychologically calm). Both approaches seem to be beneficial.

On the other hand, a **Type A personality** was originally developed by cardiologists Friedman and Rosenman (1974) when they noticed that certain personalities appeared to be more prone to heart disease. They used a particular kind of interview technique called a *structured interview* that standardized the questions and order of presentation when they spoke with their patients. Their approach included a *behavioral interview* that included observing their patients' nonverbal behaviors such as time-checking, speaking quickly, interrupting, and general restlessness. People high in a Type A personality are impatient and don't seem to manage stress well because they internalize it, leading to poor heart health. Subsequent research has focused on the central emotional experience of stress-induced hostility as the predictor of heart disease (Everson-Rose & Lewis, 2005).

A Healthy Environment.
One increasing stressor on all living creatures is due to climate change, the instability it creates, and its consequences for our health. We look at this alarming pattern in a separate application mini-chapter, but scientists already understand some of the connections between environmental abuse and health.

For example, Wells, Evans, and Cheek (2016) have accumulated evidence about the negative health effects of damaged environments such as disrupted housing, crowding, noise, chaos, and technological as well as natural disasters. Researchers no longer have to look very far into the future to predict outbreaks of infectious disease due to climate change. For example, Swaminathan, Viennet, McMichael, and Harley (2017) predict a continuing increase in the distribution, transmission, and survival of microbes due to climate change. This change is facilitated because changing climates require microbes,

Hardy personality: A personality type where individuals cope effectively with stress because their thinking style keeps their physiology calm.

Resilient personality: A personality type where individuals react appropriately to stress because they are able to cope positively with adversity.

Type A personality: A personality type characterized by competitiveness, the tendency to be impatient, and hostility, where individuals do not manage stress well because they internalize it, leading to poor health.

REUTERS/Pawel Kopczynski

whose only interest is in surviving, to find new vectors of transmission and new hosts to increase the distribution of disease. A changing climate encourages the transmission and spread of diseases.

We are very good at dealing with stress, but wouldn't it be nice if we could devote more energy to lowering the human-created strains on the environment rather than becoming better at coping with them? That is why another entire mini-chapter considers social psychology and the environment.

The Main Ideas

- Stress occurs when an individual's assessment of the current environment exceeds his or her coping abilities or resources and therefore threatens his or her well-being. The theory called general adaption syndrome suggests that when stressors continue, our health may be compromised.

- When stress leads to severe symptoms, people may suffer from posttraumatic stress disorder. Various methods and scales have been created to measure stress.

- Several variables have also been investigated in terms of managing stress. Various techniques or ideas include mindfulness, social support, personality types, and a healthy environment.

⚡ CRITICAL THINKING CHALLENGE

- One population of people who are more likely to suffer from posttraumatic stress disorder are military veterans. What is the government's responsibility to care for the psychological well-being of veterans? How can the care provided to this important population be improved?

- Imagine you've just experienced a personal crisis. When you consider the types of social support listed in Table C.4, which do you think will be the most important? Rank-order them by importance based on the following different types of crisis: (1) you are fired from your job, (2) your long-time relationship partner breaks up with you, and (3) you become stranded without a telephone, form of identification, or money in a foreign country.

HOW CAN SOCIAL PSYCHOLOGY FACILITATE ADHERENCE TO MEDICAL ADVICE?

LO 2: Apply persuasion tactics toward increasing adherence to medical advice.

You don't need to be religious to recognize the wisdom of the famous prayer used in many addiction treatment centers: "Grant me the serenity to accept what I cannot change, the courage to change what I can, and the wisdom to know the difference." The social psychology of health asks a more specific question: Why don't people who "know the difference" still not change their behaviors? More broadly, social psychology can offer insight regarding why people ignore the advice of their doctors. Why don't people take their pills as prescribed? Why don't they do their rehabilitation exercises? Why don't they regularly get screened for cancer? These are all questions regarding **treatment adherence**, or following the advice of a health care provider.

Treatment adherence: When an individual follows the advice of a health care provider.

Nonadherence Is a Big Problem

When presented with any social problem—such as lack of treatment adherence—it is useful first to get some sense of the size of the problem. **Epidemiology** is the statistical analysis of patterns of disease. As you probably suspected, statistical rates of nonadherence depend on many factors. For example, a physician may recommend anything from drinking more water to a dramatic drug intervention to exercising three times per week—those recommendations are likely to produce wide variations of adherence. One of the relatively easier ways to get a measured picture of nonadherence is to assess medication adherence.

© istockphoto.com/GMVozd

Nonadherence to Prescribed Medicines. For example, many people with schizophrenia require tightly managed adherence to their prescribed antipsychotic medications. Failure to take medications increases the risk of making their illness worse and subsequent rehospitalization. A review of 10 reports of medication usage among people with schizophrenia found an average nonadherence rate of 41.2% (Lacro, Dunn, Dolder, Leckband, & Jeste, 2002).

You would expect people diagnosed with the memory-related disorder of cognitive impairment (CI) to have higher rates of nonadherence. They simply forget to take their meds. However, when Smith and her colleagues (2017) reviewed 15 studies of medication adherence among people with CI, they found that the range of nonadherence was from 10% to 38%. That was somewhat lower than what Lacro et al. (2002) found among people with schizophrenia. That difference may be because their review of people with CI included studies that surveyed patients with and without caregiver supports—people who could encourage adherence. That, in turn, reinforces (a) the value of social support and (b) the idea that there is more to nonadherence that just not remembering to take your pills.

A study of 195,930 e-prescriptions counted only whether the e-prescriptions were not filled—in other words, the script was ordered by the physician but never picked up by the patient (Fischer et al., 2010). Here, 28% of the prescriptions were not even filled—but the fine print is important. The highest rates of nonadherence (as defined in this study) were for chronic conditions such as hypertension (28.4%), hyperlipidemia (28.2%), and diabetes (31.4%). Nonadherence is especially expensive (and dangerous) when it aggravates existing illnesses, as is likely with chronic diseases.

Nonadherence Is a Persuasion Problem. Nonadherence is often a problem of how to change behavior. For example, nonadherence to medical advice was higher for behavioral interventions such as losing weight or exercising (see DiMatteo, 2004). Becoming effective persuaders is therefore important to people in the medical field. Haynes and colleagues (Haynes, Ackloo, Sahota, McDonald, & Yao, 2008) estimated that "effective ways to help people follow medical treatments could have far larger effects on health than any treatment itself" (p. 20). Brannon, Feist, and Updegraff (2013) summarized (see Table C.5) some of the reasons patients gave for not adhering to medical advice.

Epidemiology: The statistical analysis of the patterns of a disease that are used to understand the disease's incidence and spread.

Use the Principles of Persuasion

Physicians probably prefer to think of themselves as healers rather than salespeople. But sometimes they are the same thing. Physicians need to become aware of what

■ **TABLE C.5** Reasons Patients Give for Not Following Doctor's Orders

It's too much trouble.	I gave some of my pills to my husband so he won't get sick.
I just didn't get the prescription filled.	The doctor doesn't know as much as my other doctor.
The medication was too expensive, so I took fewer pills to make them last.	The medication makes me sick.
The medication didn't work very well. I was still sick, so I stopped taking it.	I don't like the way that doctor treats me, and I'm not going back.
The medication worked after only 1 week, so I stopped taking it.	I feel fine. I don't see any reason to take something to prevent illness.
I have too many pills to take.	I don't like my doctor. He looks down on people without insurance.
I won't get sick. God will save me.	I didn't understand my doctor's instructions and was too embarrassed to ask her to repeat them.
I forgot.	I don't like the taste of nicotine chewing gum.
I don't want to become addicted to pills.	I didn't understand the directions on the label.

SOURCE: Brannon et al. (2013).

does—and does not—persuade people to take their medications, adopt an exercise program, and generally comply with medical advice. Fortunately, social influence tactics and the theory of planned behavior (described in Chapter 6) both describe how the persuasion process can be applied to increase adherence to medical advice. But these strategies don't just happen. They need people (perhaps you?) who can understand and apply scientifically developed principles of persuasion to help people take their medicines as directed.

You'll learn more by doing social psychology than by reading or thinking about it. So try treating the challenge of medical persuasion as a game. You are playing the role of psychological consultant to a medical clinic. Your job is to take the principles of persuasion you already know and apply them to the problem described below. You'll learn more by creating (and criticizing) your own intervention.

You are now the high-priced consultant. Here is the cast of characters for this exercise:

Physician: Dr. X. She has been seeing every member of the family below for about 5 years and is worried about everyone's health, but for slightly different reasons. The medical records indicate that, except for the youngest daughter, they all are overweight and getting worse. Dr. X does not want to "body shame" anyone; she acknowledges prejudice against people who are both "too thin" and "too big," but her concern is purely from a health perspective. She has talked to each of them and doesn't know what else to do. But she has heard you give a talk about cognitive dissonance at a medical conference and has talked the clinic into paying you for a consultation.

The family:

Father: Carl is 41 years old, 5'11", and weighs 255 pounds. Carl is a warehouse manager whose job also occasionally requires some physical labor. Dr. X has told him that he is "prediabetic" and needs to lose weight. His hours are more predictable than his wife's hours so he does most of the school pickups, after-school activities, doctor's appointments, and so forth.

Mother: Linda is 39 years old, 5'2", and weighs 186 pounds. Linda works for a medical recruiting firm and spends much of her workday online and making phone calls. Her overall health is good and she has stopped smoking, but she is obese, partly because she loves to bake.

Son: Ray is 13 years old, 5′6″, and weighs 169 pounds. Ray is big for his age; he is already being recruited by the J.V. football coach even though he is not especially active or interested in athletics. He prefers to play first-person shooter video games.

Daughter: Melody is 10 years old, 5′1″, and weighs 74 pounds. Melody is rail thin but doesn't think she has an eating disorder—she says she just isn't hungry. She is a conscientious student and enjoys spending time with her close group of female friends.

Persuasion Tactic: Create Cognitive Dissonance.

The theory of cognitive dissonance (see Chapter 6) proposes that people are motivated to change when they hold incompatible beliefs and behaviors. Smoking is an example that many people can understand. If you believe that smoking is bad for you but you continue to smoke, then you will be motivated (more or less) to change. You could try to resolve your dissonance by trying to convince yourself that smoking is actually good for you (a hard sell, cognitively). On the other hand, you could resolve your dissonance by quitting smoking (a hard sell, physiologically).

For example, in Chapter 6, you learned about some sorority sisters who struggled with eating disorders (Becker et al., 2008). Their symptoms lessened after they were recruited to give talks to incoming first-year students about the dangers of eating disorders. To resolve the dissonance between the advice they gave to first-year students and their own behavior, they changed their own behavior and began (and continued) to eat a more normal, healthy diet.

Questions:

1. Based on the cognitive dissonance approach, what do you advise Dr. X to say to her patients?

2. What could go wrong with this plan?

3. How well does this sorority research (Becker et al., 2008) map onto the family?

4. Should Dr. X try to influence the entire family together or try different approaches for each individual in the family?

5. Dr. X is not being paid for anything except office visits. Does she have any responsibility to try to play the role of social psychologist—or does the responsibility for health management rest solely with the family?

6. How will you know whether your intervention has been successful? In other words, what does success look like? How will you operationalize better health?

Alternative Persuasion Tactics.

Cognitive dissonance is only one of many social psychological persuasion tactics. Select or combine the tactics listed here to create an intervention that might help the family. How can these ideas apply to health psychology?

1. Intuition versus Logic (see Chapter 4): People make decisions based on both emotional or intuitive reasons and for systematic, logical reasons.

2. The theory of planned behavior (see Chapter 6):

    a. Attitude change → Influences the strength and value of underlying beliefs

    b. Subjective norms → Influence beliefs about what others believe

    c. Perceived control → Influences beliefs about the degree of control

3. Common persuasion tactics (see Chapter 6):

   a. Foot-in-the-door → People are more likely to comply with a large request if they first agree to a small request.

   b. Reciprocity → People feel obliged to give back to others who have first given to them ("return the favor"), such as the door-in-the-face technique.

   c. Liking → People prefer to say yes to other people whom they like.

   d. Consensus → People tend to behave according to how they believe others are behaving.

   e. Authority → People trust those who are credited with superior knowledge or wisdom.

Evaluation and Assessment. "The surgery was successful, but the patient died." It's an old but grim joke about a boastful surgeon who had the wrong criteria for assessing the outcome of a surgery. Assessment is important. As a consultant, you want to know whether your great ideas actually worked. Assessments designed to give meaningful feedback that will help you learn how to improve are called **formative assessments**. Assessments designed to evaluate whether your intervention was successful are called **summative assessments** (see Dunn, Baker, Mehrotra, Landrum, & McCarthy, 2013). Formative assessment is the feedback you get on a rough draft of a paper; summative assessment is your grade on the final version.

An assessment plan needs to be part of the original design of any intervention—it's important that you specify, ahead of time, what success looks like. Making assessment part of your original design from the very beginning offers many advantages. It ensures that you and your client:

1. agree on the goals of your consultancy,

2. know what success (and failure) look like,

3. can discover new ways to use your services,

4. learn how to create a better intervention next time, and

5. do not dispute whether you have earned your fee.

Assessment is a critical part of all biopsychosocial health care interventions. Assessment also represents a career path that psychology students are already on, even though they sometimes fail to recognize that their background in critical thinking and research design makes them perfect for this type of task (see Heinzen, Landrum, Gurung, & Dunn, 2015).

The Main Ideas

- The combined product of biological, psychological, and social forces on health behaviors is called the biopsychosocial model.

- One application of the biopsychosocial model is the attempt to increase treatment adherence, or following the advice of a health care provider. Several persuasion techniques from social psychology might be applied to increase patients' likelihood to follow medical advice.

- Assessment of medical interventions requires operationalization of success in advance.

Formative assessments:
Assessments designed to give meaningful feedback to help an individual learn how to improve.

Summative assessments:
Assessments design to evaluate whether an intervention was successful.

⚡ CRITICAL THINKING CHALLENGE

- If you were consciously aware that a medical practitioner was attempting to persuade you using psychological techniques, would that make you less likely to be persuaded? Why or why not?

- Should medical schools require at least one class on health or social psychology, or how psychology will influence relationships between health practitioners and patients? Again, why or why not?

Visit **edge.sagepub.com/heinzen** to help you accomplish your coursework goals in an easy-to-use learning environment.

- Mobile-friendly **eFlashcards**
- **Video** and **multimedia content**
- EXCLUSIVE! Access to full-text **SAGE journal articles**

PRACTICE AND APPLY WHAT YOU'VE LEARNED

▶ **edge.sagepub.com/heinzen**

Social Psychology and Happiness: Positive Psychology

1. What is positive psychology?

2. What are historical and upcoming topics in positive social psychology?

1. Describe how positive psychology represents a distinctive approach to psychology.

2. Compare and contrast topics from early research on positive social psychology and topics likely to be important in the future.

Juanita stood in my [Tom's] open office doorway. "I got in. And they offered me a scholarship." She wasn't crying, but she was close.

Born in the United States, Juanita [not her real name] experienced an uncertain back-and-forth childhood between the United States and Mexico. When she was 12, her family surprised her by staying in the United States and enrolled her in a high school with only one other Spanish-speaking student. It was an awkward transition for a teenager who did not speak English.

Juanita was lost in a school full of rules she did not understand. A school psychologist helped her design achievable goals and get the tutoring help she needed to achieve them. With that support, she accomplished what her parents had been hoping for: She graduated from high school. That same school psychologist guided Juanita first to a community college and later to my university. And now she was saying goodbye once again. She was going to graduate school to become a school psychologist.

Like other first-generation college students, Juanita faced challenges that people more familiar with the system take in stride. For example, experienced people and families understand that the Free Application for Federal Student Aid (FAFSA) is the doorway to money for education. But for an immigrant family of a first-ever college student, the FAFSA looks like a request for private information that might be used against them. Some first-generation college students do not get across the finish line of graduation. Juanita, however, was among those who persisted and was now planning to attend graduate school. She understood that she was starting a tradition of higher . . . and higher . . . education that would load the achievement dice for her siblings, cousins, and generations to come. How many 22-year-olds can look so far into their futures and with such purpose? Such students are much smarter than their standardized test scores might suggest. Juanita's story is full of positive psychology.

WHAT IS POSITIVE PSYCHOLOGY?

LO 1: Describe how positive psychology represents a distinctive approach to psychology.

Positive psychologists try to understand people like Juanita, the school psychologist who guided her, and the institutions that supported her. Positive psychologists are more interested, for example, in how students succeed than why they fail. **Positive psychology** is the scientific study of what ordinary humans keep doing extraordinarily well, including achievement, happiness, and more (see Compton, 2005; Seligman & Csikszentmihalyi, 2000). Positive psychology and social psychology are not the same thing. But they often share similar ambitions to help people thrive and reach their full potential. Let's look at three important concepts of positive psychology: positive subjective experiences, positive individual traits, and positive institutions.

Positive psychology: The scientific study of human strengths, virtues, positive emotions, and achievements.

Three Pillars of Positive Psychology

Juanita's life benefited from what Seligman and Csikszentmihalyi (2000) called the "three pillars of positive psychology": positive subjective experiences, positive individual traits, and positive institutions. Of course, Juanita did not experience her life within these neat categories. Positive psychology exerts its greatest influence when these three pillars are aligned so that they create the kind of cycle displayed in Figure D.1. Each pillar strengthens the others.

Positive Subjective Experiences. Positive **subjective experiences** are events that can be interpreted in a variety of ways by the person involved. Juanita's subjective experience could have been profoundly negative. It is difficult to imagine what it must have felt like for a 12-year-old to arrive in a strange classroom full of different-looking people who spoke a new language. Seligman and Csikszentmihalyi (2000) described this pillar in their seminal article in *American Psychologist*:

> The field of positive psychology at the subjective level is about valued subjective experiences: well-being, contentment, and satisfaction (in the past); hope and optimism (for the future); and flow and happiness (in the present). (p. 5)

Did Juanita "value" these kinds of subjective experiences? Probably. She looked at her past as a series of obstacles she had to overcome and family satisfactions that, despite many difficulties, she still treasured. She certainly expressed hope and optimism about her future as a graduate student and school psychologist. And she was definitely happy about her present, having just heard about being accepted into graduate school and receiving a scholarship.

Positive Individual Traits. Seligman and Csikszentmihalyi (2000) describe the second pillar as well:

> At the individual level, [positive psychology] is about positive individual traits: the capacity for love and vocation, courage, interpersonal skill, aesthetic sensibility, perseverance, forgiveness, originality, future mindedness, spirituality, high talent, and wisdom. (p. 5)

■ FIGURE D.1 The three pillars of positive psychology

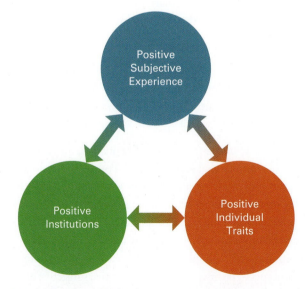

SOURCE: Seligman, M. E. P., & Csikszentmihalyi, M. (2000). Positive psychology: An introduction. *American Psychologist, 55*(1), 5-14.

Subjective experiences: The way individuals mentally experience and perceive events in their life.

Juanita also displayed the collection of positive individual traits. Her desire to become a school psychologist was much more than an intellectual choice; it was a vocation born of gratitude for how another school psychologist had intervened in her life. And getting to this point had required a quality of perseverance that is difficult for others to appreciate if they had grown up in settled homes and secure communities.

Positive Institutions. The third pillar of positive psychology is that people must be surrounded by organizations and institutions that provide respect and opportunity. Seligman and Csikszentmihalyi (2000) write,

> At the group level, [positive psychology] is about the civic virtues and the institutions that move individuals toward better citizenship: responsibility, nurturance, altruism, civility, moderation, tolerance, and work ethic. (p. 5)

You have to read between the lines of Juanita's story to appreciate the importance of positive institutions. First, a school psychologist was present and aware of her needs. Second, the school psychologist had the time to devote to a student with particular needs. Third, publicly funded higher education had served her well. Fourth, some anonymous donors had given money to funds that provided her—and many others—with the money to pursue her vocation. Finally, Juanita had strong emotional support from her family. They did not fully understand the potential risks and rewards of the decisions their daughter was making, but they decided to support her anyway.

In Juanita's case, the three pillars of positive psychology describe a social psychological formula for academic success. But it is much more. It is a formula for the kind of meaningful, positive life and career that positive psychologists hope all of us can achieve.

Subjective Well-Being: Shifting From Negative to Positive Psychology

Much of psychology's history has focused on human weaknesses. By contrast, positive psychology emphasizes human strengths and virtues. The starting point is called **subjective well-being** and refers to what people perceive and feel about their lives and psychological health.

The historical, negative approach to psychology is adapted from the **disease model** that medicine uses to assess and treat deficits in functioning. This model attempts to diagnose people's problems and eliminate those problems, bringing the person back to a state of neutrality or "normalcy." The disease model has many benefits, and it was desperately needed after World War II. The disease model is also profitable (see Seligman, 2002). Clinical practitioners have clients. Funding agencies support researchers. The pharmaceutical industry investigates drug interventions. And we all are better off understanding the causes and cures related to specific forms of human suffering.

Notice that the disease model aims to bring people back to a place where they are "not sick," a neutral or average baseline. Being "not sick" is not the same thing as being healthy, just as being "not sad" is not the same thing as being happy. Positive psychology aims to fill out the positive side of the normal curve of human experience (see Figure D.2).

After World War II, the Hungarian psychologist Csikszentmihalyi (pronounced "Cheek-sent-me-hali"; Seligman & Csikszentmihalyi, 2000, p. 9) glimpsed the importance of positive psychology when he noticed two things. First, many of the war's survivors were struggling emotionally. "Without jobs, money, or status, they were reduced to empty shells." Second, there were exceptions. "Yet there were a few who kept their integrity and purpose despite the surrounding chaos. Their serenity was a beacon that

Subjective well-being: Individuals' cognitive and emotional evaluation of their life (see *PERMA approach*).

Disease model: The model medicine uses to assess and treat deficits in functioning that attempts to diagnose people's problems and eliminate those problems, bringing the person back to a state of neutrality or "normalcy."

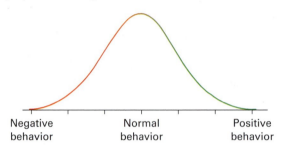

■ FIGURE D.2 Psychology is best known for paying attention to extreme behavior on the left side of the curve: mental illness, prejudice, ostracism, aggression, and so on. However, positive psychology focuses on the right side of the curve, helping people thrive and grow.

kept others from losing hope." These are the kind of people positive psychologists want to know better.

Social psychology was likewise caught up in the focus on the negative—and with good reason. The urgent postwar demand to social psychologists was to somehow "fix"—or at least start to understand—a world that was skilled at creating new weapons of mass destruction but less practical about solving social conflicts. Positive psychology had to overcome decades of attention given to the negative in order to gain traction in the psychology community.

In 1998, Martin Seligman, then serving as president of the American Psychological Association, issued a formal call for psychologists to turn their attention to the sources of well-being. He urged psychologists to explore positive, adaptive thoughts, feelings, and behaviors. The result was that psychology suddenly had many new (or newly empha-sized) research questions. They included, "What kinds of families result in children who flourish, what work settings support the greatest satisfaction among workers, what pol-icies result in the strongest civic engagement, and how people's lives can be most worth living" (Seligman & Csikszentmihalyi, 2000, p. 5).

The general approach has been to start asking questions related to the three pillars described earlier. Experimental social psychologists Gable and Haidt describe the change represented by positive psychology as an expansion rather than a replacement. A great deal of previous psychological research had focused on "how to bring people up from negative eight to zero." Its mission under positive psychology was to understand "how people rise from zero to positive eight" (Gable & Haidt, 2005, p. 103).

Positive Psychology Is Not "Pop Psychology"

It is important to not confuse positive psychology with **pop psychology**, the vague and superficial application of untested, temporarily popular, and sometimes exotic ideas. Pop psychology promises simple cures for complex problems, and these cures sometimes take on a "fad" feeling. Want to improve your memory? Rub these essential oils on your forehead. Feeling blue? Wave some crystals around. Interested in becoming a criminal profiler? Plan a career guided by television crime dramas. An alarming number of popu-lar beliefs about psychology are myths, placebo effects, superstitions, and self-deceptions (see Lilienfeld et al., 2011).

Placebo Effects. Pop psychology is the modern equivalent of what were called "pat-ent medicines" in the 1920s; they were homemade concoctions that circulated freely through an unregulated society. No matter what they claimed to cure, many patent medicines contained just enough alcohol (or other drugs, such as cocaine) to make you

Pop psychology: The vague and superficial application of untested, temporarily popular, and sometimes exotic ideas to everyday life.

feel good. Pop psychology promises similar "cures" such as remembering "past lives" to explain your problems, relieve your depression, calm your nerves, or improve your mood.

Pop psychology is full of **placebo effects** that occur when the strength of your belief leads you to experience the expected benefits of a medical or psychological treatment. The placebo has no independent effect on you. Anything can be a placebo: a nasty-tasting drink, a colorful rock, a pleasant aroma, or even an accidental gesture. They all have the potential to produce the perception that it is responsible for any improvement in your well-being—if you will only believe. They all are merely potential *confounding variables* that briefly can make you feel better if you believe in them.

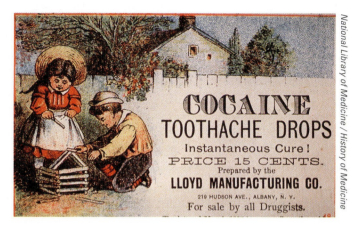

Pop psychology refers to fads that claim to make your life better without any scientific evidence, just like these "medical treatments" claimed to do for problems like rheumatism and toothaches.

The Peer Review Process. Normally, the **peer review process** is how the scientific community uses multiple people to decide whether a journal should publish a paper and to ensure publications are of high quality. If someone wants to publish research findings, the article is first reviewed by several other, well-respected people in the field (the "peers") before it sees the light of day. But in the case of positive psychology, there was so much enthusiasm for its possibilities that the peer review process was very slow at catching some obvious errors (Brown, Sokal, & Friedman, 2014; Fredrickson, 2013; Fredrickson & Losada, 2005), leading to some unfortunate crossover between positive and pop psychology at the beginning of positive psychology's growth.

We need a scientific approach to separate the effects of confounding variables from the real thing. Thus, the conscious intention of positive psychology is now to avoid pop psychology by systematically testing hypotheses and building a scientific foundation one study at a time. A scientific foundation, especially one based on peer review, is guaranteed to slow things down. Science requires measuring the underlying *constructs*—and that means testing every new measure for *reliability* and *validity*. Seligman and Csikszentmihalyi (2000) wanted to put positive psychology on a scientific as well as a conceptual foundation. They wanted to move past a "self-help" or "do-it-yourself" mentality to an authentic scientific approach. They proposed the PERMA approach to measure the concepts of positive psychology.

The PERMA Approach

Earlier psychologists (such as Jung and Maslow) had proposed concepts similar to those in positive psychology. This time around, however, Seligman and Csikszentmihalyi (2000) developed the PERMA approach.

The **PERMA approach** represents positive psychology's first efforts to measure, or *operationalize,* the central concepts of positive psychology summarized by the phrase "subjective well-being." PERMA refers to Positive emotions, Engagement, Relationship to others, Meaning and purpose, and Achievement. The evolving strategy for measuring PERMA is slightly different for every component.

- Positive emotions (happiness): Measured by a language assessment of the ratio of positive to negative words someone (or a group) uses when interacting with others.
- Engagement (or "flow," meaning truly experiencing events): Identifying and measuring our signature strengths and challenges.

Placebo effect: Occurs when the strength of individuals' belief in a medical or psychological treatment leads them to experience the expected benefits of the treatment, even though it has no independent effect on them.

Peer review process: How the scientific community uses multiple people to decide whether a journal should publish a paper to ensure publications are of high quality.

PERMA approach: An approach to measuring subjective well-being, which considers an individual's positive emotions, engagement, relationship to others, meaning and purpose, and achievement.

■ TABLE D.1 Four Possible Responses to Good News From a Spouse

	Constructive Responses	Destructive Responses
Active responses	"Congratulations and well done! I bet it was your last data analysis that convinced them. It was a clear, thoughtful presentation."	"Well, you certainly got lucky. There were several more deserving candidates. When will I see a bump in your paycheck?"
Passive responses	"That's great."	"Now you can buy better food at the grocery store, so maybe your cooking will improve."

NOTE: Positive psychology says that responses to good news from someone in our social world should be both constructive and active.

- Relationship to others (social interactions): Measured by how we habitually respond to good news. Our response tendencies can be summarized in the table in Table D.1 that isolates the response of positive psychology as both constructive and active. Imagine, for example, all the different things that a husband might say in response to learning that his wife was just promoted to be the head of research at her job.

- Meaning and purpose: Measured by the degree of commitment to some long-lasting cause to something meaningful that is bigger than yourself (e.g., joining the military to support your country, donating time or money to Habitat for Humanity, providing scholarship support for students).

- Achievement: Measured by our level of determination and tenacity; sometimes referred to as "grit." High levels of achievement also require significant self-discipline and the ability to delay gratification.

The Main Ideas

- Positive psychology is the scientific study of what ordinary humans keep doing extraordinarily well, such as happiness and achievement. Three "pillars" of positive psychology are positive subjective experiences, positive individual traits, and positive institutions.

- While much of psychology (at least, in the past) focused on moving people from having mental illnesses or problems to a state of neutrality, positive psychology attempts to move people from a state of neutrality to achieving happiness and their full potential.

- Pop psychology is the vague and superficial application of untested, temporarily popular, and sometimes exotic ideas to improve everyday life. Positive psychology is not pop psychology because it uses scientific methods and evidence to back up claims.

- One approach to positive psychology is called PERMA, which stands for the measurement of Positive emotions, Engagement, Relationship to others, Meaning and purpose, and Achievement.

⚡ CRITICAL THINKING CHALLENGE

- Think about the idea that much of psychology (such as clinical and counseling) hopes to move people from negative to neutral, while positive psychology hopes to move people from neutral to positive. When subjective well-being is placed on a normal bell curve like this, which "half" of the curve do you think is more important? Should research and focus in psychology stick to the "negative" half, attempting to help people avoid depression and low self-esteem, or should it help people move up on the "positive" half? Certainly, both are important—but which is *more* important?

- Imagine that you see a news article claiming that a new pill increases happiness. How can you investigate this claim to see if it comes from pop psychology versus scientific, positive psychology? What will you look for in the fine print?

WHAT ARE HISTORICAL AND UPCOMING TOPICS IN POSITIVE SOCIAL PSYCHOLOGY?

LO 2: Compare and contrast topics from early research on positive social psychology and topics likely to be important in the future.

Is positive psychology a new approach to psychology? No. Here's why.

The publication history displayed in Figure D.3 represents the dramatic growth of positive psychology. The starting period (1998) co-occurs with Seligman's call for more attention to positive psychology. The growth is so dramatic that it sparks the worry that positive psychology is merely a temporary intellectual distraction (see Ellickson & Brown, 1990). There may indeed be some fad appeal to positive psychology. However, the history of positive psychology is much longer than Figure D.3 suggests. The three pillars (positive subjective experiences, positive individual traits, and positive institutions) were often defined by different terms such as self-actualization, need for achievement, and peak experiences.

The Early History of Positive Psychology

Seligman and Csikszentmihalyi (2000) recognized that "William James, Carl Jung, Gordon Allport, and Abraham Maslow were interested in exploring spiritual ecstasy, play, creativity, and peak experiences" (p. 10). They were not the only ones who recognized the deep historical roots of positive psychology (see Froh, 2004). The long history of creativity research also testifies to psychologists' desire to understand what

■ FIGURE D.3 Frequency of References to "Positive Psychology" in PsycINFO by Year

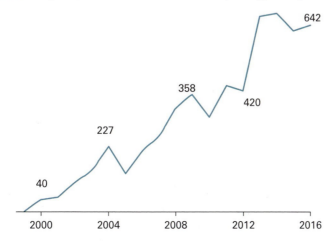

SOURCE: Data from the American Psychological Association.

kinds of people and circumstances seemed to encourage, support, and inspire innovation, group creativity, and original thinking (see Albert & Runco, 1999). Compton (2005) traces the early roots of positive psychology to both philosophy and religion.

The distinguishing characteristic of the modern positive psychology movement is the development of its scientific foundations. As Seligman and Csikszentmihalyi (2000) recognized from the outset,

> We well recognize that positive psychology is not a new idea. It has many distinguished ancestors, and we make no claim of originality. However, these ancestors somehow failed to attract a cumulative, empirical body of research to ground their ideas. (p. 13)

The First Positive Psychology Experiment: Triplett and Sport Psychology.

The seeds of a positive scientific psychology were planted more than a century earlier. We introduced you to Triplett (1898) in Chapter 8. Triplett was the researcher who conducted what was probably social psychology's first experiment. He wanted to know why bicycle racers performed better in the presence of others—he wanted a scientific explanation for peak performance. And that experiment made him the world's first scientific social psychologist, the first empirically minded positive psychologist, and the first sport psychologist (Strube, 2005).

Triplett might be surprised by the mark he left on history. In addition, Triplett might reject those honorary titles because his own article referenced a previous study by E. B. Turner. Turner had used a similar (probably archival) approach to analyzing the same question about bicycle racing. (Turner's general concerns were more about the effects of cycling on health than they were about social or positive psychology.) Triplett's work in sport psychology is the basis for the study of peak performance, ethics interventions, and slumping athletes, which are discussed next.

Peak Performance, Ethics Interventions, and Slumping Athletes.

Peak performance remains the calling card for many sport psychologists, which means that sport psychology and positive psychology have a lot of overlap. Modern **sport psychology** focuses on what the American Psychological Association (APA, 2017) describes as the scientific study of how psychology influences both participant and performance of sports, exercise, and any type of physical activity.

In general, the APA presents a positive, forward-looking, achievement-oriented agenda for sport psychologists—a good fit for positive psychologists. Unlike other areas of psychology, sport psychologists already focus on many of the positive aspects of sports. Sport psychologists gravitate to topics such as peak achievement, team building, and learning how to win and lose with grace.

Gable and Haidt (2005) emphasize that "positive psychology's aim is not the denial of the distressing, unpleasant, or negative aspects of life, nor is it an effort to see them through rose-colored glasses" (p. 105). Likewise, the values of the Association for Applied Sport Psychology (AASP, 2017) assert that members' first responsibility is to promote ethics, not peak performance. The modern sport industry offers a long list of opportunities to address ethics issues that correspond to the three pillars of positive psychology:

- Positive Subjective Experience: Reducing fan expressions of race prejudice will improve the subjective experience of targeted players.
- Positive Individual Traits: Reducing the use of performance-enhancing drugs (PEDs) will create fairness for players who kept their integrity by not using PEDs.
- Positive Institutions: Correcting how colleges and universities profit from athletics will promote institutional integrity and respect from students.

Sport psychology: The scientific study of how athletic and/or physical activity participation and performance are influenced by psychological concepts.

One recurring ethical concern within sport psychology involves the problem of a **dual relationship** that occurs when a professional takes on incompatible roles with a client. A professor should not serve as a student's therapist (there are exceptions, but they are rare). In the same way, it is inappropriate for a sport psychologist to also serve as coach (Ellickson & Brown, 1990). Even with the best of intentions, a positive institution will not allow dual relationships to develop that encourage ethical compromises.

A different kind of opportunity emerges because positive psychologists emphasize the importance of a positive subjective experience. Steepe (1995) used interviews to capture the difficult process of athletes coming out of a slump. It was ultimately a positive experience, but getting out of a slump was emotionally difficult. It involved "owning" the slump, enduring a wide range of negative emotions (including frustration, fear, self-doubt, low self-esteem), refocusing on basics, and simplified workouts. Sport psychology is an early example of positive psychology that developed an empirical base of evidence. It continues to offer significant opportunities for anyone interested in what it means to maximize performance.

Dual relationship: Occurs when a professional takes on incompatible roles with a client (for instance, if a sport psychologist also serves as a coach or if a professor serves as a student's therapist).

The Future of Positive Social Psychology

Positive psychology is harnessing the energies of social psychologists who all want to use science to have a positive social impact. Like sport psychology, positive psychology and social psychology have always been aligned with applied psychology. Researchers in these fields are the intellectual offspring of Kurt Lewin in that they want to do something useful with the skills and insights that they have acquired in social psychology. Just a few of the career opportunities (and challenges) for future positive psychologists are related to clinical psychology, military training, game-based assessments, the controversy over "life coaches," and health.

de:Benutzer:Hase, CC BY-SA 3.0

Lance Armstrong eventually admitted that he had used performance-enhancing drugs to help him win the Tour de France seven times. A positive sport psychologist would be interested in comparing his subjective experience to athletes who preserved their integrity by resisting the temptation to use this kind of drug.

Clinical Applications: Building Resilience.
Building a scientific foundation for positive psychology will require many clinicians to think differently about their own successes and failures. Seligman and Csikszentmihalyi (2000) emphasize that health practitioners need to focus on amplifying strengths in their patients, not just repairing weaknesses. Positive psychology has brought particular attention to personal resilience.

Juanita, the woman described at the beginning of this mini-chapter, probably would agree with findings from an example study related to resilience and positive psychology. It examined the beliefs of 131 Mexican American college students (Vela, Lenz, Sparrow, & Gonzalez, 2017). They found that two predictors stood out when trying to understand what helped their participants as teenagers to maintain resilience as they pushed forward in their education: hope and family. Hope and family were more important (they were *statistically significant*) than competing variables that included subjective happiness, meaning in life, and a college self-efficacy scale. Hope and family kept Juanita persevering when she could not understand any of the words spoken in her new school, and hope and family guided her along the path toward graduate school.

Military Training. Resilience also affects soldiers. One research team helped create an assessment tool for the army to measure resilience training (Vie, Scheier, Lester, & Seligman, 2016). The impetus, unfortunately, was once again related to war. There has been a sharp increase in depression, posttraumatic stress disorder (PTSD), and alcohol use among soldiers returning from battles in Iraq and Afghanistan. Thus, many health initiatives have been inspired or influenced by positive psychology. The treatment focus on depression, for example, adds more attention on building positive coping skills that lead to subjective well-being (psychology's term for "happiness"). Therapy is about increasing strengths that can make therapeutic gains permanent. For example, positive psychology has clarified the value of physical exercise for depressed individuals (Lambert, D'Cruz, Schlatter, & Barron, 2016).

Game-Based Assessments. Another expression of positive psychology is emerging from the world of assessment, especially from human-computer interactions (HCI). There are many types of assessments but, like a multiple-choice exam, they often focus on what a student has done wrong rather than right. You may have been frustrated by taking something like a multiple-choice exam that asked you specific questions leading to a poor grade when you felt that you had not gotten the opportunity to truly display what you had learned.

Bellotti and colleagues (Bellotti, Kapralos, Lee, Moreno-Ger, & Berta, 2013) and several others are pioneering ways to capture authentic strengths and weaknesses through more creative ways to assess learning. People provide such information as they engage in designed activities, including playing games that encourage peak performance (see Heinzen, Landrum, Gurung, & Dunn, 2015; Shute & Ventura, 2013). Their general recognition is that we have been systematically missing much of the most important data when we focus on what participants have *not* done well instead of measuring what they have done well. An important element of that, to a game designer, is the game mechanic referred to as "failing forward" that recognizes the importance of learning through failure.

The Controversy of Life Coaches. One of the emerging careers that belong more or less under the umbrella of positive psychology is that of the life coach. A **life coach** works with individuals as they make career and personal decisions, but often people in this career do not have formal education or credentials related to counseling. The range of descriptions sometimes used to describe a life coach suggests both its role and criticisms of its role: "Friend for hire" is at the positive end and "a fraud psychologist working without a license" at the negative end. Meanwhile, a more formal discussion of the work, its gendered nature, and the popularity of life coaching as a career has led to richer discussions about if and how to legitimatize life coaching (George, 2013). For now, this career is very controversial as many professional psychologists believe that "life coaches" are not particularly well trained to offer advice or guidance to people struggling, compared to licensed practitioners who have advanced degrees.

Health. Long before Seligman's appeal for a positive psychology, its principles already were being applied to health and health promotion. For example, Aspinwall and Tedeschi (2010) have documented early empirical work on optimism and posttraumatic growth. They also expressed concerns about the damaging effects of popular psychology weakening the scientific base of positive psychology. Others have focused on heart disease and the opportunities for positive psychology to encourage better health habits (Huffman et al., 2016). The specific mechanisms that promote health remain unclear—which means that science just doesn't know yet whether we are dealing with placebo effects. This is, therefore, an area where more people and more research are needed.

Life coach: A career based in positive psychology—although with little formal education or credentials—where individuals work with others as they make career and personal decisions.

Positive Psychology's Strange Definition of Success.

Positive psychologists have a strange definition of success. If everyone in the field is successful in their goal of making humans happy, healthy, and successful, then positive psychologists put themselves out of business. If this happens, Gable and Haidt (2005) bluntly assert that "the future of positive psychology is just plain psychology" (p. 108). Positive psychology is a corrective measure, a returning to our roots, and a way to expand the range of topics and possibilities within psychology. If the positive psychology movement is successful, then it will disappear.

The Main Ideas

- Positive psychology is not new in the field; topics were simply studied under different terms or subfields. An example is Triplett's research on peak performance in cyclists that was covered in Chapter 8.

- One area that has a lot of overlap with positive psychology is sport psychology. Other areas where positive psychology crosses over to influence research are clinical psychology, military training, game-based assessments, the controversy of "life coaches," and health.

Everett Collection Inc. / Alamy Stock Photo

Tony Robbins is a successful life coach and best-selling author.

⚡ CRITICAL THINKING CHALLENGE

- What do you think about the career path known as "life coaching"? Do you think you or your friends would benefit from a paid life coach? Should people in this career have certain educational requirements, licenses, background checks, and so on?

- What other areas of psychology do you think would benefit from having more overlap with positive psychology? Explain your answer.

- Do you think that positive psychology will continue to grow in popularity? Will there ever be a point when positive psychology is no longer needed, because people in the field have successfully elevated humanity to the point of great happiness and achievement?

Social Psychology and Behavioral Economics

1. What is behavioral economics?
2. How is behavioral economics applied to everyday situations?

1. Articulate how economics and psychology share the goal of understanding human behavior.
2. Describe various everyday applications of behavioral economics.

Underline Y for "yes" or N for "no":

- **Y   N**   If you were eating at a restaurant in a strange city, and you knew you would never return to this location, would you leave a tip for your waiter?
- **Y   N**   Does a five-dollar pill somehow cure your headache faster than a five-cent pill?
- **Y   N**   Would you be unhappy about a surprise 10% raise in salary if you also found out that your coworker received a surprise 15% raise?
- **Y   N**   Do you spend more money shopping with a credit card than when shopping with cash?
- **Y   N**   Would you be happier winning two lottery tickets worth $50 and $25 each, compared to winning one lottery ticket worth $75 and one worth nothing?

If you answered "yes" to any of the questions above, then you have started across the invisible psychological boundary from rational to irrational economic thinking. Retailers are familiar with this boundary because they use all sorts of psychological tricks to influence us to buy stuff that we do not need. For example, you really only need one pair of shoes—you can't wear more than one at a time. Three pairs might seem reasonable if you need shoes for different purposes. But how many pairs of shoes do you own—and how have you been persuaded that each pair is somehow necessary to your life?

WHAT IS BEHAVIORAL ECONOMICS?

LO 1: Articulate how economics and psychology share the goal of understanding human behavior.

Behavioral economics is the study of how economic decisions are influenced by psychological factors that indicate what we value and how much we value it (see Ariely, 2008; deCremer, Zeelenberg, & Murninghan, 2006; Harmon-Jones, 2007; Politser, 2008; Schwartz, 2008). **Rational economic thinking** relies on the strict rules of supply and demand; it assumes that we will always go for the best deal. **Irrational economic thinking** is influenced by mental shortcuts, misperceptions, and emotional biases; it recognizes that humans often ignore the rules of supply and demand.

The first economists understood that economic decisions could be influenced by human passions such as greed, empathy, selfishness, and forgiveness—or even the simple impulse to grab at the last cookie on the plate. As economics and psychology each developed, economists and psychologists built different paths to the same goal of understanding how humans influence one another. But they each learned different things on their separate journeys to that goal. The current excitement caused by behavioral economics is the result of these two rich disciplines joining forces once again.

Behavioral economics: The study of how economic decisions are influenced by psychological factors that indicate what individuals value and how much they value it.

Rational economic thinking: The idea that consumers will act rationally according to the strict rules of supply and demand, leading them to always go for the best deal.

Irrational economic thinking: The idea that consumers' decisions are often irrational because they are influenced by mental shortcuts, misperceptions, and emotional biases that often ignore the rules of supply and demand.

A Brief History of Behavioral Economics

Psychology did not formally exist when Adam Smith, the Scottish founder of economic philosophy, described his views of human behavior in his book *The Theory of Moral Sentiments* (Smith, 1759). In Smith's (1776) more famous book, *The Wealth of Nations,* he described how supply and demand acted like an invisible guiding hand that directed economic behavior. But Smith also recognized that economic behavior was influenced by **loss aversion**, the tendency for potential losses to be more psychologically influential than potential gains.

In 1759, Smith wrote that "our sympathy with sorrow is generally a more lively sensation than our sympathy with joy" (p. 60). That is why most people dislike losing $50 more than they like finding $50, an illogical cognitive bias that Smith predicted. Despite their meant-to-be-together beginnings, psychology and economics took different paths for many decades—and they only started "dating" again in the last half of the 20th century.

Psychology tried (but failed) to influence economics at a critical moment in human history through an economic theory about forgiveness. Forgiveness had its chance in 1918 starting at 11 a.m. of the 11th day of the 11th month: The Great War, soon to be called World War I, was finally over. There was a window of opportunity between that morning's peaceful silence and the vindictive Treaty of Versailles 7 months later. After 16 million deaths, the victors gathered at Versailles on June 28, 1919, were in no mood to forgive Germany. Yet one economist, John Maynard Keynes, urged the victors to forgive Germany its many debts. His economic argument was based on psychology.

Keynes warned that the bitterly *un*forgiving economic terms under consideration at the Treaty of Versailles would inspire a "vengeance . . . before which the horrors of the late German war will fade into nothing" (Keynes, 1920, p. 268). The victorious allies ignored his advice—they wanted Germany to pay dearly for all the blood they had spilled. When he could not convince the victors about the wisdom of forgiveness, Keynes resigned his position as Chancellor of the Exchequer. He then published a book bluntly titled *The Economic Consequences of the Peace.* Keynes could see the small cloud of psychological consequences forming in the dark ink of the punishing economic "peace" treaty.

Sadly, Keynes's unhappy predictions started becoming the world's history during Germany's hyperinflation in 1923. A frustrated painter-turned-politician named Adolph Hitler kept reminding the German people of the unforgiving terms of the Treaty of Versailles. Keynes understood that humiliation, vengeance, and embarrassment are social psychological passions with predictable economic consequences. Germany's experience after World War I led to the horrors of World War II (around 60 million deaths). Effective public policies require the united wisdom of both psychology *and* economics: behavioral economics.

Loss aversion: The tendency for potential losses to be more psychologically influential than potential gains.

Behavioral Economics Maps the Boundary Between Rational and Irrational Behavior

Psychology and economics went their separate ways after World War II. For about 50 years, economists focused on the implications of rational principles of

Watercolor of St. Charles Church in Vienna, painted by Adolf Hitler (signed in the lower left-hand corner).

Behrouz Mehri / AFP / Getty Images

"supply and demand." Psychologists, on the other hand, focused on cognitive thought processes, new treatments for mental illness, and social psychology. But economics and psychology were still meant for each other.

For example, according to the law of supply and demand, no one would leave a tip for a meal in a strange city. It's throwing away money that won't result in any kind of benefit. Yet most people (in a tipping culture) will leave a tip. Here are some of the psychological reasons why most people will leave some money on the table: Tipping is

- A habit, an automatic behavior
- Conforming to a social norm
- Feeling sympathy for the server
- Performing a good deed for an imaginary audience
- Trying to make the world a little more just
- A way to avoid imagined social embarrassment
- Validating your self-image as a good or generous person

Psychology and the Nobel Prize in Economics.

Psychology and economics finally started to recognize each other again around 1978, when the Nobel Prize in economics was awarded to psychologist Herbert Simon. Simon's work was the theory of **bounded rationality**, the idea that there is a natural cognitive limit on our ability to make rational economic decisions (see Jones, 1999). He was establishing that there was a boundary between rational and irrational reasoning, and this boundary was only understood when economics and psychology were combined.

In 2002, psychologist Daniel Kahneman also won the Nobel Prize in economics. Kahneman and his long-time collaborator Amos Tversky developed Simon's theory into **prospect theory**, the idea that people make predictable kinds of mistakes when trying to weigh outcomes and probabilities. Kahneman and Tversky (2000) were mapping the boundary areas where rational decision making slipped into the kind of irrational decisions that Herbert Simon had first discovered.

You can recognize the boundary between rational and irrational decision making by imagining your behavior in the following scene: You have found an expensive, fancy-looking car at an unusually low price. The owner tells you that the car may or may not have spent some time under water following a severe flood. (This happened frequently after Hurricane Katrina and Superstorm Sandy.) However, the car *looks* great and . . . it has a sunroof and a superior sound system. Will you buy it? Your rational decision-making warning system is flashing red lights: "This is a lemon. Do not buy!" But your irrational desire for a sunroof and a sound system is flashing green. If you go back and forth trying to decide, then you're straddling the boundary between rational and irrational economic decision making.

Psychology Guides the Behavioral Economic Model.

The separation of psychology and economics was always awkward. Psychological variables didn't fit easily into the traditional economic approach called the **standard economic model** (SEM). The SEM describes how people should behave *if* they were making rational decisions, *if* they always pursued the best financial deal, *if* they were not influenced by the strange economic biases, and *if* they were not influenced by a variety of social passions.

Bounded rationality: The idea that there is a natural cognitive limit on people's ability to make rational economic decisions.

Prospect theory: The idea that people make predictable kinds of mistakes when trying to weigh outcomes and probabilities.

Standard economic model (SEM): A model for understanding economic behavior that describes how people behave if they always make the most sound, rational decisions. This model is not based on psychological theory (see *rational economic thinking*).

Psychologists, on the other hand, recognize that many of our decisions are *not* rational and sometimes leave us muttering, "What in the world was I thinking when I bought six pairs of shoes?" because a sign promised "Buy five and get one free." The psychological description of irrational economic decision making is called the **behavioral economic model** (BEM). The BEM embraces insights from social cognition: We are often sloppy thinkers who, as we learned in Chapter 4, rely on mental shortcuts, perceptual biases, and heuristic habits of reasoning. The BEM recognizes that many of our automatic economic decisions are not the best deal.

The SEM and the BEM are not necessarily in conflict. Wilkinson (2008) argues that psychology's focus on cognitive processes during the 1980s (De Cremer, Zeelenberg, & Murninghan, 2006, p. 5) put economic theory on "more realistic psychological foundations" (Camerer & Lowenstein, 2004, p. 3). For a side-by-side comparison of the SEM and BEM, see Table E.1.

■ TABLE E.1 Some Assumptions of the Standard Economic Model (SEM) and the Behavioral Economic Model (BEM)

Standard Economic Model (SEM) People are . . .	Behavioral Economic Model (BEM) People are . . .
Always rational	Frequently irrational
Motivated to maximize gains and limit losses	More influenced by losses than by gains
Governed by narrow self-interests	Influenced by inarticulate social self-interests

The Main Ideas

- Behavioral economics studies how economic decisions are influenced by psychological factors that indicate what we value and how much we value it.

- The standard economic model (SEM) is based on the assumption that people make logical, rational decisions. The behavioral economic model (BEM) extends the SEM by including predictably irrational decision making.

- Behavioral economics explores the boundary between rational and irrational decision making.

⚡ CRITICAL THINKING CHALLENGE

- Form an argument about why, if we already have disciplines of psychology and economics, we should develop a field that blends the two disciplines.

- Think of four things you buy frequently. Try to identify two items you believe you choose based on the standard economic model (you follow the most logical route) and two items you believe you choose based on the behavioral economic model (perhaps your choices aren't the most rational in the world).

HOW IS BEHAVIORAL ECONOMICS APPLIED TO EVERYDAY SITUATIONS?

LO 2: Describe various everyday applications of behavioral economics.

Psychology and economics learned a great deal as they developed independently during much of the 20th century. However, they always shared the common goal of

Behavioral economic model (BEM): A model for understanding economic behavior that describes how psychology influences irrational economic decision making (see *irrational economic thinking*).

understanding how we influence one another. Just as two roads sometimes merge into one major highway that expands the number of lanes available to drive in, economics and psychology are currently merging in ways that open new possibilities.

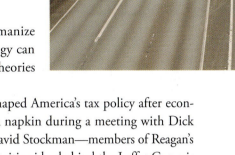

The Psychology of Tax Policy: The Laffer Curve

Letting psychology inform economics can humanize economic policies. By the same token, psychology can learn from economics about how to construct theories that can be applied to public policies.

In the 1970s, President Ronald Reagan reshaped America's tax policy after economist Arthur Laffer allegedly drew a curve on a napkin during a meeting with Dick Cheney, Donald Rumsfeld, Jude Waniski, and David Stockman—members of Reagan's staff (Laffer, 2004). The controversial, counterintuitive idea behind the Laffer Curve is sometimes called **supply side economics**, the belief that lowering taxes can increase tax revenues by stimulating the economy.

For example, imagine how much money the government collects under two extremely different tax policies: a tax rate of 0% and a tax rate of 100%. Neither of those rates produces revenue for the government, but for different reasons. At a 0% tax assessment, the government doesn't even try to tax people. So the government collects nothing at all and cannot build roads, construct sewers, resolve property disputes, or protect its citizens. At a 100% tax assessment, people don't get to keep any of their money. So, they will either refuse to work or refuse to pay—and the government still collects nothing.

According to supply side economics, there is a tax policy somewhere between 0% and 100% that (a) motivates people to work *and* (b) maximizes tax revenues; see Figure E.1. However, the Laffer Curve does not specify where that point is. The economic debate

■ FIGURE E.1 The Laffer Curve.

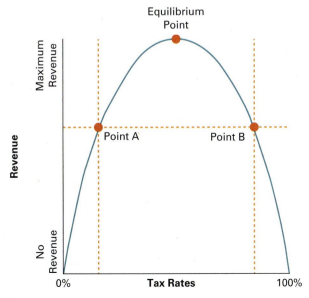

SOURCE: Laffer (2004).

Supply side economics:
The belief that lowering taxes can increase tax revenues by stimulating the economy.

is really a psychological challenge to find the high point of the curve that motivates people to work hard *and* pay their taxes. The most efficient tax policy is based on understanding the psychology of human motivation.

Game Theory Predicts Interactions Between Economics and Psychology

Game theory is a research approach that uses interdependent decision making to test people's values of cooperation versus competition. **Interdependent decision making** means that the outcome of your decision depends on someone else's decision, which is at the heart of game theory (Wilkinson, 2008). Imagine, for example, that you propose marriage. You may want to get married—but the outcome of your decision will certainly depend on whether the other person wants the same thing. Game theory can force our internal values to the surface of behavior by creating situational conflicts with uncertain outcomes. If you're not sure how the other person is going to respond, will you still propose?

In the marriage proposal dilemma, **standard game theory** (based on the SEM) predicts that you will make a rational decision to go ahead and propose marriage now because (a) being rejected won't cost you very much money, and (b) the sooner you find out, the faster you can move on to someone else. It's cold but rational. In contrast, **behavioral game theory** (based on the BEM) predicts that all kinds of psychological variables will influence your behavior. For example, you may be tempted to not propose marriage because (a) the pain of being rejected may be greater than the joy of being accepted, (b) you might be labeled a "loser," and (c) you will feel socially humiliated. Which theory provides the best description of how (you think) you would behave in this uncertain situation: standard game theory or behavioral game theory?

There are two well-known specific game scenarios studied in psychology: the prisoner's dilemma and the ultimatum game.

The Prisoner's Dilemma. If you watch any television cop shows, then you probably have seen many variations on the **prisoner's dilemma**. As a research approach, the prisoner's dilemma is an innovative way to test someone's core values of competition versus cooperation, as well as qualities such as loyalty and a sense of reciprocity. The setup of the game

Game theory: A research approach that uses interdependent decision making to test people's values of cooperation versus competition.

Interdependent decision making: Occurs when the outcome of an individual's decision depends on another individual's decision (see *game theory*).

Standard game theory: A predictor of interdependent decision-making behavior based on the standard economic model, which states that individuals will make rational decisions that consider the economic losses one would have to endure if they lost, as well as the potential for new, better deals to be made in the future (see *standard economic model* and *rational economic thinking*).

Behavioral game theory: A predictor of interdependent decision-making behavior based on the behavioral economic model, which states that individuals will make decisions based on a number of psychological variables, such as the pain of losing and the desire to conform to social norms, that may make their behavior seem irrational (see *behavioral economic model* and *irrational economic thinking*).

Prisoner's dilemma: A research approach within game theory that tests cooperation versus competition values by asking participants to imagine they are prisoners who must choose between confession (which betrays one's partner but results in a shorter sentence for you) or silence (which shows loyalty but risks betrayal by the other person).

■ FIGURE E.2 Game theory and the prisoner's dilemma. To snitch or not to snitch? That is the question.

| | | Prisoner B | |
		Confess	Keep Quiet
Prisoner A	Confess	Both go to jail for 5 years	Prisoner B goes to jail for 10 years, Prisoner A goes free
	Keep Quiet	Prisoner A goes to jail for 10 years, Prisoner B goes free	Both go to jail for 1 year

asks two players to imagine they are guilty of a crime. They've been arrested and are now being interrogated by the police in separate rooms. There's not much hard evidence, so the police are hoping that one or both suspects will confess to the crime (see Figure E.2).

If neither prisoner confesses (keeps quiet), then the prosecutor can only convict each individual of minor offences that will lead to a 1-year sentence for each of them. If only one confesses (betrays his or her partner), then the thief who did not confess receives a 10-year sentence while the "snitch" goes free. If they both confess (betray each other), then they will both receive a 5-year prison sentence. So, each prisoner's outcome depends on what the other prisoner decides to do.

■ TABLE E.2 The Prisoner's Dilemma and Behavioral Economics

	Brandon decides to split.	Brandon decides to steal.
Alicia decides to split.	Brandon gets $50,000. Alicia gets $50,000.	Brandon gets $100,000. Alicia gets $0.
Alicia decides to steal.	Brandon gets $0. Alicia gets $100,000.	Brandon gets $0. Alicia gets $0.

NOTE: If one partner cooperates but the other partner competes, their decisions shift from win-win to win-lose.

In Table E.2, you can see how the prisoner's dilemma can be applied to economic situations. In addition to being a research model and a dramatic plot device, the logic behind the prisoner's dilemma provides reliable gameshow entertainment. For example, *Golden Balls* (check it out on YouTube) offers a large pot of money, say $100,000, and two people have to decide either to "split" the money or to try to "steal" the money. If they both decide to split, then each gets $50,000. If one splits and the other steals, then the "stealer" takes it all. If they both try to steal, then they both go home with nothing.

In each of these situations, the logical choice is to cooperate; each player is guaranteed a win. However, many people will be tempted to change their play at the last minute to double their money. People also don't want to look foolish if they're tricked by the other player—so the temptation to compete rather than cooperate can be very strong. Variations on the prisoner's dilemma have kept a lot of behavioral economists busy. For example, are you more likely to cooperate with a friend than with a stranger? What happens when you play the game for several rounds? The next game helps us understand what happens when you get a reputation as a cheat.

The Ultimatum Game: Quantifying Fairness.
Is fairness important to you? In our experience, students are happy to stretch their intellects and expand their skills in a course that is difficult—if the professor is fair. It's the same with video games, sporting events, or pie-eating contests. There is no reason to play if the game is rigged ahead of time. But how important is fairness to you, personally? The **ultimatum game** uses monetary decisions to measure exactly how much you value fairness.

The rules are simple and the game is short. Two players can split a financial prize, say $100, but only one person (the Proposer) can make an offer about *how* to split the $100. A second person (the Decider) decides whether or not to accept the deal. The Decider only has authority to (a) accept the deal or (b) reject the deal. There's no negotiation. But here's the game mechanic that makes this game so engaging: If the Decider rejects the deal, then neither player gets any money. The Proposer could offer anything: $50 for the Proposer and $50 for the Decider, $60/$40, $80/$20, $99/$1, or even $20/$80 if they were feeling generous.

In other words, the Decider is in a position to punish the Proposer for being greedy—but at a personal cost, because then *neither* party gets any money. No matter

Ultimatum game: A research approach that tests individuals' values concerning money and fairness by requiring them to make an interdependent decision in this situation: Two players can split a financial prize, but only one person (the Proposer) can make an offer about how to split the money, while a second person (the Decider) can only decide whether or not to accept the deal. The Proposer can make the deal as unfair as he or she wants, but if the Decider rejects the deal, neither player gets any money.

what decision the Decider makes, the game is over. What would you do? Isn't getting any amount of money—even when it's not evenly distributed—better than nothing? The ultimatum game forces you to come up with an actual number that represents your hidden value of how much fairness means to you. Clever, right? It's even more fun if you do it as a class demonstration when you can play several times and with multiple partners because everyone quickly develops a reputation as a cheater (who should be punished) or a cooperator (who can be trusted . . . and therefore taken advantage of).

Standard game theory (based on the SEM) predicts that self-interest will direct the Proposer to offer the other person just enough money to get him or her to accept the deal, even just one dollar. Rationally, the Decider should accept even one dollar because he or she still would have $1 more than at the beginning of the game. Behavioral game theory (based on the BEM), on the other hand, predicts that the psychological variable of perceived fairness will worm its way into this decision.

How do people actually behave in the ultimatum game? Nowak, Page, and Sigmund's (2000) review in *Science* reported that if an offer came in at $70/$30 or less, then about half the responders rejected the offer. Many people prefer not to gain *any* of the prize money if they judge that the distribution of that money is too unfair. They valued fairness so much that they punished the Proposer even though it cost them (on average) about $30 to administer the punishment. But what happens over several rounds of play?

One research team (Nowak, Page, & Sigmund, 2000) allowed people to play the game many times with the same people—and to share information about how people had played the ultimatum game in the past. When a player's reputation was at stake, their behavior quickly evolved toward 50-50 fairness. Deciders stopped letting Proposers take advantage of them and Proposers stopped offering what the group considered an unfair deal.

In other words, we value fairness, in part, because we can anticipate that the surrounding community will punish us if we don't play fair. Both the prisoner's dilemma and the ultimatum game demonstrate how economic decisions force psychological variables like trust and reputation to the surface of our behavior.

The Main Ideas

- The Laffer Curve is a historical example of how behavioral economics has been used to influence government policy.

- Game theory evolved as a model that describes the interaction between economics and psychology. Two examples of game theory are the prisoner's dilemma and the ultimatum game.

- Standard game theory, based on the SEM, predicts we will always make rational decisions. Behavioral game theory, based on the BEM, takes irrational decisions and psychology into account for our decisions.

⚡ CRITICAL THINKING CHALLENGE

- If you were going to play either the prisoner's dilemma or the ultimatum game, do you think you would be more likely to cooperate to receive the best possible outcome for both people, or would you be more likely to compete to gain an advantage over the other person? Why?

- Can you identify other historical events that were, at least, in part, influenced by the combination of economics and psychology? Explain how ideas from this mini-chapter could be used to explain the event and its outcome.

- Do you think your own financial decisions are logical (and therefore align more with the standard economic model) or are more based on emotions or interpretations (and therefore align more with the behavioral economic model)? List three specific examples.

Visit **edge.sagepub.com/heinzen** to help you accomplish your coursework goals in an easy-to-use learning environment.

- Mobile-friendly **eFlashcards**
- **Video** and **multimedia content**
- EXCLUSIVE! Access to full-text **SAGE journal articles**

$SAGE edge™

Social Psychology and Relationship Violence

Core Questions

1. What are different types of relationship violence?

2. What is the psychology of people experiencing relationship violence?

3. How can survivors heal and move forward?

Learning Objectives

1. Describe various forms of relationship violence and how different research methods led to different answers to this question.

2. Analyze how romantic myths, cognitive dissonance, and affective forecasting apply to victims of relationship violence.

3. Apply research on stages of escape, narrative therapy, and posttraumatic growth to survivors of relationship violence.

Relationship violence may be the greatest contradiction in human psychology. Intimate, committed relationship partners can be—and often are—loving, supportive, and a source of joy. So, something has gone terribly wrong when relationships turn abusive—and it happens more often than you might imagine.

More than one in three women in the United States have been the victim of rape, physical violence, and/or stalking in their lives (National Intimate Partner and Sexual Violence Survey [NISVS], 2010). Women are 15 times more likely to be killed by a man they know than by a stranger (Violence Policy Center, 2015). And while women are more commonly the targets of relationship violence, men are not immune. About 30% of partner homicides are women killing men (Browne, Williams, & Dutton, 1999), and one in four men in the United States has experienced rape, physical violence, or stalking from a partner—with the majority of these crimes being physical violence (NISVS, 2010).

The stereotype of relationship violence focuses on physical abuse. But it can also come in the form of psychological and emotional abuse—and some research shows that psychological abuse can be even more harmful (Follingstad, Rutledge, Berg, Hause, & Polek, 1990). The topic of relationship violence is a harsh, depressing one. But it is a problem that doesn't seem to be going away, and ignoring it doesn't help anyone. Fortunately, social psychologists have been a source of information, understanding, and activism regarding relationship violence. However, the profession of psychology could devote more attention and resources to (a) understanding this societal problem, (b) helping communities know what victims and survivors endure, and (c) helping to prevent relationship violence from happening in the first place.

WHAT ARE DIFFERENT TYPES OF RELATIONSHIP VIOLENCE?

LO 1: Describe various forms of relationship violence and how different research methods led to different answers to this question.

This research story begins with an argument over terminology: What do we call people who have endured these crimes? Some argue that the word *victim* should never be used because it connotes "helplessness and pity" (Helloflo.com, 2017; Kirkwood, 1993). Many people with this perspective believe that the term *survivor* should be used to refer to all targets of violence because *survivor* implies someone with the strength to get past the violence—a more empowering idea. For the purpose of this chapter, both terms will be used from a pragmatic view. *Victim* will be used when referring to someone who is still experiencing a violent relationship, while *survivor* will refer to someone who has successfully escaped the violence. It's not a perfect way to resolve the problem, but it gets us started.

Relationship violence is a relatively new area of research, simply because for many years, people thought that it would be too difficult to get honest responses. There were two related problems: (1) the measurement problem of *social desirability* and (2) the "too personal" nature of the questions researchers had to ask. Sure enough, when researchers finally turned their attention to the topic that polite society did not want to talk about, a controversy immediately erupted—and it all had to do with research methodology. As often happens in science, the controversy turned out to be helpful to the unfolding research story.

The Importance of Choosing Research Methodology: Surveys Versus Archival Data

In Chapter 2, we discussed two very different options for collecting data: One option asked people to complete *self-report surveys*. A second option involved gathering information from *archival data* (sources of data originally created for another purpose). The definition and understanding of relationship violence also began as a highly charged controversy simply because different people chose each option—and these different sources each told a very different story (see Johnson, 1995, 2007).

Archival Data. Think of your home community. Where would you go to gather information about relationship violence? Frequent sources of data, especially in early research, came from police records, domestic violence shelters, hospital emergency rooms, and divorce court records (Johnson, 2007). Patterns from these sources indicated that (a) women were almost always the victims of male perpetrators; (b) violence escalated over time, sometimes reaching deadly levels; (c) perpetrators often had other criminal behaviors, such as public intoxication or violence outside of the home; and (d) violence was physical, emotional, and psychological. This conclusion fits many people's stereotypes of "domestic abuse" or "wife battery." That was the story emerging from the archival data.

Self-Report Surveys. However, the results from other sources, including *self-report surveys* and *interviews,* painted a very different picture. The first large-scale, national, anonymous survey that collected data on relationship violence was the National Family Violence Survey, which included responses from 2,143 people in 1975 and from 6,002 people in 1985 (NFVS, 1975, 1985, as cited in Johnson, 1995). Results from these surveys were controversial. Understanding *why* these data were controversial will sensitize you to how the study of relationship violence challenges stereotypes that you also might have about relationship violence.

These data were controversial for two reasons. First, they claimed that relationship violence was much more common than previously thought; about 16% of participants said they had experienced abuse. The frequency of relationship violence violated one stereotype. In comparison to how dangerous relationship violence can be, these incidents were not particularly severe; they included slapping and shoving, for example. But it was still something of a shock to people who preferred to believe some alternative story. A second controversy in these surveys was that both men and women are perpetrators and victims of relationship violence—something that went against the story the archival data had told. Claims that husbands were frequent victims of relationship violence were met with heated skepticism (see Dobash & Dobash, 1992). Both results violated stereotypes about what happened inside relationships. So, which version of relationship violence was true?

JOHN MACDOUGALL / AFP / Getty Images

There's a surprise in the answer: both. In two groundbreaking articles that went far in settling the debate about the face of relationship violence, Johnson (1995, 2007) laid out a framework for two separate forms or types of violence. By acknowledging that both forms of violence exist, both researchers and community members gain insight into how relationship violence can come in different forms (Leone, Johnson, & Cohan, 2007). Let's take a closer look at these forms of violence.

Type 1: Intimate Terrorism. The stereotypical "wife battery" form of relationship violence seen in police files, domestic violence shelters, and emergency rooms is what Johnson (1995, 2007) calls **intimate terrorism**. In his original article, Johnson called this form "patriarchal terrorism" because it is more common to be perpetrated by men against women instead of vice versa or in same-sex couples. Later he changed the name to intimate terrorism, partially to acknowledge that it is possible to have this phenomenon occur regardless of the sex or gender of the couple members involved.

Intimate terrorism includes severe forms of physical violence that may require police or medical intervention, but it also includes psychological, emotional, and sexual violence. Johnson notes that intimate terrorism often includes dynamics suggested in the "power and control wheel" first suggested by Pence and Paymar (1993), shown in Figure F.1. Thus, this type of relationship violence includes economic abuse (such as disallowing

Intimate terrorism: A type of relationship violence that occurs when one couple member controls the other couple member through severe forms of physical violence as well as psychological, emotional, and sexual violence.

■ FIGURE F.1 Power and Control Wheel

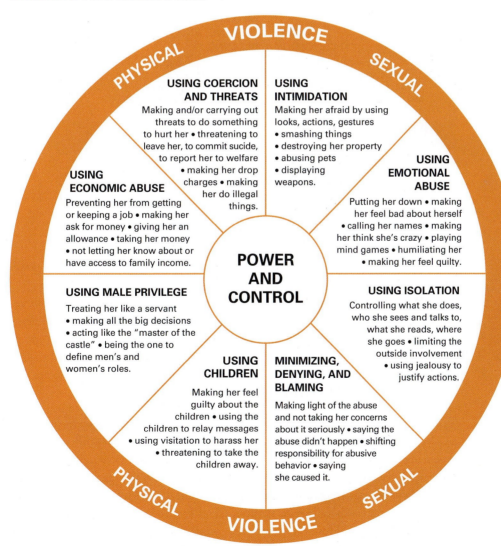

SOURCE: Pence and Paymar (1993).

COERCION AND THREATS

Making and/or carrying out threats to hurt you; Threatening to transfer or leave school; Threatening to commit suicide; Making you do illegal activities; Forcing you to drink alcohol or use illicit drugs against your will.

EMOTIONAL ABUSE

Putting you down; Not letting you study or do assignments; Keeping you up all night before an exam; Calling you names; Making you fell guilty for things that are not your fault.

GENDER PRIVILEGE

Treating you like you are inferior or his/her subordinate; Making all the big decisions; Defining and requiring rigid gender roles.

ISOLATION

Deleting contacts from your phone/email; Keeping you from roommates, family, and friends; Stopping you from joining organizations or clubs; Encouraging you stay with him/her over breaks; Using jealously to justify his/her actions.

COLLEGE POWER AND CONTROL

ECONOMIC ABUSE

Controlling how you spend your money; Having you pay his/her tuition, rent, etc.; Controlling your financial aid, personal income, flex, meal plan, CrimsonCash, etc.

INTIMIDATION

Making you afraid by using looks, actions, and gestures; Destroying your books, work, computer, etc.; Displaying weapons; Sharing plans to harm you/others, threatening pets/children.

USING TECHNOLOGY

Demanding passwords to online accounts; Texting/calling you constantly; Monitoring your social network sites; Using tracking system, GPS, and/or spyware to monitor your activity.

MINIMIZING, DENYING, AND BLAMING

Blames you for the abuse ("If you wouldn't __ I wouldn't hit you"); Denies abuse is taking place; Minimizes extent of abuse ("I don't hit you, that's real abuse, not yelling.")

SOURCE: Haven Project (2017).

someone access to money), intimidation, threats, and more. A second version of the power and control wheel designed for college relationships can be seen in Figure F.2.

The violence in intimate terrorism typically escalates over time in terms of both frequency and severity, and victims often feel completely powerless. Leone and colleagues (Leone et al., 2007) note that this form of relationship violence is more likely to appear in shelter and court records because it leads to dramatic outcomes that often require intervention—and that it's less likely to appear in *self-report surveys* because victims fear that honest answers will result in retaliation from their abuser.

Type 2: Situational Couple Violence. On the other hand, the survey responses are also *valid* representations of relationship violence; they show a very different type of experience. **Situational couple violence** is defined by Johnson (1995, 2007) as occasions when couple members argue, but neither attempts to take general control and the incidents are relatively minor (although still unhealthy). Here, fights escalate out of everyday conflicts about specific situations, and *both* couple members reciprocate in perpetrating violence. However, situational couple violence usually does not include psychological or emotional abuse, and physical abuse is typically restricted to actions

Situational couple violence: A type of relationship violence that occurs when couple members argue violently, but neither attempts to take general control and incidents are relatively minor, although still unhealthy. Situational couple violence is typically perpetrated by both couple members and includes short-term physical violence but not psychological or emotional abuse.

that do not lead to lasting injury. Johnson (2007) believes that this form of relationship violence is much more common than intimate terrorism.

In a study that directly compared couples experiencing each type of violence (Leone et al., 2007), results showed that compared to situational couple violence:

- Victims of intimate terrorism were older, in longer relationships, and less likely to be employed.
- Violence in intimate terrorism was significantly more severe (physically), more likely to increase in both frequency and severity over time, more likely to result in injury, and more likely to lead to depression and posttraumatic stress disorder symptoms in victims.
- Victims of intimate terrorism were twice as likely to call the police and four times as likely to seek medical help after a violent incident.

Male Victims

Most researchers of relationship violence agree that the type of violence described as intimate terrorism is more likely to be perpetrated by men toward women than in any other form. Some articles don't even acknowledge the possibility of male victims, or they quickly discount violence against men as being minimally important or harmful (Campbell, 2002; Johnson, 2007; Kilpatrick, 2004; Klein, Campbell, Soler, & Ghez, 1997). However, consider again the sources of information about intimate terrorism: police records, hospitals, and domestic violence shelters. For all three sources, male victims are significantly less likely to seek help after being victimized by a relationship partner, due to social stigmatization (Arnocky & Vaillancourt, 2014).

A study focusing on this question (Arnocky & Vaillancourt, 2014) asked participants to complete a social stigma scale regarding stereotypes and victim blaming

■ **TABLE F.1** Partner Violence Stigma Scale

Men/women who are abused by their romantic partners should be ashamed of themselves.
Men/women who are abused by their romantic partners are weak.
Men/women who stay with abusive partners deserve what they get.
Men/women who are abused by their romantic partners probably cannot attract anyone better.
Men/women who are abused by their romantic partners are not men/women I want to be friends with.
Many men/women who say they are abused by their romantic partners are probably lying or exaggerating.
When a woman/man hits her/his partner, it is most likely self-defense.
When a woman/man hits her/his partner, it was most likely provoked.

SOURCE: Arnocky and Vaillancourt (2014).

NOTE: Participants responded to each item on a 1 to 7 scale, with 1 indicating "I strongly disagree" and 7 indicating "I strongly agree."

within relationship violence scenarios (see Table F.1 for the items used). Participants were *randomly assigned* to answer the questions in terms of either male or female victims (sex of the victim was the *independent variable*); the items were presented as being about *just* male or *just* female victims. Average scores on the stigma scale were the *dependent variable*. Results showed that male victims were judged significantly more negatively than female victims—and this was true even for participants who had experienced relationship violence themselves. In addition, follow-up *surveys* revealed that male participants said they were much less likely to seek help or to admit to violence when it happened.

Stigmatization and lack of understanding is compounded when a man is a victim of violence within a gay relationship and thus might already be struggling with stereotyping, harassment, and discrimination (West, 1998). Gay victims may also fear that reporting violence will further enforce negative views of gay couples from outsiders as unhealthy or dysfunctional (Elliot, 1996; Hart, 1986). Still, violence in same-sex couples is prevalent; one study reported the highest rates of violence within lesbian couples (48%), then gay male couples (38%), then heterosexual couples (28%; Straus, 1979).

In one study that *interviewed* 25 gay men who had been in violent relationships (Cruz, 2003), the top three reasons men reported temporarily staying in the relationship (after it had become violent) were (1) financial dependence on their partner, (2) inexperience with same-sex couple dynamics, and (3) feelings of love despite the violence. Another study focused on forms of abuse within same-sex couples that do not appear in heterosexual couples (West, 1998), such as "homophobic control" or threatening to "out" a partner without his or her consent. Like all topics regarding gay, lesbian, transgender, and queer individuals, more research attention is needed—and more research acknowledging male victims in general is warranted as well.

Main Ideas

- Research attempting to describe relationship violence found different answers depending on the method used to collect data; different patterns emerge in self-report surveys and interviews compared to archival data using sources such as police and shelter records.

- Two forms of relationship violence are (1) intimate terrorism, which includes more severe physical violence as well as psychological, emotional, and sexual violence, and (2) situational couple violence, which occurs when both members of the couple are physically aggressive toward each other, but levels of violence are relatively small.

- The controversy about relationship violence for male victims and within gay or lesbian couples is still a subject of debate and research.

CRITICAL THINKING

- Ideas of relationship violence differed depending on whether people focused on patterns found from self-report survey and interviews versus archival records. Can you think of other areas of psychology that might be viewed differently if different research methods were used to collect data?

- Consider the different forms of psychological abuse shown in the "power and control" wheels of this section. Which two forms of abuse do you think would be the most damaging to a typical victim and why?

- The stigma toward male victims of relationship violence appears to be relatively strong. In addition, resources for male victims are scare (e.g., there are very few emergency shelters for male victims). Do you think that more resources should be devoted specifically for male victims—or would that simply take away focus and attention from female victims? How can empathy and prosocial behaviors toward male victims be increased using social psychological concepts?

WHAT IS THE PSYCHOLOGY OF PEOPLE EXPERIENCING RELATIONSHIP VIOLENCE?

LO 2: Analyze how romantic myths, cognitive dissonance, and affective forecasting apply to victims of relationship violence.

"Why doesn't she [or he] just leave?" is an unfortunate question; many researchers note that it blames the victim for experiencing abuse (see Barnett, Miller-Perrin, & Perrin, 1997; Cruz, 2003; Goetting, 1999; Jones, 2000). Victims of relationship violence don't enjoy abuse and don't deserve to be treated disrespectfully. Being involved in violence is complicated, and while most victims do eventually escape, sometimes the process takes time. We want to understand the psychological perspective of people while they are still victims—before they become survivors. This will increase our empathy and enable us to provide practical help for the needs of each individual enduring relationship violence. Several lines of research have thus attempted to explore psychological perceptions of relationship violence victims.

Cycle of violence: A theory for understanding relationship violence that states that relationship violence occurs in three cyclic phases: (1) tension building, in which an abuser becomes increasingly upset; (2) explosion, in which abuse occurs; and (3) contrition, in which the abuser apologizes and makes promises to stop his or her behavior.

The Cycle of Violence

Early research attempting to understand the psychology of people experiencing relationship violence produced a theory called the **cycle of violence** (Walker, 1979, 1984). The cycle theoretically has three phases: (1) tension building, in which an abuser becomes increasingly upset; (2) explosion, in which abuse occurs; and (3) contrition, in which the abuser apologizes and makes promises to stop his or her behavior. Other researchers have supported the idea of a cycle in violent relationships (e.g., Dutton, 1998) and suggested that victims sincerely hope and believe their partner's promises in the contrition phase. It is only after going through the full cycle multiple times that some victims realize that their partner's behaviors probably will not change—at least not anytime soon. Even if physically violent behaviors decrease in older adulthood (e.g., after retirement), emotional and psychological abuse will likely remain.

Pictorial Press Ltd/Alamy

Does the *Beauty and the Beast* fairytale encourage women to fall in love with men who treat them badly?

Romantic Myths

Rosen (1996) *interviewed* 22 women who had experienced (or were still experiencing) violence to see how they were initially attracted to and pulled into violent relationships, what she calls "processes of seduction." In her interviews, several of the women discussed **romantic myths**, or cultural messages regarding what romance is "supposed" to look like in traditional gendered ideas or social roles. Other research has defined romantic myths as "forms of popular culture [that] provide young girls with 'texts of meaning' of femininity and heterosexuality" regarding what to expect in relationships (Jackson, 2001, p. 306; see Davies, 1989; Jackson, 1993).

Rosen identified two specific romantic myths that encouraged "seduction" in violent relationships. The first is what she calls the **Cinderella fantasy**; this is the idea that a man who is a relative stranger can enter a woman's life and transform it by removing fears and saving her from problems (Rosen, 1996). Rosen points out that this myth encourages patriarchal power dynamics in which "Prince Charming" controls his wife's life and she is defined by him. The second romantic myth identified by Rosen is the **Beauty and the Beast fantasy**, in which women are told that patient, self-sacrificing love can turn a "beast" who is troubled and violent into a loving and sensitive partner. Unfortunately, Rosen notes that too often, beasts remain beasts.

Cognitive Dissonance and Minimization

Earlier in this book (see Chapter 6), we introduced the theory of cognitive dissonance. Cognitive dissonance is the idea that it makes us anxious or uncomfortable to maintain two conflicting beliefs, or to behave in a way that conflicts with our values or self-concept. Victims of relationship violence mostly likely do not believe that abuse in relationships is acceptable. Simultaneously, however, they may not be able to leave at a certain time due to financial dependency, fear, a motivation to protect children, and so on. This may cause dissonance.

Some research suggests that one way current victims can decrease dissonance is to perceive the abusive behaviors as nonabusive. In other words, victims may minimize their partner's behaviors by denying it occurred, downplaying the significance or severity of what occurred, or providing some kind of justification for the behaviors. Dunham and Senn (2000) found that women who experienced relationship violence often omit information about it when discussing their relationship with others—and that omission occurred more as the severity of abuse increased (a *positive correlation*).

One intriguing study found that victims might acknowledge the specific behaviors that occurred but interpret them in ways that avoid labeling them as "abusive" or "violent." Arriaga (2002) discovered that when victims were given the opportunity to say that a partner's physically violent actions were "just a joke," many of them agreed with this interpretation—even when the behaviors were as severe as being kicked, beat up, or struck with a weapon. Follow-up research that *interviewed* women at a domestic violence shelter asked women to recall a particularly violent incident, then explain why it happened (Goodfriend et al., 2017). When the women were still highly committed to their partners and planned to return to the relationship, cognitive dissonance would prevent them from blaming their abuser. Instead, the women blamed themselves, claimed their partner had an uncontrollable problem such as alcoholism, or said that violence was so common that leaving would be pointless.

Faulty Affective Forecasting

A fourth explanation to understand some victim's hesitancy to immediately leave a violent relationship is a lack of accurate **affective forecasting**. Affective forecasting (sometimes called **hedonic forecasting**) is when someone tries to predict how he or she will feel in the future—and several studies have shown that we are not particularly good at

Romantic myths: Cultural messages regarding what romance is supposed to look like that support traditional gendered ideas or social roles and can encourage seduction into violent relationships.

Cinderella fantasy: A romantic myth in which a man who is a relative stranger can enter a woman's life and transform it by removing fears and saving her from problems (see *romantic myths*).

Beauty and the Beast fantasy: A romantic myth in which women are told that patient, self-sacrificing love can turn a "beast" who is troubled and violent into a loving and sensitive partner (see *romantic myths*).

Affective forecasting: Occurs when an individual tries to predict how he or she will feel in the future; most individuals aren't able to do so effectively.

Hedonic forecasting: see *affective forecasting*.

■ FIGURE F.3 Research on "affective forecasting" finds that people are not very good at predicting their own future emotions.

it (Buehler & McFarland, 2001; Gilbert, Pinel, Wilson, Blumberg, & Wheatley, 1998; Hoerger, Quirk, Lucas, & Carr, 2010). This appears to be true of victims of relationship violence as well.

Arriaga and her colleagues (Arriaga, Capezza, Goodfriend, Rayl, & Sands, 2013) conducted a *longitudinal study* in which they first asked victims to predict how happy they would be if their relationship ended. Several months later, about one fourth of the relationships had ended. Once the relationship (and abuse) was over, people who were now survivors were significantly happier than they had predicted they would be. The study concluded that "expecting doom without a partner functions to maintain a relationship, even when life without an aggressive partner turns out to be better than expected" (p. 681).

Main Ideas

- Research shows that one reason some victims of violence don't immediately leave is because of a cycle of violence with three phases: (1) tension building, (2) explosion, and (3) contrition or apologies from the abuser.

- Romantic myths, such as the belief that a "beast" can turn into a prince with enough love and patience, may also contribute to the psychology of victims.

- A third reason current victims of violence may not realize their situation is abusive is because of cognitive dissonance and cognitive minimization.

- Finally, victims of violence may have trouble escaping abuse because of faulty affective forecasting, or the ability to predict how we'll feel in the future.

⚡ CRITICAL THINKING

- If romantic myths contribute to the perpetuation of violence, how can children—both boys and girls—be taught to appreciate these fairytales for their positive aspects but warned against learning the types of lessons that may lead to acceptance of relationship violence?

- Consider the four psychological experiences described in this section and imagine you are a therapist working with a client who is currently experiencing relationship violence. What are specific exercises you could ask your client to do that could help him or her work through these challenges to perceiving the situation objectively and thus helping progress toward escape?

HOW CAN SURVIVORS HEAL AND MOVE FORWARD?

LO 3: Apply research on stages of escape, narrative therapy, and posttraumatic growth to survivors of relationship violence.

Ideally, researchers would be able to understand relationship violence enough to prevent it from happening in the first place. When people working on this problem consider prevention efforts, they are typically broken up into three types of intervention (Cathey & Goodfriend, 2012). **Primary prevention** reaches people to stop violence before it begins on an individual level; again, this is the ideal. Primary prevention occurs through education and empowerment; for example, a program might teach middle schoolers what potential warning signs of violence might be within their own relationships. However, the reality of the current world is that millions of people experience relationship violence every day. Thus, two additional types of intervention are also needed.

Secondary prevention intervenes after relationship violence has begun and provides victims with resources and knowledge to prevent it from happening again. Finally, **tertiary prevention** involves educating the larger community, such as a college or university campus or a given town, regarding dynamics of relationship violence to increase empathy and understanding (Cathey & Goodfriend, 2012). Most research on response to relationship violence occurs at the secondary level. How can victims escape and become survivors instead?

Primary prevention: The prevention of relationship violence before the violence begins through education and empowerment.

Secondary prevention: Interventions that occur after relationship violence has begun, including providing victims with the resources and knowledge to prevent the violence from happening again.

Tertiary prevention: Educating the larger community, such as a college or university campus or a given town, regarding dynamics of relationship violence to increase empathy and understanding.

Escape: From Victims to Survivors

In her book *Leaving Abusive Partners,* Kirkwood (1993) *interviewed* a diverse group of 30 women who had successfully escaped violent relationships. These survivors noted that there were several obstacles that each needed to be overcome in order for them to successfully escape; these included the following:

- Finding housing and economic resources
- Obtaining medical aid for both short-term and long-term needs
- Obtaining safety and protection from their ex-partners
- Dealing with a dramatic change of circumstances

Another study interviewed 22 survivors (Rosen & Stith, 1997) and identified the "disentanglement process" (p. 174) many of them went through to get out of the relationship. In this study, there were five distinct steps the victims took to leave. First, they experienced "seeds of doubt," meaning that they were no longer able to deny or

Viviane Moos / Corbis Historical / Getty Images

minimize what was happening to them; the victims finally acknowledged that they were in abusive relationships. Second, they experienced a "turning point"; this was sometimes a small cognitive or psychological shift in how they interpreted behaviors from their partner.

A third step (Rosen & Stith, 1997) was "objective reappraisals," or the process of seeing what was happening from a more objective view. Here, victims reevaluated themselves and their partners and realized that (a) they were in real danger, (b) their partners did not truly love them, (c) the violence was not going to stop, and/or (d) they had options to escape. The fourth step toward escape in this study was "self-reclaiming actions," such as seeking counseling or building a supportive network of friends. The fifth and final step identified in this study was "last straw events," or moments that provided a catalyst for finally leaving permanently.

Healing and Moving Forward

Once victims become survivors, it still can be difficult to psychologically move forward. Some survivors—especially those subjected to severe intimate terrorism—have both physical and emotional scars. Treatment programs for survivors vary widely, and there are many approaches to helping people deal with trauma. In fact, jobs in what is now known as **trauma psychology** are growing; this field helps people recover from any severely stressful event that impairs long-term psychological functioning (see, e.g., the description on psychologyschoolguide.net, which also lists schools that offer relevant master's degree programs). Consider two examples of research on how survivors can find closure and heal.

Narrative Therapy. One option for individuals who want to heal from the trauma of relationship violence is called **narrative therapy**, which is the process of writing down autobiographical events in a therapeutic setting (Cathey & Goodfriend, 2012). Traditionally, the narratives are chronological stories, like a typical autobiography, but they could also come in the form of poems, drawings, or anything else useful to the survivor.

A series of studies by Pennebaker (see Pennebaker, 1997, for a review) showed that when people who have survived a trauma write about it, there are both psychological and physical benefits. In a review of 13 studies on narrative therapy, Smyth (1998) found that people who wrote about traumas showed significant improvements in mental health, physical health, and general functioning (such as academic grades and work absenteeism). In a summary of the benefits of narrative therapy, Cathey and Goodfriend (2012) noted that it helps survivors feel closure, helps them process what happened in manageable pieces, and provides an avenue for self-expression.

In my [Wind's] book with colleague Pamela Cathey (Cathey & Goodfriend, 2012), we worked with 10 relationship violence survivors who wrote their stories in both individual and group therapy sessions over about a year. Those stories are published in the book and represent a wide variety of experiences, including childhood sexual trauma, college dating violence, and domestic violence. In addition, three of the stories are from male survivors. The book, titled *Voices of Hope,* has also been condensed into a 1-hour theatrical performance that can be performed as a fundraiser and educational intervention for communities or universities. The play is available free of charge and has already been performed at several universities around the country.

Posttraumatic Growth. Many victims of severe trauma experience posttraumatic stress disorder (PTSD; e.g., Street & Arias, 2001). However, other research has

Trauma psychology: A field of psychology that focuses on helping people recover from any severely stressful event that impairs long-term psychological functioning.

Narrative therapy: The process of writing down autobiographical events in a therapeutic setting.

attempted to discover whether survivors of trauma such as relationship violence can heal to the point of becoming even stronger than they were before the abusive relationship started (Tedeschi & Calhoun, 1996). In this way, survivors can feel that even though what they experienced was inexcusable, they have grown past it and the violence no longer defines who they are (see Table F.2).

■ TABLE F.2 Selected Items From the Posttraumatic Growth Inventory

I changed my priorities about what is important in life.
I have a greater appreciation for the value of my own life.
I developed new interests.
I have a greater feeling of self-reliance.
I have a better understanding of spiritual matters.
I more clearly see that I can count on people in times of trouble.
I established a new path for my life.
I have a greater sense of closeness with others.
I am more willing to express my emotions.
I know better that I can handle difficulties.

SOURCE: Tedeschi and Calhoun (1996); full scale is 21 items.

One attempt to capture this empowering attitude is the development of a scale to measure **posttraumatic growth**, or feelings of positive psychological change and resilience as a result of trauma and adversity. The idea of posttraumatic growth is that after a trauma, individuals should not hope to return to the same level of self-esteem or empowerment they had beforehand; instead, they should strive to become even stronger. You can see some of the items from the scale developed by Tedeschi and Calhoun (1996, 2004) to measure posttraumatic growth. Every year, thousands of people create new lives by moving from victim to survivor to personal growth (Boals & Schuler, 2017). For researchers, therapists, and individuals, social psychology might be able to help survivors escape from their violent relationships safely, heal from their physical and psychological wounds, and become empowered.

Main Ideas

- Prevention of relationship violence can come in three levels: primary, which tries to stop violence before it begins; secondary, which attempts to prevent further violence after it starts; and tertiary, which involves educating the larger community.

- Research on escape from violent relationships shows that it occurs over several steps, such as cognitive reappraisals and self-empowerment actions.

- Research on healing from the trauma of relationship violence shows that healing can occur through interventions such as narrative therapy (writing one's story) and that this type of effort can eventually lead to posttraumatic growth.

Posttraumatic growth: Feelings of positive psychological change and resilience as a result of trauma and adversity.

⚡ CRITICAL THINKING QUESTIONS

- Some people will be able to heal from the trauma of relationship violence more quickly or more effectively than others. Identify two variables that you think might be associated with an individual's ability to experience posttraumatic growth, then explain how you might scientifically test your hypothesis. What would be the procedure of your study? How would you operationalize your variables? What statistical tests would you need to use to analyze your data?

- Most schools engage in prevention and education programs focused on relationship violence. Identity three programs, offices, staff, faculty, training opportunities, talks, performances, or anything else your college or university offers regarding education and prevention of relationship violence, then explain where each of these three people, programs, or offices fall on the framework of primary, secondary, and tertiary prevention.

Visit **edge.sagepub.com/heinzen** to help you accomplish your coursework goals in an easy-to-use learning environment.

- Mobile-friendly **eFlashcards**
- **Video** and **multimedia content**
- EXCLUSIVE! Access to full-text **SAGE journal articles**

$SAGE edge™

Social Psychology of Work: Industrial/Organizational Psychology

1. What is industrial/organizational (I/O) psychology, and what is its history?

2. What content areas are included in industrial/organizational psychology?

1. Define I/O psychology, including its history and demand for tests related to personnel selection.

2. Explain some of the major content areas within I/O psychology.

This application mini-chapter focuses your attention on industrial and organizational psychology, the application of psychological theories to the workplace. Your working life will take up only about 30% of your time as an adult. Sleeping will consume about another 33%, and during the remainder of a typical week, you'll probably spend some time preparing food and eating, shopping, visiting with friends, exercising, watching television, and so forth. If you are a parent, then your schedule becomes consumed with raising your children at every possible free moment. But, for most of us, the money we earn at work leverages the effectiveness, quality, and comforts of all the other timed parts of our lives.

You can see, then, why the psychology of the workplace is so important from a personal perspective. But the psychology of the workplace is also important from a socioeconomic perspective. From a social psychological perspective, our working life is often the public stage that presents how our thoughts, feelings, and behaviors influence—and are influenced by—other people. And, our working life also influences the economies of our towns, regions, and even the gross national product.

WHAT IS INDUSTRIAL/ORGANIZATIONAL PSYCHOLOGY, AND WHAT IS ITS HISTORY?

LO 1: Define industrial/organizational (I/O) psychology, including its history and demand for tests related to personnel selection.

Industrial/organizational psychology applies psychological theories to meet the needs of organizations and individuals in the workplace. Usually shortened to just "I/O psych," the field is guided by the **scientist-practitioner model**, just like clinical psychology or medical science. Scientists discover as much as they can about how organizations work and then apply those insights to solve real organizational problems.

If you're an I/O psychologist, then you're applying I/O science to problems such as employee morale, selecting better employees, or evaluating training programs. You need to be skilled at both theory and application—at understanding the insights from I/O science and applying them to groups of people.

I/O's Pioneer: Walter Dill Scott

There have been several colorful personalities in the history of I/O psychology. For example, prior to World War II, Hugo Münsterberg dominated headlines and popular magazines with a wide range of psychological pronouncements: advice to parents, his

Industrial/organizational psychology: The academic study of people in the workplace, where researchers apply psychological theory to meet the needs of organizations and employees.

Scientist-practitioner model: A method for approaching a field of study where individuals are trained to use their understanding of basic science in real-world applications.

thoughts about law, and just about anything else that crossed his busy, restless brain. Münsterberg was instrumental in helping to popularize psychology and make psychology's case to the general public. Because he applied many psychological ideas to educational and business settings, he could be considered one of the very first I/O psychologists. However, Münsterberg's fame and high regard from others did not endure, partially because he often defended Germany's actions during World War II.

In contrast, Walter Dill Scott kept his eyes on the prize of using psychology to make work life better. Even though he never published his experiences in an academic paper or had his picture on the cover of national magazines, Scott could be considered one of the most important pioneers in I/O psychology—and he got started with the sudden demands of an underprepared U.S. military in World War I (see Schultz & Schultz, 2016).

The Origins of Psychological Testing.

Many thousands of new soldiers needed to be processed and trained for the kinds of jobs needed by the U.S. military. Scott's plan was to use large-scale psychological testing to route personnel to the most appropriate job and to help identify "quick-thinking recruits" for special assignments. It was a massive undertaking. Professor Scott presented his plan to administer mass psychological tests to Brigadier General Joseph Kuhn.

General Kuhn didn't want plans; he wanted results—and he especially did not like professors with fancy theories (see von Mayrhauser, 1989, p. 65). When Scott began speaking, the general:

Chicago History Museum / Archive Photos / Getty Images

Walter Dill Scott, President of Northwestern University, buying a snack from a food truck (Chicago, 1926).

almost exploded with rage. He said it was his function to see that college professors did not get in the way of progress, that we are at war with Germany, and that we had no time to fool with experiments; that many people felt that the Army was a great dog on which to try experiments, and that he would see that no college professor did that. (von Mayrhauser, 1989, p. 65)

The Science-Practitioner Gap.

This part of the interaction between Scott and Kuhn captures an interesting element of the story of I/O psychology. General Kuhn did not want any psychologists getting in the way of progress, and he was right to be concerned. There has been a longstanding, deep divide between theory-minded academic psychologists and problem-solving practicing psychologists. The academics, as General Kuhn had experienced them, tended to spend their lives testing and refining theories that people outside of the academy had never heard of or cared about.

Meanwhile, the people working in the military and in corporations were in desperate need of a way to solve their everyday personnel problems; they needed some good theories. They were too busy meeting their current responsibilities and dealing with thousands of recruits to figure out which theories might be able to make their lives easier, their organizations more productive, and their efforts more effective. They weren't paid to theorize; they were paid to get things done. The people who needed psychologists the most had no practical guidance from the academics.

Walter Dill Scott, however, was not a traditional academic. Here's what happened as General Kuhn finished complaining about college professors. First, Scott allowed the general to rant until he exhausted and somewhat embarrassed himself. Then they went to lunch. It is not clear what they talked about, but it must have included the testing plan Scott had brought with him. "Three days after blowing up at Scott, Kuhn recommended . . . to the Chief of Staff . . . the primary service of the psychologists as 'classifying the personnel in order that the aptitude and capabilities of any individual may be known'" (von Mayrhauser, 1989, p. 65).

Psychological testing probably would have eventually found its way into the military without this incident. But now psychological testing was going to be a fact of life in the military for generations to come—and the practice would spread to other industries and workplaces. When Scott published a book about I/O psychology a few years later, he wrote,

> The old idea of thinking of men as so many kilograms of muscular energy, to be both exploited, and scrapped when occasion demands, is reaping the harvest it richly deserves. Burst, likewise, is the bubble of paternalism which sought to determine for labor what was good for it and feed it accordingly. (Scott & Hayes, 1921, p. iii)

The time between the wars was an opportunity for change. Even though they were writing a century earlier, Scott and Hayes (1921) anticipated what that change would look like:

> Their workers are not a bulk mass but a group of individuals. They are recognizing that these workers differ in the things they are fitted to do and capable of doing; that they differ, likewise, in their interests, ambitions, and the things that seem to them desirable; and that as men of different capacities and desires they require individual adjustment to the opportunities offered them in the field of industry. (p. iii)

The interaction between Professor Scott and General Kuhn provides a vivid summary of the origins of I/O psychology. First, both World War I and World War II created a demand for a wide variety of skills from social and I/O psychologists. Second, many of those skills were about testing large numbers of people in a very short time: personnel selection. Third, once psychology got its foot in the door and proved itself useful, the army kept finding new ways to use psychologists' skills.

■ **TABLE G.1** Some Types of Tests Used in I/O Psychology

Type of Test	Test Measures	Advantages	Disadvantages
Specific skills	Typing speed, ability to use software or mechanical tools, etc.	Less likely to have results biased by prejudice (sexism, etc.)	Requires previous experience; some knowledge continues to change (e.g., software needs)
Personality	Traits relevant to different jobs, such as extraversion or conscientiousness	Cost-effective to measure	May not be predictive of actual behaviors; results subject to impression management attempts
Cognitive abilities	Logic, reasoning, reading comprehension, math ability	Results not influenced by attempts at impression management	Results subject to stereotype threat, nerves, etc.
Integrity	Honest, reliability, cooperation, prosocial behaviors	Sends potential employees message that integrity matters in the organization	Results may be manipulated by test taker for impression management
Physical abilities	Physical fitness, ability to carry/haul heavy objects, run quickly, etc.	Relevant for many jobs (police, firefighters, etc.)	May be discriminatory, especially if used inappropriately

SOURCE: Modified from the website for the Society for Industrial and Organizational Psychology (2017).

Modern Psychological Tests

That's an outline of the backstory about testing in I/O psychology. The need for mass psychological testing grew larger as the quality of psychological tests gradually improved. And the guidelines for those improvements were two familiar ideas: *reliability* and *validity*. A trustworthy test must produce consistent results (reliability) and measure whatever it was intended to measure (validity). Using tests to determine the best use of workers (both from the company's view and from the workers' view) is still popular—and it's one of the things that I/O psychologists now can do fairly well. For example, the Career Services office on your campus probably has access to a variety of career inventories that can help point you toward careers that other people like you seem to enjoy. To further understand some of the types of the testing that I/O psychologists have developed and that are used by many industries and organizations today, see Table G.1.

Main Ideas

- Industrial/organizational psychology (usually called "I/O psych") applies psychological theories to meet the needs of organizations and individuals in the workplace. It is guided by the scientist-practitioner model.

- I/O psychology got its start by helping officers in the military develop and use tests designed to assess the best placements for personnel, based on criteria such as personality, cognitive abilities, and physical abilities.

⚡ CRITICAL THINKING

- General Joseph Kuhn wasn't the first or the last person to criticize academics for conducting research that is never applied to the general public. Most research studies are only accessible through expensive journals and are written only for other academics to understand. Discuss at least three specific ways that this system causes problems in "real-world" contexts, such as military officers not having access to personality tests, corporate managers not understanding the psychology of their employees, and so on. Identify three examples on your own.

- While personality and other types of tests are commonly used by corporations and organizations to better understand potential employees, some people have criticized these tests. One problem is that some of them lack the ability to predict any kind of actual behavior and that social desirability is high in these settings. What are two ways I/O psychologists could attempt to improve the way tests are used in this particular context?

WHAT CONTENT AREAS ARE INCLUDED IN INDUSTRIAL/ ORGANIZATIONAL PSYCHOLOGY?

LO 2: Explain some of the major content areas within I/O psychology.

Employee morale and productivity was one of the early interests of I/O psychologists. The most famous (and still controversial) set of experiments was conducted at the Hawthorne Works Western Electric plant in Illinois (see Bramel & Friend, 1981; Mayo, 1933, 1945). While the experiments were designed to see what kind of workplace changes would increase productivity, the results were surprising: *Any* form of attention from management appeared to increase productivity. This finding is now called the **Hawthorne effect**: People temporarily change their behavior because they are aware they are being observed. One explanation for the improvement was that being observed was interpreted by workers in a particular way: "the company cares about my welfare." Whatever the explanation for the Hawthorne effect, people will tend to work harder when they know the boss is watching.

The Hawthorne experiments represented a fundamental shift from the scientific management view intended to get maximum productivity out of each employee. Gradually, new employees were viewed as valued human resources. In fact, the name of the office that processes employee benefits, trains new employees, and so forth is usually called "Human Resources." There are several ways to organize the range of activities and roles performed by modern I/O psychologists. The following overview focuses first on activities intended to help employees and then on activities intended to help the organization.

How I/O Psychologists Help Employees

Positive psychology reminds us that the workplace is an environment in which people can become their best selves. People with awkward social skills in their home might be confident, assertive, and appropriate in their work environment. The challenge is to find the "best fit" between the job and the individual's personality and creative talents. On the other hand, sometimes people bring their problems from home into the workplace. In general, the goals of an I/O psychologist align most closely with positive psychologists who are always on the lookout for ways to help both the employees and organization perform at a higher level.

Employee Morale and Employee Satisfaction.
There are many influences on morale, and many of them are beyond the reach of the organization. For example, a new employee may love the job but still have low morale because the commute is so long. A formal survey to assess morale is tricky because of the social desirability problem. On the other hand, if you rely on informal gossip to assess the morale of an organization, then be careful. Gossip is more likely to carry bad news than good news, to criticize the culture than to praise it, and to generally give more attention to the negative. Gossip is difficult to ignore, but that doesn't mean that the gossiped views represent those of the larger community. The I/O psychologist will have been trained in what predicts positive and negative morale, how those features can be implemented, and how to gather the evaluation data that will tell everyone whether an intervention to improve morale was successful.

Performance Appraisal.
Individuals' work performance is often evaluated, and the evaluation process may be fraught with anxiety. The purpose, however, is not to punish (usually) but to improve performance. The I/O psychologist will help establish the benchmarks for what a positive or negative appraisal looks like. Psychology can help an organization decide how to best motivate people for good performance (e.g., additional compensation vs. public praise such as "employee of the month") and help the organization deliver poor performance evaluations in ways that will be helpful to employees instead of simply depressing or negative.

Compensation.
An I/O psychologist may also spend significant time devising compensation packages, in part because they are such an important part of what motivates employees. In some industries, it is common to reward people with a salary and then

Hawthorne effect: Occurs when individuals in a workplace setting temporarily change their behavior because they are aware of being observed (see *social desirability effect*).

supplement it with an annual bonus. The I/O psychologist, especially someone with social psychological sensibilities, might be more sensitive to the perceptions of fairness and their effects on workplace morale. Different industries, however, may also have different definitions of what "fairness" means. The I/O psychologist needs to be aware of those differences when contributing to discussions about compensation (annual bonus vs. more vacation days, hourly versus salary pay, etc.).

Work/Life Balance. The I/O psychologist may be able to help define what a healthy work/life balance actually means. That also may vary from one organizational culture to the next. A well-known soft-drink company declares that "we want to hire people who give ulcers, not people who get ulcers." Their view of work/life balance is tipped toward constant, driving work. The classic Silicon Valley startup, on the other hand, brings playthings to work and encourages free time, yoga, and ping-pong in the interest of increasing creativity.

Employee Assistance Programs (EAPs). The I/O psychologist, depending on his or her particular training and licensing, may get involved in either providing or directing people with emotional, behavioral, or personal problems to a counseling service. It is more common for the I/O psychologist to *not* play the role of a therapist at work but to know how to refer people to mental health professionals. Note, too, that to avoid ethical violations, an I/O psychologist should not fill conflicting roles in the organization. If an I/O psychologist is helping determine bonus packages, for example, it would violate the code of ethics for her or him to also be aware of confidential concerns or troubles that employees are experiencing.

How I/O Psychologists Help the Organization

The I/O psychologist's efforts to help individuals also help the organization to run more effectively. So the line between personal and organizational assistance is not always well defined. What an I/O psychologist actually does on any given day may weave back and forth several times. However, many activities of the I/O psychologist's role clearly relate to the development of the organization (rather than to the individual employees).

Job Analysis. A **job analysis** contributes to better performance by specifying what is expected in a particular job. Those expectations should be clear from the job description when a job is advertised. An I/O psychologist might be called in to help describe the job and then write the advertisement. A job analysis will clarify what starting education and skills are expected, what additional training might be needed, what personal growth trajectories a new employee can hope for, and what kind of compensation package is expected. It leans toward a "no surprises" approach to hiring and promotion. Here are two examples of online job descriptions from the website indeed.com. The first is for a babysitter; the second is for a college intern in marketing:

Job 1: Babysitter

Our family is interested in hiring a full-time babysitter to supervise our children for 40 hours a week during business hours. We are seeking an experienced, caring professional who truly enjoys spending time with kids. The successful applicant will be responsible for picking up our children from school (half-day kindergarten), engaging them with fun, developmentally-appropriate activities, keeping us updated on events throughout the day and alerting us immediately if there are any problems. This position

Job analysis: The process of creating and advertising the description of a particular job. The job analysis specifies what education, skills, and training may be needed, what growth trajectories are expected, and what compensation packages may be available.

will require some weekend and evening work, but with at least one week notice when possible. No holiday work required.

The responsibilities for the job are also listed in ways that make it difficult to misunderstand what they are:

> Pick up the children from school at 1:00 p.m. and bring the children home or to appointments that will be set up well in advance
>
> Alert the parents immediately if there are any issues at home
>
> Assist children with any school projects that may be required
>
> Engage children with fun activities, such as games, puzzles, or pretend play
>
> Answer incoming phone calls and take messages for the family

Job 2: College internship in marketing.

Our growing, family-owned Internet company would like to bring on a Marketing Intern for next summer. The successful candidate will be enrolled full-time in a major university or college and studying marketing or communications. We're looking for a driven, ambitious individual who wants to create a career in social media and content marketing. We're offering a flexible schedule if you continue to take classes in the summer or you wish to pursue other opportunities simultaneously. We provide extensive training, guidance and support, as well as the opportunity to experience the industry from the inside and gain valuable work experience.

The job responsibilities for this position are also specific.

> Enrollment in a bachelor's degree program required
>
> Familiarity with social media strategies and platforms
>
> Ability to multitask and take initiative
>
> Flexible work schedule
>
> Hardworking and dedicated outlook
>
> Ability to take direction and absorb information quickly
>
> Experience with content creation a plus, even if not professionally

Personnel Needs Assessment. Assessing personnel needs may require an I/O psychologist to conduct internal surveys and interviews. The goal is to discover the organization's or department's mission and to identify personnel gaps between the mission and the reality. It may be similar to a job analysis because the I/O psychologist needs to identify what jobs are needed to fulfill the mission, find out whether the organization already has the talent to meet those needs, and how to go get that talent, if necessary. Selecting the appropriate personnel may depend on organizational culture and correct use of testing.

Organizational Development. Organizations, like people, are constantly changing, if only because they are growing older. In addition, new competitors will come on the scene, the product may begin to look tired, and large-scale economic changes will affect a particular industry for good or ill. The problem faced by the I/O psychologist is not whether the organization will change but how it will be a productive change. Even the largest, most successful companies go out of business. The I/O psychologist may be involved in preparing employees for coming changes, helping discover what changes are most needed, or estimating whether some proposed changes are very good or very bad ideas.

Organizational Structure. Some organizations evolve to be "flat" organizations in which almost everyone has easy access to higher levels of management. Others are "hierarchical" with strict reporting criteria along formal lines of command and authority. The I/O psychologist needs to understand why an organization is structured in a particular way, whether that structure is appropriate for its evolving industry, and what changes might be necessary for the company to succeed in the future.

Evaluation and Assessment. Authentic improvement for both individuals and organizations requires authentic evaluation and assessment. We need to know, before we start to make a change, what we think success will look like. For the I/O psychologist evaluating whether the organization should renew a $3 million contract for training, success means whether the specific purposes of the training program have been achieved. And that means more measurement challenges and outcomes assessments—the kind of thinking that is a standard part of graduate training for both social and I/O psychologists.

Leadership. Social psychologist Kurt Lewin studied leadership after he immigrated to the United States from Germany. He wanted to learn what happened under authoritarian, democratic, and laissez-faire leadership styles. The modern I/O literature is full of leadership studies, the exploration of different types of leadership, leadership teams, and the short-term and long-term effects of leadership styles on organizations facing particular circumstances. If you become an I/O psychologist, you can study current theories of leadership—and be on your way to becoming a leader yourself.

Careers in Social Psychology and I/O Psychology

There are significant overlaps between social psychology and I/O psychology. Testing, leadership, and evaluation are among the most obvious. But the most striking similarities are related to the mental training each discipline provides, rather than their content. You're going to be a competent statistician if you earn a graduate degree in either field, but not because of your skills with numbers. Computer programs will take care of that for you. Instead, your value will be in your ability to recognize *confounding variables* and to question reliability and validity when reaching conclusions.

You will recognize, for example, whether increased employee productivity was due to higher levels of light in the work area or the fact that someone was finally paying attention to, and perhaps caring about, employees. You'll also know how to question whether such studies reached valid conclusions. In short, a career in social or I/O psychology prepares you for difficult, meaningful, creative work within an organization. You could become a positive force for science in some organizational setting that needs your habits of clear, critical thinking.

Main Ideas

- The Hawthorne effect is that people temporarily change their behavior because they are aware they are being observed. If employees know they are being watched, their work will temporarily improve.

- I/O psychologists have many duties, which can be divided based on whether attention is on benefiting individual employees (e.g., employee morale) or on benefiting the larger organization (e.g., an analysis of the organization's internal structure).

⚡ CRITICAL THINKING

- Write a job analysis for a job or duty that you've had at some point in your life. Make sure to explicitly explain what the duties are, any required background or education, potential areas of growth or promotion, and so on.

- It was noted that to avoid ethical problems, I/O psychologists should not fill conflicting roles in the organization. However, this mini-chapter laid out duties based on looking after employees as separate from duties looking after the good of the organization. Ideally, these two goals are the same—an organization should want its employees to be healthy and happy. But what should an I/O psychologist do if those two goals conflict (e.g., paying employees more hurts the profit margin of the company)? How can an I/O psychologist resolve these potential ethical dilemmas?

Visit **edge.sagepub.com/heinzen** to help you accomplish your coursework goals in an easy-to-use learning environment.

- Mobile-friendly **eFlashcards**
- **Video** and **multimedia content**
- EXCLUSIVE! Access to full-text **SAGE journal articles**

⑤SAGE edge™

Social Psychology of Volunteerism and Internships

1. Why do people volunteer?

2. How do internships provide career guidance?

1. To discuss how personality, job hunting, health benefits, and life satisfaction motivate volunteering.

2. To describe how internships can influence short-term decision making and long-term career planning.

What do you want to do with your life?

Such a simple question . . . yet it can be surprisingly difficult to answer. Answering this question has fueled many counseling sessions designed to help people discover their goals and to achieve them (Gelatt, 1989). Volunteerism and internships are two practical ways to start answering that question. It's a simple formula: Try something—you might like it. If you don't, then you'll still learn something about yourself.

Most colleges and universities provide many opportunities for students to get off campus to experience the larger world. This might come in the form of student clubs or organizations that provide community service, such as a club that helps walk dogs in a local shelter, work with children in an after-school program, or collect non-perishable foods to donate to a food bank. More formally, colleges and universities may even offer credit toward graduation for internships with companies looking for new people and fresh ideas. While many of these internships are not paid—and thus could be considered volunteering—they often lead to full-time, permanent jobs after graduation.

What does social psychology offer to help understand the world of volunteering and relevant internships?

WHY DO PEOPLE VOLUNTEER?

■ LO 1: To discuss how personality, job hunting, health benefits, and life satisfaction motivate volunteering.

Volunteerism is engaging in a planned, long-term, prosocial behavior (see Snyder & Omoto, 2008). While this book includes an entire chapter on the motivations behind prosocial and helping behaviors (see Chapter 10), here we focus specifically on volunteering and internships.

Volunteering benefits both the people who volunteer and the causes or organizations they support. In the long term, volunteering is associated with a variety of personal health benefits and public quality-of-life benefits. In the short term, volunteering requires effort that could be spent on other, more obviously self-serving activities. So, it is not surprising that social psychologists are interested in what motivates volunteers. Why will highly motivated individuals work for free?

Personality

Personality traits help explain volunteerism. Carlo and colleagues (Carlo, Okun, Knight, & de Guzman, 2005) tested almost 800 college students for personality traits, assessed their prosocial motivations to volunteer, and finally measured their

Volunteerism: Freely engaging in a planned, long-term, prosocial behavior.

■ FIGURE H.1 The personality path to volunteering.

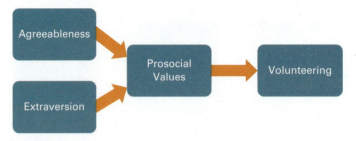

■ FIGURE H.1 The personality path to volunteering.

SOURCE: Carlo et al. (2005).

actual volunteering behaviors. They used a statistical technique called **path analysis** (shown in a simplified form in Figure H.1), which uses relationships among variables to hypothesize causal connections. The personality traits of agreeableness and extraversion predicted prosocial value motivation that, in turn, predicted actual volunteering. Both agreeableness and extraversion suggest a person with social skills that make it easier for someone to network into and then enjoy a volunteering experience. Volunteering is more likely when these personality variables are associated with having prosocial values in the first place.

Personality variables that predict volunteerism can, in theory, help us determine who is most likely to volunteer and how to target our efforts when recruiting volunteers. However, accurately assessing someone's personality in a short period of time is tricky business. Most volunteer organizations do not have the time or resources to provide extensive screening—they are more likely doing everything they can to get *anyone* to volunteer, not just particular personality types. And when we try to quickly assess— or "read"—other people's personalities, we should remember what we discovered in Chapter 5. We tend to be (a) highly confident in our ability to read other people and (b) not very good at it.

Relying on personality as a predictor of volunteerism is interesting but generally has little practical value for organizations that need volunteers. However, it might be more useful in selecting from among those volunteers who might be appropriate at the next level, such as choosing leaders for volunteer groups or even hiring someone and compensating them (paid employment).

Job Hunting

Volunteering to increase your job prospects increases your odds of success—especially for certain people. Volunteering as a path to employment is more likely in a tight job market, when people will volunteer just to get their foot in the door. A study sponsored by the Corporation for National and Community Service (Spera, Ghertner, Nerino, & DiTommaso, 2013) compared data from 2003 through 2012 and found a stable pattern: People who volunteered were about 5% more likely to get hired. Volunteering was especially helpful for people in rural areas or with no education past high school; it seems that volunteering helped level the playing field "for these individuals who typically have a more difficult time finding employment, especially during a recession" (p. 18).

Health Benefits

Volunteering appears to provide significant health benefits. Harris and Thoresen (2005) surveyed more than 7,500 people older than 70 years and discovered that volunteering was associated with a lower risk of mortality. The personal health

Path analysis: A statistical technique that uses relationships among variables to hypothesize causal connections.

benefits seem to produce social and pragmatic benefits as well, including friendships with other volunteers and lower health care costs (see Glass et al., 2004). Powell (2013) advocates for treating the social aspects of aging and volunteerism as a business enterprise that can yield both personal and social benefits.

However, many of these studies also share a familiar methodological problem: *correlation does not imply causation*. Volunteering might be good for our health and longevity, but it is just as reasonable to believe that sick people are less likely to volunteer and more likely to die sooner. Nevertheless, there is a rich literature connecting volunteering to a variety of health benefits, especially for older people (Anderson et al., 2014). These data are convincing because they are based on multiple studies using multiple methods and conducted by independent researchers. Anderson's review of the literature on volunteerism and health reported that:

Some research shows a *positive correlation* between volunteering and health, including longer life (Harris & Thoresen, 2005; Powell, 2013).

> data from *descriptive, cross-sectional, and prospective cohort studies*, along with *randomized controlled trials*, most consistently reveal that volunteering is associated with reduced symptoms of depression, better self-reported health, fewer functional limitations, and lower mortality. (p. 1505)

Life Satisfaction

Psychologists sometimes refer to the idea of "life satisfaction" with other terms: "well-being," "personal fulfillment," "a sense of accomplishment," "self-actualization," and even plain old "happiness." In short, **life satisfaction** is a sense of contentment and gratification with one's path, self-concept, social connections, and direction in life overall. Seeking improved life satisfaction seems to be the most consistent motivation for volunteering.

The importance of life satisfaction in volunteering comes from studies that look at volunteerism at different life stages. Yamashita, Keene, Lu, and Carr (2017) surveyed more than 1,000 volunteers in nonprofit organizations. They found three commonalities across these groups: community service, career advancement, and well-being. However, there was a slightly different emphasis for people at different life stages. Older adults wanted to give something back to their communities; they wanted a sense of generativity and to leave a positive legacy. However, social networking was a stronger motive among early and middle-aged adults. What makes life satisfying tends to be slightly different at different stages of our lives.

A second research team found a similar pattern, but it was expressed in slightly different language. They found that for volunteers, there was a strong statistical path from intrinsic motivation to needs being satisfied through volunteering that, in turn, produced life satisfaction (Kwok, Chui, & Wong, 2013). The end of both studies produced similar results: a sense of well-being and life satisfaction. What makes the combination of these two studies most interesting is that the first study was conducted in Nevada, in the western United States. The second study was conducted in Hong Kong, a densely populated city on the other side of the planet from Nevada. The motivational "pull" that attracts and sustains volunteers in different cultures and at different life stages seems to be the same: seeking and finding greater life satisfaction.

Life satisfaction: A sense of contentment and gratification with one's path, self-concept, social connections, and direction in life overall.

Altruistic Service Versus Overjustification

Chapter 10 explores the complex motives behind prosocial behavior. In volunteerism, psychologists have been most interested in the prosocial behavior directed at local, community-based organizations trying to meet the needs of particular populations. This suggests a human service motivation behind such volunteering—and not just to distant others, but to people in your home community. People tend to volunteer for causes that are dear to their hearts. However, as we learned in the chapter about prosocial behavior, volunteering also allows us to psychologically pat ourselves on the back for being such a "good person."

This research ties volunteerism to the question of whether prosocial behaviors are motived by egoistic values or by altruistic values. Another way to ask this question is to consider whether volunteers have **intrinsic motivation** (behaviors are done without expectation of any external reward, because the reward is something internal such as life satisfaction) or **extrinsic motivation** (behaviors are done because some kind of external reward is expected). On the surface, people who volunteer seem to have intrinsic motivation most of the time; they are giving up time or putting in effort when they aren't being paid or sometimes even thanked for their work.

However, a line of research warns how quickly motivation might change from intrinsic to extrinsic—or how volunteering could switch from altruistic motives to egoistic. When people are doing something for free, simply because they enjoy doing it—and you then start rewarding or compensating them—their motivation might become focused on the external rewards instead. This unfortunate tendency is called the **overjustification effect**. When you pay people to play with fun puzzles, they stop playing when the money stops; when you reward children for playing with markers, they don't want to play anymore when the play turns into work done for a reward (see Boggiano, Harackiewicz, Bessette, & Main, 1985; Deci & Ryan, 1985, 1991; Deci, Reis, Johnston, & Smith, 1977).

Overjustification in volunteers has been found in several studies (see Batson, Coke, Jasnoski, & Hanson, 1978; Batson, Harris, McCaul, Davis, & Schmidt, 1979; Kunda & Schwartz, 1983). One *quasi-experimental* study (Pearce, 1983) compared groups of volunteers in various settings (a student newspaper, poverty relief agency, family planning clinic, and rural fire department) to paid employees at parallel settings. Results showed that compared to their paid counterparts, the volunteers reported (a) higher levels of motivation due to social interactions, (b) greater job satisfaction, (c) less intent to leave the group, and (d) a belief that their work was more praiseworthy and useful. The network of many studies using varied methodologies leads to a fairly convincing but ironic insight. Paying people seems to make many of them less satisfied than they would be if they were doing the same work simply because they thought the work was intrinsically rewarding and worthwhile—a volunteering perspective.

Intrinsic motivation: When behaviors are performed without expectation of any external reward because the reward is something internal, such as life satisfaction.

Extrinsic motivation: When behaviors are performed because some kind of external reward, such as being paid or praised, is expected.

Overjustification effect: Occurs when individuals are rewarded or compensated for completing a task they previously did due to intrinsic motivators, which then changes the individuals' focus to the external reward, limiting or even eliminating their intrinsic motivation.

The Main Ideas

- Volunteerism is engaging in a planned, long-term, prosocial behavior.

- Four variables that are related to likelihood to volunteer are personality (especially agreeableness and extraversion), job hunting, health benefits, and life satisfaction.

- Ironically, providing extrinsic rewards (such as money) for engaging in tasks that people originally volunteered to do makes people's motivation to engage in the task lower. This phenomenon is called overjustification.

- Consider two specific times in the past when you have volunteered to help an organization or group. Do the four motivations listed in this section cover the reasons why you volunteered? If not, what is missing from this list?

- Overjustification has been applied to motivating children to read or do well in school in general. If parents provide rewards such as money or gifts when children get good grades or read, overjustification predicts that the children's intrinsic motivation for these tasks will decrease. Given this research, how should parents motivate their children to read or achieve in school?

HOW DO INTERNSHIPS PROVIDE CAREER GUIDANCE?

LO 2: To describe how internships can influence short-term decision making and long-term career planning.

An **internship** is a supervised work experience that gives students opportunities to reflect on a possible career (see O'Neill, 2010). The internship experience we will discuss is designed for undergraduate students, not for graduate students. While many of the goals overlap, the purposes of an internship for graduate students are to (a) build your skills within your chosen profession (see Kuther & Morgan, 2007), (b) secure practice hours for future certification, and (c) gain practical experience for future career and life decision making. The primary purpose of an undergraduate internship is to test whether what you think you might want to do with your life really is what you want to do with your life.

There are many ways to organize the literature about internships. For example, there are multiple stakeholders such as the student interns, the supervisors, the academic institutions, employers, and the mentors. It also can be organized around the sponsoring disciplines, the job requirements, particular skill sets, and so forth (Maertz, Stoeberl, & Marks, 2014). Our focus is to try to give the information that undergraduate students most need to know.

High-Impact Internships

Internships provide students with many benefits. It's a way to gain on-the-job experience in a short-term, mentored, learning environment. O'Neill (2010), working with

■ TABLE H.1 Benefits of College Internships

Internships can . . .
1. Help different kinds of students at different stages of career and life planning
2. Provide academic guidance about what to study
3. Help students learn about specific jobs and careers they did not know existed
4. Help students learn what it means to develop professional work habits
5. Help students discover what they do not want to do with their careers
6. Clarify what students want to do with their careers and how to get there
7. Help students apply what they have been learning in the classroom
8. Help students develop a personal network of contacts for the future

SOURCE: O'Neill (2010).

Internship: A supervised work experience that gives individuals, especially students, the opportunity to reflect on a possible career in that line of work.

the American Association of Colleges and Universities, is ready to sing the praises of a great internship experience, noting especially that they can serve different purposes for each individual student. To see her list of internship benefits, see Table H.1.

It would be a missed opportunity to think of an internship as an "easy A" or a way to fill out some general credits. The actual experience will vary with each institution and academic department. Still, no matter how it is organized—or even if it is hardly organized at all—an internship can still provide a rare opportunity. It allows you to check out particular career paths at a time of life when you are about to make several highly consequential life decisions. O'Neill (2010) asserts that:

> for those students just beginning to figure out their choice of major and career interests, an internship can help them to become aware of the many different kinds of organizations comprising "the world of work," build early professional experience, and sometimes discover what they *don't* want to do. For those students who are clearer about their career interests and academic pursuits, an internship can help them apply what they are learning in "real world" settings, gain more substantial professional experience, and begin to develop a network of people in fields that interest them. (p. 4)

A high-impact internship represents the ideal internship—how to get the most out of your internship experience. The only thing lacking in the following list would be a job offer leading to a great career. In our experience, about two thirds of internship students are offered a job and—more important—they know whether they want to accept it. A **high-impact internship** includes the following characteristics:

1. Internships are effortful. Students will devote considerable time and effort and invest themselves in the activity of the internship.

2. Internships build relationships. Frequent interactions with the sponsoring professor and the onsite supervisor will help create a spirit of mentorship and support.

3. Internships engage diversity. Exposure to diverse ideas, life stages, circumstances, and people will challenge students in novel ways that push intellectual and emotional growth.

4. Internships provide rich feedback. Both the quantity and quality of feedback from formal and informal sources will create a continuous feedback loop of meaningful experiences, especially if the student is in close proximity to their supervisor.

5. Internships inspire self-reflection. Opportunities for personal growth will be a by-product of reflecting on personal values, beliefs, ethics, and behavioral choices as students come to understand how the work of their internship fits into a larger picture.

Diversify Your Experience

To get the most career guidance out of an internship, you will want to pay attention to the practices of effective internships described above. That way you will have a better sense of whether you really want to devote many years to working in that particular industry. There is a caution, however. Your experience as an intern may not be representative of the entire industry. For example, if you are interested in a career as a school

High-impact internship:
An ideal, mutually beneficial internship. The intern devotes time, effort, and intelligence to the organization. The organization provides authentic mentoring, regular feedback, diverse experiences, and opportunities for self-reflection and growth.

psychologist, then you may want to try to create internship experiences at different schools and serving different age groups.

You want the diversity of experience because the actual work that people do under the job title of "school psychologist" will mean different things in different districts, buildings, and age groups. In one district, you might end up being the superintendent's go-to person for data and writing reports for the Board of Education. In another district, that job title will mean that you spend most of your day as a substance abuse counselor. In a third district, you might be the leader on a student evaluation team or spend most of your time administering tests—and then explaining the meaning of various psychometric tests to parents. As you make career judgments, be cautious about generalizing your experience to an entire industry.

■ TABLE H.2 Data From the American Community Survey Regarding Business-Relevant Jobs

	Overall	Business Majors	Nonbusiness Majors	With Internship Experience	Without Internship Experience
Interview rate (%)	16.6	17	16.2	18.4	16.1
No. of observations	9,396	5,189	4,207	2,335	7,061

An Internship on Your Resume

Having an internship on your resume appears to give you an advantage, at least in terms of being interviewed. Table H.2 displays data that may not be especially dramatic, but they are definitely encouraging for nonbusiness majors, including psychology students (Nunley, Pugh, Romero, & Seals, 2016). Overall, business majors, on average, had a slight edge over nonbusiness majors when applying for a job in business (17% vs. 16.2%). However, this difference was not *statistically significant*. The more interesting finding was that having an internship gave you a bigger edge in the probability of being called for an interview, regardless of your college major. Again, it was not a huge difference, but this time it was *statistically significant* (18.4% vs. 16.1%).

It is important to recognize that your choice of major is not a job title. In fact, these data suggest that for jobs in business, what you major in does not matter very much. Every academic major will serve you well—but only if you take it seriously. Each major will teach you critical thinking, for example, but focused on their particular topic. They all will teach you how to communicate clearly, but with a content emphasis related to their major. They all will expect some minimal level of training in their fields. But even Stanley Milgram never took a psychology course until the summer before he entered graduate school.

Abuse of Interns

For all the wonderful things that an internship can do for your life, you need to be aware that internships are sometimes abused by employers who regard you as free, volunteer labor and have no interest in mentoring you or providing you with a meaningful experience. In short, there is a justified worry that some unpaid internships are really just jobs that people are doing for free instead of a growth experience (see Greenvald, 2016).

The line between volunteering and internships is not always clear, and it gives room for abuse by employers. The problem is especially acute in certain industries where providing free labor has become an informal expectation if you wish to enter the industry. It is a larger problem than you might expect. For example, the debate also involves college athletes who generate significant institutional income for what many consider "slave" wages (see Ontiveros, 2015; Perlin, 2012) and movie studios (see Greenhouse, 2013) where free labor at the start of a career has become an industry standard. Writing for the *Indiana Law Review,* Gessner (2014) has described why the situation is so dicey for interns:

> Internships are incredibly valuable to interns in terms of gaining experience, securing job references, and expanding their professional network. Thus, it is not surprising to learn that intern lawsuits . . . are only recent developments in the legal realm. Interns have been reluctant, for good reason, to risk labeling themselves as a whistleblower within their desired job industry. (p. 1055)

There is a new assertiveness among interns and internship coordinators as stories of abuse invite closer regulations. Gessner (2014) presents the legal issue as revolving around the meaning of an "employee" versus a "trainee" while acknowledging that it still is more complicated than that. But whether you are considered a volunteer, intern, trainee, or employee, you have very little power. Gessner advocates for flexibility in a regulated environment. The problem with too many standardized regulations is that they will be arbitrary across situations and personalities that vary significantly across industries, institutions, and individuals. For example, students seeking internships in social services will confront a vast bureaucracy that is usually composed of many local cultures. One internship in child welfare may have you filing alone in a back room, but another child welfare internship may take you on site visits to families in need and ask you to participate in some group treatment discussions.

In the face of so much diversity of the internship experience, we encourage you to speak candidly with your academic supervisor. For example, at the end of one internship experience, a student confided that he believed that the social service agency where he interned was "billing for bodies" rather than providing services. If someone walked in the door, that social service agency sent to its funders phony evidence that they were providing personal counseling and job assistance. It is probably wise to check out both volunteering and internship opportunities with multiple, independent sources before you make a commitment.

Reevaluate Your Prior Decisions

Here is a tale of two internships.

Anita wanted to become an elementary school teacher. "My parents, aunts, and uncles . . . they're almost all teachers," she told her internship class. She insisted that her internship be in an elementary school. Near the end of the semester, the class gathered to tell their stories. When it was Anita's turn, she bluntly declared, "I hated it. I thought all these little kids were going to hug me and say, 'I love you' and 'thank you, Miss Anita,' but I spent all day wiping their little noses, looking for lost boots, and dealing with crabby, unreasonable parents." An odd question helped Anita focus on alternative careers—but only briefly.

"What course, if any, have you taken that you loved but were surprised by how much you loved it?"

"That's easy," Anita replied. "Anatomy and physiology." She then kept the class spellbound with a beautiful mini-lecture about what it was like to have "magic eyes" that allowed her to see inside the arm as muscles, tendons, and fingers all cooperated in the simple act of throwing a ball. "It's beautiful," she concluded. She could probably go into physical therapy.

"Then why aren't you a biology major?" one of the students asked her.

"Oh," she replied, "I hate science."

Anita was going to graduate in a month, and she had no intention of going back to "boring college" and spending any more money on tuition. Plus, her extended family of teachers had informally arranged to have a teaching job waiting for her. But if Anita is burnt out before she starts her career as a teacher, then what kind of teacher will she be in 20 years? Will she be happy? Will she train yet another generation of girls to "hate science"?

That was a failed internship.

Pamela had a more successful internship, but the ending was still uncertain.

In the first class, Pamela took about 10 minutes to admit that she didn't really want an internship in psychology. "What I really want," she finally admitted, "is to work in the fashion industry." She got lucky; a friend knew a friend who knew a friend at a major fashion magazine. One week later, Pamela had one of the most coveted internships in that industry. Four weeks later, she came back and said, "Fail me for the course. I'm not going back. Those are the ugliest human beings I have ever met. They are. . . ." She went on about their many faults for a while and then repeated. "Go ahead and fail me. I refuse to go back."

She was startled by the reply. "But that's been a successful internship. You want to find out sooner rather than later if a career that you thought you might love is really not the right career for you."

That was a successful internship.

When an internship experience goes well, it forces you to rethink your plans and recalibrate your ambitions. You may have another 50 years of employment in front of you. You want to get started on a path that you like—and sometimes the path will surprise you.

The Main Ideas

- An internship is a supervised work experience that gives students opportunities to reflect on a possible career; a high-impact internship provides an ideal setting.

- Having a diversity of experience with internships is likely to enhance your resume. However, some organizations abuse interns, so be careful when choosing internship experiences.

⚡ CRITICAL THINKING

- Describe your ideal future career, then identify three potential organizations or sponsors of internships that could help you gain experience. Provide contact information for each of those potential sponsors that might actually help you talk with someone there about an internship.

- This section discusses several benefits of internships, but it also touched on at least one possible drawback of internships (being abused by a potential employer). Are there other potential disadvantages to engaging in internships? Find two people who have actually completed internships and interview them about the two best parts of their experience and the two worst parts. If you were to complete an internship, how could you proactively avoid those negative experiences?

Abel, S. M., Krever, E. M., & Alberti, P. W. (1990). Auditory detection, discrimination and speech processing in ageing, noise-sensitive and hearing-impaired listeners. *Scandinavian Audiology, 19*(1), 43–54.

Ackerman, J. (2015). Persuasion by proxy: Vicarious self-control use increases decision compliance. In K. Diehl & C. Yoon (Eds.), *ACR North American advances* (pp. 68–73). Duluth, MN: Association for Consumer Research.

Adhikary, A. K. (1984a). Hunters and gatherers in India: A preliminary appraisal of their structure and transformation. *Journal of the Indian Anthropological Society, 19*(1), 8–16.

Adhikary, A. K. (1984b). *Society and world view of the Birhor: A nomadic hunting and gathering community of Orissa*. Calcutta, India: Anthropological Survey of India.

Adler, A. (1930). Individual psychology. In C. Murchison (Ed.), *Psychologies of 1930* (pp. 395–405). Worcester, MA: Clark University Press.

Adorjan, M., Christensen, T., Kelly, B., & Pawluch, D. (2012). Stockholm syndrome as vernacular resource. *The Sociological Quarterly, 53*(3), 454–474.

Adorno, T. W., Frenkel-Brunswik, D. J., Levinson, D. J., & Sanford, R. N. (1950). *The authoritarian personality*. New York, NY: Harper & Row.

Aggarwal, P., & O'Brien, C. L. (2008). Social loafing on group projects: Structural antecedents and effect on student satisfaction. *Journal of Marketing Education, 30*(3), 255–264.

Agnew, C. R., Loving. T. J., Le, B., & Goodfriend, W. (2004). Thinking close: Measuring relational closeness as perceived self-other inclusion. In D. Mashek & A. Aron (Eds.), *Handbook of closeness and intimacy* (pp. 103–115). Mahwah, NJ: Lawrence Erlbaum.

Agnew, C. R., Van Lange, P. M., Rusbult, C. E., & Langston, C. A. (1998). Cognitive interdependence: Commitment and the mental representation of close relationships. *Journal of Personality and Social Psychology, 74*(4), 939–954.

Agthe, M., Spörrle, M., & Maner, J. K. (2010). Don't hate me because I'm beautiful: Anti-attractiveness bias in organizational evaluation and decision making. *Journal of Experimental Social Psychology, 46*(6), 1151–1154.

Aguinis, H., Pierce, C. A., & Quigley, B. M. (1995). Enhancing the validity of self-reported alcohol and marijuana consumption using a bogus pipeline procedure: A meta-analytic review. *Basic and Applied Social Psychology, 16*(4), 515–527.

Ainsworth, M. S. (1979). Infant–mother attachment. *American Psychologist, 34*(10), 932–937.

Aitchison, J. (2003). *Words in the mind: An introduction to the mental lexicon*. Oxford, UK: Blackwell.

Ajzen, I. (1991). The theory of planned behavior. *Organizational Behavior and Human Decision Processes, 50*(2), 179–211.

Ajzen, I., & Fishbein, M. (1980). *Understanding attitudes and predicting social behavior*. Upper Saddle River, NJ: Prentice Hall.

Alain, C., McDonald, K. L., Ostroff, J. M., & Schneider, B. (2004). Aging: A switch from automatic to controlled processing of sounds? *Psychology and Aging, 19*(1), 125–133.

Albert, R. S., & Runco, M. A. (1999). A history of research on creativity. *Handbook of Creativity, 2,* 16–31.

Alexander, M. G., & Fisher, T. D. (2003). Truth and consequences: Using the bogus pipeline to examine sex differences in self-reported sexuality. *Journal of Sex Research, 40*(1), 27–35.

Alicke, M. D., LoSchiavo, F. M., Zerbst, J., & Zhang, S. (1997). The person who out performs me is a genius: Maintaining perceived competence in upward social comparison. *Journal of Personality and Social Psychology, 73*(4), 781–789.

Al-khatib, B. A. (2012). The effect of using brainstorming strategy in developing creative problem solving skills among female students in Princess Alia University College. *American International Journal of Contemporary Research, 2*(10), 29–38.

Allee, W. C., Collias, N. E., & Lutherman, C. Z. (1939). Modification of the social order in flocks of hens by the injection of testosterone propionate. *Physiological Zoology, 12*(4), 412–440.

Allport, F. H. (1920). The influence of the group upon association and thought. *Journal of Experimental Psychology, 3*(3), 159–182.

Allport, G. W. (1935). Attitudes. In C. Murchison (Ed.), *Handbook of social psychology* (Vol. 2, pp. 798–844). Worcester, MA: Clark University Press.

Allport, G. W. (1937). *Personality: A psychological interpretation*. New York, NY: Holt.

Allport, G. W. (1954). *The nature of prejudice*. New York, NY: Addison.

Allport, G. W. (1966). Traits revisited. *American Psychologist, 21*(1), 1–10.

Allport, G. W. (1979). *The nature of prejudice*. New York, NY: Basic Books.

Allport, G. W., & Vernon, P. E. (1933). *Studies in expressive movement*. New York, NY: Haffner.

Allred, K. D., & Smith, T. W. (1989). The hardy personality: Cognitive and physiological responses to evaluative threat. *Journal of Personality and Social Psychology, 56*(2), 257–266.

Altemeyer, B. (1981). *Right-wing authoritarianism*. Winnipeg, Canada: University of Manitoba Press.

Altemeyer, B. (1990). Altemeyer replies. *Canadian Psychology, 31*(4), 393–396.

Altemeyer, B. (1994). Reducing prejudice in right-wing authoritarians. In M. P. Zanna & J. M. Olson (Eds.), *The psychology of prejudice: The Ontario symposium* (Vol. 7, pp. 131–148). Hillsdale, NJ: Lawrence Erlbaum.

Alter, A. L., Oppenheimer, D. M., Epley, N., & Eyre, R. N. (2007). Overcoming intuition: Metacognitive difficulty activates analytic reasoning. *Journal of Experimental Psychology, 136*(4), 569–576.

Alter, A. L., Oppenheimer, D. M., & Zemla, J. C. (2010). Missing the trees for the forest: A construal level account of the illusion of explanatory depth. *Journal of Personality and Social Psychology, 99*(3), 436–451.

Amato, P. R. (1983). Helping behavior in urban and rural environments: Field studies based on a taxonomic organization of helping episodes. *Journal of Personality and Social Psychology, 45*(3), 571–586.

Ambady, N., Hallahan, M., & Conner, B. (1999). Accuracy of judgments of sexual orientation from thin slices of behavior. *Journal of Personality and Social Psychology, 77*(3), 538–547.

Ambady, N., & Rosenthal, R. (1993). Half a minute: Predicting teacher evaluations from thin slices of nonverbal behavior and physical attractiveness. *Journal of Personality and Social Psychology, 64*(3), 431–441.

American Psychological Association. (2017). *Sport psychology.* Retrieved from http://www.apa.org/ed/graduate/specialize/sports.aspx

Amir, T. (1984). The Asch conformity effect: A study in Kuwait. *Social Behavior and Personality, 12*(2), 187–190.

Amir, Y. (1976). The role of intergroup contact in change of prejudice and race relations. In P. A. Katz (Ed.), *Towards the elimination of racism* (pp. 245–280). New York, NY: Pergamon.

Andersen, S. M., Lepper, M. R., & Ross, L. (1980). Perseverance of social theories: The role of explanation in the persistence of discredited information. *Journal of Personality and Social Psychology, 39*(6), 1037–1049.

Anderson, C. A. (1987). Temperature and aggression: Effects on quarterly, yearly, and city rates of violent and nonviolent crime. *Journal of Personality and Social Psychology, 52*(6), 1161–1173.

Anderson, C. A. (1989). Temperature and aggression: Ubiquitous effects of heat on occurrence of human violence. *Psychological Bulletin, 106*(1), 74–96.

Anderson, C. A., Shibuya, A., Ihori, N., Swing, E. L., Bushman, B. J., Sakamoto, A., Rothstein, H. R., & Saleem, M. (2010). Violent video game effects on aggression, empathy, and prosocial behavior in Eastern and Western countries: A meta-analytic review. *Psychological Bulletin, 136*(2), 151–173.

Anderson, J. R. (1984). The development of self-recognition: A review. *Developmental Psychobiology, 17*(1), 35–49.

Anderson, K. B., Cooper, H., & Okamura, L. (1997). Individual differences and attitudes toward rape: A meta-analytic review. *Personality and Social Psychology Bulletin, 23*(3), 295–315.

Anderson, N. D., Damianakis, T., Kröger, E., Wagner, L. M., Dawson, D. R., Binns, M. A., . . . Cook, S. L. (2014). The benefits associated with volunteering among seniors: A critical review and recommendations for future research. *Psychological Bulletin, 140*(6), 1505–1533.

Anderson-Hanley, C., Snyder, A. L., Nimon, J. P., & Arciero, P. J. (2011). Social facilitation in virtual reality-enhanced exercise: Competitiveness moderates exercise effort of older adults. *Clinical Interventions in Aging, 6,* 275–280.

Andrews, B., Brewin, C. R., Rose, S., & Kirk, M. (2000). Predicting PTSD symptoms in victims of violent crime: The role of shame, anger, and childhood abuse. *Journal of Abnormal Psychology, 109*(1), 69–73.

Angell, J. R. (1909). The influence of Darwin on psychology. *Psychological Review, 16*(3), 152–169.

Arad, A., Tolmach, M., & Ziskin, L. (Producers), & Webb, M. (Director). (2012). *The amazing Spider-Man* [Motion picture]. United States: Marvel Entertainment.

Archer, J. (2004). Sex differences in aggression in real-world settings: A meta-analytic review. *Review of General Psychology, 8*(4), 291–322.

Archer, J. (2006). Cross-cultural differences in physical aggression between partners: A social-role analysis. *Personality and Social Psychology Review, 10*(2), 133–153.

Archer, J., & Birring, S. S., & Wu, F. C. (1998). The association between testosterone and aggression among young men: Empirical findings and a meta-analysis. *Aggressive Behavior, 24*(6), 411–420.

Ariely, D. (2008). *Predictably irrational: The hidden forces that shape our decisions.* New York, NY: HarperCollins.

Armstrong, K. (2000). *The battle for God: Fundamentalism in Judaism, Christianity, and Islam.* New York, NY: Knopf.

Arnocky, S., & Vaillancourt, T. (2014). Sex differences in response to victimization by an intimate partner: More stigmatization and less help-seeking among males. *Journal of Aggression, Maltreatment & Trauma, 23*(7), 705–724.

Arnold, D. L., Jackson, R. W., Waterfield, N. R., & Mansfield, J. W. (2007). Evolution of microbial virulence: The benefits of stress. *TRENDS in Genetics, 23*(6), 293–300.

Aron, A., Aron, E. N., & Norman, C. (2001). Self-expansion model of motivation and cognition in close relationships and beyond. In G. Fletcher & M. Clark (Eds.), *Blackwell handbook of social psychology: Interpersonal processes* (pp. 478–501). Hoboken, NJ: Blackwell.

Aron, A., Aron, E. N., & Smollan, D. (1992). Inclusion of Other in the Self Scale and the structure of interpersonal closeness. *Journal of Personality and Social Psychology, 63*(4), 596–612.

Aron, E. N., & Aron, A. (1996). Love and the expansion of the self: The state of the model. *Personal Relationships, 3*(1), 45–58.

Aronson, E. (1999). Dissonance, hypocrisy, and the self-concept. In E. Harmon-Jones J. Mills (Eds.), *Cognitive dissonance: Progress on a pivotal theory in social psychology* (pp. 103–126). Washington, DC: American Psychological Association.

Aronson, E., & Mills, J. (1959). The effect of severity of initiation on liking for a group. *The Journal of Abnormal and Social Psychology, 59*(2), 177–181.

Arora, M. (2017, May 22). From filthy to fabulous: Mumbai beach undergoes dramatic makeover. *CNN.* Retrieved from http://www.cnn.com/2017/05/22/asia/mumbai-beach-dramatic-makeover/index.html

Arriaga, X. B. (2002). Joking violence among highly committed individuals. *Journal of Interpersonal Violence, 17*(6), 591–610.

Arriaga, X. B., Capezza, N. M., Goodfriend, W., Rayl, E. S., & Sands, K. J. (2013). Individual well-being and relationship maintenance at odds: The unexpected perils of maintaining a relationship with an aggressive partner. *Social Psychological and Personality Science, 4*(6), 676–684.

Arthur, N., & Lee, C. (2008). Young Australian women's aspirations for work, marriage and family: 'I guess I am just another person who wants it all'. *Journal of Health Psychology, 13*(5), 589–596.

Asch, S. E. (1946). Forming impressions of personality. *Journal of Abnormal and Social Psychology, 41*(3), 258–290.

Asch, S. E. (1951). Effects of group pressure upon the modification and distortion of judgments. In H. Guetzkow (Ed.), *Groups, leadership and men; research in human relations* (pp. 177–190). Oxford, UK: Carnegie Press.

Asch, S. E. (1952). Effects of group pressure on the modification and distortion of judgments. In G. E. Swanson, T. M. Newcomb, & E. L. Hartley (Eds.), *Readings in social psychology* (2nd ed.). New York, NY: Holt.

Asch, S. E. (1955). Opinions and social pressure. *Scientific American, 193*(5), 31–35.

Asch, S. E. (1956). Studies of independence and conformity: I. A minority of one against a unanimous majority. *Psychological Monographs: General and Applied, 70*(9, Whole No. 416), 1–70.

Asch, S. E. (1957). An experimental investigation of group influence. In *Symposium on preventive and social psychiatry* (pp. 15–17). Washington, DC: Walter Reed Army Institute of Research.

Ascher, W., & Brown, S. R. (2014). Technologies of mediation: An assessment of methods for the mediation of international conflicts. *Contributions of Technology to International Conflict Resolution, 1987,* 95–103.

Aspinwall, L. G., & Tedeschi, R. G. (2010). The value of positive psychology for health psychology: Progress and pitfalls in examining the relation of positive phenomena to health. *Annals of Behavioral Medicine, 39*(1), 4–15.

Association for Applied Sport Psychology. (2017). *Home.* Retrieved from http://www.appliedsportpsych.org/

Attanasio, P., McGraw, P., McGraw, J., Falvey, J., Frank, D., Goffman, M., . . . Garcia, R. (Producers). (2016). *Bull* [Television series]. United States: CBS Television Distribution.

Avnet, J., & Kerner, J. (Producers), & Herek, S. (Director). (1992). *The mighty ducks* [Motion picture]. USA: Walt Disney Pictures, Avent-Kerner Productions, The Kerner Entertainment Company, & Buena Vista Pictures.

Babad, E., Avni-Babad, D., & Rosenthal, R. (2004). Prediction of students' evaluations from brief instances of professors' nonverbal behavior in defined instructional situations. *Social Psychology of Education, 7*(1), 3–33.

Bachman, J. G., & O'Malley, P. M. (1986). Self-concepts, self-esteem, and educational experiences: The frog pond revisited (again). *Journal of Personality and Social Psychology, 50*(1), 35–46.

Bakan, D. (1966). *The duality of human existence: An essay on psychology and religion.* Oxford, UK: Rand McNally.

Baker, S. M., & Petty, R. E. (1994). Majority and minority influence: Source-position imbalance as a determinant of message scrutiny. *Journal of Personality and Social Psychology, 67*(1), 5–19.

Bandura, A. (1977). *Social learning theory.* Oxford, UK: Prentice-Hall.

Bandura, A. (1986). *Social foundations of thought and action: A social cognitive theory.* Englewood Cliffs, NY: Prentice-Hall.

Bandura, A., Ross, D., & Ross, S. A. (1961). Transmission of aggression through imitation of aggressive models. *Journal of Abnormal and Social Psychology, 63*(3), 575–582.

Bandura, A., Ross, D., & Ross, S. A. (1963a). Imitation of film-mediated aggressive models. *Journal of Abnormal and Social Psychology, 66*(1), 3–11.

Bandura, A., Ross, D., & Ross, S. A. (1963b). Vicarious reinforcement and imitative learning. *Journal of Abnormal and Social Psychology, 67*(6), 601–607.

Bargh, J. A. (1997). The automaticity of everyday life. In R. S. Wyer Jr. (Ed.), *Advances in social cognition* (Vol. 10, pp. 1–61). Mahwah, NJ: Lawrence Erlbaum.

Bargh, J. A., & Chartrand, T. L. (1999). The unbearable automaticity of being. *American Psychologist, 54*(7), 462–479.

Bargh, J. A., Chen, M., & Burrows, L. (1996). Automaticity of social behavior: Direct effect of trait construct and stereotype activation. *Journal of Personality and Social Psychology, 71*(2), 230–244.

Bargh, J. A., & McKenna, K. Y. A. (2004). The Internet and social life. *Annual Review of Psychology, 55,* 573–590.

Bargh, J. A., & Williams, E. L. (2006). The automaticity of social life. *Current Directions in Psychological Science, 15*(1), 1–4.

"Barkley is arrested after Orlando bar fight." (1997, October 27). *The Washington Post.* Retrieved from https://www.washingtonpost.com/archive/sports/1997/10/27/barkley-is-arrested-after-orlando-bar-fight/27787d5d-d345-4641-b019-f8e7952a75f8/?utm_term=.88be893efcce

Barnes, C. D., Brown, R. P., & Osterman, L. L. (2012). Don't tread on me: Masculine honor ideology in the U.S. and militant responses to terrorism. *Personality and Social Psychology Bulletin, 38*(8), 1018–1029.

Barnett, J., & Coulson, M. (2010). Virtually real: A psychological perspective on massively multiplayer online games. *Review of General Psychology, 14*(2), 167–179.

Barnett, O. W., Miller-Perrin, C. L., & Perrin, R. D. (1997). *Family violence across the lifespan: An introduction.* Thousand Oaks, CA: Sage.

Baron, R. A. (1972). Aggression as a function of ambient temperature and prior anger arousal. *Journal of Personality and Social Psychology, 21*(2), 183–189.

Baroni, C., & Orombelli, G. (1996). The Alpine "Iceman" and Holocene climactic change. *Quaternary Research, 46*(1), 78–83.

Barr, J., Malbran, P., Berko, A., Lockett, A., & Kostura, J. (2012). Hazing trend involves horrifying violation of young athletes. *ESPN.* Retrieved from http://www.espn.com/espn/feature/story/_/id/17507010/otl-investigation-trend-sodomy-hazing

Barrett, D. W., Wosinska, W., Butner, J., Petrova, P., Gornik-Durose, M., & Cialdini, R. B. (2004). Individual differences in the motivation to comply across cultures: The impact of social obligation. *Personality and Individual Differences, 37*(1), 19–31.

Barsky, A. (2014). Response to article on 'Abused mothers' safety concerns and court mediators' custody recommendations. *Journal of Family Violence, 29*(4), 357–358.

Bartholomew, K., & Horowitz, L. M. (1991). Attachment styles among young adults: A test of a four-category model. *Journal of Personality and Social Psychology, 61*(2), 226–244.

Bartholow, B. D., & Heinz, A. (2006). Alcohol and aggression without consumption: Alcohol cues, aggressive thoughts, and hostile perception bias. *Psychological Science, 17*(1), 30–37.

Bartlett, F. C. (1932). *Remembering.* Cambridge, UK: Cambridge University Press.

Basner, M., Babisch, W., Davis, A., Brink, M., Clark, C., Janssen, S., & Stansfeld, S. (2014). Auditory and non-auditory effects of noise on health. *The Lancet, 383*(9925), 1325–1332.

Bass, B. M. (1998). *Transformational leadership: Industrial, military, and educational impact.* Mahwah, NJ: Lawrence Erlbaum.

Bassili, J. N. (2003). The minority slowness effect: Subtle inhibitions in the expression of views not shared by others. *Journal of Personality and Social Psychology, 84*(2), 261–276.

Batool, S., & Malik, N. I. (2010). Role of attitude similarity and proximity in interpersonal attraction among friends. *International Journal of Innovation, Management and Technology, 1*(2), 142–146.

Batson, C. D. (1990). How social an animal? The human capacity for caring. *American Psychologist, 45*(3), 336–346.

Batson, C. D. (1991). *The altruism question: Toward a social-psychological answer.* Hillsdale, NJ: Lawrence Erlbaum.

Batson, C. D. (1998). Altruism and prosocial behavior. In D. T. Gilbert, S. T. Fiske, & G. Lindzey (Eds.), *The handbook of social psychology* (Vols. 1–2, 4th ed., pp. 282–316). New York, NY: McGraw-Hill.

Batson, C. D., Bolen, M. H., Cross, J. A., & Neuringer-Benefiel, H. E. (1986). Where is the altruism in the altruistic personality? *Journal of Personality and Social Psychology, 50*(1), 212–220.

Batson, C. D., Coke, J. S., Jasnoski, M. L., & Hanson, M. (1978). Buying kindness: Effect of an extrinsic incentive for helping on perceived altruism. *Personality and Social Psychology Bulletin, 4*(1), 86–91.

Batson, C. D., Duncan, B. D., Ackerman, P., Buckley, T., & Birch, K. (1981). Is empathic emotion a source of altruistic motivation? *Journal of Personality and Social Psychology, 40*(2), 290–302.

Batson, C. D., & Gray, R. A. (1981). Religious orientation and helping behavior: Responding to one's own or the victim's needs? *Journal of Personality and Social Psychology, 40*(3), 511–520.

Batson, C. D., Harris, A. C., McCaul, K. D., Davis, M., & Schmidt, T. (1979). Compassion or compliance: Alternative dispositional attributions for one's helping behavior. *Social Psychology Quarterly, 42*(4), 405–409.

Batson, C. D., Kobrynowicz, D., Dinerstein, J. L., Kampf, H. C., & Wilson, A. D. (1997). In a very different voice: Unmasking moral hypocrisy. *Journal of Personality and Social Psychology, 72*(6), 1335–1348.

Batson, C. D., Naifeh, S. J., & Pete, S. (1978). Social desirability, religious orientation, and racial prejudice. *Journal for the Scientific Study of Religion, 17*(1), 31–41.

Batson, C. D., Schoenrade, P., & Ventis, W. L. (1993). *Religion and the individual: A social-psychological perspective.* New York, NY: Oxford University Press.

Batson, C. D., Thompson, E. R., & Chen, H. (2002). Moral hypocrisy: Addressing some alternatives. *Journal of Personality and Social Psychology, 83*(2), 330–339.

Baumeister, R. F. (1986). *Identity: Cultural change and the struggle for the self.* Oxford, UK: Oxford University Press.

Baumeister, R. F. (1989). The optimal measure of illusion. *Journal of Social and Clinical Psychology, 8*(2), 176–189.

Baumeister, R. F. (1998). The self. In D. T. Gilbert, S. T. Fiske, & G. Lindzey (Eds.), *Handbook of social psychology* (Vol. 2, 4th ed., pp. 680–740). New York, NY: McGraw-Hill.

Baumeister, R. F., Campbell, J. D., Krueger, J. I., & Vohs, K. D. (2003). Does high self-esteem cause better performance, interpersonal success, happiness, or healthier lifestyles? *Psychological Science in the Public Interest, 4*(1), 1–44.

Baumeister, R. F., & Leary, M. R. (1995). The need to belong: Desire for interpersonal attachments as a fundamental human motivation. *Psychological Bulletin, 117*(3), 497–529.

Baumeister, R. F., Smart, L., & Boden, J. M. (1996). Relation of threatened egotism to violence and aggression: The dark side of high self-esteem. *Psychological Review, 103*(1), 5–33.

Baumrind, D. (1964). Some thoughts on ethics of research: After reading Milgram's "behavioral study of obedience." *American Psychologist, 19*(6), 421–423.

Baxter, L. A., & West, L. (2003). Couple perceptions of their similarities and differences: A dialectical perspective. *Journal of Social and Personal Relationships, 20*(4), 491–514.

BBC News. (2008). Hindus opposing EU swastika ban. *BBC News,* International version. Retrieved from http://news.bbc.co.uk/2/hi/europe/6269627.stm

Becker, C. B., Bull, S., Schaumberg, K., Cauble, A., & Franco, A. (2008). Effectiveness of peer-led eating disorders prevention: A replication trial. *Journal of Consulting and Clinical Psychology, 76*(2), 347–354.

Becker, E. (1973). *The denial of death.* New York, NY: Academic Press.

Beckerman, S., & Feitschans, B. (Producers), & Milius, J. (Director). (1984). *Red dawn* [Motion picture]. USA: United Artists, Valkyrie Films, & MGM/UA Entertainment Company.

Beer, J. S., John, O. P., Scabini, D., & Knight, R. T. (2006). Orbitofrontal cortex and social behavior: Integrating self-monitoring and emotion-cognition interactions. *Journal of Cognitive Neuroscience, 18*(6), 871–879.

Begany, J. J., & Milburn, M. A. (2002). Psychological predictors of sexual harassment: Authoritarianism, hostile sexism, and rape myths. *Psychology of Men & Masculinity, 3*(2), 119–126.

Begue, L. (2005). Self-esteem regulation in threatening social comparison: The roles of belief in a just world and self-efficacy. *Social Behavior and Personality, 33*(1), 69–76.

Belavkin, R. V. (2001). The role of emotion in problem solving. In *Proceedings of the AISB'01: Symposium on emotion, cognition and affective computing* (pp. 49–57). Heslington, England: AISB Press.

Bellisario, D. P., Glasberg, G., Brennan, S., Johnson, C. F., Horowitz, M., Harmon, M., . . . Drewe, A. C. (Producers). (2003–). *NCIS* [Television series]. United States: Bellisarius Productions.

Bellotti, F., Kapralos, B., Lee, K., Moreno-Ger, P., & Berta, R. (2013). Assessment in and of serious games: An overview. *Advances in Human-Computer Interaction, 2013*(2), 1–11.

Belz, M., Pyritz, L. W., & Boos, M. (2013). Spontaneous flocking in human groups. *Behavioural Processes, 92,* 6–14.

Bem, D. J. (1967). Self-perception: An alternative interpretation of cognitive dissonance phenomena. *Psychological Review, 74*(3), 183–200.

Bem, D. J. (1972). Self-perception theory. In L. Berkowitz (Ed.), *Advances in experimental social psychology* (Vol. 6, pp. 1–62). New York, NY: Academic Press.

Bem, D. J., & McConnell, H. K. (1970). Testing the self-perception explanation of dissonance phenomena: On the salience of premanipulation attitudes. *Journal of Personality and Social Psychology, 14*(1), 23–31.

Benjamin, L. T., & Crouse, E. M. (2002). The American Psychological Association's response to *Brown v. Board of Education:* The case of Kenneth B. Clark. *American Psychologist, 57*(1), 38–50.

Belo, J. (1935). The Balinese temper. *Journal of Personality, 4*(2), 120–146.

Bennett, J. W. (1967). *Hutterian brethren: The agricultural economy and social organization of a communal people.* Stanford, CA: Stanford University Press.

Berg, J., Komarnicki, T., & Robertson, S. (Producers), & Favreau, J. (Director). (2003). *Elf* [Motion picture]. United States: New Line Cinema.

Berkowitz, L. T. (1983). Aversively stimulated aggression: Some parallels and differences in research with animals and humans. *American Psychologist, 38*(11), 1135–1144.

Berkowitz, L. T. (1988). Frustrations, appraisals, and aversively stimulated aggression. *Aggressive Behavior, 14*(1), 3–11.

Berkowitz, L. T. (1989). Frustration-aggression hypothesis: Examination and reformulation. *Psychological Bulletin, 106*(1), 59–73.

Berkowitz, L. T., Cochran, S. T., & Embree, M. C. (1981). Physical pain and the goal of aversively stimulated aggression. *Journal of Personality and Social Psychology, 40*(4), 687–700.

Berkowitz, L. T., & LePage, A. (1967). Weapons as aggression-eliciting stimuli. *Journal of Personality and Social Psychology, 7*(2), 202–207.

Bernstein, D. M., Erdfelder, E., Meltzoff, A. N., Peria, W., & Loftus, G. R. (2011). Hindsight bias from 3 to 95 years of age. *Journal of Experimental Psychology: Learning, Memory, and Cognition, 37*(2), 378–391.

Bernstein, M. J., Sacco, D. F., Brown, C. M., Young, S. G., & Claypool, H. M. (2010). A preference for genuine smiles following social exclusion. *Journal of Experimental Social Psychology, 46*(1), 196–199.

Berry, D. S., Jones, G. M., & Kuczaj, S. A. (2000). Differing states of mind: Regional affiliation, personality judgement, and self-view. *Basic and Applied Social Psychology, 22*(1), 43–56.

Berry, J. W. (1967). Independence and conformity in subsistence-level societies. *Journal of Personality and Social Psychology, 7*(4, Pt. 1), 415–418.

Berscheid, E., & Regan, P. C. (2005). *The psychology of interpersonal relationships.* Upper Saddle River, NJ: Pearson Prentice Hall.

Betsch, C., Bohm, R., & Korn, L. (2013). Inviting free-riders or appealing to prosocial behavior? Game-theoretical reflections on communicating herd immunity in vaccine advocacy. *Health Psychology, 32*(9), 978–985.

Bettelheim, B. (1943). Individual and mass behavior in extreme situations. *Journal of Abnormal and Social Psychology, 38*(4), 417–452.

Bhattacharyya, A. (1953). An account of the Birhor of Palamau. *Bulletin of the Department of Anthropology (India), 2,* 1–16.

Bhopal, K. (2011). 'Education makes you have more say in the way your life goes': Indian women and arranged marriages in the United Kingdom. *British Journal of Sociology of Education, 32*(3), 431–447.

Bianchi, A., & Phillips, J. G. (2005). Psychological predictors of problem mobile phone use. *CyberPsychology & Behavior, 8*(1), 39–51.

Bierhoff, H. W., Klein, R., & Kramp, P. (2006). Evidence for the altruistic personality from data on accident research. *Journal of Personality, 59*(2), 263–280. (Original work published in 1991).

Bilewicz, M., & Krzeminski, I. (2010). Anti-semitism in Poland and Ukraine: The belief in Jewish control as a mechanism of scapegoating. *International Journal of Conflict and Violence, 4*(2), 235–243.

Billig, M., & Tajfel, H. (1973). Social categorization and similarity in intergroup behavior. *European Journal of Social Psychology, 3*(1), 27–52.

Binder, J., Zagefka, H., Brown, R., Funke, F., Kessler, T., Mummendey, A., . . . Leyens, J. (2009). Does contact reduce prejudice or does prejudice reduce contact? A longitudinal test of the contact hypothesis among majority and minority groups in three European countries. *Journal of Personality and Social Psychology, 96*(4), 843–856.

The biology of beauty. (1996, June 2). Retrieved from http://www.newsweek.com/biology-beauty-178836

Biringer, F., Anderson, J. R., & Strubel, D. (1988). Self-recognition in senile dementia. *Experimental Aging Research, 14*(4), 177–180.

Birney, R. C., Burdick, H., & Teevan, R. C. (1969). *Fear of failure.* New York, NY: Van Nostrand-Reinhold.

Bisson, M. A., & Levine, T. R. (2009). Negotiating a friends with benefits relationship. *Archives of Sexual Behavior, 38*(1), 66–73.

Blair, K. L. (2016, November 10). A 'basket of deplorables'? A new study finds that Trump supporters are more likely to be Islamaphobic, racist, transphobic and homophobic. Retrieved from http://blogs.lse.ac.uk/usappblog/2016/10/10/a-basket-of-deplorables-a-new-study-finds-that-trump-supporters-are-more-likely-to-be-islamophobic-racist-transphobic-and-homophobic

Blanc, A. K. (2001). The effect of power in sexual relationships on sexual and reproductive health: An examination of the evidence. *Studies in Family Planning, 32*(3), 189–213.

Blanck, P. D., Rosenthal, R., Hart, A. J., & Bernieri, F. (1990). The measure of the judge: An empirically-based framework for exploring trial judges' behavior. *Iowa Law Review, 75,* 653–684.

Blanton, H., Jaccard, J., Klick, J., Mellers, B., Mitchell, G., & Tetlock, P. E. (2009). Strong claims and weak evidence: Reassessing the predictive validity of the IAT. *Journal of Applied Psychology, 94*(3), 567–582.

Blass, T. (2004). *The man who shocked the world.* New York, NY: Basic Books.

Blomqvist, J. (2007). Self-change from alcohol and drug abuse: Often-cited classics. In H. Klingemann & L. C. Sobell (Eds.), *Promoting self-change from addictive behaviors: Practical implications for policy, prevention, and treatment* (pp. 31–57). New York, NY: Springer.

Blood, R. J. (1967). *Love match and arranged marriage: A Tokyo-Detroit comparison.* New York, NY: Free Press.

Boals, A., & Schuler, K. L. (2017). Reducing reports of illusory posttraumatic growth: A revised version of the Stress-Related Growth Scale (SRGS-R). *Psychological Trauma: Theory, Research, Practice, and Policy.* Advance online publication.

Boehler, M. L., Rogers, D. A., Schwind, C. J., Mayforth, R., Quin, J., Williams, R. G., & Dunnington, G. (2006). An investigation of medical student reactions to feedback: A randomised controlled trial. *Medical Education, 40*(8), 746–749.

Boggiano, A. K., Harackiewicz, J. M., Bessette, J. M., & Main, D. S. (1985). Increasing children's interest through performance-contingent reward. *Social Cognition, 3*(4), 400–411.

Bologna, S. M., & Camp, C. J. (1997). Covert versus overt self-recognition in late stage Alzheimer's disease. *Journal of the International Neuropsychological Society, 3*(2), 195–198.

Bond, C. F., & Titus, L. J. (1983). Social facilitation: A meta-analysis of 241 studies. *Psychological Bulletin, 94*(2), 265–292.

Bond, R., & Smith, P. B. (1996). Culture and conformity: A meta-analysis of studies using Asch's (1952b, 1956) line judgment task. *Psychological Bulletin, 119*(1), 111–137.

Boninger, D. S., Gleicher, F., & Strathman, A. (1994). Counterfactual thinking: From what might have been to what may be. *Journal of Personality and Social Psychology, 67*(2), 297–307.

Bonta, B. D. (1997). Cooperation and competition in peaceful societies. *Psychological Bulletin, 121*(2), 299–320.

Bontempo, R., Lobel, S., & Triandis, H. (1990). Compliance and value internalization in Brazil and the U.S.: Effects of allocentrism and anonymity. *Journal of Cross-Cultural Psychology, 21*(2), 200–213.

Book, A. S., Starzyk, K. B., & Quinsey, V. L. (2001). The relationship between testosterone and aggression: A meta-analysis. *Aggression and Violent Behavior, 6*(6), 579–599.

Bosson, J. K., Swann, W. B. Jr., & Pennebaker, J. W. (2000). Stalking the perfect measure of implicit self-esteem: The blind men and the elephant revisited? *Journal of Personality and Social Psychology, 79*(4), 631–643.

Boulette, T. R., & Andersen, S. M. (1986). "Mind control" and the battering of women. *Cultic Studies Journal, 3*(1), 25–35.

Bouts, P., Spears, R., & van der Pligt, J. (1992). Counterfactual processing and the correspondence between events and outcomes: Normality versus value. *European Journal of Social Psychology, 22*(4), 387–396.

Bowlby, J. (1958). The nature of the child's tie to his mother. *The International Journal of Psychoanalysis, 39,* 350–373.

Bowlby, J. (1982). Attachment and loss: Retrospect and prospect. *American Journal of Orthopsychiatry, 52*(4), 664–678.

Bowlby, J. (1988). Defensive processes in response to stressful separation in early life. In E. J. Anthony & C. Chiland (Eds.), *The child in his family, Vol. 8: Perilous development: Child raising and identity formation under stress* (pp. 23–30). Oxford, UK: John Wiley.

Bramel, D., & Friend, R. (1981). Hawthorne, the myth of the docile worker, and class bias in psychology. *American Psychologist, 36*(8), 867–878.

Brandstätter, E. (2000). Comparison based satisfaction: Contrast and empathy. *European Journal of Social Psychology, 30*(5), 673–703.

Brannigan, A. (2013). Stanley Milgram's obedience experiments: A report card 50 years later. *Society, 50*(6), 623–628.

Brannigan, A., Nicholson, I. A. M., & Cherry, F. (2015). Introduction to the special issue: Unplugging the Milgram machine. *Theory & Psychology, 25*(5), 551–563.

Brannon, L., Feist, J., & Updegraff, J. A. (2013). *Health psychology: An introduction to behavior and health.* Boston, MA: Cengage Learning.

Brase, G. L., Adair, L., & Monk, K. (2014). Explaining sex differences in reactions to relationship infidelities: Comparisons of the roles of sex, gender, beliefs, attachment, and sociosexual orientation. *Evolutionary Psychology, 12*(1), 73–96.

Braun, M. F., & Bryan, A. (2006). Female waist-to-hip and male waist-to-shoulder ratios as determinants of romantic partner desirability. *Journal of Social and Personal Relationships, 23*(5), 805–819.

Brennan, K. A., Clark, C. L., & Shaver, P. R. (1998). Self-report measurement of adult attachment: An integrative overview. In J. A. Simpson & W. S. Rholes (Eds.), *Attachment theory and close relationships* (pp. 46–76). New York, NY: Guilford.

Brewer, M. B. (1991). The social self: On being the same and different at the same time. *Personality and Social Psychology Bulletin, 17*(5), 475–482.

Briggs, J. L. (1994). "Why don't you kill your baby brother?" The dynamics of peace in Canadian Inuit camps. In L. E. Sponsel & T. Gregor (Eds.), *The anthropology of peace and nonviolence* (pp. 155–181). Boulder, CO: Lynne Rienner.

Brink, A., Eller, C. K., & Gan, H. (2015). Reporting fraud: An examination of the bystander effect and evidence strength. In D. B. Schmitt (Eds.), *Advances in accounting behavioral research* (pp. 125–154). Bingley, UK: Emerald Group Publishing.

Brockner, J. (1984). Low self-esteem and behavioral plasticity: Some implications for personality and social psychology. In L. Wheeler (Ed.), *Review of personality and social psychology* (Vol. 4, pp. 237–271). Beverly Hills, CA: Sage.

Brown, B. B. (1982). The extent and effects of peer pressure among high school students: A retrospective analysis. *Journal of Youth and Adolescence, 11*(2), 121–133.

Brown, N. L., Sokal, A. D., & Friedman, H. L. (2014). Positive psychology and romantic scientism. *American Psychologist, 69*(6), 636–637.

Brown, R. (1965). *Social psychology.* Oxford, UK: Free Press of Glencoe.

Brown v. Board of Education of Topeka, 347 U.S. 483 (1954).

Brown v. Mississippi, 297 U.S. 278, 56 S. Ct. 461, 80 L. Ed. 682, 1936 U.S. LEXIS 527 (U.S. Feb. 17, 1936).

Browne, A., Williams, K. R., & Dutton, D. G. (1999). Homicide between intimate partners. In M. D. Smith & M. A. Zahn (Eds.), *Studying and preventing homicide: Issues and challenges* (pp. 55–78). Thousand Oaks, CA: Sage.

Bruck, M., & Ceci, S. J. (2009). Reliability of child witnesses' reports. In J. L. Skeem & S. O. Lilienfeld (Eds.), *Psychological science in the courtroom: Consensus and controversy* (pp. 149–171). New York, NY: Guilford.

Bruckheimer, J., & Oman, C. (Producers), & Yakin, B. (Director). (2000). *Remember the Titans* [Motion picture]. United States: Walt Disney Pictures and Buena Vista Pictures.

Brummett, B. R., Wade, J. C., Ponterotto, J. G., Thombs, B., & Lewis, C. (2007). Psychosocial well-being and a multicultural personality disposition. *Journal of Counseling & Development, 85*(1), 73–81.

Bruner, J. S., & Tagiuri, R. (1954). The perception of people. In G. Lindzey (Ed.), *Handbook of social psychology* (Vol. 2). Cambridge, MA: Addison Wesley.

Bruza, B., Welsh, M., Navarro, D., & Begg, S. (2011). Does anchoring cause overconfidence only in experts? Retrieved from chrome-extension://oemmndcbldboiebfnladdacbdfmadadm/http://csjarchive.cogsci.rpi.edu/proceedings/2011/papers/0443/paper0443.pdf

Brysbaert, M., Stevens, M., Mandera, P., & Keuleers, E. (2016). How many words do we know? Practical estimates of vocabulary size dependent on word definition, the degree of language input and the participant's age. *Frontiers in Psychology, 7*(1116), 1–11.

Bucchianeri, M. M., & Corning, A. F. (2012). An experimental test of women's body dissatisfaction reduction through self-affirmation. *Applied Psychology: Health and Well-Being, 4*(2), 188–201.

Buchner, E. F. (1910). Psychological progress since 1909. *Psychological Bulletin, 7*(1), 1–16.

Buck, R. (1980). Nonverbal behavior and the theory of emotion: The facial feedback hypothesis. *Journal of Personality and Social Psychology, 38*(5), 811–824.

Buehler, R., Griffin, D., & Ross, M. (1994). Exploring the "planning fallacy": Why people underestimate their task completion times. *Journal of Personality and Social Psychology, 67*(3), 366–381.

Buehler, R., & McFarland, C. (2001). Intensity bias in affective forecasting: The role of temporal focus. *Personality and Social Psychology Bulletin, 27*(11), 1480–1493.

Burleson, K., Leach, C. W., & Harrington, D. M. (2005). Upward social comparison and self-concept: Inspiration and inferiority among art students in an advanced programme. *British Journal of Social Psychology, 44*(1), 109–123.

Burnstein, E., Crandall, C., & Kitayama, S. (1994). Some neo-Darwinian decision rules for altruism: Weighing cues for inclusive fitness as a function of the biological importance of the decision. *Journal of Personality and Social Psychology, 67*(5), 773–789.

Bushman, B. J. (2002). Does venting anger feed or extinguish the flame? Catharsis, rumination, distraction, anger, and aggressive responding. *Personality and Social Psychology Bulletin, 28*(6), 724–731.

Bushman, B. J., & Anderson, C. A. (2001). Is it time to pull the plug on hostile versus instrumental aggression dichotomy? *Psychological Review, 108*(1), 273–279.

Bushman, B. J., Baumeister, R. F., & Phillips, C. M. (2001). Do people aggress to improve their mood? Catharsis beliefs, affect regulation opportunity, and aggressive responding. *Journal of Personality and Social Psychology, 81*(1), 17–32.

Bushman, B. J., Baumeister, R. F., & Stack, A. D. (1999). Catharsis, aggression, and persuasive influence: Self-fulfilling or self-defeating prophecies? *Journal of Personality and Social Psychology, 76*(3), 367–376.

Bushman, B. J., & Whitaker, J. L. (2010). Like a magnet: Catharsis beliefs attract angry people to violent video games. *Psychological Science, 21*(6), 790–792.

Buss, A. H. (1961). *The psychology of aggression.* New York, NY: John Wiley.

Buss, A. H., & Perry, M. (1992). The aggression questionnaire. *Journal of Personality and Social Psychology, 63*(3), 452–459.

Buss, D. M. (1985). Human mate selection. *American Scientist, 73*(1), 47–51.

Buss, D. M. (1989). Sex differences in human mate preferences: Evolutionary hypotheses tested in 37 cultures. *Behavioral and Brain Sciences, 12*(1), 1–49.

Buss, D. M. (1994). *The evolution of desire: Strategies of human mating.* New York, NY: Basic Books.

Buss, D. M. (2005). *The murderer next door: Why the mind is designed to kill.* New York, NY: Penguin.

Buss, D. M. (2016). Human mating strategies. In R. J. Sternberg, S. T. Fiske, & D. J. Foss (Eds.), *Scientists making a difference: One hundred eminent behavioral and brain scientists talk about their most important contributions* (pp. 383–388). New York, NY: Cambridge University Press.

Buss, D. M., & Duntley, J. D. (2006). The evolution of aggression. In M. Schaller, J. A. Simpson, & D. T. Kenrick (Eds.), *Evolution and social psychology* (pp. 263–285). New York, NY: Psychology Press.

Buss, D. M., & Kenrick, D. T. (1998). Evolutionary social psychology. In D. T. Gilbert, S. T. Fiske, & G. Lindzey (Eds.), *The handbook of social psychology* (Vols. 1–2, 4th ed., pp. 982–1026). New York, NY: McGraw-Hill.

Buss, D. M., Larsen, R. J., Westen, D., & Semmelroth, J. (1992). Sex differences in jealousy: Evolution, physiology, and psychology. *Psychological Science, 3*(4), 251–255.

Bussey, K., & Bandura, A. (1999). Social cognitive theory of gender development and differentiation. *Psychological Review, 106*(4), 676–713.

Butera, P. C., Wojcik, D. M., & Clough, S. J. (2010). Effects of estradiol on food intake and meal patterns for diets that differ in flavor and fat content. *Physiology & Behavior, 99*(1), 142–145.

Butz, D. A., & Yogeeswaran, K. (2011). A new threat in the air: Macroeconomic threat increases prejudice against Asian Americans. *Journal of Experimental Social Psychology, 47*(1), 22–27.

Byers, J. (2004). *Last letters home.* New York, NY: CDS.

Byrne, S., & Pease, K. (2003). Crime reduction and community safety. *Handbook of Policing,* 286–310.

Cacioppo, J. T., & Petty, R. E. (1982). The need for cognition. *Journal of Personality and Social Psychology, 42*(1), 116–131.

Cacioppo, J. T., Petty, R. E., Feinstein, J., & Jarvis, W. B. G. (1996). Dispositional differences in cognitive motivation: The life and times of individuals varying in need for cognition. *Psychological Bulletin, 119*(2), 197–253.

Cacioppo, J. T., Petty, R. E., & Kao, C. F. (1984). The efficient assessment of need for cognition. *Journal of Personality Assessment, 48*(3), 306–307.

Calhoun, J. B. (1962a). A behavioral sink. In E. Bliss (Ed.), *Roots of behavior.* New York, NY: Harper.

Calhoun, J. B. (1962b). Population density and social pathology. *Scientific American, 206*(2), 139–150.

Camerer, C. F., & Lowenstein, G. (2004). Behavioral economics: Past, present, future. In C. F. Camerer, G. Lownstein, & M. Rabin (Eds.), *Advances in behavioral economics* (pp. 3–51). New York, NY: Russell Sage Foundation.

Cameron, C. D., Brown-Iannuzzi, J. L., & Payne, B. K. (2012). Sequential priming measures of implicit social cognition: A meta-analysis of associations with behavior and explicit attitudes. *Personality and Social Psychology Review, 16*(4), 330–350.

Campbell, A. (2008). The morning after the night before: Affective reactions to one-night stands among mated and unmated women and men. *Human Nature, 19*(2), 157–173.

Campbell, D., & Stanley, J. (1966). *Experimental and quasi-experimental designs for research* (N. Gage, Ed.). Chicago, IL: Rand McNally.

Campbell, J. C. (2002). Health consequences of intimate partner violence. *The Lancet, 359*(9314), 1331–1336.

Caplan, P. J. (1994). *Lifting a ton of feathers: A woman's guide for surviving in the academic world.* Toronto, Ontario: University of Toronto Press.

Carey, B. (2009, July 27). In battle, hunches prove to be valuable. *New York Times.*

Carlo, G., Koller, S. H., Eisenberg, N., Da Silva, M. S., & Frohlich, C. B. (1996). A cross-national study on the relations among prosocial moral reasoning, gender role orientations, and prosocial behaviors. *Developmental Psychology, 32*(2), 231–240.

Carlo, G., Okun, M. A., Knight, G. P., & de Guzman, M. T. (2005). The interplay of traits and motives on volunteering: Agreeableness, extraversion and prosocial value motivation. *Personality and Individual Differences, 38*(6), 1293–1305.

Carlsmith, K. M., Wilson, T. D., & Gilbert, D. T. (2008). The paradoxical consequences of revenge. *Journal of Personality and Social Psychology, 95*(6), 1316–1324.

Carney, R. M., & Freedland, K. E. (2007). Depression and coronary heart disease: More pieces of the puzzle. *The American Journal of Psychiatry, 164*(9), 1307–1309.

Carr, P. L., Szalacha, L., Barnett, R., Caswell, C., & Inui, T. (2003). A 'ton of feathers': Gender discrimination in academic medical careers and how to manage it. *Journal of Women's Health, 12*(10), 1009–1018.

Carretta, T. R., & Moreland, R. L. (1982). Nixon and Watergate: A field demonstration of belief perseverance. *Personality and Social Psychology Bulletin, 8*(3), 446–453.

Cartsonis, S., McG, & Viola, M. (Producers), & Sandel, A. (Director). (2015). *The DUFF* [Motion picture]. United States: Vast Entertainment.

"Case closed: Rape and human rights in the Nordic countries." (2010). Retrieved from https://web.archive.org/web/20131020202147/http://www.amnesty.dk/sites/default/files/mediafiles/44/case-closed.pdf

Cathey, P., & Goodfriend, W. (2012). *Voices of hope: Breaking the silence of relationship violence.* Storm Lake, IA: Institute for the Prevention of Relationship Violence.

Ceci, S. J., & Bruck, M. (1995). The pros and (mostly) cons of using anatomically detailed dolls. In *Jeopardy in the courtroom: A scientific analysis of children's testimony* (pp. 161–186). Washington, DC: American Psychological Association.

Cervone, D. (2004). The architecture of personality, *Psychological Review, 111*(1), 183–204.

Cervone, D., & Peake, P. K. (1986). Anchoring, efficacy, and action: The influence of judgmental heuristics on self-efficacy judgments and behavior. *Journal of Personality and Social Psychology, 50*(3), 492–501.

Chadha, G., & Nayar, D. (Producers), & Chadha, G. (Director). (2002). *Bend it like Beckham* [Motion picture]. Germany: Bend It Films.

Chagnon, N. A. (1983). *Yanomamö: The fierce people* (3rd ed.). New York, NY: Holt, Rinehart, & Winston.

Chaiken, S. (1980). Heuristic versus systematic information processing in the use of source versus message cues in persuasion. *Journal of Personality and Social Psychology, 39*(5), 752–766.

Chance, S. E., Brown, R. T., Dabbs, J. M., & Casey, R. (2000). Testosterone, intelligence and behavior disorders in young boys. *Personality and Individual Differences, 28*(3), 437–445.

Chandra, S. (1973). The effects of group pressure in perception: A cross-cultural conformity study. *International Journal of Psychology, 8*(1), 37–39.

Chapin, J. R., & Coleman, G. (2012). Optimistic bias about dating/relationship violence among teens. *Journal of Youth Studies, 15*(5), 645–655.

Chapman, G. B., & Johnson, E. J. (2002). Incorporating the irrelevant: Anchors in judgments of belief and value. In T. Gilovich, D. Griffin, & D. Kahneman (Eds.), *Heuristics and biases: The psychology of intuitive judgment* (pp. 120–138). Cambridge, UK: Cambridge University Press.

Chen, J. M., Kim, H. S., Mojaverian, T., & Morling, B. (2012). Culture and social support provision: Who gives what and why. *Personality and Social Psychology Bulletin, 38*(1), 3–13.

Chen, S., & Chaiken, S. (1999). The heuristic-systematic model in its broader context. In S. Chaiken & Y. Trope (Eds.), *Dual-process theories in social psychology* (pp. 73–96). New York, NY: Guilford.

Cherry, F. (1995). *The 'stubborn particulars' of social psychology: Essays on the research process.* Florence, KY: Taylor & Frances/Routledge.

Chiesa, A., & Serretti, A. (2009). Mindfulness-based stress reduction for stress management in healthy people: A review and meta-analysis. *Journal of Alternative and Complementary Medicine, 15*(5), 593–600.

Chou, H. G., & Edge, N. (2012). 'They are happier and having better lives than I am': The impact of using Facebook on perceptions of others' lives. *Cyberpsychology, Behavior, and Social Networking, 15*(2), 117–120.

Chuck, E. (2016, March 31). Fact sheet: Who has nuclear weapons, and how many do they have? *NBC News.* Retrieved from http://www.nbcnews.com/news/world/fact-sheet-who-has-nuclear-weapons-how-many-do-they-n548481

Chung, H., & Zhao, X. (2003). Humour effect on memory and attitude: Moderating role of product involvement. *International Journal of Advertising, 22*(1), 117–144.

Cialdini, R. B. (2001). *Influence: Science and practice* (4th ed.). Boston, MA: Allyn & Bacon.

Cialdini, R. B. (2007). *Influence: Science and practice* (5th ed.). Boston, MA: Allyn & Bacon.

Cialdini, R. B., Bordern, R. J., Thorne, A., Walker, M. R., Freeman, S., & Sloan, L. R. (1976). Basking in reflected glory: Three (football) field studies. *Journal of Personality and Social Psychology, 34*(3), 366–373.

Cialdini, R. B., Kallgren, C. A., & Reno, R. R. (1991). A focus theory of normative conduct: A theoretical refinement and reevaluation of the role of norms in human behavior. *Advances in Experimental Social Psychology, 24*, 201–234.

Cialdini, R. B., Levy, A., Herman, C. P., Kozlowski, L. T., & Petty R. E. (1976). Elastic shifts of opinion: Determinants of direction and durability. *Journal of Personality and Social Psychology, 34*(4), 633–672.

Cialdini, R. B., & Trost M. R. (1998). Social influence: Social norms, conformity, and compliance. In D. T. Gilbert, S. T. Fiske, & G. Lindzey (Eds.), *The handbook of social psychology* (Vols. 1–2, 4th ed., pp. 151–192). New York, NY: McGraw-Hill.

Cialdini, R. B., Vincent, J. E., Lewis, S. K., Datalan, J., Wheeler, D., & Darby, B. L. (1975). Reciprocal concessions procedure for inducing compliance: The door-in-the-face technique. *Journal of Personality and Social Psychology, 31*(2), 206–215.

Ciucci, E., Caussi, P., Menesini, E., Mattei, A., Petralli, M., & Orlandini, S. (2011). Weather daily variation in winter and its effect on behavior and affective states in day-care children. *International Journal of Biometeorology, 55*(3), 327–337.

Clark, M. S., & Mills, J. (1979). Interpersonal attraction in exchange and communal relationships. *Journal of Personality and Social Psychology, 37*(1), 12–24.

Clark, R. D., & Hatfield, E. (1989). Gender differences in receptivity to sexual offers. *Journal of Psychology & Human Sexuality, 2*(1), 39–55.

Clarkson, M. (2010). The long and short of it: Leg length, aggression and the evolution of the human mind. *Australian Archaeology, 70,* 81.

Clement, R. W., & Krueger, J. (2002). Social categorization moderates social projection. *Journal of Experimental Social Psychology, 38*(3), 219–231.

Clement, R. W., Sinha, R. R., & Krueger, J. (1997). A computerized demonstration of the false consensus effect. *Teaching of Psychology, 24*(2), 131–135.

Clifford, M. M., & Walster, E. (1973). Research note: The effect of physical attractiveness on teacher expectations. *Sociology of Education, 46*(2), 248–258.

Cohen, A. H., & Krueger, J. S. (2016). Rising mercury, rising hostility: How heat affects survey response. *Field Methods, 28*(2), 133–152.

Cohen, D., Nisbett, R. E., Bowdle, B. F., & Schwarz, N. (1996). Insult, aggression, and the Southern culture of honor: An "experimental ethnography." *Journal of Personality and Social Psychology, 70*(5), 945–960.

Coker, A. L., Smith, P. H., McKeown, R. E., & King, M. J. (2000). Frequency and correlates of intimate partner violence by type: Physical, sexual, and psychological battering. *American Journal of Public Health, 90*(4), 553–559.

Cole, S., & Dioso-Villa, R. (2006). CSI and its effects: Media, juries, and the burden of proof. *New England Law Review, 41*(3), 435–470.

Collins, L. (Producer), & Stanton, A. (Director). (2016). *Finding Dory* [Motion picture]. United States: Walt Disney Studios Motion Pictures.

Collins, S. (2008). *The hunger games.* New York, NY: Scholastic Press.

Collins, S. (2009). *Catching fire.* New York, NY: Scholastic Press.

Collins, S. (2010). *Mockingjay.* New York, NY: Scholastic Press.

Comacho, L. M., & Paulus, P. B. (1995). The role of social anxiousness in group brainstorming. *Journal of Personality and Social Psychology, 68*(6), 1071–1080.

Compton, W. C. (2005). *Introduction to positive psychology.* Belmont, CA: Thomson Wadsworth.

Conley, T. D., Moors, A. C., Matsick, J. L., Ziegler, A., & Valentine, B. A. (2011). Women, men, and the bedroom: Methodological and conceptual insights that narrow, reframe, and eliminate gender differences in sexuality. *Current Directions in Psychological Science, 20*(5), 296–300.

Conley, T. D., Moors, A. C., Ziegler, A., & Karathanasis, C. (2012). Unfaithful individuals are less likely to practice safer sex than openly nonmonogamous individuals. *Journal of Sexual Medicine, 9*(6), 1559–1565.

Connolly, T., Routhieaux, R. L., & Schneider, S. K. (1993). On the effectiveness of group brainstorming: Test of an underlying cognitive mechanism. *Small Group Research, 24*(4), 490–503.

Cooper, W. H. (1981). Ubiquitous halo. *Psychological Bulletin, 90*(2), 218–244.

Corey, S. (1937). Professed attitudes and actual behavior. *Journal of Educational Psychology, 28*(4), 271–280.

Correll, J., Park, B., Judd, C. M., & Wittenbrink, B. (2002). The police officer's dilemma: Using ethnicity to disambiguate potentially threatening individuals. *Journal of Personality and Social Psychology, 83*(6), 1314–1329.

Cosmides, L., & Tooby, J. (1992). Cognitive adaptations for social exchange. In L. Cosmides & J. Tooby (Eds.), *The adapted mind: Evolutionary psychology and the generation of culture* (pp. 163–228). New York, NY: Oxford University Press.

Costanzo, M., & Krauss, D. (2015). *Forensic and legal psychology.* London, UK: Macmillan.

Cottrell, C. A., & Neuberg, S. L. (2005). Different emotional reactions to different groups: A sociofunctional threat-based approach to prejudice. *Journal of Personality and Social Psychology, 88*(5), 770–789.

Cottrell, N. B., Wack, D. L., Sekerak, G. J., & Rittle, R. H. (1968). Social facilitation of dominant responses by the presence of an audience and the mere presence of others. *Journal of Personality and Social Psychology, 9*(3), 245–250.

Craik, F. I., & Lockhart, R. S. (1972). Levels of processing: A framework for memory research. *Journal of Verbal Learning & Verbal Behavior, 11*(6), 671–684.

Crall, P., & Goodfriend, W. (2016). "She asked for it": Statistics and predictors of rape myth acceptance. *Modern Psychological Studies, 22,* 15–27.

Cramer, R. J., Miller, A. K., Amacker, A. M., & Burks, A. C. (2013). Openness right-wing authoritarianism and antigay prejudice in college students: A meditational model. *Journal of Counseling Psychology, 60*(1), 64–71.

Crandall, C. S. (1994). Prejudice against fat people: Ideology and self-interest. *Journal of Personality and Social Psychology, 66*(5), 882–894.

Crandall, C. S., & Eshleman, A. (2003). A justification-suppression model of the expression and experience of prejudice. *Psychological Bulletin, 129*(3), 414–446.

Cranney, J., & Dunn, D. S. (2011). *The psychologically literate citizen: Foundations and global perspectives.* New York, NY: Oxford University Press.

Crawford, J. T., Brandt, M. J., Inbar, Y., & Mallinas, S. R. (2016). Right-wing authoritarianism predicts prejudice equally toward "gay men and lesbians" and "homosexuals." *Journal of Personality and Social Psychology, 111*(2), 31–45.

Creswell, J. D., Dutcher, J. M., Klein, W. M. P., Harris, P. R., & Levine, J. M. (2013). Self-affirmation improves problem-solving under stress. *PLoS One, 8*(5), e62593.

Creswell, J. D., Welch, W. T., Taylor, S. E., Sherman, D. K., Gruenewald, T. L., & Mann, T. (2005). Affirmation of personal values buffers neuroendocrine and psychological stress responses. *Psychological Science, 16*(11), 846–851.

Crocker, J., & Luhtanen, R. K. (1990). Collective self-esteem and ingroup bias. *Journal of Personality and Social Psychology, 58*(1), 60–67.

Crocker, J., Luhtanen, R., Blaine, B., & Broadnax, S. (1994). Collective self-esteem and psychological well-being among White, Black, and Asian college students. *Personality and Social Psychology Bulletin, 20*(5), 503–513.

Crocker, J., & Major, B. (1989). Social stigma and self-esteem: The self-protective properties of stigma. *Psychological Review, 96*(4), 608–630.

Crocker, J., & Major, B. (2003). The self-protective properties of stigma: Evolution of a modern classic. *Psychological Inquiry, 14*(3–4), 232–237.

Crocker, J., & Nuer, N. (2003). The insatiable quest for self-worth. *Psychological Inquiry, 14*(1), 31–34.

Crocker, J., Thompson, L. L., McGraw, K. M., & Ingerman, C. (1987). Downward comparison, prejudice, and evaluations of others: Effects of self-esteem and threat. *Journal of Personality and Social Psychology, 52*(5), 907–916.

Cropley, D. H., Cropley, A. J., Kaufman, J. C., & Runco, M. A. (2010). *The dark side of creativity.* New York, NY: Cambridge University Press.

Crowder, K., & Goodfriend, W. (2012). Good monkey see, good monkey do: Children's imitative prosocial behavior. *Journal of Psychological Inquiry, 17*(2), 7–16.

Crowne, D. P., & Marlowe, D. (1960). A new scale of social desirability independent of psychopathology. *Journal of Consulting Psychology, 24*(4), 349–354.

Cruz, J. M. (2003). 'Why doesn't he just leave?': Gay male domestic violence and the reasons victims stay. *The Journal of Men's Studies, 11*(3), 309–323.

Cunningham, W. A., Johnson, M. K., Raye, C. L., Gatenby, J. C., Gore, J. C., & Banaji, M. R. (2004). Separable neural components in the processing of black and white faces. *Psychological Science, 15*(12), 806–813.

Curhan, J. R., & Pentland, A. (2007). Thin slices of negotiation: Predicting outcomes from conversational dynamics within the first 5 minutes. *Journal of Applied Psychology, 92*(3), 802–811.

The current situation of gender equality in Sweden—country profile. (2013). Retrieved from http://ec.europa.eu/justice/gender-equality/files/epo_campaign/131006_country-profile_sweden.pdf

Cyders, M. A., Dzemidzic, M., Eiler, W. J., & Kareken, D. A. (2016). An fMRI study of responses to sexual stimuli as a function of gender and sensation seeking: A preliminary analysis. *Journal of Sex Research, 53*(8), 1020–1026.

Damasio, A. (2010). *Self comes to mind: Constructing the conscious brain.* New York, NY: Pantheon/Random House.

Damon, W., & Hart, D. (1988). *Self-understanding in childhood and adolescence.* Cambridge, England: Cambridge University Press.

Dardis, C. M., Murphy, M. J., Bill, A. C., & Gidycz, C. A. (2016). An investigation of the tenets of social norms theory as they relate to sexually aggressive attitudes and sexual assault perpetration: A comparison of men and their friends. *Psychology of Violence, 6*(1), 163–171.

Darley, J. M., & Batson, C. D. (1973). 'From Jerusalem to Jericho': A study of situational and dispositional variables in helping behavior. *Journal of Personality and Social Psychology, 27*(1), 100–108.

Darley, J. M., & Latané, B. (1968). Bystander intervention in emergencies: Diffusion of responsibility. *Journal of Personality and Social Psychology, 8*(4, Pt. 1), 377–383.

Darwin, C. R. (1859). *On the origin of the species by means of natural selection.* London, UK: John Murray. Retrieved from http://darwin-online.org.uk/content/frameset?itemID=F373&viewtype=text&pageseq=1

Darwin, C. R. (1871). The descent of man. *The Great Books of the Western World, 49,* 320.

Darwin, C. R. (1872). *The expression of the emotions in man and animals.* London, UK: John Murray.

Darwin, C. R. (1877). A biographical sketch of an infant. *Mind, 2,* 85–94.

Davidson, A. R., & Jaccard, J. J. (1979). Variables that moderate the attitude-behavior relation: Results of a longitudinal survey. *Journal of Personality and Social Psychology, 37*(8), 1364–1376.

Davies, B. (1989). *Frogs and snails and feminist tales: Preschool children and gender.* Sydney, Australia: Allen & Unwin.

Davies, B. (1992). Women's subjectivity and feminist stories. In C. Ellis & M. Flaherty, *Investigating subjectivity: Research on lived experience* (pp. 53–76). Newbury Park, CA: Sage.

Davies, M. F. (1982). Self-focused attention and belief perseverance. *Journal of Experimental Social Psychology, 18*(6), 595–605.

Davis, C. G., & Lehman, D. R. (1995). Counterfactual thinking and coping with traumatic life events. In N. J. Roese & J. M. Olson (Eds.), *What might have been: The social psychology of counterfactual thinking* (pp. 353–374). Hillsdale, NJ: Lawrence Erlbaum.

Davis, C. G., Lehman, D. R., Silver, R. C., Wortman, C. B., & Ellard, J. H. (1996). Self-blame following a traumatic event: The role of perceived avoidability. *Personality and Social Psychology Bulletin, 22*(6), 557–567.

Davis, C. G., Lehman, D. R., Wortman, C. B., Silver, R. C., & Thompson, S. C. (1995). The undoing of traumatic life events. *Personality and Social Psychology Bulletin, 21*(2), 109–124.

Dawes, R. M. (1989). Statistical criteria for establishing a truly false consensus effect. *Journal of Experimental Social Psychology, 25*(1), 1–17.

Dawes, R. M., & Mulford, M. (1996). The false consensus effect and overconfidence: Flaws in judgments or flaws in how we study judgment? *Organizational Behavior and Human Decision Processes, 65*(3), 201–211.

Dawkins, R. (1976). *The selfish gene.* New York, NY: Oxford University Press.

de Castro, J. M. (2000). Eating behavior: Lessons from the real world of humans. *Nutrition, 16*(10), 800–813.

De Cremer, D., Zeelenberg, M., & Murnighan, J. K. (2006). Social animals and economic beings: On unifying social psychology and economics. In D. De Cramer, M. Zeelenberg, & J. K. Murnighan (Eds.), *Social psychology and economics* (pp. 3–14). Part Drive, UK: Taylor and Francis Ltd.

de Geus, E., Eijzenga, W., Menko, F. H., Sijmons, R. H., de Haes, H. C. J. M., Aalfs, C. M., & Smets, E. M. A. (2016). Design and feasibility of an intervention to support cancer genetic counselees in informing their at-risk relatives. *Journal of Genetic Counseling, 25*(6), 1179–1187.

de Waal, F. B., Aureli, F., & Judge, P. G. (2000). Coping with crowding. *Scientific American, 282*(5), 76–81.

Dean, G. W., & Kelly, I. W. (2003). Is astrology relevant to consciousness and PSI? *Journal of Consciousness Studies, 10*(6–7), 175–198.

Deci, E. L., Reis, H. T., Johnston, E. J., & Smith, R. (1977). Toward reconciling equity theory and insufficient justification. *Personality and Social Psychology Bulletin, 3*(2), 224–227.

Deci, E. L., & Ryan, R. M. (1985). *Intrinsic motivation and self-determination in human behavior.* New York, NY: Plenum.

Deci, E. L., & Ryan, R. M. (1991). A motivational approach to self: Integration in personality. In R. A. Dienstbier (Ed.), *Nebraska symposium on motivation, 1990: Perspectives on motivation* (pp. 237–288). Lincoln: University of Nebraska Press.

Deets, L. E. (1931). The origins of conflict in the Hutterische communities. *Publications of the American Sociological Society, 25*, 125–135.

Delfour, F., & Marten, K. (2001). Mirror image processing in three marine mammal species: Killer whales (*Orcinus orca*), false killer whales (*Pseudorca crassidens*) and California sea lions (*Zalophus californianus*). *Behavioural Processes, 53*(3), 181–190.

DeLongis, A., Folkman, S., & Lazarus, R. S. (1988). The impact of daily stress on health and mood: Psychological and social resources as mediators. *Journal of Personality and Social Psychology, 54*(3), 486–495.

DeNault, L. K., & McFarlane, D. A. (1995). Reciprocal altruism between male vampire bats, *Desmodus rotundus. Animal Behaviour, 49*(3), 855–856.

DeNeys, W. (2006). Dual processing in reasoning: Two systems but one reasoner. *Psychological Science, 17*(5), 428–433.

Dennis, I., Newstead, S. E., & Wright, D. E. (1996). A new approach to exploring biases in educational assessment. *British Journal of Psychology, 87*(4), 515–534.

DePaulo, B. M., Kashy, D. A., Kirkendol, S. E., Wyer, M. M., & Epstein, J. A. (1996). Lying in everyday life. *Journal of Personality and Social Psychology, 70*(5), 979–995.

Dereli, E., & Karakuş, Ö. (2011). An examination of attachment styles and social skills of university students. *Electronic Journal of Research in Educational Psychology, 9*(2), 731–744.

Deutsch, M. (1972). Review of encounter groups: Basic readings. *Contemporary Psychology, 17*(6), 358.

Deutsch, M., & Gerard, H. B. (1955). A study of normative and informational social influences upon individual judgment. *Journal of Abnormal and Social Psychology, 51*(3), 629–636.

Deutsch, F. M., & Lamberti, D. M. (1986). Does social approval increase helping? *Personality and Social Psychology Bulletin, 12*(2), 149–157.

DeVries, D. L., & Ajzen, I. (1971). The relationship of attitudes and normative beliefs to cheating in college. *Journal of Social Psychology, 83*(2), 199–207.

Dhiaulhaq, A., De Bruyn, T., & Gritten, D. (2015). The use and effectiveness of mediation in forest and land conflict transformation in Southeast Asia: Case studies from Cambodia, Indonesia and Thailand. *Environmental Science & Policy, 45,* 132–145.

Didion, J. (2005). *The year of magical thinking* (Book club kit). New York, NY: Knopf.

Diehl, M., & Strobe, W. (1987). Productivity loss in idea-generating groups: Toward the solution of a riddle. *Journal of Personality and Social Psychology, 53*(3), 497–509.

Diekman, A. B., & Eagly, A. H. (2000). Stereotypes as dynamic constructs: Women and men of the past, present, and future. *Personality and Social Psychology Bulletin, 26*(10), 1171–1188.

Diekman, A. B., & Goodfriend, W. (2006). Rolling with the changes: A role congruity perspective on gender norms. *Psychology of Women Quarterly, 30*(4), 369–383.

Diener, E. (1979). Deindividuation, self-awareness, and disinhibition. *Journal of Personality and Social Psychology, 37*(7), 1160–1171.

Diener, E., Fraser, S. C., Beaman, A. L., & Kelem, R. T. (1976). Effects of deindividuation variables on stealing among Halloween trick-or-treaters. *Journal of Personality and Social Psychology, 33*(2), 178–183.

Dietrich, D. M., & Berkowitz, L. (1997). Alleviation of dissonance by engaging in prosocial behavior or receiving ego-enhancing feedback. *Journal of Social Behavior & Personality, 12*(2), 557–566.

Dietrich, D. M., & Schuett, J. M. (2013). Culture of honor and attitudes toward intimate partner violence in Latinos. *Sage Open, 3*(2), 1–11.

DiMatteo, M. R. (2004). Variations in patients' adherence to medical recommendations: A quantitative review of 50 years of research. *Medical Care, 42*(3), 200–209.

Dion, K. L. (2000). Group cohesion: From "field of forces" to multidimensional construct. *Group Dynamics: Theory, Research, and Practice, 4*(1), 7–26.

Dion, K., Berscheid, E., & Walster, E. (1972). What is beautiful is good. *Journal of Personality and Social Psychology, 24*(3), 285–290.

Disney, W. (Producer), & Sharpsteen, B., & Luske, H. (Directors). 1940. *Pinocchio* [Motion picture]. United States: Walt Disney Productions.

Disney, W., & Walsh, B. (Producers), & Stevenson, R. (Director). (1964). *Mary Poppins* [Motion picture]. United States: Walt Disney Productions.

Dixson, A. F., Halliwell, G., East, R., Wignarajah, P., & Anderson, M. J. (2003). Masculine somatotype and hirsuteness as determinants of sexual attractiveness to women. *Archives of Sexual Behavior, 32*(1), 29–39.

Dobash, R. E., & Dobash, R. P. (1992). *Women, violence and social change.* New York, NY: Routledge.

Dobuzinskis, A. (2017, May 29). Two men stabbed to death on Oregon train trying to stop anti-Muslim rant. *Reuters.* Retrieved from http://www.reuters.com/article/us-usa-muslims-portland-idUSKBN18N080

Dockery, T. M., & Bedeian, A. G. (1989). "Attitudes versus actions": LaPiere's (1934) classic study revisited. *Social Behavior and Personality, 17*(1), 9–16.

Dodge, K. A., Lochman, J. E., Harnish, J. D., Bates, J. E., & Pettit, G. S. (1997). Reactive and proactive aggression in school children and psychiatrically impaired chronically assaultive youth. *Journal of Abnormal Psychology, 106*(1), 37–51.

Dollard, J., Miller, N. E., Doob, L. W., Mowrer, O. H., & Sears, R. R. (1939). *Frustration and aggression.* New Haven, CT: Yale University Press.

Donahue, M. J. (1985). Intrinsic and extrinsic religiousness: The empirical research. *Journal for the Scientific Study of Religion, 24*(4), 418–423.

Donnellan, M. B., Trzesniewski, K. H., Robins, R. W., Moffitt, T. E., & Caspi, A. (2005). Low self-esteem is related to aggression, antisocial behavior, and delinquency. *Psychological Science, 16*(4), 328–335.

Donnerstein, E., & Donnerstein, M. (1976). Research in the control of interracial aggression. In R. G. Green & E. C. O'Neal (Eds.), *Perspectives on aggression* (pp. 133–168). New York, NY: Academic Press.

Doosje, B., & Branscombe, N. R. (2003). Attributions for the negative historical actions of a group. *European Journal of Social Psychology, 33*(2), 235–248.

Doosje, B., Branscombe, N. R., Spears, R., & Manstead, S. R. (1998). Guilty by association: When one's group has a negative history. *Journal of Personality and Social Psychology, 75*(4), 872–886.

Dougherty, M. R. P., Gettys, D. F., & Ogden, E. E. (1999). MINERVA-DM: A memory process model of judgments of likelihood. *Psychological Review, 106*(1), 180–209.

Dovidio, J. F., & Morris, W. N. (1975). Effects of stress and commonality of fate on helping behavior. *Journal of Personality and Social Psychology, 31*(1), 145–149.

Dovidio, J. F., & Penner, L. A. (2001). Helping and altruism. In G. J. O. Fletcher & M. S. Clark (Eds.), *Blackwell handbook of social psychology: Interpersonal processes* (pp. 162–195). New York, NY: Blackwell.

Downes, D., Rock, P., Chinkin, C., & Gearty, C. (Eds.). (2013). *Crime, social control and human rights: From moral panics to states of denial, essays in honour of Stanley Cohen.* Abingdon, UK: Routledge.

Downey, G., & Feldman, S. I. (1996). Implications of rejection sensitivity for intimate relationships. *Journal of Personality and Social Psychology, 70*(6), 1327–1343.

Downey, J. L., & Christensen, L. (2006). Belief persistence in impression formation. *North American Journal of Psychology, 8*(3), 479–488.

Doyen, S., Klein, O., Pichon, C., & Cleeremans, A. (2012). Behavioral priming: It's all in the mind, but whose mind? *PLoS ONE, 7*(1), e29081.

Drouin, M., & Landgraff, C. (2012). Texting, sexting, and attachment in college students' romantic relationships. *Computers in Human Behavior, 28*(2), 444–449.

Dubner, S. J., & Levitt, S. D. (2006, November 5). The way we live now: Freakonomics; the price of climate change. *New York Times.* Retrieved March 7, 2007, from http//:www.nytimes.com

Duckitt, J., & Sibley, C. G. (2010). Right-wing authoritarianism and social dominance orientation differentially moderate intergroup effects on prejudice. *European Journal of Personality, 24*(7), 583–601.

Dugosh, K. L., Paulus, P. B., Roland, E. J., & Yang, H-C. (2000). Cognitive stimulation in brainstorming. *Journal of Personality and Social Psychology, 79*(5), 722–735.

Dunbar, R. I. M. (1998). The social brain hypothesis. *Brain, 9*(10), 178–190.

Duncan, L. E., Peterson, B. E., & Winter, D. G. (1997). Authoritarianism and gender roles: Toward a psychological analysis of hegemonic relationships. *Personality and Social Psychology Bulletin, 23*(1), 41–49.

Dunham, K., & Senn, C. Y. (2000). Minimizing negative experiences: Women's disclosure of partner abuse. *Journal of Interpersonal Violence, 15*(3), 251–261.

Dunn, D. S., Baker, S. C., Mehrotra, C. M., Landrum, R. E., & McCarthy, M. A. (2013). An overview of assessment: Demonstrating effective teaching and learning. In *Assessing teaching and learning in psychology: Current and future perspectives* (pp. 1–7). New York, NY: Wadsworth.

Dunn, M., Thomas, J. O., Swift, W., & Burns, L. (2012). Elite athletes' estimates of the prevalence illicit drug use: Evidence for the false consensus effect. *Drug and Alcohol Review, 31*(1), 27–32.

Dunnette, M. D., Campbell, J., & Jaastad, K. (1963). The effect of group participation on brainstorming effectiveness for 2 industrial samples. *Journal of Applied Psychology, 47*(1), 30–37.

Dunning, D., & Madey, S. F. (1995). Comparison processes in counterfactual thought. In N. J. Roese & J. M. Olson (Eds.), *What might have been: The social psychology of counterfactual thinking* (pp. 103–131). Hillsdale, NJ: Lawrence Erlbaum.

Dunning, D., & Parpal, M. (1989). Mental addition and subtraction in counterfactual reasoning: On assessing the impact of actions and life events. *Journal of Personality and Social Psychology, 57*(1), 5–15.

Dutton, D. G. (1998). *The abusive personality: Violence and control in intimate relationships.* New York, NY: Guilford.

Dutton, D. G., & Aron, A. P. (1974). Some evidence for heightened sexual attraction under conditions of high anxiety. *Journal of Personality and Social Psychology, 30*(4), 510–517.

Dutton, D. G., & Painter, S. (1993). The battered woman syndrome: Effects of severity and intermittency of abuse. *American Journal of Orthopsychiatry, 63*(4), 614–622.

Dworkin, S. L., & O'Sullivan, L. (2005). Actual versus desired initiation patterns among a sample of college men: Tapping disjunctures within traditional male sexual scripts. *The Journal of Sex Research, 42*(2), 150–158.

Eagly, A. H. (1987). *Sex differences in social behavior: A social role interpretation.* Hillsdale, NJ: Lawrence Erlbaum.

Eagly, A. H. (2009). The his and hers of prosocial behavior: An examination of the social psychology of gender. *American Psychologist, 64*(8), 644–658.

Eagly, A. H., & Chaiken, S. (1993). *The psychology of attitudes.* Fort Worth, TX: Harcourt Brace Jovanovich.

Eagly, A. H., & Chaiken, S. (2007). The advantages of an inclusive definition of attitude. *Social Cognition, 25*(5), 582–602.

Eagly, A. H., Wood, W., & Chaiken, S. (1978). Causal inferences about communicators and their effect on opinion change. *Journal of Personality and Social Psychology, 36*(4), 424–435.

Eagly, A. H., Wood, W., & Diekman, A. B. (2000). Social role theory of sex differences and similarities: A current appraisal. In T. Ekes & H. M. Trautner (Eds.), *The developmental social psychology of gender* (pp. 123–174). Mahwah, NJ: Lawrence Erlbaum.

Echols, L., & Graham, S. (2013). Birds of a different feather: How do cross-ethnic friends flock together? *Merrill-Palmer Quarterly, 59*(4), 461–488.

Eden, D. (1990). *Pygmalion in management: Productivity as a self-fulfilling prophecy.* Lexington, MA: Lexington Books.

Education Advisory Board. (2016, November 3). 7 colleges welcome their first black presidents. Retrieved from https://www.eab.com/daily-briefing/2016/11/03/7-colleges-welcome-their-first-black-presidents

Edwards, K. M., Gidycz, C. A., & Murphy, M. J. (2015). Leaving an abusive dating relationship: A prospective analysis of the investment model and theory of planned behavior. *Journal of Interpersonal Violence, 30*(16), 2908–2927.

Einhorn, H. J., & Hogarth, R. M. (1986). Judging probable cause. *Psychological Bulletin, 99*(1), 3–19.

Einstein, A. (1955). A new form of the general relativistic field equations. *Annals of Mathematics, 62*(1), 128–138.

Eisenberg, N. I., Fabes, R., & Shea, C. (1989). Gender differences in empathy and prosocial moral reasoning: Empirical investigations. In M. M. Brabeck (Ed.), *Who cares? Theory, research, and educational implications of the ethic of care* (pp. 127–143). New York, NY: Praeger.

Eisenberg, R. (2016). Home visiting quality and parent involvement: Examining mediation in home visiting. *Dissertation Abstracts International Section A, 76.* Retrieved from http://preserve.lehigh.edu/etd/2583

Eisenberger, N. I., & Lieberman, M. D. (2005). Why it hurts to be left out: The neurocognitive overlap between physical and social pain. In K. D. Williams, J. P. Forgas, & W. von Hippel (Eds.), *The social outcast: Ostracism, social exclusion, rejection, and bullying* (pp. 109–130). New York, NY: Psychology Press.

Eisenberger, N. I., Lieberman, M. D., & Williams, K. D. (2003). Does rejection hurt? An fMRI study of social exclusion. *Science, 302*(5643), 290–292.

Ekman, P. (2006). *Darwin and facial expression: A century of research in review.* Cambridge, MA: Malor Books.

Ekman, P., & Frank, M. G. (1993). Lies that fail. In M. Lewis & C. Saarni (Eds.), *Lying and deception in everyday life* (pp. 184–200). New York, NY: Guilford.

Ekman, P., & Friesen, W. V. (1969). Nonverbal leakage and clues to deception. *Psychiatry, 32*(1), 88–97.

Ekman, P., & Friesen, W.V. (1971). Constants across cultures in the face and emotion. *Journal of Personality and Social Psychology, 17*(2), 124–129.

Ekman, P., & Friesen, W. V. (1974). Detecting deception from body or face. *Journal of Personality and Social Psychology, 29*(3), 288–298.

Ekman, P., & O'Sullivan, M. (2006). From flawed self-assessment to blatant whoppers: The utility of voluntary and involuntary behavior in detecting deception. *Behavioral Sciences & the Law, 24*(5), 673–686.

Ekman, P., O'Sullivan, M., & Frank, M. G. (1999). A few can catch a liar. *Psychological Science, 10*(3), 263–266.

Ekman, P., O'Sullivan, M., & Matsumoto, D. (1991). Confusions about context in the judgment of facial expression: A reply to 'The contempt expression and the relativity thesis'. *Motivation and Emotion, 15*(2), 169–176.

Ellickson, K. A., & Brown, D. R. (1990). Ethical considerations in dual relationships: The sport psychologist-coach. *Journal of Applied Sport Psychology, 2*(2), 186–190.

Elliot, P. (1996). Shattering illusions: Same-sex domestic violence. *Journal of Gay & Lesbian Social Services, 4*(1), 1–8.

Ellis, J. (1976). *Eye-deep in Hell: Trench warfare in WW I.* Baltimore, MD: Johns Hopkins University Press.

Ellison, N. B., Steinfield, C., & Lampe, C. (2007). The benefits of Facebook 'friends:' Social capital and college students' use of online social network sites. *Journal of Computer-Mediated Communication, 12*(4), 1143–1168.

Emswiller, T., Deaux, K., & Willits, J. E. (1971). Similarity, sex, and requests for small favors. *Journal of Applied Social Psychology, 1*(3), 284–291.

Engel, G. L. (1977). The need for a new medical model: A challenge for biomedicine. *Science, 196*(4286), 129–136.

Epley, N. (2004). A tale of tuned decks? Anchoring as accessibility and anchoring as adjustment. In D. J. Koehler & N. Harvey (Eds.), *Blackwell handbook of judgment and decision making* (pp. 240–257). Malden, MA: Blackwell.

Epley, N., Boaz, K., & Van Boven, L. (2004). Perspective taking as egocentric anchoring and adjustment. *Journal of Personality and Social Psychology, 87,* 447–460.

Epley, N., & Gilovich, T. (2001). Putting adjustment back in the anchoring and adjustment heuristic: Differential processing of self-generated and experimenter-provided anchors. *Psychological Science, 12,* 391–396.

Epley, N., & Gilovich, T. (2004). Are adjustments insufficient? *Personality and Social Psychology Bulletin, 30*(4), 447–460.

Epley, N., & Gilovich, T. (2006). The anchoring-and-adjustment heuristic: Why the adjustments are insufficient. *Psychological Science, 17*(4), 311–318.

Epley, N., Keysar, B., Van Boven, L., & Gilovich, T. (2004). Perspective taking as egocentric anchoring and adjustment. *Journal of Personality and Social Psychology, 87*(3), 327–339.

Epstein, J., Noel, J., Finnegan, M., & Watkins, K. (2016). Bacon brains: Video games for teaching the science of addiction. *Journal of Child & Adolescent Substance Abuse, 25*(6), 504–515.

Essock-Vitale, S. M., & McGuire, M. T. (1985). Women's lives viewed from an evolutionary perspective. II. Patterns of helping. *Ethology and Sociobiology, 6*(3), 155–173.

Etcheverry, P. E., & Agnew, C. R. (2004). Subjective norms and the prediction of romantic relationship state and fate. *Personal Relationships, 11*(4), 409–428.

Everson-Rose, S. A., & Lewis, T. T. (2005). Psychosocial factors and cardiovascular diseases. *Annual Review of Public Health, 26,* 469–500.

Farmer, R. F., & Sundberg, N. D. (2010). Buffering hypothesis. In *Corsini encyclopedia of psychology.* New York, NY: John Wiley.

Fazio, R. H. (1987). Self-perception theory: A current perspective. In M. P. Zanna, J. M. Olson, & C. P. Herman (Eds.), *Social influence: The Ontario symposium* (pp. 129–150) Hillsdale, NJ: Lawrence Erlbaum.

Feely, T. H. (2002). Evidence of halo effects in student evaluations of communication instruction. *Communication Education, 51*(3), 225–236.

Feige, K. (Producer), & Johnston, J. (Director). (2011). *Capitan American: The first avenger* [Motion picture]. United States: Marvel Studios.

Feige, K. (Producer), & Whedon, J. (Director). (2012). *The avengers* [Motion picture]. USA: Marvel Studios & Walt Disney Studios.

Fein, S., & Spencer, S. J. (1997). Prejudice as self-image maintenance: Affirming the self through derogating others. *Journal of Personality and Social Psychology, 73*(1), 31–44.

Feinberg, M., & Willer, R. (2011). Apocalypse soon? Dire messages reduce belief in global warming by contradicting just-world beliefs. *Psychological Science, 22*(1), 34–38.

Feingold, A. (1992). Good-looking people are not what we think. *Psychological Bulletin, 111*(2), 304–341.

Feshbach, S. (1964). The function of aggression and the regulation of aggressive drive. *Psychological Review, 71*(4), 257–272.

Festinger, L. (1954). A theory of social comparison processes. *Human Relations, 7*(2), 117–140.

Festinger, L. (1957). *A theory of cognitive dissonance.* Stanford, CA: Stanford University Press.

Festinger, L., & Carlsmith, J. M. (1959). Cognitive consequences of forced compliance. *The Journal of Abnormal and Social Psychology, 58*(2), 203–210.

Festinger, L., & Maccoby, N. (1964). On resistance to persuasive communication. *Journal of Abnormal and Social Psychology, 68*(4), 359–366.

Festinger, L., Pepitone, A., & Newcomb, T. (1952). Some consequences of deindividuation. *The Journal of Abnormal and Social Psychology, 47*(2), 382–389.

Festinger, L., Riecken, H. W., & Schachter, S. (2008). *When prophecy fails: A social and psychological study of a modern group that predicted the destruction of the world.* Minneapolis: University of Minnesota Press. (Original work published 1956)

Festinger, L., Schachter, S., & Back, K. W. (1950). *Social pressures in informal groups: A study of human factors in housing.* New York, NY: Harper & Bros.

Feyereisen, P. (2006). Review of nonverbal communication across disciplines. Volume 1: Culture, sensory interaction, speech, conversation. Volume 2: Paralanguage, kinesics, silence, personal and environmental interaction. Volume 3: Narrative literature, theater, cinema, translation. *Gesture, 6*(2), 273–282.

Fiedler, F. E. (1967). *A theory of leadership effectiveness.* New York, NY: McGraw Hill.

Fiedler, F. E. (1996). Research on leadership selection and training: One view of the future. *Administrative Science Quarterly, 41*(2), 241–250.

Fiedler, K., Freytag, P., & Meiser, T. (2009). Pseudocontingencies: An integrative account of an intriguing cognitive illusion. *Psychological Review, 116*(1), 187–206.

Filindra, A., & Pearson-Merkowitz, S. (2013). Together in good times and bad? How economic triggers condition the effects of intergroup threat. *Social Science Quarterly, 94*(5), 1328–1345.

Fincher, D., Spacey, K., Roth, E., Donen, J., Brunetti, D., Davies, A., . . . Wright, R. (Producers). (2013–). *House of cards* [Television series]. United States: Media Rights Capital.

Findlay, L. C., & Coplan, R. J. (2008). Come out and play: Shyness in childhood and organized sports participation. *Canadian Journal of Behavioural Science, 40*(3), 153–161.

Finkel, N. J. (2000). But it's not fair! Commonsense notions of unfairness. *Psychology, Public Policy, and Law, 6*(4), 898–952.

Firestone, I. J., Kaplan, K. J., & Russell, J. C. (1973). Anxiety, fear, and affiliation with similar-state versus dissimilar-state others: Misery sometimes loves nonmiserable company. *Journal of Personality and Social Psychology, 26*(3), 409–414.

The first 9/11 backlash fatality: The murder of Balbir Singh Sodhi. (2011, August 30). Retrieved from http://saldef.org/issues/balbir-singh-sodhi/#.WTJDBRPyuRs

Fischer, P., & Greitemeyer, T. (2013). The positive bystander effect: Passive bystanders increase helping in situations with high expected negative consequences for the helper. *The Journal of Social Psychology, 153*(1), 1–5.

Fischhoff, B. (1975). Hindsight is not equal to foresight: The effect of outcome knowledge on judgment under uncertainty. *Journal of Experimental Psychology: Human Perception and Performance, 1*(3), 288–299.

Fischhoff, B. (2002). For those condemned to study the past: Heuristics and biases in hindsight. In D. J. Levitin (Ed.), *Foundations of cognitive psychology: Core readings* (pp. 621–636). Cambridge, MA: MIT Press.

Fischhoff, B. (2007). An early history of hindsight research. *Social Cognition, 25*(1), 10–13.

Fishbein, M., & Cappella, J. N. (2006). The role theory in developing effective health communications. *Journal of Communication, 56*(1), S1–S17.

Fischer, M. A., Stedman, M. R., Lii, J., Vogeli, C., Shrank, W. H., Brookhart, M. A., & Weissman, J. S. (2010). Primary medication non-adherence: Analysis of 195,930 electronic prescriptions. *Journal of General Internal Medicine, 25*(4), 284–290.

Fisher, T. D., & Brunell, A. B. (2014). A bogus pipeline approach to studying gender differences in cheating behavior. *Personality and Individual Differences, 61–62*, 91–96.

Fiske, S. T., Cuddy, A. J., Glick, P., & Xu, J. (2002). A model of (often mixed) stereotype content: Competence and warmth respectively follow from perceived status and competition. *Journal of Personality and Social Psychology, 82*(6), 878–902.

Fiske, S. T., Kenny, D. A., & Taylor, S. E. (1982). Structural models for the mediation of salience effects on attribution. *Journal of Experimental Social Psychology, 18*(2), 105–127.

Fleder, G., Kankiewicz, C., & Milchan, A. (Producers), & Fleder, G. (Director). (2003). *Runaway jury* [Motion picture]. United States: 20th Century Fox.

Fleming, J. S., & Courtney, B. E. (1984). The dimensionality of self-esteem: II. Hierarchical facet model for revised measurement scales. *Journal of Personality and Social Psychology, 46*(2), 404–421.

Fogelson, A. (Producer), & Gottlieb, L. (Director). (1985). *Just one of the guys* [Motion picture]. USA: Colombia Pictures, Summa Entertainment Group, & Triton.

Follingstad, D. R., Rutledge, L. L., Berg, B. J., Hause, E. S., & Polek, D. S. (1990). The role of emotional abuse in physically abusive relationships. *Journal of Family Violence, 5*(2), 107–120.

Fonda, H., Rose, R., & Donnelly, T. A. (Producers), & Lumet, S., & Friedkin, W. (Directors). (1997). *12 angry men* [Motion picture]. United States: Orion-Nova Productions and MGM Television. (Original work published 1957).

Fontana, D. (2003). *The secret language of symbols: A visual key to symbols and their meanings.* San Francisco, CA: Chronicle Books.

Forgas, J. P. (1998). On being happy and mistaken: Mood effects on the fundamental attribution error. *Journal of Personality and Social Psychology, 75*(2), 318–331.

Forsyth, D. R. (2010). *Group dynamics* (5th ed.). Belmont, CA: Wadsorth/Cengage.

Forsyth, D. R., Lawrence, N. K., Burnette, J. L., & Baumeister, R. F. (2007). Attempting to improve the academic performance of struggling college students by bolstering their self-esteem: An intervention that backfired. *Journal of Social and Clinical Psychology, 26*(4), 447–459.

Fox, N. A., & Davidson, R. J. (1988). Patterns of brain electrical activity during facial signs of emotion in 10-month-old infants. *Developmental Psychology, 24*(2), 230–236.

Francis, C., & Barber, J. (2013). A framework for understanding noise impacts on wildlife: An urgent conservation priority. *Frontiers in Ecology and the Environment, 11*(6), 305–313.

Frank, M. G., & Gilovich, T. (1988). The dark side of self- and social perception: Black uniforms and aggression in professional sports. *Journal of Personality and Social Psychology, 54*(1), 74–85.

Frederick, D., & Fales, M. (2016). Upset over sexual versus emotional infidelity among gay, lesbian, bisexual, and heterosexual adults. *Archives of Sexual Behavior: The Official Publication of the International Academy of Sex Research, 45*(1), 175–191.

Fredrickson, B. L. (2013). Updated thinking on positivity ratios. *American Psychologist, 68*(9), 814–822.

Fredrickson, B. L., & Losada, M. F. (2005). Positive affect and the complex dynamics of human flourishing. *American Psychologist, 60*(7), 678–686.

Freedman, J. L., & Fraser, S. C. (1966). Compliance without pressure: The foot-in-the-door technique. *Journal of Personality and Social Psychology, 4*(2), 195–202.

Fridlund, A. J. (1994). *Human facial expression.* San Diego, CA: Academic Press.

Friedemann, V. M., & Morgan, M. K. (1985). *Interviewing sexual abuse victims using anatomical dolls: The professional's guidebook.* Eugene, OR: Shamrock Press.

Friedman, M., & Rosenman, R. (1974). *Type A behavior and your heart.* New York, NY: Knopf.

Friedman, S. T. (1964). Parental child-rearing attitudes and social behavior of children. *Dissertation Abstracts, 24*(8), 3415.

Friend, R., Rafferty, Y., & Bramel, D. (1990). A puzzling misinterpretation of the Asch 'conformity' study. *European Journal of Social Psychology, 20*(1), 29–44.

Frieze, I. H., Olson, J. E., & Russell, J. (1991). Attractiveness and income for men and women in management. *Journal of Applied Social Psychology, 21*(13), 1039–1057.

Froh, J. J. (2004). The history of positive psychology: Truth be told. *NYS Psychologist, 16*(3), 18–20.

Fulero, S. M., & Wrightsman, L. S. (2008). *Forensic psychology.* Boston, MA: Cengage Learning.

Fultz, J., Schaller, M., & Cialdini, R. B. (1988). Empathy, sadness, and distress: Three related but distinct vicarious affective responses to another's suffering. *Personality and Social Psychology Bulletin, 14*(2), 312–325.

Furley, P., Schweizer, G., & Bertrams, A. (2015). The two modes of an athlete: Dual-process theories in the field of sport. *International Review of Sport and Exercise Psychology, 8*(1), 106–124.

Furnham, A. (1995). The just world, charitable giving and attitudes to disability. *Personality and Individual Differences, 19*(4), 577–583.

Furnham, A. (2003). Belief in a just world: Research progress over the past decade. *Personality and Individual Differences, 34*(5), 795–817.

Furnham, A., & Dowsett, T. (1993). Sex differences in social comparison and uniqueness bias. *Personality and Individual Differences, 15*(2), 175–183.

Furnham, A., & Gunter, B. (1984). Just world beliefs and attitudes towards the poor. *British Journal of Social Psychology, 23*(3), 265–269.

Gable, S. L., & Haidt, J. (2005). What (and why) is positive psychology? *Review of General Psychology, 9*(2), 103–110.

Gagnon, J. H., & Simon, W. (1987). The sexual scripting of oral genital contacts. *Archives of Sexual Behavior, 16*(1), 1–25.

Gakhal, B., & Senior, C. (2008). Examining the influence of fame in the presence of beauty: An electrodermal 'neuromarketing' study. *Journal of Consumer Behavior, 7*(4–5), 331–341.

Galanter, M. (2005). The hundred-year decline of trials and the thirty years war. *Stanford Law Review, 57*(5), 1255–1274.

Gallup, G. J. (1968). Mirror-image stimulation. *Psychological Bulletin, 70*(6, Pt. 1), 782–793.

Gamble, J. L., & Hess, J. J. (2012). Temperature and violent crime in Dallas, Texas: Relationships and implications of climate change. *Western Journal of Emergency Medicine, 13*(3), 239–246.

Gana, K., Alaphilippe, D., & Bailly, N. (2004). Positive illusions and mental and physical health in later life. *Aging & Mental Health, 8*(1), 58–64.

Gangestad, S. W., Thornhill, R., & Yeo, R. A. (1994). Facial attractiveness, developmental stability, and fluctuating asymmetry. *Ethology & Sociobiology, 15*(2), 73–85.

Gannon, T. A., Keown, K., & Polaschek, D. L. (2007). Increasing honest responding on cognitive distortions in child molesters: The bogus pipeline revisited. *Sexual Abuse: Journal of Research and Treatment, 19*(1), 5–22.

Gansberg, M. (1964, March 27). 37 who saw murder didn't call the police. *New York Times.*

Gawronski, B., & Bodenhausen, G. V. (2006). Associative and propositional processes in evaluation: An integrated review of implicit and explicit attitude change. *Psychological Bulletin, 132*(5), 692–731.

Geen, R. G. (1989). Alternative conceptions of social facilitation. In P. B. Paulus (Ed.), *Psychology of group influence* (2nd ed., pp. 15–51). Hillsdale, NJ: Lawrence Erlbaum.

Gelatt, H. B. (1989). Positive uncertainty: A new decision-making framework for counseling. *Journal of Counseling Psychology, 36*(2), 252–256.

Gelb, B. D., & Zinkhan, G. M. (1986). Humor and advertising effectiveness after repeated exposures to a radio commercial. *Journal of Advertising, 15*(2), 15–34.

Gendron, M., Roberson, D., van der Vyver, J. M., & Barrett, L. F. (2014). Cultural relativity in perceiving emotion from vocalizations. *Psychological Science, 25*(4), 911–920.

Gentile, D. A., Coyne, S., & Walsh, D. A. (2011). Media violence, physical aggression, and relational aggression in school age children: A short-term longitudinal study. *Aggressive Behavior, 37*(2), 193–206.

George, K. M., & Basavarajappa. (2016). Impact of brainstorming on creativity among middle school children. *Journal of the Indian Academy of Applied Psychology, 42*(2), 320–327.

George, M. (2013). Seeking legitimacy: The professionalization of life coaching. *Sociological Inquiry, 83*(2), 179–208.

Gerber, A. S., Huber, G. A., Doherty, D., Dowling, C. M., & Panagopoulos, C. (2013). Big five personality traits and responses to persuasive appeals: Results from voter turnout experiments. *Political Behavior, 35*(4), 687–728.

Gergen, K. J., Gergen, M. M., & Barton, W. H. (1973). Deviance in the dark. *Psychology Today, 7*(5), 129–130.

Geronimus, A. T. (1992). The weathering hypothesis and the health of African-American women and infants: Evidence and speculations. *Ethnicity & Disease, 2*(3), 207–221.

Gessner, J. (2014). How railroad brakemen derailed unpaid interns: The need for a revised framework to determine FLSA coverage for unpaid interns. *Indiana Law Review, 48,* 1053.

Gettleman, J. (2011, December 28). For Somali women, pain of being a spoil of war. *New York Times,* p. A1.

Ghaemi, S. N. (2009). The rise and fall of the biopsychosocial model. *The British Journal of Psychiatry, 195*(1), 3–4.

Giarraputpo, J., Golin, S., Juvonen, N. (Producers), & Segal, P. (Director). (2004). *50 first dates* [Motion picture]. United States: Columbia Pictures.

Gibbons, F. X., & Buunk, B. P. (1999). Individual differences in social comparison: Development of a scale of social comparison orientation. *Journal of Personality and Social Psychology, 76*(1), 129–142.

Gibbons, F. X., Lane, D. J., Gerrard, M., Reis-Bergan, M., Lautrup, C. L., Pexa, N. A., & Blanton, H. (2002). Comparison-level preferences after performance: Is downward comparison theory still useful? *Journal of Personality and Social Psychology, 83*(4), 865–880.

Gilbert, D. T. (1991). How mental systems believe. *American Psychologist, 46*(2), 107–119.

Gilbert, D. T., Giesler, R. B., & Morris, K. A. (1995). When comparisons arise. *Journal of Personality and Social Psychology, 69*(2), 227–236.

Gilbert, D. T., & Gill, M. J. (2000). The momentary realist. *Psychological Science, 11*(5), 394–398.

Gilbert, D. T., & Hixon, J. G. (1991). The trouble of thinking: Activation and application of stereotypic beliefs. *Journal of Personality and Social Psychology, 60*(4), 509–517.

Gilbert, D. T., & Malone, P. S. (1995). The correspondence bias. *Psychological Bulletin, 117*(1), 21–38.

Gilbert, D. T., Pinel, E. C., Wilson, T. D., Blumberg, S. J., & Wheatley, T. P. (1998). Immune neglect: A source of durability bias in affective forecasting. *Journal of Personality and Social Psychology, 75*(3), 617–638.

Gillath, O., Adams, G., & Kunkel, A. (2012). *Relationship science: Integrating evolutionary, neuroscience, and sociocultural approaches.* Washington, DC: American Psychological Association.

Gilovich, T. (1983). Biased evaluation and persistence in gambling. *Journal of Personality and Social Psychology, 44*(6), 1110–1126.

Gilovich, T., Kerr, M., & Medvec, V. H. (1993). Effect of temporal perspective on subjective confidence. *Journal of Personality and Social Psychology, 64*(4), 552–560.

Glass, T. A., Freedman, M., Carlson, M. C., Hill, J., Frick, K. D., Ialongo, N., . . . Wasik, B. A. (2004). Experience corps: Design of an intergenerational program to boost social capital and promote the health of an aging society. *Journal of Urban Health, 81*(1), 94–105.

Gleick, E. (1997, February 10). Marine blood sports. *Time,* p. 30.

Glick, P., & Fiske, S. T. (1996). The ambivalent sexism inventory: Differentiating hostile and benevolent sexism. *Journal of Personality and Social Psychology, 70*(3), 491–512.

Glick, P., & Fiske, S. T. (2001). An ambivalent alliance: Hostile and benevolent sexism as complementary justifications for gender inequality. *American Psychologist, 56*(2), 109–118.

Glick, P., Sakalli-Ugurlu, N., Ferreira, M. C., & de Souza, M. A. (2002). Ambivalent sexism and attitudes toward wife abuse in Turkey and Brazil. *Psychology of Women Quarterly, 26*(4), 292–297.

Goethals, G. R. Messick, D. M., & Allison, S. T. (1991). The uniqueness bias: Studies of constructive social comparison. In J. Suls & T. A. Wills (Eds.), *Social comparison: Contemporary theory and research* (pp. 149–176). New York, NY: Lawrence Erlbaum.

Goetting, A. (1999). *Getting out: Life stories of women who left abusive men.* New York, NY: Columbia University Press.

Goetzman, G., Hanks, T., & Wilson, R. (Producers), & Jones, K. (Director). (2002). *My big fat Greek wedding 2* [Motion picture]. United States: Gold Circle Films.

Goetzman, G., Hanks, T., & Wilson, R. (Producers), & Zwick, J. (Director). (2002). *My big fat Greek wedding* [Motion picture]. United States: Gold Circle Films.

Goff, P. A., Jackson, M. C., Di Leone, B. A. L., Culotta, C. M., & DiTomasso, N. A. (2014). The essence of innocence: Consequences of dehumanizing Black children. *Journal of Personality and Social Psychology, 106*(4), 526–545.

Goffman, E. (1959). *The presentation of self in everyday life.* Oxford, UK: Doubleday.

Goffman, E. (1963). *Stigma: Notes on the management of spoiled identity.* Englewood Cliffs, NJ: Prentice Hall.

Golding, W. (1954). *Lord of the flies.* London, UK: Faber and Faber.

Goldsman, A., Milchan, A., & Foster, L. (Producers), & Liman, D. (Director). (2005). *Mr. & Mrs. Smith* [Motion picture]. United States: 20th Century Fox.

Goldstein, A. L., Wall, A. M., Wekerle, C., & Krank, M. (2013). The impact of perceived reinforcement form alcohol and involvement in leisure activities on adolescent alcohol use. *Journal of Child & Adolescent Substance Abuse, 22*(4), 340–363.

Goldstein, J. (1968). Psychoanalysis and jurisprudence: On the relevance of psychoanalytic theory to law. *The Psychoanalytic Study of the Child, 23*(1), 459–479.

Goldstein, J. H., Davis, R. W., & Herman, D. (1975). Escalation of aggression: Experimental studies. *Journal of Personality and Social Psychology, 31*(1), 162–170.

Gonsalkorale, K., & Williams, K. D. (2007). The KKK won't let me play: Ostracism even by a despised outgroup hurts. *European Journal of Social Psychology, 37*(6), 1176–1186.

Goodfriend, W. (2005). Partner-esteem: Romantic partners in the eyes of biased beholders. *Dissertation Abstracts International.*

Goodfriend, W. (2008). The social psychology of the Justice League of America. In R. Rosenberg & J. Canzoneri (Eds.), *Psychology of superheroes* (pp. 19–28). Dallas, TX: BenBella.

Goodfriend, W. (2009). Proximity and attraction. In H. T. Reis & S. Sprecher (Eds.), *Encyclopedia of human relationships* (pp. 1297–1299). Thousand Oaks, CA: Sage.

Goodfriend, W. (2012). Sexual script or sexual improv? Nontraditional sexual paths. In M. Paludi (Ed.), *The psychology of love* (Vol. 1, pp. 59–71). Santa Barbara, CA: Praeger.

Goodfriend, W., & Agnew, C. R. (2008). Sunken costs and desired plans: Examining different types of investments in close relationships. *Personality and Social Psychology Bulletin, 34*(12), 1639–1652.

Goodfriend, W., Agnew, C. R., & Cathey, P. (2017). Understanding commitment and partner-serving biases in close relationships. In J. Fitzgerald (Ed.), *Foundations for couples' therapy: Research for the real world* (pp. 51–60). New York, NY: Routledge.

Goodfriend, W., & Formichella-Elsden, A. (2017). Multiple identities, multiple selves? Diana Prince's actual, ideal, & ought selves. In T. Langley & M. Wood (Eds.), *Wonder Woman psychology: Lassoing the truth* (pp. 139–149). New York, NY: Sterling.

Goodman, W. (1997, May 27). Turning a sex abuse case around. *New York Times.* Retrieved from http://www.nytimes.com/1997/05/27/arts/turning-a-sex-abuse-case-around.html

Gordon, A. K., & Kaplar, M. E. (2002). A new technique for demonstrating the actor-observer bias. *Teaching of Psychology, 29*(4), 301–303.

Gordon, R. A. (1996). Impact of ingratiation on judgments and evaluations: A meta-analytic investigation. *Journal of Personality and Social Psychology, 71*(1), 54–70.

Gorn, G. J., & Goldberg, M. E. (1980). Children's responses to repetitive television commercials. *Journal of Consumer Research, 6*(4), 421–424.

Gosling, S. D., Ko, S. J., Mannarelli, T., & Morris, M. E. (2002). A room with a cue: Personality judgments based on offices and bedrooms. *Journal of Personality and Social Psychology, 82*(3), 379–398.

Grammer, K., & Thornhill, R. (1994). Human (Homo sapiens) facial attractiveness and sexual selection: The role of symmetry and averageness. *Journal of Comparative Psychology, 108*(3), 233–242.

Grasten, R., Grasten, T., Hussain, A., Schwartzman, Y., & Vorhies, A. J. (Producers), & Grasten, P. (Director). (2016). *37* [Motion Picture]. United States: Regner Grasten Film.

Graves, N. B., & Graves, T. D. (1985). Creating a cooperative learning environment. In R. Slavin (Ed.), *Learning to cooperate, cooperating to learn* (pp. 403–436). New York, NY: Plenum.

Grazer, B., Moosekian, V., Sackheim, D., Baum, S., Nevins, D., . . . Maeder, S. (Producers). (2009–2011). *Lie to me* [Television series]. United States: 20th Television.

Grazer, B. (Producer), & Shadyac, T. (Director). (1997). *Liar liar* [Motion picture]. United States: Universal Pictures.

Greenhouse, S. (2013). Judge rules that movie studio should have been paying interns. *New York Times*, p. B1.

Greenvald, J. (2016). The ongoing abuse of unpaid interns: How much longer until I get paid. *Hofstra Law Review, 45,* 673.

Greenwald, A. G., Banaji, M. R., Rudman, L. A., Farnham, S. D., Nosek, B. A., & Mellott, D. S. (2002). A unified theory of implicit attitudes, stereotypes, self-esteem, and self-concept. *Psychological Review, 109*(1), 3–25.

Greenwald, A. G., & Farnham, S. D. (2000). Using the Implicit Association Test to measure self-esteem and self-concept. *Journal of Personality and Social Psychology, 79*(6), 1022–1038.

Greitemeyer, T., & Mügge, D. O. (2013). Rational bystanders. *British Journal of Social Psychology, 52*(4), 773–780.

Greitemeyer, T., & Mügge, D. O. (2015). 'Video games do affect social outcomes: A meta-analytic review of the effects of violent and prosocial video game play': Corrigendum. *Personality and Social Psychology Bulletin, 41*(8), 1164.

Griffit, W., & Veitch, R. (1971). Hot and crowded: Influence of population density and temperature on interpersonal affective behavior. *Journal of Personality and Social Psychology, 17*(1), 92–98.

Griggs, R. A., & Whitehead, G. I. (2015). Coverage of Milgram's obedience experiments in social psychology textbooks: Where have all the criticisms gone? *Teaching of Psychology, 42*(4), 315–322.

Griskevicius, V., Tybur, J. M., Gangestad, S. W., Perea, E. F., Shapiro, J. R., & Kenrick, D. T. (2009). Aggress to impress: Hostility as an evolved context-dependent strategy. *Journal of Personality and Social Psychology, 96*(5), 980–994.

Grobman, A., Landes, D., & Milton, S. (1983). *Genocide, critical issues of the Holocaust: A companion volume to the film,* Genocide. Springfield, NJ: Behrman House, Inc.

Grøntvedt, T. V., & Kennair, L. O. (2013). Age preferences in a gender egalitarian society. *Journal of Social, Evolutionary, and Cultural Psychology, 7*(3), 239–249.

Grossman, P., Niemann, L., Schmidt, S., & Walach, H. (2004). Mindfulness-based stress reduction and health benefits: A meta-analysis. *Journal of Psychosomatic Research, 57*(1), 35–43.

Gruber-Baldini, A. L., Schaie, K. W., & Willis, S. L. (1995). Similarity in married couples: A longitudinal study of mental abilities and rigidity-flexibility. *Journal of Personality and Social Psychology, 69*(1), 191–203.

Gruter, M., & Masters, R. D. (1986). Ostracism as a social and biological phenomenon: An introduction. *Ethology and Sociobiology, 7*(3–4), 149–158.

Guenther, C. L., & Alicke, M. D. (2008). Self-enhancement and belief perseverance. *Journal of Experimental Social Psychology, 44*(3), 706–712.

Guerin, B. (2001). Replacing catharsis and uncertainty reduction theories with descriptions of historical and social context. *Review of General Psychology, 5*(1), 44–61.

Guild, P. D., Strickland, L. H., & Barefoot, J. C. (1977). Dissonance theory, self-perception and the bogus pipeline. *European Journal of Social Psychology, 7*(4), 465–476.

Guimond, S., Branscombe, N. R., Brunot, S., Buunk, A. P., Chatard, A., Désert, M., . . . Yzerbyt, V. (2007). Culture, gender, and the self: Variations and impact of social comparison processes. *Journal of Personality and Social Psychology, 92*(6), 1118–1134.

Gulati, R., & Puranam, P. (2009). Renewal through reorganization: The value of inconsistencies between formal and informal organizations. *Organization Science, 20*(2), 422–440.

Gunnell, J. J., & Ceci, S. J. (2010). When emotionality trumps reason: A study of individual processing style and juror bias. *Behavioral Sciences & the Law, 28*(6), 850–877.

Guthrie, R. (2004). *Even the rat was white: A historical view of psychology.* New York, NY: Harper & Row. (Original work published 1976).

Habashi, M. M., Graziano, W. G., & Hoover, A. E. (2016). Searching for the prosocial personality: A big five approach to linking personality and prosocial behavior. *Personality and Social Psychology Bulletin, 42*(9), 1177–1192.

Hafer, C. L., Begue, L., Choma, B. L., & Dempsey, J. L. (2005). Belief in a just world and commitment to long-term deserved outcomes. *Social Justice Research, 18*(4), 429–444.

Hair, M., Renaud, K. V., & Ramsay, J. (2007). The influence of self-esteem and locus of control on perceived email-related stress. *Computers in Human Behavior, 23*(6), 2791–2803.

Halpern, D. F. (2010). *Undergraduate education in psychology: A blueprint for the future of the discipline.* Washington, DC: American Psychological Association.

Halsey, L. G., Huber, J. W., Bufton, R. J., & Little, A. C. (2010). An explanation for enhanced perceptions of attractiveness after alcohol consumption. *Alcohol, 44*(4), 307–313.

Haney, C., Banks, W., & Zimbardo, P. (1973). Interpersonal dynamics in a simulated prison. *International Journal of Criminology and Penology, 1*(1), 69–97.

Hansen, C. H., & Hansen, R. D. (1988). Finding the face in the crowd: An angry superiority effect. *Journal of Personality and Social Psychology, 54*(6), 917–924.

Hansen, D. E., Vandenberg, B., & Patterson, M. L. (1995). The effects of religious orientation on spontaneous and nonspontaneous helping behaviors. *Personality and Individual Differences, 19*(1), 101–104.

Hansen, R. D. (1980). Commonsense attribution. *Journal of Personality and Social Psychology, 39*(6), 996–1009.

Hanson, H., Josephson, B., Nathan, S., Toynton, I., Kettner, C., Collier, J., Peterson, M., & Zisk, R. (Producers), & Reichs, K., Deschanel, E., Boreanaz, A., Hong, G. (Directors). (2005–2017). *Bones* [Television series]. United States: Josephson Entertainment.

Hardin, G. (1968). The tragedy of the commons. *Science, 162,* 1243–1248.

Hardy, C. J., & Latane, B. (1988). Social loafing in cheerleaders: Effects of team membership and competition. *Journal of Sport and Exercise Psychology, 10*(1), 109–114.

Harmon-Jones, E. (2007). Asymmetrical frontal cortical activity, affective valence, and motivational direction. In E. Harmon-Jones & P. Winkielman (Eds.), *Social neuroscience: Integrating biological and psychological explanations of social behavior* (pp. 137–156). New York, NY: Guilford.

Harper, C. (2007). *Intersex.* Oxford, UK: Berg.

Harrigan, J. A., & O'Connell, D. M. (1996). How do you look when feeling anxious? Facial displays of anxiety. *Personality and Individual Differences, 21*(2), 205–212.

Harris, A. H., & Thoresen, C. E. (2005). Volunteering is associated with delayed mortality in older people: Analysis of the longitudinal study of aging. *Journal of Health Psychology, 10*(6), 739–752.

Hart, B. (1986). Lesbian battering: An examination. In K. Lobel (Ed.), *Naming the violence: Speaking out about lesbian battering* (pp. 173–189). Seattle, WA: Seal Press.

Harvey, J. H., & McGlynn, R. P. (1982). Matching words to phenomena: The case of the fundamental attribution error. *Journal of Personality and Social Psychology, 43*(2), 345–346.

Harvey, J. H., Town, J. P., & Yarkin, K. L. (1981). How fundamental is the fundamental attribution error? *Journal of Personality and Social Psychology, 40*(2), 346–349.

Haselton, M. G., & Funder, D. C. (2006). The evolution of accuracy and bias in social judgment. In M. Schaller, J. A. Simpson, & D. T. Kenrick (Eds.), *Evolution and social psychology* (pp. 15–37). Madison, CT: Psychosocial Press.

Haslam, S. A., Reicher, S. D., & Birney, M. E. (2016). Questioning authority: New perspectives on Milgram's 'Obedience' research and its implications for intergroup relations. *Current Opinion in Psychology, 11,* 6–9.

Haslam, S. A., Reicher, S. D., Millard, K., & McDonald, R. (2015). "Happy to have been of service": The Yale archive as a window into the engaged followership of participants in Milgram's "obedience" experiments. *British Journal of Social Psychology, 54*(1), 55–83.

Haslam, S. A., Ryan, M. K., Postmes, T., Spears, R., Jetten, J., & Webley, P. (2006). Sticking to our guns: Social identity as a basis for the maintenance of commitment to faltering organizational projects. *Journal of Organizational Behavior, 27*(5), 607–628.

Haven Project. (2017). *The college power and control wheel.* Retrieved from http://www.iup.edu/haven/news/

Haynes, R. B., Ackloo, E., Sahota, N., McDonald, H. P., & Yao, X. (2008). Interventions for enhancing medication adherence. *Cochrane Database of Systematic Reviews, 2,* CD000011.

Hazan, C., & Shaver, P. (1987). Romantic love conceptualized as an attachment process. *Journal of Personality and Social Psychology, 52*(3), 511–524.

Hearst, P. C., & Moscow, A. (1998). *Patty Hearst: Her own story.* New York, NY: Avon Books.

Heider, F. (1958). *The psychology of interpersonal relations.* Hoboken, NJ: John Wiley.

Heinzen, T. E. (1995). Commentary: The ethical evaluation bias. *Creativity Research Journal, 8*(4), 417–422.

Heinzen, T. E., Gordon, M. S., Landrum, R. E., Gurung, R. A. R., Dunn, D. S., & Richman, S. (2015). A parallel universe: Psychological science in the language of game design. In T. Reiners & L. C. Wood (Eds.), *Gamification in education and business* (pp. 133–149). New York, NY: Springer.

Heinzen, T. E., Landrum, R. E., Gurung, R. A., & Dunn, D. S. (2015). Game-based assessment: The mash-up we've been waiting for. In *Gamification in education and business* (pp. 201–217). Cham, Switzerland: Springer International.

Helloflo.com. (2017). *Home.* Retrieved from http://helloflo.com/

Henchy, T., & Glass, D. C. (1968). Evaluation apprehension and the social facilitation of dominant and subordinate responses. *Journal of Personality and Social Psychology, 10*(4), 446–454.

Henriksen, D., & Dayton, E. (2006). Organizational silence and hidden threats to patient safety. *Health Services Research, 41*(4, Pt. 2), 1539–1554.

Herek, G. M. (1987). Religious orientation and prejudice: A comparison of racial and sexual attitudes. *Personality and Social Psychology Bulletin, 13*(1), 34–44.

Hewitt, P. L., & Genest, M. (1990). The ideal self: Schematic processing of perfectionistic content in dysphoric university students. *Journal of Personality and Social Psychology, 59*(4), 802–808.

Higgins, C. A., Judge, T. A., & Ferris, G. R. (2003). Influence tactics and work outcomes: A meta-analysis. *Journal of Organizational Behavior, 24*(1), 89–106.

Higgins, E. T. (1987). Self-discrepancy: A theory relating self and affect. *Psychological Review, 94*(3), 319–340.

Higgins, E. T. (2002). How self-regulation creates distinct values: The case of promotion and prevention decision making. *Journal of Consumer Psychology, 12*(3), 177–191.

Hill, L. K., Hoggard, L. S., Richmond, A. S., Gray, D. L., Williams, D. P., & Thayer, J. F. (2017). Examining the association between perceived discrimination and heart rate variability in African Americans. *Cultural Diversity and Ethnic Minority Psychology, 23*(1), 5–14.

Hilton, A., Potvin, L., & Sachdev, I. (1989). Ethnic relations in rental housing: A social psychological approach. *Canadian Journal of Behavioral Science, 21*(2), 121–131.

Hilton, L., Hempel, S., Ewing, B. A., Apaydin, E., Xenakis, L., Newberry, S., . . . Maglione, M. A. (2016). Mindfulness meditation for chronic pain: Systematic review and meta-analysis. *Annals of Behavioral Medicine, 51*(2), 199–213.

Hirschberger, G. (2006). Terror management and attributions of blame to innocent victims: Reconciling compassionate and defensive responses. *Journal of Personality and Social Psychology, 91*(5), 832–844.

Hirschberger, G., Florian, V., & Mikuliner, M. (2005). Fear and compassion: A terror management analysis of emotional reactions to physical disability. *Rehabilitation Psychology, 50*(3), 246–257.

Hoch, S. J. (1987). Perceived consensus and predictive accuracy: The pros and cons of projection. *Journal of Personality and Social Psychology, 53*(2), 221–234.

Hochschild, A. (2011). *To end all wars: A story of loyalty and rebellion, 1914–1918.* New York, NY: Houghton Mifflin Harcourt.

Hoerger, M., Quirk, S. W., Lucas, R. E., & Carr, T. H. (2010). Cognitive determinants of affective forecasting errors. *Judgment and Decision Making, 5*(5), 365–373.

Hogg, M. A. (2016). Social identity theory. In S. McKeown, R. Haji, & N. Ferguson (Eds.), *Understanding peace and conflict through social identity theory: Contemporary global perspectives* (pp. 3–17). New York, NY: Springer.

Hoigaard, R., Fuglestad, S., Peters, D. M., Cuyper, B. D., Backer, M. D., & Boen, F. (2010). Role satisfaction mediates the relation between role ambiguity and social loafing among elite women handball players. *Journal of Applied Sport Psychology, 22*(4), 408–419.

Hollingdale, J., & Greitemeyer, T. (2013). The changing face of aggression: The effect of personalized avatars in a violent video game on levels of aggressive behavior. *Journal of Applied Social Psychology, 43*(9), 1862–1868.

Holmes, D. S. (1968). Dimensions of projection. *Psychological Bulletin, 69*(4), 248–268.

Holmes, D. S. (1978). Projection as a defense mechanism. *Psychological Bulletin, 85*(4), 677–688.

Holmes, T. H., & Rahe, R. H. (1967). The social readjustment rating scale. *Journal of Psychosomatic Research, 11*(2), 213–218.

Hornberger, R. H. (1959). The differential reduction of aggressive responses as a function of interpolated activities. *American Psychologist, 14*(7), 354.

Hoshino-Browne, E., Zanna, A. S., Spencer, S. J., Zanna, M. P., Kitayama, S., & Lackenbauer, S. (2005). On the cultural guises of cognitive dissonance: The case of Easterners and Westerners. *Journal of Personality and Social Psychology, 89*(3), 294–310.

Hosoda, M., Stone-Romero, E. F., & Coats, G. (2003). The effects of physical attractiveness on job-related outcomes: A meta-analysis of experimental studies. *Personnel Psychology, 56*(2), 431–462.

Hovland, C. I., Janis, I. L., & Kelley, H. H. (1953). *Communication and persuasion: Psychological studies of opinion change.* New Haven, CT: Yale University Press.

Hovland, C. I., & Sears, R. R. (1940). Minor studies in aggression: VI. Correlation of lynchings with economic indices. *Journal of Psychology, 9*(2), 301–310.

Howe, L. E. A. (1989). Hierarchy and equality: Variations in Balinese social organization. *Bijdragen tot de Taal, Land-en Volkenkunde, 145*(1), 47–71.

Howell, S. (1984). *Society and cosmos: Chewong of peninsular Malaysia.* Oxford, UK: Oxford University Press.

Hua, M., & Tan, A. (2012). Media reports of Olympic success by Chinese and American gold medalists: Cultural differences in causal attribution. *Mass Communication & Society, 15*(4), 546–558.

Huesmann, L. R. (2010). Nailing the coffin shut on doubts that violent video games stimulate aggression: Comment on Anderson et al. (2010). *Psychological Bulletin, 136*(2), 179–181.

Huffman, J. C., Millstein, R. A., Mastromauro, C. A., Moore, S. V., Celano, C. M., Bedoya, C. A., . . . Januzzi, J. L. (2016). A positive psychology intervention for patients with an acute coronary syndrome: Treatment development and proof-of-concept trial. *Journal of Happiness Studies, 17*(5), 1985–2006.

Hugo, V. (1831). *The hunchback of Notre-Dame.* Paris, France: Gosselin.

Human Rights Watch. (2002). *"We are not the enemy:" Hate crimes against Arabs, Muslims, and those perceived to be Arab or Muslim after September 11.* Retrieved from https://www.hrw.org/report/2002/11/14/we-are-not-enemy/hate-crimes-against-arabs-muslimsand-those-perceived-be-arab-or

Hume, D. (1888). *A treatise of human nature* (L. Selby-Bigge Sir, Ed.). Oxford, UK: Clarendon.

Hunsberger, B. (1995). Religion and prejudice: The role of religious fundamentalism, quest, and right-wing authoritarianism. *Journal of Social Issues, 51*(2), 113–129.

Huntley, M., & Goodfriend, W. (2012). Stress from physical conflicts based upon sex, masculinity, and color perception. *Journal of Psychological Inquiry, 17,* 29–35.

Hust, S. T., Marett, E. G., Lei, M., Ren, C., & Ran, W. (2015). *Law & Order, CSI,* and *NCIS:* The association between exposure to crime drama franchises, rape myth acceptance, and sexual consent negotiation among college students. *Journal of Health Communication, 20*(12), 1369–1381.

Hutz, C. S., De Conti, L., & Vargas, S. (1994). Rules used by Brazilian students in systematic and nonsystematic reward allocation. *The Journal of Social Psychology, 134*(3), 331–338.

Ian, D. (2007). Halo effects in grading student projects. *Journal of Applied Psychology, 92*(4), 1169–1176.

Iedema, J., & Poppe, M. (1999). Expectations of others' social value orientations in specific and general populations. *Personality and Social Psychology Bulletin, 25*(12), 1443–1450.

Ingham, A. G., Levinger, G., Graves, J., & Peckham, V. (1974). The Ringelmann effect: Studies of group size and group performance. *Journal of Experimental Social Psychology, 10*(4), 371–384.

Insko, C. A., Turnbull, W., & Yandell, B. (1974). Facilitative and inhibiting effects of distraction on attitude change. *Sociometry, 37*(4), 508–528.

Isaac, S., & Juvonen, N. (Producers), & Gosnell, R. (Director). (1999). *Never been kissed* [Motion picture]. United States: 20th Century Fox.

Isaacson, W. (2014). *The innovators: How a group of hackers, geniuses, and geeks created the digital revolution.* New York, NY: Simon & Schuster.

Isenberg, D. (1986). Group polarization: A critical review and meta-analysis. *Journal of Personality and Social Psychology, 50*(6), 1141–1151.

Iyengar, S., & Westwood, S. J. (2015). Fear and loathing across party lines: New evidence on group polarization. *American Journal of Political Science, 59*(3), 690–707.

Izard, E. C. (1990). Facial expressions and the regulation of emotions. *Journal of Personality and Social Psychology, 58*(3), 487–498.

Izuma, K., Saito, D. N., & Sadato, N. (2010). Processing of the incentive for social approval in the ventral striatum during charitable donation. *Journal of Cognitive Neuroscience, 22*(4), 621–631.

Jack, R. E., Garrod, O. B., Yu, H., Caldara, R., & Schyns, P. G. (2012). Facial expressions of emotion are not culturally universal. *PNAS Proceedings of the National Academy of Sciences of the United States of America, 109*(19), 7241–7244.

Jackson, J. M., & Williams, K. D. (1985). Social loafing on difficult tasks: Working collectively can improve performance. *Journal of Personality and Social Psychology, 49*(4), 937–942.

Jackson, R. M. (2006). Opposing forces: How, why, and when will gender inequality disappear? In F. D. Blau, M. C. Brinton, & D. B. Grusky (Eds.), *The declining significance of gender?* (pp. 215–244). New York, NY: Russell Sage Foundation.

Jackson, S. (1993). Women and the family. In D. Richardson & V. Robinson (Eds.), *Thinking feminist: Key concepts in women's studies* (pp. 177–200). New York, NY: Guilford.

Jackson, S. (2001). Happily never after: Young women's stories of abuse in heterosexual love relationships. *Feminism & Psychology, 11*(3), 305–321.

Jacobs, R. C., & Campbell, D. T. (1961). The perpetuation of an arbitrary tradition through several generations of a laboratory microculture. *The Journal of Abnormal and Social Psychology, 62*(3), 649–658.

Jacobson, N. S., & Gottman, J. M. (1998). *When men batter women: New insights into ending abusive relationships.* New York, NY: Simon & Schuster.

Janes, L. M., & Olson, J. M. (2000). Jeer pressures: The behavioral effects of observing ridicule of others. *Personality and Social Psychology Bulletin, 26*(4), 474–485.

James, W. (1890). *The principles of psychology.* New York, NY: Henry Holt.

Janis, I. L. (1972). *Victims of groupthink: A psychological study of foreign-policy decisions and fiascoes.* Boston, MA: Houghton Mifflin.

James, W. (1983). *Talks to teachers on psychology and to students on some of life's ideals* (Vol. 12). New York, NY: Henry Holt. (Original work published 1899).

Jansma, J. M., Ramsey, N. F., Slagter, H. A., & Kahn, R. S. (2001). Functional anatomical correlates of controlled and automatic processing. *Journal of Cognitive Neuroscience, 13*(6), 730–743.

Jennings, J. R., Pardini, D. A., & Matthews, K. A. (2017). Heart rate, health, and hurtful behavior. *Psychophysiology, 54*(3), 399–408.

Jhally, S., Ericsson, S., & Talreja, S. (Producers), & Jhally, S. (Director). (1999). *Tough guise: Violence, media, and the crisis in masculinity* [Motion picture]. United States: Media Education Foundation.

Jin, Y., & Li, J. (2017). When newbies and veterans play together: The effect of video game content, context and experience on cooperation. *Computers in Human Behavior, 68,* 556–563.

John, O. P., & Srivastava, S. (1999). The big five trait taxonomy: History, measurement, and theoretical perspectives. In L. A. Pervin & O. P. John (Eds.), *Handbook of personality: Theory and research* (2nd ed., pp. 102–138). New York, NY: Guilford.

Johnson, B. T., & Eagly, A. H. (1989). Effects of involvement on persuasion: A meta-analysis. *Psychological Bulletin, 106*(2), 290–314.

Johnson, D., & Lewis, G. (1999). Do you like what you see? Self-perceptions of adolescent bullies. *British Educational Research Journal, 25*(5), 665–677.

Johnson, D. J., & Rusbult, C. E. (1989). Resisting temptation: Devaluation of alternative partners as a means of maintaining commitment in close relationships. *Journal of Personality and Social Psychology, 57*(6), 967–980.

Johnson, J. M., & Pettigrew, T. F. (2005). Kenneth B. Clark (1914–2005). *American Psychologist, 60*(6), 649–651.

Johnson, M. P. (1995). Patriarchal terrorism and common couple violence: Two forms of violence against women. *Journal of Marriage and the Family, 57*(2), 283–294.

Johnson, M. P. (2007). The intersection of gender and control. In L. O'Toole, J. R. Schiffman, & M. L. K. Edwards (Eds.), *Gender violence: Interdisciplinary perspectives* (2nd ed., pp. 257–268). New York: New York University Press.

Johnson, R. D., & Downing, L. L. (1979). Deindividuation and valence of cues: Effects on prosocial and antisocial behavior. *Journal of Personality and Social Psychology, 37*(9), 1532–1538.

Johnston, E. (2001). The repeated reproduction of Bartlett's Remembering. *History of Psychology, 4*(4), 341–366.

Johnston, L. (2002). Behavioral mimicry and stigmatization. *Social Cognition, 20*(1), 18–35.

Johnston, R. (2005). *Analytic culture in the U.S. intelligence community: An ethnographic study.* Washington, DC: Government Printing Office.

Joly, D. (Ed.). (2016). *Scapegoats and social actors: The exclusion and integration of minorities in Western and Eastern Europe*. Basingstoke, UK: Macmillan.

Jonas, E., Martens, A., Niesta Kayser, D., Fritsche, I., Sullivan, D., & Greenberg, J. (2008). Focus theory of normative conduct and terror-management theory: The interactive impact of mortality salience and norm salience on social judgment. *Journal of Personality and Social Psychology, 95*(6), 1239–1251.

Jones, A. (2000). *Next time, she'll be dead: Battering and how to stop it*. Boston, MA: Beacon.

Jones, B. D. (1999). Bounded rationality. *Annual Review of Political Science, 2*(1), 297–321.

Jones, E. E. (1979). The rocky road from acts to dispositions. *American Psychologist, 34*(2), 107–117.

Jones, E. E., & Davis, K. E. (1965). From acts to dispositions: The attribution process in person perception. In L. Berkowitz (Ed.), *Advances in experimental social psychology* (Vol. 2, pp. 219–266). New York, NY: Academic Press.

Jones, E. E., & Harris, V. A. (1967). The attribution of attitudes. *Journal of Experimental Social Psychology, 3*(1), 1–24.

Jones, E. E., & Pittman, T. S. (1982). Toward a general theory of strategic self-presentation. In J. Suls (Ed.), *Psychological perspectives on the self* (Vol. 1, pp. 231–262). Hillsdale, NJ: Lawrence Erlbaum.

Jones, T. F., Craig, A. S., Hoy, D., Gunter, E. W., Ashley, D. L., Barr, D. B., . . . Schaffner, W. (2000). Mass psychogenic illness attributed to toxic exposure at a high school. *The New England Journal of Medicine, 342*(2), 96–100.

Jordan, C. H., Spencer, S. J., & Zanna, M. P. (2005). Types of high self-esteem and prejudice: How implicit self-esteem relates to ethnic discrimination among high explicit self-esteem individuals. *Personality and Social Psychology Bulletin, 31*(5), 693–702.

Jussim, L., & Harber, K. D. (2005). Teacher expectations and self-fulfilling prophecies: Knowns and unknowns, resolved and unresolved controversies. *Personality and Social Psychology Review, 9*(2), 131–155.

Kahneman, D. (2003). A perspective on judgment and choice: Mapping bounded rationality. *American Psychologist, 58*(9), 697–720.

Kahneman, D. (2011). *Thinking, fast and slow*. New York, NY: Farrar, Straus and Giroux.

Kahneman, D., & Frederick, S. (2005). A model of heuristic judgment. In K. J. Holyoak & R. G. Morrison (Eds.), *The Cambridge handbook of thinking and reasoning* (pp. 267–293). Cambridge, UK: Cambridge University Press.

Kahneman, D., & Riis, J. (2005). Living, and thinking about it: Two perspectives on life. In *The science of well-being* (pp. 285–304). New York, NY: Oxford University Press.

Kahneman, D., & Tversky, A. (1979). On the interpretation of intuitive probability: A reply to Jonathan Cohen. *Cognition, 7*(4), 409–411.

Kahneman, D., & Tversky, A. (1982). The simulation heuristic. In D. Kahneman, P. Slovic, & A. Tversky (Eds.), *Judgment under uncertainty: Heuristics and biases* (pp. 201–208). Cambridge, UK: Cambridge University Press.

Kahneman, D., & Tversky, A. (2000). *Choices, values, and frames*. New York, NY: Cambridge University Press.

Kamat, S. S., & Kanekar, S. (1990). Prediction of and recommendation for honest behavior. *The Journal of Social Psychology, 130*(5), 597–607.

Kameda, T., & Tindale, R. S. (2006). Groups as adaptive devices: Human docility and group aggregation mechanisms in evolutionary context. In M. Schaller, J. Simpson, & D. Kenrick (Eds.), *Evolution and social psychology* (pp. 317–341). New York, NY: Psychology Press.

Kandel, E. R. (2006). *In search of memory: The emergence of a new science of mind*. New York, NY: Norton.

Kandler, C., Bleidorn, W., & Riemann, R. (2012). Left or right? Sources of political orientation: The roles of genetic factors, cultural transmission, assortative mating, and personality. *Journal of Personality and Social Psychology, 102*(3), 633–645.

Karatzias, A., Power, K. G., & Swanson, V. (2002). Bullying and victimisation in Scottish secondary schools: Same or separate entities? *Aggressive Behavior, 28*(1), 45–61.

Karau, S. J., & Williams, K. D. (1993). Social loafing: A meta-analytic review and theoretical integration. *Journal of Personality and Social Psychology, 65*(4), 681–706.

Kärtner, J., Keller, H., & Chaudhary, N. (2010). Cognitive and social influences on early prosocial behavior in two sociocultural contexts. *Developmental Psychology, 46*(4), 905–914.

Kassin, S. M. (1997). The psychology of confession evidence. *American Psychologist, 52*(3), 221.

Kassin, S. M. (1998). Eyewitness identification procedures: The fifth rule. *Law and Human Behavior, 22*(6), 649–653.

Kassin, S. M. (2015). The social psychology of false confessions. *Social Issues and Policy Review, 9*(1), 25–51.

Kassin, S. M., & Kiechel, K. L. (1996). The social psychology of false confessions: Compliance, internalization, and confabulation. *Psychological Science, 7*(3), 125–128.

Kassin, S. M., & Sukel, H. (1997). Coerced confessions and the jury: An experimental test of the "harmless error" rule. *Law and Human Behavior, 21*(1), 27–46.

Kassin, S. M., Williams, L. N., & Saunders, C. L. (1990). Dirty tricks of cross-examination: The influence of conjectural evidence on the jury. *Law and Human Behavior, 14*(4), 373–384.

Kassin, S. M., & Wrightsman, L. S. (1985). Confession evidence. In S. M. Kassin & L. S. Wrightsman (Eds.), *The psychology of evidence and trial procedure* (pp. 67–94). Thousand Oaks, CA: Sage.

Kassin, S. M., & Wrightsman, L. S. (1988). *The American jury on trial: Psychological perspectives*. New York, NY: Taylor & Francis.

Katz, D., Allport, F. H., & Jenness, M. B. (1931). *Students' attitudes; A report of the Syracuse University reaction study*. Oxford, UK: Craftsman Press.

Katz, J., & Wigderson, S. (2012). 'Put out or get out': Understanding young women's experiences of verbal sexual coercion by male dating partners. In M. A. Paludi (Ed.), *The psychology of love* (pp. 113–129). Santa Barbara, CA: Praeger/ABC-CLIO.

Keating, C. F., Pomerantz, J., Pommer, S. D., Ritt, S. J., Miller, L. M., & McCormick, J. (2005). Going to college and unpacking hazing: A functional approach to decrypting initiation practices among undergraduates. *Group Dynamics: Theory, Research, Practice, 9*(2), 104–126.

Keating, J., Van Boven, L., & Judd, C. M. (2016). Partisan underestimation of the polarizing influence of group discussion. *Journal of Experimental Social Psychology, 65*, 52–58.

Kelley, H. H. (1950). The warm-cold variable in first impressions of persons. *Journal of Personality, 18*(4), 431–439.

Kelley, H. H. (1955). Salience of membership and resistance to change of group-centered attitudes. *Human Relations, 8*(3), 275–289.

Kelley, H. H. (1967). Attribution theory in social psychology. *Nebraska Symposium on Motivation, 15*, 192–238.

Kelley, H. H. (1973). The processes of causal attribution. *American Psychologist, 28*(2), 107–128.

Kelman, H. C., & Hamilton, V. L. (1989). *Crimes of obedience: Toward a social psychology of authority and responsibility*. New Haven, CT: Yale University Press.

Keltner, D., & Shiota, M. N. (2003). New displays and new emotions: A commentary on Rozin and Cohen (2003). *Emotion, 3*(1), 86–91.

Kemmelmeier, M., Jambor, E. E., & Letner, J. (2006). Individualism and good works: Cultural variation in giving and volunteering across the United States. *Journal of Cross-Cultural Psychology, 37*(3), 327–344.

Kennedy, B. (2013). The hijacking of foreign policy decision making: Groupthink and presidential power in the post-9/11 world. *Southern California Interdisciplinary Law Journal, 21*, 633–680.

Kerr, N. L., & Bruun, S. E. (1981). Ringelmann revisited: Alternative explanations for the social loafing effect. *Personality and Social Psychology Bulletin, 7*(2), 224–231.

Keynes, J. (1920). *The economic consequences of the peace*. New York, NY: Harcourt, Brace and Howe.

Kiesler, S. B., & Mathog, R. B. (1968). Distraction hypothesis in attitude change: Effects of effectiveness. *Psychological Reports, 23*(3), 1123–1133.

Kilpatrick, D. G. (2004). What is violence against women? Defining and measuring the problem. *Journal of Interpersonal Violence, 19*(11), 1209–1234.

Kim, H., & Markus, H. R. (1999). Deviance or uniqueness, harmony or conformity? A cultural analysis. *Journal of Personality and Social Psychology, 77*(4), 785–800.

Kim, K. J., & Sundar, S. S. (2013). Can interface features affect aggression resulting from violent video game play? An examination of realistic controller and large screen size. *Cyberpsychology, Behavior, and Social networking, 16*(5), 329–334.

Kim, Y. J., & Na, J. H. (2007). Effects of celebrity athlete endorsement on attitude towards the product: The role of credibility, attractiveness and the concept of congruence. *International Journal of Sports Marketing and Sponsorship, 8*(4), 23–33.

King, E. B., Shapiro, J. R., Hebl, M. R., Singletary, S. L., & Turner, S. (2006). The stigma of obesity in customer service: A mechanism for remediation and bottom-line consequences of interpersonal discrimination. *Journal of Applied Psychology, 91*(3), 579–593.

Kinsey, A. C., Pomeroy, W. B., & Martin, C. E. (1948). *Sexual behavior in the human male*. Oxford, UK: Saunders.

Kirkwood, C. (1993). *Leaving abusive partners: From the scars of survival to the wisdom for change*. Thousand Oaks, CA: Sage.

Kitayama, S., Snibbe, A. C., Markus, H. R., & Suzuki, T. (2004). Is there any "free" choice? Self and dissonance in two cultures. *Psychological Science, 15*(8), 527–533.

Kite, M. E., Deaux, K., & Haines, E. L. (2007). Gender stereotypes. In F. L. Denmark & M. A. Paludi (Eds.), *Psychology of women: A handbook of issues and theories* (2nd ed., pp. 205–236). Westport, CT: Praeger/ Greenwood.

Klein, E., Campbell, J., Soler, E., & Ghez, M. (1997). *Ending domestic violence: Changing public perceptions/halting the epidemic*. Thousand Oaks, CA: Sage.

Kleinke, C. L., & Meyer, C. (1990). Evaluation of rape victim by men and women with high and low belief in a just world. *Psychology of Women Quarterly, 14*(3), 343–353.

Klump, K. L., Keel, P. K., Sisk, C., & Burt, S. A. (2010). Preliminary evidence that estradiol moderates genetic influences on disordered eating attitudes and behaviors during puberty. *Psychological Medicine, 40*(10), 1745–1753.

Klump, K. L., McGue, M., & Iacono, W. G. (2003). Differential heritability of eating attitudes and behaviors in prepubertal versus pubertal twins. *International Journal of Eating Disorders, 33*(3), 287–292.

Knickmeyer, R., & Baron-Cohen, S. (2006). Topical review: Fetal testosterone and sex differences in typical social development and in autism. *Journal of Child Neurology, 21*(10), 825–845.

Koehler, D. J., & Poon, C. S. K. (2006). Self-predictions overweight strength of current intentions. *Journal of Experimental Social Psychology, 42*(4), 517–524.

Koocher, G. P. (1977). Bathroom behavior and human dignity. *Journal of Personality and Social Psychology, 35*(2), 120–121.

Kopelson, A., & Carlyle, P. (Producers), & Fincher, D. (Director). (1995). *Seven* [Motion picture]. United States: New Line Cinema.

Korde, R., & Paulus, P. B. (2017). Alternating individual and group idea generation: Finding the elusive synergy. *Journal of Experimental Social Psychology, 70*, 177–190.

Kraut, R. E., & Johnson, R. E. (1979). Social and emotional messages of smiling: An ethological approach. *Journal of Personality and Social Psychology, 37*(9), 1539–1553.

Kravitz, D. A., & Martin, B. (1986). Ringelmann rediscovered: The original article. *Journal of Personality and Social Psychology, 50*(5), 936–941.

Kressel, N. J. (2012). *"The sons of pigs and apes": Muslim anti-Semitism and the conspiracy of silence*. Washington, DC: Potomac Books.

Kressel, N. J., & Kressel, D. (2002). *Stack and sway: The new science of jury consulting*. Boulder, CO: Westview.

Kretschmar, J. M., & Flannery, D. J. (2007). Substance abuse and violent behavior. In D. J. Flannery, A. T. Vazsonyi, & I. D. Waldman (Eds.), *The Cambridge handbook of violent behavior and aggression* (pp. 647–663). Cambridge, UK: Cambridge University Press.

Krosnick, J. A., & Petty, R. E. (1995). Attitude strength: An overview. In R. E. Petty & J. A. Krosnick (Eds.), *Attitude strength: Antecedents and consequences* (pp. 1–24). Mahwah, NJ: Lawrence Erlbaum.

Krueger, J. I., & Clement, R. W. (1994). The truly false consensus effect: An ineradicable and egocentric bias in social perception. *Journal of Personality and Social Psychology, 67*(4), 596–610.

Krueger, J. I., Vohs, K. D., & Baumeister, R. F. (2008). Is the allure of self-esteem a mirage after all? *American Psychologist, 63*(1), 64–65.

Krueger, J. I.., & Zeiger, J. S. (1993). Social categorization and the truly false consensus effect. *Journal of Personality and Social Psychology, 65*(4), 670–680.

Krueger, R. F., Hicks, B. M., & McGue, M. (2001). Altruism and antisocial behavior: Independent tendencies, unique personality correlates, distinct etiologies. *Psychological Science, 12*(5), 397–402.

Kruse, H., Smith, S., van Tubergen, F., & Maas, I. (2016). From neighbors to school friends? How adolescents' place of residence relates to same-ethnic school friendships. *Social Networks, 44,* 130–142.

Kteily, N. S., Sidanius, J., & Levin, S. (2011). Social dominance orientation: Cause or 'mere effect'? Evidence for SDO as a causal predictor of prejudice and discrimination against ethnic and racial outgroups. *Journal of Experimental Social Psychology, 47*(1), 208–214.

Kubany, E. S., Leisen, M. B., Kaplan, A. S., & Kelly, M. P. (2000). Validation of a brief measure of posttraumatic stress disorder: The Distressing Event Questionnaire (DEQ). *Psychological Assessment, 12*(2), 197–209.

Kulik, J. A., & Mahler, H. I. (1989). Stress and affiliation in a hospital setting: Preoperative roommate preferences. *Personality and Social Psychology Bulletin, 15*(2), 183–193.

Kulik, J. A., Mahler, H. I., & Moore, P. J. (1996). Social comparison and affiliation under threat: Effects on recovery from major surgery. *Journal of Personality and Social Psychology, 71*(5), 967–979.

Kulish, N. (2008, March 20). Efforts to restore shine to medal tarnished by Nazis. *New York Times International,* p. A4.

Kumru, A., Carlo, G., Mestre, M. V., & Samper, P. (2012). Prosocial moral reasoning and prosocial behavior among Turkish and Spanish adolescents. *Social Behavior and Personality, 40*(2), 205–214.

Kunda, Z., & Schwartz, S. H. (1983). Undermining intrinsic moral motivation: External reward and self-presentation. *Journal of Personality and Social Psychology, 45*(4), 763–771.

Kurdek, L. A., & Schmitt, J. P. (1987). Partner homogamy in married, heterosexual cohabiting, gay, and lesbian couples. *Journal of Sex Research, 23*(2), 212–232.

Kuther, T., & Morgan, R. (2007). *Careers in psychology: Opportunities in a changing world* (2nd ed.). Pacific Grove, CA: Wadsworth/Thomson.

Kwok, Y. Y., Chui, W. H., & Wong, L. P. (2013). Need satisfaction mechanism linking volunteer motivation and life satisfaction: A mediation study of volunteers subjective well-being. *Social Indicators Research, 114*(3), 1315–1329.

Labroo, A. A., Mukhopadhyay, A., & Dong, P. (2014). Not always the best medicine: Why frequent smiling can reduce wellbeing. *Journal of Experimental Social Psychology, 53,* 156–162.

Lac, A., Crano, W. D., Berger, D. E., & Alvaro, E. M. (2013). Attachment theory and theory of planned behavior: An integrative model predicting underage drinking. *Developmental Psychology, 49*(8), 1579–1590.

Lacro, J. P., Dunn, L. B., Dolder, C. R., Leckband, S. G., & Jeste, D. V. (2002). Prevalence of and risk factors for medication nonadherence in patients with schizophrenia: A comprehensive review of recent literature. *The Journal of Clinical Psychiatry, 63*(10), 892–909.

Laffer, A. B. (2004). The Laffer curve: Past, present, and future. *Heritage Foundation Backgrounder: Policy, Research, & Analysis, 1765,* 1176–1196.

LaForge, I., & Goodfriend, W. (2012). Developing a new device for measuring preferred body shapes. *Journal of Psychological Inquiry, 17,* 45–49.

LaFrance, M., & Woodzicka, J. A. (1998). No laughing matter: Women's verbal and nonverbal reactions to sexist humor. In J. K. Swim & C. Stangor (Eds.), *Prejudice: The target's perspective* (pp. 61–80). San Diego, CA: Academic Press.

Laird, J. D. (1974). Self-attribution of emotion: The effects of expressive behavior on the quality of emotional experience. *Journal of Personality and Social Psychology, 29*(4), 475–486.

Lake, B. M., Ullman, T. D., Tenenbaum, J. B., & Gershman, S. J. (2016). Building machines that learn and think like people. *Behavioral and Brain Sciences.* Retrieved from https://arxiv.org/pdf/1604.00289.pdf

Lamb, C. S., & Crano, W. D. (2014). Parents' beliefs and children's marijuana use: Evidence for a self-fulfilling prophecy effect. *Addictive Behaviors, 39*(1), 127–132.

Lambert, L., D'Cruz, A., Schlatter, M., & Barron, F. (2016). Using physical activity to tackle depression: The neglected positive psychology intervention. *Middle East Journal of Positive Psychology, 2*(1), 42–60.

Lang, B. (2017). 'Wonder Woman' breaks records: biggest live-action box office hit by female director. *Variety.* Retrieved August 23, 2017, from http://variety.com/2017/film/box-office/wonder-woman-box-office-female-directors-1202477406/

Langer, E. J., & Rodin, J. (1976). The effects of choice and enhanced personal responsibility for the aged: A field experiment in an institutional setting. *Journal of Personality and Social Psychology, 34*(2), 191–198.

Langlois, J. H., & Roggman, L. A. (1990). Attractive faces are only average. *Psychological Science, 1*(2), 115–121.

Langlois, J. H., Roggman, L. A., & Musselman, L. (1994). What is average and what is not average about attractive faces? *Psychological Science, 5*(4), 214–220.

LaPiere, R. T. (1934). Attitudes vs. actions. *Social Forces, 13*(2), 230–237.

Larrick, R. P., Timmerman, T. A., Carton, A. M., & Abrevaya, J. (2011). Temper, temperature, and temptation: Heat-related retaliation in baseball. *Psychological Science, 22*(4), 423–428.

Larsen, K. S. (1974). Conformity in the Asch experiment. *Journal of Social Psychology, 94*(2), 303–304.

Larsen, K. S. (1982). Cultural conditions and conformity: The Asch effect. *Bulletin of the British Psychological Society, 35,* 347.

Larsen, K. S. (1990). The Asch conformity experiment: Replications and transhistorical comparisons. *Social Behavior and Personality, 5*(4), 163–168.

Latané, B., & Darley, J. (1970). *The unresponsive bystander why doesn't he help? Century Psychology Series.* New York, NY: Appleton-Century Crofts.

Laumann, E. O., Gagnon, J. H., Michael, R. T., & Michaels, S. (1994). *The social organization of sexuality: Sexual practices in the United States.* Chicago, IL: University of Chicago Press.

Launer, D., & Schiff, P. (Producers), & Lynn, J. (Director), (1992). *My cousin Vinny* [Motion picture]. United States: 20th Century Fox.

Lawrence, J. E. (1974). Science and sentiment: Overview of research on crowding and human behavior. *Psychological Bulletin, 81*(10), 712–720.

Lazarus, R., & Folkman, S. (1984). *Stress, appraisal, and coping.* New York, NY: Springer.

Le, B., & Agnew, C. R. (2003). Commitment and its theorized determinants: A meta-analysis of the investment model. *Personal Relationships, 10*(1), 37–57.

Le, B., Dove, N. L., Agnew, C. R., Korn, M. S., & Mutso, A. A. (2010). Predicting nonmarital romantic relationship dissolution: A meta-analytic synthesis. *Personal Relationships, 17*(3), 377–390.

Leach, J. K., & Patall, E. A. (2013). Maximizing and counterfactual thinking in academic major decision making. *Journal of Career Assessment, 21*(3), 414–429.

Learman, L. A., Avorn, J., Everitt, D. E., & Rosenthal, R. (1990). Pygmalion in the nursing home: The effects of caregiver expectations on patient outcomes. *Journal of the American Geriatrics Society, 38*(7), 797–803.

Leary, M. R., Tate, E. B., Adams, C. E., Batts Allen, A., & Hancock, J. (2007). Self-compassion and reactions to unpleasant self-relevant events: The implications of treating oneself kindly. *Journal of Personality and Social Psychology, 92*(5), 887–904.

Lee, E., Sitze, G., & Logan, J. R. (2003). Social support to parents-in-law: The interplay of gender and kin hierarchies. *Journal of Marriage and Family, 65*(2), 396–403.

Lee, J. (1993). *Facing the fire: Experiencing and expressing anger appropriately.* New York, NY: Bantam.

Lee, J. G., & Thorson, E. (2008). The impact of celebrity-product incongruence on the effectiveness of product endorsement. *Journal of Advertising Research, 48*(3), 433–449.

Lee, Y. H., & Mason, C. (1999). Responses to information incongruency in advertising: The role of expectancy, relevancy, and humor. *Journal of Consumer Research, 26*(2), 156–169.

Lee, Y. T., & Ottati, V. (1995). Perceived in-group homogeneity as a function of group membership salience and stereotype threat. *Personality and Social Psychology Bulletin, 21*(6), 610–619.

Le Hénaff, B., Michinov, N., Le Bohec, O., & Delaval, M. (2015). Social gaming is inSIDE: Impact of anonymity and group identity on performance in a team game-based learning environment. *Computers & Education, 82*, 84–95.

Lehmiller, J. J. (2010). Differences in relationship investments between gay and heterosexual men. *Personal Relationships, 17*(1), 81–96.

Lehmiller, J. J. (2014). *The psychology of human sexuality.* Hoboken, NJ: Wiley-Blackwell.

Lehmiller, J. J., VanderDrift, L. E., & Kelly, J. R. (2011). Sex differences in approaching friends with benefits relationships. *Journal of Sex Research, 48*(2–3), 275–284.

Leippe, M. R., & Elkin, R. A. (1987). When motives clash: Issue involvement and response involvement as determinant of persuasion. *Journal of Personality and Social Psychology, 52*(2), 269–278.

Leone, J. M., Johnson, M. P., & Cohan, C. L. (2007). Victim help seeking: Differences between intimate terrorism and situational couple violence. *Family Relations: An Interdisciplinary Journal of Applied Family Studies, 56*(5), 427–439.

Leonhardt, D., & Quealy, K. (2015, May 15). How your hometown affects your chances of marriage. *New York Times.*

Lerner, M. J. (1965). Evaluation of performance as a function of performer's reward and attractiveness. *Journal of Personality and Social Psychology, 1*(4), 355–360.

Lerner, M. J. (1980). *The belief in a just world: A fundamental delusion.* New York, NY: Plenum.

Lerner, M. J., & Miller, D. T. (1978). Just world research and the attribution process: Looking back and ahead. *Psychological Bulletin, 85*(5), 1030–1051.

Lerner, M. J., & Simmons, C. H. (1966). The observer's reaction to the "innocent victim": Compassion or rejection? *Journal of Personality and Social Psychology, 4*(2), 203–210.

Levenson, H., Burford, B., Bonno, B., & Davis, L. (1975). Are women still prejudiced against women? A replication and extension of Goldberg's study. *Journal of Psychology, 89*(1), 67–71.

Levine, M., Prosser, A., Evans, D., & Reicher, S. (2005). Identity and emergency intervention: How social group membership and inclusiveness of group boundaries shape helping behavior. *Personality and Social Psychology Bulletin, 31*(4), 443–453.

Levy, R. I. (1973). *Tahitians: Mind and experience in the Society Islands.* Chicago, IL: University of Chicago Press.

Levy, R. I. (1978). Tahitian gentleness and redundant controls. In A. Montagu (Ed.), *Learning non-aggression: The experience of non-literate societies* (pp. 222–235). Oxford, UK: Oxford University Press.

Lewan, P. C., & Stotland, E. (1961). The effects of prior information on susceptibility to an emotional appeal. *Journal of Abnormal and Social Psychology, 62*(2), 450–453.

Lewin, K. (1936) *Principles of topological psychology.* New York: McGraw-Hill.

Lewin, K. (1939). Field theory and experiment in social psychology: Concepts and methods. *American Journal of Sociology, 44*(6), 868–896.

Lewin, K. (1948). *Resolving social conflicts.* New York, NY: Harper & Row.

Lewin, K. (1951). *Field theory in social science: Selected theoretical papers* (D. Cartwright, Ed.). Oxford, UK: Harpers.

Li, N. P., Yong, J. C., Tov, W., Sng, O., Fletcher, G. O., Valentine, K. A., . . . Balliet, D. (2013). Mate preferences do predict attraction and choices in the early stages of mate selection. *Journal of Personality and Social Psychology, 105*(5), 757–776.

Lick, D. J., Cortland, C. I., & Johnson, K. L. (2016). The pupils are the windows to sexuality: Pupil dilation as a visual cue to others' sexual interest. *Evolution and Human Behavior, 37*(2), 117–124.

Liden, R. C., Wayne, S. J., Jaworski, R. A., & Bennett, N. (2004). Social loafing: A field investigation. *Journal of Management, 30*(2), 285–304.

Lieberman, M. D. (2000). Intuition: A social cognitive neuroscience approach. *Psychological Bulletin, 126*(1), 109–137.

Lightdale, J. R., & Prentice, D. A. (1994). Rethinking sex differences in aggression: Aggressive behavior in the absence of social roles. *Personality and Social Psychology Bulletin, 20*(1), 34–44.

Lilienfeld, S. O., Lynn, S. J., Ruscio, J., & Beyerstein, B. L. (2011). *50 great myths of popular psychology: Shattering widespread misconceptions about human behavior.* Hoboken, NJ: John Wiley.

Lindstrom, M. (2011). *Brandwashed: Tricks companies use to manipulate our minds and persuade us to buy.* New York, NY: Crown Business.

Lobel, M., Cannella, D. L., Graham, J. E., DeVincent, C., Schneider, J., & Meyer, B. A. (2008). Pregnancy-specific stress, prenatal health behaviors, and birth outcomes. *Health Psychology, 27*(5), 604–615.

Loftus, E. F. (1975). Leading questions and the eyewitness report. *Cognitive Psychology, 7*(4), 560–572.

Loftus, E. F., & Ketcham, K. (1996). *The myth of repressed memory: False memories and allegations of sexual abuse.* New York, NY: St. Martin's Griffin.

Loftus, E. F., & Palmer, J. C. (1974). Reconstruction of automobile destruction: An example of the interaction between language and memory. *Journal of Verbal Learning and Verbal Behavior, 13*(5), 585–589.

Loftus, E. F., & Palmer, J. C. (1996). Reconstruction of automobile destruction: An example of the interaction between language and memory. In S. Fein & S. Spencer (Eds.), *Readings in social psychology: The art and science of research* (pp. 143–147). Boston, MA: Houghton Mifflin.

Loftus, E. F., & Zanni, G. (1975). Eyewitness testimony: The influence of the wording of a question. *Bulletin of the Psychonomic Society, 5*(1), 86–88.

Lopez, M. H., & Gonzalez-Barrera, A. (2014, March 6). Women's college enrollment gains leave men behind. *Pew Research Center.* Retrieved from http://www.pewresearch.org/fact-tank/2014/03/06/womens-college-enrollment-gains-leave-men-behind/

Lough, J. W. H. (2006). *Weber and the persistence of religion: Social theory, capitalism, and the sublime.* New York, NY: Routledge.

Love, L., & Waldman, E. (2016). The hopes and fears of all the years: 30 years behind and the road ahead for the widespread use of mediation. *Ohio St. Journal on Dispute Resolution, 31,* 123.

Luo, Z., Qu, H., & Marnburg, E. (2013). Justice perceptions and drives of hotel employee social loafing behavior. *International Journal of Hospitality Management, 33,* 456–464.

MacDonald, G., Zanna, M. P., & Holmes, J. G. (2000). An experimental test of the role of alcohol in relationship conflict. *Journal of Experimental Social Psychology, 36*(2), 182–193.

Macmillan, M. (2000). *An odd kind of fame: Stories of Phineas Gage.* Cambridge, MA: MIT Press.

Madathil, J., & Benshoff, J. M. (2008). Importance of marital characteristics and marital satisfaction: A comparison of Asian Indians in arranged marriages and Americans in marriages of choice. *The Family Journal, 16*(3), 222–230.

Maertz, C. J., Stoeberl, P. A., & Marks, J. (2014). Building successful internships: Lessons from the research for interns, schools, and employers. *The Career Development International, 19*(1), 123–142.

Maisonneuve, N., Stevens, M., Niessen, M. E., & Steels, L. (2009). NoiseTube: Measuring and mapping noise pollution with mobile phones. In I. N. Athanasiadis,

P. A. Mitkas, A. E. Rizzoli, & J. Marx Gómez (Eds.), *Information technologies in environmental engineering* (pp. 215–228). Berlin, Germany: Springer.

Major, B., Carrington, P. I., & Carnevale, P. J. (1984). Physical attractiveness and self-esteem: Attributions for praise from an other-sex evaluator. *Personality and Social Psychology Bulletin, 10*(1), 43–50.

Major, B., Sciacchitano, A. M., & Crocker, J. (1993). In-group versus out-group comparisons and self-esteem. *Personality and Social Psychology Bulletin, 19*(6), 711–721.

Mankiewicz, R. (2000). *The story of mathematics.* Princeton, NJ: Princeton University Press.

Manning, R., Levine, M., & Collins, A. (2007). The Kitty Genovese murder and the social psychology of helping: The parable of the 38 witnesses. *American Psychologist, 62*(6), 555–562.

Marino, L. (2002). Convergence of complex cognitive abilities in cetaceans and primates. *Brain, Behavior and Evolution, 59*(1–2), 21–32.

Marks, G. (1984). Thinking one's abilities are unique and one's opinions are common. *Personality and Social Psychology Bulletin, 10*(2), 203–208.

Markus, H. R. (1977). Self-schemata and processing information about the self. *Journal of Personality and Social Psychology, 35*(2), 63–78.

Markus, H. R., & Kitayama, S. (1991). Culture and the self: Implications for cognition, emotion, and motivation. *Psychological Review, 98*(2), 224–253.

Markus, H. R., & Kitayama, S. (1994). A collective fear of the collective: Implications for selves and theories of selves. *Personality and Social Psychology Bulletin, 20*(5), 568–579.

Marrow, A. (1969). *The practical theorist: The life and work of Kurt Lewin.* New York, NY: Basic Books.

Marrow, J. (2002). Demonstrating the anchoring-adjustment heuristic and the power of the situation. *Teaching of Psychology, 29*(2), 129–132.

Marsh, H. A., Malik, F., Shapiro, E., Omer, S. B., & Frew, P. M. (2014). Message framing strategies to increase influenza immunization uptake among pregnant African American women. *Maternal and Child Health Journal, 18*(7), 1639–1647.

Marsh, H. W., Köller, O., & Baumert, J. (2001). Reunification of East and West German school systems: Longitudinal multilevel modeling study of the big-fish-little-pond effect on academic self-concept. *American Educational Research Journal, 38*(2), 321–350.

Marsh, H. W., & Richards, G. E. (1988). Tennessee self-concept scale: Reliability, internal structure, and construct validity. *Journal of Personality and Social Psychology, 55*(4), 612–624.

Marshall, F., Crowley, P., & Sangberg, P. L. (Producers), & Greengrass, P. (Director). (2007). *The Bourne ultimatum* [Motion picture]. United States: Universal Pictures.

Marshall, T. C., Bejanyan, K., Di Castro, G., & Lee, R. A. (2013). Attachment styles as predictors of Facebook-related jealousy and surveillance in romantic relationships. *Personal Relationships, 20*(1), 1–22.

Martijn, C., Sheeran, P., Wesseldijk, L. W., Merrick, H., Webb, T. L., Roefs, A., & Jansen, A. (2013). Evaluative conditioning makes slim models less desirable as standards for comparison and increases body satisfaction. *Health Psychology, 32*(4), 433–438.

Martin, R. C., Coyier, K. R., VanSistine, L. M., & Schroeder, K. L. (2013). Anger on the Internet: The perceived value of rant-sites. *Cyberpsychology, Behavior, and Social Networking, 16*(2), 119–122.

Martini, M. (1994). Peer interactions in Polynesia: A view from the Marquesas. In J. Roopnarine, J. E. Johnson, & F. H. Hooper (Eds.), *Children's play in diverse cultures* (pp. 74–122). Albany: State University of New York Press.

Marx, G. (2007). *The Groucho letters: Letters from and to Groucho Marx.* New York, NY: Simon & Schuster.

Mashek, D., Cannaday, L. W., & Tangney, J. P. (2007). Inclusion of community in self scale: A single-item pictorial measure of community connectedness. *Journal of Community Psychology, 35*(2), 257–275.

Masser, B. M., & Abrams, D. (2004). Reinforcing the glass ceiling: The consequences of hostile sexism for female managerial candidates. *Sex Roles, 51*(9), 609–615.

Masters, N. T., Casey, E., Wells, E. A., & Morrison, D. M. (2013). Sexual scripts among young heterosexually active men and women: Continuity and change. *Journal of Sex Research, 50*(5), 409–420.

Matheny, D., & Miller, K. (2000, January 4). A magical land where all the pets are above average. *Minneapolis Star-Tribune,* p. E1.

Matheson, M. P., Stansfeld, S. A., & Haines, M. M. (2003). The effects of chronic aircraft noise exposure on children's cognition and health: 3 field studies. *Noise and Health, 5*(19), 31–40.

Matsumoto, D. (2009). Culture and emotional expression. In R. S. Wyer, C. Chiu, & Y. Hong (Eds.), *Understanding culture: Theory, research, and application* (pp. 271–287). New York, NY: Psychology Press.

Matsumoto, D., & Willingham, B. (2009). Spontaneous facial expressions of emotion of congenitally and noncongenitally blind individuals. *Journal of Personality and Social Psychology, 96*(1), 1–10.

Mattingly, B. A., & Lewandowski, G. J. (2013). An expanded self is a more capable self: The association between self-concept size and self-efficacy. *Self and Identity, 12*(6), 621–634.

Mattingly, B. A., & Lewandowski, G. J. (2014). Broadening horizons: Self-expansion in relational and non-relational contexts. *Social and Personality Psychology Compass, 8*(1), 30–40.

Matusitz, J., & Breen, G. M. (2012). An examination of pack journalism as a form of groupthink: A theoretical and qualitative analysis. *Journal of Human Behavior in the Social Environment, 22*(7), 896–915.

Matz, D. C., Hofstedt, P. M., & Wood, W. (2008). Extraversion as a moderator of the cognitive dissonance associated with disagreement. *Personality and Individual Differences, 45*(5), 401–405.

Mayo, E. (1933). *The human problems of an industrial civilization.* New York, NY: Macmillan.

Mayo, E. (1945). *The social problems of an industrial civilization.* Oxford, UK: Graduate School of Business Administration.

Mbaeze, I. C., Ukwandu, E., & Ndubuisi, N. O. (2011). Effect of wrestling films and gender on children's aggressiveness. *Pakistan Journal of Social Sciences, 8*(5), 262–270.

McCall, M., & Nattrass, K. (2001). Carding for the purchase of alcohol: I'm tougher than other clerks are! *Journal of Applied Social Psychology, 31*(10), 2184–2194.

McConahay, J. B. (1983). Modern racism and modern discrimination: The effects of race, racial attitudes, and context on simulated hiring decisions. *Personality and Social Psychology Bulletin, 9*(4), 551–558.

McConahay, J. B. (1986). Modern racism, ambivalence, and the modern racism scale. In J. F. Dovidio & S. L. Gaertner (Eds.), *Prejudice discrimination, and racism* (pp. 91–125). San Diego, CA: Academic Press.

McCormick, C. T. (1992). *Handbook of the law of evidence* (4th ed.). St. Paul, MN: West.

McCrae, R. R., & Costa, P. T. (1987). Validation of the five-factor model of personality across instruments and observers. *Journal of Personality and Social Psychology, 52*(1), 81–90.

McDermott, R. C., & Lopez, F. G. (2013). College men's intimate partner violence attitudes: Contributions of adult attachment and gender role stress. *Journal of Counseling Psychology, 60*(1), 127–136.

McFarland, S. G. (1989). Religious orientations and the targets of discrimination. *Journal for the Scientific Study of Religion, 28*(3), 324–336.

McGloin, R., Farrar, K. M., & Fishlock, J. (2015). Triple Whammy! Violent games and violent controllers: Investigating the use of realistic gun controllers on perceptions of realism, immersion, and outcome aggression. *Journal of Communication, 65*(2), 280–299.

McGovern, D. J. (2011). *Eliza undermined: The romanticism of Shaw's* Pygmalion. Retrieved September 26, 2011, from http://mro.massey.ac.nz/bitstream/handle/10179/2414/02_whole.pdf?sequence=1

McGovern, T. V., Corey, L., Cranney, J., Dixon, W. J., Holmes, J. D., Kuebli, J. E., . . . Walker, S. J. (2010). Psychologically literate citizens. In D. F. Halpern (Ed.), *Undergraduate education in psychology: A blueprint for the future of the discipline* (pp. 9–27). Washington, DC: American Psychological Association.

McGuire, W. J. (1964). Inducing resistance to persuasion: Some contemporary approaches. In L. Berkowitz (Ed.), *Advances in experimental social psychology* (Vol. 1, pp. 191–229). New York, NY: Academic Press.

McGuire, W. J. (1985). Attitudes and attitude change. In G. Lindzey & E. Aronson (Eds.), *Handbook of social psychology* (Vol. 2, 3rd ed., pp. 233–346). New York, NY: Random House.

McKelvie, S. J. (2000). Quantifying the availability heuristic with famous names. *North American Journal of Psychology, 2*(2), 347–356.

McMillen, D. L., & Austin, J. B. (1971). Effect of positive feedback on compliance following transgression. *Psychonomic Science, 24*(2), 59–61.

Mealy, M., Stephan, W., & Urrutia, I. C. (2007). The acceptability of lies: A comparison of Ecuadorians and Euro-Americans. *International Journal of Intercultural Relations, 31*(6), 689–702.

Mecca, A. M., Smelser, N. J., & Vasconcellos, J. (1989). *The social importance of self-esteem.* Berkeley: University of California Press.

Mehrabian, A., & Stefl, C. A. (1995). Basic temperament components of loneliness, shyness, and conformity. *Social Behavior and Personality, 23*(3), 253–263.

Meltzoff, A. N., & Moore, M. K. (1977). Imitation of facial and manual gestures by human neonates. *Science, 198*(4312), 75–78.

Meltzoff, A. N., & Moore, M. K. (1989). Imitation in newborn infants: Exploring the range of gestures imitated and the underlying mechanisms. *Developmental Psychology, 25*(6), 954–962.

Mendel, R., Traut-Mattausch, E., Jonas, E., Leucht, S., Kane, J. M., Maino, K., . . . Hamann, J. (2011). Confirmation bias: Why psychiatrists stick to wrong preliminary diagnoses. *Psychological Medicine, 41*(12), 2651–2659.

Merali, N. (2012). Arranged and forced marriage. In M. A. Paludi (Ed.), *The psychology of love* (pp. 143–168). Santa Barbara, CA: Praeger/ABC-CLIO.

Merton, R. K. (1948). The self-fulfilling prophecy. *Antioch Review, 8*(2), 193–210.

Mesagno, C., Harvey, J. T., & Janelle, C. M. (2012). Choking under pressure: The role of fear of negative evaluation. *Psychology of Sport and Exercise, 13*(1), 60–68.

Messner, M. A. (1988). Sports and male domination: The female athlete as contested ideological terrain. *Sociology of Sport Journal, 5*(3), 197–211.

Michaels, J. W., Blommel, J. M., Brocato, R. M., Linkous, R. A., & Rowe, J. S. (1982). Social facilitation and inhibition in a natural setting. *Replications in Social Psychology, 2,* 21–24.

Michaels, L., Doumanian, J., & Ebersol, D. (Producers), & King, D. R., Wilson, D., Miller, P., & McCarthy-Miller, B. (Directors). (1975–). *Saturday night live* [Television series]. United States: Broadway Video.

Michaels, L. (Producer), & Waters, M. (Director). (2004). *Mean girls* [Motion picture]. USA: M. G. Films, Broadway Video, & Paramount Pictures.

Michinov, N. (2007). Social comparison and affect: A study among elderly women. *The Journal of Social Psychology, 147*(2), 175–189.

Middlemist, R. D., Knowles, E. S., & Matter, C. F. (1976). Personal space invasions in the lavatory: Suggestive evidence for arousal. *Journal of Personality and Social Psychology, 33*(5), 541–546.

Middlemist, R. D., Knowles, E. S., & Matter, C. F. (1977). What to do and what to report: A reply to Koocher. *Journal of Personality and Social Psychology, 35*(2), 122–124.

Milchan, A., Grisham, J., Nathanson, M., & Lowry, H. (Producers), & Schumacher, J. (Director). (1996). *A time to kill* [Motion picture]. United States: Regency Enterprises and Warner Bros.

Milgram, S. (1963). Behavioral study of obedience. *The Journal of Abnormal and Social Psychology, 67*(4), 371–378.

Milgram, S. (1970). The experience of living in cities. *Science, 167*(3924), 1461–1468.

Milgram, S. (1974). *Obedience to authority: An experimental view.* New York, NY: Harper & Row.

Milgram, S., Bickman, L., & Berkowitz, L. (1969). Note on the drawing power of crowds of different size. *Journal of Personality and Social Psychology, 13*(2), 79–82.

Milgram, S., & Sabini, J. (1978). On maintaining urban norms: A field experiment in the subway. In A. Baum & J. E. Singer (Eds.), *Advances in environmental psychology* (Vol. 1, pp. 31–40). Mahwah, NJ: Lawrence Erlbaum.

Miller, D. T., & Ross, M. (1975). Self-serving biases in the attribution of causality: Fact or fiction? *Psychological Bulletin, 82,* 213–225.

Miller, R. S., & Perlman, D. (2009). *Intimate relationships* (5th ed.). New York, NY: McGraw-Hill.

Miranda, J. P., & Kanekar, S. (1993). Estimated willingness to help as a function of help-seeking contexts, cost of helping, and subject's sex and involvement. *Revue Internationale de Psychologie Sociale, 6,* 105–120.

Mita, T. H., Dermer, M., & Knight, J. (1977). Reversed facial images and the mere-exposure hypothesis. *Journal of Personality and Social Psychology, 35*(8), 597–601.

Mitchell, W. E. (1990). Why Wape men don't beat their wives. *Pacific Studies, 13,* 141–150.

Mixon, D. (1972). Instead of deception. *Journal for the Theory of Social Behavior, 2*(2), 145–177.

Møller, A. P., & Petrie, M. (2002). Condition dependence, multiple sexual signals, and immunocompetence in peacocks. *Behavioral Ecology, 13*(2), 248–253.

Monahan, J. L., Murphy, S. T., & Zajonc, R. B. (2000). Subliminal mere exposure: Specific, general, and diffuse effects. *Psychological Science, 11*(6), 462–466.

Monin, B., & Norton, M. I. (2003). Perceptions of a fluid consensus: Uniqueness bias, false consensus, false polarization and pluralistic ignorance in a water conservation crisis. *Personality and Social Psychology Bulletin, 29*(5), 559–567.

Monroe, B. M., & Read, S. J. (2008). A general connectionist model of attitude structure and change: The ACS (attitude as constraint satisfaction) model. *Psychological Review, 115*(3), 733–759.

Mooradian, T. A., Davis, M., & Matzler, K. (2011). Dispositional empathy and the hierarchical structure of personality. *The American Journal of Psychology, 124*(1), 99–109.

Morgan, S. E., Movius, L., & Cody, M. J. (2009). The power of narratives: The effect of entertainment television organ donation storylines on the attitudes, knowledge, and behaviors of donors and nondonars. *Journal of Communication, 59*(1), 135–151.

Moritz, H. H., & Jaffe, T. (Producers), & Wiseman, L. (Director). (2012). *Total recall* [Motion picture]. United States: Columbia Pictures.

Morling, B. (2015). *Research methods in psychology: Evaluating a world of information* (2nd ed.). New York, NY: Norton.

Morris, M. W., & Peng, K. (1994). Culture and cause: American and Chinese attributions for social and physical events. *Journal of Personality and Social Psychology, 67*(6), 949–971.

Morrison, K. R., & Miller, D. T. (2008). Distinguishing between silent and vocal minorities: Not all deviants feel marginal. *Journal of Personality and Social Psychology, 94*(5), 871–882.

Morrock, R. (2010). *The psychology of genocide and violent oppression: A study of mass cruelty from Nazi Germany to Rwanda.* Jefferson, NC: McFarland.

Morry, M. M. (2005). Relationship satisfaction as a predictor of similarity ratings: A test of the attraction-similarity hypothesis. *Journal of Social and Personal Relationships, 22*(4), 561–584.

Morry, M. M. (2007). The attraction-similarity hypothesis among cross-sex friends: Relationship satisfaction, perceived similarities, and self-serving perceptions. *Journal of Social and Personal Relationships, 24*(1), 117–138.

Moscovici, S., & Zavalloni, M. (1969). The group as a polarizer of attitudes. *Journal of Personality and Social Psychology, 12*(2), 125–135.

Moskowitz, D. A., Turrubiates, J., Lozano, H., & Hajek, C. (2013). Physical, behavioral, and psychological traits of gay men identifying as Bears. *Archives of Sexual Behavior, 42*(5), 775–784.

Mullen, B., Johnson, C., & Salas, E. (1991). Productivity loss in brainstorming groups: A meta-analytic integration. *Basic and Applied Social Psychology, 12*(1), 3–23.

Münsterberg, H. (1908). *On the witness stand: Essays on psychology and crime.* New York, NY: McClure.

Murphy, C. M., & O'Farrell, T. J. (1996). Marital violence among alcoholics. *Current Directions in Psychological Science, 5*(6), 183–186.

Murphy, D., DeSanto, T., di Bonaventura, L., Bryce, I., & Spielberg, S. (Producers), & Bay, M. (Director). (2007). *Transformers* [Motion picture]. USA: Di Bonaventura Pictures, DreamWorks Pictures, & Paramount Pictures.

Murphy, Y., & Murphy, R. (1974). *Women of the forest.* New York, NY: Columbia University Press.

Murray, A. A., Wood, J. M., & Lilienfeld, S. O. (2012). Psychopathic personality traits and cognitive dissonance: Individual differences in attitude change. *Journal of Research in Personality, 46*(5), 525–536.

Murray, J. D., Spadafore, J. A., & McIntosh, W. D. (2005). Belief in a just world and social perception: Evidence for automatic activation. *The Journal of Social Psychology, 145*(1), 35–47.

Murray, S. L., Holmes, J. G., & Griffin, D. W. (1996a). The benefits of positive illusions: Idealization and the construction of satisfaction in close relationships. *Journal of Personality and Social Psychology, 70*(1), 79–98.

Murray, S. L., Holmes, J. G., & Griffin, D. W. (1996b). The self-fulfilling nature of positive illusions in romantic relationships: Love is not blind, but prescient. *Journal of Personality and Social Psychology, 71*(6), 1155–1180.

Mussweiler, T., & Strack, F. (2001). "Considering the impossible": Explaining the effects of implausible anchors. *Social Cognition, 19,* 145–160.

Myers, D. G. (1975). Discussion-induced attitude polarization. *Human Relations, 28*(8), 699–714.

Myers, D. G., & Diener, E. (1995). Who is happy? *Psychological Science, 6*(1), 10–19.

Nandedkar, A., & Midha, V. (2012). It won't happen to me: An assessment of optimism bias in music piracy. *Computers in Human Behavior, 28*(1), 41–48.

Naquin, C. E., Kurtzberg, T. R., & Belkin, L. Y. (2010). The finer points of lying online: E-mail versus pen and paper. *Journal of Applied Psychology, 95*(2), 387–394.

National Intimate Partner and Sexual Violence Survey. (2010). *NISVS summary reports.* Retrieved from https://www.cdc.gov/violenceprevention/nisvs/index.html

Neff, K., & Vonk, R. (2009). Self-compassion versus global self-Esteem: Two different ways of relating to oneself. *Journal of Personality, 77*(1), 23–50.

Nenkov, G. Y., Morrin, M., Ward, A., Schwartz, B., & Hulland, J. (2008). A short form of the maximization scale: Factor structure, reliability and validity studies. *Judgment and Decision Making, 3*(5), 371–388.

Nesse, R. M. (2001). *Evolution and the capacity for commitment.* New York, NY: Russell Sage Foundation.

Neta, M., & Tong, T. T. (2016). Don't like what you see? Give it time: Longer reaction times associated with increased positive affect. *Emotion, 16*(5), 730–739.

Neuman, J. H., & Baron, R. A. (2011). Social antecedents of bullying: A social interactionist perspective. In S. Einarsen, H. Hoel, D. Zapf, & C. Cooper (Eds.), *Bullying and harassment in the workplace: Developments in theory, research, and practice* (pp. 201–225). Boca Raton, FL: CRC Press.

Neumann, R., & Strack, F. (2000). Mood contagion: The automatic transfer of mood between persons. *Journal of Personality and Social Psychology, 79*(2), 211–223.

Newman, D. M. (2007). *Identities and inequalities: Exploring the intersections of race, class, gender, and sexuality.* Boston, MA: McGraw-Hill.

Newton, N. A., Khanna, C., & Thompson, J. (2008). Workplace failure: Mastering the last taboo. *Consulting Psychology Journal: Practice and Research, 60*(3), 227–245.

Nichol, F. D. (1944). *The midnight cry: A defense of William Miller and the Millerites.* Washington, DC: Review and Herald.

Nicholson, I. A. M. (2011). 'Torture at Yale': Experimental subjects, laboratory torment and the 'rehabilitation' of Milgram's 'obedience to authority'. *Theory & Psychology, 21*(6), 737–761.

Nicholson, I. A. M. (2015). The normalization of torment: Producing and managing anguish in Milgram's 'Obedience' laboratory. *Theory & Psychology, 25*(5), 639–656.

Nicholson, I. R. (2011). New technology, old issues: Demonstrating the relevance of the Canadian Code of Ethics for Psychologists to the ever-sharper cutting edge of technology. *Canadian Psychology/Psychologie Canadienne, 52*(3), 215–224.

Nickerson, R. S. (1998). Confirmation bias: A ubiquitous phenomenon in many guises. *Review of General Psychology, 2*(2), 175–220.

Nier, J. A. (2004). Why does the 'above average effect' exist? Demonstrating idiosyncratic trait definition. *Teaching of Psychology, 31*(1), 53–54.

Nier, J. A., Bajaj, P., McLean, M. C., & Schwartz, E. (2013). Group status, perceptions of agency, and the correspondence bias: Attributional processes in the formation of stereotypes about high and low status groups. *Group Processes & Intergroup Relations, 16*(4), 476–487.

Nisbett, R. E., Caputo, C., Legant, P., & Marecek, J. (1973). Behavior as seen by the actor and as seen by the observer. *Journal of Personality and Social Psychology, 27*(2), 154–164.

Nisbett, R. E., Krantz, D. H., Jepson, C., & Kunda, Z. (1983). The use of statistical heuristics in everyday inductive reasoning. *Psychological Review, 90*(4), 339–363.

Nisbett, R. E., & Kunda, Z. (1985). Perception of social distributions. *Journal of Personality and Social Psychology, 48*(2), 297–311.

Nisbett, R. E., & Ross, L. (1980). *Human inference: Strategies and shortcomings of social judgment.* Englewood Cliffs, NJ: Prentice Hall.

Nisbett, R. E., & Wilson, T. D. (1977). Telling more than we can know: Verbal reports on mental processing. *Psychological Review, 84,* 231–259.

Noelle-Neumann, E. (1993). *Spiral of silence.* Chicago, IL: University of Chicago Press.

Norenzayan, A., & Nisbett, R. E. (2000). Culture and causal cognition. *Current Directions in Psychological Science, 9*(4), 132–135.

Norman, D. (2013). *The design of everyday things: Revised and expanded edition.* New York, NY: Basic Books.

Nowak, M. A., Page, K. M., & Sigmund, K. (2000). Fairness versus reason in the ultimatum game. *Science, 289*(5485), 1773–1775.

Nunley, J. M., Pugh, A., Romero, N., & Seals, R. A. (2016). College major, internship experience, and employment opportunities: Estimates from a résumé audit. *Labour Economics, 38,* 37–46.

Nye, J. (2008). *The powers to lead.* New York, NY: Oxford University Press.

Obermaier, M., Fawzi, N., & Koch, T. (2016). Bystanding or standing by? How the number of bystanders affects the intention to intervene in cyberbullying. *New Media & Society, 18*(8), 1491–1507.

O'Brien, B. (2009). Prime suspect: An examination of factors that aggravate and counteract confirmation bias in criminal investigations. *Psychology, Public Policy, and Law, 15*(4), 315–334.

O'Connor B. P., & Dyce, J. (1993). Appraisals of musical ability in bar bands: Identifying the weak link in the looking-glass self chain. *Basic and Applied Social Psychology, 14*(1), 69–86.

Öhman, A., & Mineka, S. (2001). Fears, phobias, and preparedness: Toward an evolved module of fear and fear learning. *Psychological Review, 108*(3), 483–522.

Oman, R. F., & King, A. C. (2000). The effect of life events and exercise program format on the adoption and maintenance of exercise behavior. *Health Psychology, 19*(6), 605–612.

O'Neill, N. (2010). Internships as a high-impact practice: Some reflections on quality. *Peer Review, 12*(4), 4–8.

Ontiveros, M. L. (2015). NCAA athletes, unpaid interns and the s-word: Exploring the rhetorical impact of the language of slavery. *Michigan State Law Review, 2015,* 1657.

Ortiz, J., & Raine, A. (2004). Heart rate level and antisocial behavior in children and adolescents: A meta-analysis. *Journal of the American Academy of Child & Adolescent Psychiatry, 43*(2), 154–162.

Osborn, A. F. (1957). *Applied imagination: Principles and procedures of creative problem solving* (3rd ed.). New York, NY: Scribner.

Ost, J., Granhag, P., & Udell, J. (2008). Familiarity breeds distortion: The effects of media exposure on false reports concerning media coverage of the terrorist attacks in London on 7 July 2005. *Memory, 16*(1), 76–85.

Overing, J. (1986). Images of cannibalism, death and domination in a "non-violent" society. In D. Riches (Ed.), *The anthropology of violence* (pp. 86–101). Oxford, UK: Blackwell.

Overing, J. (1989). The aesthetics of production: The sense of community among the Cubeo and Piaroa. *Dialectical Anthropology, 14*(3), 159–175.

Parlamis, J. D., Allred, K. G., & Block, C. (2010). Letting off steam or just steaming? The influence of venting target and offender status on attributions and anger. *International Journal of Conflict Management, 21*(3), 260–280.

Park, J. W., & Hastak, M. (1994). Memory based product judgments: Effect of involvement at encoding and retrieval. *Journal of Consumer Research, 21*(3), 534–547.

Parmesan, C. (2006). Ecological and evolutionary responses to recent climate change. *Annual Review of Ecology, Evolution, and Systematics, 37*(1), 637–669.

Parnes, S. J., & Meadow, A. (1959). Effects of "brainstorming" instructions on creative problem solving by trained and untrained subjects. *Journal of Educational Psychology, 50*(4), 171–176.

Patrick, C. J., & Verona, E. (2007). The psychophysiology of aggression: Autonomic, electrocortical, and neuro-imaging findings. In D. J. Flannery, A. T. Vazsonyi, & I. D. Waldman (Eds.), *The Cambridge handbook of violent behavior and aggression* (pp. 111–150). Cambridge, UK: Cambridge University Press.

Paul, E. L., & Hayes, K. A. (2002). The causalities of 'casual' sex: A qualitative exploration of the phenomenology of college students' hookups. *Journal of Social and Personal Relationships, 19*(5), 639–661.

Paul, E. L., McManus, B., & Hayes, A. (2000). 'Hookups': Characteristics and correlates of college students' spontaneous and anonymous sexual experiences. *Journal of Sex Research, 37*(1), 76–88.

Paulus, P. B., Nakui, T., Putman, V. L., & Brown, V. R. (2006). Effects of task instructions and brief breaks on brainstorming. *Group Dynamics: Theory, Research, and Practice, 10*(3), 206–219.

Pearce, J. L. (1983). Job attitude and motivation differences between volunteers and employees from comparable organizations. *Journal of Applied Psychology, 68*(4), 646–652.

Pedersen, W. C., Miller, L. C., Putcha-Bhagavatula, A. D., & Yang, Y. (2002). Evolved sex differences in the number of partners desired? The long and short of it. *Psychological Science, 13*(2), 157–161.

Peetz, J., & Kammrath, L. (2011). Only because I love you: Why people make and why they break promises in romantic relationships. *Journal of Personality and Social Psychology, 100*(5), 887–904.

Pence, E., & Paymar, M. (1993). *Education groups for men who batter: The Duluth model.* New York, NY: Springer.

Penkal, J. L., & Kurdek, L. A. (2007). Gender and race differences in young adults' body dissatisfaction. *Personality and Individual Differences, 43*(8), 2270–2281.

Pennebaker, J. W. (1997). Writing about emotional experiences as a therapeutic process. *Psychological Science, 8*(3), 162–166.

Perlin, R. (2012). Intern nation: How to earn nothing and learn little in the brave new economy. *Contemporary Sociology, 42*(3), 454–454.

Perloff, R. M., & Brock, T. C. (1980). And thinking makes it so: Cognitive responses to persuasion. In M. Roloff & G. Miller (Eds.), *Persuasion: New directions in theory and research* (pp. 67–100). Beverly Hills, CA: Sage.

Perrett, D. I., May, K. A., & Yoshikawa, S. (1994). Facial shape and judgements of female attractiveness. *Nature, 368*(6468), 239–242.

Perrin, S., & Spencer, C. P. (1981). Independence or conformity in the Asch experiment as a reflection of cultural and situational factors. *British Journal of Social Psychology, 20*(3), 205–210.

Perry, D. G., & Bussey, K. (1979). The social learning theory of sex differences: Imitation is alive and well. *Journal of Personality and Social Psychology, 37*(10), 1699–1712.

Perry, G. (2013). *Behind the shock machine: The untold story of the notorious Milgram psychology experiments.* New York, NY: New Press.

Pessin, J. (1933). The comparative effects of social and mechanical stimulation on memorizing. *The American Journal of Psychology, 45*(2), 263–270.

Pessoa, F. (2002). *The book of disquiet*. London, UK: Penguin.

Peterson, C. K., & Harmon-Jones, E. (2012). Anger and testosterone: Evidence that situationally-induced anger relates to situationally-induced testosterone. *Emotion, 12*(5), 899–902.

Petty, R. E., & Cacioppo, J. T. (1979). Effects of forewarning of persuasive intent and involvement on cognitive responses. *Personality and Social Psychology Bulletin, 5*(2), 173–176.

Petty, R. E., & Cacioppo, J. T. (1986). *Communication and persuasion: Central and peripheral routes to attitude change*. New York, NY: Springer-Verlag.

Petty, R. E., & Cacioppo, J. T. (1996). *Attitudes and persuasion: Classic and contemporary approaches*. Boulder, CO: Westview.

Petty, R. E., Cacioppo, J. T., & Haugtvedt, C. P. (1992). Ego-involvement and persuasion: An appreciative look at the Sherifs' contribution to the study of self-relevance an attitude change. In D. Granberg & G. Sarup (Eds.), *Social judgment and intergroup relations: Essays in honor of Muzifer Sherif* (pp. 147–175). New York, NY: Springer-Verlag.

Petty, R. E., Harkins, S. G., Williams, K., & Latane, B. (1977). The effects of group size on cognitive effort and evaluation. *Personality and Social Psychology Bulletin, 3*(4), 579–582.

Petty, R. E., & Wegener, D. T. (1998). Attitude change: Multiple roles for persuasion variables. In D. T. Gilbert, S. T. Fiske, & G. Lindzey (Eds.), *The handbook of social psychology* (Vol. 1, 4th ed., pp. 323–390). New York, NY: McGraw-Hill.

Phillips, J. G., Butt, S., & Blaszczynski, A. (2006). Personality and self-reported use of mobile phones for games. *Cyberpsychology & Behavior, 9*(6), 753–758.

Phillips, M. L., Howard, R., & David, A. S. (1996). 'Mirror, mirror on the wall, who. . .?': Towards a model of visual self-recognition. *Cognitive Neuropsychiatry, 1*(2), 153–164.

Pieters, R., Warlop, L., & Wedel, M. (2002). Breaking through the clutter: Benefits of advertisement originality and familiarity for brand attention and memory. *Management Science, 48*(6), 765–781.

Pinker, S. (2002). *The blank slate: The modern denial of human nature*. New York, NY: Viking.

Pinker, S. (2011). *The better angels of our nature: Why violence has declined*. New York, NY: Viking.

Pinter, B., & Greenwald, A. G. (2005). Clarifying the role of the 'other' category in the self-esteem IAT. *Experimental Psychology, 52*(1), 74–79.

Pittinsky, T. L. (2010). A two-dimensional model of intergroup leadership: The case of national diversity. *American Psychologist, 65*(3), 194–200.

Plotnik, J. M., de Waal, F. B., & Reiss, D. (2006). Self-recognition in an Asian elephant. *PNAS Proceedings of the National Academy of Sciences of the United States of America, 103*(45), 17053–17057.

Pluralism Project at Harvard University. (2013). *Research report: Post 9/11 hate crime trends: Muslims, Sikhs, Hindus and Jews in the U.S. (2013)*. Retrieved from http://pluralism.org/research-report/post-9-11-hate-crime-trends-muslims-sikhs-hindus-and-jews-in-the-u-s/

Podnar, O. (2007, July 25). The day Yugoslav soccer died: Croats celebrate the 15th anniversary of the beginning of the Patriotic War . . . on the soccer field! *Soccerphile*. Retrieved from http://www.soccerphile.com/soccerphile/news/balkans-soccer/football-war.html

Politser, P. (2008). *Neuroeconomics: A guide to the new science of making choices*. New York, NY: Oxford University Press.

Polman, E. (2010). Why are maximizers less happy than satisficers? Because they maximize positive and negative outcomes. *Journal of Behavioral Decision Making, 23*(2), 179–190.

Popper, K. (1959). The logic of scientific discovery. *Physics Today, 12*(11), 53–54.

Porter, E. S. (Producer & Director). (1903). *The great train robbery* [Motion picture]. United States: Warner Bros.

Porter, S., ten Brinke, L., & Wallace, B. (2012). Secrets and lies: Involuntary leakage in deceptive facial expressions as a function of emotional intensity. *Journal of Nonverbal Behavior, 36*(1), 23–37.

Post, J. M., & Panis, L. K. (2011). Crimes of obedience: "Groupthink" at Abu Ghraib. *International Journal of Group Psychotherapy, 61*(1), 48–66.

Powell, J. (2013). *Volunteering, aging and business*. New York, NY: Nova.

Poyatos, F. (2002a). *Nonverbal communication across disciplines. Volume 1: Culture, sensory interaction, speech, conversation*. Amsterdam, Netherlands: John Benjamins.

Poyatos, F. (2002b). The nature, morphology and functions of gestures, manners and postures as documented by creative literature. *Gesture, 2*(1), 99–117.

Pratkanis, A. R., & Aronson, E. (2001). *Age of propaganda: The everyday use and abuse of persuasion*. New York, NY: Freeman.

Pratto, F., Sidanius, J., Stallworth, L. M., & Malle, B. F. (1994). Social dominance orientation: A personality variable predicting social and political attitudes. *Journal of Personality and Social Psychology, 67*(4), 741–763.

Praxmarer, S. (2011). How a presenter's perceived attractiveness affects persuasion for attractiveness-unrelated products. *International Journal of Advertising, 30*(5), 839–865.

Prentice-Dunn, S., & Rogers, R. W. (1982). Effects of public and private self-awareness on deindividuation and aggression. *Journal of Personality and Social Psychology, 43*(3), 503–513.

Priester, J. R., & Petty, R. E. (1996). The gradual threshold model of ambivalence: Relating the positive and negative bases of attitudes to subjective ambivalence. *Journal of Personality and Social Psychology, 71*(3), 431–449.

Provine, R. (1992). Contagious laughter: Laughter is sufficient stimulus for laughs and smiles. *Bulletin of the Psychonomic Society, 30*(1), 1–4.

Provine, R. (1996). Laughter. *American Scientist, 84*(1), 38–47.

Pryor, J. H., Hurtado, S., DeAngelo, L. E., Blake, L. P., & Tran, S. (2010). *The American freshman: National norms fall 2009*. Berkeley: University of California Press.

Puckett, J. M., Petty, R. E., Cacioppo, J. T., & Fisher, D. L. (1983). The relative impact of age and attractiveness stereotypes on persuasion. *Journal of Gerontology, 38*(3), 340–343.

Pyszczynski, T., Greenberg, J., & Holt, K. (1985). Maintaining consistency between self-serving beliefs and available data: A bias in information evaluation. *Personality and Social Psychology Bulletin, 11*(2), 179–190.

Pyszczynski, T., Greenberg, J., & Solomon, S. (1999). A dual-process model of defense against conscious and unconscious death-related thoughts: An extension of terror management theory. *Psychological Review, 106*(4), 835–845.

Pyszczynski, T., Greenberg, J., Solomon, S., Arndt, J., & Schimel, J. (2004). Converging toward an integrated theory of self-esteem: Reply to Crocker and Nuer (2004), Ryan and Deci (2004), and Leary (2004). *Psychological Bulletin, 130*(3), 483–488.

Pyszczynski, T., Wicklund, R. A., Floresku, S., Koch, H., Gauch, G., Solomon, S., & Greenberg, J. (1996). Whistling in the dark: Exaggerated consensus estimates in response to incidental reminders of mortality. *Psychological Science, 7*(6), 332–336.

Ramsden, E., & Adams, J. (2009). Escaping the laboratory: The rodent experiments of John B. Calhoun & their cultural influence. *Journal of Social History, 42*(3), 761–792.

Raven, B. H. (1958). Legitimate power, coercive power, and the observability in social influence. *Sociometry, 21*(2), 83–97.

Ray, J. J. (1990). Comment on "right-wing authoritarianism." *Canadian Psychology, 31*(4), 392–393.

Reeder, G. D. (1982). Let's give the fundamental attribution error another chance. *Journal of Personality and Social Psychology, 43*(2), 341–344.

Reiber, C., & Garcia, J. R. (2010). Hooking up: Gender differences, evolution, and pluralistic ignorance. *Evolutionary Psychology, 8*(3), 390–404.

Reis, H. T., Maniaci, M. R., Caprariello, P. A., Eastwick, P. W., & Finkel, E. J. (2011). Familiarity does indeed promote attraction in live interaction. *Journal of Personality and Social Psychology, 101*(3), 557–570.

Remmers, H. H. (1934). Reliability and halo effect of high school and college students' judgments of their teachers. *Journal of Applied Psychology, 18*(5), 619–630.

Reston, J. (2007). *The conviction of Richard Nixon: The untold story of the Frost/Nixon interviews.* New York, NY: Harmony Books.

Rhodes, N., & Wood, W. (1992). Self-esteem and intelligence affect influenceability: The mediating role of message reception. *Psychological Bulletin, 111*(1), 156–171.

Richardson, J. T., & Bellanger, F. (Eds.). (2016). *Legal cases, new religious movements, and minority faiths.* Abingdon, UK: Routledge.

Ringelmann, M. (1913). Recherches sur les moteurs animes: Travail de l'homme [Research on animate sources of power: The work of man]. *Annales de l'Institut National Agronomique, 12*(1), 1–40.

Rivenburgh, N. K. (2000). Social identity theory and news portrayals of citizens involved in international affairs. *Media Psychology, 2*(4), 303–329.

Robins, L. N. (1974). A follow-up study of Vietnam veterans' drug use. *Journal of Drug Use, 4*(1), 61–63.

Robins, L. N. (1993). Vietnam veterans' raid recovery from heroin addiction: A fluke or normal expectation? *Addiction, 88*(8), 1041–1054.

Rochat, P., & Striano, T. (2002). Who's in the mirror? Self-other discrimination in specular images by four- and nine-month-old infants. *Child Development, 73*(1), 35–46.

Rockström, J., Steffen, W., Noone, K., Persson, A., Chapin, F. S. III, Lambin, E. F., . . . Foley, J. A. (2009). A safe operating space for humanity. *Nature, 461*, 472–475.

Rodin, J., & Langer, E. J. (1977a). Long-term effects of a control-relevant intervention with the institutionalized aged. *Journal of Personality and Social Psychology, 35*(12), 897–902.

Rodin, J., & Langer, E. J. (1977b). Erratum to Rodin and Langer. *Journal of Personality and Social Psychology, 36*(5), 462.

Roese, N. J. (1997). Counterfactual thinking. *Psychological Bulletin, 121*(1), 133–148.

Rosen, K. H. (1996). The ties that bind women to violent premarital relationships: Processes of seduction and entrapment. In D. D. Cahn & S. A. Lloyd (Eds.), *Family violence from a communication perspective* (pp. 151–176). Thousand Oaks, CA: Sage.

Rosen, K. H., & Stith, S. M. (1997). Surviving abusive dating relationships: Processes of leaving, healing and moving on. In G. Kantor & J. Jasinski (Eds.), *Out of the darkness: Contemporary perspectives on family violence* (pp. 170–182). Thousand Oaks, CA: Sage.

Rosenberg, M. (1965). Rosenberg self-esteem scale (RSE). *Acceptance and Commitment Therapy: Measures Package, 61,* 52.

Rosenberg, M. (1979). *Conceiving the self.* New York, NY: Basic Books.

Rosenberg, R. S., & Canzoneri, J. (Eds.). (2008). *The psychology of superheroes: An unauthorized exploration.* Dallas, TX: BenBella Books.

Rosenthal, R. (1994). Interpersonal expectancy effects: A 30-year perspective. *Current Directions in Psychological Science, 3*(6), 176–179.

Rosenthal, R. (2002). Covert communication in classrooms, clinics, courtrooms, and cubicles. *American Psychologist, 57*(11), 839–849.

Rosenthal, R., & Fode, K. (1963). The effect of experimenter bias on the performance of the albino rat. *Behavioral Science, 8*(3), 183–189.

Rosenthal, R., & Jacobsen, L. (1968). *Pygmalion in the classroom: Self-fulfilling prophecies and teacher expectations.* New York, NY: Holt, Rhinehart, and Winston.

Roser, M. (2017). Homicides. *Our World in Data.* Retrieved from https://ourworldindata.org/homicides/

Ross, L. D. (1977). The intuitive psychologist and his shortcomings: Distortions in the attribution process. In L. Berkowitz (Ed.), *Advances in experimental social psychology* (Vol. 10, pp. 173–220). San Diego, CA: Academic Press.

Ross, L. D., & Nisbett, R. E. (1991). *The person and the situation: Perspectives of social psychology.* New York, NY: McGraw-Hill.

Roth, V. (2011). *Divergent.* New York, NY: Katherine Tegen Books.

Rothman, A. J., & Hardin, C. D. (1997). Differential use of the availability heuristic in social judgment. *Personality and Social Psychology Bulletin, 23*(2), 123–138.

Rotter, J. B. (1954). *Social learning and clinical psychology.* Englewood Cliffs, NJ: Prentice-Hall.

Rotter, J. B. (1990). Internal versus external control of reinforcement: A case history of a variable. *American Psychologist, 45*(4), 489–493.

Rotton, J., Frey, J., Barry, T., Milligan, M., & Fitzpatrick, M. (1979). The air pollution experience and physical aggression. *Journal of Applied Social Psychology, 9*(5), 397–412.

Rowatt, W. C., & Franklin, L. M. (2004). Christian orthodoxy, religious fundamentalism, and right-wing authoritarianism as predictors of implicit racial prejudice. *The International Journal for the Psychology of Religion, 14*(2), 125–138.

Rowling, J. K. (1997). *Harry Potter and the sorcerer's stone.* New York, NY: Scholastic.

Rowling, J. K. (1998). *Harry Potter and the chamber of secrets.* New York, NY: Scholastic.

Rowling, J. K. (1999). *Harry Potter and the prisoner of Azkaban.* New York, NY: Scholastic.

Rowling, J. K. (2000). *Harry Potter and the goblet of fire.* New York, NY: Scholastic.

Rowling, J. K. (2003). *Harry Potter and the order of the phoenix.* New York, NY: Scholastic.

Rowling, J. K. (2005). *Harry Potter and the half-blood prince.* New York, NY: Scholastic.

Rowling, J. K. (2007). *Harry Potter and the deathly hallows.* New York, NY: Scholastic.

Royet, J. P., Plailly, J., Delon-Martin, C., Kareken, D. A., & Segebarth, C. (2003). fMRI of emotional responses to odors: Influence of hedonic valence and judgment, handedness, and gender. *Neuroimage, 20*(2), 713–728.

Rubin, Z., & Peplau, L. A. (1975). Who believes in a just world? *Journal of Social Issues, 31*(3), 65–89.

Rusbult, C. E. (1980). Commitment and satisfaction in romantic associations: A test of the investment model. *Journal of Experimental Social Psychology, 16*(2), 172–186.

Rusbult, C. E., & Buunk, B. P. (1993). Commitment processes in close relationships: An interdependence analysis. *Journal of Social and Personal Relationships, 10*(2), 175–204.

Rusbult, C. E., & Martz, J. M. (1995). Remaining in an abusive relationship: An investment model analysis of nonvoluntary dependence. *Personality and Social Psychology Bulletin, 21*(6), 558–571.

Rusbult, C. E., Martz, J. M., & Agnew, C. R. (1998). The investment model scale: Measuring commitment level, satisfaction level, quality of alternatives, and investment size. *Personal Relationships, 5*(4), 357–391.

Russell, B. L., & Trigg, K. Y. (2004). Tolerance of sexual harassment: An examination of gender differences, ambivalent sexism, social dominance, and gender roles. *Sex Roles, 50*(7), 565–573.

Russell, G. (2008). *Aggression in the sports world: A social psychological perspective.* New York, NY: Oxford University Press.

Russo, A. (Producer), & Landis, J. (Director). (1983). *Trading places* [Motion picture]. United States: Paramount Pictures.

Sampson, E. E. (1988). The debate on individualism. *American Psychologist, 43*(1), 15–22.

Sandler, K., & Studlar, G. (1999). *Titanic: Anatomy of a blockbuster.* New Brunswick, NJ: Rutgers University Press.

Sanna, L. J. (1992). Self-efficacy theory: Implications for social facilitation and social loafing. *Journal of Personality and Social Psychology, 62*(5), 774–786.

Sarnoff, I., & Zimbardo, P. G. (1961). Anxiety, fear, and social isolation. *The Journal of Abnormal and Social Psychology, 62*(2), 356–363.

Saucier, D. A., Stanford, A. J., Miller, S. S., Martens, A. L., Miller, A. K., Jones, T. L., . . . Burns, M. D. (2016). Masculine honor beliefs: Measurement and correlates. *Personality and Individual Differences, 94,* 7–15.

Saucier, D. A., Till, D. F., Miller, S. S., O'Dea, C. J., & Andres, E. (2015). Slurs against masculinity: Masculine honor beliefs and men's reactions to slurs. *Language Sciences, 52,* 108–120.

Saunders, B. A., Kelly, E., Cohen, N. P., & Guarino, C. (2016). Right-wing authoritarianism and social dominance orientation indirectly predict support for New York City's stop-&-frisk policy through prejudice. *Current Psychology, 35*(1), 92–98.

Savin-Williams, R. C., Cash, B. M., McCormack, M., & Rieger, G. (2017). Gay, mostly gay, or bisexual leaning gay? An exploratory study distinguishing gay sexual orientations among young men. *Archives of Sexual Behavior, 46*(1), 265–272.

Scanlan, T. P. (2015). *Influences of CSI effect, Daubert ruling, and NAS report on forensic science practices.* Doctoral dissertation, Walden University.

Schachter, S. (1959). *The psychology of affiliation: Experimental studies of the sources of gregariousness.* Stanford, CA: Stanford University Press.

Schaller, M., & Cialdini, R. B. (1988). The economics of empathic helping: Support for a mood management motive. *Journal of Experimental Social Psychology, 24*(2), 163–181.

Schaller, M., & Cialdini, R. B. (1990). Happiness, sadness, and helping: A motivational integration. In E. T. Higgins & R. M. Sorrentino (Eds.), *Handbook of motivation and cognition: Foundations of social behavior* (Vol. 2, pp. 265–296). New York, NY: Guilford.

Schippers, M. C. (2014). Social loafing tendencies and team performance: The compensating effect of agreeableness and conscientiousness. *Academy of Management Learning & Education, 13*(1), 62–81.

Schmale, A., & Iker, H. (1966). The psychological setting of uterine cervical cancer. *Annals of the New York Academy of Sciences, 125*(1), 807–813.

Schnabel, K., Asendorpf, J. B., & Greenwald, A. G. (2008). Assessment of individual differences in implicit cognition: A review of IAT measures. *European Journal of Psychological Assessment, 24*(4), 210–217.

Schnall, S., & Laird, J. D. (2003). Keep smiling: Enduring effects of facial expressions and postures on emotional experience and memory. *Cognition and Emotion, 17*(5), 787–797.

Schneider, B. A., & Pichora-Fuller, M. K. (2001). Age-related changes in temporal processing: Implications for speech perception. *Seminars in Hearing, 22*(3), 227–240.

Schneider, D. (1973). Implicit personality theory: A review. *Psychological Bulletin, 79*(5), 294–309.

Schneider, W., & Shiffrin, R. M. (1977). Controlled and automatic human information processing: I. Detection, search, and attention. *Psychological Review, 84*(1), 1–66.

Schultz, D. P., & Schultz, S. E. (2016). *Theories of personality*. Boston, MA: Cengage Learning.

Schwartz, B., Ward, A., Monterosso, J., Lyubormirsky, S., White, K., & Lehman, D. R. (2002). Maximizing versus satisficing: Happiness is a matter of choice. *Journal of Personality and Social Psychology, 83*(5), 1178–1197.

Schwartz, H. H. (2008). *A guide to behavioral economics.* Reston, VA: Higher Education Publications.

Schwarz, N. (1998). Accessible content and accessibility experiences: The interplay of declarative and experiential information in judgment. *Personality and Social Psychology Review, 2*(2), 87–99.

Schwarz, S., & Hassebrauck, M. (2012). Sex and age differences in mate-selection preferences. *Human Nature, 23*(4), 447–466.

Schweingruber, D., Cast, A. D., & Anahita, S. (2008). 'A story and a ring': Audience judgments about engagement proposals. *Sex Roles, 58*(3–4), 165–178.

Scott, W., & Hayes, M. (1921). *Science and common sense in working with men.* Oxford, UK: Ronald.

Scull, M. T. (2013). Reinforcing gender roles at the male strip show: A qualitative analysis of men who dance for women (MDW). *Deviant Behavior, 34*(7), 557–578.

Sears, D. O., & Henry, P. J. (2005). Over thirty years later: A contemporary look at symbolic racism. In M. P. Zanna (Ed.), *Advances in experimental social psychology* (Vol. 37, pp. 95–150). San Diego, CA: Academic Press.

Sedikides, C., & Skowronski, J. J. (1997). The symbolic self in evolutionary context. *Personality and Social Psychology Review, 1*(1), 80–102.

Seibert, S. E., & Goltz, S. M. (2001). Comparison of allocations by individuals and interacting groups in an escalation of commitment Situation1. *Journal of Applied Social Psychology, 31*(1), 134–156.

Seligman, M. E. P. (1975). *Helplessness.* San Francisco, CA: Freeman.

Seligman, M. E. P. (1998). Treatment becomes prevention & treatment. *Prevention & Treatment, 1*(2), 1e.

Seligman, M. E. P. (2002). Positive psychology, positive prevention, and positive therapy. In C. R. Snyder & S. J. Lopez (Eds.), *Handbook of positive psychology* (pp. 3–9). New York, NY: Oxford University Press.

Seligman, M. E. P., & Csikszentmihalyi, M. (2000). Positive psychology: An introduction. *American Psychologist, 55*(1), 5–14.

Selye, H. (1973). The evolution of the stress concept: The originator of the concept traces its development from the discovery in 1936 of the alarm reaction to modern therapeutic applications of syntoxic and catatoxic hormones. *American Scientist, 61*(6), 692–699.

Shaheen, J. G. (2003). Reel bad Arabs: How Hollywood vilifies a people. *The Annals of the American Academy of Political and Social Science, 588*(1), 171–193.

Shapiro, S. L., Schwartz, G. E., & Bonner, G. (1998). Effects of mindfulness-based stress reduction on medical and premedical students. *Journal of Behavioral Medicine, 21*(6), 581–599.

Sharp, F. C. (1928). *Ethics.* New York, NY: Century Company.

Shedler, J., & Manis, M. (1986). Can the availability heuristic explain vividness effects? *Journal of Personality and Social Psychology, 51*(1), 26–36.

Sheldon, K. M., King, L. A., Houser-Marko, L., Osbaldiston, R., & Gunz, A. (2007). Comparing IAT and TAT measures of power versus intimacy motivation. *European Journal of Personality, 21*(3), 263–280.

Shepperd, J. A., & Koch, E. J. (2005). Pitfalls in teaching judgment heuristics. *Teaching of Psychology, 32*(1), 43–46.

Sherif, C. W., Sherif, M., & Nebergall, R. E. (1965). *Attitude and attitude change: The social judgment-involvement approach.* Philadelphia, PA: Saunders.

Sherif, M. (1935). A study of some social factors in perception. *Archives of Psychology, 187,* 60.

Sherif, M. (1936). *The psychology of social norms.* Oxford, UK: Harper.

Sherif, M. (1956). Experiments in group conflict. *Scientific American, 195,* 54–58.

Sherif, M. (1966a). *Group conflict and cooperation: Their social psychology.* London, UK: Routledge & Kegan Paul.

Sherif, M. (1966b). *In common predicament: Social psychology of intergroup conflict and cooperation.* Boston, MA: Houghton Mifflin.

Sherif, M., Harvey, O. J., White, B. J., Hood, W. R., & Sherif, C. W. (1961). *The Robbers Cave experiment: Intergroup conflict and cooperation.* Norman: University of Oklahoma Book Exchange.

Sherif, M., & Sherif, C. W. (1969). Ingroup and intergroup relations: Experimental analysis. In M. Sherif & C. W. Sherif (Eds.), *Social psychology* (pp. 221–266). New York, NY: Harper & Row.

Sherman, D. K., & Cohen, G. L. (2002). Accepting threatening information: Self-affirmation and the reduction of defensive biases. *Current Directions in Psychological Science, 11*(4), 118–123.

Sherman, J. W., Gawronski, B., & Trope, Y. (2014). *Dual-process theories of the social mind.* New York, NY: Guilford.

Sherman, S. J., Chassin, L., Presson, C. C., & Agostinelli, G. (1984). The role of the evaluation and similarity principles in the false consensus effect. *Journal of Personality and Social Psychology, 47*(6), 1244–1262.

Shute, V., & Ventura, M. (2013). *Stealth assessment: Measuring and supporting learning in video games.* Cambridge, MA: MIT Press.

Silveira, J. M., & Hudson, M. W. (2015). Hazing in the college marching band. *Journal of Research in Music Education, 63*(1), 5–27.

Silver, J., Hill, G., Wachowski, A., & Wachowski, L. (Producers), & McTeigue, J. (Director). (2005). *V for Vendetta* [Motion picture]. United States: Warner Bros. Pictures.

Silverstein, M., Gans, D., & Yang, F. M. (2006). Intergenerational support to aging parents: The role of norms and needs. *Journal of Family Issues, 27*(8), 1068–1084.

Silvia, P. J., & Gendolla, G. E. (2001). On introspection and self-perception: Does self-focused attention enable accurate self-knowledge? *Review of General Psychology, 5*(3), 241–269.

Simmons, C. H., & Lerner, M. J. (1968). Altruism as a search for justice. *Journal of Personality and Social Psychology, 9*(3), 216–225.

Simon, H. A. (1955). A behavioral model of rational choice. *Quarterly Journal of Economics, 69*(1), 99–118.

Simon, H. A. (1956). Rational choice and the structure of the environment. *Psychological Review, 63*(2), 129–138.

Simon, J. B., Nail, P. R., Swindle, T., Bihm, E. M., & Joshi, K. (2017). Defensive egotism and self-esteem:

A cross-cultural examination of the dynamics of bullying in middle school. *Self and Identity, 16*(3), 270–297.

Simon, J. R. (1990). The effects of an irrelevant directional cue on human information processing. In R. W. Proctor & T. G. Reeve (Eds.), *Stimulus-response compatibility: An integrated perspective* (pp. 31–86). Oxford, UK: North-Holland.

Simon, M., & Devlin, D. (Producers), & Bill, T. (Director). (1980). *My bodyguard* [Motion picture]. USA: Melvin Simon Productions & 20th Century Fox.

Simons, S. H., Cillessen, A. N., & de Weerth, C. (2017). Associations between circadian and stress response cortisol in children. *Stress: The International Journal on the Biology of Stress, 20*(1), 52–58.

Simpson, J. A., Gangestad, S. W., & Lerma, M. (1990). Perception of physical attractiveness: Mechanisms involved in the maintenance of romantic relationships. *Journal of Personality and Social Psychology, 59*(6), 1192–1201.

Singh, D. (1993a). Adaptive significance of female physical attractiveness: Role of waist-to-hip ratio. *Journal of Personality and Social Psychology, 65*(2), 293–307.

Singh, D. (1993b). Body shape and women's attractiveness: The critical role of waist-to-hip ratio. *Human Nature, 4*(3), 297–321.

Singh, D., & Randall, P. K. (2007). Beauty is in the eye of the plastic surgeon: Waist-hip ratio (WHR) and women's attractiveness. *Personality and Individual Differences, 43*(2), 329–340.

Siy, J. O., & Cheryan, S. (2016). Prejudice masquerading as praise: The negative echo of positive stereotypes. *Personality and Social Psychology Bulletin, 42*(7), 941–954.

Skitka, L. J., Bauman, C. W., & Lytle, B. L. (2009). Limits on legitimacy: Moral and religious convictions as constraints on deference to authority. *Journal of Personality and Social Psychology, 97*(4), 567–578.

Skodol, A. E. (2010). The resilient personality. In J. W. Reich, A. J. Zautra, & J. S. Hall (Eds.), *Handbook of adult resilience* (pp. 112–125). New York, NY: Guilford.

Sloman, L. (2000). The syndrome of rejection sensitivity: An evolutionary perspective. In P. Gilbert & K. Bailey (Eds.), *Genes on the couch: Explorations in evolutionary psychotherapy* (pp. 257–275). Hove, East Sussex, UK: Brunner-Routledge.

Slusher, M. P., & Anderson, C. A. (1989). Belief perseverance and self-defeating behavior. In R. C. Curtis (Ed.), *Self-defeating behaviors: Experimental research, clinical impressions, and practical implications* (pp. 11–40). New York, NY: Plenum.

Smith, A. (1759). *The theory of moral sentiments.* London, UK: Printed for Andrew Millar, Alexander Kincaid and J. Bell.

Smith, C. T., & Nosek, B. A. (2011). Affective focus increases the concordance between implicit and explicit attitudes. *Social Psychology, 42*(4), 300–313.

Smith, D., Lovell, J., Weller, C., Kennedy, B., Winbolt, M., Young, C., . . . Chen, K. (2017). A systematic review of medication non-adherence in persons with dementia or cognitive impairment. *PLoS ONE, 12*(2), e0170651.

Smith, P. B., & Bond, M. H. (1993). *Social psychology across cultures: Analysis and perspectives.* Hertfordshire, UK: Harvester Wheatsheaf.

Smrt, D. L., & Karau, S. J. (2011). Protestant work ethic moderates social loafing. *Group Dynamics: Theory, Research, and Practice, 15*(3), 267–274.

Smyth, J. M. (1998). Written emotional expression: Effect sizes, outcome types, and moderating variables. *Journal of Consulting and Clinical Psychology, 66*(1), 174–184.

Snyder, M., & Miene, P. K. (1994). Stereotyping of the elderly: A functional approach. *British Journal of Social Psychology, 33*(1), 63–82.

Snyder, M., & Omoto, A. M. (2008). Volunteerism: Social issues perspectives and social policy implications. *Social Issues and Policy Review, 2*(1), 1–36.

Society for Industrial and Organizational Psychology. (2017). *Science for a smarter workplace.* Retrieved from https://www.siop.org/

Solomon, J. D., Genovese, W., Jacobson, M., & Valva, M. (Producers), & Solomon, J. D. (Director). (2016). *The witness* [Motion picture]. United States: FilmRise.

Sommer, R. (1983). Spatial behavior. *Small Groups and Social Interaction, 1,* 9–15.

Son Hing, L. S., Bobocel, D. R., Zanna, M. P., & McBride, M. V. (2007). Authoritarian dynamics and unethical decision making: High social dominance orientation leaders and high right-wing authoritarianism followers. *Journal of Personality and Social Psychology, 92*(1), 67–81.

Soussignan, R. (2002). Duchenne smile, emotional experience, and autonomic reactivity: A test of the facial feedback hypothesis. *Emotion, 2*(1), 52–74.

Souza, M. G. T. C., Roazzi, A., & Souza, B. C. (2011). When killing is a legitimate course of action: A multidimensional investigation into the culture of honor as an explanation for homicides in northeastern Brazil. In Y. Fisher & I. A. Friedman (Eds.), *New horizons for facet theory: Searching for structure in content spaces and measurement* (pp. 85–98). Washington, DC: FTA Publications.

Sparks, E. A., Ehrlinger, J., & Eibach, R. P. (2012). Failing to commit: Maximizers avoid commitment in a way that contributes to reduced satisfaction. *Personality and Individual Differences, 52*(1), 72–77.

Spence, J. T., & Buckner, C. E. (2000). Instrumental and expressive traits, trait stereotypes, and sexist attitudes. *Psychology of Women Quarterly, 24*(1), 44–62.

Spencer, S. J., Fein, S., Wolfe, C. T., Fong, C., & Dunn, M. A. (1998). Automatic activation of stereotypes: The role of self-image threat. *Personality and Social Psychology Bulletin, 24*(11), 1139–1152.

Spencer, S. J., Steele, C. M., & Quinn, D. M. (1999). Stereotype threat and women's math performance. *Journal of Experimental Social Psychology, 35*(1), 4–28.

Spera, C., Ghertner, R., Nerino, A., & DiTommaso, A. (2013). *Volunteering as a pathway to employment does volunteering increase odds of finding a job for the out of work?* Washington, DC: Office of Research & Evaluation, Corporation for National and Community Service.

Spilka, B., Hood, R. W., Hunsberger, B., & Gorsuch, R. (2003). *The psychology of religion: An empirical approach.* New York, NY: Guilford.

Spohn, C. (2014). Twentieth-century sentencing reform movement: Looking backward, moving forward. *Criminology & Public Policy, 13*(4), 535–545.

Stanglin, D., & Gross, E. (1997, March 31). Oprah: A heavenly body. *US News and World Report,* p. 18.

Stanovich, K. E., & West, R. F. (2000). Individual differences in reasoning: Implications for the rationality debate? *Behavioral and Brain Sciences, 23*(5), 645–665.

Stanovich, K. E., & West, R. F. (2002). Individual differences in reasoning: Implications for the rationality debate? In T. Gilovich, D. Griffin, & D. Kahneman (Eds.), *Heuristics and biases: The psychology of intuitive judgment* (pp. 421–440). New York, NY: Cambridge University Press.

Starbuck, W. H. (1963). Level of aspiration. *Psychological Review, 70*(1), 51–60.

Starks, T., Castro, M., Castiblanco, J., & Millar, B. (2017). Modeling interpersonal correlates of condomless anal sex among gay and bisexual men: An application of attachment theory. *Archives of Sexual Behavior: The Official Publication of the International Academy of Sex Research, 46*(4), 1089–1099.

State of Arizona v. Frank Silva Roque. (2006). No. CR-03-0355-AP, Arizona Supreme Court. Retrieved September 26, 2009, from http://www.supreme.state.az.us/opin/pdf2006/CR030355AP.pdf

Steblay, N. M. (1987). Helping behavior in rural and urban environments: A meta-analysis. *Psychological Bulletin, 102*(3), 346–356.

Steele, C. M. (1988). The psychology of self-affirmation: Sustaining the integrity of the self. In L. Berkowitz (Ed.), *Advances in experimental social psychology* (Vol. 21, pp. 261–302). New York, NY: Academic Press.

Steele, C. M. (1997). A threat in the air: How stereotypes shape intellectual identity and performance. *American Psychologist, 52*(6), 613–629.

Steele, C. M., & Aronson, J. (1995). Stereotype threat and the intellectual performance of African Americans. *Journal of Personality and Social Psychology, 69*(5), 797–811.

Steepe, T. P. (1995). *The professional athlete's experience of moving out of a slump.* Chicago, IL: Urban Ministries, Inc.

Steiner, I. D. (1972). *Group process and productivity.* New York, NY: Academic Press.

Steinfeldt, J. A., Foltz, B. D., Kaladow, J. K., Carlson, T. N., Pagano, L. A., Benton, E., & Steinfeldt, M. C. (2010). Racism in the electronic age: Role of online forums in expressing racial attitudes about American Indians. *Cultural Diversity and Ethnic Minority Psychology, 16*(3), 362–371.

Stenico, C., & Greitemeyer, T. (2015). 'The others will help: The presence of multiple video game characters reduces helping after the game is over': Corrigendum. *The Journal of Social Psychology, 155*(1), 91.

Stevens, C. K., & Kristof, A. L. (1995). Making the right impression: A field study of applicant impression management during job interviews. *Journal of Applied Psychology, 80*(5), 587–606.

Stone, J., & Cooper, J. (2001). A self-standards model of cognitive dissonance. *Journal of Experimental Social Psychology, 37*(3), 228–243.

Stoner, J. A. F. (1961). *A comparison between individual and group decisions involving risk.* Unpublished master's thesis, Massachusetts Institute of Technology.

Stoner, J. A. F. (1968). Risky and cautious shifts in group decisions: The influence of widely held values. *Journal of Experimental Social Psychology, 4*(4), 442–459.

Stout, H. A. F. (2011). *Portrayals of relational aggression in popular teen movies: 1980–2009.* Master's thesis, Brigham Young University.

Strack, F., Martin, L. L., & Stepper, S. (1988). Inhibiting and facilitating conditions of the human smile: A non-obtrusive test of the facial feedback hypothesis. *Journal of Personality and Social Psychology, 54*(5), 768–777.

Strack, F., & Mussweiler, T. (1997). Explaining the enigmatic anchoring effect: Mechanisms of selective accessibility. *Journal of Personality and Social Psychology, 73*(3), 437–446.

Straus, M. A. (1979). Measuring intrafamily conflict and violence: The conflict tactics (CT) scales. *Journal of Marriage and the Family, 41*(1), 75–88.

Straus, S. G., Parker, A. M., & Bruce, J. B. (2011). The group matters: A review of processes and outcomes in intelligence analysis. *Group Dynamics: Theory, Research, and Practice, 15*(2), 128–146.

Street, A. E., & Arias, I. (2001). Psychological abuse and posttraumatic stress disorder in battered women: Examining the roles of shame and guilt. *Violence and Victims, 16*(1), 65–78.

Strick, M., van Baaren, R. B., Holland, R. W., & van Knippenberg, A. (2009). Humor in advertisements enhances product liking by mere association. *Journal of Experimental Psychology: Applied, 15*(1), 35–45.

Strömwall, L., Alfredsson, H., & Landström, S. (2013). Blame attributions and rape: Effects of belief in a just world and relationship level. *Legal and Criminological Psychology, 18*(2), 254–261.

Stroud, N. J. (2010). Polarization and partisan selective exposure. *Journal of Communication, 60*(3), 556–576.

Strube, M. J. (2005). What did Triplett really find? A contemporary analysis of the first experiment in social psychology. *The American Journal of Psychology, 118*(2), 271–286.

Subra, B., Muller, D., Bègue, L., Bushman, B. J., & Delmas, F. (2010). Automatic effects of alcohol and aggressive cues on aggressive thoughts and behaviors. *Personality and Social Psychology Bulletin, 36*(8), 1052–1057.

Sue, D. W. (2003). *Overcoming our racism: The journey to liberation.* San Francisco, CA: Jossey-Bass.

Sue, D. W. (2010). *Microaggressions in everyday life: Race, gender, and sexual orientation.* Hoboken, NJ: John Wiley.

Sue, D. W., Capodilupo, C. M., Torino, G. C., Bucceri, J. M., Holder, A. M. B., Nadal, K. L., & Esquilin, M. (2007). Racial microaggressions in everyday life: Implications for clinical practice. *American Psychologist, 62*(4), 271–286.

Suls, J., & Green, P. (2003). Pluralistic ignorance and college student perceptions of gender-specific alcohol norms. *Health Psychology, 22*(5), 479–486.

Suls, J., & Wan, C. K. (1987). In search of the false-uniqueness phenomenon: Fear and estimates of social consensus. *Journal of Personality and Social Psychology, 52*(1), 211–217.

Suls, J., & Wheeler, L. (2000). *Handbook of social comparison: Theory and research.* Dordrecht, Netherlands: Kluwer Academic.

Sundaram, C. S. (2013). Stockholm syndrome. In *Salem press encyclopedia.* Hackensack, NY: Salem Press.

Sundie, J. M., Kenrick, D. T., Griskevicius, V., Tybur, J. M., Vohs, K. D., & Beal, D. J. (2011). Peacocks, Porsches, and Thorstein Veblen: Conspicuous consumption as a sexual signaling system. *Journal of Personality and Social Psychology, 100*(4), 664–680.

Surowiecki, J. (2005). *The wisdom of crowds*. New York, NY: Anchor.

Sutphin, S. T. (2010). Social exchange theory and the division of household labor in same-sex couples. *Marriage & Family Review, 46*(3), 191–206.

Swami, V., Nader, I. W., Pietsching, J., Stieger, S., Tran, U. S., & Voracek, M. (2012). Personality and individual difference correlates of attitudes toward human rights and civil liberties. *Personality and Individual Differences, 53*(4), 443–447.

Swaminathan, A., Viennet, E., McMichael, A. J., & Harley, D. (2017). Climate change and the geographical distribution of infectious diseases. In E. Petersen, L. H. Chen, & P. Schlagenhauf-Lawlor (Eds.), *Infectious diseases: A geographic guide* (p. 470). Chichester, UK: John Wiley.

Swann, W. J., & Buhrmester, M. D. (2012). Self as functional fiction. *Social Cognition, 30*(4), 415–430.

Swann, W. J., Chang-Schneider, C., & Larsen McClarty, K. (2007). Do people's self-views matter? Self-concept and self-esteem in everyday life. *American Psychologist, 62*(2), 84–94.

Swinkels, A. (2003). An effective exercise for teaching cognitive heuristics. *Teaching of Psychology, 30*(2), 120–122.

Tagler, M. J. (2010). Sex differences in jealousy: Comparing the influence of previous infidelity among college students and adults. *Social Psychological and Personality Science, 1*(4), 353–360.

Tajfel, H. M. (1970). Experiments in intergroup discrimination. *Scientific American, 223*(5), 96–102.

Tajfel, H. M. (1981). *Human groups and social categories: Studies in social psychology.* Cambridge, UK: Cambridge University Press.

Tajfel, H. M. (1982). Social psychology of intergroup relations. *Annual Review of Psychology, 33*(1), 1–39.

Tajfel, H. M., Billig, M. G., Bundy, R. P., & Flament, C. (1971). Social categorization and intergroup behaviour, *European Journal of Social Psychology, 1*(2), 149–178.

Tajfel, H. M., & Turner, J. C. (1979). An integrative theory of intergroup conflict. *The Social Psychology of Intergroup Relations, 33*(47), 33–47.

Tajfel, H. M., & Turner, J. C. (1986). The social identity theory of intergroup behavior. In S. Worchel & W. G. Austin (Eds.), *Psychology of intergroup relations* (pp. 7–24). Chicago, IL: Nelson-Hall.

Tal-Or, N., & Papirman, Y. (2007). The fundamental attribution error in attributing fictional figures' characteristics to the actors. *Media Psychology, 9*(2), 331–345.

Tarullo, A. R., St. John, A. M., & Meyer, J. S. (2017). Chronic stress in the mother-infant dyad: Maternal hair cortisol, infant salivary cortisol and interactional synchrony. *Infant Behavior & Development, 47,* 92–102.

Tatum, B. D. (1997). *Why are all the Black kids sitting together in the cafeteria?* New York, NY: Basic Books.

Taubman-Ben-Ari, O., & Findler, L. (2006). Motivation for military service: A terror management perspective. *Military Psychology, 18*(2), 149–159.

Taufique, S., Lee, D., Ragussis, D., & Walker, T. (Producers), & Ragussis, D. (Director). (2016). *Imperium* [Motion picture]. United States: Lionsgate Premiere.

Tavris, C., & Aronson, E. (2007). *Mistakes were made (but not by me): Why we justify foolish beliefs, bad decisions, and hurtful acts.* New York, NY: Harcourt.

Taylor, S. E. (1981). The interface of cognitive and social psychology. In J. Harvey (Ed.), *Cognition, social behavior, and the environment* (pp. 189–211). Hillsdale, NJ: Lawrence Erlbaum.

Taylor, S. E. (1998). The social being in social psychology. In D. T. Gilbert, S. T. Fiske, & G. Lindzey (Eds.), *The handbook of social psychology* (Vol. 1, 4th ed., pp. 58–95). New York, NY: McGraw Hill.

Taylor, S. E. (2002). *The tending instinct: How nurturing is essential to who we are and how we live.* New York, NY: Henry Holt.

Taylor, S. E., & Fiske, S. T. (1978). Salience, attention, and attribution: Top of the head phenomena. In L. Berkowitz (Ed.), *Advances in experimental and social psychology* (Vol 11, pp. 249–288). New York, NY: Academic Press.

Taylor, S. E., & Gonzaga, G. C. (2006). Evolution, relationships, and health: The social shaping hypothesis. In M. Schaller, J. A. Simpson, & D. T. Kenrick (Eds.), *Evolution and social psychology* (pp. 211–236). New York, NY: Psychology Press.

Taylor, S. E., Kemeny, M. E., Reed, G. M., Bower, J. E., & Gruenewald, T. L. (2000). Psychological resources, positive illusions, and health. *American Psychologist, 55*(1), 99–109.

Taylor, S. E., & Thompson, S. C. (1982). Stalking the elusive "vividness" effect. *Psychological Review, 89*(2), 155–181.

Tedeschi, R. G., & Calhoun, L. G. (1996). The posttraumatic growth inventory: Measuring the positive legacy of trauma. *Journal of Traumatic Stress, 9*(3), 455–471.

Tedeschi, R. G., & Calhoun, L. G. (2004). Posttraumatic growth: Conceptual foundations and empirical evidence. *Psychological Inquiry, 15*(1), 1–18.

Teigen, K. H. (1994). Yerkes-Dodson: A law for all seasons. *Theory & Psychology, 4*(4), 525–547.

Teigen, K. H., & Jensen, T. K. (2011). Unlucky victims or lucky survivors? Spontaneous counterfactual thinking by families exposed to the Tsunami disaster. *European Psychologist, 16*(1), 48–57.

ten Brinke, L., & Porter, S. (2012). Cry me a river: Identifying the behavioral consequences of extremely high-stakes interpersonal deception. *Law and Human Behavior, 36*(6), 469–477.

Tennen, H., & Herzberger, S. (1987). Depression, self-esteem, and the absence of self-protective attributional biases. *Journal of Personality and Social Psychology, 52*(1), 72–80.

Tetlock, P. E. (1992). The impact of accountability on judgment and choice: Toward a social contingency model. In M. P. Zanna (Ed.), *Advances in experimental social psychology* (Vol. 25, pp. 331–376). San Diego, CA: Academic Press.

Thaler, R. H., & Sunstein, C. R. (2008). *Nudge: Improving decisions about health, wealth, and happiness.* London, UK: Penguin.

Thibaut, J. W., & Kelley, H. H. (1959). *The social psychology of groups.* Oxford, UK: John Wiley.

Thompson, M. M., Zanna, M. P., & Griffin, D. W. (1995). Let's not be indifferent about (attitudinal) ambivalence. In R. Petty & J. Krosnick (Eds.), *Attitude strength: Antecedents and consequences* (pp. 361–386). Hillsdale, NJ: Lawrence Erlbaum.

Thornberg, R., & Knutsen, S. (2011). Teenagers' explanations of bullying. *Child & Youth Care Forum, 40*(3), 177–192.

Thornhill, R., & Gangestad, S. W. (1994). Human fluctuating asymmetry and sexual behavior. *Psychological Science, 5*(5), 297–302.

Todd, S., & Todd, J. (Producers), & Nolan, C. (Director). (2000). *Memento* [Motion picture]. United States: Newmarket.

Toi, M., & Batson, C. D. (1982). More evidence that empathy is a source of altruistic motivation. *Journal of Personality and Social Psychology, 43*(2), 281–292.

Tottenham, N., Phuong, J., Flannery, J., Gabard-Durnam, L., & Goff, B. (2013). A negativity bias for ambiguous facial-expression valence during childhood: Converging evidence from behavior and facial corrugator muscle responses. *Emotion, 13*(1), 92–103.

Travis, C. B., Phillippi, R. H., & Tonn, B. E. (1989). Judgment heuristics and medical decisions. *Patient Education and Counseling, 13*(3), 211–220.

Triandis, H. C. (1989). The self and social behavior in differing cultural contexts. *Psychological Review, 96*(3), 506–520.

Triandis, H. C. (1996). The psychological measurement of cultural syndromes. *American Psychologist, 51*(4), 407–415.

Triplett, N. (1898). The dynamogenic factors in pacemaking and competition. *American Journal of Psychology, 9*(4), 507–533.

Trope, Y., & Gaunt, R. (2000). Processing alternative explanations of behavior: Correction or integration? *Journal of Personality and Social Psychology, 79*(3), 344–354.

Tsaousis, I. (2016). The relationship of self-esteem to bullying perpetration and peer victimization among schoolchildren and adolescents: A meta-analytic review. *Aggression and Violent Behavior, 31,* 186–199.

Tsintsadze-Maass, E., & Maass, R. W. (2014). Groupthink and terrorist radicalization. *Terrorism and Political Violence, 26*(5), 735–758.

Tullis, T., & Albert, B. (2013). *Measuring the user experience: Collecting, analyzing, and presenting usability metrics.* Amsterdam, Netherlands: Elsevier.

Tulving, E., & Pearlstone, Z. (1966). Availability versus accessibility of information in memory for words. *Journal of Verbal Learning & Verbal Behavior, 5*(4), 381–391.

Turner, C. W., Layton, J. F., & Simons, L. S. (1975). Naturalistic studies of aggressive behavior: Aggressive stimuli, victim visibility, and horn honking. *Journal of Personality and Social Psychology, 31*(6), 1098–1107.

Turner, J. C., & Tajfel, H. (1986). The social identity theory of intergroup behavior. In S. Worchel & W. G. Austin (Eds.), *Psychology of intergroup relations* (pp. 7–24). Chicago, IL: Nelson.

Tversky, A., & Kahneman, D. (1973). Availability: A heuristic for judging frequency and probability. *Cognitive Psychology, 5*(2), 207–232.

Tversky, A., & Kahneman, D. (1974). Judgment under uncertainty: Heuristics and biases. *Science, 185*(4157), 1124–1131.

Twenge, J. M. (2006). What is the interface between culture and self-esteem? In M. H. Kernis (Ed.), *Self-esteem issues and answers: A sourcebook of current perspectives* (pp. 389–395). New York, NY: Psychology Press.

Ubbiali, A. Donati, D., Chiorri, C., Bregani, V., Cattaneo, E. Maffei, C., & Visintini, R. (2008). The usefulness of the multidimensional health locus of control form C (MHLC-C) for HIV + subjects: An Italian study. *AIDS Care, 20*(4), 495–502.

Uchino, B. N. (2004). *Social support and physical health: Understanding the health consequences of relationships.* New Haven, CT: Yale University Press.

Uchino, B. N., Bowen, K., Carlisle, M., & Birmingham, W. (2012). Psychological pathways linking social support to health outcomes: A visit with the 'ghosts' of research past, present, and future. *Social Science & Medicine, 74*(7), 949–957.

Untied, A. S., & Dulaney, C. L. (2015). College students' perceived risk of sexual victimization and the role of optimistic bias. *Journal of Interpersonal Violence, 30*(8), 1417–1431.

Uniyal, S., Paliwal, R., Kaphaliya, B., & Sharma, R. K. (2016). Human overpopulation: Impact on environment. *Environmental Issues Surrounding Human Overpopulation, 738*(632), 1–11.

Unzueta, M. M., Everly, B. A., & Gutierrez, A. S. (2014). Social dominance orientation moderates reactions to Black and White discrimination claimants. *Journal of Experimental Social Psychology, 54*(2), 81–88.

U.S. Bureau of Labor Statistics. (2009). Retrieved from https://www.bls.gov/

U.S. Census Bureau. (2010). *2010 Census data.* Retrieved from https://www.census.gov/2010census/data/

U.S. Department of Veterans Affairs. (2017). *PTSD: National center for PTSD.* Retrieved from https://www.ptsd.va.gov/

Vallacher, R. R., Coleman, P. T., Nowak, A., & Bui-Wrzosinska, L. (2010). Dynamical foundations of intractable conflict: Introduction to the special issue. *Peace and Conflict: Journal of Peace Psychology, 16*(2), 113–125.

Vallacher, R. R., & Solodky, M. (1979). Objective self-awareness, standards of evaluation, and moral behavior. *Journal of Experimental Social Psychology, 15*(3), 254–262.

Valor-Segura, I., Exposito, F., & Moya, M. (2011). Victim blaming and exoneration of the perpetrator in domestic violence: The role of beliefs in a just world and ambivalent sexism. *The Spanish Journal of Psychology, 14*(1), 195–206.

Van Beest, I., & Williams, K. D. (2006). When inclusion costs and ostracism pays, ostracism still hurts. *Journal of Personality and Social Psychology, 91*(5), 918–928.

van Bommel, M., van Prooijen, J. W., Elffers, H., & Van Lange, P. A. M. (2014). Intervene to be seen: The power of a camera in attenuating the bystander effect. *Social Psychological and Personality Science, 5*(4), 459–466.

van Bommel, M., van Prooijen, J. W., Elffers, H., & Van Lange, P. A. M. (2016). The lonely bystander: Ostracism leads to less helping in virtual bystander situations. *Social Influence, 11*(3), 141–150.

Van den Berghe, P. L., & Peter, K. (1988). Hutterites and Kibbutzniks: A tale of nepotistic communism. *Man, 23*(3), 522–539.

van der Klink, J. L., Blonk, R. B., Schene, A. H., & van Dijk, F. H. (2001). The benefits of interventions for work-related stress. *American Journal of Public Health, 91*(2), 270–276.

Van Goozen, S. H. M., Cohen-Kettenis, P. T., Gooren, L. J. G., Frijda, N. H., & Van De Poll, N. E. (1995). Gender differences in behaviour: Activating effects of cross-sex hormones. *Psychoneuroendocrinology, 20*(4), 343–363.

Van Horn, K. R., Arnone, A., Nesbitt, K., Desilets, L., Sears, T., Giffin, M., & Brudi, R. (1997). Physical distance and interpersonal characteristics in college students' romantic relationships. *Personal Relationships, 4*(1), 25–34.

Van Lange, P. A. M., Rusbult, C. E., Semin-Goossens, A., Gorts, C. A., & Stalpers, M. (1999). Being better than others but otherwise perfectly normal: Perceptions of uniqueness and similarity in close relationships. *Personal Relationships, 6*(3), 269–289.

van Osch, Y., Breugelmans, S. M., Zeelenberg, M., & Bölük, P. (2013). A different kind of honor culture: Family honor and aggression in Turks. *Group Processes & Intergroup Relations, 16*(3), 334–344.

Van Vugt, M., & Van Lange, P. A. M. (2006). The altruism puzzle: Psychological adaptations for prosocial behavior. In M. Schaller, J. A. Simpson, & D. T. Kenrick (Eds.), *Evolution and social psychology* (pp. 237–261). Madison, CT: Psychosocial Press.

Vaughan, G., & Guerin, B. (1997). A neglected innovator in sports psychology: Norman Triplett and the early history of competitive performance. *International Journal of the History of Sport, 14*(2), 82–99.

Veblen, T. (1918). *The theory of the leisure class: An economic study in the evolution of institutions.* New York, NY: B. W. Huebsch. (Original work published 1899).

Vela, J. C., Lenz, A. S., Sparrow, G. S., & Gonzalez, S. L. (2017). Using a positive psychology and family framework to understand Mexican American adolescents' college-going beliefs. *Hispanic Journal of Behavioral Sciences, 39*(1), 66–81.

Velanova, K., Lustig, C., Jacoby, L. L., & Buckner, R. L. (2007). Evidence for frontally mediated controlled processing differences in older adults. *Cerebral Cortex, 17*(5), 1033–1046.

Venkatesh, S. A. (1997). The social organization of street gang activity in an urban ghetto. *American Journal of Sociology, 103*(1), 82–111.

Venkatesh, S. A. (2008). *Gang leader for a day: A rogue sociologist takes to the streets.* New York, NY: Penguin.

Verona, E., & Sullivan, E. A. (2008). Emotional catharsis and aggression revisited: Heart rate reduction following aggressive responding. *Emotion, 8*(3), 331–340.

Vicary, A., & Zaikman, Y. (2017). The CSI effect: An investigation into the relationship between watching crime shows and forensic knowledge. *North American Journal of Psychology, 19*(1), 51–64.

Vidyasagar, P., & Mishra, H. (1993). Effect of modeling on aggression. *Indian Journal of Clinical Psychology, 20*(1), 50–52.

Vie, L. L., Scheier, L. M., Lester, P. B., & Seligman, M. P. (2016). Initial validation of the U.S. Army global assessment tool. *Military Psychology, 28*(6), 468–487.

Viki, G. T., & Abrams, D. (2002). But she was unfaithful: Benevolent sexism and reactions to rape victims who violate traditional gender role expectations. *Sex Roles, 47*(5), 289–293.

Violence Policy Center. (2015). *Research, investigation, analysis & advocacy for a safer America.* Retrieved from http://www.vpc.org/

Vohra, N., & Singh, M. (2005). Mental traps to avoid while interpreting feedback: Insights from administering feedback to school principals. *Human Resource Quarterly, 16*(1), 139–147.

von Mayrhauser, R. T. (1989). Making intelligence functional: Walter Dill Scott and applied psychological testing in World War I. *Journal of the History of the Behavioral Sciences, 25*(1), 60–72.

von Stülpnagel, R., & Steffens, M. C. (2010). Prejudiced or just smart?: Intelligence as a confounding factor in the IAT effect. *Zeitschrift für Psychologie/Journal of Psychology, 218*(1), 51–53.

Wadsworth, M. E. J. (1976). Delinquency, pulse rates and early emotional deprivation. *British Journal of Criminology, 16*(3), 245–256.

Wagenmakers, E. J., Beek, T., Dijkhoff, L., Gronau, Q. F., Acosta, A., Adams, R. B., Jr., . . . Zwaan, R. A. (2016). Registered replication report: Strack, Martin, & Stepper (1988). *Perspectives on Psychological Science, 11*(6), 917–928.

Wainwright, D. (2015, November 26). Football banning orders fall as figures reveal bad behaviour. *BBC News.* Retrieved from http://www.bbc.com/news/uk-england-34936495

Wajda-Johnston, V. A., Handal, P. J., Brawer, P. A., & Fabricatore, A. N. (2001). Academic dishonesty at the graduate level. *Ethics & Behavior, 11*(3), 287–305.

Walker, L. E. (1979). Behind the closed doors of the middle-class wifebeater's family. *Contemporary Psychology, 24*(5), 404–405.

Walker, L. E. (1980). *The battered woman.* New York, NY: Harper & Row.

Walker, L. E. (1984). Battered women, psychology, and public policy. *American Psychologist, 39*(10), 1178–1182.

Wallach, M. A., & Kogan, N. (1965). The roles of information, discussion, and consensus in group risk-taking. *Journal of Experimental Social Psychology, 1*(1), 1–19.

Waller, W. (1937). The rating and dating complex. *American Sociological Review, 2*(5), 727–734.

Walther, J. B., & Bazarova, N. N. (2007). Misattribution in virtual groups: The effects of member distribution on self-serving bias and partner blame. *Human Communication Research, 33*(1), 1–26.

Wang, J., Leu, J., & Shoda, Y. (2011). When the seemingly innocuous "stings": Racial microaggressions and their emotional consequences. *Personality and Social Psychology Bulletin, 37*(12), 166–1678.

Wang, S. S., Moon, S., Kwon, K. H., Evans, C. A., & Stefanone, M. A. (2010). Face off: Implications of visual cues on initiating friendship on Facebook. *Computers in Human Behavior, 26*(2), 226–234.

Wang, Q. (2006). Relations of maternal style and child self-concept to autobiographical memories in Chinese, Chinese immigrant, and European American 3-year-olds. *Child Development, 77*(6), 1794–1809.

Wang, Q., Koh, J. K., Song, Q., & Hou, Y. (2015). Knowledge of memory functions in European and Asian American adults and children: The relation to autobiographical memory. *Memory, 23*(1), 25–38.

Wann, D. L. (2006). Understanding the positive social psychological benefits of sport team identification: The team identification-social psychological health model. *Group Dynamics: Theory Research, and Practice, 10*(4), 272–296.

Warner, J. L. (Producer), & Cukor, G. (Director). (1964). *My fair lady* [Motion picture]. United States: Warner Bros.

Wasserman, L. H. (2007). The correlation between brain development, language acquisition, and cognition. *Early Childhood Education Journal, 34*(6), 415–418.

Waters, M. (Producer), & Michaels, L. (Director). (2004). *Mean girls* [Motion picture]. United States: Paramount Pictures.

Wayne, K., O'Dwyer, A., Barry, D., Dillard, L., Polo-Neil, H., & Warriner, M. (2011). The burden of combat: Cognitive dissonance in Iraq war veterans. In D. C. Kelly, S. Howe-Barksdale, & D. Gitelson (Eds.), *Treating young veterans: Promoting resilience through practice and advocacy* (pp. 33–79). New York, NY: Springer.

Weber, C., Dunaway, J., & Johnson, T. (2012). It's all in the name: Source cue ambiguity and the persuasive appeal of campaign ads. *Political Behavior, 34*(3), 561–584.

Webster, A. (2016, June 2). Review: "The witness," a brother's quest to put Kitty Genovese case to rest [Review of the film *The witness,* by J. Solomon]. *New York Times.* Retrieved from https://www.nytimes.com/2016/06/03/movies/the-witness-review-kitty-genovese.html?mcubz=1&_r=0

Wegener, D. T., & Petty, R. E. (1998). The naive scientist revisited: Naive theories and social judgment. *Social Cognition, 16*(1), 1–7.

Wei, M., Russell, D. W., Mallinckrodt, B., & Vogel, D. L. (2007). The experiences in close relationship scale (ECR)–short form: Reliability, validity, and factor structure. *Journal of Personality Assessment, 88*(2), 187–204.

Weinstein, N. D. (1980). Unrealistic optimism about future life events. *Journal of Personality and Social Psychology, 39*(5), 806–820.

Weldon, M. S., Blair, C., & Huebsch, P. D. (2000). Group remembering: Does social loafing underlie collaborative inhibition? *Journal of Experimental Psychology: Learning, Memory, and Cognition, 26*(6), 1568–1577.

Wells, N. M., Evans, G. W., & Cheek, K. A. (2016). Environmental psychology. In H. Franklin (Ed.), *Environmental health: From global to local* (pp. 203–230). San Francisco, CA: John Wiley.

West, C. M. (1998). Leaving a second closet: Outing partner violence in same-sex couples. In J. L. Jasinski & L. M. Williams (Eds.), *Partner violence: A comprehensive review of 20 years of research* (pp. 163–183). Thousand Oaks, CA: Sage.

West, L. J. (1993). A psychiatric overview of cult-related phenomenon. *Journal of the American Academy of Psychoanalysis, 21*(1), 1–19.

Wheeler, S. C., & Petty, R. E. (2001). The effects of stereotype activation on behavior: A review of possible mechanisms. *Psychological Bulletin, 127*(6), 797–826.

Whiteley, P., Sy, T., & Johnson, S. K. (2012). Leaders' conceptions of followers: Implications for naturally occurring Pygmalion effects. *The Leadership Quarterly, 23*(5), 822–834.

Whitley, B. E., & Kite, M. E. (2010). *The psychology of prejudice and discrimination.* Belmont, CA: Wadsworth Cengage Learning.

Whitman, M. (1993). Removing a badge of slavery: The record of *Brown v Board of Education. Choice Reviews Online, 31*(1), 20.

Wicker, A. W. (1969). Attitudes versus actions: The relationship of verbal and overt behavioral responses to attitude objects. *Journal of Social Issues, 25*(4), 41–78.

Wieman, C., & Welsh, A. (2016). The connection between teaching methods and attribution errors. *Educational Psychology Review, 28*(3), 645–648.

Wignall, A. E., Heiling, A. M., Cheng, K., & Herberstein, M. E. (2006). Flower symmetry preferences in honeybees and their crab spider predators. *Ethology, 112*(5), 510–518.

Wilkinson, G. S. (1984). Reciprocal food sharing in the vampire bat. *Nature, 308*(5955), 181–184.

Wilkinson, G. S. (1990). Food sharing in vampire bats. *Scientific American, 262*(2), 76–82.

Wilkinson, N. (2008). *An introduction to behavioral economics.* Basingstoke, UK: Palgrave Macmillan.

Williams, K. D. (2002). *Ostracism: The power of silence.* New York, NY: Guilford.

Williams, L. M., Gatt, J. M., Schofield, P. R., Olivieri, G., Peduto, A., & Gordon, E. (2009). 'Negativity bias' in risk for depression and anxiety: Brain-body fear circuitry correlates, 5-HTT-LPR and early life stress. *Neuroimage, 47*(3), 804–814.

Willoughby, T., Adachi, P. J. C., & Good, M. (2012). A longitudinal study of the association between violent video game play and aggression among adolescents. *Developmental Psychology, 48*(4), 1044–1057.

Wilson, D. K., Friend, R., Teasley, N., Green, S., Reaves, I. L., & Sica, D. A. (2002). Motivation versus social cognitive interventions for promoting fruit and vegetable intake and physical activity in African American adolescents. *Annals of Behavioral Medicine, 24*(4), 310–319.

Wilson, T. D., Houston, C. E., Etling, K. M., & Brekke, N. (1996). A new look at anchoring effects: Basic anchoring and its antecedents. *Journal of Experimental Psychology: General, 125*(4), 387–402.

Wilson, T. D., Lindsey, S., & Schooler, T. Y. (2000). A model of dual attitudes. *Psychological Review, 107*(1), 101–126.

Winslow, D. (1999). Rights of passage and group bonding in the Canadian Airborne. *Armed Forces and Society, 25*(3), 429–457.

Wise, R. (Producer & Director). (1965). *The sound of music* [Motion picture]. United States: 20th Century Fox.

Wolf, D., & Stern, J. (Producers). (1990–2010). *Law and order* [Television series]. United States: Wolf Films.

Woloch, N. (1996). *Muller v. Oregon: A brief history with documents (Bedford series in history and culture).* Boston, MA: Bedford Books of St. Martin's Press.

Woodzicka, J. A., & LaFrance, M. (2005). The effects of subtle sexual harassment on women's performance in a job interview. *Sex Roles, 53*(1–2), 67–77.

Worringham, C. J., & Messick, D. M. (1983). Social facilitation of running: An unobtrusive study. *The Journal of Social Psychology, 121*(1), 23–29.

Wrightsman, L. S., & Kassin, S. (1993). *Confessions in the courtroom.* Thousand Oaks, CA: Sage.

Wrightsman, L. S., Nietzel, M. T., & Fortune, W. H. (1994). *Psychology and the legal system* (3rd ed.). Belmont, CA: Thomson Brooks/Cole.

Yamada, S., Cappadocia, M. C., & Pepler, D. (2014). Workplace bullying in Canadian graduate psychology programs: Student perspectives of student-superior relationships. *Training and Education in Professional Psychology, 8*(1), 58–67.

Yamashita, T., Keene, J. R., Lu, C. J., & Carr, D. C. (2017). Underlying motivations of volunteering across life stages. *Journal of Applied Gerontology: The Official Journal of the Southern Gerontological Society.* Advance online publication.

Yates, A., & Terr, L. C. (1988). Anatomically correct dolls: Should they be used as the basis for expert testimony? *Journal of the American Academy of Child & Adolescent Psychiatry, 27*(2), 254–257.

Yi, J. P., Vitaliano, P. P., Smith, R. E., Yi, J. C., & Weinger, K. (2008). The role of resilience on psychological adjustment and physical health in patients with diabetes. *British Journal of Health Psychology, 13*(2), 311–325.

Ying, X., Li, H., Jiang, S., Peng, F., & Lin, Z. (2014). Group laziness: The effect of social loafing on group performance. *Social Behavior and Personality: An International Journal, 42*(3), 465–471.

Yoon, C. (2011). Theory of planned behavior and ethics theory in digital piracy: An integrated model. *Journal of Business Ethics, 100*(3), 405–417.

Yoshida, E., Peach, J. M., Zanna, M. P., & Spencer, S. J. (2012). Not all automatic associations are created equal: How implicit normative evaluations are distinct from implicit attitudes and uniquely predict meaningful behavior. *Journal of Experimental Social Psychology, 48*(3), 694–706.

Yu, R. F., & Wu, X. (2015). Working alone or in the presence of others: Exploring social facilitation in baggage X-ray security screening tasks. *Ergonomics, 58*(6), 857–865.

Yukl, G., & Tracey, J. B. (1992). Consequences of influence tactics used with subordinates, peers, and the boss. *Journal of Applied Psychology, 77*(4), 525–535.

Yunus, M. (2007). *Banker to the poor: Micro-lending and the battle against world poverty.* New York, NY: PublicAffairs.

Zadro, L., Williams, K. D., & Richardson, R. (2004). How long can you go? Ostracism by a computer lowers belonging, control, self-esteem, and meaningful existence. *Journal of Experimental Social Psychology, 40*(4), 560–567.

Zajonc, R. B. (1965). Social facilitation. *Science, 149*(3681), 269–274.

Zajonc, R. B., Heingartner, A., & Herman, E. M. (1969). Social enhancement and impairment of performance in the cockroach. *Journal of Personality and Social Psychology, 13*(2), 83–92.

Zajonc, R. B., & Sales, S. M. (1966). Social facilitation of dominant and subordinate responses. *Journal of Experimental Social Psychology, 2*(2), 160–168.

Zawadzki, B. (1948). Limitations of the scapegoat theory of prejudice. *The Journal of Abnormal and Social Psychology, 43*(2), 127–141.

Zillmann, D. (1994). Cognition-excitation interdependencies in the escalation of anger and angry aggression. In M. Potegal & J. F. Knutson (Eds.), *The dynamics of aggression: Biological and social processes in dyads and groups* (pp. 45–71). Hillsdale, NJ: Lawrence Erlbaum.

Zimbardo, P. G. (1960). Involvement and communication discrepancy as determinants of opinion conformity. *Journal of Abnormal and Social Psychology, 60*(1), 86–94.

Zimbardo, P. G. (1970). The human choice: Individuation, reason and order versus deindividuation, impulse, and chaos. In W. J. Arnold & D. Levine (Eds.), *Nebraska symposium on motivation* (Vol. 18). Lincoln: University of Nebraska Press.

Zimbardo, P. G. (1973). On the ethics of intervention in human psychological research: With special reference to the Stanford prison experiment. *Cognition, 2*(2), 243–256.

Zimbardo, P. G. (2007). *The Lucifer effect: Understanding how good people turn evil.* New York, NY: Random House.

Zimmermann, D. H., & West, C. (1996). Sex roles, interruptions and silences in conversation. *Amsterdam Studies in the Theory and History of Linguistic Science Series, 4,* 211–236.

Zinsser, W. (1991). *On writing well.* New York, NY: HarperCollins.

Zuiker, A. E., Petersen, W., Bruckheimer, J., Donahue, A., Fink, K., Shankar, N., & Cannon, D. (Producers). (2000–2015). *CSI: Crime scene investigation* [Television series]. United States: Jerry Bruckheimer Television.

Action research: The application of scientific principles to social problem solving in the real world.

Actor-observer bias: An individual's tendency to think of personality when explaining other people's behavior but external, situational causes when explaining their own behavior.

Actual self: An individual's current self-concept, including strengths and weaknesses.

Adaptive categorization: The idea that the instinct to group and label other people and things in the environment arose because it was a benefit to survival.

Affect blend: When two or more contradictory emotions are shown on different parts of an individual's face, making it difficult to accurately understand his or her expression.

Affective forecasting: Occurs when an individual tries to predict how he or she will feel in the future; most individuals aren't able to do so effectively.

Ageism: Negative stereotypes and discrimination experienced by older individuals, which often leads to stress.

Agency: A stereotypically male-oriented pattern of behavior that emphasizes being masterful, assertive, competitive, and dominant.

Aggression: Behavior intended to harm others who do not wish to be harmed.

Agreeableness: A personality trait that includes the willingness to be flexible, to cooperate, and to try to please other people; people high in this trait are also less likely to be social loafers.

Alcohol disinhibition hypothesis: The idea that alcohol interferes with the brain's ability to suppress violent behavior by lowering anxiety and harming an individual's ability to accurately assess a situation.

Algorithm: A systematic, logical method of searching for a solution to a problem or question.

Alternatives: The actual number and quality of other relationship options individuals would have if they ended their current romantic relationship.

Altruism: Helping others purely out of selfless concern for their well-being.

Ambivalent sexism: A combination of hostile and benevolent sexism that occurs when an individual views "good" women from a benevolent perspective but is hostile to women who fail to meet these standards.

American Psychological Association (APA): A large organization of professional psychologists who provide those in the field with information in the form of scholarly publications, citation style guidelines, and ethical standards for research.

Analysis of variance (ANOVA): A statistical test that uses both the mean and the standard deviation to compare the differences between three or more groups.

Anchoring and adjustment heuristic: Occurs when an individual makes a decision using information within a problem that unduly influences his or her final answer. The tendency to adjust little when a plausible estimate, or anchor, has been provided, despite not knowing whether the information is reliable.

Anthropology: The study of culture and human behavior over time.

Anxious/ambivalent attachment: A type of attachment style produced by inconsistent parents, which translates into high levels of jealousy and low self-esteem within adult relationships. Individuals with an anxious/ambivalent attachment style tend to have turbulent relationships.

Applied researchers: Psychologists who translate the findings of basic researchers into social action and apply psychological ideas to the real world.

Archival data: Stored information that was originally created for some other purpose not related to research that can later be used by psychologists, such as census data.

Arranged marriage: A marriage that was decided on by the couple members' families for pragmatic reasons, such as a good match in terms of socioeconomic status.

Assortative mating: The process by which organisms that are similar tend to mate with each other, meaning an individual is more likely to mate with someone who shares his or her features and interests (see *similarity-attraction hypothesis*).

Attachment theory: A framework for understanding relationships that focuses on how an individual's familial environment during the formative years affects his or her ability to begin and maintain normal, adult relationships.

Attitude inoculation: The process of building up resistance to attempts at persuasion.

Attitude object: The object, person, place, or idea an individual explicitly or implicitly evaluates and directs his or her attitude toward.

Attitudes: An inner tendency to judge or evaluate something or someone either positively or negatively.

Attribution theory: The idea that individuals attempt to understand the behavior of those around them by forming commonsense explanations for the cause of others' behavior.

Attributional ambiguity: Confusion individuals have concerning the cause of the way others treat them, experienced most often by members of stigmatized groups.

Attributions: How individuals explain the causes of others' actions and events.

Auction fever: The tendency for individuals to overbid the value of an item in a socially competitive environment.

Authentic confession: A false confession that is given by accused individuals who honestly believe they committed the crime they have confessed to, even though they didn't. An authentic confession may be coerced, such as if the confessor gradually comes to believe she or he is guilty due to the use of certain interrogation techniques, or voluntary, such as if the confessor is delusional or mentally ill.

Authoritarian personality: A personality characterized by three major behavioral tendencies: submission to authority, discipline toward those who defy authority, and the tendency to conform to conventional beliefs.

Auto-kinetic effect: An optical illusion that occurs when an individual perceives a stationary object as moving. Degree of perceived movement can be influenced through conformity.

Availability heuristic: The tendency to overestimate the frequency or importance of information based on how easily it comes to mind. Occurs when an individual makes a decision using the most easily available information.

Average face: A computer-generated composite face created by combining several individual faces, so that it does not contain any unusual or strange features. Averages faces are often perceived as more attractive than individual faces.

Avoidant/fearful attachment: A type of attachment style produced by consistently unsupportive parents, which translates into a general lack of trust and isolating behaviors within adult relationships. Individuals with an avoidant/fearful attachment style tend to isolate themselves from consistent relationships.

Basic researchers: Psychologists who increase our understanding of psychology by creating and improving the theories that predict social behavior.

Basking in reflected glory: A method of self-enhancement that involves affiliating with an ingroup when that group has been successful.

Beauty and the Beast fantasy: A romantic myth in which women are told that patient, self-sacrificing love can turn a "beast" who is troubled and violent into a loving and sensitive partner (see *romantic myths*).

Behavioral economic model (BEM): A model for understanding economic behavior that describes how psychology influences irrational economic decision making (see *irrational economic thinking*).

Behavioral economics: The study of how economic decisions are influenced by psychological factors that indicate what individuals value and how much they value it.

Behavioral game theory: A predictor of interdependent decision-making behavior based on the behavioral economic model, which states that individuals will make decisions based on a number of psychological variables, such as the pain of losing and the desire to conform to social norms, that may make their behavior seem irrational (see *behavioral economic model* and *irrational economic thinking*).

Behavioral interview: A type of interview where the interviewer observes participants' nonverbal behaviors, such as time checking, rate of speaking, interrupting, and general restlessness.

Benevolent prejudice: The perception that members of certain groups have positive qualities that should be praised and valued; however, this positive evaluation typically includes condescending attitudes that result in unfair standards and maintain oppression of the outgroup.

Between-participants design: An experimental research design where the levels or conditions of the independent variable are different for each group of participants; patterns are found by comparing the responses between groups.

Big 5 Model: A model of personality that posits that five fundamental personality traits differentiate between people and predict behaviors: openness to experience, conscientiousness, extraversion, agreeableness, and neuroticism.

Bilateral symmetry: When the two halves of an object, face, or body perfectly match. Faces with bilateral symmetry are often deemed more attractive than those without bilateral symmetry.

Biopsychosocial model: The idea that human health is the combined product of biological, psychological, and social forces.

BIRGing: See *basking in reflected glory*.

Bogus feedback: False information given to participants in an experiment that is designed to show the effect an individual's expectations can have on outcomes.

Bogus pipeline: A fake lie detector machine used to circumvent social desirability bias.

Bounded rationality: The idea that there is a natural cognitive limit on people's ability to make rational economic decisions.

Brain imaging study: The use of neurological measurement machines to measure the structure or function of the brain to understand neural activity. Examples include functional magnetic resonance imaging (fMRI), computed tomography (CT), positron emission tomography (PET), and electroencephalography (EEG).

Brainstorming: A group approach to problem solving that emphasizes nonevaluative creative thinking where members generate lots of ideas, encourage wild ideas, don't judge any idea, and actively modify or expand other people's ideas.

Buffering hypothesis: The idea that social support provides critical resources needed to overcome environmental stressors.

Bystander effect: A phenomenon in which the likelihood of being helped in an emergency is negatively correlated with the number of people who witness that emergency.

Case study: A type of research where scientists conduct an in-depth study on a single example of an event or a single person to test a hypothesis.

Catharsis hypothesis: The idea that purposefully engaging in aggressive behavior releases built-up aggression, reducing aggressive thoughts and behaviors overall.

Causal variable: The variable in an experiment that causes change in a second variable (see *independent variable*).

Central path: A type of persuasion in which appeals are direct, elaborate, and systematic; requires close attention and careful evaluation of alternatives by the individual being persuaded.

Central trait: A major characteristic of an individual's personality that indicates the presence of several associated traits, together creating a unified impression about the entire person.

Cherry-picking data: Occurs when people select only the data that support what they want to believe and ignore contradicting data.

Cinderella fantasy: A romantic myth in which a man who is a relative stranger can enter a woman's life and transform it by removing fears and saving her from problems (see *romantic myths*).

Classical conditioning: A process that occurs when individuals learn to associate one thing in their environment with another due to personal experience.

Clinical or counseling psychology: A subfield of psychology that helps people who have maladaptive or problematic thoughts and behaviors.

Coerced confession: A confession that is given as a result of using force, such as torture or prolonged, intense interrogation, on an accused individual. Coerced confessions are not always reliable.

Cognitive dissonance: A state of psychological discomfort that occurs when an individual tries to maintain conflicting beliefs and behaviors.

Cognitive load: The amount of information that an individual's thinking systems can handle at one time.

Cognitive load shifting: When an individual's two thinking systems interact by smoothly shifting back and forth between intuition and logic.

Cognitive miser: The tendency for humans to take mental shortcuts to minimize cognitive load.

Cognitive neoassociation analysis: A theory that predicts aggression is based on both negative emotional reactions and cognitive, logical interpretations of our environment.

Collaborative law: An approach used in divorce proceedings that requires that lawyers and clients work exclusively toward settlement, signaling their willingness to give up potential profits for shared benefits such as a faster settlement, relative peace, and practical cooperation.

Collective self-esteem: Individuals' evaluation of the worth of the social groups of which they are a member.

Commitment: An individual's decision to stay in a romantic relationship for the long term.

Communal orientation: An approach to relationships that occurs when the couple members aren't concerned with perfect balance or fairness; they don't "keep track" of good and bad experiences and are willing to give without the condition of receiving, which often leads to more forgiveness.

Communication-persuasion matrix: A model for understanding persuasion that proposes that there are six steps in the persuasion process—attention, comprehension, learning, acceptance, retention, and conclusion—which build on each other due to exposure to the four elements of persuasion—the source, the message, the recipient, and the context—resulting in attitude change.

Communion: A stereotypically female-orientated pattern of behavior that emphasizes being friendly, unselfish, other oriented, and emotionally expressive.

Comparative social psychology: Species-level comparisons of social behavior usually used to determine the uniqueness of human behavior.

Comparison group: A group of participants in an experiment who receive either no treatment or an alternative treatment (see *control group*).

Comparison level: Individuals' abstract idea concerning what an "average" relationship's ratio of rewards to costs might be based on relationships the individuals have previously seen, including their own past relationships, the relationships of their parents and their friends, or relationships seen in the media.

Comparison level for alternatives: The perceived next-best relationship people could have if they ended their current relationship.

Compliance: A type of explicit social influence where an individual behaves in response to a direct or indirect request.

Composite face: See *average face*.

Compulsive hoarding syndrome: A type of mental disorder that occurs when an individual has a distressing inner demand to save objects in order to reduce anxiety.

Confederate: An individual who assists a researcher by pretending to be a participant in an experiment.

Confirmation bias: Occurs when individuals only search for evidence that confirms their beliefs while ignoring evidence that contradicts their beliefs.

Conformity: A type of implicit social influence where individuals voluntarily change their behavior to imitate the behavior of others.

Confounding variables: Co-occurring influences that make it impossible to logically determine causality. Confounding variables, such as bad weather or the inability to concentrate on a survey due to illness, provide alternate explanations for the outcome of an experiment that make it impossible to know whether the results are due to the independent variable (see *internal validity*).

Conscientiousness: A personality trait that includes striving for achievement, attention to detail, and a sense of responsibility; people high in this trait are also less likely to be social loafers.

Consensus: The dimension of Kelly's covariation model of attribution that refers to whether other people tend to act the same way toward the target person in the situation.

Consistency: The dimension of Kelly's covariation model of attribution that refers to whether the same actor and same target always act the same way when together.

Conspicuous consumption: Publicly displaying the use of expensive products in an attempt to impress others.

Construction hypothesis: The idea that memories are constructed as needed at the time an individual is asked to use them, making recollection of specific memories subject to bias, stereotypes, probabilities, and wishes.

Constructs: Theoretical ideas that cannot be directly observed, such as attitudes, personality, attraction, or how we think.

Contact hypothesis: The idea that increasing contact or exposure may reduce prejudice if the groups' members perceive themselves to be of equal status, group members interact on an individual level, authority figures appear to be supportive, and the groups have common goals.

Context variables: Characteristics concerning how a persuasive message is delivered that can make it more or less persuasive, including distraction, forewarning, and repetition.

Contingency theory of leadership: The idea that there is no one best leadership style; different types of people, environments, and situations call for different kinds of leaders.

Control group: A group of participants in a true experiment that serves as a neutral or baseline group that receives no treatment.

Converging evidence: Occurs when different types of studies from independent researchers using different methods reach the same conclusions.

Coordination loss: When a lack of cooperation and communication weakens a group's effectiveness, leading to a loss of productivity.

Correlation: A type of statistical test that determines whether two or more variables are systematically associated with each other by identifying linear patterns in data.

Correlation coefficient: A number that indicates the relationship or association between two quantitative variables. It ranges from −1.00 to +1.00.

Correlational design: A research design where scientists analyze two or more variables to determine their relationship or association with each other.

Counterfactual thinking: The tendency to imagine alternative facts or events that would have led to a different future; imagining "what might have been."

Covariation model of attribution: The idea that individuals make attributions concerning the cause of an event between two people, the actor and the target, by assessing these three dimensions: whether other people typically act that way toward the target (consensus), whether the actor typically behaves that way (distinctiveness), and whether the actor and target always act this way together (consistency).

Covary: To vary or happen in correlation with another event.

Cover story: A believable but incorrect story a researcher tells participants in an experiment to mask the true nature of the researcher's hypothesis (see *deception*).

Credibility: How believable or trustworthy a source or person is.

Critical thinking: The ability to analyze, apply, and explore ideas in new and open-minded ways.

Cross-sectional study: A type of research design in which qualitative data are gathered via observation to describe a specific feature of a group of people at a specific point in time.

Crowding: The subjective sense that there are too many people in a given space.

CSI effect: The unrealistic expectations of forensic science that are created by watching fictional television.

Culture: A collection of shared beliefs, customs, attitudes, values, social norms, and intellectual pursuits that distinguishes one group of people from another.

Culture of honor: A culture where individuals, especially men, tend to perceive insults as a threat to their reputation for masculine courage, pride, and virtue that must be restored through dominance and aggression.

Following an insult, individuals from a culture of honor are more likely to feel threatened, be emotionally upset, become physiologically primed for aggression, and engage in aggressive or dominant behaviors.

Cultureme: Culture-specific nonverbal communication such as inside jokes, religious symbols, official government seals, and corporate branding that represent cultural communication not understood by those outside of the culture and convey widely shared social impressions.

Current outcomes: An individual's perception of the total combined positive and negative outcomes of a relationship, which can be represented as a ratio of rewards to costs.

Cycle of violence: A theory for understanding relationship violence that states that relationship violence occurs in three cyclic phases: (1) tension building, in which an abuser becomes increasingly upset; (2) explosion, in which abuse occurs; and (3) contrition, in which the abuser apologizes and makes promises to stop his or her behavior.

Debriefing: Additional details given to participants after participation in an experiment, including information about the hypotheses, an opportunity to ask questions, an opportunity to see the results, and an explanation of any deception.

Deception: Hiding the true nature of an experiment from a participant to prevent a change in how the participant would respond.

Decisional forgiveness: A change in an individual's behavioral intentions toward a transgressor, such as deciding to communicate with him or her more.

Default decision: The decision that is made if an individual chooses to do nothing.

Defensive attribution: Attributions made by individuals to avoid feeling fear about the potential for future negative events.

Dehumanize: When an individual cognitively perceives another individual as lacking positive human qualities but as retaining negative, animalistic qualities.

Deindividuation: A psychological process that occurs when self-awareness is replaced by a social role or group identity, resulting in the loss of individuality.

Density: An objective numerical calculation of how many people occupy a particular space, expressed as number of people per quantifiable amount of space.

Dependent variable: The measured outcome of an experiment that is affected by the independent variable.

Derogation of alternatives: The tendency for individuals who are highly committed to a current partner to downgrade possible alternatives, thus avoiding temptation.

Descriptive norm: What an individual perceives to be the behavior of most people in a specific situation; what most people do, or what is commonly done.

Descriptive study: A type of study in which a researcher gathers data about the participants or phenomenon being studied in an effort to describe their basic characteristics, not to discern statistical patterns.

Diffusion of responsibility: When an individual feels less responsible for an outcome due to the presence of others.

Discrimination: Unfair behaviors toward a particular group or members of a group based on a stereotype or prejudice.

Disease model: The model medicine uses to assess and treat deficits in functioning that attempts to diagnose people's problems and eliminate those problems, bringing the person back to a state of neutrality or "normalcy."

Distinctiveness: The dimension of Kelly's covariation model of attribution that refers to whether the actor in the situation tends to act the same way toward everyone.

Distress: Stress due to negative stressors, such as a death in an individual's family.

Door-in-the-face: A persuasion technique that occurs when compliance is gained by first making a large request, which is usually refused, and then following it with a smaller request, which is usually accepted.

Double-barreled item: A scale item that includes more than one basic idea, making it difficult for individuals to know how to respond if they agree with one of the ideas but not the other.

double-blind experiment: A tool used by psychologists to reduce bias where neither the participants nor the researchers know whether the participants are in the control group or the experimental group. This reduces the likelihood that hopes or expectations can influence outcomes.

Downward counterfactuals: Imagined outcomes that are worse than reality.

Downward social comparison: When individuals compare themselves to someone who is worse than they are, often to help them feel better about themselves.

Dual attitudes: When an individual holds contrasting positive and negative beliefs about the same attitude object.

Dual processing: The ability to process information using both intuition and logic.

Dual relationship: Occurs when a professional takes on incompatible roles with a client (for instance, if a sport psychologist also serves as a coach or if a professor serves as a student's therapist).

Duchenne smile: A genuine, felt smile.

Duping delight: The facial smirk that appears when people think that they have gotten away with a lie.

Effort justification: The tendency for individuals to convince themselves that a group they belong to is wonderful if they have gone through embarrassing, difficult, or expensive efforts to gain membership in the group.

Egoistic altruism: Helping others in exchange for some kind of personal benefit.

Elaboration likelihood model (ELM): A model for understanding how an individual can be persuaded that proposes that there are two paths to persuasion: a direct, explicit, "central" route that requires deliberate, logical thinking and an indirect, implicit, "peripheral" route that relies on emotional appeals (see *heuristic-systematic model*).

Emotional forgiveness: A replacement of negative, unforgiving emotions about a transgressor with positive, other-oriented emotions.

Empathy-altruism hypothesis: The idea that feelings of empathy and compassion create a purely altruistic motivation to help.

Endowment effect: See *mere ownership effect*.

Entitlement: A short-term impression management tactic where a person takes credit for positive events he or she was not a part of.

Environmental psychology: The psychological study of the interplay between individuals and their surroundings, including natural environments, structural and architectural design, and social settings.

Epidemiology: The statistical analysis of the patterns of a disease that are used to understand the disease's incidence and spread.

Escalation of aggression effect: The tendency for aggression between individuals to spiral into increasingly more aggressive exchanges from which the antagonists are seemingly unable to free themselves.

Escalation trap: When individuals increase their commitment to a failing situation to justify previous investments of time, effort, or resources.

Eustress: Stress due to positive events, such as a wedding or a promotion at work.

Evaluation apprehension hypothesis: The idea that individuals' anxiety about being judged by others is what causes physiological arousal and consequential changes in behavior, accounting for the tendency to improve on simple tasks in the presence of others, but flounder on difficult or new tasks.

Evaluative belief: See *attitudes*.

Exchange orientation: An approach to relationships that occurs when the couple members prefer direct reciprocity; they tend to "keep track" of good and bad experiences and act similarly in return, which often leads to less forgiveness.

Excitation transfer effect: The tendency for individuals to transfer their excitement over a situation to excitement about another person (see *misattribution of arousal*).

Experiment: A research design where scientists randomly assign participants to groups and systematically compare changes in behavior. Experiments allow scientists to control confounding variables and establish cause-effect relationships.

Experimenter bias: When an experimenter unconsciously affects the outcome of a study, such as when the experimenter subtly changes how he or she treats people in the different experimental groups.

Explicit attitudes: Attitudes that are the product of controlled, conscious beliefs about an attitude object.

Explicit expectations: Clearly and formally stated expectations for social behavior.

External attributions: Explanations for an individual's behavior that are based on factors that are outside of the person's control, such as getting sick, the weather, or bad luck.

External locus of control: The general belief that one's future is up to fate, chance, powerful other people, or some higher power, rather than within that person's own control.

External validity: The extent to which results of any single study could apply to other people or settings (see *generalizability*).

Extrinsic motivation: When behaviors are performed because some kind of external reward, such as being paid or praised, is expected.

Extrinsic religiosity: When an individual is religious because of social or practical rewards.

Face validity: When a scale or test obviously appears to measure what it is intended to measure.

Facial feedback hypothesis: The idea that individuals infer their own emotions based on the facial expression they are making.

Facial leakage: Occurs whenever concealed emotions are betrayed by automatic muscle responses.

Factorial design: A type of experiment where each participant is exposed to a combination of two or more independent variables.

False confession: A confession given for a crime the accused individual did not commit.

False dichotomy: A situation presented as two opposing and mutually exclusive options when both options may work together, such as the role of nature and nurture in determining human behavior.

False negative: Occurs when an individual or test says an event or condition is not present when it is.

False positive: Occurs when an individual or test says an event or condition is present when it is not.

False uniqueness bias: The belief that we are more unique than others when it comes to socially desirable traits.

False-consensus effect: The false assumption that other people share our values, perceptions, and beliefs.

Falsification: Testing whether a hypothesis can be disproved. A skeptical approach taken by psychologists used to determine the accuracy of an idea based upon eliminating all other possibilities.

Field experiment: An experiment that occurs in a natural environment instead of in a lab setting (see *naturalistic observation*).

Field of eligibles: The potential dates and mates available for an individual not in a committed romantic relationship, based on that individual's criteria for a romantic partner.

Foot-in-the-door: A persuasion technique that occurs when agreeing to a small, initial request makes an individual more likely to later agree to a much larger request.

Forensic psychology: The application of psychological theory to legal processes, such as suspect interrogations, criminal evidence evaluation, personal evaluation for jury duty or competency, family law, workplace assessment, and policy evaluation.

Forgiveness: An internal process that occurs when individuals consciously choose to release negative thoughts they have toward another individual for past wrong or harm, accepting—though not forgetting—what happened.

Formative assessments: Assessments designed to give meaningful feedback to help an individual learn how to improve.

Framing: The process of changing the way information is presented to make it more persuasive, especially concerning individuals' tendency to be persuaded more by positively worded messages than negatively worded messages.

Free riders: People who gain more benefits from the group than they contribute to the group; social loafers or "slackers."

Friends with benefits: A type of relationship where an individual has casual sex repeatedly with the same person over time, remaining friends with that person instead of starting an official romantic relationship.

Friendship contacts: Individual, positive, personal interactions that reduce prejudice.

Frustration-aggression theory: The idea that individuals' frustration builds a physical and psychological tension that they feel must be let out, frequently in the form of aggression toward "weaker" targets.

Functional distance: The tendency for people who are in close proximity due to the geographic and architectural design of an environment to be more likely to develop a cohesive group, such as a friendship or a romantic relationship.

Fundamental attribution error: The tendency to overestimate the influence of personality and underestimate the power of the situation when making attributions about other people's behaviors.

Fundamentalism: A form of religiosity in which people believe their chosen faith is the only true faith, that religious texts should be taken literally, and that forces of evil are active and present all around them.

Fungibility: The degree of interchangeability one item has with another item. For instance, money is fungible because it is easily interchanged for many items and services.

Game theory: A research approach that uses interdependent decision making to test people's values of cooperation versus competition.

Game-designed social dilemma: A situation that tempts an individual to choose personal gain by behaving in a way that would be harmful if everyone else behaved the same way (see *game theory* and *prisoner's dilemma*).

Gender socialization: The expected patterns of behavior deemed appropriate for men and women by rewarding each sex for doing what is considered socially acceptable.

General adaptation syndrome: A three-stage theory concerning how organisms respond to stress, which proposes that persistent stress can deplete a body's resources, making an individual vulnerable to disease.

Generalizability: How much the results of a single study can apply to the general population (see *external validity*).

Generational influence: A cultural belief or norm that transcends the replacement of people; when individuals continue to conform even when the originator of the behavior is no longer present.

Genetic determinism: The idea that genetic influence alone determines behavioral outcomes.

Good subject bias: A type of social desirability bias that occurs when participants respond in the way they think the researcher wants them to respond to support the hypothesis.

Group: When two or more individuals interact with one another or are joined together by a common fate.

Group cohesiveness: The degree to which members of a group feel connected to one another.

Group dynamics: The social roles, hierarchies, communication styles, and culture that naturally form when groups interact.

Group norms: See *social norms*.

Group polarization: When a group makes more extreme decisions than the average of individual decisions, toward either a more or less risky position.

Groupthink: The tendency for people in groups to minimize conflict by thinking alike and publicly agreeing with each other, especially in groups with high group cohesiveness, strong and directive leadership, and a stressful situation to resolve.

Halo effect: When an entire social perception of a person is constructed around a single trait.

Hamilton's inequality: A formula that predicts when people benefit from prosocial behavior that considers how closely related someone is to the helper, as well as costs and benefits to the helper.

Hardy personality: A personality type where individuals cope effectively with stress because their thinking style keeps their physiology calm.

Hawthorne effect: Occurs when individuals in a workplace setting temporarily change their behavior because they are aware of being observed (see *social desirability effect*).

Hazing: Whenever members of a group establish arbitrary rituals for new members that may cause physical or emotional harm, which can be a type of escalation trap for aspiring members (see *effort justification*).

Hedonic forecasting: See *affective forecasting*.

Hedonic treadmill: A metaphor that describes how an individual's happiness, despite a changing reference point, somehow remains approximately the same.

Herd mentality: The tendency to blindly follow the direction your group is moving toward; when group norms encourage individuals to conform to those around them, especially when it comes to their beliefs.

Heuristic: A mental shortcut that makes it easier for an individual to solve difficult problems by facilitating the mental accessibility of certain ideas. Examples include the anchoring and adjustment heuristic, the availability heuristic, and the representativeness heuristic.

Heuristic-systematic model (HSM): A model for understanding how an individual can be persuaded, which proposes that there are two paths to persuasion: a direct, systematic path and an indirect, heuristic path (see *elaboration likelihood model*).

High-impact internship: An ideal internship where the intern devotes considerable time and effort to the learning experience, has frequent interactions with sponsors and supervisors, is exposed to diverse ideas and novel challenges, is provided with quality feedback on his or her performance, and has the opportunity for self-reflection and personal growth.

Hindsight bias: Occurs when an individual believes they could have predicted the outcome of a past event, but only after they already know what happened; the false belief that they "knew it all along."

Hookup: One-time sexual interactions that are typically focused on sexual pleasure rather than fostering personal, psychological bonds.

Hostile aggression: An impulsive, emotion-based reaction to perceived threats.

Hostile sexism: When an individual exhibits overtly aggressive behavior toward or dispenses harsh judgment toward women who do not fit prescribed gender stereotypes.

Human factors: An academic discipline within psychology devoted to designing products or systems that best cater to human needs (see *user experience*).

Hypothesis: A specific statement made by a researcher before conducting a study about the expected outcome of the study based on prior observation. Hypotheses are falsifiable statements that researchers believe to be true (see *falsification*).

Ideal self: The person an individual wants to be in the future, including maximized strengths and minimized weaknesses.

Implicit Association Test (IAT): An indirect way to measure the strength of particular beliefs or constructs by analyzing reaction times. Faster reaction times suggest a strong mental connection.

Implicit attitudes: Attitudes based on automatic, unconscious beliefs about an attitude object.

Implicit expectations: Unspoken rules enforced by group norms that influence an individual's behavior.

Implicit methodologies: Indirect ways of measuring topics that may be skewed by social desirability bias, which produce more reliable, valid responses than direct, explicit, self-report approaches to collecting data (see *Implicit Association Test*).

Impression management: See *self-presentation theory*.

Inclusion of the other in the self (IOS) scale: A scale used to measure psychological inclusion of others in the self-concept where people circle one of many pairs of circles with increasing overlap between "self" and "other" to indicate how much their self-concept includes a specified other person.

Inclusive fitness: The probability that our genetic heritage will be preserved in the offspring of relatives.

Independent self-construal: When an individual's ideal self is largely based on internal, personal qualities.

Independent variable: A variable that is manipulated at the beginning of an experiment to determine its effect on the dependent variable.

Industrial/organizational psychology: The academic study of people in the workplace, where researchers apply psychological theory to meet the needs of organizations and employees.

Informational belief: A fact-based belief that includes no positive or negative judgment.

Informational social influence: When individuals voluntarily conform to group standards because they are uncertain about the correct answer or behavior.

Informed consent: Participants' right to be told what they will be asked to do and whether there are any potential dangers or risks involved before a study begins.

Ingroup: Any group in which an individual is a member; these groups can be based on chosen or nonchosen characteristics such as race, nationality, sex, sexual orientation, club membership, favorite sports team, or where an individual went to college.

Ingroup heterogeneity: The tendency for individuals to see wide diversity within their ingroups.

Initiation effect: See *effort justification*.

Injunctive norm: What an individual perceives to be the socially acceptable behavior in a specific situation; what is socially sanctioned, or what society says people are supposed to do.

Institutional review boards (IRBs): Committees of people who consider the ethical implications of any study before giving the researcher approval to begin formal research.

Instrumental aggression: A thoughtful, reason-based decision to harm others in order to gain resources such as territory, money, self-esteem, or social status.

Instrumental confession: A false confession that is given purposefully by the accused individual, even though he or she doesn't believe the confession to be true. An instrumental confession may be coerced, such as to end an interrogation, or voluntary, such as to protect someone else or to gain notoriety.

Insufficient justification: Occurs when individuals engage in a behavior that does not match their attitudes or self-concept and cannot rationalize the behavior; this discrepancy creates cognitive dissonance.

Interactionist perspective: The idea that personality and situation jointly affect an individual's social behavior.

Interactions: The combination of several influences on an outcome, such as the influence of both personality and environment on behavior.

Interdependence theory: A model for understanding romantic relationships that suggests that relationship stability is predicted by commitment, which is, in turn, predicted by a combination of satisfaction within the relationship and the potential for quality alternative relationships.

Interdependent decision making: Occurs when the outcome of an individual's decision depends on another individual's decision (see *game theory*).

Interdependent self-construal: When an individual's ideal self is largely based on social qualities, especially relationships with others.

Internal attributions: Explanations for an individual's behavior that are based on factors that are within the person's control, such as an individual's personality or conscious choices.

Internal locus of control: The general belief that an individual is in control of his or her own fate.

Internal validity: The level of confidence researchers have that patterns of data are due to what is being tested, as opposed to flaws in how the experiment was designed.

Internship: A supervised work experience that gives individuals, especially students, the opportunity to reflect on a possible career in that line of work.

Interview: A method for obtaining data about an individual or group of individuals by eliciting verbal responses to questions (see *one-shot case study*).

Intimate terrorism: A type of relationship violence that occurs when one couple member controls the other couple member through severe forms of physical violence as well as psychological, emotional, and sexual violence.

Intrinsic motivation: When behaviors are performed without expectation of any external reward because the reward is something internal, such as life satisfaction.

Intrinsic religiosity: When individuals hold sincere belief in their faith's teachings and attempt to apply those principles to everyday behaviors.

Intuition: The ability to know something quickly and automatically; a "gut feeling" that takes little mental effort.

Investment model: A statistical model for understanding romantic relationships that includes all three predictors of commitment: satisfaction, alternatives, and investments.

Investments: The amount of time, energy, and resources put into a relationship that would be lost if the relationship were to end.

Irrational economic thinking: The idea that consumers' decisions are often irrational because they are influenced by mental shortcuts, misperceptions, and emotional biases that often ignore the rules of supply and demand.

Jigsaw classroom: A technique used by teachers where students are first divided into "expert groups" that learn a certain set of information and then are mixed such that the second set of teams, the "jigsaw groups," each include one member from the expert groups. Jigsaw requires that the members rely on each other to learn the material.

Job analysis: The process of creating and advertising a description for a particular job that clearly denotes what education and skills are expected, what training may be needed, what personal growth trajectories a new employee can hope for, and what compensation package can be expected.

Just world hypothesis: The idea that individuals have a need to believe that they live in a world where people generally get what they deserve, which can lead to incorrect internal attributions for others' behavior.

Kernel of truth theory: The idea that stereotypes can be at least somewhat based on truth, even though they contain other fictitious elements, may be exaggerated, and/or are out of date.

Kinship selection: The evolutionary urge to favor those with closer genetic relatedness.

Lake Woebegone effect: See *false uniqueness bias*.

Life coach: A career based in positive psychology— although with little formal education or credentials— where individuals work with others as they make career and personal decisions.

Life satisfaction: A sense of contentment and gratification with one's path, self-concept, social connections, and direction in life overall.

Logic: The ability of humans to use reason, think systematically, and carefully consider evidence about possible futures.

Longitudinal study: A study that occurs over time or multiple sessions where researchers repeatedly observe the same set of participants to analyze change.

Loss aversion: The tendency for potential losses to be more psychologically influential than potential gains.

Lowball technique: A persuasion technique where an incentive is offered at the beginning of a deal, such as a low price, but then is later removed due to the terms of the agreement being changed. Despite the change, cognitive and emotional commitment to the item from the original deal often leads to acceptance of the new, less attractive deal.

Machiavellianism: A personality trait that describes people who are manipulative, distrustful of others, and egocentric.

Magical thinking: Beliefs based on assumptions that do not hold up to reality, such as "if only" thinking, counterfactual thinking, and optimistic bias.

Maltreatment effects: When hazing elicits social dependency that promotes allegiance to the group.

Mass psychogenic illness: A form of social contagion where physical symptoms of an illness appear within a cohesive social group, although the illness appears to have no physical cause.

Matched pairs: A type of experimental research design where participants are grouped according to shared characteristics, such as IQ, age, or gender, instead of through random assignment to condition.

Maximizer: An individual who engages a heavier cognitive load by exhaustively examining criteria when making decisions.

Memory structures: The cognitive structures that form the mind and organize and interpret social information, namely, schemas, scripts, and stereotypes.

Mental accessibility: The ease with which an idea comes to mind.

Mental accounting: How individuals mentally manipulate money when making economic decisions.

Mental availability: The information already salient in one's mind.

Mental structures: See *memory structures*.

Mere exposure: The tendency for individuals to prefer familiar objects and individuals, especially as exposure to them increases.

Mere ownership effect: The tendency for individuals to evaluate objects they own—or perceive to own—more favorably just because they own them.

Mere presence hypothesis: The idea that being in the presence of others, even if they aren't watching, will increase an individual's physiological arousal, and this arousal will help performance on easy tasks and hinder performance on difficult tasks.

Message variables: Characteristics of a message that can make it more or less persuasive, including whether the listener personally cares about the topic and how the message is presented.

Message-learning approach: The idea that there are four elements to the persuasion process: the source (who is doing the persuading), the message (the persuasive information), the recipient (who they are persuading), and the context (how they are persuading).

Meta-analysis: A study that summarizes and statistically combines many individual studies on a particular topic.

Microaggressions: Statements or behaviors that subtly insult a marginalized group by expressing an aggressor's prejudice and discrimination, with or without their conscious intent to do so. Microaggressions include microinsults, microassaults, and microinvalidations.

Micro-expression: An involuntary flash of emotional honesty.

Mindfulness: A meditative focus on the present that is often used to lessen stress.

Minimal group paradigm: An experimental method to create groups based on meaningless categories to study intergroup dynamics.

Minimization: Occurs when a victim of relationship violence attempts to perceive abusive behavior as nonabusive by denying it occurred, downplaying the significance or severity of what occurred, or by providing some kind of justification for the behaviors.

Mirror self-recognition test: A scientific paradigm where a mark is placed on an animal's forehead and it is placed in front of a mirror. The animal is assumed to have self-recognition if it touches the mark on its forehead.

Misattribution of arousal: The tendency for individuals to misattribute physiological reactions to environmental stimuli as attraction (see *excitation transfer effect*).

Misinformation effect: Occurs when exposure to false information or leading questions about an event leads to errors in an individual's ability to recall the original event.

Model of dual attitudes: A model for understanding attitudes that proposes that new attitudes override, rather than replace, old attitudes.

Modern-symbolic prejudice: A form of prejudice where individuals think of themselves as valuing equality and respect for all people while they simultaneously oppose social change that would allow equality to occur.

Moral hypocrisy: Occurs when individuals desire to appear moral while avoiding the costs of behaving morally.

Moral integrity: Occurs when individuals are motivated to live up to their own standards of morality and ethics, resulting in an increase in altruistic behavior.

Moral panic: The widespread belief that a particular group of people pose an urgent threat to society, based on accusations of a moral nature.

Mortality salience: When researchers make the idea of death, especially an individual's own unavoidable death, more vivid.

Narcissism: Excessive self-love based on unwarranted belief in one's specialness relative to others.

Narrative therapy: The process of writing down autobiographical events in a therapeutic setting.

Naturalistic observation: A research design where scientists gather data by observing people in the environment within which the behavior naturally occurs (for instance, observing leadership styles in a corporate office).

Nature: Influences on our thoughts and behaviors that come from biology or physiology, such as genetics, hormones, or brain differences.

Negative correlation: A negative correlation occurs when the correlation coefficient is between -0.01 and -1.00. In this case, as one variable increases, the other decreases.

Negative state relief model: The idea that seeing another person in need causes individuals emotional distress, and helping decreases those negative emotions (see *egoistic altruism*).

Negativity bias: The automatic tendency to notice and remember negative information better than positive information.

Neural circuitry of reward: A set of brain neurons that respond to both actual and anticipated rewards.

Nonverbal communication: The many ways individuals communicate through body language, tone of voice, and facial expressions.

Norm of reciprocity: The idea that individuals respond in kind to courtesies and concessions from others.

Normative social influence: When individuals publicly conform to gain social acceptance and avoid rejection.

Nurture: Influences on our thoughts and behaviors that come from our life circumstances, how we were raised, experiences we've had, and our environment in general.

Obedience: A type of explicit social influence where individuals behave in a particular way because someone of higher status ordered them to do so.

Old-fashioned prejudice: Obvious, overt prejudice that is considered inappropriate by most social standards today, such as forcing people of a specified race to drink only from a certain water fountain.

One-group pretest-posttest design: A type of preexperimental research design in which the expected outcome is measured both before and after the treatment to assess change.

One-shot case study: A type of preexperimental research design that explores an event, person, or group in great detail by identifying a particular case of something or trying a technique once, then observing the outcome.

Operant conditioning: A process that occurs when individuals learn to predict the outcomes of given behaviors based on the outcomes they've experienced for those same behaviors in the past.

Operationalize: The process of specifying how a construct will be defined and measured.

Opinion conformity: A short-term impression management tactic where people endorse the opinion of others to increase liking and attraction and gain social influence.

Opportunity cost: The cost of not pursuing alternative opportunities. For example, the opportunity cost of going to college includes the actual expenses incurred as well as the loss of potential income from employment.

Optimal distinctiveness theory: The idea that individuals can simultaneously achieve the advantages of being seen as a unique and important individual and of being in a group by being an identifiable member of a small and elite group.

Optimal margin theory: Psychological theory that proposes a slight to moderate range of healthy distortions of reality improves psychological and physiological well-being.

Optimistic bias: The unrealistic expectation that things will turn out well.

Order effects: Variations in participants' responses due to the order in which materials or conditions are presented to them.

Other-enhancement: A short-term impression management tactic where people compliment another person and seem to admire them to increase liking and attraction and gain social influence.

Ought self: The person that individuals think others expect them to be. This changes depending on the reference group.

Outgroup: Any group in which an individual is not a member.

Outgroup homogeneity: The perception that all members of a particular outgroup are identical to each other.

Overjustification effect: Occurs when individuals are rewarded or compensated for completing a task they previously did due to intrinsic motivators, which then changes the individuals' focus to the external reward, limiting or even eliminating their intrinsic motivation.

Pansexual: Sexual attraction based on individuals' personal characteristics, regardless of their sex, gender, or gender identity.

Parental investment: The amount of time, effort, and physical resources needed for an individual to produce and raise genetic offspring.

Participant observation: A technique used during naturalistic observation where scientists covertly disguise themselves as people belonging in an environment in an effort to observe more authentic social behaviors.

Participant observer: A type of qualitative data collection method where the researcher acts as a participant in a study while observing the actions of the true participants.

Paternity uncertainty: Anxiety experienced by men due to doubt about whether a child is genetically theirs.

Path analysis: A statistical technique that uses relationships among variables to hypothesize causal connections.

Payment decoupling: A type of mental accounting that separates payment from consumption, leading to changes in how an individual spends money. For instance, the instant gratification of obtaining items with a credit card can skew rational spending behavior because payment occurs later.

Peer review process: How the scientific community uses multiple people to decide whether a journal should publish a paper to ensure publications are of high quality.

Perceived control: The amount of control individuals believe they have over themselves and their environment, which, in combination with attitudes and social norms, predicts intended behavior.

Peripheral path: A type of persuasion in which appeals are indirect, implicit, and emotion based; requires little effort by the individual being persuaded, leading to quick and easy conclusions.

PERMA approach: An approach to measuring subjective well-being, which considers an individual's positive emotions, engagement, relationship to others, meaning and purpose, and achievement.

Person perceptions: People's perceptions of one another based on initial impressions of their behavior and assumptions concerning what characteristics correspond with that behavior.

Personal importance: Individuals' tendency to put more effort into processing persuasive messages when they think the issue is important or personally relevant.

Personal space: The individual boundary around an individual's body that gives that person a sense of control over his or her environment.

Physical distance: A moderator of exposure dictated by the physical distance between two places (for example, the number of steps an individual would have to take to get from one apartment to another).

Placebo effect: Occurs when the strength of individuals' belief in a medical or psychological treatment leads them to experience the expected benefits of the treatment, even though it has no independent effect on them.

Planning fallacy: The unjustified confidence that one's own project, unlike similar projects, will proceed as planned.

Pluralistic ignorance: When a majority of individuals in a group get the false impression that others do not share their private perspective, making them less likely to express their opinion.

Political orientation: An attitude held by an individual concerning matters of politics and government often characterized by the possession of liberal or conservative ideas.

Polyamory: When individuals have multiple committed relationships at once.

Polyandry: A type of polyamorous relationship in which one man has multiple female partners.

Polygamy: When the individuals in a polyamorous relationship are legally married.

Polygyny: A type of polyamorous relationship in which one woman has multiple male partners.

Pop psychology: The vague and superficial application of untested, temporarily popular, and sometimes exotic ideas to everyday life.

Positive correlation: A positive correlation occurs when the correlation coefficient is between +0.01 and +1.00. In this case, as one variable increases, the other also increases.

Positive illusions: Beliefs that depart from reality in ways that help us to remain optimistic, especially in relation to the belief we can control our own lives more than we can, the tendency to have an unrealistically optimistic view of the future, and the desire to discover meaning in critical life events.

Positive psychology: The scientific study of how human strengths and virtues influence feelings, thoughts, and behaviors.

Positive stereotype: Overgeneralized or oversimplified beliefs about a group that are in a favorable direction or valence; positive stereotypes still lead to negative outcomes.

Post hoc matched groups design: This technique is used when random assignment to condition is not possible. Researchers select an experimental group based on a single variable, then select a control/comparison group as similar as possible in every way except for that variable.

Posttest-only control group design: A type of true experiment where the dependent variable is measured for two or more groups, including a control group, only after the experimental manipulation.

Posttraumatic growth: Feelings of positive psychological change and resilience as a result of trauma and adversity.

Preexperiment: A research design in which a single group of people is tested to see whether some kind of treatment has an effect, such as a one-shot case study or a one-group pretest-posttest.

Prejudice: Emotion-centered judgments or evaluations about people based on their perceived membership in a particular group.

Presupposition: Wording that assumes a condition in a specific situation is present. When used in a survey or interview, presuppositions can make individuals more likely to suppose that the assumed condition was present.

Pretest-posttest control group design: A type of true experiment where the dependent variable is tested both before and after the experimental manipulation.

Primary prevention: The prevention of relationship violence before the violence begins through education and empowerment.

Priming: Initial activation of a concept within a semantic network that allows related ideas to come more easily to mind.

Principle of noncommon effects: The idea that individuals make attributions by looking for a single factor that seems to account for what occurred based on its degree of difference from the other possible factors.

Principle of parsimony: The tendency for individuals to prefer the simplest answer that explains the most evidence.

Prisoner's dilemma: A research approach within game theory that tests cooperation versus competition values by asking participants to imagine they are prisoners who must choose between confession (which betrays one's partner but results in a shorter sentence for you) or silence (which shows loyalty but risks betrayal by the other person).

Private conformity: Conforming thoughts or behaviors that are kept to oneself and are felt genuinely by the individual (see *public conformity*).

Proactive aggression: See *instrumental aggression*.

Procedural artifact: A finding that results from how a researcher conducted the experiment, rather than introduction of the independent variable.

Process loss: The reduction of effort—and thus productivity—in group settings that comes from a lack of motivation, often due to social loafing.

Promiscuity: The number of casual sexual partners one has.

Propinquity effect: See *proximity effect*.

Prosocial behavior: Any action performed to help others, either on an individual level or a group level.

Prosocial moral reasoning: An individual's ability to analyze moral dilemmas in which two or more people's needs conflict with each other and where formal rules are absent.

Prospect theory: The idea that people make predictable kinds of mistakes when trying to weigh outcomes and probabilities.

Prospective cohort study: A type of research design in which researchers intermittently gather data over a long period of time from several groups of individuals (cohorts) who differ with respect to a certain variable.

Protestant work ethic: A set of personality traits that includes valuing discipline, honoring commitments, and doing a good job in any setting; people high in this trait are also less likely to be social loafers.

Proximity effect: The tendency for individuals to like people who are in close geographic proximity to themselves, due to the mere exposure effect (see *mere exposure*).

PsycINFO database: The most comprehensive database of research books and journal articles across psychological subdisciplines.

Public conformity: Conforming thoughts or behaviors shared with others; these actions may not be genuinely endorsed (see *private conformity*).

Pure altruism: See *altruism*.

***p* value:** A number that indicates the probability or likelihood that a pattern of data would have been found by random chance. Commonly seen as a variation of "$p < .05$," which, in this example, means there is a less than 5% probability the patterns are due to chance.

Qualitative data: Results in subjective forms such as the content of essays or interviews.

Quantitative data: Results in numerical form, such as scores on self-report measures or the percentage of people who act a certain way.

Quasi-experiment: A research design where outcomes are compared across different groups that have not been formed through random assignment but instead occur naturally.

Random assignment to experimental condition: A solution to the problem of confounding variables wherein each person in an experiment has an equal chance of being randomly assigned to either the experimental condition or the control condition. By randomly assigning participants to a condition, confounding variables are assumed to be distributed equally across groups, making the groups essentially identical.

Random assignment to groups: A technique in which every participant in an experiment has equal probability of being assigned to each group. This means that extraneous variables are also likely to be evenly distributed.

Random sampling: A sampling technique used to increase a study's generalizability and external validity wherein a researcher randomly chooses people to participate from a larger population of interest.

Randomized controlled trial: A type of research design in which participants are randomly assigned to one of several experimental conditions or interventions, including a control condition that receives no intervention.

Rational economic thinking: The idea that consumers will act rationally according to the strict rules of supply and demand, leading them to always go for the best deal.

Rationalization trap: Progressively larger self-justifications that lead to harmful, stupid, and immoral outcomes.

Reactive aggression: See *hostile aggression*.

Reactivity: When people change their behavior simply because they're being observed (see *social desirability bias* and *good subject bias*).

Realistic conflict theory: The idea that prejudice results from the justifications we create to determine that our ingroup should receive an unfair amount of limited resources.

Recipient variables: Characteristics of the people receiving a persuasive message that make them more or less likely to be persuaded, such as their attitude strength, intelligence, personality, self-esteem, and need for cognition.

Reciprocal altruism: Altruistic behavior that occurs because individuals expect that their helpfulness now will be returned in the future.

Reconciliation: A social process that leads to a friendly reunion between former opponents. While forgiveness is private, reconciliation is public.

Reference point: A point in an individual's mental accounting system that all other options for a specific situation are compared to in order to estimate value.

Rejection sensitivity: The fear of social rejection and ostracism.

Relationship personality: Behavior patterns that describe an individual's habitual interpersonal dynamic with others.

Reliability: Consistency of measurement, over time or multiple testing occasions. A study is said to be reliable if similar results are found when the study is repeated.

Religion as quest: A form of religiosity in which people view religion from a philosophical and spiritual stance, involving skepticism, doubt, and exploration.

Religiosity: The degree to which one is religious and why.

Replication: The process of conducting the same experiment using the same procedures and the same materials multiple times to strengthen reliability, internal validity, and external validity.

Representativeness heuristic: Occurs when individuals make a decision based on how closely their observations resemble the "typical" case. The tendency to classify observations according to a preexisting, typical case and using that process to come to a conclusion.

Research paradigm: A method of or approach for doing research.

Resilient personality: A personality type where individuals react appropriately to stress because they are able to cope positively with adversity.

Restorative justice method: A method for obtaining justice that intends to help people heal, forgive, and reconcile to achieve a better future by focusing on truth and togetherness.

Retributive justice method: A method for obtaining justice that intends to punish people so that they can suffer equally to the people whom they harmed.

Reverse scoring: A technique used to encourage careful reading of each item on a scale by wording questions negatively as well as positively, which reverses the direction of the scoring.

Right to withdraw: The right participants have to stop being in a study at any time, for any reason, or to skip questions on a survey if they are not comfortable answering them.

Risky shift: The tendency of groups to make riskier or more daring decisions than the average of individuals (see *group polarization*).

Romantic myths: Cultural messages regarding what romance is supposed to look like that support traditional gendered ideas or social roles and can encourage seduction into violent relationships.

Satisfaction: An individual's perception of whether a romantic relationship is better or worse than average.

Satisficing: A practical solution to the problem of information overload that occurs when an individual takes mental shortcuts to make decisions; criteria are not exhaustively examined but are deemed "good enough" under the circumstances.

Scapegoat theory: The idea that prejudice is the result of one group blaming another innocent group for its problems (see *frustration-aggression theory*).

Scatterplot: A graph that demonstrates the relationship between two quantitative variables by displaying plotted participant responses.

Schema: A cognitive and memory structure for organizing the world.

Scientific method: A systematic way of creating knowledge by observing, forming a hypothesis, testing a hypothesis, and interpreting the results. The scientific method helps psychologists conduct experiments and formulate theories in a logical and objective manner.

Scientist-practitioner model: A method for approaching a field of study where individuals are trained to use their understanding of basic science in real-world applications.

Script: A memory structure or type of schema that guides common social behaviors and expectations for particular types of events; scripts provide individuals with an order of events for common situations and expectations for others' behavior.

Secondary prevention: Interventions that occur after relationship violence has begun, including providing victims with the resources and knowledge to prevent the violence from happening again.

Secure attachment: A type of attachment style produced by consistently supportive parents, which translates into healthy, trusting, long-term adult relationships. Individuals with a secure attachment style tend to have relatively high self-esteem and aren't overly jealous or anxious.

Self: Individuals' internal narrative about themselves.

Self-affirmation theory: The idea that individuals try to impress themselves to preserve their sense of worth and integrity; they focus their thoughts and attitudes on what makes them feel good about themselves.

Self-awareness: The understanding that we are a separate entity from other people and objects in our world; a state of being conscious of our own existence.

Self-compassion: An orientation to care for oneself.

Self-concept: The personal summary of who we believe we are, including our assessment of our positive and negative qualities, our relationships to others, and our beliefs and opinions.

Self-discrepancy: When a mismatch exists between an individual's actual, ideal, and ought selves.

Self-efficacy: The degree to which individuals believe that they are capable of completing a specific task or achieving a particular goal.

Self-enhancements: A short-term impression management technique where people imply that their actual accomplishments are more significant than they first appear to be.

Self-esteem: Individuals' subjective, personal evaluation of their self-concept, including judgments made about self-worth.

Self-expansion theory: The idea that all humans have a basic motivation to grow, improve, and enhance our self-concept, specifically through close social relationships.

Self-fulfilling prophecy: When an individual's expectations about someone else change his or her behavior, which then changes the other person's behaviors such that they fulfill the first individual's expectations.

Self-insight: Individuals' ability to self-observe and evaluate their own behavior.

Self-justification: The desire to explain one's actions in a way that preserves or enhances a positive view of the self.

Self-monitor: Individuals' ability to notice and adjust their own behavior in an attempt to fit in.

Self-perception theory: The theory that individuals form their self-concept by observing their own behavior and trying to infer their own motivations, attitudes, values, and core traits.

Self-presentation theory: The tendency to adjust the self and perform in slightly different ways for varying others to gain social influence.

Self-recognition: See *self-awareness*.

Self-report scale: A type of survey item where participants give information about themselves by selecting their own responses (see *survey*).

Self-schema: A way to think about how the self-concept is formed whereby memory structures that summarize and organize our beliefs about self-relevant information create a cognitive framework within which individuals interpret the events of their lives.

Self-serving cognitive biases: Cognitive distortions that enhance people's self-concept by making them perceive that they are a little better than they actually are.

Semantic network: A collection of mental concepts that are connected by common characteristics.

Sense of individual identity: How individuals perceive themselves to uniquely fit into a larger group. Such social comparisons and group role development contribute to individuals' self-concept.

Shadow of the future: Describes how an awareness of possible future events influences individuals' present decisions, especially their desire to cooperate.

Similarity-attraction hypothesis: The idea that people tend to form relationships, romantic and otherwise, with others who have the same attitudes, values, interests, and demographics as themselves (see *assortative mating*).

Single-blind experiment: A tool used by psychologists to reduce bias where the participants do not know whether they are in the control group or the experimental group. This reduces the likelihood that hopes or expectations can influence outcomes.

Situational couple violence: A type of relationship violence that occurs when couple members argue violently, but neither attempts to take general control and incidents are relatively minor, although still unhealthy. Situational couple violence is typically perpetrated by both couple members and includes short-term physical violence but not psychological or emotional abuse.

Social agents: Individuals who send messages about cultural beliefs and expectations that help transmit ideas from one generation to the next; social agents include any source that transmits information, such as parents and the media (see *social learning theory*).

Social cognition: The study of how people combine intuition and logic to process social information.

Social comparison theory: The use of social comparisons to construct the self-concept when no other objective standard is available.

Social contagion: The spontaneous distribution of ideas, attitudes, and behaviors among larger groups of people.

Social desirability bias: The tendency for participants to provide dishonest responses so that others have positive impressions of them.

Social dominance orientation: Individuals with a tendency to exhibit outgroup prejudice due to a desire for social hierarchy and power within a situation.

Social exchange: The evolution of prosocial resource trading that strengthens the group, from sharing food in early societies to exchanging money for goods today. Social exchanges encourage prosocial behaviors in humans by offering reproductive and survival advantages to individuals and groups who use them.

Social exchange theory: See *interdependence theory*.

Social facilitation: When individuals exhibit improved effort and individual performance in the presence of others.

Social identity theory: The idea that individuals have an automatic tendency to categorize each other and to form ingroups and outgroups that validate their perceptions of themselves in flattering and useful ways.

Social influence: How an individual's thoughts, feelings, and behaviors respond to their social world, including tendencies to conform to others, follow social rules, and obey authority figures.

Social leader: A type of leader who focuses on the people involved and invests time in building teamwork, facilitating interactions, and providing support.

Social learning theory: The idea that individuals observe what others do and copy them, especially when those behaviors lead to success or rewards.

Social loafing: When people working in a group reduce their individual level of effort.

Social norms: Rules that indicate how people are expected to behave in particular social situations, which, in combination with attitudes and perceived control, often predict intended behavior.

Social psychology: The scientific study of how people influence each other's thoughts, feelings, and behaviors

Social responsibility norm: The idea that each individual has a duty to improve the world by helping those in need.

Social role theory: The idea that stereotypes form when individuals observe the roles that different kinds of people occupy in the world and then reinforce those roles by assuming the people occupying them are well suited to the roles.

Social roles: A type of implicit social influence regarding how certain people are supposed to look and behave.

Social support: The degree to which an individual is embedded in a network of people who can provide various kinds of assistance, if needed.

Sociology: The study of human society and social behavior at the group level.

Source variables: Characteristics of individuals that make their message more or less persuasive, including their level of credibility, their attractiveness, and their social power.

Specificity principle: Proposes that the link between attitudes and behaviors is strong when the attitude and the behavior are measured at the same level of specificity.

Spiral of silence: When fear of rejection leads people to keep silent about a private opinion, misperceive the louder opinion as a majority opinion, and therefore become even less likely to express their private opinion.

Sport psychology: The scientific study of how athletic and/or physical activity participation and performance are influenced by psychological concepts.

Stages of provocation model: A model for understanding aggression within which an individual's thoughts, feelings, and behaviors collectively contribute to the escalation of aggression in three stages.

Standard deviation: The amount of variability in a distribution. In other words, how widely dispersed the data are.

Standard economic model (SEM): A model for understanding economic behavior that describes how people behave if they always make the most sound, rational decisions. This model is not based on psychological theory (see *rational economic thinking*).

Standard game theory: A predictor of interdependent decision-making behavior based on the standard economic model, which states that individuals will make rational decisions that consider the economic losses one would have to endure if they lost, as well as the potential for new, better deals to be made in the future (see *standard economic model* and *rational economic thinking*).

Statistical significance: The likelihood that the results of an experiment are due to the independent variable, not chance (see *p value*).

Statistics: Mathematical analyses that reveal patterns in data, such as correlations, *t* tests, and analyses of variance.

Stereotype: A type of oversimplified and overgeneralized schema that occurs when an individual assumes that everyone in a certain group has the same traits.

Stereotype content model: The idea that two categories of judgment, warmth and competence, interact to form four different types of prejudice: paternalistic prejudice (high warmth, low competence), admiration prejudice (high warmth, high competence), contemptuous prejudice (low warmth, low competence), and envious prejudice (low warmth, high competence).

Stereotype threat: When an individual feels at risk for confirming a negative stereotype about his or her group; this anxiety can be distracting and can ironically cause the stereotype to come true as a type of self-fulfilling prophecy.

Stockholm syndrome: When hostages develop affection for their captors.

Strange situation: Refers to either the experimental paradigm in which a mother and child are observed in a room as the mother leaves and returns or to the room itself in which this occurs.

Strategic forgiveness: A degree of forgiveness calculated to signal to a competitor an individual's willingness to cooperate.

Stress: When individuals' assessment of the current environment exceeds their coping abilities or resources and therefore threatens their well-being.

Structured interview: A type of interview where the interviewer standardizes the questions and their order of presentation for each participant in an effort to create a similar, neutral experience for each interviewee.

Subjective age: How old individuals feel compared to their chronological age.

Subjective experiences: The way individuals mentally experience and perceive events in their life.

Subjective well-being: Individuals' cognitive and emotional evaluation of their life (see *PERMA approach*).

Sufficient justification: Occurs when individuals are able to rationalize a behavior that does not match with their attitudes, which leads to a low level of cognitive dissonance.

Summative assessments: Assessments designed to evaluate whether an intervention was successful.

Sunken cost fallacy: See *escalation trap*.

Superordinate goals: Objectives that cannot be achieved without the cooperation of an outgroup; superordinate goals often result in overcoming personal differences for a shared reward and therefore can reduce prejudice.

Supply side economics: The belief that lowering taxes can increase tax revenues by stimulating the economy.

Survey: A research design where researchers collect data by asking participants to respond to questions or statements.

Sustainable environment: A state in which the resources of the world are not overtaxed, allowing living things, including humans, to adapt and survive now and in the future.

Task leader: A type of leader who focuses on completing assignments, achieving goals, and meeting deadlines.

Terror management theory: The idea that an awareness of our own mortality terrifies individuals, forcing them to cling to comforting beliefs.

Tertiary prevention: Educating the larger community, such as a college or university campus or a given town, regarding dynamics of relationship violence to increase empathy and understanding.

Theory of informational and normative influence: The idea that there are two ways that social norms cause conformity (see *informational social influence* and *normative social influence*).

Theory of planned behavior: The idea that attitudes are only one of three categories of belief—attitudes, subjective norms, and perceived control—that together predict behavioral intentions, which then predict behavior.

Threshold: A point that must be exceeded for a certain effect or consequence to occur.

Threshold effects: Consequences that occur as a result of exceeding a certain limit. In the case of environmental psychology, consequences of going past the Earth's capacity for pollution, overcrowding, or other concerns.

Tragedy of the commons: The idea that individuals, in their attempt to benefit themselves, will collectively harm society.

Transactional leader: A type of leader who uses rewards and punishments to motivate group members; these leaders help to maintain the status quo.

Transformational leader: A type of leader who uses inspiration and group cohesiveness to motivate group members; these leaders are useful for challenging established rules or procedures.

Trauma psychology: A field of psychology that focuses on helping people recover from any severely stressful event that impairs long-term psychological functioning.

Treatment adherence: When an individual follows the advice of a health care provider.

Trial consultant: An individual who tries to influence the outcome of a trial in three ways: (1) by helping to select a sympathetic jury, (2) by developing trial strategies, and (3) by assisting in witness preparation.

True experiment: See *experiment*.

Truly false consensus effect: Occurs when individuals believe that others share their beliefs, even after they have objective, statistical information that contradicts that belief.

***t* test:** A statistical test that uses both the mean and the standard deviation to compare the difference between two groups.

Twin study: A study in which sets of twins are compared to each other, which can help quantify the interacting influences of nature and nurture.

Type A personality: A personality type characterized by competitiveness, the tendency to be impatient, and hostility, where individuals do not manage stress well because they internalize it, leading to poor health.

Typologies: Categorical systems that help individuals think more clearly about complex but related events.

Ultimatum game: A research approach that tests individuals' values concerning money and fairness by requiring them to make an interdependent decision in this situation: Two players can split a financial prize, but only one person (the Proposer) can make an offer about how to split the money, while a second person (the Decider) can only decide whether or not to accept the deal. The Proposer can make the deal as unfair as he or she wants, but if the Decider rejects the deal, neither player gets any money.

Uni-valenced decision: A decision based on an attitude about an attitude object that is either good or bad but not both.

Universality hypothesis: The idea that nonverbal facial expressions are universal, regardless of culture.

Upward counterfactuals: Imagined outcomes that are better than reality.

Upward social comparison: When individuals compare themselves to someone who is better than they are, often to improve on a particular skill.

Urban overload hypothesis: The idea that people in cities avoid social interactions with strangers simply because they are overwhelmed by the number of people they encounter each day.

User experience: How consumers engage with and experience their everyday environments. Some psychologists study the user experience to make products that are more consumer-friendly.

Volunteerism: Freely engaging in a planned, long-term, prosocial behavior.

Waist-to-hips ratio: The ratio comparing the circumference of the waist to the circumference of the hips, which often plays a role in determining female body attractiveness.

Waist-to-shoulders ratio: The ratio comparing the circumference of the waist to the circumference of the shoulders, which often plays a role in determining male body attractiveness.

Weapons effect: The tendency for the presence of weapons to prime aggressive thoughts, feelings, and behaviors.

Weathering: The idea that the cumulative effects of chronic stressors and high-effort coping predispose individuals to physical deterioration, premature aging, and chronic diseases.

What-is-beautiful-is-good effect: When physical attractiveness creates a halo effect such that individuals who are beautiful are also perceived to have several other positive characteristics.

White privilege: The social benefits of being White in White-centric societies.

Wisdom of crowds: Using the collective insights of many people to test, develop, and refine new ideas, products, and services; also called "crowdsourcing."

Within-participants design: An experimental research design where the same group of participants all experience each experimental condition; patterns are found by comparing responses for each condition.

Worldview: The way an individual perceives and approaches the world.

Yerkes-Dodson law: An empirical relationship between stress and performance that predicts that moderate amounts of stress are associated with optimal performance.

D'Cruz, A., 454
Dean, G. W., 120
DeAngelo, L. E., 317
Death penalty, 418 (table)
Death thoughts, 148, 150
Deaux, K., 316, 324
Debriefing, 51
De Bruyn, T., 425
de Castro, J. M., 244, 245 (figure)
Deception, 51, 139–143, 142 (figure), 310
    See also Lying; Milgram studies
Deceptions of kindness, 142 (figure)
Deci, E. L., 494
Decision-making process
    ethical decisions, 221, 221 (table)
    group decision-making, 254–256
    individual influences, 254–258
    interdependent decision making, 462
    medical treatment adherence, 440
    rational versus irrational decision-making, 459
    uni-valenced decisions, 165
De Conti, L., 319
De Cremer, D., 457, 460
Deets, L. E., 361 (table)
Defensive attributions, 148–149
de Geus, E., 261
de Guzman, M. T., 491
    See also Carlo, G.
de Haes, H. C. J. M.. See de Geus, E.
Dehumanization, 349–350
Deindividuation, 211–215, 212 (figure), 213 (figure), 213 (table)
Delaval, M., 247
Delayed gratification, 450
    See also PERMA approach
Delfour, F., 59
Deliberate lying, 142 (figure)
Delmas, F., 357
DeLongis, A., 431
Delon-Martin, C., 121
Dempsey, J. L., 146
DeNault, L. K., 306
DeNeys, W., 94
Dennis, I., 130
Density, 411–412
Denying behaviors, 469 (figure), 470 (figure)
DePaulo, B. M., 140
Dependency, 239, 239 (figure)
Dependent variables, 36, 37 (table), 83, 186 (figure), 307
Depression, 431, 454, 471
Dereli, E., 383
Dermer, M., 371
Derogation of alternatives, 390
DeSanto, T.. See Murphy, D.
Deschanel, E.. See Hanson, H.
Descriptive norms, 204
Desegregation, 6, 276
Désert, M.. See Guimond, S.
Desilets, L.. See Van Horn, K. R.
de Souza, M. A., 290
Destructive responses, 450, 450 (table)
Determination, 450
    See also PERMA approach
Deutsch, F. M., 312
Deutsch, M., 202
DeVincent, C., 431
Devlin, D., 355
DeVries, D. L., 169
de Waal, F. B., 59, 411, 414

de Weerth, C., 41
Dhiaulhaq, A., 425
di Bonaventura, L.. See Murphy, D.
Di Castro, G., 383
Didion, J., 105–106
Diehl, M., 260
Diekman, A. B., 275, 317, 318, 394
Diener, E., 74, 211, 212
Dietrich, D. M., 309, 346
Difficult-to-get-into groups, 236–237, 252
Diffusion of responsibility, 250–251, 252, 322–323
Dijkhoff, L.. See Wagenmakers, E. J.
Di Leone, B. A. L., 349
Dillard, L.. See Wayne, K.
DiMatteo, M. R., 438
Dinerstein, J. L., 315
Dion, K. L., 131, 232
Dioso-Villa, R., 424
Direct aggression, 334 (table), 335, 341, 355
Discrimination
    basic concepts, 270, 270 (table)
    blackness bias, 349–350
    doll studies, 276
    forensic psychology, 418 (table)
    microaggressions, 335
    minimal group paradigm, 271–273
    mitigation strategies, 291–296
    post-9/11 violence, 269
    racial discrimination, 307–308
    same-sex relationships, 397
    scapegoat theory, 279–280
    stereotype content model, 281, 281 (table)
    stress-related health problems, 431
    See also Prejudice; Stereotypes
Disease model, 447
Disentanglement process, 476–477
Dishonesty, 31, 78, 140–141
Disinhibition, 212 (figure), 212–215
Dismissing attachment style, 383, 384 (figure), 386
Disney, W., 132, 511
Disobedience, 220, 220 (figure)
Dispositional attributions, 146, 152–155
Dispute mediation, 418 (table), 425–426
Dissociation, 142 (figure)
Dissonance
    See also Cognitive dissonance
Distinctiveness, 149
Distractions, 187, 276
Distress, 435
DiTomasso, N. A., 349
DiTommaso, A., 492
Divergent (Roth), 15
Diversity
    gender diversity, 6–7
    internships, 497
Divorce mediation, 426
Dixon, W. J.. See McGovern, T. V.
Dixson, A. F., 379
DNA evidence, 418 (table)
Dobash, R. E., 468
Dobash, R. P., 468
Dobuzinskis, A., 310
Dockery, T. M., 166
Dodge, K. A., 335
Dog breeds, 340, 340 (photo)
Doherty, D., 187
Dolder, C. R., 438
    See also Lacro, J. P.

Emotions
  cognitive dissonance, 181–182
  micro-expressions, 140–141
  negative state relief, 308–309
  PERMA approach, 449–450, 450 (table)
  positive versus negative emotions, 141
  stereotype content model, 281, 281 (table)
  universality hypothesis, 138 (photo), 138–139
  vulnerability, 239, 239 (figure)
  See also Aggressive behaviors
Empathy-altruism hypothesis, 304 (table), 309–311, 312
Employee assistance programs (EAPs), 486
Employee morale and satisfaction, 485
Emswiller, T., 324
Engagement, 449
  See also PERMA approach
Engel, G. L., 429, 430 (figure)
Enola Gay, 333
Entitlements, 69
Envious prejudice, 281 (table)
Environmental factors
  aggressive behaviors, 355–357
  nature versus nurture debate, 9–10
  noise-induced stress, 410–411
  overpopulation impacts, 411–414
  personality-environmental interactions, 9
  stress and health issues, 429–437
  threshold effects, 405–409, 406 (table)
  tragedy of the commons, 414
Environmental psychology, 405
Epidemiology, 438
Epley, N., 95, 110, 116, 513
Epstein, J., 355
Epstein, J. A., 140
Equal and fair treatment, 307–308
Erdfelder, E., 121
Ericsson, S., 345
Escalation of aggression effect, 336
Escalation trap, 237
Eshleman, A., 288
ESPN, 237
Esquilin, M.. See Sue, D. W.
Essock-Vitale, S. M., 305
Esteem, 61, 61 (figure)
Etcheverry, P. E., 392
Ethical considerations
  actor-observer attribution bias, 153
  decision-making matrix, 221, 221 (table)
  employee assistance programs, 486
  Milgram studies, 221 (table), 221–222
  research methods, 17, 49–51, 307
  sport psychology, 452–453
Ethnicity, 176 (table), 176–177, 278, 279 (figure)
Etling, K. M., 116
Eustress, 435
Evaluation apprehension hypothesis, 247, 261
Evaluation research, 418 (table), 426
Evaluations and assessments
  industrial/organizational psychology, 488
  medical treatment adherence, 441
  positive psychology practices, 454
Evaluative beliefs, 164–165
Evans, C. A., 131
Evans, D., 324
  See also Levine, M.
Evans, G. W., 436
Evergreen tree (symbol), 144 (table)
Everitt, D. E., 135

Everly, B. A., 284
Everson-Rose, S. A., 436
Evidence-based thinking, 13
Evidence evaluation, 418 (table)
Evil. See Good versus evil
Ewing, B. A.. See Hilton, L.
Exception-finding scripts, 101
Excitation transfer effect, 375
Exclusion, social, 240–242
Exclusive groups, 236 (photo), 236–237
Exotic effect, 378
Expectancy effect, 130, 133
Expectations, 130–131, 133–134, 134 (figure), 197–198, 198 (figure)
Experience, 110 (figure), 112–113, 172–173, 497
Experimental groups, 203, 238
Experimental tools and techniques, 15–17, 111, 213, 213 (table)
Experimenter bias, 133
Expertise, 186
Explicit attitudes, 164–165, 175–176
Explicit expectations, 198, 198 (figure)
Explicit prejudice, 288
Explicit self-esteem, 78
Exposito, F., 146
  See also Valor-Segura, I.
External attributions, 146, 152–155, 154 (figure)
External locus of control, 148
External validity, 48, 135–137
Extinction rates, 406 (table)
Extraversion, 313, 313 (table), 492, 492 (figure)
Extrinsic motivation, 494
Extrinsic religiosity, 285
Eyewitness testimony, 418 (table), 422–423
Eyre, R. N., 95

F
Fabes, R., 316
Fabricatore, A. N., 84
Facebook, 75, 117, 131, 256
Face validity, 78
Facial expressions
  facial feedback hypothesis, 167–168, 168 (figure)
  lying behaviors, 139–143, 142 (figure)
  universality hypothesis, 138, 138 (photo)
Facial feedback hypothesis, 167–168, 168 (figure)
Facial leakage, 140
Facilitation. See Social facilitation
Factitious disorders, 142 (figure)
Factorial designs, 213, 213 (table), 271, 315
Failed prophecies, 179–180
Failing forward, 454
Fairness, 463–464, 486
Fake lie detection, 175–176
Fake smiles, 140–141
Fales, M., 398
False beliefs, 146
False compliments, 142 (figure)
False confessions, 151, 420–421, 421 (table)
False consensus bias, 156
False dichotomy, 10, 392
False memories, 118–120, 119 (figure)
False negative, 418
False positive, 418
False uniqueness bias, 156
Falsification principle, 16–17
Falvey, J.. See Attanasio, P.
Family law, 418 (table)
Family relationships, 453
Farmer, R. F., 435

norm of reciprocity, 190–191
practical applications, 407–408
Pessin, J., 246
Pessoa, F., 72
Pete, S., 504
Peter, K., 361 (table)
Peters, D. M.. *See* Hoigaard, R.
Petersen, W.. *See* Zuiker, A. E.
Peterson, B. E., 283
Peterson, C. K., 344
Peterson, M.. *See* Hanson, H.
Petralli, M.. *See* Ciucci, E.
Petrie, M., 69
Petrova, P.. *See* Barrett, D. W.
Pettigrew, T. F., 276
Pettit, G. S., 335
Petty, R. E., 97, 145, 164, 165, 183, 186, 187, 188, 248, 276
See also Cialdini, R. B.
Pexa, N. A.. *See* Gibbons, F. X.
Phillippi, R. H., 117
Phillips, C. M., 360
Phillips, J. G., 81
Phillips, M. L., 70
Phony smiles, 140
Phuong, J., 141
Physical abuse, 469 (figure), 470 (figure)
See also Relationship violence
Physical aggression, 334 (table)
Physical attraction. *See* Attraction
Physical attractiveness
average faces, 377–378, 378 (figure)
bilateral symmetry, 376 (photo), 376–377, 377 (photo)
universal traits, 375–376
waist-to-hips/waist-to-shoulders ratios, 378–379, 379 (figure), 393
"what-is-beautiful-is-good" effect, 131, 186, 376
Physical distance, 371
Physical maturity-birth date relationship, 136 (table), 136–137
Physiological arousal, 374–375
Physiological research, 41
Piaroa society, 361 (table)
Pichon, C., 111
Pichora-Fuller, M. K., 96
Pierce, C. A., 176
Pieters, R., 185
Pietsching, J.. *See* Swami, V.
Pinel, E. C., 475
Pinker, S., 73, 210, 337, 363, 412
Pinocchio (motion picture), 103, 132
Pinter, B., 78
Pit bulls, 340 (photo)
Pitt, Brad, 369, 373, 376, 387, 390, 394
Pittinsky, T. L., 254
Pittman, T. S., 168
Placebo effects, 449, 454
Plailly, J., 121
Planned behavior theory, 169 (figure), 169–170, 408, 439, 440
Planning fallacy, 109
Plotnik, J. M., 59
Pluralism Project at Harvard University, 269
Pluralistic ignorance, 258, 325
Podnar, O., 345
Polarization, group, 254–256
Polaschek, D. L., 176
Polek, D. S., 467
Policy compliance, 418 (table)
Policy evaluation, 418 (table)
Political orientation, 172
Politser, P., 457

Polman, E., 105
Polo-Neil, H.. *See* Wayne, K.
Polyamory, 388
Polyandry, 388
Polygamy, 388
Polygyny, 388
Pomerantz, J.. *See* Keating, C. F.
Pomeroy, W. B., 392
See also Kinsey, A. C.
Pommer, S. D.. *See* Keating, C. F.
Ponterotto, J. G., 78
Poon, C. S. K., 108
Pope, Alexander, 361
Poppe, M., 156
Popper, K., 16
Pop psychology, 448–449, 454
Popular culture
attachment theory, 385
Captain America, 309
correlation-causation relationship, 40
counterfactual thinking, 108
group dynamics, 252
Kitty Genovese, 321
misattribution of arousal, 374
persuasion models, 184
prejudice reduction, 294
relational aggression in teen movies, 355
self-discrepancy theory, 67
self-fulfilling prophecies, 132
social conformity, 207
Population density, 411–412
Porter, E. S., 32, 353
Porter, S., 142
Positive attitudes, 166, 169, 172, 174
Positive correlations, 44–45, 45 (figure)
Positive emotions, 141, 449
Positive illusions, 73–74
Positive individual traits, 446 (figure), 446–447, 452
Positive institutions, 446 (figure), 447, 452, 453
Positive psychology
basic concepts, 3, 445
clinical applications, 453–455
historical perspective, 451–453
peer review process, 449
PERMA approach, 449–450, 450 (table)
publication growth, 451 (figure)
subjective well-being, 447–448, 448 (figure)
three pillars, 446 (figure), 446–447
Positive social roles, 213 (table), 213–214
Positive stereotypes, 213, 213 (table), 278
Positive subjective experiences, 446, 446 (figure), 452, 453
Post, J. M., 258
Post-9/11 violence, 269
Post hoc matched groups design, 307
Postmes, T.. *See* Haslam, S. A.
Posttest-only control group design, 37–38
Posttraumatic growth, 477–478, 478 (table)
Posttraumatic stress disorder (PTSD), 410–411, 431–433, 432 (table), 454, 471, 477–478
Potvin, L., 278
Powell, J., 493, 493 (photo)
Powell, Lew, 163
Power, K. G., 82
Power and control wheels, 469 (figure), 470 (figure)
Poyatos, F., 143
Pratkanis, A. R., 180
Pratto, F., 284
Praxmarer, S., 186